A MEDITERRANEAN SOCIETY

S. D. GOITEIN and
PAULA SANDERS

A Mediterranean Society

THE JEWISH COMMUNITIES OF THE ARAB WORLD
AS PORTRAYED IN THE DOCUMENTS OF THE CAIRO GENIZA

. . . .

VOLUME VI

Cumulative Indices

UNIVERSITY OF CALIFORNIA PRESS
Berkeley • Los Angeles • London

University of California Press
Berkeley and Los Angeles, California

University of California Press, Ltd.
London, England

First Paperback Printing 1999

Library of Congress Cataloging-in-Publication Data
(Revised for vol. 6)

Goitein, S. D., 1900–
A Mediterranean society.
"Published under the auspices of the Near Eastern Center, University of California, Los Angeles."
Includes bibliographical references and index.
Contents: v. 1. Economic foundations – v. 2. The community – [etc.] – v. 6. Cumulative indices.
1. Jews–Islamic Empire–Civilization. 2. Islamic Empire–Civilization. 3. Cairo Genizah. I. Gustave E. von Grunebaum Center for Near Eastern Studies. II. Title.
D199.3.G58 956′.00492401822 67-22430
ISBN 0-520-08136-6 (cl. : alk. paper)
ISBN 0-520-22164-8 (pbk. : alk. paper)

Printed in the United States of America

08 07 06 05 04 03 02 01 00 99

10 9 8 7 6 5 4 3 2 1

The paper used in this publication meets the minimum requirements of ANSI/NISO Z39.48-1992 (R 1997) (*Permanence of Paper*). ♾

Contents

PREFACE vii

GENERAL INDEX 1

INDEX OF GENIZA TEXTS 127

INDEX OF SCRIPTURAL, RABBINIC, AND MAIMONIDEAN CITATIONS 226

Preface

This volume contains cumulative indices to the five volumes of the late S. D. Goitein's *A Mediterranean Society*. Professor Goitein intended for the cumulative indices to supplement and supersede the individual volume indices, which do not include material from the notes and appendices. Furthermore, with the exception of volume 1, the geniza texts themselves were not indexed in the individual volumes. Professor Goitein often said that he thought the notes were the most important part of the books, and he regretted that the voluminous information contained in them was not made accessible in a more systematic way to researchers. In typical fashion, he began the preparations to produce a cumulative volume long before he approached the University of California Press with the idea. He had successive research assistants index all citations of geniza texts and other material from the notes and appendices on note cards. These note cards were stored in fifteen shoe boxes, kept inside and on top of the metal cabinets that held his large collection of photographs of geniza documents.

The note cards and published indices of the individual volumes form the basis for these cumulative indices. I have attempted here to reconcile the inevitable inconsistencies in spelling and citation that creep into a work published over a period of some twenty years. To the extent possible, all references for particular individuals, terms, places, or topics are consolidated in a single entry, with cross-references to variants in spelling, citation, or nomenclature. Especially large entries for important cities or people have been broken down into more detailed subentries. Technical terms appear in both Judeo-Arabic and English and are cross-referenced. In addition, brief definitions for Judeo-Arabic terms are included when those usages differ from conventional Arabic or Hebrew meanings.

The Index of Geniza Texts is arranged alphabetically by collection and follows largely the order established in volume 1. However, experienced readers of *A Mediterranean Society* will notice several differences between the cumulative Index of Geniza Texts and the index in volume 1. First, the order of classmarks in the collections of the Cambridge University Library, which comprise the major part of the geniza documents cited in Goitein's work, has been changed

to follow that established in Stefan Reif's *Published Material from the Cambridge Genizah Collections: A Bibliography 1896–1980* (Cambridge, 1988), an invaluable reference work which users of this index will certainly consult. In addition, the citations in this index have been checked against Reif's citations, and corrections have been noted and cross-referenced. I have not, however, reconciled Goitein's method for citing geniza documents from the Taylor-Schechter Collection with that employed by Reif. As explained to me in an electronic mail communication by Stefan Reif (March 30, 1992), Goitein's custom was to use "f." within classmarks to refer to the running number and not to the actual folio. For example, what appears in Reif's bibliography as 10J5.1 appears in Goitein's work as 10J5, f.1 (where "f." is the running number and not the folio number). Second, the plus signs and asterisks after classmarks, included in the notes for volume 1 through volume 4, have been dropped. These marks were used to indicate documents that had been edited in M. Michael's *Nahray b. Nissim,* or documents edited and to be included in Goitein's *India Book* or his *Mediterranean People,* two long-term projects that remain unpublished. A fuller description and explanation of these two projects may be found in volume 1, pages ix, xviii, xxii, and xxiv. Third, references to the *Responsa* of Abraham and Moses Maimonides have been moved to the Index of Scriptural, Rabbinic, and Maimonidean Citations. Finally, I have not employed the use of "*r*" to indicate *recto.* Readers should take *recto* as the default in citations; references to the *verso* only of a document are indicated by "*v.*"

Readers should also note that references are given differently in the Index of Geniza Texts than in the General Index and the Index of Scriptural, Rabbinic, and Maimonidean Citations. In the Index of Geniza Texts, references are cited by chapter, section, subsection, and note number. Sections or subsections of a chapter are separated by semicolons; chapters are separated by periods. References to appendices precede those to notes, following the order established in the volumes. Lowercase plain roman numerals indicate chapters; uppercase bold roman numerals indicate volumes. In the General Index and the Index of Scriptural, Rabbinic, and Maimonidean Citations, references are cited by volume and page number. Uppercase bold roman numerals indicate volumes; plain Arabic numerals indicate page numbers. Readers should note that an item may appear more than once on the indicated page.

It gives me pleasure to acknowledge the assistance and advice that colleagues and friends have given over the many years in which these

indices were being prepared. Ralph Hattox, Shaun Marmon, and Amy Singer provided invaluable assistance of varying kinds during the years when we were graduate students together at Princeton. Anne Hartstein Pace did much of the indexing necessary for the Index of Scriptural, Rabbinic, and Maimonidean Citations and provided other assistance. Stefan Reif, director of the Taylor-Schechter Research Unit at the Cambridge University Library, answered my queries via electronic mail. Elliott Shore, Librarian of the Historical Studies and Social Science Library of the Institute for Advanced Study in Princeton, New Jersey, generously provided space and an assistant to me during the year after Professor Goitein's death. The Department of Near Eastern Studies of Princeton University has continued to provide substantial support to this project.

Many of Professor Goitein's colleagues and disciples in Geniza studies have provided assistance, but I wish to thank three in particular. Mordechai Friedman offered valuable advice in the early stages of the project and made numerous corrections to the Index of Scriptural, Rabbinic, and Maimonidean Citations. Avrom Udovitch has been a constant source of support and has contributed significantly to every part of this volume. I owe a special debt to Mark Cohen for his friendship and good counsel throughout this project. He also read the final manuscript in its entirety and made countless suggestions and corrections. Finally, I acknowledge with gratitude the continued cooperation and material support of S. D. Goitein's children, Elon Goitein, Ayala Gordon, and Ofra Rosner.

Paula Sanders

General Index

References are given by volume and page number. Upper case bold roman numerals indicate volumes; plain Arabic numerals indicate page numbers. Reader should note that an item may appear more than once on the indicated page.

A

Aaron, biblical, **I**, 56; **II**, 157
Aaron, cantor, **II**, 454
Aaron, the cantor, son of Ephraim, the scribe, **II**, 476, 597
Aaron Abuʾl-Ḥasan, **II**, 537
Aaron Ibn al-ʿAmmānī. *See* Aaron b. Yeshūʿā
Aaron Ben-Meir's sister's son, **III**, 25
Aaron (=Ḥalfon) b. Ephraim b. Ṭarsōn, **II**, 568, 571; **V**, 618
Aaron b. Fuhayd, **I**, 414
Aaron, the ḥāvēr, son of Rabbi Ḥiyyā, **IV**, 443
Aaron b. Joseph, elder, **II**, 430
Aaron b. Joseph ha-Kohen b. Sarjādo, scholar, **V**, 386, 615
Aaron b. Joshua ha-Kohen, **V**, 154
Aaron b. Moses Ben-Asher, **V**, 372
Aaron b. Peraḥyā, **V**, 563
Aaron al-Qalaʿī, **II**, 497
Aaron Ibn Ṣaghīr, **III**, 75
Aaron b. Ṣedāqā b. Aaron al-ʿAmmānī, **II**, 245, 576
Aaron b. Yeshūʿā Ibn al-ʿAmmānī, **II**, 245, 258, 259, 264, 320, 576, 580, 596, 602; **III**, 478; **V**, 460–461, 506, 513
Abacus, **II**, 557
Abattoirs. *See* Slaughterhouses
ʿAbbādān(ī), **IV**, 128, 384; **V**, 551
abbā mārī (Aram., "Dad, my lord," intimate form of address), **III**, 25, 432
abbār, needle-maker, **I**, 421
Abbasid(s), **I**, 22; **II**, 243, 316; **IV**, 125, 162
ʿabd. *See* Slave
ʿAbd, House of, Muslim postal agency, **I**, 286, 288, 293
ʿAbdallah (Ibn) Barābik ("Tales"), **II**, 496, 505
ʿAbd al-ʿAẓīm al-Mundhirī, Islamic theologian, **V**, 477
ʿAbd al-ʿAzīz, common Jewish name, **II**, 505
ʿAbd al-Bāqī, the perfumer, **I**, 441
ʿAbd al-Dāʾim, common Jewish name, **II**, 464
ʿAbd al-Jabbār, **V**, 606, 608
ʿAbd al-Karīm, common Jewish name, **II**, 464, 505
ʿAbd al-Laṭīf, physician, **IV**, 60, 71
ʿAbd al-Muʾmin, Almohad caliph, **I**, 234; **V**, 59, 60, 521
ʿAbd al-Muṭṭalib, Dr., **I**, 470
ʿAbd al-Salām, **I**, 308
Abdel Tawwab, modern author, **IV**, 55
ʿAbd al-Wāḥid, common Jewish name, **II**, 505
Abī Bishr Jacob Ibn Joseph, **V**, 572
al-ʿabīd al-taṣdīr, **II**, 612
Abī Jacob Joseph Ibn Jacob, **V**, 572
Abiʾl-Ḥay Ṣalḥūn, **V**, 597
Abiʾl-ʿIzz, banker, **II**, 494
ʿabīr, a perfume, **I**, 420
Abiʾl-Riḍā, banker, **II**, 494
Abī Saʿīd, teacher, **II**, 465, 559
ʿAbla, house of, **II**, 120
Ablutions, **II**, 435, 552
abnāʾ al-nās, persons from a good family. See *ben ṭōvīm*
Al-ʾab rabb, "The father is like God," **III**, 79
Abraham, biblical, **III**, 27; **V**, 514, 602
Abraham, *parnās*, **II**, 449
Abraham b. Aaron, scribe, **II**, 344
Abraham b. Aaron *ha-mumḥe* b. Ephraim, **II**, 443, 444, 597; **III**, 455, 458, 466
Abraham b. Abiʾl-Ḥayy, **III**, 43
Abraham b. Abuʾl-Rabīʿ. *See* Abraham the Pious

Abraham al-ʿAdanī, II, 497
Abraham b. Amram, I, 434; V, 557
Abraham b. ʿAṭā (Nathan), Nagid, II, 24, 244; V, 566
Abraham Ben Yijū, I, 435; II, 20, 480; III, 6, 29, 55-56, 137, 138, 239, 470; IV, 400, 420, 439; V, 35, 191, 229-230, 231, 240, 247, 519, 562, 570, 572, 575, 589, 604
Abraham b. Burayk, Abū Isḥāq, I, 258
Abraham b. Daʾūd, V, 280
Abraham II b. David, Nagid, II, 524, 526, 529-530, 605. *See also* Abraham Maimonides
Abraham b. David b. Sighmār, III, 183
Abraham b. David of Provence, III, 185
Abraham Dustarī. *See* Abū Saʿd al-Tustarī
Abraham Dyer, II, 451
Abraham Ibn Ezra, poet, II, 592; III, 431; V, 15, 45, 119, 382, 405, 448, 587, 615, 621, 627
Abraham b. Hananel al-Amshāṭī, III, 188, 466
Abraham b. Ḥayy, II, 555
Abraham (Burayh) b. Isaac, II, 471, 472
Abraham b. Isaac the Scholar, I, 238-239, 242, 244, 363, 459; II, 476, 512, 522, 565, 566, 567; III, 75, 91, 137, 266, 507; IV, 110, 377; V, 266-267, 443, 540, 580
Abraham II b. Isaac II b. Abraham I b. Daniel b. Isaac I, III, 12-13
Abraham b. Isaac b. Furāt, physician, II, 243, 246, 604, 610; III, 118, 451; V, 195, 236-237, 242, 257, 263-264, 284, 299, 321, 562, 597, 625
Abraham b. Jacob, III, 430
Abraham b. Jacob Derʿī, judge, I, 407; III, 481; IV, 399; V, 591
Abraham b. Joseph, V, 573
Abraham b. Joseph al-Siqillī, I, 407
Abraham b. Judah, banker, V, 401
Abraham ha-Kohen, V, 150, 264
Abraham Kohen b. Daniel, I, 362
Abraham Levi b. Samuel, II, 597
Abraham Maimonides (Maimuni), Nagid, II, 46, 48, 51, 52, 98, 142, 496, 508, 514, 515, 524, 532, 546, 553; III, 307, 479, 492; IV, 12, 20, 21, 38, 87, 154, 157, 165, 230, 281, 350, 366, 372, 433, 436, 448; V, 185, 505, 510, 515, 537, 548, 555, 572, 585, 628, 640; administration of social services, II, 103, 111, 133, 420, 429, 449, 461, 466, 492, 542, 559; biographical details, II, 39-40, 583; III, 62, 473; V, 476-477, 492, 493; cases brought before, I, 88, 255, 366, 491; II, 397; III, 72; commentary, III, 229; contributions to charity, II, 486, 487; controversy and opposition, II, 21, 26, 141, 208, 220, 406-407, 485; and Dammuh sanctuary, V, 22-23; and father, V, 197-198, 477; illness, II, 493; V, 111, 113-114, 493; instructions of, I, 57, 101; II, 111; judgments and duties of, II, 217, 326; III, 331; V, 138, 485-493; judicial procedure, II, 341; *Kifāya* (The Complete Guide for the Pious), II, 168; V, 8, 198, 475-476, 477-481, 493, 494-495; letters of, II, 96, 534, 578; III, 258, 268-269; V, 481-482, 484-485, 489; letters to, I, 63; II, 44, 49, 111, 576, 579; III, 271, 302, 494; V, 39, 88, 483-484; medical career, II, 244, 250, 264; V, 492; and *muqaddams*, II, 36, 74, 75; as Nagid, II, 21, 26, 32, 33, 391, 526, 529, 600; III, 443, 489; opinions on marriage questions, III, 23, 58, 80, 101, 268-269; personality, V, 475, 482, 495; pietism, II, 156, 166, 217, 406, 555; V, 8, 9, 478-484, 491-492, 494-495, 502; and poll tax, II, 383, 391, 466; queries and responsa, I, 14, 134, 136, 141, 146, 177, 258, 428; II, 36, 37, 39-40, 293, 301, 326, 338, 383, 401, 526; III, 101; scholarship, V, 474-475; on slaves, I, 136, 141, 146; solicitations to assist needy, II, 96, 135, 136; on use of Muslim judiciary, II, 401
Abraham II Maimonides, II, 560
Abraham Maimuni. *See* Abraham Maimonides
Abraham b. Mevassēr, *al-sāgūl* ("The Cherished"), II, 475
Abraham b. Mevassēr, notary, III, 466
Abraham b. Moses, V, 615
Abraham al-Najīb. *See* Abraham b. Yaḥyā ha-Levi al-Najīb
Abraham b. Nathan. *See* Abraham b. ʿAṭā (Ibn ʿAṭā)
Abraham III b. Nathan āv II, judge in Cairo, II, 405, 425, 434, 512, 573, 538, 597, 598; III, 90, 302, 445, 469, 483, 493, 500, 502; V, 113, 197, 204, 327, 553, 564, 596, 624
Abraham b. Nathan the Seventh, I, 84; II, 586, 587, 589; III, 256, 473, 483; V, 590
Abraham b. Nathan b. Abraham āv, II, 597; III, 327; IV, 282, 384
Abraham II b. Nathan I b. Abraham I. *See* Abraham b. Nathan b. Abraham āv
Abraham the Pious, I, 366; II, 429, 451; IV, 399; V, 8, 79, 80, 346, 459-460, 481, 527, 641
Abraham the proselyte, II, 306

Abraham Qābisī, Gaon, **II**, 522
Abrahams, Israel, **II**, 82, 84
Abraham b. Saadya, **II**, 572
Abraham b. Sahlān, banker. *See* Barhūn b. Sahlān
Abraham b. Sahlān, head of the Babylonian congregation, **II**, 455, 471, 511, 614; **III**, 486; **V**, 120, 553
Abraham (Ibrahīm) b. Salām, **III**, 215
Abraham b. Samuel al-Andalusī, **III**, 294
Abraham b. Samuel al-Derʿī, **II**, 429
Abraham, the scholar, son of Moses, the teacher, **V**, 573
Abraham b. Shabbetay, grandfather of the *muqaddam*, **II**, 47
Abraham b. Shabbetay, *muqaddam*, **II**, 45, 47, 342; **V**, 372, 611, 622
Abraham b. Shemaʿya *he-ḥāvēr*, judge, **II**, 268, 512, 565, 572; **III**, 507; **V**, 212, 553
Abraham b. Solomon b. Judah Gaon, **II**, 15, 58, 200, 522; **V**, 369
Abraham Son of the Scholar, judge. *See* Abraham b. Isaac the Scholar
Abraham al-Tāhertī, **II**, 475
Abraham Ṭaḥṭāḥī (probably Tunisian), **II**, 475
Abraham Ibn Tībān, **III**, 252
Abraham (Barhūn) b. Yaḥyā Fāsī, **V**, 536, 575
Abraham b. Yaḥyā ha-Levi al-Najīb, **II**, 419, 543; **V**, 269, 510, 511, 564, 581
Abraham b. Yashar. *See* Abū Saʿd al-Tustarī
Abramson, Sheraga, **I**, 4
Absentmindedness, **V**, 242–243
Abū (Bū), **I**, 357
Abū ʿAbdallah b. al-Baʿbāʿ, **I**, 477
Abuʾl-ʿAlā, the banker, **I**, 241
Abuʾl-ʿAlā, head of the congregations, **II**, 538
Abuʾl-ʿAlā, sheikh, **V**, 56, 188, 454, 460
Abū ʿAlā Japheth b. Maṣlīʾaḥ, **III**, 350
Abuʾl-ʿAlā b. Joseph, **I**, 366
Abuʾl-ʿAlā al-Kohen, **II**, 561
Abuʾl-ʿAlā al-Maʿarrī, **I**, 143, 434; **II**, 278; **III**, 10; **V**, 601
Abuʾl-ʿAlā b. Mufaḍḍal Ibn al-Marāwiḥī, **II**, 495
Abuʾl-ʿAlā Musallam b. Sahl, **IV**, 318
Abuʾl-ʿAlā b. al-Nafīs, **II**, 490
Abuʾl-ʿAlā b. Shaʿyā, banker, **II**, 455
Abuʾl-ʿAlā Ibn Shaʿya Ibn Tadmurī, **II**, 508
Abuʾl-ʿAlā b. Tammām, **V**, 149
Abuʾl-ʿAlā Yūsuf b. Dāʾūd Ibn Shaʿyā, **III**, 428
Abū ʿAlī, banker, **II**, 425
Abū ʿAlī, "brother-in-law" of Abraham Yijū, **II**, 480
Abū ʿAlī. *See* Japheth b. Abraham
Abū ʿAlī b. Abū ʿAmr, **V**, 245, 574
Abū ʿAlī Ibn Baruch, *parnās*, **II**, 448, 459
Abū ʿAlī Ezekiel b. Nethanel ha-Levi, **II**, 262; **IV**, 251, 444, 448; **V**, 454, 575, 590
Abū ʿAlī Ibn Faḍlān I, banker of Baghdad, **II**, 525; **V**, 263, 264
Abū ʿAlī II Ibn Faḍlān, **II**, 18
Abū ʿAlī Ḥasan, **II**, 538
Abū ʿAlī Ḥasan b. ʿAlī al-Baṣrī. *See* Japheth b. Eli
Abū ʿAlī Ḥasan b. ʿImrān, **IV**, 438; **V**, 574, 598
Abū ʿAlī *al-qazzāz* b. Khalaf, **III**, 465
Abū ʿAlī b. al-Raqqī, **IV**, 429
Abū ʿAlī b. Shekhanyā, cantor, **V**, 159
Abū ʿAlī b. al-Sukkārī, **V**, 159
Abuʾl-Bahā, elder and scholar, **II**, 495; **IV**, 446
Abū Bakr, the Almoravid, **I**, 235
Abū Bakr al-Rashīdī, **I**, 372
Abuʾl-Barakāt, physician, **III**, 354
Abuʾl-Barakāt, silk-weaver, **V**, 150–151
Abuʾl-Barakāt, tailor, **V**, 27
Abuʾl-Barakāt al-Baghdādī, **II**, 592
Abuʾl-Barakāt b. Joseph Lebdī, **II**, 479; **IV**, 19, 286, 321
Abuʾl-Barakāt II b. Joseph III al-Lebdī, **V**, 544
Abuʾl-Barakāt b. Ḥārith, merchant, **V**, 289, 587
Abuʾl-Barakāt Hibat Allah, "The Unique," **II**, 302, 380
Abuʾl-Barakāt *al-kātib al-sadīd*, **II**, 605
Abuʾl-Barakāt *al-kātib*, Yehuda ha-Kohen, **II**, 355, 604; **IV**, 397
Abuʾl-Barakāt al-Lebdī, sugar maker, **V**, 135, 543
Abuʾl-Barakāt Mevōrākh al-Ḥalabī b. Solomon, **III**, 491
Abuʾl-Barakāt *al-mūrid*, **II**, 505
Abuʾl-Barakāt Ibn al-Quḍāʿī, **II**, 603
Abuʾl-Barakāt Ibn Shaʿyā, **III**, 501
Abuʾl-Barakāt Solomon b. Elijah. *See* Solomon b. Elijah
Abuʾl-Bayān b. Abū Naṣr al-Ḥalabī, *parnās*, **II**, 94, 417, 422, 448, 542
Abuʾl-Bayān Isaac b. Baruch, cantor, **III**, 220–221
Abuʾl-Bishr al-Kirmānī, **IV**, 100
Abuʾl-Bishr Mevassēr ha-Kohen b. Salmān, **II**, 605
Abuʾl-Bishr Salmān, **I**, 93
Abū Dirham Ismaʿīl, **II**, 538
Abūʾl-Faḍāʾil Ibn al-Nāqid, **IV**, 286

Abu'l-Faḍl, silk-weaver, V, 150–152
Abu'l-Faḍl Ben al-Baṣrī, V, 579
Abu'l-Faḍl Ibn al-Dhahabī Joseph b. Joshiah, III, 504; IV, 373; V, 104
Abu'l-Faḍl b. Elazar, V, 34
Abu'l-Faḍl *he-ḥāvēr*. *See* Mevōrākh b. Saadya
Abu'l-Faḍl Ibn al-Kallām, II, 579
Abu'l-Faḍl Mevōrākh b. Abraham, *parnās*, II, 449, 455
Abu'l-Faḍl the Persian, characteristic name, II, 508
Abu'l-Faḍl b. Qaṭā'if, II, 507
Abu'l-Faḍl al-Ṣabbāgh b. Abu'l-ʿIzz al-Jabbān, V, 544
Abu'l-Faḍl Ibn Ṣaghīr, II, 474
Abu'l-Faḍl b. Sahl, V, 626
Abu'l-Faḍl Sahl (Heb. Shelah) b. Yūshaʿ Ibn Shaʿyā, III, 9; V, 375
Abu'l-Faḍl Ṣāliḥ Tāhertī, I, 444
Abu'l-Faḍl Shēlā ha-Levi, IV, 325
Abu'l-Fakhr, nephew of Ḥalfōn b. Nethanel, III, 230–231
Abu'l-Fakhr al-Jabbān b. Saadya, V, 544
Abu'l-Fakhr Saadya b. Abraham, II, 498, 582
Abu'l-Faraj, I, 241, 338, 357
Abu'l-Faraj, II, 461
Abu'l-Faraj, physician, IV, 438
Abu'l-Faraj b. Abi'l-Saʿīd, Karaite banker, IV, 99
Abu'l-Faraj b. Abū Mufaḍḍal Ibn al-Marāwiḥī, II, 495
Abu'l-Faraj b. Ghazāl al-Qaysarānī, III, 191
Abu'l-Faraj Hārūn, V, 372
Abu'l-Faraj Hibat Allah, V, 36
Abu'l-Faraj al-Iṣfahānī, V, 425
Abu'l-Faraj al-Jubaylī, IV, 135
Abu'l-Faraj b. Joseph, the Spaniard, I, 321
Abu'l-Faraj b. al-Kallām, merchant, II, 579; V, 445–446, 447
Abu'l-Faraj b. Khalaf, III, 470
Abu'l-Faraj b. Maḥfūẓ, *parnās* and beadle, II, 430, 444, 449, 451
Abu'l-Faraj Ibn Maʿmar al-Sharābī, shopkeeper. *See* Nethanel ha-Levi b. Amram
Abu'l-Faraj of Mosul, I, 473
Abu'l-Faraj b. al-Nafīs, II, 490
Abu'l-Faraj b. Qasāsā, III, 465; V, 168
Abu'l-Faraj Ibn al-Ramlī, Kohen, V, 148–149
Abu'l-Faraj b. al-Rayyis. *See* Elijah b. Zechariah
Abu'l-Faraj Sulaymān, I, 444
Abu'l-Faraj Ibn al-Tinnīsī, I, 436
Abu'l-Faraj Yeshūʿā ha-Talmīd b. Ṣedāqā al-Ramlī, II, 435
Abu'l-Fatḥ Naṣr b. Ibrāhīm, Muslim scholar, II, 562
Abu'l-Futūḥ b. Abu'l-Ḥasan, II, 502
Abu Ghālib, Christian physician, V, 315
Abu'l-Ḥajjāj Joseph b. Elazar, III, 255
Abū Ḥanīfa, IV, 151
Abū Hārūn (Moses) Ibn Ezra, V, 627
Abu'l-Ḥasan, son of Sheikh Abu'l-Faḍl the silk-weaver, V, 150
Abu'l-Ḥasan, V, 253
Abu'l-Ḥasan, V, 440
Abu'l-Ḥasan, son of Sumr, V, 357–358
Abu'l-Ḥasan, spondle-maker, V, 170
Abu'l-Ḥasan, the glassmaker, II, 502
Abu'l-Ḥasan Ibn Abū Saʿd, II, 481
Abu'l-Ḥasan b. Abū Sahl, III, 479; IV, 325, 457
Abu'l-Ḥasan Adōnīm, III, 10
Abu'l-Ḥasan b. Ayyūb, V, 169, 553
Abu'l-Ḥasan Eli b. Isaac ha-Kohen, II, 540
Abu'l-Ḥasan *al-dihqān*, V, 581
Abu'l-Ḥasan al-Ḥalabī, banker, V, 168
Abu'l-Ḥasan Ibrahīm al-Zayyāt, V, 528
Abu'l-Ḥasan b. Mūsā *al-fāṣid* ("the bloodletter"), II, 585
Abu'l-Ḥasan *al-ṣayrafī*, III, 505
Abu'l-Ḥasan Ibn Ṭībān, III, 482
Abu'l-Ḥasan *al-wazzān* ("the weigher"), II, 479
Abū Ḥayyūn, carpenter, II, 461
Abu'l-Ḥusayn, brother-in-law of Nahray b. Nissīm, V, 523
Abu'l-Ḥusayn ʿAmīd al-Dawla Yiḥye b. Abraham Segullat ha-yeshiva, III, 488
Abu'l-Ḥusayn al-Ḥalabī, II, 478; III, 288
Abu'l-Ḥusayn Hārūn b. Yeshūʿā, I, 441
Abu'l-Ḥusayn Ibn Nufayʿ, characteristic name, II, 508
Abu'l-Ḥusayn b. Solomon, V, 544
Abu'l-Ḥusayn (Aaron b. Yeshūʿā) al-Tinnīsī, IV, 43–44
Abū Ibrahīm Ibn Barōn, V, 463, 637
Abū Ibrahīm Ismaʿīl b. Barhūn, V, 282
Abū Ibrahīm (Isḥāq) Ibn al-Sahl, V, 211, 566
Abū ʿImrān, referring to Moses Maimonides, V, 633. *See also* Moses Maimonides
Abū ʿImrān al-Bāḥir b. al-Muwaffaq, IV, 355
Abū ʿImrān Mūsā Ibn al-Majjānī, I, 162, 168–169, 232, 277, 371; V, 281
Abū ʿImrān Mūsā, merchant. *See* Mūsā b. Abi'l-Ḥayy
Abū ʿImrān al-Ṣā'igh b. Joseph, III, 482

Abū Isḥāq, *allūf* (= Abraham b. Sahlān), **II**, 614
Abū Isḥāq, silk worker, **II**, 427
Abū Isḥāq b. Abu'l-Rabīᶜ, elder, **II**, 429
Abū Isḥāq Ibrāhīm b. ᶜAlī, **I**, 444
Abū Isḥāq al-Ilbīrī, **IV**, 418
Abū Isḥāq b. Muᶜṭī, **V**, 466
Abū Isḥāq b. Ṣalḥān, **V**, 170
Abū Isḥāq b. Sayyid al-Ahl al-Abzārī, **IV**, 372
Abū Isḥāq b. Ṭībān, banker, **I**, 461; **II**, 477, 478
Abū Isḥāq b. Wāzī, **V**, 464
Abu'l-ᶜIzz, *rayyis*, **IV**, 446
Abu'l-ᶜIzz b. Abu'l-Maᶜānī, sugar merchant, **II**, 580
Abu'l-ᶜIzz al-Levi, **V**, 511
Abu'l-Jūd Tobias, physician, **V**, 458
Abū Kallabūṣ, **IV**, 357; **V**, 511
Abu'l-Karam, banker, **V**, 135
Abu'l-Karam b. Abu'l-Munā Isaac b. Judah, **I**, 363
Abu'l-Karam Nādīv ha-Levi b. Saᶜadya, **IV**, 375
Abū Kathīr. *See* Ephraim b. Shemarya
Abu'l-Khayr, government supplier, **V**, 15, 84–86, 135, 136
Abu'l-Khayr, partner in lead workshop, **I**, 363
Abu'l-Khayr ("Mr. Good"), the proselyte, **II**, 306–307, 478, 504, 592
Abu'l-Khayr Ben Nahum, **V**, 553
Abu'l-Khayr Faraḥ, **V**, 507
Abu'l-Khayr Mubārak, **V**, 377
Abu'l-Khayr b. Saadya, **III**, 464
Abu'l-Khayr Ṣedāqā Ṣamō'aḥ b. Sāsōn, **V**, 606
Abu'l-Khayr Tāhertī, *ḥāvēr*, **I**, 444; **III**, 430, 463
Abukir (Abūqīr), **I**, 323
Abu'l-Maᶜālī, *ṣayrafī*, **I**, 248
Abu'l-Maᶜālī al-Dhahabī Solomon b. Yākhīn, **V**, 543
Abu'l-Maᶜālī b. Judah, known as Ben Asad, **III**, 9, 296–297, 299, 488; **V**, 145, 268, 357–358, 545, 546, 581, 605
Abu'l-Maᶜānī, **V**, 57
Abu'l-Maḥāsin b. al-Asᶜad Abu'l-Ḥasan al-Ṣafī, **II**, 435
Abu'l-Maḥāsin Japheth b. Joshiah, physician, **II**, 580
Abu'l-Majd, milkman, **II**, 459
Abu'l-Majd Meir b. Yākhīn. *See* Abu'l-Majd *ha-Mēvīn*
Abu'l-Majd *ha-Mēvīn*, cantor, **II**, 136, 220, 420–421, 430, 461, 503, 505, 546, 548, 553, 569, 570; **III**, 475; **V**, 515, 537, 548
Abu'l-Majd Uzziel, teacher, **II**, 533, 559
Abu'l-Makārim, notable, **II**, 280
Abu'l-Makārim, *parnās*, **II**, 427
Abu'l-Makārim b. Bu'l-Ḥasan Ibn al-Kirmānī, **IV**, 375
Abu'l-Makārim Moses b. Japheth ha-Levi, **II**, 587
Abu'l-Makārim Nādīv, perfumer, **I**, 412; **II**, 422
Abu'l-Makārim b. Nissīm, **II**, 479
Abu'l-Makārim al-Sadīd b. Bu'l-Dimm al-Ṭabīb, **II**, 609
Abū Manṣūr b. Ayyūb, **III**, 505
Abū Manṣūr of Damascus, **I**, 243
Abū Manṣūr Elazar b. Yeshūᶜā ha-Levi, **III**, 278
Abū Manṣūr b. Eli, physician, **II**, 576–577
Abu'l-Manṣūr Ibn al-Muᶜallima ("Son of the Schoolmistress"), **III**, 356
Abū Manṣūr Kohen b. Qasāsā, **III**, 465, 495
Abū Manṣūr ha-Levi b. Abraham al-Dimashqī, **II**, 427
Abu'l-Manṣūr b. al-Rayyis Abu'l-Faraj, **III**, 484
Abū Manṣūr Samuel b. Hananya. *See* Samuel b. Hananya, Nagid
Abū Manṣūr Ṣemaḥ b. Japheth b. Ṭiqvā, **IV**, 318
Abū Manṣūr Tustarī, **I**, 183
Abū Manṣūr b. Zaffān, **II**, 508
Abu'l-Maᶜrūf Ṣadaqa, **III**, 504
Abū Mufaḍḍal (Moses), *rayyis*, judge and merchant, **I**, 275; **II**, 442, 477, 478, 503
Abu'l-Mufaḍḍal b. Peraḥya, **III**, 290
Abū Muḥammad ᶜAbdallah, **III**, 432
Abū Muḥammad b. Abū Rajā', vizier, **V**, 464
Abu'l-Munā, druggist, **V**, 153
Abu'l-Munā, financier, **V**, 251
Abu'l-Munā, kunya, **II**, 457, 582
Abu'l-Munā, the *ghulām*, **I**, 132
Abu'l-Munā, sheikh. *See* Tiqwa b. Amram
Abu'l-Munā b. Dā'ūd. *See* Yeshūᶜā b. Jacob
Abu'l-Munā b. Sābiq, **III**, 502
Abu'l-Munā Isaac b. Judah, **I**, 363
Abu'l-Munā Jacob b. David, **II**, 262
Abu'l-Munajjā Kohen (al-Zārīz), **II**, 423
Abu'l-Munajjā Solomon b. Saadya, **III**, 482
Abu'l-Munajjā Solomon b. Ṣedāqā, **I**, 462; **V**, 149
Abu'l-Munajjā Solomon b. Shaᶜya, **II**, 356, 358, 377, 604; **III**, 10, 11; **IV**, 436; **V**, 566

Abū Munajjā b. Abū Sahl Thiqat al-Mulk, **II**, 356–357; **IV**, 237; **V**, 212, 257
Abu'l-Munā al-Kohen al-ʿAṭṭār, **II**, 265
Abu'l-Munā al-Kohen Ibn Jāzuliyya, **II**, 482
Abu'l-Munē Yaʿqūb b. Banīn, **II**, 561
Abū Mūsā Hārūn b. al-Muʿallim Yaʿqūb, **IV**, 438; **V**, 574, 598
Abūn, **I**, 407
Abūn b. Ṣadaqa (Ṣedāqā) al-Maghribī, **I**, 292; **III**, 476, 484; **IV**, 446; **V**, 52, 303–304, 519, 572, 574, 596, 623
Abū Najāḥ. *See* "Monk, The"
Abu'l-Najm, physician, **II**, 502
Abu'l-Najm, *rayyis*, **II**, 459
Abu'l-Najm Hilāl, **V**, 158
Abū Naṣr, the banker, **I**, 246
Abū Naṣr b. Abraham, **I**, 455; **II**, 587; **III**, 480; **V**, 573, 635
Abū Naṣr of Aleppo, merchant, and wife, **V**, 152–155
Abū Naṣr of Alexandria, **II**, 304
Abū Naṣr Elazar b. Abraham b. Elisha, **I**, 366
Abū Naṣr b. Elisha, **V**, 575
Abū Naṣr Joseph b. Ḥasan, **III**, 505
Abū Naṣr Judah, of Damascus, **V**, 126
Abū Naṣr ha-Kohen Ibn al-Kāmukhī, **III**, 351
Abū Naṣr b. Mevōrākh, **III**, 443
Abū Naṣr b. Mukhtār, *ṣaydanī*, **II**, 581
Abū Naṣr Musāfir, **I**, 407
Abū Naṣr Ibn Ṣaghīr, **III**, 290
Abū Naṣr b. Sahl Tustarī, **III**, 456, 497; **V**, 534
Abū Naṣr Salāma b. Saʿīd Ibn Nufayʿ, **V**, 125
Abū Naṣr Samuel, **II**, 492; **V**, 516
Abū Naṣr b. Shālōm *he-ḥāvēr*, **II**, 456
Abū Naṣr Tustarī, **I**, 183, 372, 387, 451; **II**, 441, 454, 473; **III**, 45, 56, 136; **IV**, 265, 438, 448; **V**, 241, 280–281, 367, 370, 454, 455, 460, 461
abū qandalāt. See *būqandalāt*
Abu'l-Qāsim, *mutawalli sikka*, **II**, 605
Abu'l-Qāsim ʿAbd al-Raḥmān, **II**, 590; **V**, 191
Abu'l-Qāsim al-Ḥalabī, sharif, **V**, 444
Abu'l-Qāsim's Ḥikāya, **IV**, 112, 113
Abu'l-Rabīʿ Solomon b. Joseph Ibn Gabbay. *See* Abraham the Pious
Abū Riḍā (Rādā), Karaite, **V**, 6009
Abū Riḍā, physician, **V**, 105
Abu'l-Riḍā, cantor, **II**, 463
Abu'l-Riḍā, the *shōmēr*, **I**, 363
Abu'l-Riḍā b. Berākhōt Ibn al-Lebdī, **I**, 367
Abu'l-Riḍā b. Judah *he-ḥāvēr*, blind man, **II**, 553
Abu'l-Riḍā Yiḥyē b. Samuel, son-in-law of the Nagid Abraham Maimuni, **I**, 367
Abu'l-Riẓā b. al-Ṣadr, *al-tājir al-Baghdādī*, **I**, 437
Abū (Bū) Saʿd. *See* Moses b. Nethanel ha-Levi
Abū Saʿd, physician, **V**, 271
Abū Saʿd, son of Wuḥsha, **III**, 349, 350, 352
Abū Saʿd b. Abu'l-Ḥusayn, **IV**, 289
Abū Saʿd b. Ḥātim, *parnās*, **II**, 416, 426, 434
Abū Saʿd Hibat Allah = Nethanel *Rōsh ha-qāhāl*, **II**, 611
Abū Saʿd Isḥāq b. Khalaf b. ʿAllūn, **II**, 610
Abū Saʿd Khalaf b. Salāma. *See* Ḥalfōn b. Solomon
Abū Saʿd Rayyis, **III**, 74
Abū Saʿd (Ibn Ṭayyib), cantor, **II**, 431
Abū Saʿd al-Tustarī, **I**, 165, 183, 347, 372, 416; **II**, 30, 351, 352, 374, 441, 473; **III**, 56, 135, 137, 357, 455; **IV**, 187; **V**, 98, 109, 300, 367
Abū Saʿd al-Zaylūsī, **II**, 477
Abū Sahl, banker, **V**, 168, 554
Abū Sahl ʿAṭā', **V**, 597
Abū Sahl ʿĒzer b. ʿAlī, **I**, 444
Abū Sahl b. Ibrāhīm, **III**, 479
Abū Sahl Ibn Kammūna, **III**, 13; **V**, 400
Abū Sahl ha-Levi b. *al-āhūv*, cantor, **II**, 433, 460, 466, 569; **V**, 87, 530
Abū Sahl Manasse b. David, **IV**, 410; **V**, 537, 584
Abū Sahl Manasse b. Eli ha-Levi, **I**, 363
Abū Sahl b. Moses. *See* Abū Sahl ha-Levi b. *al-āhūv*
Abū Saʿīd b. Abū Naṣr b. Isaiah, **II**, 545; **V**, 610
Abū Saʿīd al-ʿAfṣī, **IV**, 442, 448
Abū Saʿīd Dā'ūd Ben Shaʿyā, **III**, 428
Abū Saʿīd b. Ghulayb, **II**, 479
Abū Saʿīd Khalaf, **II**, 590
Abū Saʿīd Ḥalfōn ha-Kohen b. Joseph, **III**, 351
Abū Saʿīd Makhlūf, **IV**, 413
Abū Saʿīd Ḥalfōn b. Manasse, cantor and clerk, **II**, 445, 447
Abū Saʿīd b. Naḥmān, **III**, 489
Abū Saʿīd b. Thābit, **IV**, 289
Abū Sargah church, **II**, 145; **IV**, 355
Abu 'Sḥāq (Abraham) of Aden, **II**, 419
Abū Sḥāq (Abraham), teacher, **II**, 451
Abū sijill (one with a document), a nickname, **II**, 479; **IV**, 434

Abū Ṣīr. *See* Būṣīr
Abū Sulaymān, III, 428
Abū Sulaymān, banker, V, 168
Abū Sulaymān b. Nuʿmān, V, 225–226, 569
Abuʾl-Surūr, V, 154
Abuʾl-Surūr, Son of ʿAṭiyya, V, 159
Abuʾl-Surūr, perfumer, IV, 321, 449
Abuʾl-Surūr, *shōmēr*, II, 448
Abuʾl-Surūr b. David, III, 482
Abuʾl-Surūr Ibn al-Qābisī, III, 442
Abū Surūr Isaac Tāhertī, I, 444
Abuʾl-Surūr ha-Levi Ibn al-Zakkār, II, 428
Abuʾl-Surūr b. Sighmār, IV, 429
Abuʾl-Surūr b. Ṭarīf, II, 481
Abuʾl-Surūr Yūshaʿ b. Nathan, II, 560
Abuʾl-Ṭāhir, V, 169, 171
Abuʾl-Ṭāhir b. Maḥfūẓ, beadle, II, 421, 431, 540; IV, 436; V, 547
Abuʾl-Ṭāhir Mevōrākh b. Shēlā *al-mūrid*, III, 483
Abuʾl-Ṭāhir b. Rajā, qadi and business agent, I, 446; II, 295, 367
Abū Ṭarib, III, 93
Abū Thābit b. al-Rayyis, V, 553
Abuʾl-Thanāʾ, physician, II, 578
Abuʾl-Thanā b. Abū Saʿd, banker, II, 431
Abuʾl-Wafā, V, 85, 529
Abū Yaḥyā. *See* Nahray b. Nissīm
Abū Yaʿqūb, V, 111
Abū Yaʿqūb, V, 210
Abū Yaʿqūb b. Ezrah, merchant, V, 466
Abū Yaʿqūb al-Ḥakīm, representative of merchants, I, 447; II, 498, 503, 507; V, 144, 145. *See also* Yekuthiel b. Moses *ha-rōfē*
Abū Yaʿqūb Ibrāhīm, II, 520
Abū Yaʿqūb Joseph of Ben Nahum family, and wife, V, 167–173, 553
Abū Yaʿqūb Joseph b. Solomon, II, 539
Abū Yaʿqūb Ibn Shāma, I, 322
Abū Yaʿqūb ʿUqbān, V, 566
Abuʾl-Yumn al-Shammās (the deacon), mason, II, 434
Abū Yūsuf Yaʿqūb Ibn Shaʿyā, III, 428
Abū Zikrī b. Elijah, physician, II, 318, 380, 462, 492; III, 30, 207, 435, 480, 494; V, 174–179, 243, 246, 257, 300, 394, 515, 540, 554, 556, 561
Abū Zikrī Ḥayyīm b. (ʿAmmār) Madīnī (of Palermo), II, 476
Abū Zikrī Judah b. Joseph ha-Kohen Sijilmāsī, I, 192, 241, 357, 380; II, 271, 479; III, 58, 282; IV, 189, 196 239, 250, 257, 369, 384, 416, 443, 444; V, 59, 240, 248, 252, 280, 576, 596
Abū Zikrī Judah b. Manasse b. David, II, 478; III, 288
Abū Zikrī Kohen. *See* Abū Zikrī Judah b. Joseph ha-Kohen Sijilmāsī
Abū Zikrī Ibn Qayyōmā, V, 293
Abū Zikrī Ibn Sighmār. *See* Judah b. Moses Ibn Sighmār
Abū Zikrī al-Ṭabīb, I, 447
Abū Zikrī Yaḥyā b. Manasse, II, 476, 479; V, 233
Abū Zikrī Yaḥyā Zuṭṭā, II, 528
Abū Zikrī Yiḥye b. Mevōrākh, V, 286–287, 562
Abyār (Ibyār), Egypt, III, 388; IV, 167, 350, 401, 403
Abyssinian, I, 138, 139, 386
abzārī, distributor of seeds, I, 438, 448; II, 427, 474
Acacia trees, II, 436
Academies, Jewish. *See* Gaon, Yeshiva
Account(s-books), I, 23, 152, 162, 166, 172, 182, 184, 197, 204–209, 216, 223, 225, 226, 231, 236, 239, 259, 355, 369, 372, 374, 381; II, 102, 135, 337, 413–437, 438–469, 543
Acknowledgment of debts (*iqrār, hōdāʾā*) I, 250; of a purchase, II, 334, 600. See also *ḥujja*
Acorns, I, 155; II, 454
Acquittance (Aram., *sheṭār avīzārya*; *ibrāʾ*), II, 600
Acre (Akko), Palestine, I, 54, 109, 127, 275, 278, 291, 293, 326, 427; III, 61, 151, 280; beneficiaries of community chest from, II, 440, 441, 442, 444, 447, 467; contributions to charity, II, 29, 202, 360, 496, 569; courts of, II, 567; communal jurisdiction, II, 330; family life, III, 196, 197, 340; ms. from, II, 526, 555, 588; III, 489; not considered part of Holy Land, V, 555; occupation by Crusaders, I, 45, 132; II, 88, 282; III, 238, 286; IV, 42, 261; port of, I, 212–213; synagogues in, II, 157, 167; taken by Mamluks, II, 393
adā, customs (paid), I, 489
adam, taking something as food additional to bread, II, 126
Adams, Robert McC., V, 630
ʿadat ēl (Heb.), assembly of God, II, 530
ʿAdāya b. Peraḥyā, IV, 427
Addresses of letters, IV, 42
Aden, South Arabia, I, 48, 51, 59, 429; III, 56, 58, 241, 431; IV, 1, 206, 384, 447; V, 514; application to Muslim authorities in, II, 405; Arabic dialect spoken in, I, 16; climate, I, 8; clothing in, IV, 166, 169, 197, 417; disrespect for Gaon's prerogatives in, II, 405; exports from, I, 100; IV, 124, 129, 134,

145, 146, 147, 149, 169, 377, 393, 403, 442; foreigner from in Cairo, **II**, 419; houses in, **IV**, 276, 370; letters to/from, **I**, 274; **II**, 70; **III**, 246; **V**, 50, 52, 67–69; medical examination of passengers arriving from India in, **I**, 351; merchants in, **I**, 7, 45, 182, 189, 335, 336, 424, 426; **II**, 26, 95, 270, 275, 323, 523, 542, 572; **III**, 55, 61, 137, 264, 482, 485; **IV**, 147, 149, 169, 257, 394; public prayers in, **II**, 21; query addressed to religious authorities in Fustat from, **I**, 421; rabbinical court of, **II**, 331; value of currency in, **IV**, 379, 404, 413
ʿadl. *See* Notary
Adler, Elkan N., **I**, 3, 4, 17, 24, 129, 395; **V**, 519
E. N. Adler Collection, New York, **III**, 96
Administration, medieval, **II**, 101, 102, 115, 117
Administration of communal property, **II**, 417, 432, 433, 543, 603
Administrator of the mosques of Cairo, **II**, 102, 543
Administrator of pious foundations, **II**, 103, 115; notes of, **II**, 93
Adoption, **III**, 248–249
"Adornments" (term for jewelry), **IV**, 201
Adult education, **II**, 192–195
Adultery, **V**, 314
Adversity: attitudes toward, **V**, 48–49, 51–53, 62–63, 72–73, 241–242, 244–245; conventions for writing about, **V**, 46–48, 51–52, 234, 236–237; God's role, **V**, 49, 52, 62–63, 326–327; and wills, **V**, 133. *See also* Death; Epidemics; Illness; Political turmoil
Aegean Sea, **IV**, 455
ʿAfāf, slave girl, **III**, 354
al-Afḍal, Fatimid vizier, **IV**, 72, 123, 183, 237, 371, 412
"Affairs with women," **III**, 83
Afghanistan, **I**, 187, 283
ʿAfīf b. Ezra, physician, **V**, 86
afīthīmūn, (Ar.-Gr.) dodder of thyme, **I**, 47; **II**, 583
afshaʿ (Ar.-Heb.), Jew who renounces faith, **II**, 300; **V**, 521. See also *pāshaʿ*
ʿafṣī, distributor of gallnuts, **I**, 438; **V**, 519
Age groups, **II**, 61–65
Age at marriage, **III**, 77, 78, 131, 141, 163, 186, 199
Aging. *See* Old age
Agriculture, **I**, 116–126, 265; **V**, 70–71
ʿagūnā (Heb., woman neither divorced nor widowed). *See* Widow, grass
aḥbālī (ropemaker), **I**, 106, 419
aḥbās al-yahūd. *See* Pious foundations
aḥdāth. *See* Young men
Aḥimaʿaṣ chronicle, **II**, 524, 575
ahl (wife), **III**, 160, 425, 461
ahliyya, **III**, 432
Aḥmad Amīn, **IV**, 175
Aḥmad al-Badawī, **V**, 19, 508
Aḥmad b. Ṭūlūn, **II**, 148; **V**, 558
"Aḥmad the wine seller," **IV**, 254
al-Aḥnaf, Arab chieftain, **IV**, 43
Ahnasiyya district, **II**, 539
aḥram (Ar.-Heb.), to ban or excommunicate, **II**, 599. *See also* Excommunication
aḥrār (blameless, lit. "free") **III**, 438
al-āhūv (Heb., "Friend [of the Yeshiva]"), **II**, 569
al-Ahwāz, **I**, 164–165, 181, 400; **III**, 289, 491; **IV**, 417
ʿāʾila, dependents, household, **III**, 425
ʿAʾisha, wife of Muhammad the Prophet, **V**, 561, 592
ʿāj. *See* Ivory
ajal (fixed end), **V**, 130–131
al-ʿAjamī, **I**, 400
ajīr (journeyman), **I**, 93
akhbār, information, police or business intelligence, **I**, 201, 271; **V**, 50, 53–54
Akhmīm, **I**, 298; **IV**, 349
Akkadian, **I**, 149, 230
ʿAkkāwī, family name from Akko, Palestine, **V**, 519
Akko. *See* Acre
akolythos (Gr., no objection), **II**, 328
Alabaster, **IV**, 146
al-ʾab rabb ("The father is the lord," Ar. maxim), **III**, 79
ʿalaltā (Aram., dowry), **III**, 453
ʿAlam al-Dawla ("Banner of the Dynasty"), **II**, 113
ʿAlam b. Maḥfūẓ, **III**, 502
ʿalāma (trademark, sign), **I**, 81; **II**, 578
aʿlāq (precious items), **I**, 101; **IV**, 201. *See also* Jewelry
ālātī. *See* Musicians
ʿAlam Ibn al-ʿUdī ("The Luminary, son of the dealer in odoriferous wood"), characteristic name, **II**, 503
Alchemists, Street of, **I**, 83
Aleppo, **I**, 20, 36, 60, 71, 129, 192, 276, 281, 291; **II**, 81, 204, 213, 535; **III**, 4, 61, 177, 306, 450, 489; **IV**, 427, 440; **V**, 433, 514; age groups in, **II**, 61; anti-semitism in, **II**, 587; architecture and

real estate in, IV, 56, 277; beneficiaries of community chest from, II, 441, 444, 447, 454, 467; as capital city, IV, 6; clothing from, IV, 170; communal officials in/from, I, 54, 271; II, 19; converts in, III, 11; donors from, II, 477, 496; family life, III, 262, 280, 288, 289, 440, 485; foreigners from, in Egypt, I, 54; II, 153, 167; IV, 45; Islamic urbanism of, IV, 3; Jewish judges in, II, 76, 509, 515; III, 29, 461; IV, 433; letters to, II, 41; IV, 245, 398; mail service, I, 294; marriage documents from, III, 98, 111, 112, 375, 379, 395, 408, 416, 438, 440; IV, 217, 429; ms. from, II, 530; merchants in, I, 69, 178, 190, 348, 416; Muslim militia in, II, 370, 608; scholars from, II, 205; spiritual leader of, II, 564; synagogues in, I, 17; II, 6, 413, 520. *See also* Ḥalabī, Ibn al-Ḥulaybī

Aleppo robe, IV, 170; V, 524

Alexandria, *passim*; synagogues in, II, 6, 54, 56, 57, 59, 77, 146, 154, 213, 217; burial in, V, 144–145, 156–157; Crusader invasion, V, 55–56; differences from Cairo, V, 82, 249; education in, V, 418; epidemics in, V, 113; hospitality in, V, 29–30, 32; Karaites in, V, 365; moral standards in, V, 249, 314; taxes on non-Muslims, V, 460; textile industry in, V, 520; troubles in, V, 50–51, 56–57, 104, 422–423

Alexius I Comnenus, I, 39; IV, 244

Alfa mats, II, 267

Algeria, I, xvii, 31, 42, 43, 64, 212, 276, 308; II, 106, 188, 559; IV, 453

Algiers (al-Jazāʾir), IV, 455

Alhambra of Granada, I, 265

ʿAlī b. Aḥmad, I, 293

ʿAlī b. Ḥassān b. Maʿālī al-Ṭarābulusī, II, 102

ʿAlī b. Ḥazqīl. *See* Eli ha-Kohen I b. Ezekiel I

ʿAlī b. Sulaymān, I, 444; III, 427

Alids, II, 19

Alimony, II, 36, 81, 544, 615; III, 83, 114, 190, 191, 199, 200, 233, 258, 268, 271, 295, 299; IV, 334, 461

ʿaliyyā (Heb., elite), I, 409

Alkali, I, 154

Alkaloid plants, IV, 140

ʿAllān b. Ḥassūn, III, 193–194; V, 221–222, 568, 573

ʿAllān b. Ibrahīm, V, 315

ʿAllān b. Nahum, V, 315

Alliance Israelite Universelle, I, 5

Allony (Alloni), Nehemia, I, 4; IV, 289; V, 386

allūf (Heb.), II, 22, 199, 536, 614

ʿAllūn b. Maʿmar. *See* Eli b. Amram

ʿAllūn b. Yaʿīsh, *parnās*. *See* Eli ha-Kohen b. Yaḥyā

ʿAllūsh b. Yeshūʿā, III, 481; V, 536

almemar ("platform"), Jewish pronounciation of *al-minbar*, II, 147

almenūt ḥayyūt (Heb., grass widow), III, 469. *See also* Widow, grass

Almeria, Spain, I, 61, 62, 64, 210, 212, 213, 215, 218, 285, 288, 302, 305, 310, 313, 325, 334, 344, 477; II, 278; IV, 169, 192, 403, 405, 408, 415

Almohads, I, 32, 40, 41, 51, 57, 65, 308; II, 300, 302, 404, 480, 591; V, 59–62, 70, 521, 522, 524, 556, 621

Almonds, I, 83, 121, 195; IV, 246, 247, 429; shelled, I, 190, 210

Almonds and raisins, recommended by Maimonides, IV, 247

Almoners, II, 102, 105, 543

Almoravids, I, 40, 41, 61, 340; II, 293; V, 59–60, 521, 524. *See also* Murābiṭ

Alms, II, 503

Alms box, II, 106

Aloe, an odoriferous wood, I, 154; IV, 389

alqāb. *See* Honorific titles

Altmann, Alexander, V, 452

Alum (potash), I, 45, 154, 334, 471; IV, 405

ʿalw (upper floor of a house), IV, 63, 70–73, 367. See also *ʿulūw* (pl.)

alwāḥ mushattiya (winterly bottoms), ships arriving in winter, I, 481

ʿAmāʾim ("[Ruler over] the turbans," i. e. the men), a woman, III, 105, 112, 187

ʿamal (work, i.e. government service), II, 355, 604

āmālaka (Sanskrit), myrobalan, emblic, II, 464, 583. *See also* Myrobalan

Amalfi (-ans), I, 40, 46, 59, 211, 214, 325, 326, 329; IV, 27, 58

Amalric, Frankish king of Jerusalem, V, 54, 604

ʿamal al-rīf, II, 531

amāra, circumstantial evidence, II, 337, 601

Amari, Michele, I, 102

Amat al-ʿAzīz, f., III, 136, 497

Amat al-Qādir, "Maidservant of the Almighty," III, 253, 330, 482, 497

Amat al-Wāḥid, III, 497

ʿambarī, dealer in ambergris, I, 438

Amber, IV, 148, 207-208, 217-221, 319, 322, 327, 383, 385, 421, 428, 455, 465; as color, IV, 126, 130; V, 523
Amber neckband, *ʿanbarīniyya*. *See* Amber
Ambergris, I, 153, 154, 155, 200; II, 78; IV, 401
ambon(e) (Lat.-Gr.-Coptic), Coptic reader's platform, II, 146-147, 149, 550. See also *anbōl*
Āmid, Iraq, II, 441, 467; IV, 146. *See also* Diyarbakir
al-ʿAmīd b. Kushik, II, 609
ʿAmīd al-Dawla ("Support of the Government"), II, 355, 376; III, 7, 428
āmidī, variety of cloth, I, 50, 153
ʿāmil, director of revenue, I, 267; II, 298, 361, 377, 378, 392, 605, 610; IV, 349, 435
Amīn al-Dawla ("Trustee of the Dynasty"), II, 113, 356, 376, 479, 531, 587, 609; V, 14
Amīn al-Mulk ("Trustee of the Government"), II, 514, 587; V, 14
amīr, I, 310; II, 63, 368, 378, 423, 428, 525; IV, 40. *See also* Governor
al-Āmir, Fatimid caliph, II, 520; IV, 183
Amīr al-Juyūsh, viceroy, II, 606. *See also* Badr al-Jamālī
ʿĀmir Ibn al-Ramlī, I, 472
al-Amjad, son of Sultan Saladin, V, 178, 556
amlaj. See *āmālakā*
Amlaj, name of an official, II, 464
ʿāmmāl, "working," employed, I, 38, 93; II, 438
ʿAmmān, I, 49, 54, 403; II, 442
ʿAmmānī family, Alexandria, II, 36, 221, 245, 576; IV, 443; V, 39, 490
ʿAmmār (*maḥras*), IV, 34, 368
ʿAmmār, son of the Head of the Congregation, I, 461
ʿAmmār b. Joseph, I, 362
ʿAmmār b. Makhlūf, III, 290
Amnon, biblical, V, 583
amōrā(s) (Aram.), II, 562; IV, 192. *See also* Broadcaster
Amram, *Nafīs*, II, 609
Amram, *shōfēṭ*, II, 596
Amram b. Elijah ha-Kohen, V, 438
Amram b. Ezra, II, 538; III, 347
Amram Gaon, II, 564; V, 540, 600
Amram b. Ḥalfōn ha-Levi, II, 431
Amram b. Isaac, V, 105, 119, 454
Amram b. Joseph, V, 540
Amram ha-Kohen b. Abuʾl-Majd Ibn al-Ṣanānīrī, V, 543
Amram b. Saʿīd Mūsā, V, 315-316
amshāṭī (comb maker), I, 416; II, 498; as family name, IV, 225; V, 86
Āmul, I, 61, 281, 400
Amulet (*maymūn*), IV, 204, 207, 218, 319, 322, 327, 329, 427, 453
ʿĀna, V, 432-433
ʿĀnān, founder of Karaism, V, 608
ʿAnān, leader of local Karaites, II, 47
ʿAnānī (Karaite), IV, 14, 351
Anatoli of Marseilles, French rabbi, I, 53, 67; II, 71, 125, 430, 466, 515, 537, 567; III, 209, 462, 470; IV, 239, 437
ʿanbariyya, chain of pieces of amber, V, 523. *See also* Amber
anbōl (Judeo-Arabic), elevated platform, II, 146, 147, 151, 177, 550, 551. See also *almemar*; *migdāl*; *al-minbar*
Ancestors and agnates, honoring of, III, 2-47; worship, III, 15
Ancient Near East(ern), III, 264, 271, 293
Andalus (-ians). *See* Spain, Spanish
Andalusī ("Native of Muslim Spain"), I, 20, 21, 50; III, 14, 293
Andreas, II, 309
Anemones (*shaqāʾiq*), IV, 209
Angels, invocations of, V, 336-337
al-ʿĀnī family, III, 28
ʿaniyyīm (Heb., the poor), II, 142, 466. *See also* Poor; Poverty
Anklet, IV, 200, 201, 221-222, 418, 429
anmāṭ. *See* Carpets
Anmāṭī (carpet dealer), IV, 123, 124, 382
Anna Comnena, IV, 244
anṣār (helpers), II, 62
ʿanṣara. *See* Pentecost
Anṣārī, I, 292-294
anshē ha-kenēsā, II, 531
anshē Torah (Heb.), II, 565. See also *baʿale Torah*; *benē Torah*
Anṭalya (Adalia), I, 214
ʿAntara, II, 120
Antimony, I, 154, 155, 197, 334
Antioch, I, 38, 178; II, 507; IV, 6
"Anti-Semitism," II, 278-283, 586-589
Antiquity, IV, 137, 159, 164, 172
antlia (Aram.-Gr., water penetrating into a ship and the pump used to draw it out), I, 483
Antonin, Archimandrite, I, 3
Antoun, Richard L., III, 27
ʿanzarūt (Sarcocolla), V, 543
Apartments, II, 414, 424, 427, 428, 429, 430, 431, 432, 545; III, 459; IV, 59, 367
Apocalyptic movements, V, 397-398
Apostasy (*pishʿūth*), II, 300, 591. *See also* Conversion

Apothecaries. *See* Druggists
apotropā (Heb.-Gr.), representative, I, 463
Appeals: to higher authority, II, 339, 471–510, 492, 544, 613; III, 77, 305, 339; individual to community, II, 107, 169–170, 323–325; public, 12, 78; II, 44, 46, 49, 53, 96, 97, 106–109, 169
Appelt, Heinrich, IV, 270
Apples, I, 121, 151; IV, 209, 217, 232; shape in jewelry, IV, 422, 432, 440
Apprenticing, II, 560; III, 25, 218, 237
Apricot (color), IV, 175, 323
ʿaqabiyya, IV, 315, 451
Aqavya b. Mahalalel, V, 623
aqdas (Judeo-Ar., to dedicate to a pious purpose), II, 99, 542. *See also* Pious foundations
aqfālī. *See* Locksmiths
Aqiba, Rabbi, V, 624; wife of, III, 322
ʿaqīd (curds, coagulated milk), II, 271
ʿaqīqa, IV, 423
aqnā (Judeo-Ar., to confer a right), II, 329, 600
ʿaqqāda (female lacemaker), I, 430
ʿAqrabā, I, 192
al-ʿAqrabānī, Ezekiel b. Masʿūd, I, 192
aqrāq. *See* Cork shoes
aqṭāʿ = *qaṭāʿī* (galleys), I, 473
Aquinas, Saint Thomas, V, 407
Āqul, Iraq, II, 441
Arab (-ia, -ians, -s), I, 30, 72, 73, 111, 131, 282; II, 6, 8, 11, 22, 259, 281, 310, 341, 355; III, 7, 8, 15, 36; IV, 45. 307; genealogies, III, 7, 8; pre-Islamic, III, 21, 315
Arabian Nights, II, 68, 85, 190, 229, 257, 302, 318, 342, 572, 580, 592; III, 162, 185, 344; V, 43, 200
Arabic characters, II, 430, 433, 438, 450, 453, 466, 467, 468, 490, 492, 494, 497, 499, 503, 504, 506, 508, 520, 523, 536, 555, 558, 568, 572, 583, 589, 602. *See also* Script: Arabic
Arabic language, I, 14–15, 16, 19, 22, 26, 52, 64, 67, 113, 160, 210, 230, 250, 282, 296, 304, 305; II, 176, 182, 190, 195, 202, 206, 207, 210, 218, 220, 235, 242, 243, 248, 249, 251, 277, 283, 303, 320, 341, 350, 352; III, 16, 25, 32, 65, 75, 103, 133, 145, 156, 189, 193, 204, 209, 249, 257, 267, 292, 319, 350; V, 299, 360, 384, 429. *See also* Middle Arabic; Script: Arabic
Arabic literature: derivation of, V, 388; drinking in, V, 39; envy in, V, 300; fortune in, V, 329; friendship in, V, 275–276, 279, 283-284, 286, 294; influence on Hebrew, V, 286, 424–425; narrative styles, V, 215; "Relief after hardship," V, 53; sexuality in, V, 308, 317–318; See also *Arabian Nights*; Poetry
Arabic names, II, 130, 237, 315
Arabic numerals, I, 209; II, 178
Arabic papyri. *See* Papyri, Arabic
Arabization, I, 41
ʿarabūn (prepayment in full), I, 199
Āraḥ b. Nathan. *See* Musāfir b. Wahb
Aramean = non-Jew, II, 586
Aramaic, I, 15, 230, 241, 250, 282, 301, 349, 435; II, 158, 164, 175, 176, 195, 206, 320, 520, 533, 539, 555; III, 22, 25, 52, 125, 132, 264, 293; IV, 50, 78, 105, 117, 150, 193, 304, 311, 459
Arbitration, board of, II, 339
archi-synagogos (Gr.), II, 76
Architecture, domestic. *See* Domestic architecture
Architectural terms of foreign origin, IV, 78
Archives, I, 1, 7–9; II, 343, 344
ʿarḍ (flax), I, 188. *See also* Flax
ʿarḍī (broad shawl), II, 529; IV, 152, 196, 416, 417, 462, 463
ʿārēl (Heb., uncircumcised, i.e. Christian), II, 278, 586. *See also* Christians; *naṣrānī*
ʿarīf. *See* Head of a profession
ʿarīf al-naqqādīn (Head of the assayers of money), I, 250. See also *naqqād*
Aristophanes, V, 593
Aristotelianism, V, 450. *See also* Greek philosophy
Arithmetic, II, 177, 178
ʿāriya (borrowing), I, 463
arjawānī. *See* Purple dye(r)
Arjīsh (town in Armenia), IV, 412
Arjīshī robe, IV, 182
Ark(s), holy, IV, 124, 136
Arles, I, 40; II, 95, 542
armala. *See* Widows
armay (Aram., Aramean, i.e. non-Jew), II, 586
Armenia(ns), I, 100; IV, 119, 123, 126, 197. 306; Little, I, 67
Armenian stone, II, 267, 583; IV, 422
Armlet: *miʿḍada*, worn on the upper arm, IV, 203, 220, 419, 428; *shāhid*, IV, 220, 428
armōn (Heb.), II, 604
Arms, manufacture and sale of, I, 109, 211
Army, I, 72; II, 610; food for, IV, 252
Arrajān(ī), I, 244, 400
arrhabōn (Gr.), I, 199

Arrears, II, 392, 414, 423, 424, 428, 450, 462, 548
Arrest, for non-payment of poll tax, II, 612
Arsenev, I, 3
Arsenic, I, 154
"Arsenic," slave girl, I, 137, 140
Art, Islamic, IV, 111
Artisans, II, 2, 113, 179, 191, 296, 297, 394. See also *ṣāniʿ*
ʿarūs (betrothed), III, 90
ʿArūs b. Joseph, Abuʾl-Afrāḥ (al-Mahdawī), I, 194, 207, 208, 243, 260, 340–342, 344, 357, 457, 459; II, 613; III, 25, 230, 233, 252, 253, 475, 482; IV, 44, 236, 355, 373, 405, 421; V, 221, 523, 568
Arye b. Judah, III, 177, 347
ʿasā (please), II, 579
ʿaṣabiyya (dedicated following, esprit de corps), II, 64
Al-Asʿad, money changer, II, 428
Al-Asʿad, physician, II, 485; V, 582
Asad b. Manṣūr b. Asad, III, 9, 497
Asʿad (al-dīn) Yaʿqūb b. Isḥāq al-Maḥallī, III, 465; V, 271, 272
ʿaṣāʾib wa-rafāʾid, IV, 386
ʿasalī. See *ʿassāl*
aṣbāghī (seller of "paints"), I, 155
Ascalon, Palestine, I, 37, 381, 461; III, 198, 340, 481; IV, 180, 193, 218, 403, 409, 445; communal officials in, II, 77, 78, 81, 214, 528, 538, 565, 566, 568; III, 24; communal strife in, II, 536; community chest, II, 416, 543; IV, 94; Crusaders in, I, 35, 36, 259; II, 500; flax prices in, I, 197; foreigners from, in Egypt, II, 441, 442, 451, 555; IV, 10; foreigners in, II, 167; IV, 45; Jewish community of, II, 530; Jewish judges in, II, 320, 596; letters from, I, 197, 333; II, 384, 523; III, 75, 503; V, 47, 54; mail service, I, 290, 293, 294; as maritime city, I, 45, 212, 316, 317, 320, 326; II, 43; IV, 193, 304; marriages in/of people from, III, 75, 76, 262, 351; IV, 218; merchants in, I, 132, 239, 268, 333; Muslim officials in, II, 348, 366, 605; ransoming of captives in, III, 356; scholars from, II, 88, 384; synagogues in, II, 18, 146
"Ascetic, The," title of prominent woman donor, II, 99, 542
Ascetic, ascesticism II, 7, 99, 542; IV, 41
ʿaṣfur (safflower), I, 120, 427
ʿashāʾ. *See* Meal, evening
aṣḥāb al-akhbār (government secret service), I, 271
aṣḥāb al-ḥaḍar (townspeople), IV, 364
aṣḥāb al-khilaʿ (ruler's entourage), II, 351
aṣḥāb al-kutub (couriers of letters), I, 284
aṣḥāb al-shawānī (pirates, raiders), I, 477
Asher, a proselyte, II, 307
ʿashīra (clan, tribe), III, 425
Ashkenaz, European Christians, V, 612
Ashmūm (Ṭanāḥ), I, 385, 468; II, 49, 468; III, 488; IV, 350, 414, 445; V, 513
Ashmūnayn, I, 243; IV, 402, 446. *See also* Ushmūn
ʿashshī (dinner cook), I, 115, 424
Ashtor, E., I, 94–95, 407–408, 453; IV, 25, 273; V, 8
Ashū, slave girl, II, 20
ashyāf (eyepowder), II, 585
Asia Minor, I, 38, 58, 124; II, 40, 147, 441, 447; III, 120, 121
ʿaṣīda (paste), IV, 248
aṣīlā (Heb., "of noble descent," attribute of bride), III, 103
ʿāṣir, I, 428. See also *ʿaṣṣār*
ʿaskar. *See* Bay window
al-ʿAskar, suburb, IV, 54
aṣl ("root," original copy of an account), I, 206, 209, 452
asmā (to pledge), II, 495, 544. *See also* Pledges
Asparagus, IV, 232, 261, 433, 447; as color, IV, 174
Assaf, Simha, I, 25, 26; II, 306; III, 96
ʿassāl. *See* Honey, seller of
ʿaṣṣār (operator of oil or wine press), I, 92, 428
ʿAṣṣār family, III, 500
Assassination attempt, IV, 136
Assassins, terrorist sect, IV, 25
Assimilation, V, 272, 390. *See also* Conversion; Muslims
Assyrian, IV, 152
Astrologer (*munajjim*), Astrology, II, 464; III, 233; V, 28, 292, 329, 330, 332, 420–422; female (*munajjima*), I, 430; V, 625. See also *ḥukm*
Astronomy, V, 383, 420
Aswan, Egypt, I, 244; II, 383; III, 8, 83, 137, 142, 426; IV, 241, 438
aswira. *See* Bracelets
Asyūṭ, IV, 439
ʿAṭā (Nathan), II, 24
ʿataba (threshold, "bridge"), type of mat, IV, 126, 128, 383, 384
ʿatal (levers), III, 468
aṭbāq (flat lamps), II, 150
ʿateret ha-sōferīm (Heb., "Pride of the Officials"), II, 532
Atfīḥ, Egypt, II, 310, 359, 594, 606
Athaliah, biblical queen, V, 637

Athārib, near Aleppo, Syria, V, 605
Athens, III, 168
ʿatīq. *See* Freedmen
ʿAṭiyya's house, II, 452
Atonement for sins, V, 48–49, 326. *See also* Day of Atonement
ʿAttābī robe, IV, 184, 412
Attachment to one's city, IV, 40–47. See also *baladiyya*
ʿaṭṭār (perfumer or druggist), II, 261–272, 484, 494, 507, 508, 581-585; III, 138. *See also* Druggist, Perfumer(s)
al-ʿAṭṭārīn, Square of the Perfumers, II, 263
ʿaṭṭārīn, residents of Square of the Perfumers, II, 508
ʿAṭṭār al-Maḥallī, II, 582
Attestation, formulas of, II, 601
Attorney, II, 335, 599, 600; power of, III, 287-288
Auction, public, I, 192 ff.; IV, 326, 456
Auditor(s), III, 290
Austrian Academy of Sciences, IV, 270
Autonomy, communal, extent of, II, 311, 402–407
Authorities, Jewish, III, 80 ff., 164, 218, 278, 293, 294; Muslim, III, 76, 79, 82, 83, 120, 200, 212, 217, 228, 257, 277, 280, 286, 287, 293, 294, 295, 335, 350
āv (Heb.). *See* President of the High Court
aval (Fr., bill of exchange), I, 241
Averroes. *See* Ibn Rushd
Avicenna. *See* Ibn Sīnā
avīzār (Aram., free of obligation), II, 600
ʿAwāḍ, I, 381
ʿAwāḍ b. Hananel, I, 439
ʿawn (salary, emoluments), I, 117; II, 605
Ayalon, David, I, 140
ʿAydhāb, Sudan, I, 42, 133, 136, 244, 269; II, 360, 606; III, 339, 485; IV, 445
ʿayn (substance, money [generally gold coin]), I, 230, 381, 382, 391, 458. *See also* Dinar
ʿayn wa-ʿarḍ (cash and kind), I, 230, 458
aytām al-aḥyā (orphans whose parents are still alive), III, 302
ʿAyyāsh b. Nissīm b. Baruch, V, 507
ʿAyyāsh b. Ṣadaqa, I, 378, 473
Ayyūb, I, 38
Ayyūb b. Tamīm, II, 25, 525
Ayyubid(s), I, xvii, xviii, 29, 38; architecture, IV, 67; continuity with Fatimid period, IV, 111; conversion to Islam under, II, 300; discrimination against Jews and Christians, II, 288, 289; different from later Middle Ages, IV, 41; Egypt a refuge under, II, 138; Geniza source for social history of, I, 19, 148, 200; gold scarce under, I, 234; government control, I, 266, 270; head of Jewish community under, II, 23, 27, 526; hospitals, II, 251; insecurity in transition from Fatimids, III, 126, 182; and *jāliya*, II, 386, 388; Jewish communal autonomy under, II, 405–407; Jewish judiciary under, II, 327; Jewish physicians, II, 380; IV, 12; judiciary and police, II, 373; less liberal than Fatimids, I, 63; mail service, I, 284; Maimonides and, IV, 12, 258; material culture, IV, 137, 147, 205, 312; Muslim law under, II, 397; Muslims transport goods to Jews, IV, 437; non-Muslims in entourage of Muslim rulers, II, 345; non-Muslim govt. officials, I, 73, 188; II, 374; petition by Jewish physician to sultan, II, 256; plunder of Fustat by, V, 524; population, IV, 46; prominence of *muḥtasib* under, II, 369; silver standard, I, 388, 390, 491; slaves under, I, 132, 134; sugar industry, I, 125; tax-farming, II, 363; topography under, IV, 29, 30, 33; women, II, 432; III, 358
Azarya, "son of the female copyist," II, 184
ʿAzaryāhū b. Ephraim, physician, V, 110–111
al-Azhar Mosque, II, 202, 209, 565; IV, 73, 128. *See also* Mosque
Azhar b. Abraham, *shōfēṭ*, II, 596
Azhar (Meir) b. Jābir, III, 439
azharōt. *See* Poems, liturgical
al-ʿAzīz, Fatimid caliph, I, 33, 232, 233, 237; II, 277, 354; III, 56, 357, 456; IV, 384. *See also* ʿAzīziyya; Nizārī coins
al-ʿAzīz, Ayyubid ruler, V, 175, 555
ʿAzīz(a), female name, I, 436
ʿAzīza b. Ḥusayn b. David, III, 426
ʿAzīziyya dinars. *See* Dinar
ʿAzīziyya dirhems. *See* Dirhem
ʿAzzūn, coinage of, I, 373

B

Baalbek, Lebanon, I, 444; II, 71, 442, 600; III, 114; IV, 437
baʿalē ha-bayit (Heb.): wife, III, 160; "masters of the house," III, 160, 461
baʿal ha-mas (Heb.) = *ṣāḥib al-jāliya*, II, 612
baʿal ha-mīlā (Heb., father of the boy [circumcision]), II, 498
baʿalē battim (Heb., scion of distinguished family), III, 2, 425

baʿalē Torah (Heb.), II, 565. See also *benē Torah*; *anshē Torah*
Bābād, I, 400
bāb al-kattān (Flax Gate), I, 448
bāb al-nisāʾ, women's door. *See* Secret door
Babshād, I, 400
bāb al-sirr. *See* Secret door
Babylonia(ns). *See* Iraq(ians)
Babylonian rite, III, 50, 93, 103, 104, 107
Bachelor, II, 577, 604; III, 24, 62, 231
Badajoz, Spain, I, 69; II, 580
al-Baddī, for al-Lebdi, V, 543. *See also* Lebdi
Badges with inscriptions, IV, 113
badhanj. *See* Wind catcher
Bādis, ruler of Tunisia, I, 291; II, 24
badla (costume), IV, 158, 398
Badr ("Full moon"), collector of rent, II, 431
Badr al-Jamālī, Fatimid vizier, I, 188, 316; II, 400, 512, 606; V, 519, 636. *See also* Amīr al-Juyūsh
badw. *See* Bedouin(s)
Bafshād, I, 400
Baghdad(ī), I, 281, 299, 422; II, 158; III, 4, 93; absence of business letters from, IV, 415; banking in, I, 61, 230, 244, 245; caliphate of, I, 131; IV, 119 (*see also* Abbasids); cantors in, II, 90, 223, 224, 569; charity for foreigners from, II, 441, 442, 444, 457, 467, 509; IV, 155; churches and synagogues in, II, 144; circulation of money in, I, 61, 242; clothing in, I, 72; IV, 162, 164, 175, 191; contributions to, I, 22, 65; discrimination against Christians in, II, 287; divorce document from, III, 260; domestic architecture in, I, 71; III, 38, 435; IV, 78; ecumenical authority, I, 65, 66; II, 94; education in, II, 180, 186, 559; excommunications of people from, II, 217, 331; exilarch, I, 92, 144; II, 17, 18, 21,26, 27, 39; family of Christian doctors in, II, 245; furnishings and housewares, IV, 131, 140, 146, 149, 175, 390; Gaons, II, 10, 11, 12–13, 14, 22, 24, 29, 52, 55, 600; III, 13, 88, 153; immigrants to/from, I, 49, 54, 117, 126, 265, 421; II, 231, 525; inquiries sent to high council of, III, 19; Jewish craftsmen in, II, 583; Jewish judiciary, II, 595; literary models, II, 557; mail service, I, 285, 287; Messianism in, III, 47; Muslim government in, I, 230; II, 10, 316; III, 36; pilgrimage to shrines in, I, 56; responsa from, I, 22, 66; II, 565; saintly woman in, III, 47, 62; Seljuks in, I, 35; II, 286; Sherira Gaon and Elhanan b. Shemarya in, II, 564; synagogue in, III, 300; weights, I, 360; yeshivas, I, 52, 53, 158, 376; II, 5, 8, 24, 28, 171, 198, 200, 203, 240, 320, 402–403; V, 383–384
Baghdad, name of girl, III, 91
Bahāʾ al-dawla, Buyid title, V, 579
Bahā b. Mufaḍḍal ha-Kohen, III, 443
Bahgat, Aly, IV, 53, 54
Bahiyya, daughter of Ibn ʿAwkal, I, 144
Bahiyya, daughter of Yaʿīsh ha-Kohen, III, 330, 501
Bahnasā (ī). *See* Flax
baḥrī (Nile boatsman), II, 506
al-baḥr al-māliḥ (the salty sea). *See* Mediterranean Sea
baḥr al-rūm (Sea of the Romans). *See* Mediterranean Sea
Baḥṭīṭ, Egypt, III, 327
Bahūdī, prominent family, II, 440, 476
bāḥūr (Heb., young man, or junior), I, 413, 433, 470; II, 61, 535, 536, 564. *See also* Young men; *ṣibyān*
baḥūrīm (Heb.). *See* Young men
Baker(y) (*khabbāz*), I, 87, 114, 254, 261, 363, 423; IV, 237–238; female (*khabbāza*), I, 129, 431
Bakers' strike, IV, 238
bakhāya dirhems. *See* Dirhem
Baking, III, 341; IV, 232
Bakhtaway, I, 400
Bakriyya, dinars issued by Amīr Abū Bakr, I, 235
balāʾ (disaster), V, 537
balad, II, 537, 543
baladī: co-citizen, IV, 45; local (silk), I, 418
baladiyya, attachment to one's city, IV, 45
Balāgh al-Munā, slave girl, I, 434
balakhsh. *See* Rubies
Balarm. *See* Palermo, Sicily
Balas stone. *See* Rubies
balaylaj (Ar.-Per.), beleric, II, 583
balda (small town), IV, 349
Baldwin, King of Jerusalem, I, 37
Bale, size of, I, 220, 226, 227, 335; bursting of, I, 487. See also *shikāra*
balligh tuʾjar ("deliver and God will reward you"), I, 284; II, 532
ballūṭī (distributor of acorns), I, 438
Balog, Paul, I, 368–387 *passim*, 390
Baltic Sea, IV, 207
Bama, Indian slave, I, 435; IV, 400, 439

Bamboo (*khayāzir, khuzūrān*), IV, 138, 386, 388
Bamboo crystals, I, 154
bāmōth, open places, II, 586
Ban. *See* Excommunication
Ban "in general terms" (*ḥerem setām*), II, 340–341, 602
al-Banā, Egypt, III, 388, 435; IV, 277, 362
Banana leaves, IV, 246, 441
Banāna, quarter in Fustat, IV, 13; prison, II, 508
Bananas, I, 80, 121
Banāt ("Girls"), name, II, 560
Banāt, daughter of Japheth Abu'l-Riḍā, III, 280
"Bandages and brassieres," IV, 131
bandar (Per.), term for western harbor of Aden, V, 523
Bandariyya, I, 320
Banditry, Bandits, I, 475; V, 23, 69, 70, 108, 162. *See also* Adversity; Political turmoil
Baneth, D.H., I, 6, 26; II, 249; V, 465, 555
Banīn b. Dā'ūd, druggist, II, 262, 582, 584
Banīn b. Jacob, V, 610
Banīna, f., III, 289
Banishment to an island, II, 309
Baniyas, Palestine, II, 6, 58, 214, 322, 440, 444, 455, 467, 566, 597
Bankers, I, 154, 261, 262, 264, 308, 376; II, 34, 38, 81, 456, 472, 477, 478, 484, 490, 492, 493, 507, 508, 545 (see also *gizbār*; *jahbadh*); court, II, 10. See also *ṣayrafī*; Money changers
Banking, I, 82, 174–175, 179, 229–266. *See also* Money; Purses of coins
Bankruptcy, I, 182, 204, 248; II, 582
bannā' (mason), I, 422
Banū Ḥujayla, I, 411
Banū Jamā'a, Shāfi'ī jurists, II, 320
Banū Maṭruḥ, rulers of Tripoli, Libya, V, 636
Banū Musaykīn, I, 441
Banū Wā'il quarter, Fustat, IV, 13
Bānyās, II, 562
Baptism in Judaism, I, 136
Baqā, f., III, 176
Baqā, *parnās*, II, 488
al-baqla ("the vegetable" = garden mallow), IV, 440
baqqāl (seller of vegetables), I, 152, 426
baqqam (brazilwood), I, 402
Baqṭas (Patti), I, 326
bar (Aram., son), II, 594
barā'a (acquittance, bill of divorce), II, 384, 611; III, 268, 485, 486
barābik ("Tales"), name, II, 496, 505
Baradānī brothers, III, 301, 493
baraka (blessings), V, 229
Barakāt, as abbreviation of Abu'l-Barakāt, V, 506
Barakāt, brother of Salmān ha-Levi b. Solomon, V, 542
Barakāt, *ṣāni'* of Ben Sālim, I, 414
Barakāt-Berākhōt, I, 357
Barakāt al-Jiblī, V, 539
Barakāt b. Joseph Lebdi, IV, 317
Barakāt b. Khulayf, merchant, V, 159
Barakāt b. Mūsā Ibn Miska, I, 365
Barakāt b. Yeshū'ā, V, 543
barbakh. *See* Pipe
Barber treating patients, II, 255
barca (I), boat. See *barqalū*
Barcelona, Spain, II, 564
barda'a. *See* Pad
"Bareheaded" (= boldfaced, irreverent), IV, 159
Barges (Nile and other), I, 295, 302, 305, 317, 320, 322
Barhūn b. Isaac Tāhertī, I, 181, 372, 373, 375, 440; IV, 264, 383–384, 410, 411; V, 191, 599
Barhūn b. Isma'īl Tāhertī, III, 22, 118
Barhūn b. Maṣlī'ah, V, 518
Barhūn b. Moses. *See* Barhūn II b. Mūsā b. Barhūn I Tāhertī
Barhūn II b. Mūsā b. Barhūn I Tāhertī, I, 375, 483; III, 42, 430; IV, 373, 402, 406, 407; V, 46, 129–130, 173, 584, 597
Barhūn (Abraham) b. Sahlān, banker, I, 463; III, 268
Barhūn b. Ṣāliḥ Tāhertī, I, 207, 377, 378, 467; III, 474; IV, 373; V, 597
Barhūn Tāhertī (the elder), I, 444; II, 590; III, 6
Bari, Italy, II, 25, 242, 245, 309
barīd, governmental courier and intelligence service, I, 282, 283, 284, 285
Bar Kokhba, V, 359
Barley, I, 118–119, 211; II, 420; IV, 243; flour, IV, 260
Bar Mitzvah, V, 28
Barnīk, I, 212
barniyya (pots, vessel, casket), II, 584; IV, 321, 323, 343, 389, 392, 454–455, 467
Baron, Salo, V, 372
Barqa, Libya, I, 318; III, 246, 247; V, 569; beneficiaries of charity from, II, 439, 440, 442, 463, 467, 468; III, 63; caravan from, I, 278; containers ex-

ported from, I, 334; famine in, IV, 242; interfaith relations in, II, 274; jewelry sent to, IV, 428; Jewish judges in, II, 274, 314, 320, 595, 596; IV, 242, 439; heiress from, III, 280, 489; importance for international commerce, I, 212; lease of house in, IV, 95; letters from, I, 378; IV, 439; marriage documents from, III, 98, 117, 190, 373, 405; merchants from/in, I, 68, 378; IV, 27, 95; Muslim pirates from, I, 327
barqalū (a small bale), I, 335, 336, 486
Bārra b. Ḥalfon, f., III, 437
barrāda, IV, 391
barrakān, IV, 182
Bartering, V, 5
Barthe, Helene, V, 506
barṭīl (bribe), I, 488
Baruch, II, 490, 491
Baruch b. Isaac of Aleppo, II, 215; III, 288; IV, 398, 431; V, 513
Barzān, Kurdish locality of Iraq, II, 496
Barzanj, I, 400
baṣalī (violet gray color of an onion cut open), I, 419
Basātīn cemetery, Fustat, I, 4, 5
Bashfulness, V, 198-199
Basil, II, 68; flower, IV, 175
Basin (*ṭast*), IV, 139, 315, 321, 385, 388, 389, 390
basīqa. *See* Pledges
Baṣīr, bell-maker, and wife, V, 472–474
Basketmaker (*qaffāṣ*), I, 416
Baskets (*khayzurāna*, *qafaṣ*, *qashwa*, *quffa*, *salla*), I, 334, 416, 486; II, 104; IV, 131–132, 315, 386, 393, 394, 452
basq (Gr. *abax*, abacus), II, 557
al-basqāt wal-dhāqat (accounting instruments), II, 557
Basra, Iraq, I, 49, 460; II, 184, 217, 304, 362; IV, 43
al-Baṣrī, renegade, II, 591
bassām (Heb.) = *ʿaṭṭār* (Ar.), II, 265
basṭa (landing), IV, 369
ʾl-baṭāla wal-qirāya, II, 565. See also *sekhar baṭṭāla*
baṭaṭī (maker of leather bottles). See *baṭṭāṭ*
Bathhouses, II, 432, 473; III, 186, 217, 343; IV, 141, 406, 455; V, 533; construction, V, 98; Muslim use, V, 96–97; for recreational health care, V, 95, 96–100; on Sabbath, V, 96; shared by Muslims and Jews, V, 96, 533; women's, IV, 22; V, 43, 97–98
Bath of the Cock, V, 96, 532
Bath of the Cook, IV, 22
Bath of al-Kaʿkī (the Pretzel-maker), V, 96, 532
Bath(house) of the Mice, II, 227, 571; IV, 30, 356; V, 533
Bathrobe (*minshafa*), IV, 191, 315, 317, 321, 324, 327, 330, 331, 416; V, 97, 533
Bathroom, IV, 138, 367
baṭlānīm, II, 211. See also *benē Torah*
Baṭrīqa b. Aaron, III, 461
baṭṭa (leather bottle), I, 422
baṭṭāl (unemployed), II, 438, 563, 565
baṭṭāṭ (maker of leather bottles), I, 422
bawāridī (maker of cooling or cold vegetables), I, 115, 424
bayʿ (sale), in Tunisia used for price of unit sold, I, 239, 453; II, 607
Baybars, sultan, II, 137
al-Baysānī, V, 444
bayit (Heb.). See *bayt*
bayt: house, family, room, II, 131, 418, 493, 552, 583, 612; III, 2, 425, 461; IV, 57, 70, 292, 362, 363; quadratic figures in the texture of a stuff, IV, 127, 384; container for Ṭabarī material, IV, 304–305
al-bayta, extended family, V, 525
al-Bayṭār (Veterinary), family name, II, 415
bayṭār. *See* Veterinarian
bayt al-māʾ (room with water). *See* Washroom
bayt al-māl (treasury), I, 458
bayt al-maqdis. *See* Jerusalem
bayt al-nisāʾ. *See* Women, gallery
bayt al-tibn (hay storeroom), IV, 368
Bay window (*rawshan*), IV, 61–62, 78, 364, 365
bayyāʿ (seller of foodstuffs), I, 152, 424, 438; IV, 296
bayyāʿāt ("saleswomen," female brokers), I, 439
bayyāt (night watchman), IV, 357
Bazaar(s), II, 529, 608, 612; IV, 3, 8, 15, 26, 57–58; V, 5, 206. *See also* Market
Bazaar, Great, II, 434, 483, 490, 548
Bazaar of the Perfumers, III, 220; IV, 15
Bazaar of the Threads, II, 483
bazbūz ("nozzle, spout"), nickname, II, 506
bazz (cloth), II, 590
bazzāz (clothier), I, 438, 448
Beadle(s) (*khādim*, *shammāsh*), I, 94; II, 54, 77, 82–87, 90, 92, 106, 115, 117, 121, 123, 124, 125, 129–130, 149, 150, 204, 211, 228, 416, 417, 418, 419, 421, 427, 430, 431, 432, 438, 439, 442, 449,

450, 459, 460, 462, 464, 488, 539, 540, 541, 572, 601, 609; III, 64, 138; IV, 124 (see also *farrāsh*); called "servant of the community" (*khādim al-jamāʿa*), II, 539; female (*khādima*), I, 130, 431; II, 85
Bead maker (*kharazī*), I, 416
Beads (*ḥabba, kharaz*), I, 99–100, 154, 334, 337; IV, 27, 202, 419, 426
Beans, substitute for bread, IV, 245
Beauty desired, IV, 129, 135, 156, 198
Becker, Carl Heinrich, V, 497
Bed cover. *See* Blanket
Bedding (*firāsh*), II, 501; IV, 107, 108, 109, 115, 129, 130, 165, 298-299, 304, 307–309, 377, 380, 450, 452, 457, 459
bedīqā, examination (of ritual purity), II, 570
Bedouin(s), *badw*, I, 35, 39, 75, 118, 279, 281, 328, 409; II, 55, 137, 281, 283, 379; IV, 150, 242, 310, 401, 439; V, 58-59, 69; levies, I, 31, 72
Bedroom, IV, 48-49, 372
Beds, pairs of, IV, 115
Bedstead (*sarīr*), IV, 106, 107, 113, 114, 117, 379
Beef, IV, 231, 443
Beehives, II, 606
Beekeeper, -ing, I, 76, 118, 125, 210, 429
Beer (*mizr*), I, 119; IV, 261, 447
"Beggars" (lower middle class), I, 79, 152, 410. See also *ṣaʿlūk*
Beirut, I, 45, 110, 293
beldār (Heb., courier), I, 282
Beleric, II, 583
Belisar, general of Justinian, III, 339
Bell, in house, IV, 61
Bellamy, James A., V, 469–470
Bell maker, I, 109, 421; II, 488
Belt (*wasaṭ*), IV, 320
Belt maker, IV, 16
bēmā (Heb.-Gr., reader's platform), II, 146. See also *anbōl*
Ben Asad. *See* Abuʾl-Maʿālī b. Judah
Benaya, scribe, II, 184
Benayah b. Mūsā, V, 562
Benayahu, Meir, V, 290, 568
Ben ʿAzzay, III, 62
Ben bat Shāʾūl, III, 426
Ben al-Bērūtī of Minya, a Karaite, V, 609
Ben Dōsā, V, 532
Ben Shekhanya. *See* Japheth b. David b. Shekhanya
Bench (*ṣuffa*), IV, 67; built-in (*maṣṭaba*), IV, 62–63, 77
benē = (*a*)*bnā*, II, 565
Benediction(s), III, 54, 87, 95, 234. *See also* Blessings
benē Torah (Heb.), students of the sacred law, II, 211, 441, 565, 572. See also *baʿalē Torah; anshē Torah*
Benhā, Egypt, I, 125, 417, 429; II, 130, 463, 606; III, 221, 472; IV, 154
Ben Hammād, IV, 438
Ben al-Ḥazzān, II, 423
Benjamin ha-Kohen, V, 436
Benjamin Nehāwendī, V, 364
Benjamin of Rosetta (Binyām al-Rashīdī), II, 585
Benjamin of Tudela, II, 45, 54, 78, 140, 523, 550; V, 431, 502
Ben Kalīlā, I, 463
Ben-Meir, Gaon, III, 25; V, 383
Ben Mesayyēm, I, 463
Ben Naḥmān, *ḥazzān*, III, 484
Ben Nahum family, V, 167, 553
Ben Phinehas house, II, 120, 422, 429, 448, 548
Ben Pinhas al-Damīrī. *See* Meshullam b. Mevassēr
Ben Pinhas house, IV, 104
Ben Ṣaghīr, "Mr. Small," III, 11, 289, 292
Ben Shaʿyā, representative of the merchants, I, 191; III, 428. *See also* Ibn Shaʿya
Ben Shekhanya. *See* Japheth b. David b. Shekhanya
Ben Sira. *See* Ecclesiasticus
Benton, John F., V, 215–216
ben ṭōvīm (Heb. = Ar. *abnāʾ al-nās*), of a good family, I, 409; II, 447
Benveniste of Narbonne, I, 34, 247; V, 514
Ben Yijū, IV, 210, 224, 423, 428, 429; V, 67, 68, 519
Ben Zabqala, II, 419
Bequests, II, 12. *See also* Wills
bē rabbānān (Aram., house of higher learning), II, 315, 595
Berachiah brothers. *See* Berechiah brothers
Berākhōt, cantor in provincial town, V, 285–286
Berākhōt al-Ashmūnī, Rabbenu, of Bilbays, V, 31
Berākhōt b. Elazar, known as Barakāt b. Abū Naṣr, I, 365
Berākhōt b. Japheth, IV, 457
Berākhōt ha-Kohen b. Aaron *ha-mumḥe*, III, 488
Berber(s), I, 31, 37, 40, 41, 44; II, 379; III, 6, 57; IV, 35
Berbera, Somalia, I, 133; IV, 129
Berechiah brothers, I, 181, 444; III, 19, 56, 430; V, 560

berīt ḥadāshā (Heb., New Covenant), **II**, 568
Berkeley symposium, 1966, **IV**, 4
Betel leaves, **I**, 154
bēth dīn (Heb., Jewish court), **I**, 465; **II**, 314, 401, 574, 595, 597, 600, 614
bēth genīza (Heb.), **I**, 1; **IV**, 369
bēth ha-malkuth (Heb., the Government house), **I**, 458
bēth ha-midrāsh (Heb.), **II**, 199, 202, 562
bēth ha-miqdāsh (Heb.), The Temple, **II**, 552
bēth kenēseth (Heb.), **II**, 165
bēth kissē (Heb., room with a chair), term for bathroom, **IV**, 367
bēth al-nisā (Heb.), women's gallery in synagogue. See *bayt al-nisā*ʾ
Beth Shearim (Shaʿarayim), **II**, 146
Betrothal(s), **III**, 54, 69, 72, 73, 74, 75, 79, 87-95, 116, 441-446 (*see also* Engagement; *qiddūshīn*; *taqdīs*); benediction, **III**, 87; cancellation of, **III**, 92-93, 133; gift, **III**, 88, 90, 91, 92 (*see also* Cup). *See also* Marriage
beʿūlā (Heb.), previously married, **III**, 447
Beverages. *See* Beer; Drinking; Potions; Wine
Bible, **I**, xvii, 49, 63, 64, 346; **II**, 2, 7, 10, 16, 20, 27, 52, 57, 62, 72, 88, 129, 146, 159, 160, 161, 167, 171, 181, 182, 183, 184, 185, 192, 193, 195, 196, 205, 206, 207, 212, 220, 238, 239, 275, 278, 304, 309, 499, 552, 598; **IV**, 197-198; **V**, 133, 140, 372, 385-386; reading of, **II**, 146, 147, 247, 499, 598. *See also* Torah. For individual verses, *see* Index of Scriptural, Rabbinic, and Maimonidean Citations
Bible codex, **III**, 184, 201, 247; price, **I**, 109, 154, 259. *See also* Torah scroll
Bible school. See *kuttāb*
Biblical times. *See* Israel, Ancient
Bibliophile, **II**, 268
Bidʿa, slave girl, **I**, 434
biḍāʿa (goods), **I**, 183, 446
Bigamy. *See* Wife, second
Bijāya (Bougie), **I**, 212, 308, 310; **V**, 521
bilā maʿīsha (without livelihood), **V**, 525
Bilbays, Egypt, cantor from, **II**, 563; charitable foundations, **II**, 546; communal jurisdiction in, **II**, 602; court records from, **III**, 77, 127, 236, 454, 477; Crusader massacre of, **I**, 36; divorce cases from, **I**, 145, 383; **III**, 262, 263; domestic architecture, **IV**, 77, 363; donations from congregation in, **II**, 97; forced conversion of Jews to Islam in, **II**, 51; foreigners in, **II**, 153; Frankish occupation of, **V**, 54-55; French rabbi in, **II**, 122, 542; heirs and orphans in, **III**, 297, 303, 442; interplay of Jewish and Muslim laws in, **II**, 400; Jewish judges of, **III**, 72, 73, 82, 297, 494; **IV**, 227; Jewish population, **II**, 45, 51; legal documents from, **I**, 256, 384; **II**, 400, 595; legal procedure, **II**, 601; letters from, **I**, 404; **II**, 308, 390, 563, 572, 601; **III**, 503; Maimonides' responsum to, **II**, 602; marriage documents from, **III**, 389, 390, 403, 411, 412, 415; *muqaddam* in, **II**, 308, 534, 572; **III**, 503; overland travel to/from, **I**, 278; *parnās* of, **II**, 81; poll-tax in, **II**, 390, 563; public appeal for French rabbis in, **II**, 122; rabbi from Yemen in, **II**, 97; sale of houses in, **III**, 327, 497; **IV**, 276, 278, 372; sale of land in, **I**, 385; synagogue of, **II**, 153; widows in, **III**, 483, 494; wine production in, **IV**, 259; women, **III**, 340, 499
bilīj (compartment on a ship), **I**, 481
billawr. *See* Crystal
Bill of exchange (*suftaja*), **I**, 208, 242-245, 247, 460, 461; **II**, 328. *See also* Promissory notes
bīmāristān (Per., "place for the sick"). *See* Hospital
bint ʿamm (wife), **III**, 27, 30
bint ʿirs (bride), **II**, 432
bint al-mara (stepdaughter), **III**, 311
Binzertī (from Bizerta), **I**, 302
biqyār. *See* Turban
biʾr (well), **II**, 552
Birds, as pets, **V**, 45
Bīr Jabr (in Alexandria), **IV**, 46, 351, 360
birkat al-ʿirāqiyyīn (pool of the Iraqians), **II**, 552
birsīm (Egyptian clover), **II**, 360
Birthday parties, **V**, 27-28
Birth register, **III**, 233
biṣabr shahrayn (two months' deferment), **I**, 449. *See also* Deferment of rent
bisbāsī (dealer in mace), **I**, 438
Bishāra, **I**, 436
Bishr, *ṣayrafī*, **I**, 374
Bishr b. Abraham, **III**, 482
Bishr b. Dāʾūd, **I**, 463
biṭār (veterinary), **II**, 532. *See also* Veterinarian
biʿtuh bil-nasiyya (delaying of payment), **I**, 449
Black, **IV**, 125, 163, 174, 176, 177, 406, 407
Black dirhem. *See* Dirhem
Blackish-blue (*kuḥlī*), **IV**, 176

Blacksmith(s) (*ḥaddād*), I, 83, 92, 421; II, 582
Blanket, bedcover (*liḥāf, muḍarraba*), IV, 115ff., 167, 308, 316, 321, 324, 327, 331, 380, 459
Blau, Joshua, I, 26
Bleeding, II, 247. *See also* Phlebotomists
Blessed, slave, I, 138
Blessing, House of, I, 195, 231
Blessing(s) over a dead or living person, III, 2, 103, 191; of and for dead, V, 6, 182-183, 409-410; of God, V, 326-328, 335-336; in letters, V, 230, 235; at meals, V, 33, 35, 40, 352; public, V, 35-36, 298-299, 352; for travel, V, 37. *See also* Prayer
Blind, II, 92, 133, 134, 161-162, 199, 454, 458, 459, 501, 553, 559
Bloodletters (cuppers, phlebotomists), Bloodletting, I, 75, 91; II, 255, 579, 585; IV, 254-255, 323; V, 100
Blue (sky-color, turquoise), IV, 117, 174-175, 177, 406
Bluish-iridescent (*fākhiṭī*), I, 419; IV, 181, 182
Blumberg, Harold, V, 407
Board of wood, tray for different dishes, IV, 145
Boaz, biblical, III, 50, V, 531
Bodleian Library, Oxford, I, 2, 5, 6, 8, 24; III, 96
Bolsters, IV, 108, 111 ff.
Bombay, I, 9
Bōne. *See* Būna
Bonine, Michael E., IV, 4
Bookbinder, I, 112, 422; II, 239
Bookish civilization, II, 237, 241, 266
Bookkeeping technique, II, 464
Book of Daniel, V, 522
Book of Jubilees, III, 169
Book of Light, III, 169
Books, II, 111, 115, 181, 194, 216, 237, 239, 241, 242, 248, 263, 528; children's exercise, II, 557; circulation, I, 64; as collateral, I, 259; II, 80; dealing in by physicians, V, 457; as heirloom, I, 266; lists, II, 206, 248; V, 3-4, 425; part of dowry, IV, 311; ransom of, V, 85, 376, 529; sale of, I, 196, 382; in synagogues, II, 53, 83, 111, 151, 152; trade in, I, 154, 379; transport of, I, 334, 335. *See also* Libraries
Bookseller, II, 189, 515, 560, 597
Borax, I, 154; describing color white, IV, 174, 378
Borders (*ʿalam*), IV, 113, 125, 127, 411, 454, 456; gilded, IV, 113
Bosworth, C. E., V, 260
Bottlemakers, lane of, I, 422
Bougie. *See* Bijāya
Bouhdiba, Abdelwahab, V, 308
Boujedra, Rachid, V, 312
Bourdieu, Paul, III, 27
Bourgeoisie, Middle Eastern, II, 2, 3, 7; III, 52, 162, 230; IV, 184, 311
Bowls, IV, 145-146, 315, 322, 393, 429, 453; as gifts, II, 529
Box: *ḥuqqa*, IV, 321, 388, 430; V, 97, 533; *safaṭ*, IV, 130-131, 316, 421
"Boy" (slave or employee), I, 93, 94, 96, 161-164
Boys, sexual abuse of, III, 208
Bracelets: four different groups, IV, 219-220; *dastaynaq*, 329, 428, 451; *dumluj*, IV, 200, 219, 220, 332, 427, 428, 460; *ḥadīda*, IV, 202, 203, 204, 208, 213, 219, 327, 419, 424, 425, 428; *siwār* or *suwār*, IV, 200, 208, 212, 219-220, 319, 322, 424, 427, 428; bulging, IV, 204; granulated, IV, 204, 212; worn in pairs, IV, 200, 219, 451
Braided ornaments, IV, 211
Brain, Robert, V, 277-278, 284
Brandenburg, Dietrich, IV, 55
Braslavsky, II, 447
Brass, IV, 140, 141, 143, 144, 145, 147, 150, 203
Braudel, Fernand, IV, 4; V, 497-498
Brauer, Erich, V, 498-499
Brazier, IV, 136
Brazilwood (dye), I, 45, 46, 165-166, 178, 184, 202, 219, 222; II, 78; IV, 173, 406
Bread, I, 229, 316; II, 543, 547, 559; IV, 142, 230, 232, 233, 234-244, 245, 434, 435 (*see also* Bakery); average weight of, IV, 244; baker, II, 590; collection of, II, 491, 498 (see also *mezōnōt*); distribution of, II, 98, 100, 108, 123, 126-130, 135, 142, 423, 436, 438-469, 476, 540, 541, 543, 544; III, 63, 65, 324; price of, II, 461; IV, 237 ff., 435, 439, 443; shapes of, IV, 243; taboo regarding, II, 307-308; "things taken together with," IV, 244-253; two types of, II, 105; unleavened barley, IV, 243; unsold, IV, 238; weekly rations, IV, 236-237
Breadwinners, number of, II, 139-140, 142
"Breast of the Falcon." *See* Anklet
Bribes, I, 185, 445; II, 318, 347, 368, 529, 607; IV, 357; V, 205-206
Bridal outfit. *See* Dowry
Bridal procession, III, 70, 116, 126, 441

Bridal trunk, bureau (*muqaddama*), **IV**, 130, 320, 321, 385, 454, 459
Bride(s), maintenance between betrothal and marriage, **III**, 94
Bride-comber (*māshiṭa*), **I**, 93, 127, 430
Briggs, Martin S., **IV**, 55
"Brightness," slave girl, **I**, 139
Brinner, William M., **V**, 53
British Museum, London, **I**, 5, 24; **II**, 183, 257
Broadcast(er), in yeshiva, **II**, 198, 202, 562
Brocade, **I**, 46, 153; **II**, 78; **IV**, 110, 115, 116, 119, 120, 124, 126, 168, 303–304, 320, 324, 377, 380, 381, 454, 455
Brokers, **I**, 160–161, 192, 252; **II**, 297; female, **I**, 129, 161, 184, 259, 265
Bronze, **IV**, 137, 202; lids, **IV**, 142
Brother(s), **III**, 15–20, 40, 47; and sisters, **II**, 399; **III**, 20–26, 183, 202, 330, 333; as guardian, **III**, 236, 283. *See also* Family feeling
Brotherly relationship, formal, of unrelated persons, **III**, 47
Brown (*asmar*), color, **IV**, 175–176, 182
Brown, Kenneth L., **V**, 75
Brown, L. Carl, **IV**, 4
Brownish-pink (eye of the partridge), color, **IV**, 175
Bū ʿAlī b. Bū ʿAmr, **III**, 485
Buʾl-Barakāt, **II**, 492
Buʾl-Faḍl b. al-Maskīl, **II**, 321
Buʾl-Ḥasan b. Buʾl-ʿAlā, **I**, 366
Buʾl-Ḥasan al-Hōd, **III**, 501
Bulyanī, **V**, 69
Buʾl-Makārim, **II**, 492
Buʾl-Makārim the Goldsmith, Joseph b. Samuel, **IV**, 328
Buʾl-Makārim, Moses b. Ezekiel, **III**, 196
Bū Manṣūr b. Solomon. *See* Samuel b. Solomon
Bū Saʿīd, **II**, 433
Bucket, **IV**, 140, 315, 317, 321, 324, 331, 390
Buckle, **IV**, 163
Budapest, **III**, 12
Budge papyrus, **IV**, 48
bū-glosson (Gr., oxtongue), **II**, 583
buhār, weight of 300 pounds, **I**, 220
Buḥayra province, **I**, 135
Buildings, maintenance of. *See* Repairs
Building operations. *See* Repairs
Bukhara, Central Asia, **IV**, 36; **V**, 517
bukhnuq (kerchiefs), **IV**, 320, 330, 401, 459, 463
Bukhtīshū family of Baghdad, **II**, 245
buldār (Heb., courier), **I**, 282
Bulyanā(ī), **V**, 523
Bulyāt (Gr. bouleutes), councillor, **II**, 541
Būna (Bōne), Algiers, **I**, 42; **II**, 452; **V**, 549
Bunāna, *maḥras*, **IV**, 34, 357
Bunāna, a sailor, **I**, 313
Bundār, a freedman, **I**, 146–147; **II**, 396
Bundār b. Moses, **III**, 26
Bunduqī. *See* Venice
bunni (maker of carp pickles), **I**, 430
būqalamūn. *See* chameleon-colored
būqandalāt. *See* Chandeliers
buqyār. *See* Turban
Būra, Egypt, **II**, 439; **III**, 64
Burayh=Abraham, **II**, 471
burayq, **IV**, 245, 440
Burckhardt, Jacob, **V**, 215–216, 496
burda (outer shawl with fringes), **IV**, 196
Bureau (*muqaddama*). *See* Bridal trunk
Burglars, **IV**, 61, 74
Burial: attire, **IV**, 155, 160, 162, 188–189, 414; **V**, 160–161; coffins, **V**, 162; expenses, **II**, 111, 135, 413, 420, 548, 588; provision for, in wills, **V**, 142, 144–145, 146, 166. *See also* Death; Funerals
burīden (Per., cutting), **I**, 282
burj (tower), **I**, 412; **II**, 422
Burma, **II**, 416
Bursa, Turkey, **IV**, 32
burseqī (Heb.-Gr., tanner), **II**, 430
Burying of coins, **I**, 265
Bushrān, an official, **I**, 249
Bushr b. Asad b. al-Salār, f., **III**, 442
Bushr-Bishr ("Good tidings"), name, **IV**, 316, 453
busht (overall), **IV**, 339, 464
Business: cash flow, **V**, 446; document style, **V**, 336; enmity in, **V**, 300; family, **V**, 127, 239–240, 393; friendship, **V**, 273–274, 277; honesty in, **V**, 205–213; honor in, **V**, 203–205; intelligence, **I**, 166, 201; in wills, **V**, 136–137; practices, **I**, 157, 192–200; principles, **I**, 200–202; seasons, **I**, 195, 207 (see also *mawsim*); volume of, **I**, 214–217; year-end debt clearing, **V**, 37, 173, 207. Mentioned *passim*. *See also* Trade
Būṣīr, Egypt, **I**, 86, 153, 165, 185, 207, 224, 227, 232, 237, 243, 253, 278, 295, 345, 372, 377, 378, 415, 418, 448, 474, 488; **II**, 387; **IV**, 351, 410. *See also* Flax
bustān (orchard), **I**, 122
busuṭ. *See* Rugs
Butcher (*jazzār*), **I**, 115, 424
Butler, Alfred J., **II**, 145, 147
Buttons, **IV**, 116, 400
Buzāʿa, Syria, **II**, 454
Buzbūz ("nozzle, spout"), nickname, **II**, 506

Buzyān, Afghanistan, IV, 305
Buzyōn, IV, 305, 316, 317, 452
Byzantine, Byzantium, I, 29, 38, 39, 40, 50, 53; IV, 1, 4, 10, 114, 124, 212, 244, 296; abolishment of office of patriarch, II, 17; attachment to, I, 63, 64; beneficiaries of charity from, I, 63; II, 441, 442, 457; III, 63, 114, 229; brocade, IV, 110, 380, 381; bureaucracy and ceremonials, II, 357; business practices, I, 45, 256; character of documents from, I, 22; charitable foundations, II, 112; commerce with, I, 45, 211; IV, 27; congregations in, II, 157; converts to Judaism from, II, 304; courier service, I, 282; emigration to/from, I, 49, 50, 53, 58, 59; II, 50, 300, 533; distributions to refugees from, II, 462; embassy, IV, 119; export of products, I, 46; and Fatimids, I, 39; fortress (*see* Fortress of the Greeks, Fustat); gold currency, III, 120; government control of foreign trade, I, 269; guilds, I, 82; Jewish glassmaker with Arabic *kunya*, II, 306; Jewish merchants living in, I, 49; III, 177; Jews captured by Muslim pirates, II, 481, 482; Karaism in, I, 65; lack of business letters from, I, 22; law, II, 289, 328; letters from, I, 58; II, 574; III, 467; mail service, I, 282, 285; maritime law, II, 89; marriage contract from, III, 98; navy, I, 328, 331; order from to Egyptian copyist, II, 238; origin of Palestinian congregations, II, 52; origin of spiritual and communal leaders, II, 70; Palestine under rule of, II, 197; physicians in, II, 242; pilgrim from, I, 63; ransom and support of captives from, II, 96; re-opening churches and synagogues, II, 435; *rūmī*, meaning Byzantine, IV, 298, 303, 377; scholar from, II, 157; III, 48, 200; scribal practices, II, 573; silk, I, 103; statute forbidding appt. of scholar from as judge, II, 66; students from in Iraqi yeshivas, II, 202; Tarsus taken by, II, 214; trade, I, 45, 46, 211, 269, 301; Tunisian merchant in, II, 385; visits by foreigners limited in, I, 59; women, I, 49; III, 210, 302. *See also* Rūm

C

Cadastre, II, 434, 436; IV, 13, 39, 350
Caesarea, Palestine, I, 45, 188, 192, 321, 350; II, 154, 447; III, 191; IV, 7, 8
Cahen, Claude, I, 272, 345; II, 319, 361; IV, 4, 5; V, 496
Cairo, *passim*
Cairo Geniza documents, I, 1-28 and *passim*. *See also* Geniza
Cairo Museum, II, 551; IV, 414
Cakes, I, 114, 254
Caldron (*qidr*), IV, 391
Caleb b. Aaron, V, 631
Calendar. *See* Era
Calendar: disputes concerning, V, 366, 383; fixing of, II, 54-55; IV, 452-453
Caliph(s), II, 12, 29, 34, 71, 72, 165, 247, 287, 312, 316, 574; III, 3, 10, 13, 315, 339, 357; IV, 11. *See also* Fatimids
Caliphal rescript. *See* Rescript of ruler
Calligraphy, II, 557, 560, 573, 575, 577, 582, 594. *See also* Script; Writing, art of
Calsana, Spain, II, 497
Cambridge, England, II, 18; III, 12, 81
Cambridge Colloquium, 1976, IV, 4
Camel loads, I, 215, 220, 227
Camels, I, 211, 270, 276, 285
Camphor (*kāfūr*), I, 154, 155; meaning dark brown, IV, 176, 462
Canal. See *khalīj*
Canard, M., I, 472
Candles, II, 421, 462, 463, 492, 493, 551; collection for, II, 98; *ṣubḥī*, IV, 133; wax, IV, 133, 321
Candlesticks (*ḥasaka*), IV, 135, 321, 324, 327, 388
Canister, IV, 143, 391, 463
Canister makers, II, 582, 584; Street of, I, 421
Cannabis (marijuana), II, 270
Canopy, IV, 117, 381; bridal, IV, 116, 307
Cantillation, II, 174-175, 562
Cantors, I, 67, 79, 170; II, 16, 74, 90, 92, 107, 152, 189, 219-224, 330, 332, 480, 499, 503, 507, 526, 533, 541, 542, 546, 565, 568-570, 595, 599; III, 59, 79, 103, 133, 187, 195, 240, 254, 259, 300, 335, 338, 429, 430, 456, 469, 479, 502; appeals and collections for, II, 106, 109, 504, 506; as *muqaddam*, II, 69, 70, 73; beneficiaries of community chest, II, 85, 122, 123, 124, 125, 222, 440, 442, 444, 447, 449, 450, 455, 459, 467; chanting of liturgy, II, 160, 161, 219-222, 534, 550; III, 220; communal responsibilities, II, 89, 115, 117, 223-224, 420, 430, 445, 454, 464; confidants of women, II, 223-224; III, 497; as head of Ṣahrajt congregation, II, 50; part of professional class, II, 172;

III, 138, 139, 189; IV, 433; read Scriptures in Babylonian congregations, II, 52; as ritual slaughterers, II, 225, 226, 228; and scholarship, II, 88, 211, 219–222; as scribes and copyists, II, 229, 231, 237, 238, 476, 538; III, 186, 472; social rank, II, 42, 77; III, 14, 138, 218; traveling, II, 135, 136, 542, 544, 553, 569; III, 220, 229
Canvas, I, 333
Cape. See *nişfiyya*
Capernaum, Palestine, II, 146
Capitals and port cities. *See* City
Captain(s), I, 157, 313, 342
Captives, ransom of I, 329–330; II, 55, 79, 96, 97, 169, 170, 216, 472, 481, 482, 486, 499, 500, 507, 539, 542, 549; III, 102, 107, 340; V, 47, 54, 353, 373–376, 457, 462–463, 604, 612, 637
Carat. See *qīrāṭ*
Caravan (*qāfila*), I, 215, 275–280, 289, 294, 337, 468, 469; II, 586; pilgrim, II, 472. See also *mawsim*
Caravanserai, I, 187–189, 267, 338, 349, 350; II, 113, 279, 496; III, 298; IV, 245. See also *dār al-wakāla*; *funduq*
Caraway, I, 199
Carcopino, J., modern author, I, 97
Cardamom (*hayl*), II, 270, 585
Carmathians, I, 131
Carnelians (*ʿaqīq*), I, 154; IV, 205–206, 221, 393, 420, 421
Carobs, I, 121, 316
Carpenter(s), I, 90, 96, 97, 113; II, 297, 434, 461, 465
Carpet, I, 210, 365; II, 52, 53, 149, 150, 474; III, 219; IV, 117 ff., 123–127, 333, 459; *kahramāna*, IV, 337, 383, 462; physician's, IV, 125; with medallions of crowned heads, IV, 121, 123. *See also* Rugs; *waṭā*; *zarbiyya*
Carpet House, IV, 123, 125
Carriages, I, 275
Carthage, North Africa, IV, 7
Carthaginians, II, 366
carthamus (Lat., safflower seed), I, 120
Carved wood, IV, 64, 65, 66, 67, 103
Casanova, Paul, IV, 28; V, 96
Cash, II, 547–548; IV, 447; scarcity of, III, 121, 123, 155
Caspian Sea, IV, 144, 452
Cassia (laxative), II, 268, 584
Cassia, daughter of Shefaṭyā, III, 32–33, 319; IV, 139
Casson, Lionel, I, 476, 484
Castile (Castilia), Spain, I, 41, 55; II, 95
"Castle of Edom," Fustat, I, 44
catarzo (Ital., floss silk). *See* Silk
Catholic (-s, -ism), III, I, 55, 158
Catholicus, Head of Nestorian church, I, 52; II, 17, 176, 287, 298
Cattawi Pasha, Joseph M., I, 5
Cattle: breeding, I, 124; trade in, I, 211
Cattle pen. See *zareba*
Ceiling, IV, 65, 365
Cellar, wine, IV, 259
Cemetery: of Fustat, V, 162–163; visits to, V, 183–186
Censer (*mijmara*), IV, 137, 388, 389. See also *mugmār*
Census, II, 460
Central Asia, I, 228, 400
Ceramics. *See* Pottery
Ceremonial of the Fatimid court, II, 374
Certificate of yeshiva, II, 212
"Certified," designation of cantors, II, 223. See also *mumḥe*
Cesspool cleaning, II, 117; IV, 36–37, 54
Ceuta (Sabta), Morocco, I, 50, 63, 64, 325; II, 307, 381, 593; V, 76, 528
Ceylon, I, 50; II, 331
Chains, IV, 205–206, 218. *See also* Necklace
Chairs, absence of, IV, 107, 108
Chameleon-colored, IV, 120, 324, 381
Chandeliers (*būqandalāt*), II, 150, 551; IV, 133, 135
Chapira, Bernard, I, 5
Character. *See* Personality
Chard (leaf beets), IV, 230, 231, 433
Chardin, Sir John, I, 160
Charitable foundations. *See* Pious foundations
Charity, II, 91–143; attitudes toward, V, 81, 92–94, 354, 358; bequests, V, 142–143; economic importance, V, 74–75, 91–92, 353–354, 358; ecumenical aspects, II, 94–97; interfaith, II, 91, 282; legal status, V, 354–358; letters requesting, V, 76-89, 227, 233–234; motivation of, II, 142; popular character of, II, 97-99; private, II, 110, 123, 143, 455, 490, 544; III, 325, 349, 353; public, II, 91–143, 310, 403, 455, 474; III, 42, 63–65, 119, 259–260, 276, 325 (*see also* Pious foundations); virtue, V, 192, 358
Chaucer, V, 604
Cheating (customs) I, 62, 344
Checks. *See* Orders of payment
Cheese, I, 46, 76, 105, 124, 188, 208, 223, 270, 366, 380, 444; II, 532; IV, 10, 251–252, 428, 429, 443, 444; V,

534. See also *ḥālūm*; *kaysī*; *makhlūṭ*; *mishsh*
Cheese maker (-ing), I, 150, 428, 437; II, 500; IV, 443
Chemicals, I, 154
Chess, II, 302; V, 44–45
Chessplayer, I, 254
Chestmakers, I, 83, 113, 423
Chests, I, 113; IV, 129–131, 316, 320, 321, 331. See also *ṣundūq*
Chewing gum, IV, 246, 248–249, 441, 442
Chicken, I, 124, 211; II, 100, 228, 420, 432, 463; III, 194; IV, 230, 232, 233, 247, 249–250; food for sick, IV, 232–233, 250, 422, 433, 434, 443
Chicken coops, IV, 250, 443
Chickpeas, I, 438; IV, 232, 245, 440
Chief of police, II, 56, 63, 68, 358, 428
Childbirth, III, 226, 230–231
Child(ren), II, 41, 42, 52, 137, 173–185; as collateral, I, 259; early participation in adult life, III, 236–237, 342; foster, III, 248–249; given wine, III, 234; grown-up, III, 240–248; labor, I, 98-99; marriage of, III, 76, 78, 79, 88, 344; neglect, III, 200; number of, III, 237–240; upbringing, III, 234–237, 247, 341; value to parents, III, 223–224. *See also* Family feeling; Parents
Child's death as atonement for father's sins, III, 227
China, Chinese, I, 67, 81, 104, 133, 222, 282, 295, 314; II, 416; III, 12, 355; IV, 106, 119, 146, 165, 192, 193, 322
China. *See* Porcelain
Chios, I, 214, 268
Choker, *ḥanak*, IV, 204, 210, 216, 319, 329; *mikhnaqa* (10–11 cy.), IV, 216, 426, 427. *See also* Necklace
Chorasin, synagogue in, II, 146
Christian(-s, -ity), I, 112, 248, 287, 345; II, 17, 18, 60, 82, 164, 264, 265, 345, 430, 434, 582, 614; III, 7, 36, 47, 60, 357; IV, 7, 8, 13, 27, 44, 45, 50, 155, 189, 198, 227; V, 6; attitudes toward slaves and slavegirls, I, 134, 142; (Coptic) calendar regulates seafaring, I, 311; character of communal life under Islam, II, 1, 2, 3, 4, 273–278; communal autonomy, II, 311, 312, 401, 402, 403, 404, 407; III, 83; communal crises and strife, II, 61, 332; conversion to/from, II, 304, 305, 308, 309, 372, 445, 592, 593; Coptic, I, 18, 98, 105, 110, 311, 317, 355; II, 19, 146, 176, 281, 305; III, 158, 260, 323, 457 (*see also* Church, Coptic; Coptic deacon; Coptic monks; Coptic numerals); countries, I, 61, 65, 66, 211; II, 37; discrimination and restrictions, I, 62; II, 143, 285–288; IV, 195; domestic architecture of, I, 71; economic activities of, I, 40, 73, 100, 110, 119, 122; II, 295, 586; III, 59; IV, 10, 181; education and scholarship, II, 176, 196, 205, 206; neighbors to Jews or Muslims, I, 110, 119; II, 114, 263, 290, 291, 292, 293, 421, 533, 545, 589; III, 243, 327; IV, 13, 16, 17, 19, 21, 46, 49, 56, 58, 60, 64, 98, 101, 279, 281, 282, 286, 295; intercommunal relations, II, 280, 281, 282, 283, 289–300; interplay of laws, parallel customs, III, 142, 168; Jacobite, IV, 99; loans by Jews to, I, 257; Melchite, III, 357; IV, 98; Nestorian(s), III, 95; partnerships with Jews, I, 385; II, 292, 295; persecutions of, I, 19, 34, 41; II, 28, 137, 299–300, 435; physicians, II, 241, 244, 245, 252, 256, 258, 578, 610; pilgrimage, I, 55, 257; II, 370, 447; and piracy, I, 327, 328, 329; III, 340; and poll tax, I, 147, 344; II, 387, 391, 392, 394; religious and communal officials, II, 217, 219; service to Muslim government, I, 31, 34, 72, 416; II, 374, 376, 378, 527; IV, 10; slave girls, I, 136 (*see also* European slavegirls; Slavegirls); social position of, I, 71; travel by, I, 345, 347; use of wine, I, 123; IV, 253, 258
Chronology, dating, I, 23, 207, 208, 289-290, 355–357, 457, 489, 491
Church(es), II, 2, 3, 9, 19, 23, 55, 82, 85, 112, 113, 143–155, 166, 185, 277, 280, 308, 309, 333, 435; IV, 3, 16, 17, 30, 32, 68, 118, 124, 133, 137; Coptic, II, 146, 146, 149, 152, 153, 164, 277, 333, 407, 554; Eastern, II, 5–6, 16, 159, 176; III, 94, 158, 276, 357; music, II, 151; property, IV, 25
Church chant, II, 175
Cinnamon, I, 44, 154, 200, 219, 337
Cipolla, Carlo M., I, 391
Circumcision, II, 89, 122, 301, 309, 485, 498, 507, 591-592; III, 20, 232–233; Coptic, III, 232–233
Cistern, IV, 68
Citrus fruit, I, 121
City, medieval Islamic, IV, 1–47, 2
Civil unrest, IV, 18, 168. *See also* Political turmoil
Claim, legal, II, 601
Class, I, 75–80; III, 129, 141

Class differences: attitudes towards, V, 80, 254–255; sexuality, V, 308–309, 321. *See also* Social rank
Cleaner, cleaning, (*ṣafy*), IV, 178, 183, 409
Cleanliness, personal, V, 100. *See also* Bathhouses
Cleopatra, Queen, I, 298
Clerks, III, 73, 80, 94, 97, 98, 108, 133, 141, 143, 170, 203, 243, 263; of private persons, II, 467
Clinton, Jerome, V, 553
Cloak, faced, IV, 181, 182; *kisā*, II, 457; IV, 188, 384, 411; *malḥafa* and *mulāʾa*, I, 90; II, 500; III, 467; IV, 116, 154, 157, 166, 179, 180, 181, 182, 188, 320, 321, 327, 333, 380, 396, 401, 408, 409, 452, 461; *mukhlaf*, IV, 189, 199, 326, 456, 463; *wiqāya*, IV, 315, 452; wool, IV, 153
"Closing of the account," I, 208
Cloth. *See* individual fabrics and textiles
Clothier(s), I, 83, 155; II, 477; III, 59
Clothing, I, 71–72, 150, 203, 210, 229 and *passim*; II, 548, 559, 591; IV, 47, 105, 150–200, 227, 450–467; abstain from changing, IV, 157; attitudes toward, IV, 150–152; cash value of, IV, 184–185ff.; care of, IV, 183–184, 412; changing for the night, IV, 157–158; changing for Sabbath and holidays, IV, 155–158; cleaning of, IV, 183; collection for, II, 109, 503; cosmopolitan aspects, IV, 190-192; custom-made, IV, 179; discrimination in, II, 286–288; distribution of, II, 100, 103, 123, 130–132, 134, 142, 418, 420, 423, 442, 444, 446, 448, 459, 500, 501; III, 65, 324; economic importance of, IV, 184-190; fabrics, IV, 164–172; "for home and street," IV, 152–153; given to orphans, IV, 190; as gift to fiancee, III, 68, 85, 109–110; handouts of, IV, 155, 190; husband obliged to provide for wife, IV, 187–188, 314; of Jewish women, IV, 198–200; lack of, V, 89–90, 102; local aspects, IV, 193; more prestigious than food, IV, 150-151; more valuable than jewelry in dowries, IV, 186–187; mourning, V, 173, 174, 177; old, II, 109; of non-Muslims, IV, 193ff., 396, 416; passed from mother to daughter, IV, 188; for paying customs, IV, 185; of the poor, IV, 151, 152, 154; price of, IV, 166; ritual, II, 599; of schoolboys (*see* Schoolboys); of scribes, II, 238; old, no collection of, II, 109; types of, IV, 158–164; used (*see* Second-hand clothes); value of houses compared with (in dowries), IV, 189-190; wife's economic security and power, IV, 185–186ff.
"Cloud," color, IV, 166, 174, 320, 323
Cloves, I, 154; IV, 183, 202, 419
Coat. See *ridāʾ*
Cobblers, I, 51, 75, 92, 111; II, 63, 536; IV, 164
Code of Law of Maimonides, II, 125, 142, 207, 313, 329, 336, 546
Codex Hammurabi, II, 257
Coffins, V, 162. *See also* Burial; Death
Cohen, Hayyim J., I, 104, 112, 119, 416; V, 308
Cohesiveness of the family, III, 4, 15
Coins. *See* Copper; Dinar; Dirhem; Money; Purses of coins
Cold, IV, 136, 153; complaints about, IV, 117. *See also* Weather
Collar, IV, 164. *See also* Turban
Collar (*miḥbas*). *See* Necklace
Collateral(s), I, 259, 262, 263, 385, 463; IV, 457
Collection fees, II, 80, 117
Collection of payment, I, 197–200. *See also* Credit; Debt
Collections, II, 429, 472–510, 543; joint, II, 534; special, II, 12, 137–138; weekly, II, 46, 100, 108. *See also* Pledges
Collectors of revenue, II, 79, 116, 539
Colocasia, IV, 232, 245, 434, 440
Colocasia, nickname, II, 454
Cologne, Germany, I, 296; II, 58
Colonnade, The. See *ṣaffayn*
Colophons, II, 181, 240
Colophony, IV, 260, 447
Colors, I, 106–107; IV, 113, 172–177, 181. *See also* Dyeing, dyers and separate listings under amber; apricot; asparagus; bitter orange; black; blackish-blue (*kuḥlī*); blue; bluish-iridescent; brown; brownish-pink (eye of the partridge); camphor; chameleon-colored; "cloud"; crimson; dark blue; dust; emerald; gazelle-blood; ginger; grayish; green; honey; honeydew; lead; *maftūḥ*; *manna*; musk; olive green; orange; peppergray; pink; pomegranate; purple; purplish-brown; *qaṭawī*; red; rose marmelade; ruby; safflower; saffron; *saḥābī* (white); sandal; sandalwood; sky blue; *ubābī*; violet; wax; white; wine; yellow
Columns in synagogues, II, 145, 147, 150

Combination lock, IV, 131
Combs, I, 99–100; IV, 224–225, 322, 430; V, 37, 515
Coming of age, III, 236–237. *See also* Puberty
Commenda (*muḍāraba, qirāḍ*), I, 163, 171–180, 183, 184, 186, 247, 384; II, 262, 294, 328, 590. *See also* Partnership
Commission, brokerage, I, 163, 169, 183–186, 191, 238–240, 243–244, 342; IV, 289
Communal accounts, IV, 37, 38, 40, 104
Communal autonomy, II, 613–615
Communal buildings: maintenance of, II, 100, 119–120; rents of, IV, 291-296; signs on, II, 121
Communal jurisdiction, II, 311–345, 395–407, 594–603
Communal officials, II, 425, 428, 430, 439, 440, 441, 451, 452, 455, 459, 460, 462, 529, 535, 537-541, 588, 595
Communal prayer. *See* Prayer, communal
Communal property. *See* Pious foundations
Communal records, II, 93
Communal services. *See* Social services
Communal treasury, II, 543
Community chest (*qōdesh*). *See* Pious foundations
Community officials, IV, 9
Companions of Prophet Muhammad, V, 557
Competition, II, 606, 608; V, 189-190, 198, 299–300; among physicians, II, 257; among teachers, II, 186, 187; economic by newcomers, II, 67–68
Complaints, attitudes toward, V, 73
Compound(s) of a city, IV, 14, 18, 35, 56, 77
Compound of the Jerusalemites, III, 324; IV, 14, 102
Compound of the poor, II, 415; IV, 14
Concealing the body, IV, 153, 161
Concubinage, II, 352; III, 143, 147, 170; V, 311, 321-322, 486-487. *See also* Slavegirls
conditum (wine with honey and spices), IV, 260
Condolence, III, 217; V, 28, 177–181
Confiscation by market police, II, 268
Congregation. *See* Local community
Congratulation(s), III, 58, 116, 118, 217; V, 27, 42, 110–111
Conjugal relations, III, 168–170, 190. *See also* Marriage; Sexual activity
Constantelos, Demetrios J., V, 74
Constantinople (Istanbul), I, 39, 43, 44, 53, 58, 84, 92, 211, 325, 326, 327; II, 54, 167, 281, 384, 463, 534; III, 177, 200; IV, 1, 19, 168, 402; V, 36. *See also* Byzantine; Silk
Consuls, Italian, I, 192
Containers of perfumes, IV, 316, 452
Containers for wine, I, 464–465, 485; IV, 256–257, 258, 259, 445, 446, 447
Contract(s), II, 546, 599, 600, 603, 613; of sale, I, 11, 123, 141, 196
Contributions, II, 440, 471–510, 580, 606; reduction of, II, 479
Conversion: attitudes toward, V, 237, 328, 461; to Islam, II, 51, 299–311, 534, 591-594, 610; III, 11, 12, 135, 200, 264, 290; IV, 287; V, 59, 60–61, 398, 399, 521; to Judaism, II, 303–311; to Sufism, V, 471–474. *See also* Apostasy
Convoys, I, 167, 277, 306, 308, 319, 321, 331
Cook(s), II, 453, 467, 529
Cooking: Coptic, IV, 234; woman not praised for, IV, 228–229
Cooling jars, IV, 320
Copper, I, 108, 154, 334, 420; IV, 131, 132, 134, 135, 138, 139, 147; basin, (*qadaḥ*), II, 584; IV, 124, 393; board of kitchen (*kab*[*a*]*ka*), IV, 144, 392; coins, I, 360, 388 (see also *fals*); covers, IV, 142; cups, IV, 142; as currency, II, 490; section of trousseau list, IV, 133, 144, 327, 450, 452; vessels, II, 584; IV, 106, 124, 139, 140, 324
Coppersmiths, I, 83, 109; IV, 123, 383, 464; Street of, IV, 28, 351
Copperware, Lebanese, IV, 135
Copt, Coptic. *See* Christian, Coptic
Coptic church. *See* Church, Coptic
Coptic deacon, III, 83, 117, 142
Coptic monks, II, 153
Coptic numerals, I, 209, 241; II, 178, 303, 421, 426, 431, 450, 456, 461, 463, 467, 483, 492, 493, 494, 495, 496, 497, 499, 508; IV, 433, 465
Copyists, II, 189, 228–240, 444, 560, 574-575; female, II, 558, 572. *See also* Scribes
Corals, I, 47, 99–100, 153, 154, 155, 177, 199, 222, 334; IV, 201, 386; merchant of (*marjānī, mirjānī*), I, 416, 438
Cordova, Spain, I, 69; II, 10, 172, 173; III, 146, 149; IV, 169, 399, 402
Coriander, II, 585; IV, 232
Cork shoes (*aqrāq*), I, 422; IV, 163, 400

Coromandel coast, India, **III**, 207
Corporation, the. See *ḥavūrā*
Correspondence, commercial and private, **I**, 11–12, 26, 162, 163 and *passim*
Corridor (*dihlīz*), **IV**, 62–63, 75, 365; usually unlit, **IV**, 136
Corvee, **II**, 393-394, 612
Cosmopolitanism, **I**, 63–64
Cost of transport, **I**, 339–346
Costume jewelry, **IV**, 202, 216
Costumes, male and female, **IV**, 153–155
Cotton (*quṭn*), **I**, 105–154, 418, 419; **IV**, 159, 165, 170–171, 177, 180, 404; worn by middle class, **IV**, 165; clothing of the poor, **IV**, 170; trader in (*qaṭṭān*), **IV**, 170, 404; clothing of, **III**, 304–305
Coulton, George Gordon, **V**, 337
"Court" (= judge), **II**, 314; **IV**, 326, 427, 457
Court clerk, **II**, 223, 229, 445
Court physicians, **IV**, 11
Court records, **I**, 9, 10, 15, 146, 162, 177, 179, 183, 184, 186, 248, 251ff., 362–367, 380, 458, 464; **II**, 313–327, 343, 522, 526, 600; **III**, 96, 125, 155, 187, 188, 191, 197, 202, 207, 214, 236, 247, 254, 262, 266, 267, 282, 288, 289, 292, 294, 332, 348, 352; **V**, 487–488; Judeo-Persian, **III**, 289
Courts, Jewish, **I**, 59, 181, 204, 251–252, 257, 259, 262, 265, 268, 273, 382, 384, 391; **II**, 8, 25, 33, 34, 58, 74, 78, 82, 83, 84, 115, 153, 186, 207, 311–345; Jewish and Muslim, **II**, 526, 596, 598, 602, 606, 613, 614; Muslim, **I**, 123, 181, 204, 251–252, 259, 260, 262, 273, 366, 384, 445; **II**, 3, 322, 398–402; **IV**, 409. *See also* Judges; Judiciary, Jewish; Law; Procedure; Qadi
Courtiers, **II**, 39, 345–354
Courtyard, central, **IV**, 11, 48, 56, 59, 62, 63, 77, 369
Cousin(s), **III**, 55
Coverlet (*muḍarraba*), **IV**, 316, 452
Cow (or Son of the Cow), family name, **III**, 12
Cowley, A. E., **I**, 6
Cowry (cowrie) shells, **I**, 154, 275, 373; **IV**, 201
Craftsmen, **I**, 49, 51, 80–116, 150, 254, 262, 264, and *passim*; **II**, 179, 297, 424, 440, 441, 466; **III**, 189, 191, 193. *See also* Artisans
Credit, **I**, 151, 197–200, 250, 262 and *passim*
Creme (*zubd*), **IV**, 233, 434
Crescent (*hilāl*), **IV**, 210, 216
Creswell, K. A. C., **IV**, 73
Creswick, H. R., **I**, 4
Crete, **I**, 38, 46, 47, 49, 124, 214, 325; **II**, 79, 130, 444; **IV**, 168, 402, 443
Criminal cases, **II**, 330
Crimson (*qirmiz*), **I**, 417; **IV**, 169, 173, 193, 406; dyer of (*qirmizīnī*), **I**, 107, 420
Cross on clothing, **IV**, 199
Crown. *See* Tiara
Crusaders, Crusades, **I**, 18, 19, 32, 35, 36, 37, 43, 45, 57, 98, 102, 104, 127, 132, 180, 259, 281, 296; **II**, 55, 88, 119, 128, 130, 137, 152, 169, 201, 277, 282, 393, 500, 501, 507; **III**, 10, 114, 190, 201, 238, 248, 286, 325, 356, 379; **IV**, 41, 42, 56, 161, 261; **V**, 49, 54, 55–56, 372–379, 612
Crypto-Jews, **II**, 300
Crystal (Rock-), **I**, 99–100
Crystal (*billawr*), **IV**, 223, 224, 319, 322, 327, 343, 430, 467; describing lustrous textile, **IV**, 174
Cubeb, **I**, 219; **IV**, 230, 433
Cucumber (*faqqūs*), **IV**, 232, 433
Cuff (*tannūr*), **IV**, 204, 319
Cup: common drinking (*kūz*), **IV**, 142, 148, 393, 394 (see also *kūz*); drunk by bride and groom at betrothal, **III**, 87, 95
Cupper. *See* Bloodletter
Curse(s), **III**, 229; **IV**, 14; **V**, 234–235. *See also* Blessings; Wife, beating and cursing
Curtains (*sitr, sutūr*), **II**, 589; **IV**, 117ff., 125, 381, 382; as portières, **IV**, 118; in synagogue, **II**, 146, 423
Cushions, **IV**, 108, 109, 111ff., 306-307; in synagogue, **II**, 149, 156. See also *miswara*
Customs duties, **I**, 345, 489; **II**, 289, 360, 589, 608, 610
Customs house, **I**, 201, 202, 218, 337, 341–346. *See also* Cheating
Customs offices, **II**, 371
Cyprus, **I**, 38, 214, 323; **II**, 230

D

(*ʿal*) *daʿat ha-qāhāl* (Heb.) = Ar. *ʿan rayʾ al-jamāʿa* ("with the consent of the community"), **II**, 542
ḍabābīr (packages, mail pouches), **I**, 389
dabāgha (tanning), **II**, 605
dābbat furāniq (courier's mount), **I**, 283
Dabīqī linen. *See* Linen

dāda (nurse for children), I, 135, 137, 434
dādhī. *See* Lichen
dafaʿ ("paid"), II, 432
daftar (booklet or account book), I, 205, 206, 209
daftar al-muwāyama (daily account book), I, 451
dahhānūn (painters in oil), I, 423
Dahrūṭ, Upper Egypt, I, 299; V, 108
Dahshūr, I, 86
dāʿī, II, 578
ḍaʿīf, poor young man, II, 415, 418, 426, 457
Dairy products, IV, 252
Dais. See *martaba*
dajājī (chicken dealer), I, 124, 410; III, 206; IV, 233
dakākīn (retail shops), IV, 58
Dakarnas, Egypt, II, 463
Dakarnasiyya, IV, 359
dakhal (returning to Fustat-Cairo or Alexandria from countryside), IV, 9
dakka (or *dikka*), sleeping bench, IV, 114, 131, 379
dalāla. *See* Commission
Dalāṣ, II, 610
Dalāta, Palestine, II, 467
dallāl (broker), I, 160–161, 439
dallāla (woman broker), I, 161, 431; III, 330, 504
ḍamān (appointment as tax-farmer), II, 361, 363, 607
Damanhūr, Egypt, III, 82
Damascus, Damascene, I, 8, 20, 35, 36, 46, 56, 58, 68, 83, 106, 129, 183, 191, 212, 244, 249; II, 217, 211, 212, 308, 357, 475, 502, 593, 600, 601; III, 30, 31, 38, 93, 94, 98, 136, 148, 198, 199, 206, 278, 280, 285, 287, 325, 405, 408, 415, 416, 428, 437, 446, 447, 448, 456, 462, 489, 491, 497, 499, 504; IV, 6, 8, 10, 15, 19, 22, 56, 57, 120, 136, 139, 140, 184, 186, 193, 215, 282, 286, 353, 362, 363, 389, 390, 391, 393, 394, 412, 426, 428, 429, 430, 456; communal officials, II, 56, 70, 78, 81, 221, 316, 320, 526, 527, 571; contributors to charity, I, 122; II, 29, 202, 211, 496; education, II, 182, 186, 559; exilarch, II, 19; beneficiaries of community chest in Fustat from, II, 439, 441, 447, 454, 461, 467; domestic architecture, IV, 71, 73, 74; foreigners from in Egypt, I, 49; II, 158, 384, 429; III, 188; Gaon, II, 18; Great Synagogue, IV, 20; hospital, II, 251; Karaites, II, 534; letters to/from, I, 82, 178, 199, 243, 291, 426; II, 182, 573; III, 26, 201, 234, 257, 468, 484; Market of the Jews, IV, 20; Market of the Laborers, IV, 20, 353; Palestinian and Babylonian congregations, II, 6; Palestinian yeshiva in, I, 257; II, 30, 201, 513; pound (weight), I, 360; relations between communities, I, 71; relations with government, II, 48, 605; siege of, II, 347; silk, I, 102; synagogues in, II, 204, 415, 416, 520; travel to/from, I, 276, 277, 278, 284, 348; II, 45; III, 340, 345; IV, 227
Damask, siglaton, I, 102, 417; IV, 116, 121 and *passim*, 455
Dāmghān, I, 400
Damietta (Dimyāṭ), Egypt, I, 20, 37, 44, 178, 179, 186, 190, 213, 233, 296, 366, 413; II, 43, 521; III, 178, 290, 295; IV, 9, 43, 167, 179, 349, 376, 401, 408; V, 55; Abuʾl-Munajjā in, II, 356, 377; V, 566; beneficiaries of community chest from, II, 468; charitable collections in, II, 506, 534; communal institutions and officials in, II, 8, 79, 231, 237, 315, 322, 444, 595, 597, 599; Crusades, I, 98; II, 79, 393; V, 535; domestic architecture, IV, 75; education in, II, 185; elders, II, 58, 597; III, 46; govt. officials in, II, 356, 366, 371, 376, 377; industries, I, 82; Muslim-Christian relations in, II, 394; Samaritans in, II, 520
ḍamīn, person for whom security is given, II, 440, 605, 606
ḍāmin. *See* Tax farmers
Damīra, Egypt, I, 404; II, 187, 384, 461, 463, 485, 533, 537, 568, 589, 601, 612; III, 284–285, 496; IV, 43
Dammūh, Egypt, I, 425; II, 42, 78, 111, 144, 151, 333, 426, 427, 429, 452, 459, 485; III, 176, 211, 337, 464; IV, 35, 36, 261; variant spellings, V, 509; synagogue of, I, 96, 462; V, 19, 20–24, 510, 511
Damsīs, Egypt, I, 61, 84, 417, 425, 426; II, 222, 438, 544, 599; III, 388, 401, 438; IV, 43, 129, 162, 215, 399, 400, 426; V, 567
Dan, a proselyte, II, 307
dānaq, one sixth of a *qīrāṭ*. *See* Money of account
Dancers, female, I, 129
Dancing, V, 22, 42, 202
Daniel, R., II, 452
Daniel b. Azariah. *See* Daniel b. Azarya
Daniel b. Azarya, Gaon and *nāsī*, I, 435;

II, 15, 19, 64, 168, 332, 436, 511–512, 515, 523, 525, 527, 528, 529, 543, 587, 604; III, 15, 31, 118, 137, 261, 292-293, 442, 447, 461, 483, 492; V, 32, 242, 258, 263–264, 298-299, 321, 395, 512, 513, 517, 519, 571, 578, 585, 596, 618, 625
Daniel b. Elazar, Gaon, II, 527
Daniel b. Ḥisday, Exilarch, I, 396; II, 18, 20, 524
Daniel Ibn Shāma, V, 573
Dāniyāl (Daniel) Ibn Shaʿyā, III, 10
Daniel al-Qūmisī, V, 361
daniyy (poor quality), I, 452
daqqāq (flour seller), I, 423
daqqāqa (female flour seller), I, 431
al-Daqqī, dealer in fine goods, II, 449
dār: house, compound, I, 83; II, 430, 542; IV, 56ff., 94, 292, 362, 363 (*see also* House); house, family, III, 425
dār al-anmāṭ. See *dār al-māṭ*
dār al-aruzz (House of Rice), storehouse and bourse for sale of rice, I, 426, 448
darb (alley, street), I, 426; IV, 14, 350, 353. *See also* Streets and quarters in Cairo; Streets and quarters in Fustat
dār al-baraka (House of Blessing), place for financial transactions, I, 458; IV, 27–28, 351. *See also* Exchange rate; *dār al-ṣarf*
darbī, II, 413
darb al-kanīs (street of the synagogue), II, 435
darb al-maqādisa. *See* Jerusalem compound
darb al-zanājiliyyīn. *See* Canister Makers, Street of
dār al-ḍarb, II, 605. *See also* Mint
dardāra (elm trunks), IV, 376
Dardīr mansion, IV, 65
dār al-Fāḍil, II, 509
Dār al-Fāʾizī, quarter in Fustat, V, 524
dargā, II, 568
dār al-ḥarīr (House of Silk), I, 448
dār al-imāra, IV, 356
ḍarīr (*ṣarīr*, *ṭarīr*), blind, II, 574
Darius, Persian king, III, 21
dār al-jadīda (New House), I, 448
dār al-jawhar. *See* Jewelry House
dār al-kattān (House of Flax), I, 448
Dark blue, IV, 126
dār al-khall (Vinegar House), I, 428
dār al-lawz (House of Almonds), I, 448
"Darling," slave girl, I, 139
dār mānak, IV, 27, 355
dār al-māṭ (House of Carpets), I, 365, 448; II, 474
dār al-muʾan (House of Dues), I, 448
al-dār al-mubāraka. See *dār al-baraka*
dārōsh, man expounding the Scriptures, II, 567
dār al-qāḍī, II, 607
ḍarra (Ar. = Heb. *ṣāra*), rival wife, III, 209
darrāb (guard), IV, 14, 35, 351
ḍarrāb (hammerer), I, 420
dār al-ṣarf (Exchange House of Fustat), I, 170, 174, 230, 238, 239; II, 348, 354, 508, 512; IV, 22, 27–28. See also *dār al-baraka*
darshān. See *dārōsh*
dār al-sukkar (House of Sugar), I, 448; II, 531
dār al-sulṭān (Sultan's palace), II, 603; IV, 356
dār al-ṭirāz, II, 376
ḍarūriyyāt (necessities), II, 559
dār al-wakāla (agency house of representative of merchants), I, 187-192, 218, 269, 446, 447; II, 45, 341, 366, 367, 376, 607, 609; IV, 26, 27. *See also* Caravanserai
dār al-zabīb (House of Raisins), I, 448
dār al-zaʿfarān (Saffron House), II, 509
dār al-zayt, I, 448
dast. *See* Bracelets; Set
dast (quire or package), I, 410
dastaynaq. *See* Bracelet
Date(s) (*tamr*, *balaḥ*, *ruṭab*, *busr*), I, 120–121; IV, 232, 247, 440, 441; gift for Day of Atonement, IV, 247; merchant, I, 155; pressed, IV, 247, 441
Date honey, IV, 247
Date palms, I, 118, 121; in house, IV, 76, 77
Dates. *See* Chronology
Dāʾūd b. Abuʾl-Faraj ʿImrān b. Levi ha-Kohen. *See* David b. Amram ha-Kohen
Dāʾūd b. Mūsā, III, 426
Dāʾūd b. Nahum, V, 573
Daughter(s), III, 24, 39, 61, 68, 227–229, 341–342; as heir, II, 395-396. *See also* Children; *karīma*; Parents
David, biblical, II, 17-19, 89, 523; V, 583, 643
David, House of, II, 458, 523
David, brother of Maimonides. *See* David Maimonides
David, man designating himself as *nāsī*, II, 458
David Ibn Abī Zimra, rabbi, III, 425
David b. Abraham al-Fāsī, V, 363, 372
David (I) b. Abraham Maimonides, Nagid, I, 261; II, 31, 32, 116, 132, 164, 190, 244, 431, 433, 492, 493, 494, 515,

526, 527–528, 529; **III**, 284, 448; **IV**, 285; **V**, 89, 513
David Allūf b. Ḥōtām, **III**, 454
David b. Amram, **II**, 26; **III**, 136, 456; **IV**, 186
David b. Azarya, brother of Daniel b. Azarya, **III**, 118, 137
David b. Daniel b. Azarya, Exilarch, **II**, 18, 19, 30, 32, 33, 39, 78, 332, 415, 442, 508, 512, 523, 528, 565, 571, 595; **III**, 136, 261, 280, 442, 481, 505; **V**, 258, 596
David b. Ephraim, **III**, 441
David al-Fāsī, **V**, 611
David b. Isaac, **II**, 472, 534; **V**, 367, 609
David (II) b. Joshua, Nagid, descendant of Maimonides, **II**, 41, 133, 245, 252; **V**, 471, 472–474
David b. Judah, **II**, 566
David Kimḥī, **V**, 615
David ha-Kohen *ha-meʿulle*, **II**, 567
David b. Maimon. *See* David Maimonides
David Maimonides, brother of Moses Maimonides, **II**, 240, 258, 448; **III**, 17, 32; **V**, 328, 393
David (I) Maimonides. *See* David (I) b. Abraham Maimonides
David (II) Maimonides. *See* David (II) b. Joshua, descendant of Maimonides
David b. Maymon. *See* David Maimonides
David b. Mevōrākh, known as Ben Khuzayr, **III**, 469, 499
David Ibn al-Muqammiṣ, a Karaite, **V**, 619
David *ha-nāsī*, **III**, 481
David *ha-nāsī* b. Daniel, **III**, 481
David the Refugee, *pālīṭ*, b. R. Joseph, **IV**, 328, 457
David b. Shekhanya, **II**, 570, 571, 600; **III**, 138, 456; **V**, 557
David b. Solomon b. David, **V**, 379
Davidson, Israel, **V**, 388–389
David b. Zakkay, **V**, 386, 614
ḍawāḥī, villages around Cairo, **II**, 468
dawātī (maker of writing cases), **I**, 416
ḍayʿa (village or farm), **I**, 117–118, 425, 426; **II**, 608; **III**, 207
Daybed. See *ṭarrāḥa*
dayn, **II**, 415
dayn ḥāll, a debt already due, **I**, 385
Day of Atonement, **II**, 106, 129, 164, 168, 351, 499, 506, 544, 568, 602; **III**, 3, 125, 351; **IV**, 156, 192, 247; **V**, 270, 349–350, 426, 603
Day of Judgment, **II**, 309, 340
dayyān (Heb.). *See* Judge
dayyān muvhāq (presiding judge), **II**, 514. *See also* Judge
dayyān al-yahūd (judge of the Jews), **II**, 326, 327, 538, 598. *See also* Judge
Dead Sea Scrolls, **I**, 17; **II**, 240, 345; **III**, 110, 169
Death: attitudes toward, **V**, 128–131; God's role, **V**, 130–131, 140–141, 155; Islamic notions, **V**, 131; life after, **V**, 129, 130, 161, 182–185, 245, 406–409, 411; notification of government office of, **III**, 277; scenes, **V**, 155–156; thoughts of, **V**, 244–245. *See also* Burial; Funerals; Deathbed declarations; Mourning; Wills
Deathbed declarations, **I**, 10, 135, 144, 152, 264; **II**, 126, 252, 413, 436, 540, 578, 593; **III**, 42, 146, 168, 227, 251–254, 255, 259, 327, 331, 382, 385, 409, 410, 411, 412, 443, 487; **IV**, 414
Debt, **I**, 96, 168, 198, 250–253, 384; **II**, 446, 529, 532, 544, 545, 607, 613, 614; of relative to be paid by family, **III**, 43; transfer of (*ḥawāla*), **I**, 241–242, 460; **II**, 488, 494, 502. *See also* Credit
Debtor, **IV**, 9
Decline of Eastern Jewry, **II**, 103, 120, 124, 128, 138, 141, 215, 219, 258, 277, 303, 321, 327, 361
Decorative covers, **IV**, 130
Deferment of rent, **I**, 449; **IV**, 294
Degree (diploma), **II**, 565
"Delight of the Yeshiva," honorific title, **II**, 543; **III**, 240, 290, 294
Delphi, Greece, **III**, 320
Demona, Sicily, **IV**, 126, 193, 383, 416
denarius (Lat.), **I**, 359. *See also* Dinar
Denia, Spain, **I**, 69, 126, 212, 213, 318; **II**, 379, 602, 610
Dental care, **V**, 101
Dentists, **II**, 255
Denunciation, **II**, 602
Deodar, **II**, 584
Deodorizing a room, **IV**, 137
Department of Antiquities, Egyptian, **IV**, 53
de Planhol, X., **IV**, 5
Depression, **III**, 222
Deputy judges, **II**, 20, 53, 70, 316, 460, 515, 596. See also *nāʾib*
Derʿa, **I**, 53. *See* Abraham b. Jacob
Derʿa, Morocco, **II**, 429, 499
derāsh. *See* Sermon
Dervish cups (*kashkūlayn*), **IV**, 424, 426
derwend (iron locks), **IV**, 376
Description de l'Egypte, **IV**, 55
Dessau, Herman, **V**, 497
Detectives, **II**, 587, 608, 610

"Dexterity," slave girl, I, 137, 138, 139
deyōdar. *See* Deodar
dhabbāḥ. *See* Ritual slaughterer
dhabīḥa, *dhabāḥa* (*dhabēḥa*). *See* Ritual slaughter
d(h)abl. *See* Tortoiseshell
dhahab. *See* Gold
Dhahab, slave girl. *See* "Gold"
dhahabī. *See* Goldsmith
dhāqāt (Gr. *deka*, tens), accounting instrument, II, 557
dhibāḥa. See *dhabīḥa*
dhimma, responsibility, III, 21
dhimmī. *See* Non-Muslim
Dhū Jibla, capital of Inner Yemen, V, 562
Dhukur ("Treasure"), f., III, 279
dhū riyāsatayn ("the man with the two commands"), II, 606
Dhuʾl-Kifl, V, 508
"Diadem," the cantor. *See* Hillel b. Eli
ḍibāb (wooden locks), I, 421; II, 485
dībāj. *See* Brocade
Dictation by the teacher, II, 210
Dietary laws, II, 224–228, 283; Jewish, IV, 141, 145; V, 352; of Muslims, II, 277
Dietetic problems, II, 578
Dietrich, Albert, I, 283; II, 270; IV, 432
dihlīz. *See* Corridor
Dihqān (Per., low gentry), family name, II, 454
dikka, *dakka* (settee), II, 584; IV, 386
dilāla (broker's fee), I, 160, 445, 449
Dimashq. *See* Damascus
al-Dimashqī, I, 20, 149–150, 157, 158; II, 578. *See also* Damascus
Dimyāṭ. *See* Damietta
Dimyāṭī linen. *See* Linen
dīn (religious virtue), V, 191-192, 333-334, 598
Dinar (gold coin), I, *passim*, 359; Adenese (Mālikī), IV, 419; ʿAdliyya, I, 231; Āghmāt(-ī), I, 235, 236; ʿAzīzī, ʿAzīziyya, I, 232; IV, 20, 353; Bakriyya, issued by Amīr Abū Bakr, I, 235; Damascus, I, 238, 387; *dīnār jayshī* (soldier's pay), II, 123, 546; exchange rate, I, 368-392; II, 46; Ḥasanī I, 207, 239; Maʿadd (Mustanṣirī), I, 234–235, 242, 459; al-Mahdiyya, dinars coined in, I, 234, 235, 236, 237, 238, 377; Miṣrī ("minted in Fustat"), I, 234; Muʿizzī, IV, 16; Muʿizziyya, quarter dinars, I, 459; Muʾminī, of Almohad caliph ʿAbd al-Muʾmin, I, 434; Murābiṭī, I, 235, 236, 239, 460; Mustanṣiriyya, I, 459, 460; *mushammasa* ("exposed to the sun" [meaning uncertain]), I, 373; Nizārī, I, 237, 240; IV, 443; *rubāʿī* (quarter dinar), I, 343, 359 and *passim*, 377, 378; II, 489; IV, 453; *rubāʿiyya* (Sicilian quarter dinar), I, 438; Tripoli, I, 207, 239. See also *ʿayn*; Dirhem; Exchange rate; Gold; Money; Money of account; *ṭarī*; *waks*
Dining. *See* Meals
Dining room, IV, 48-49
Diocesan organization of the diaspora, II, 22, 28, 29, 403, 524. *See also* Gaons
diōknē (Heb.). *See* Bill of exchange
Dioscorides, pharmaceutical handbook, II, 258, 264, 266, 583
Dipper (*karnīb*), IV, 140, 315, 321, 331
Director of coinage, II, 605
Director of finance, II, 284, 298
Director of the Mint, II, 605
Dirge(s), III, 234, 357; on daughter, II, 184
dirham. *See* Dirhem
Dirhem (silver coin), I, 360 and *passim*; II, 37; IV, 419; ʿAzīziyya, I, 370; *bakhāya* dirhems, II, 123, 449, 546; "cut-up," I, 385, 491; IV, 438, 446; *dirham aswad* (black dirhem), I, 387, 388; dirhem *fulūs*, IV, 276; *fiḍḍa*, I, 360; II, 389, 501; fractional, I, 369–389; Kāmilī, I, 386; Muʿizz (Fatimid caliph), I, 370; Nāṣiriyya, I, 386; *niṣf fiḍḍa* (half dirhem), I, 367; Nizāriyya, I, 233, 237, 240, 458, 460; *nuqra*, I, 253, 256, 360, 377, 386, 387, 388, 390, 391, 458; II, 465, 490, 494; III, 78, 285, 451, 467, 490; IV, 372; *qarawiyya*, Qayrawān dirhems, I, 375; Ẓāhiriyya, IV, 443; as weight, I, 360 and *passim*; IV, 419. *See also* Dinar; Exchange rate; *fals*; *kesāfīm*; Silver
dirra, mat as wall hanging, IV, 385
Disabled persons, II, 92, 133, 438
Disciplinary problems, II, 182, 183
Discounts, I, 196-197, 199. See also *samāḥa*
Discrimination against non-Muslims, II, 27, 143, 273–289, 380
Discriminatory badges, II, 27, 38
Disk (*qurṣa*), IV, 427
Displaced persons. *See* Foreigners; Refugees
Display of riches, IV, 151
Dispositions in contemplation of death, III, 96, 253; IV, 449
Disrobing, IV, 188
Distinctive clothing self-imposed, IV, 195

District of the Prisons, quarter in Alexandria, IV, 282
Diversification, merchants', I, 153–155
Division of labor, I, 99–115, 240
Divorce, I, 58, 383, 386; II, 16, 27, 36, 50, 72, 84, 122, 215, 224, 230, 231, 311, 318, 343, 400, 458, 515, 527, 531, 539, 540, 591, 595, 596, 598; III, 61, 63, 69, 74, 77, 79, 81, 82, 101, 104, 119, 123, 133, 138, 144, 156, 176, 177, 182, 184, 188, 190, 205, 216, 217–218, 260–272, 369, 378, 380, 381, 383, 385, 388, 391, 409, 410, 412, 422, 446, 451, 457, 481–488; IV, 44, 66; V, 228, 313. See also *iftidāʾ*
Divorce, bills of, I, 10; III, 260, 262, 264–265, 268, 458, 466; identical for same couple, III, 269; conditional, III, 144, 155, 189, 190, 192, 195; V, 218, 567. See also *geṭ*
Divorcee, II, 318, 539, 540; III, 267, 270–271, 274, 334
dīwān (government office), I, 267, 269, 467; II, 361; IV, 33, 356
dīwān al-kharāj (tax office), II, 609
dīwān al-mawārīth (office of inheritance), II, 582
dīwān al-nafaqāt (office of expenditure), I, 249
dīwān al-taḥqīq (accounting office), III, 428
ḍiyāfa (hospitality), II, 136
diyāna, II, 546
Diyār Baḥrī, I, 427
Diyarbakir, Turkey, IV, 146
diyār al-mashriq (the eastern regions), I, 401
Diyār Qays, I, 327
diyār al-sukna. *See* Neighborhood, residential
Djerba. *See* Jerba
dmwy, spelling of Dammūh, V, 509. *See also* Dammūh
Documents admitted as evidence, II, 337
Domestic architecture, IV, 47–82; general character, IV, 47–49, 77–78
Domestic help, I, 129–130, 147
Domicile, type desired, IV, 91
Donations, II, 92-99, 163, 426, 429, 434, 471–510, 520, 593, 609; of buildings, II, 415, 429, 433, 435, 436, 534, 545; to schools, II, 11–12, 22, 53, 65, 201, 203. *See also* Charity; Pious foundations
Donkeys, I, 211, 270, 271, 276, 381; II, 256, 279; IV, 263, 264, 265
Donna Jamīla, V, 115
Door, IV, 61, 66, 118; main (*bāb zimām*), IV, 80. *See also* Secret door
Dōsā, mother of, V, 570
Dōsā family, II, 440; V, 568
Dōsā b. Joshua al-Ḥāvēr al-Lādhiqī, V, 224, 569
Dōsā b. Saadya, Gaon, II, 14, 15, 522; V, 128
Double standards, II, 297
"Downers," I, 100
Downtown, IV, 15
Dowry, II, 389, 399, 613; III, 2, 67, 68, 77, 85, 86, 99, 100, 104, 105, 106, 123–131, 140–141, 143, 145, 180–183, 187, 188, 192, 214, 218, 282, 447, 448, 452, 453, 454, 456; IV, 105ff. and *passim*, 452; assessment of, III, 86, 98, 124–126, 129; of childless woman, II, 519; doubling prices in assessment, III, 127; house part of, II, 113; and marriage gift of husband, III, 130–131; V, 141, 151; not in money, III, 130; of orphan or poor girl, II, 135, 413; receipts, III, 126, 128. See also *jahāz*; *nedunyā*; *raḥl*; *shuwār*; Trousseau lists
drachme (Gr.), I, 360. *See also* Dirhem
Dragoman (*turgeman*), II, 198, 213, 562
Drainpipes, IV, 36, 54, 361, 372
Draperies, IV, 105–106, 117ff., 184; borrowing of, IV, 122
Dressing gown (*muzarra*), IV, 116, 299, 320, 324, 332, 380, 381, 454, 460
Dressing table, IV, 222–226
Dressmaker, I, 128; female (*khayyāṭa*), I, 430; II, 506
Dried fruit (*naql*), I, 121, 154; IV, 246, 441. See also *naqliyyīn*
Drinking: with Gentiles, V, 39–40; parties, V, 39–41; during Ramadan, V, 40, 223; restraint, V, 94–95, 223; sociability, V, 38-39; women, V, 42–43. *See also* Beer; Beverages; Potions; Wine
Drinking vessels, IV, 147, 256–257. See also *jarra*; *ṭamāwiya*; *ṭāsa*
Drinking water, III, 192
Dropsie College, I, 3, 5, 6
Dropsy, II, 501, 579
Drower, Lady Ethel Stefana, V, 516
Druggist, I, xvii, 179, 384, 78 and *passim*; II, 46, 261–272, 532, 581–585; IV, 10, 15. See also *ʿaṭṭār*; Pharmaceutical products; Prescriptions
Drugstore, I, xvii, 173–174, 175, 177
duʿāʾ, special prayer service, V, 537. *See also* Prayer
ḍuʿafā. *See* Poor

dūdī (little worm), **I**, 482
dukhrān (Aram.). *See* Memorial lists
dukhūl (entering), consummation of marriage, **III**, 70, 441
dukkān (workshop, office), **I**, 238, 416, 417; **II**, 253, 321; **IV**, 355
dukkān al-ʿiṭr (perfumery), **II**, 262
dukkān ṣabgh wa-ḥarīr: store for dyeing and selling silk, **I**, 366
dūlāb (wheel), machinery in factory, **II**, 492; **IV**, 386; "cupboard," **IV**, 386
Dulūk (Doliche), Asia Minor, **II**, 545
al-Dulūkī, from Dulūk, **II**, 545
Dumbarton Oaks symposium, 1976, **IV**, 4
dumluj. *See* Bracelet
Dumūh. *See* Dammūh
dūn (poor quality), **I**, 452
Dunash Ibn Labrāt, and wife, **V**, 468-469
Dūqī, Norman gold of Messina, **I**, 256
Durability of materials, **III**, 140
Dura-Europos, **II**, 151
Duress, document written under, **III**, 79
durj, high wooden case with a cover, **II**, 584
durj. *See* Jewel box
dūrqāʿa, **IV**, 67, 366
Durrī ("Gem"), slave, **I**, 133, 409; **II**, 483
Dust color, **IV**, 174
dustūr bīmāristānī ("Hospital Handbook"), **II**, 264
duwayra. *See* Houses, small
duwayrat al-miqwā ("the little house of the ritual bath"), **II**, 552
duwwāma ("whipping-top"), nickname of ship, **I**, 477, 480
Dyeing, dyers, **I**, 51, 72, 78, 84, 87, 89, 92, 100, 106-108, 153, 154, 210, 362, 365, 366, 415; **II**, 46, 62, 98, 113, 119, 433, 439, 453, 467, 483, 486, 492, 502, 532, 544, 583; **IV**, 20, 172; of clothes, **IV**, 183, 412; of hair, **IV**, 151; house of, **II**, 426; Street of, **II**, 483. See also *misṭāḥ*
Dyes, **IV**, 171-172; blackish or deep blue, **IV**, 173
Dying young, **III**, 4, 23
Dysentery, **II**, 578

E

"Early installment." *See* Marriage gift of husband, first installment
Earrings (*ḥilaq*), **IV**, 203, 209, 210, 211, 214-215, 319, 322, 426; Isfahān type, **III**, 162; *khurṣ*, *khirṣ*, **IV**, 215, 426, 465; *mukhammas*, **IV**, 214-215; *shunūf*, **IV**, 215; *turk* (pl. *atrāk*, *tarākī*), **IV**, 215, 315, 426
"Ears" (= handles), **IV**, 139
Earthenware. *See* Pottery
Earthquake, **II**, 290
East Africa, **I**, 133
Eastern church. *See* Church, Eastern
Easterners, Jews of Babylonia, **II**, 6
Eastern Europe, **III**, 121, 305
Eating: in public, **V**, 40; moderately, **IV**, 229, 433. *See also* Food
"Eating on one table," **III**, 39
Ecclesiasticus, Book of, **I**, 4; commentaries on, **V**, 386-387
Economic life, attitudes toward, **V**, 72
Economic opportunities, **IV**, 6
ʿēd (Heb.). *See* Notary
ēdā (Heb., assembly), **II**, 538
Edfu, Lake of, **I**, 341
ʿēdīm neʾemānīm (Heb. = Ar. *ʿudūl*). *See* Notary
Edom: "the Roman Empire," **II**, 157; designating Crusaders, **V**, 595. *See also* Crusaders; Europe(an)
Education, **II**, 171-211, 403, 555-568; **IV**, 10, 30; adult, **II**, 561; aims of, **II**, 175-183; elementary, **II**, 72, 173-183, 556-560; faulty theories of, **II**, 174; general, **V**, 426-430; of girls, **II**, 558; **III**, 303, 349, 354; higher, **II**, 561-565; organization of elementary, **II**, 185-190; of poor children, **II**, 421, 463, 465; secular, **II**, 172, 210, 403. *See also* Scholarship; Yeshivas
ʿēdūth (*ber*)*ūrā* (well-attested witness), **II**, 601
Eggplant, **IV**, 230, 245, 439
Eggs, **IV**, 250, 443
Egypt, mentioned *passim*. *See also* individual place-names
Egyptians, ancient, **IV**, 108, 114, 165, 189, 212, 223, 225, 233
Elazar, Abū Ghālib, **I**, 249
Elazar, Great Rav of Alexandria, **V**, 44
Elazar, old man of Tripoli, **V**, 121
Elazar b. Elazar, **III**, 278
Elazar b. Ismāʿīl. *See* Elazar b. Samuel
Elazar b. Jacob ha-Bavli, **V**, 582
Elazar b. Judah b. Elazar, **V**, 528
Elazar b. Judah ha-Kohen, **V**, 82
Elazar ha-Levi Abū Naṣr Abuʾl-Ḥasan, **V**, 543
Elazar ha-Levi b. Ṭiqva, **III**, 488
Elazar b. Michael, **V**, 445, 634
Elazar b. Samuel, **I**, 387; **V**, 594

Elazar *ha-shōfēṭ*, III, 489
Elazar b. Tobias, II, 428
Elazar b. Yeshūʿā ha-Levi, IV, 367
Eleazar Kallir, V, 614
Elder (*shaykh, zāqēn*), I, xvii and *passim*; III, 427, 428; IV, 24; "the (righteous)," I, 4–5, 176, 182, 187; honorific title, III, 91, 310; trusted slave called, I, 132, 432
"Elder of the congregations," II, 279–280
"Elder of the Diaspora," II, 29, 526
Elders of the community, II, 16, 42, 44, 58–61, 77, 102, 103, 342, 403, 416, 423, 428, 435, 476, 495, 535, 538, 543, 544, 597; III, 74, 77, 75, 79, 188, 197, 200, 247, 257, 260
Elections, no formal, II, 31
Elegy. *See* Funerals, speeches
eleison (Gr., "have mercy"), II, 147, 499
Elephantine, Egypt, III, 264
Elephantine archives, II, 345
El-Garh, Muhammad, I, 364, 485
Elhanan b. Shemarya, judge, I, 48; II, 29, 51, 202, 203, 204, 213, 331–332, 455, 511, 521, 526, 533, 562–563, 564, 568, 594, 598, 600, 601; III, 486, 495; IV, 333; V, 578, 618
Eli-ʿAlī, I, 357
Eli-ʿAllūn, *parnās*, II, 609
Eli b. Amram, judge, II, 64, 136, 218, 230, 236, 504, 511–512, 527, 533, 535, 536, 542, 548, 566, 568, 574; III, 183, 468, 483, 489; V, 264, 552, 571, 625
Eli b. David, III, 495
Eli b. Ezekiel ha-Kohen, V, 507
Eli b. Hillel b. Eli, II, 610; IV, 349; V, 518, 574
Eli b. Ḥiyya, II, 573
Eli b. Isaac ha-Kohen Ghazāl, I, 463; II, 540
Eli (I) ha-Kohen b. Ezekiel (I), I, 292; II, 415, 467, 528, 579; III, 197-198, 51; V, 525, 542, 609, 610
Eli (II) ha-Kohen b. Ezekiel (II), II, 575; III, 429
Eli ha-Kohen b. Yaḥyā (or Yaʿīsh-Ḥayyim), *parnās*, II, 78, 83, 129, 414, 415, 423, 444, 501, 522, 523, 535, 539, 609, 610; III, 207, 266, 330, 358, 469, 481, 501; IV, 368, 383; V, 134, 213, 285, 531, 542, 586, 609
Eli ha-Levi b. Nethanel, II, 513
Eli b. Mevassēr, I, 363
Eli b. Nathan, II, 530
Eli b. Nathanel, V, 305
Eli b. Samuel Ben Asad, III, 296
Eli b. Shemarya b. Ḥalfōn, III, 481
Eli *ha-mumḥē* b. Abraham, I, 472–473; II, 555; III, 456
Eliezer, II, 497
Elijah, biblical, I, 56; II, 350; V, 511
Elijah, Gaon of Jerusalem, I, 238
Elijah, judge, II, 449, 462, 466, 492, 532, 550, 567, 615
Elijah b. Abraham ha-Kohen, II, 563
Elijah Bashyatchi, V, 364, 608
Elijah b. Judah b. Yaḥyā, IV, 411
Elijah ha-Kohen b. Abraham, V, 432–438, 631
Elijah ha-Kohen b. Solomon, Gaon, II, 14, 15, 573; III, 234, 280, 476, 479, 489; V, 128, 443
Elijah the Rūmī, II, 462
Elijah b. Zacharia(h). *See* Elijah b. Zechariah
Elijah b. Zechariah, judge, I, 64, 287, 366; II, 104, 195, 308, 327, 338, 380, 397, 515, 537, 563, 569, 578; III, 72–73, 245, 302, 303, 428, 468, 473, 476, 494; IV, 241, 297, 427, 438; V, 13–14, 88, 174–175, 178, 188, 243, 279, 305, 515, 540, 559, 560, 574, 584
Elimelech Kohen, II, 497
Elisha, biblical, IV, 108; V, 536
Elkana, biblical, III, 109
Elōhīm (Heb., God), II, 569
Elvira, Spain, IV, 418
Embezzlement, II, 319
Emblic, II, 267, 271, 583
Embroiderer, I, 85, 128, 363; II, 499. See also *raqqām(a)*
Embroidery. *See* Needlework
Embroidery, silk, IV, 403
Emerald, IV, 206, 421; as color, IV, 117
emeth (Heb., truth), II, 233, 500, 544
EMeTH, superscription denoting charity, II, 500, 544
"Eminent member," title of dignitary. See *meʿulle*
Emissaries, II, 569
Emoluments (*ʿawn*), II, 605
Employees, II, 133, 185, 191
Employment: general and industrial, I, 92-99, 129, 170; II, 142, 296; commercial, I, 161–164; contracts of, I, 11, 94, 249
emūnā (Heb., trust), II, 586
Encrusted with gold and niello, IV, 139
Endogamy, III, 26–33, 55
Engagement, I, 383, 387; III, 65–76, 79, 84, 87, 95; broken off, III, 72, 86, 157; contract, III, 157, 311; IV, 317-321; fines for non-fulfillment of, IV, 319. *See also* Betrothal(s); Marriage
England, medieval, II, 373; IV, 138, 153

Enmity: toward addressees, V, 237–238, 296; forgiveness, V, 340–341; gloating, V, 303–305; and slander, V, 300–303, 307; social importance, V, 297-299; standard phrases, V, 235, 297, 299, 306. *See also* Competition
Ennen, Edith, IV, 10, 32, 43
Entertainers, V, 21, 42
Entrance to living quarters, separate, IV, 58
Envoys of yeshivas, Nagids, II, 223
Envy, V, 299–300. *See also* Competition; Enmity
Ephraim, II, 526
Ephraim b. Eli ha-Kohen, II, 535
Ephraim b. Ḥalfōn Ibn al-Zaffān, III, 460; V, 4, 505
Ephraim *he-ḥāvēr* b. Eli b. Ṭarsōn, II, 511
Ephraim b. Isaac, V, 76-79, 527
Ephraim b. Jacob, I, 407, 408
Ephraim b. Joseph ha-Levi, III, 500
Ephraim ha-Kohen b. Abraham, II, 472, 515
Ephraim b. Maḥfūẓ. *See* Ephraim b. Shemarya
Ephraim b. Meshullām, scribe and judge, II, 483, 513, 549, 555; III, 138, 154, 456, 460; V, 358
Ephraim b. Shemarya, I, 293; II, 22, 58, 59, 66, 71, 76, 88, 190, 227, 264, 415, 435, 438, 472, 504, 511, 527, 533, 535, 536, 537, 538, 566, 571, 574, 582, 595, 613, 614; III, 43–44, 301, 436, 492, 495, 501; V, 610
Ephraim *ha-shōfēṭ*, II, 595
Epidemic diseases, V, 71–72, 112–116, 373–374. *See also* Illness; Plague
Epiphany, II, 285; IV, 14
Epistolary practice, imitation of Muslim, V, 628. *See also* Wedding poem; Writing, art of Epithalamium
epi-thymon (Gr., dodder of thyme). See *afithīmūn*
epitropos (Gr.). *See* Proxy
Era of Copts, III, 100, 233
Era of the Creation, I, 355; II, 548; IV, 437
Era of the Documents (Seleucid Era), I, 355; IV, 314, 451
Era of the Greeks. *See* Era of the Documents
Era of Jews, III, 100, 233
Era of Muslims, III, 233
ērūsīn (Heb.). *See* Betrothal(s)
Ess, J. van, V, 398
Estates, II, 279, 395, 396; III, 278–302; V, 158–160, 166–172. *See also* Wills
Esther, biblical, as model, III, 170–171, 317
Esther, Book of, II, 177, 550
Etan ha-Ezraḥi, cantor, III, 221; V, 586
Ethiopian, IV, 219
Ethiopic language, II, 283; III, 169
etrōg (Heb., citrus medica), I, 121
Ettinghausen, Richard, I, 51, 422; III, 109; V, 515
Eucharist, II, 19
Euphrates, IV, 398
Europe(an), I, 51, 70, 149, 159, 160, 231; II, 25, 68, 101, 111, 131, 157, 178, 210, 242, 434, 563, 611; III, 184, 185, 220, 239, 245, 260, 272; IV, 230, 432, 452; beneficiaries of community chest, II, 95, 127, 128, 441, 442, 443, 444, 457; books ordered from, II, 528; commerce with, I, 22, 31, 33, 44–47, 103, 154, 178, 188, 210, 211; IV, 173; communal officials in, II, 25, 222, 224; contrasts to Geniza society, I, 72, 75, 82, 117; III, 240, 357; IV, 128; charitable appeals and institutions, II, 112, 403, 464, 499, 506; education, II, 197, 200, 206; Jew in/from, II, 104, 275, 277, 353; proselytes, II, 129, 304, 306, 310; refugees from Crusades, II, 130; religious life in, II, 176, 200, 226; slaves, slavegirls, I, 132, 135, 136, 138, 139, 142; III, 331; sources of communal revenue, II, 104; universities, II, 228, 235. *See also* Rūm
Evans-Pritchard, E., V, 499
Evening lessons, II, 193, 220
"Ever-living," houseleek as decoration on earrings, IV, 209
Evyatar b. Elijah b. Solomon ha-Kohen, Gaon, II, 15, 573; III, 468, 479, 481; V, 284–285, 519
Evyatar al-Kohen al-Āmidī, II, 600; V, 642
Evyatar Scroll, II, 592
Ewer, IV, 139, 315, 321, 324, 331
Excavations, IV, 12, 49, 53–55
Exchange, House of. See *dār al-ṣarf*
Exchange rate (of dirhems, dinars), I, 220, 239, 240, 359, 368-392; II, 584. *See also* Dinar; Dirhem; Money
Exchange marriages, III, 32. *See also* Marriage
Excommunication (*ḥerem, niddūy*), ban, I, 69, 259; II, 16, 27, 35, 65, 74, 75, 115, 224, 306, 331, 332, 333, 503, 536, 551, 562, 570, 571, 592, 599, 600, 602, 614; III, 82, 83, 195, 209, 335, 351; IV, 198; V, 22, 185–186, 369. *See also* Ban "in general terms"
Executor(s), III, 292–301

Exercise books, II, 178
Exilarch. *See* Head of the Diaspora
"Expert," designation of cantors, II, 223. See also *mumḥe*
Expulsion from a yeshiva, II, 522
Extended family, III, 1–47, 139, 231, 235, 334, 425–437; economic aspects, III, 33–35, 40, 69; joint domicile of, III, 35–40, 86
Eye care, V, 100–101
Eye powder, II, 585
Ezekiel, biblical, I, 56; tomb of, V, 18, 30
Ezekiel (II) ha-Kohen he-Ḥāvēr b. Eli he-Ḥāvēr, II, 522; V, 567
Ezekiel b. Nathan, V, 358
Ezekiel b. Nethanel ha-Levi, brother of Ḥalfōn b. Nethanel, I, 380; II, 262, 338; III, 231; V, 331, 595, 610
Ezra, biblical, I, 56; II, 90
Ezra, the Scribe, V, 18, 19, 24
Ezra b. Ismaʿīl b. Ezra, V, 572
Ezrah family, as distinguished from Ibn Ezra family, V, 638

F

Face, uncovering of, III, 305, 324
Factions, II, 61–65
Factories, I, 80–82; II, 492, 494. *See also* Paper; Sugar
Factotum. See *ghulām*
Faḍāʾil b. ʿAwāʾid, II, 427
al-Fāḍil, *qāḍī*, II, 609
Fāḍil al-Baysānī, qadi of Saladin, II, 229, 509
faḍl (superiority), V, 194-196
Faḍl Allāh b. Berakhōt Ibn al-Lebdī, I, 367
Faḍl Allāh al-ʿOmarī, II, 526
al-Faḍl al-Tustarī, V, 333
Fahd, *al-wakīl*, I, 446
Fahda ("Cheetah"), f., III, I, 45
fāʾida. *See* Revenue, sources of
fāʾida mutaʿayyin(a) (fixed profit), I, 384
Fairs, IV, 7
Fāʾiza ("Favorite"), f., III, 45, 157, 446
Fāʾiza, d. of Solomon b. Nathanel, III, 268, 486
fākhitī. *See* Bluish-iridescent
fakhkhār (clay worker), I, 110, 422
Fakhr ("Glory"), f., III, 278. *See also* Sitt al-Fakhr
Fakhr, the cheese maker, II, 500
Fakhr al-ʿArab, I, 310; IV, 432, 447
Fakhr al-Dawla, title, II, 589
Fakhr al-Dīn Taṭṭar, V, 175, 555
Fakhr al-Mulk, II, 63
Fakhr al-Ṣanāʿi, Samaritan official, II, 520
Fakhri, Ahmad (Ahmed), modern author, I, 473; IV, 59
fākhūrānī. See *fākhkhār*
fākhūrī. See *fākhkhār*
falka, I, 486
fals (copper coin), IV, 433, 434. *See also* Copper; Dirhem
fāmī (grocer, keeper of grain store), I, 152, 426, 438
Families, influential, IV, 10
Family, I, 27, 73, 77-79, 130; II, 75, 126, 245; extended, III, 2
Family feeling: business concerns, V, 127, 239–240, 393; expressed in letters, V, 3; importance, V, 216; Maimonides family, V, 197-198, 398, 477; parent-child relations, V, 117, 122–126, 141–142, 180–181, 185, 222, 224–226; in wills, V, 141–142. *See also* Children; Parents; Partnerships
Family honor, III, 28, 43
Family house, IV, 59. See also *bayt*; House(s)
Family names, I, 155, 357; III, 8, 12, 102, 170; derived from occupations or places of origin, III, 13–14; derived from the mother's name, III, 12
Family planning, III, 230
Famine, II, 39, 111, 130, 141, 283; III, 208; IV, 124, 239, 240, 242, 247, 439; V, 29, 71, 115. *See also* Food
Fāmiya (Afāmiya), II, 587
"Famous," said of a house, IV, 18
fanāʾ (pest), V, 537. *See also* Plague; *wabāʾ*
Fans, I, 99–100; IV, 149. See also *ma-rāwiḥī*
faqīh: lower Muslim official, II, 431, 590; Muslim doctor of law, II, 280, 346, 367, 431, 590, 591
Far East, I, 32
Faraḥ, I, 380
Faraḥ, II, 101
Faraḥ b. Abuʾl-ʿAlā, I, 364
Faraḥ b. ʿAṭiyya, IV, 443
Faraḥ b. ʿAyyāsh, V, 213
Faraḥ b. Dunash, I, 49
Faraḥ b. Ibrahīm, II, 454
Faraḥ b. Ismaʿīl b. Faraḥ, I, 387, 460; III, 479, 480; IV, 355, 400; V, 565
Faraḥ b. Joseph, III, 469
Faraḥ b. Joseph b. Faraḥ, IV, 429
Faraj, freedman of Barhūn, I, 436
Faraj, teacher from Mosul, II, 441
Faraj ("Relief"), widow of Yeshūʿā b. Joseph, Nagid, III, 211

Faraj Allah ("God has helped"), characteristic name, II, 496, 501; IV, 367
Faraj b. Nahum, III, 484
Farājī Kohen b. Joseph the Sicilian, IV, 251
farajiyya (open robe with wide sleeves), IV, 425. *See also* Robe
Farajiyya b. Ṣedāqā, IV, 275
farānisa. See *parnās* (welfare official)
Faraskūr, IV, 349
Faraskūr family, II, 439; IV, 359
farāwiz (ornamented bands), IV, 382
Farewell, gestures of, V, 33–34
Fares, Bichr, V, 200
Farisī, I, 400
Farjiyyah b. Sahlān, III, 470–471
farkha. *See* Robe
Farming of revenue, I, 12, 382; II, 358, 360, 416, 422, 427, 430, 606; from communal houses, II, 80, 83, 115. *See also* Tax-farmers
farrān (oven man), I, 254, 423; II, 129
farrāsh (mosque attendant, Muslim beadle), II, 82. *See also* Beadle
farsh (carpet), IV, 126. *See also* Carpets
Faruk, I, 331
fasāsārī, IV, 182
fashshāṭ (one who boasts), II, 471
Fāsī, I, 20; V, 566. *See also* Fez
fāṣid, faṣṣād. *See* Phlebotomist
faṣṣ. *See* Semi-precious stones
Fasting, III, 93, 193, 196, 221; private, II, 301, 307; public, II, 53, 97, 165, 462. *See also* Ramaḍān
Father(s), III, 21, 23, 24, 34, 39, 61, 66, 68, 69, 73, 74, 75, 76, 78, 79, 87, 88, 92, 99, 102, 130, 216, 243, 244, 245. *See also* Paternal family
Father-in-law, III, 83, 129, 171, 201
Fathi, Hassan, IV, 56
Fatima, I, 30
Fatimids, I, 2, 19, 22, 65, 279, 327, 328, 349, 478; II, 23, 33, 138, 149, 150, 251, 263, 277; III, 185, 198, 272, 278, 290, 356, 357; IV, 59, 76, 128, 137, 175, 200, 370, 384, 417, 455, 459; administration, I, 249, 261, 270, 272, 284, 299; II, 320, 363, 365, 369, 373, 394, 527, 573, 608; III, 110, 126, 135; IV, 28, 40; commerce, I, 148, 194, 222, 266, 269, 270; communal autonomy under, I, 62; II, 404; III, 277; and Crusades, I, 45; destruction of churches and synagogues, I, 21; discrimination against non-Muslims, I, 71, 345; II, 285, 286, 300; Fustat under, IV, 33, 46; historical survey, I, 29–39, 40; industry, I, 125; Jewish community under, II, 12, 27, 28, 30, 202, 244, 245, 327, 345, 347, 394, 405, 525, 537; IV, 195; Jewish physicians under, II, 27, 30, 243, 244, 245, 345, 347; IV, 265; mail service, I, 284, 286, 294; money and banking, I, 61, 233, 234, 235, 236, 240, 249, 359, 368, 388, 391; II, 571; IV, 28, 202; Muslim communal strife, II, 165; non-Muslims in govt. service, I, 68, 73, 165, 188, 281; II, 288, 345, 374; III, 10, 126; IV, 187; poll-tax, II, 386; propaganda, II, 194, 202, 349, 603; public prayer, II, 165; relations with Gaons, II, 12; silk, I, 222, 245; slaves and slavegirls, I, 132, 137
Fat tail of sheep, IV, 227, 230, 231, 234, 433
fatwā (legal opinion), I, 13; II, 325, 367, 567, 598
fayj (courier), I, 284-291, 372, 470, 471
fayj ṭayyār (express courier), I, 290
faylam, IV, 385
Fayrūz, slave, I, 138, 433, 435
Fayyūm, Egypt, I, 20, 53, 84, 103, 118, 135, 240, 269, 372; II, 35, 361, 362, 539; III, 207-208, 214-215, 270, 301, 470; IV, 238, 247, 436, 441; V, 506. *See also* Flax
Feast of breaking fast (of Ramadan). See *ʿīd al-fiṭr*
Feast of sacrifice. See *ʿīd al-kabīr*
Feast of Tabernacles. *See* Sukkot
Feast of the Cross. See *ʿīd al-ṣalīb*
"Feathered" (*murāyash*). See *murayyash*
Fellahs, I, 75, 118
"Fellow designate," II, 213
Felt, II, 446; IV, 155, 411
Fennel, I, 155; distributor of (*shamārī*), I, 438
Fenton, Paul, V, 515, 568
Fernea, Elizabeth Warnock, IV, 228–229
Fez, Morocco, I, 20, 49, 53, 61, 83, 84, 166, 181, 210, 277, 289; II, 9, 278, 370, 478; III, 19, 31, 429; IV, 3, 405, 408
fi'a (denomination), II, 534
fiḍḍa, full silver coin. *See* Dirhem
fiḍḍī (merchant in silver, "silverman"), I, 420, 438. *See also* Silver
"Fidelity," slave girl, I, 139
"Fifth," contribution to the yeshiva, II, 12
Fighting, V, 41, 305–306. *See also* Banditry and other acts of violence
Figs, I, 121

Figures: of animals, IV, 113, 120, 121, 137, 382, 423; of birds, IV, 113, 137, 139, 210, 378, 423
Figurines (*tamāthīl*), IV, 224, 430, 467
Filial piety, IV, 41, 44
Filigree, IV, 209, 211–212, 219, 223, 322, 424, 425, 427, 428, 458
Financiers, II, 525
Fines, II, 12, 38, 53, 100, 110, 330, 331, 332, 358, 388, 389, 534, 599, 611, 612; III, 66, 78, 85, 86, 87, 92, 114, 144, 148, 174, 187, 188, 247
Finger ring: *dabla*, ring without stone, IV, 204, 208, 211, 212, 220–221, 429; *khātam*, pronounced *khātim*, IV, 221, 420, 342, 466. *See also* Ring
Firanga (Heb., Land of the Franks), I, 43
firāsh. *See* Bedding
Fire, IV, 12, 70
Fire damage, absence of, IV, 103–104
Fire-pot, brazier or coal pan (*kānūn*), IV, 136, 388
Firkovitch Collection, Leningrad, I, 5, 13, 25; II, 343
"Firms," of artisans, I, 84; of merchants, I, 181–182
firnās. See *parnās*
Firstborn, in Jewish and Muslim law, II, 398–399; son, III, 20, 37, 279–280
First cousins, marriage between, III, 27–33, 87, 103. *See also* Marriage
Fir trees (*shūhāt*), II, 434
Fish, IV, 250–251, 443
Fishermen, II, 492; Street of (al-Ṣayyādīn), IV, 444
Fish-mongers, I, 27, 126, 167
fisqiyya (basin with fountain), IV, 65, 366, 367. *See also* Fountain
Fittings for jewelry, IV, 201
Five Books of Moses. *See* Bible
Fizyōn. *See* Buzyōn
Flax (*kattān*), I, 20, 45, 46, 76, 86, 98, 104–105, 153, 154, 157, 165, 184, 188, 191, 193-194, 195, 196, 197, 198, 199, 200, 201, 210, 214, 216, 218, 219, 220, 222, 224–228, 249, 252, 254, 265, 267, 295, 302, 333, 335, 337, 338, 343, 345, 372, 375, 418; II, 45, 378, 531, 590; III, 198, 217; IV, 10, 26, 29, 165, 167, 168, 179, 193, 242, 355, 400, 402, 410; varieties of: Aqfāṣ (Aqfahs), I, 455; Ashmūnī I, 226, 456; Asyūṭī, I, 227, 456; Atfīḥī, I, 456; Bahnasā (ī), I, 135, 276, 456; III, 53; IV, 119–120, 121, 242, 382, 402; Barrānī, I, 456, 457; IV, 416; Būsh, I, 157, 456; II, 606; Būṣīr, I, 226, 456; Dallāṣ, I, 456; Fayyūmī, I, 224, 226, 456; Fīsha (Fīshiyya), I, 456; *kāmil(ī)* ("complete"), I, 456; *kattān laythī* (Laythi flax, i.e., variety of flax traded in Laythī weight), I, 227, 361, 456, 457 (see also *laythī qinṭār*); *kattān manfūsh* (hatchelled flax), I, 418; Mālāl, I, 224, 226, 456, 457; *mamshūṭ* (combed flax), I, 418; Mīsārī, I, 224, 456; *qimāṭ* ("bandage," "swaddle"), I, 456, 457; Qissīs, I, 225, 456; Sanbūṭī, I, 456; Sāwī, I, 456; IV, 416; Ṭamāwī, I, 457; Ṭansāwī, I, 79, 311, 457; Ṭanṭāwī, I, 457; Tfīḥī, I, 224, 456. See also *bāb al-kattān*; *dār al-kattān*; Linen; *mashshāṭ*; *mushāqa*; *mustaʿmil kattān*; *sūq al-kattānīn*
Flax-workers, II, 455, 502
Fleischer, Ezra, V, 389, 408, 556, 586, 623
Fleurs-de-lis, decorating marriage contract(s), III, 112
Flight of population, IV, 242. *See also* Migrations
Flogging, IV, 36
Floors (of a house). See *ṭabaqa*
Florence, I, 345
Florentine ducats, III, 181
Flour, II, 465; IV, 236, 243
Flowers, floral designs, IV, 112, 123; vases for, 150
Flyswatter (*midhabba*), IV, 149, 394
Folding doors, IV, 64, 65
Folktale(s), III, 358
fondaco, *fondago* (Heb., inn), I, 349. See also *funduq*
Fonduk. See *funduq*
Food, II, 529; IV, 47, 226–253, 314; cosmopolitan character, IV, 253; Geniza taciturn about, IV, 226–229, 244; Jewish, enjoyed by Muslims, IV, 227; gift to fiancee, III, 66; more sumptuous than reflected in Geniza, IV, 244; lack of, V, 88-89; preparation of, I, 100–101, 113–115, 129, 152; price of, V, 71; prohibitions, V, 619; provisions for a holiday, IV, 230–231; storage and cooking of, IV, 141–144; trade in, I, 151; vendors of, II, 486; weekly distribution for the poor, II, 432, 465, 501; IV, 443. *See also* Famine
Food industry, II, 467
Footmen, II, 608
Footwear, IV, 162–164. *See also* Shoes; Slippers
Foreign trade, influence of, V, 6–7
Foreigners, I, 49, 51, 62, 68, 85; II, 67, 70, 79, 81, 88, 92, 95, 97, 100, 126,

134, 154, 187, 188, 216, 384, 394, 429, 432, 438, 440, 441, 442, 444, 447, 449, 459, 461, 462, 463, 466, 467, 468, 481, 496, 499, 506, 508, 536, 539, 542, 543, 551, 564, 599, 611; III, 81, 220; IV, 8, 14
Forgiveness, V, 340–341. *See also* Enmity
Formularies, II, 344, 527, 603
Fortress of the Candles. *See* Fortress of the Greeks, Fustat
Fortress of the Greeks, Fustat, I, 265; II, 264; III, 243, 326; IV, 12, 13, 16, 17, 18, 19, 22, 29, 37, 70, 91, 98, 278, 281, 321, 350, 352, 377; V, 146, 546, 547; towers used as apartments, IV, 12, 87
Fortress of the Rūm. *See* Fortress of the Greeks, Fustat
Forty. *See* Spiritual perfection
Fountain, IV, 48, 68. See also *fisqiyya*; *zarrāqāt*
Fractional dirhems. *See* Dirhems
France, French, I, 22, 29, 32, 40, 43, 52, 53, 65, 66, 67, 110, 191, 214, 258; II, 11, 66, 67, 70, 71, 188, 202, 212, 221, 317, 366, 542, 559, 591; IV, 10, 153, 154, 158; V, 29. *See also* Franks
Frankfort am Main, V, 597, 632
Frankfort Municipal Library, I, 5
Frankincense, I, 154
Franks, I, 35, 36, 43, 53–54; II, 281, 549; land of the, II, 136; *See also* Crusaders; Europeans; France
Frederic II, German emperor, I, 40
Freedmen (*ʿatīq*, *meshuḥrār*), freedman, I, 48, 78, 144–147, 436; II, 545, 591. *See also* Freedwomen; Slaves
Freedom of contract, I, 87; II, 328
Freedom of movement, III, 153–156, 174, 190, 191, 216–217
Freedwomen, I, 144–146, 368; II, 441, 449; III, 102, 262, 368, 370, 373, 395, 447. *See also* Slavegirls
Freer, Charles L., I, 5
Freer Gallery of Art, Washington, D.C., I, 5; II, 297
Freight, cost of, I, 341–344
French Jewish immigrants, III, 162
French rabbis, II, 97, 207, 406
"Fresh" coins. See *ṭarī*
Freshening appliances, IV, 138
Friday, Muslim weekly holiday, I, 365; II, 19, 296
Friday night, III, 168, 221, 222. *See also* Sabbath
Friedenberg, Daniel M., V, 357, 605
Friedman, Milton. *See* Friedman, Mordechai
Friedman, Mordechai, II, 345; III, 96, 101, 147–149, 153, 264, 267; IV, 217; V, 313, 487, 507, 550, 595
Friendship: in business, V, 273–274, 277; comradeship in struggle, V, 10, 273; estrangement, V, 292-297; formal, I, 164–169 (*see also* Informal cooperation; Partnership; *ṣuḥba*); V, 274, 275–276; God's role, V, 273, 292; in literary pursuits, V, 285–289; nature of, V, 5, 272–273, 278–283, 292, 427–428; in religious study, V, 283–285, 289–292; terminology, V, 277, 279; unrequited, V, 285–286
Fringes, IV, 113, 152, 196-198, 378, 417. See also *murayyash*; *sakākīn*; Tassels
Frjlh. *See* Faraj Allah
Fromm, Erich, V, 597
Front and entrance, IV, 59ff.
Frontlets, IV, 207
Frugality of diet, IV, 253. *See also* Eating
Fruits, IV, 234, 246, 440, 441
Fruit trees. *See* Orchard
Frying pans, IV, 143, 391
Fuḍayl b. Manasse, II, 592
Fugitive from the poll tax, II, 382. See also *hārib*; Poll tax
Fuks, L., I, 13
Fulayfil ("little peppercorn"), nickname, II, 506
Fulled cloth (*maqṣūr*), IV, 178
Fuller, fulling (*qaṣṣār*, *ṭaffāl*), II, 540; III, 341; IV, 178, 179, 183, 232, 407, 412, 434
Fuller's earth (*ṭafl*, *ṭufāl*), II, 540; III, 341; IV, 178, 407
fulūs = dirhems, II, 432, 491. *See also* Dirhems
Fumigation, II, 269; IV, 137–138, 149
Fumigator (*mibkhara*), IV, 137, 388
funduq, I, 189, 349, 350, 490; II, 113, 114, 135, 154, 420, 429, 434, 465, 545, 548; IV, 17, 29–30, 36, 351, 437. *See also* Caravanserai
funduqānī (proprietor of caravanserai), I, 189; II, 548
funduqiyya, prostitute, I, 350
Funerals, II, 125, 216, 285, 372; accounts, IV, 160; expenses, II, 426, 449; memorial service, V, 115; music, V, 157; participation, V, 156–157; payment for, V, 152, 157–158, 160, 162–163, 171–172; personnel, V, 153, 163–164, 165; speeches, II, 567, 576; V, 164–165. *See also* Burial; Death; Mourning
Funeral oration. *See* Funerals, speeches

Fūq, maidservant, **V**, 547
fuqqāʿ (honey sherbet), **II**, 531; **IV**, 261. *See also* Potions
fuqqāʿa (bottle for honey sherbet), **I**, 474, 485; **II**, 271, 585; **IV**, 261, 447
fuqqāʿī (seller of honey sherbet), **II**, 531, 585; **IV**, 447; **V**, 517
furāniq (Per., courier), **I**, 283, 286, 470
Furayj b. Suhayl Ibn Abu'l-Gharīb, **III**, 482
Furaykh ("Little Chick"), characteristic name, **II**, 501
furnāq (furnace in bathhouse), **V**, 99, 533
Furnishings, furniture, **I**, 46, 113; **II**, 584; **IV**, 105-138
Furrayj ("pullet"), name, **II**, 606
Furriers, **II**, 608; Street of, **IV**, 56
Furs, **IV**, 129; trade in, **I**, 154
furush. *See* Bedding
fustat miṣr (Fustat of Egypt), mentioned *passim*; burning of in 1168, **II**, 141; **V**, 528; designations of, **IV**, 6; history of, **V**, 20; perception of by outsiders, **V**, 309-310
fuṣūl (chapters, courses), **II**, 561. See also *perāqīm*
fūṭa (sari-like cloth), **II**, 131, 448; **IV**, 155, 403
Fuwwa, Egypt, **I**, 295, 297, 299, 492; **II**, 279, 606; **IV**, 406

G

gabbāʾē ṣedāqā. *See* Almoner(s)
Gabes, Tunisia, **I**, 102, 278, 279, 469; **II**, 9, 256, 320, 337, 522, 596; **III**, 6, 183, 203; **IV**, 117, 168, 402
Gable roof (*gamalūn*), **II**, 145, 436; **IV**, 74, 369
Gabriel, unpopular name among Jews of Islam, **V**, 599
Gabriel, Albert, **IV**, 53, 54, 65, 74
Gaeta, **I**, 40
Gala costume (*ḥulla*), **IV**, 154, 326, 327, 401, 455. *See also* Robe of honor
Galen, **II**, 249
Galilee, **II**, 89, 144, 146, 234
Galleys (*ghurāb, qaṭāʿi*), **I**, 295, 306-307, 308
Gallnuts (*ʿafṣ*), **I**, 154, 155, 213; **IV**, 405
Gamaliel, **III**, 8
gamalūn. *See* Gable roof
Gambling, **II**, 47, 531, 532; **V**, 44-45
Games, **V**, 13, 21-22
Gamliel b. Moses, poet, **V**, 537
Gamliel b. Simḥa, judge, **I**, 366, 382
ganj (Per., storehouse or treasure), **I**, 1
Gaon, Head of Academy, **I**, 25, 53, 60, 68, 144, 258, 330; **II**, 4, 5-22, 24, 30, 31, 39, 52, 55, 58, 59, 60, 64-67, 70, 71, 76, 89, 90, 107, 158, 164, 198, 226, 322, 331, 333, 365, 401, 511, 512, 519-524, 527, 535, 541, 554, 562, 597, 602, 609; **III**, 4, 14, 25, 61, 133, 137, 166, 186, 199, 245, 323, 358; **V**, 571, 618
Gaon designate, **II**, 15, 522
Garbage removal, **IV**, 23, 35-36, 357
Garcin, Jean-Claude, **V**, 523
Garden, **IV**, 48, 56-57, 63, 72, 76-77
Garden mallow (*mulūkhiyya*), **IV**, 230, 231, 232, 234, 245, 440
Garlic, **IV**, 209, 230, 232, 245, 422, 426, 433
Gate, **IV**, 60, 67
Gatekeepers, **I**, 341-342; **II**, 454; **IV**, 62
Gate of the Breach (*kharq*), **II**, 497
Gate of the Well, **II**, 431
Gauze, **IV**, 166
Gaza (Ghaza), Palestine, **I**, 116, 119, 212, 426; **II**, 59, 62, 167, 308, 441, 467, 496, 511, 535, 537; **III**, 44, 301, 304; **IV**, 45, 360, 413
"Gazelle," slave girl, **I**, 138, 139
Gazelle-blood (color), **IV**, 182
gedōl ha-ḥavērīm, **II**, 566
gedōl ha-yeshīvā, **II**, 566
Geertz, Clifford, **V**, 497, 500
Gelzer, Matthias, **V**, 497
gemār = *gemāra*, **II**, 561, 564. *See also* Talmud
Gems. *See* Precious stones
Gems, House of, **II**, 509
Genealogy, **II**, 567; **III**, 3, 4-5, 7, 8, 103, 239-240, 425-427
Generosity, **V**, 193-194. *See also* Charity
Geniza: function of, **V**, 92; Karaite papers in, **V**, 371-372; literary texts, **I**, 13-15; source, **I**, 1-28 and *passim*; **V**,4, 499. *See also* Letters
Geniza synagogue. *See* Synagogue of the Palestinians
Genoa, Italy, **I**, 32, 40, 43, 45, 46, 59, 211, 308, 309, 317, 318, 325; **IV**, 1
Gentile (*goy*, i.e. Muslim), **II**, 275, 278, 586, 587, 591, 606
"Gentile writ," **II**, 615
Georgia, **I**, 49
gēr (Heb., proselyte), **II**, 307, 592, 594. *See also* Proselyte
gērashtō (Heb., repudiation), **III**, 485. *See also* Divorce
German(ic), **I**, 13, 160

Germany, medieval, I, 258; II, 68; IV, 153
Gervers, Veronika, IV, 118
geṭ (Heb., bill of divorce), II, 230–231; III, 268, 486, 487. *See also* Divorce, bills of
Geveret ʿAlāmōt (Heb., "Queen of the Girls"), III, 136
gevīr ha-mevīnīm ("Master of the Discerning"), uncommon title, II, 578; V, 605
ha-gevīrā ("the dowager"), III, 31
gezozṭrā (Heb.), IV, 365. *See also* Bay window
*ghadā*ʾ. *See* Meal, morning
ghaḍāʾirī. *See* Porcelain, maker of
ghaḍār. *See* Porcelain
ghafīr (watchman), II, 464. *See also* Nightwatchmen
ghāʾib, *ghāb* (absent), II, 457
ghalāʾilī (manufacturer of women's undergarments), I, 108. See also *ghilāla*
ghalaq (wooden lock), I, 421
Ghālib b. Ḥalfōn al-Zayyāt, III, 437
ghāliya (perfume), IV, 226, 431. *See also* Perfume(r)
ghallāq (maker of wooden locks), I, 421; as family name, IV, 363
ghalq (place that can be locked), IV, 363, 368
gharābiliyya (makers of sieves), I, 416
gharbal al-turāb (sifting earth), II, 424
Gharbiyya province, II, 468
ghāsilat al-Rūm (female washer for the Rūm), I, 43
ghaṭāʾ wa-waṭāʾ (cover and bedding), IV, 298, 299. *See also* Bedding
Ghayfa, Egypt, II, 439; III, 64
Ghayfī, IV, 359
ghayr mustaqill (incompetent), II, 538
al-Ghazāl ("Gazelle"), V, 36
al-Ghazālī, Muslim theologian, I, 65, 202; II, 318; III, 153; V, 397
ghazzāl (spinner), I, 416
Ghetto, absence of, I, 71–73; IV, 21, 46
ghifāra (protection). See *khifāra*
ghifāra (pl. *ghafāʾir*). *See* Mantle
ghilāla (women's undergarment), I, 108; III, 463; IV, 154, 166, 315, 396, 401, 412. See also *ghalāʾilī*
ghilmān (armed slaves), II, 607. See also *ghulām*
ghilmān al-ʿāmil (the young men of the tax collector), I, 414
ghīṭān (fields). *See* Vineyard
ghulām (slave, freedman or employee), I, 93, 132, 133, 144, 432; II, 298, 440, 453, 454, 463, 467, 483 (*see also* Freedmen; Slave; "Young man"); apprentice, I, 93
Ghulayb b. Moses, II, 537
al-Ghumūr, I, 32
ghurāb (galley), I, 306, 307, 476–477; (raven), I, 306, 477
ghurfa (room on upper floor), IV, 76, 81, 370
Ghuzz. *See* Seljuks
Gibb, Hamilton, V, 256
Gibraltar, Straits of, I, 41; V, 521
Gibson, McGuire, V, 630
Gifts, I, 449; II, 529, 537, 543, 546, 599, 608; anonymous, II, 495, 505; at childbirth, III, 22; from husband, III, 167–168; to business friends, I, 167. See also *hiba*
Gil, Moshe, II, 118; IV, 102, 291-292; V, 74
Gilded, IV, 163 and *passim*, 378
Ginger, I, 44; IV, 260; color, IV, 402; vases, IV, 138
Ginzberg, Louis, I, 25
Girgenti, I, 330
Girls, II, 183–185; III, 62, 102, 200, 226–229, 235, 236, 242, 342; puberty of, III, 68, 71, 236
Giza. *See* Gizeh
gizbār (Heb., treasurer), I, 249; III, 136. See also *jahbadh*
Gizeh, Egypt, I, 5, 276, 327; II, 144, 262, 285, 591; IV, 448; V, 23
Glass, II, 78; IV, 16, 106; meaning translucent, IV, 174; vessels, IV, 131, 133, 148; weights, 110, 360; window, II, 145
Glassmaker, I, 51, 71, 85, 87, 88, 93, 94, 95, 100, 109–110, 153, 254, 334, 363, 365, 428; II, 110, 113, 140, 296, 306, 456, 502, 504, 545
Glassmaker, House of the, II, 420, 434
Gloating over an enemy, V, 303–305
Glutton (*mujalliḥ*) IV, 229. *See also* Eating
Goblets (*sāghar*) IV, 148
God, III, 5, 16, 17, 18-19, 34, 35, 42, 44, 52, 53, 60, 62, 66, 79, 117, 190, 194, 196, 198, 202, 205, 213, 217, 219, 221, 222–223, 226, 239, 241, 242, 244, 259, 303, 304, 338, 351, 353; V, 49, 52, 62–63, 130–131, 140–141, 155, 273, 292, 323–347, 451–452. *See also* Judaism; Prayer; Religion
gōʾēl (Heb., the Redeemer), II, 568
Goethe, Johann Wolfgang von, V, 2, 514
Golb, Norman, I, 4; II, 306; IV, 9; V, 20

"Gold," slave girl, **I**, 135, 139, 433; **V**, 547
Gold, **I**, 78, 99-100, 155, 200, 223, 267, 301, 368; **II**, 471, 476, 478, 482, 287, 508, 529, 609; **IV**, 139 and *passim*, 417, 419, 455; "the Gold" as term for jewelry, **IV**, 201; as main material for jewelry, **IV**, 202-203, 419; payments connected with marriage contract made in, **I**, 391; **III**, 119-120; red, **IV**, 196. *See also* Dinar; Money; *mufaṣṣala*
Goldberg, Harvey, **III**, 27
Golden rim, **IV**, 148, 208, 327
Gold luster, **IV**, 148
Goldsmith(s, -ing), **I**, 51, 87, 108, 420; **II**, 80, 296, 413, 486, 490, 493; **IV**, 201, 211
Goldstein, Bernard R., **V**, 420
Gold threads, **IV**, 124, 125, 166, 187, 320, 323, 327, 329, 378, 409, 425, 456
"Gold water." *See* Tin
Goldziher, I., **V**, 19, 191-192
gombaria (Heb.), **I**, 306
Good deeds, **III**, 224
Good wishes, **III**, 107-108
Government, **I**, 81-82, 90, 93, 97, 115-116, 260, 264, 266-272, 294, 302, 310, 342, 379; **II**, 7, 10, 16, 22, 26, 27, 29, 30, 31, 32, 35, 47, 59, 60, 63, 65, 69, 113, 126, 137, 274, 284, 288, 341, 345-380, 603; administration, **IV**, 14; agents, **II**, 2, 351, 354-358; banker (see *jahbadh*); clerks, **II**, 229; office (see *dīwān*); officials, **I**, 255, 265 and *passim*; **II**, 2, 18, 38, 42, 46, 98, 166, 173, 179, 242, 345-358, 421, 463, 472, 477, 520, 523, 530, 604-607; **III**, 2, 11, 14, 206, 208, 240, 282, 299, 357; **IV**, 11, 19; officials, non-Muslim, **II**, 374, 609-610; papers (letter of appointment), **II**, 405-406, 614-615; provider of municipal services, **IV**, 33-40; service, **II**, 172, 308 (see also *khidma*); unattractive, **II**, 375
Governor, **II**, 29, 45, 48, 56, 62, 71, 243, 304, 312, 365, 405, 576, 604; **IV**, 238
Gown with sleeves (*jubba*), **IV**, 154, 315, 333, 404, 460
goy (Heb.), gentile, i.e., Muslim. *See* Gentile
Grabar, Oleg, **IV**, 3, 76
Grace, "taking permission at," **II**, 20
Grace after meals, **II**, 524
Grain. *See* Wheat
Grain speculation, **IV**, 235, 435
Granada, Spain, **I**, 41, 52, 57, 69, 77; **II**, 25, 95, 353, 542; **IV**, 169, 402
Grandfather, **III**, 3, 6, 7, 8, 13, 39, 44, 103, 201, 292, 425, 492
Grandmother, **II**, 188, 477; **III**, 77, 130, 232, 291
Grandson, **III**, 7, 224
Granulation, "beaded," **IV**, 212, 219, 428
Grapes, **II**, 414, 529; **IV**, 257
Gratitude, expression of, **V**, 35-36
Gravedigger, **II**, 306, 449, 453, 456; **V**, 165
Grayish, **IV**, 166, 320, 323, 327, 330
Great Bazaar, in Fustat, **II**, 114, 140, 227, 263, 434; **IV**, 13, 17, 29, 30, 31, 281, 350
Great Fast. *See* Day of Atonement
Great Market. *See* Great Bazaar
Great Mosque (Mosque of ʿAmr), **II**, 263; **IV**, 13, 26, 28. *See also* Mosque
Great Sanhedrin, **II**, 71. *See also* Yeshiva
Great Synagogue. *See* Synagogue of the Palestinians
Greece, Greek, **I**, 102, 111, 417; **II**, 2, 65, 167, 241, 249, 251, 253, 573; **III**, 119, 153, 355; **IV**, 29, 48, 78, 115, 116, 118, 140, 143, 150, 159, 172, 176, 178, 202, 205, 209, 212, 223, 224, 229, 248, 252, 256, 259, 347, 408, 453; **V**, 7, 10, 276, 285, 363, 387, 407, 409, 419-420, 450-451, 475, 481, 495; language, **I**, 4, 38, 49, 53, 64, 349; sciences, **II**, 265; titles, **II**, 87
Green (*masannī* [bright green], pistachio), **IV**, 117, 166, 174, 175, 406. *See also* Emerald
Greenberg, Moshe, **V**, 583
Grief. *See* Mourning
Grierson, P., **I**, 370, 377
Grillwork, **II**, 551-552
Grocery store, **IV**, 143
Grohmann, Adolf, **I**, 13; **II**, 392; **IV**, 86
Grooming, **IV**, 222, 429
Ground rent (*ḥikr*), **II**, 116, 429, 432; **IV**, 37-38, 358
Ground tax. *See* Ground rent
Group consciousness, **II**, 273-289
Guardhouse, **II**, 609
Guardian(s), **III**, 292, 297; flogging of, **III**, 294
Guardianships, **II**, 36
"Guards" (of ritual purity), **II**, 85, 225, 226
Guide of the Perplexed. *See* Moses Maimonides
Guilds, Islamic, **I**, 82-83, 84
Gum arabic, **I**, 154
Gush Halav (Heb.). *See* al-Jīsh
gwzēhy (Heb.). *See* Nutmeg

Gypsum, II, 424, 428, 552

H

ḥābār, II, 589
ḥabba (grain or one-third of a *qīrāṭ*). *See* Money of account
ḥabbāl. See *aḥbālī*
ḥabr. See *ḥāvēr*
ḥabs. See Pious foundations
ḥabs (prison), II, 508; IV, 34, 357
ḥaddād. See Blacksmith
ḥadhdhā'. See Shoemaker
ḥadīda. See Bracelet
Ḥadīth, on shame, V, 199
hadiyya. See Gift
Hadramaut, Arabia, IV, 55
hadrat (abbrev., *hd*) ("His Eminence"), title of Nagid, II, 496
hadrath ha-rōfe'īm, II, 577
ḥaffāfa (hair removal specialist), I, 430
al-Ḥāfiẓ, Fatimid caliph, II, 342; IV, 167, 306
Ḥāfiẓī linen, IV, 306
Ḥāfiẓiyya, imperial guard, IV, 167, 401
Haftara (lections from the Prophets), II, 151
Hagar, biblical, III, 210
Haifa, Palestine, I, 127, 305; II, 440, 444, 454, 459, 467; V, 555
ḥā'ik. See Weaver
Haim-Kedouri, Sylvia, IV, 164
Hair ornaments, IV, 211, 214, 424, 455
ḥāja ("what is needed," i.e., spices). *See* Spices
ḥajala (canopy), IV, 381
ḥajalī (eye of the partridge). *See* Brownish-pink
ḥajar fiḍḍa (silver stone, silver ingot), I, 388. *See also* Silver
ḥajar nuqra (silver stone, silver ingot), I, 388, 389. *See also* Silver
ḥājib (vizier in Spain), I, 310
ḥajj (Muslim pilgrimage to Mecca), I, 55, 404; II, 422, 588. *See also* Pilgrimage
ḥājj (Muslim pilgrim to Mecca), I, 55; II, 422, 472. See also *ḥajj*
al-Ḥajjāj, viceroy of Iraq, I, 283; II, 165, 190
ḥajjār. See Stonecutter
hajm (a large drinking bowl), type of ship, I, 477
ḥakīm (man of philosophical erudition), II, 172, 246, 315, 316, 477, 507, 601
al-Ḥakīm ("The Doctor"). *See* Jekuthiel b. Moses
al-Ḥākim, Fatimid caliph, I, 18, 21, 34, 71, 270; II, 12, 28-29, 53, 55, 86, 112, 145, 202, 284, 286, 293, 299, 300, 350, 354, 356, 387, 473, 562, 591; III, 357; IV, 14, 130, 174, 185, 261, 376, 440; V, 211, 213, 521, 549, 578, 630
Ḥākimiyya, IV, 130
Ḥalabī, I, 20, 246, 357; II, 81. *See also* Aleppo
al-Ḥalabī, Abu'l-Ḥusayn, I, 248
halak ("died"), II, 457
ḥālāl (Heb.), III, 440
halaylaj. See Myrobalan
Half-cloak, IV, 327, 330
Half-holiday. See *mō'ēd*
Ḥalfōn ("Substitute"), name, V, 618
Ḥalfōn, *ḥāvēr,* V, 580
Ḥalfōn b. Elazar ha-Kohen, II, 485, 597
Ḥalfōn b. Ghālib, cantor and scribe, II, 597
Ḥalfōn b. Maḍmūn, Nagid of Yemen, II, 26
Ḥalfōn b. Manasse, court clerk, I, 425, 433, 464; II, 177, 231, 240, 344, 425, 436, 442, 452, 479, 545, 558, 569, 572, 582, 597; III, 22, 73, 80, 98, 105, 112, 116, 127, 133, 145, 174, 216, 239, 279, 329, 430, 432, 434, 435, 441, 445, 446, 448, 449, 453, 457, 458, 460, 466, 467, 471, 479, 482, 483, 487, 490, 491, 500, 501, 502, 504, 505, 506; IV, 349, 352, 375, 385, 407, 413, 456; V, 132, 133, 140, 159, 422, 518, 534, 539, 542, 548, 549, 553, 598, 604, 618, 625, 626
Ḥalfōn b. Manasse Ibn al-Qaṭā'if ha-Levi. *See* Ḥalfōn b. Manasse
Ḥalfōn b. Nethanel (ha-Levi), India trader, I, 213, 256, 297, 380; II, 209, 303, 513; III, 19, 58, 61–62, 231, 239, 339, 440, 449; IV, 251, 350, 404, 415, 448; V, 10, 16, 119, 195-196, 205, 241, 244, 273, 280–281, 287–288, 300, 305, 393, 426, 453–459, 463–467, 507, 535, 562, 573, 575, 586, 587, 589, 590, 595, 598, 634, 637, 638
Ḥalfōn b. Solomon, IV, 441
Ḥalfōn Dimyāṭī. *See* Ḥalfōn b. Nethanel
Ḥalfōn ha-Levi b. Daniel b. Bundār, III, 497
Ḥalfōn ha-Kohen, V, 159
Ḥalfōn ha-Levi b. Joseph, V, 578, 579
Ḥalfōn (= Khalaf) ha-Levi b. Solomon, II, 597
ḥalīṣā (Heb.), ceremony based on Deuteronomy 25:9, II, 452, 570
ḥallā' (maker of ornaments, jeweler), I, 108, 420. See also *jawhar(ī)*
ḥallāb (milkman), I, 428

al-Ḥallāj, Sufi, V, 493-494
Hall of Ḥammūd, II, 434
Hallway. *See* Corridor
ḥalqa (circle), for auctioning, I, 188, 192
ḥālūm (salted cheese), I, 367, 429. *See also* Cheese
Ḥamā, Syria, III, 11
ḥamaḍ (appetizer), II, 584
Hamadhān, I, 400
al-Hamadhānī, Badīᶜ al-Zamān, I, 324
Hamadhānī, poet, IV, 69, 367
ḥamāʾilī ornaments (necklace with flowers or small coins), IV, 320, 454
Haman, biblical, II, 74, 299, 393; III, 171
ḥāmās (Heb.) *al-Rīf* (sufferings of *muqaddams* in the countryside), II, 74; IV, 349
al-Hamdānī, II, 583
ḥāmil (meal carrier), IV, 390, 394
ḥāmi ʾl-ḥāra (guard of the quarter), II, 608; IV, 14, 35. *See also* Police; Quarter of a city; *ṣāḥib al-rubᶜ*
Ḥammād b. Muḥammad, I, 473
Ḥammū al-Barghawāṭī, I, 377
Ḥammūdid, I, 371, 374
Ḥammūdiyya, near Damascus, I, 425
Ḥammūriyya, Syria, II, 423; IV, 20
ḥamūd (Heb., "delight," i.e., son), expression of parental affection, III, 225, 249, 474
hanāʾ (congratulation reception), III, 116
hanāʾat ha-shewāqīm, II, 543
ḥanak. *See* Choker
Hananel b. Samuel, judge, I, 433; II, 421, 485, 487, 488, 515, 598, 612; IV, 349; V, 22, 23, 114, 268, 418, 419, 510, 538
Hananel b. Hushiel, II, 25, 203, 338, 563
Hananiah b. Manṣūr b. Ezra, V, 379
Hananel of Qayrawān, I, 52; II, 613; V, 557
ḥanbal, type of rug, III, 472; IV, 126–127, 384
Handwriting, I, 7, 22
Hangings as decoration, II, 151
ḥanīn (feeling of family attachment), III, 425. *See also* Family feeling
ḥannāṭ (dealer in wheat), I, 119
Hanukkah, II, 187, 559; III, 204; V, 16, 350, 352, 395, 604
ḥānūt (shop), IV, 263
hanbāzayn (pincers), II, 609
"Happiness," slave girl, I, 138, 140
haqāṣ(*īn*), II, 607
ḥaqq al-taᶜlīm, II, 556
ḥāra. *See* Quarter of a city
harāʾisī (preparer of *harīsa*), I, 424
ḥaramiyya. See *ḥarīm*
ḥarāmōt. *See* Excommunication
ḥārāsh (Heb.), I, 420
harash (bursting of a bale and subsequent damage), I, 487
al-ḥarbī. *See* Warships
Harbonah, biblical, nickname, III, 64
Hardwood or heartwood. *See* Wood
hārib (fugitive), II, 382, 607
ḥarīm (women's quarters), I, 71; IV, 60–61. *See also* Seclusion of women; Women
ḥarīr. *See* Silk
al-ḥarīr al-fayrūzī (silk dyed to turquoise blue), I, 420. *See also* Silk
ḥarīrī. *See* Silk, worker
ḥarīrī (silken). *See* Silk
al-Ḥarīrī, I, 409; IV, 381, 412
ḥarīr quṣṭanṭīnī (Constantinople silk). *See* Constantinople; Silk
harīs(*a*) (dough stuffed with meat, fat, spices), I, 72, 115, 424; IV, 227, 243, 249, 431, 433
al-Ḥarīzī, Judah, poet, I, 324; IV, 69
Harkavy, Abraham, orientalist, I, 25; II, 521; V, 629
Harness, IV, 262, 264
Ḥarrān, northwest Mesopotamia, I, 192
Ḥarrānī, street in Fustat, IV, 283, 284
harrās (preparer of *harīsa*), I, 115, 424
ḥars. See *ḥirāsa*
Hārūn, Arabic form of Aaron, V, 548
Hārūn, elder, II, 428
Hārūn b. Khulayf b. Hārūn, III, 479
Hārūn al-Rashīd, I, 427
Hārūnī Ṭabarī, IV, 304, 306
ḥāsab (to make an account), II, 580. *See also* Accounts
Ḥasab ("Distinction"), f., III, 278
Ḥasab, wife of a cheesemaker, V, 544
ḥasaka. *See* Candlesticks
al-Ḥasan b. ᶜAbd al-Raḥmān, I, 293
Ḥasan b. Abū Saᶜd al-Tustarī, I, 362; III, 135–136, 455; IV, 187, 414
Ḥasan b. Bundār, V, 34
Ḥasan b. Maḥmūd al-Ḥadramī, II, 590
al-Ḥasan b. Muḥammad, I, 293
Ḥasan the Persian, II, 441, 455
Ḥasday b. Nathan, *parnās*, III, 471
ḥāṣēr (courtyard, house), IV, 56ff., 362. *See also* Courtyard, central
Hāshim, coinage of, I, 373
ḥāshir (rallier), II, 379, 610
Ḥashīsh, family name, II, 480
ḥashshāsh (maker of cesspools), I, 423
ḥasīdīm, II, 214; V, 480–481, 482–483. *See also* Pietism
Haskins, Charles Homer, V, 216

Hasmonean(s), **III**, 8
Ḥasnā, d. of Ezekiel b. Masʿūd al-ʿAqrabānī, **III**, 335
Ḥāṣōr, Palestine, **III**, 409
Ḥassān b. Ibrāhīm b. Azhar, **III**, 435; **IV**, 354
Ḥassūn of Ascalon, **III**, 349, 350–351
Ḥassūn b. Kushik, **III**, 428
ḥaṭāṭ, ḥaṭīṭa (small discount). See *samāḥa*
Ḥātimiyya family, **III**, 466
Havdala ceremony at termination of Sabbath, **II**, 430
ḥāvēr (Heb., member of the yeshiva), **I**, 92, 424, 466; **II**, 8, 22, 28, 29, 64, 69, 70, 76, 80, 172, 189, 211, 212, 214, 217, 218, 224, 332, 382, 456, 464, 476, 490, 492, 495, 496, 498, 505, 535, 538, 539, 565, 566, 567, 569, 571, 574, 575, 589, 597, 602, 614; **III**, 19, 20, 257, 430, 431, 434, 442, 451, 458, 460, 468, 489, 502. *See also* individuals bearing title
ḥavūrat ha-ṣedeq (the Righteous Corporation), **II**, 196, 561, 566
ḥawāla. See Debt, transfer of
ḥawānīt. See Stores
ḥawḍ (water reservoir), **II**, 586
hāwinī (maker of mortars), **I**, 421. *See also* Mortar and pestle
Hay Gaon, **V**, 127–128, 390, 395-396, 404–405, 419, 437
hayāmina. See Trustees
hayba (respect), **II**, 35
Hayfāʾ ("Slender"), d. of Sulaymān Ibn al-ʿArīq, **III**, 196
Hay Gaon, **I**, 52–53; **II**, 10, 15, 17, 24, 25, 29, 177, 298, 337, 338, 344, 521, 526, 558, 564, 603; **III**, 261, 270, 300; **V**, 520, 570, 585, 616
haykal (Coptic, sanctuary). *See* Church, Coptic
hayl. See Cardamom
haymana (Judeo-Ar., office of trustee), **II**, 80, 539. *See also* Trustees
ḥayr(ī). See *majlis*
Ḥayyīm b. ʿAmmār al-Madīnī, **I**, 374, 455, 484; **II**, 525; **III**, 339–340, 442, 503; **IV**, 184, 410; **V**, 303, 519, 574, 583
Ḥayyīm Ḥabshūsh, **IV**, 458
Ḥayyīm Ḥubāra, **I**, 413
Ḥayyīm b. Jacob. *See* Khalaf b. Jacob
Ḥayyīm the Lame, **V**, 252–253, 576
Ḥayyīm (II) b. Sahlawayh (II) b. Ḥayyīm, **III**, 290, 439, 491
ḥāz (occupying part of a house), **IV**, 372
Hazelnuts, **I**, 121; **IV**, 441; seller of, **II**, 467
ḥaẓẓ (favor), **II**, 604; **III**, 440
ḥazzām (packer), **I**, 486. *See also* Packing
ḥazzān. See Cantor
al-ḥazzān al-gādōl. See Cantor, chief
ḥazzān ha-keneseth (cantor of the synagogue), **II**, 223, 569
ḥazzān al-majlis (cantor of the audience hall), cantor of Nagid's private synagogue, **II**, 223, 569
ḥazzānūth. See Poetry, liturgical
Headband, **IV**, 323, 324, 327, 330
Headcover, ornamenting face, **IV**, 159; required constantly, **IV**, 158–160
Head of Academy. *See* Gaon
Head of a profession, **I**, 84; **IV**, 434
"Head of the Assembly," title in Iraqian yeshivas, **II**, 472
Head of the Community, **III**, 26, 100, 108, 146, 196. *See also* Gaon, Nagid
Head of the Congregation(s), **II**, 24, 75–77, 434, 538, 542, 566, 598
Head of the Diaspora (*raʾs al-jālūt*), **I**, 54, 92, 144; **II**, 17, 18, 24, 25, 26, 27, 28, 31, 39, 287, 519–524, 588; **IV**, 413
Head of the Jews (*raʾīs al-yahūd*), **I**, 260, 379, 381; **II**, 23, 26, 27, 31, 32, 33, 34, 35, 36, 37, 38, 39, 64, 83, 211, 244, 417, 429, 442, 458, 493, 494, 524, 526, 527, 528, 529, 565. *See also* Nagid; *shaykh al-yahūd*
"Head of the synagogue," **II**, 58, 76; **III**, 4, 94
Head of the yeshiva. *See* Gaon
Health: hygiene, **V**, 94–101; wishes for good, **V**, 46. *See also* Illness; Physicians
Heat, **IV**, 117
Heating appliances, **IV**, 136
Hebrew, **I**, 1, 4, 5, 15, 19, 64, 68, 230, 250, 282, 284, 296, 304, 305, 425; **II**, 162, 164, 190, 195, 207, 210, 218, 248, 249, 277, 281, 283, 309, 310, 320, 323, 341, 350, 355; **III**, 16, 52, 88, 136, 143, 145, 156, 189, 193, 199, 204, 209, 220; **IV**, 47, 69, 78, 117, 122, 123, 150, 154, 162, 175, 178, 197, 311, 409; calligraphy, **II**, 174, 180, 184, 229, 234; characters used to write Arabic, **II**, 231–232, 253, 254, 266, 294, 303, 499, 512, 520, 533, 555, 574, 583, 588; **IV**, 50; cursive script, **II**, 234–235, 250, 346; documents, **I**, 254; **III**, 292; **IV**, 24, 37, 89, 172, 265; feelings about, **V**, 348–349, 386; Karaites, **V**, 364–365, 372; known by educated Jews, **I**, 52; language of synagogue service, **II**, 220; names, **II**, 130, 237, 315; **III**, 319; numerals, **II**, 178, 447, 491; phrases in Arabic context, **I**, 16; **IV**, 42, 122, 162;

poetry, II, 159; V, 320 (*see also* Poetry, liturgical); as secret code, I, 60, 265, 271; IV, 239, 242; study of linguistics, V, 372, 380-382, 424, 429; studied with Bible, II, 206; titles, I, 249; II, 352; use in letters, V, 309, 422-423, 434; use for emphasis, V, 612; women's knowledge, V, 468, 470. *See also* Script: Hebrew
Hebrew-German (Old Yiddish), I, 397
Hebron, Palestine, I, 113; II, 56, 73, 122, 146, 167, 284, 446, 447, 502, 536, 555; IV, 45, 264
Heirlooms, IV, 105
Heirs, II, 613; III, 277-292. *See also* Inheritance
hēkhāl (Heb.). *See* Holy ark
Helena, mother of Constantine, I, 350
"Heliopolis stone," IV, 103
Hell, V, 410. *See also* Satan
Hellas, III, 15, 321
Hellen(ist)ic, I, 20, 73, 77; IV, 3 and *passim*
Helper (in workshop), I, 94-98, 113
hēmān (Aram.), trustee, II, 80, 539. *See also* Trustee
Hemp, I, 86, 105
Hems, ornamental (*mudhayyal*), IV, 324, 455
Hen, IV, 230, 231
Henna, I, 155; III, 443; IV, 389, 406 (see also *ḥinnāwī*); ceremony, III, 71, 116
heqdēsh (Heb.). *See* Pious foundations
Herald, II, 87
Herāt, IV, 305
Heredity: influence of, II, 597; principle of, II, 87-91, 162, 319, 541; of public office, III, 4
ḥerem (Heb.) *See* Excommunication
ḥerem setām (Heb.). *See* Ban "in general terms"
ḥerem ha-yishūv (Heb.), term not found in Geniza papers, II, 68
Herlihy, David, III, 131; IV, 4
Herodotus, 282; III, 21
Herzfeld, Ernst, IV, 125, 306; V, 516
Ḥesed. *See* Abū Naṣr Tustarī
Hezekiah b. Benjamin, Karaite, IV, 314, 316
Hezekiah b. David, Exilarch and Gaon, II, 17, 87, 564; V, 197, 563
hiba (gift), I, 449. *See also* Gift
Hiba, II, 427
Hiba, rent collector, V, 551
Hiba b. Bishr, I, 363
Hiba b. Israel, III, 197-198
Hiba b. Nīsān, teacher, V, 377
Hiba al-Zakī, I, 365
Hibat Allah, orphan, IV, 275
Hibat Allāh, II, 576. *See also* Nethanel b. Moses ha-Levi
Hibat Allāh b. Futūḥ Ibn al-ʿAmmānī, III, 117
ḥibba (love and affection), expected from husband, IV, 451. See also *ḥīsa*; *maḥabba*
ḥibbūr (Heb., joining [of two sheets of paper]), II, 573
al-ḥibbūr, term used by Oriental Jews for *Mishneh Torah*, V, 641
ḥibrā' (ladies' dark veil), I, 108. *See also* Veil
ḥibrāwī (maker of ladies' dark veil), I, 108, 420
Hides, I, 111-112, 153, 154, 333; IV, 129
"Hierocratic" organization, II, 54, 56, 80
Higgins, R. A., IV, 202, 212
High Court of the Yeshiva, II, 9 and *passim*. *See also* Yeshiva
Higher studies, organization of, II, 195-210
High Holidays, II, 34, 60, 108, 122; III, 204, 308, 337
High priest(s) of Jerusalem, III, 7, 8; IV, 192
Ḥijāz(ī), I, 54, 56, 180; II, 387, 441, 442, 447, 588. *See also* Qayrawān
ḥikr. *See* Ground rent
Hilāla b. Hiba, III, 502
Hilāl and Sulaym, I, 32, 41, 57, 235, 281, 327, 377
Hilāl b. Nissīm, IV, 438
Hilāl b. Thābit (= Heb. Yākhīn) b. Munīr (= Heb. Meir), II, 583; V, 37
ḥilaq. *See* Earrings
Hillel, the sage, V, 81
Hillel, *parnās*, II, 504
Hillel, *ṣāḥib* of Ibn al-Sukkarī, I, 441
Hillel b. Eli, scribe and cantor, I, 363, 405, 425, 443, 462, 463, 465, 466; II, 111, 222, 231, 234, 237, 240, 344, 415, 430, 446, 501, 541, 569, 570, 572-573, 576, 582, 597; III, 233, 348, 350, 351, 437, 470, 482, 483, 504, 505; IV, 368, 423, 428; V, 213, 292, 542, 543, 557, 566, 567, 588, 625; daughter of, V, 574
Hillel b. Isaac, II, 471
Hillel b. Joseph b. Jacob Ibn ʿAwkal, V, 35, 194
Hillel b. Naḥmān, III, 435
Hillel b. Zadok, V, 358
ḥiml (camel load), I, 220, 486
Hindu, II, 277
ḥinnā'. *See* Henna

ḥinnāwī (dealer in henna), **I**, 438; family name, **II**, 506
Hippocrates, **II**, 249, 252; oath of, **II**, 244
ḥirāsa (fee for police protection), **IV**, 35, 37, 357
ḥirz (charm written for protection), **III**, 226
ḥīsā (Heb., love and considerateness), expected from wife, **III**, 437; **IV**, 451. See also *ḥibba*; *maḥabba*
ḥisba (tax for store licenses), **I**, 270. *See also* Market police; Market supervision
Ḥisday, leader of Karaite community, **III**, 204
Ḥisday Ibn Shaprūṭ, **I**, 191; **V**, 468, 638
ḥiṣrim muna'na' (grape juice flavored with mint), **II**, 584
ḥiṣṣa. *See* Houses, shares in
Ḥiwwī, biblical name, **V**, 616
Ḥiwwī al-Balkhī, **V**, 388-389
Ḥiyyā b. Isaac, the Spaniard, judge, **II**, 513, 549; **III**, 284, 490; **IV**, 289, 328; **V**, 57-58, 358, 521
ḥizāna. *See* Poetry, liturgical
ḥizb (faction), **II**, 64
Ḥmtyh, place name, **II**, 606
Hoarding, **I**, 263-266; **III**, 140
hōd ha-malkūth (Heb.). *See* Bahā' al-dawla
Hōd (*ha-yeshiva*) (Splendor [of the Yeshiva]), **II**, 525, 535
hōdā'ā (Heb.). *See* Acknowledgment of debts
Hoffman, Lois Wladis, **III**, 223-225
Holidays, **I**, 164, 348, 350, 357; **II**, 96, 97, 99, 159, 193, 219, 222, 224, 431, 455, 457, 463, 465, 501, 506, 532, 533, 542, 544, 559, 569, 598; **III**, 18, 115, 125, 236, 283, 337; **IV**, 10, 21, 155-158; as terms for payment, **I**, 254, 256, 258, 260; business on, **V**, 16-17; Messianism and, **V**, 394-395; Muslim, **II**, 590, 591; occasion for charity, **V**, 75, 87-89; religious spirit, **V**, 349-352; socializing, **V**, 14-17. *See also* Sabbath and individual holidays
Holy ark, **II**, 145, 146, 147, 149, 153, 156, 306, 423, 424, 532
Holy City. *See* Jerusalem
Holy Land. *See* Palestine
Holy Scriptures. *See* Bible
Holy Sepulchre, **I**, 18
Homelessness, **V**, 90-91
ḥōmesh (Heb., "the fifth"), fixed charge, **II**, 521. See also *khums*; *ḥoq*
Homosexuality: female, **V**, 316; male, **V**, 21, 202, 311-312, 319-320
Honesty, **V**, 204-214
Honey, **I**, 46, 125, 219; **II**, 46; **IV**, 233, 246, 260 (see also *'aṣīda*); seller of (*'assāl, mu'assil*), **I**, 429; **II**, 474. See also *shahd*
Honey and vinegar, syrup of, **I**, 151; **II**, 267, 268, 271. *See also* Oxymel
Honey bee, **IV**, 248
Honey, color, **IV**, 175, 194, 195
Honeydew, color, **IV**, 177, 407
Honey made of dates, **IV**, 247
Honey sherbet. See *fuqqā'*
Honor, **V**, 200-204
Honorific titles (*alqāb*), **I**, 78, 84, 358, 414, 442 and *passim*; **II**, 17, 20, 52, 55, 60, 75, 77, 162, 172, 246, 355, 356, 432, 478, 480, 508, 512, 513, 514, 515, 520, 523, 525, 531-532, 533, 534, 541, 553, 554, 577, 587, 605, 609, 612; **III**, 44; **V**, 10, 260-272, 430, 578
Hood (*kṣy*) with garment, **IV**, 117, 320, 323, 330, 454
"Hooks for the kitchen," **IV**, 144
Hoops (*ṭārāt*), **IV**, 133, 423, 424
Hopkins, Simon, **V**, 640
ḥoq (fixed charge), **II**, 521. See also *ḥōmesh*; *khums*
Horant and Hilde, **I**, 13
Hormshir, **I**, 400
Horoscope(s), **III**, 233
Horses, **I**, 211, 285
Hospice. See *funduq*
Hospitality. *See* Charity; Visiting
Hospitals (*bīmāristān, māristān*), **II**, 251, 257, 508, 528, 547, 577, 578; government, **II**, 39, 133, 172, 249, 250, 256; **IV**, 70, 367
Hostess, **IV**, 228
Hourani, Albert H., **IV**, 4
House(s), **I**, 261, 264, 382, 385, 386, 391; **II**, 46, 68, 86, 189, 245, 262, 560, 591, 602; **IV**, 37, 47, 189-190; adjacent, **IV**, 16; adjoining the synagogue, **II**, 152-153; as augury or omen, **IV**, 90, 101; belonging to Church, **IV**, 25; billeting in, **IV**, 24; "built-up," **IV**, 23; changing hands between Muslims, Christians and Jews, **II**, 263, 292; **IV**, 98-99; changing names of, **II**, 119; as collateral, **I**, 259; **IV**, 85, 273, 276, 278, 279, 280; deeds of sale, **I**, 196, 449; **II**, 531; **IV**, 49-52, 67, 76; descriptions of, **II**, 573; **IV**, 78-82; designation in Ar. and Heb., **IV**, 56; disputes over, **II**, 318; **IV**, 52; divided vertically, **IV**, 71; durability and maintenance, **IV**, 97ff.; = family, **II**, 546; **IV**, 59; form of investment,

IV, 83-85; foundations of, IV, 23; garden, IV, 56-57; general character, IV, 77-78; gift, IV, 49-52, 88; ground floor of (see *qāʿa*); ill-omened, III, 34; in Delta, IV, 59, 294; in Ṣanʿa, Yemen, IV, 71; interior, IV, 48, 105, 313 and *passim* (*see also* Furnishings); for jewelry, carpets, apples, etc., bazaars, IV, 26, 27, 34, 57-58; large, IV, 56, 79-80; lease of, IV, 52; life stories of, IV, 98-100; maintenance, IV, 101; materials used in construction, IV, 102ff.; middle floors, IV, 59; Mediterranean, III, 38; mobility within, IV, 48; multistoried, IV, 2, 54, 55, 58-59, 81-82; names of, II, 545; IV, 85; number of occupants, IV, 97; open spaces outside, IV, 60; "opening for the wind," IV, 62; occupied by different parties, IV, 83-84; one within another, IV, 57; owned in both Fustat and Cairo, IV, 11; ownership of, IV, 82-86; partnership in, I, 170, 252; II, 615; IV, 83; pillars, IV, 23; and pious foundations, II, 97, 99, 101, 102, 103, 110, 112, 118-119, 133, 155, 413-437; IV, 52-53, 88 and *passim*; prices, II, 50, 572; IV, 18, 51, 86-87, 273-290; for progeny, IV, 85-86; references in Ar. papyri, IV, 53; rent collected according to Muslim calendar, I, 270, 356; rents low, IV, 85; repairs of, II, 102, 111, 116, 145, 414-437, 533, 605; IV, 85, 100; revenue from, I, 263; II, 360, 413-437; right of repurchase of sold, IV, 87-88, 278, 279, 285; shares in (*ḥiṣṣa*), I, 266, 446; II, 245, 430, 433; IV, 51, 82-83, 371, 449; small, I, 252; IV, 56ff., 276, 363, 365; socio-economic aspects of, IV, 82-104; store-top (see *ʿulūw*); structural changes, IV, 102; tilting, IV, 38, 60; traditional Egyptian, IV, 48-56, 63; transfer of, II, 400; IV, 89; types of, IV, 56-59; upper floors, IV, 59, 63, 80; vacancies, II, 114; with three inner courts, IV, 16; of women, II, 396, 532, 545; IV, 85 and *passim*, 276, 280, 281, 282; workmen employed in, IV, 102; in Yemen, I, 71. *See also* Donation of buildings; *manzil*; Residence

"House" = wife, III, 164

House of ʿAblā, II, 434

House of Blessing. See *dār al-baraka*

House of the Daughter of Nafīs *al-sharābī*, V, 580

House of David, III, 25, 135

House of Exchange. See *dār al-ṣarf*

House of the Glassmaker, IV, 293

House of Hiba al-Abzārī ("dealer in seeds"), II, 427

House of the Pious, II, 421, 429

House of the She-camel, II, 426

Household: bills, II, 269; goods, II, 584, 585; joint, III, 39-40, 250

Housekeeper, female, II, 292

Houseleek, IV, 209, 423, 426

Housewares, IV, 138-150, 450

Housing. *See* Residence

ḥōv (Heb., debt), delayed installment of marriage gift, III, 104. *See also* Marriage gift of husband

Ḥubārah, Joseph, III, 36

Ḥudayjī street, Fustat, IV, 18, 19, 22, 280, 284, 352, 353, 372

Hughes, Graham, IV, 226

ḥujja ([Muslim document] of acknowledgement), I, 251-260; II, 401, 614. *See also* Acknowledgement of debt

ḥujra (chamber, room), meaning separate building, III, 479; IV, 363, 370

ḥukm (astrologer's conclusion from astral phenomena), V, 626

ḥulayqāt (ringlets), I, 423

ḥulla. *See* Gala costume

Ḥulwān, I, 400

Humility, V, 196-199

ḥummuṣ. *See* Chickpeas

Hungarian Academy of Sciences, I, 3, 5

Hunger, IV, 226, 239-240. *See also* Famine; Food

ḥuqqa. *See* Box

Ḥurayfīsh ("little vagabond"), nickname, II, 506

ḥurrayq (nettles), wild herb, I, 483; IV, 245

hurrās. See *harrās*

ḥūs (Heb., to pity), III, 437

Ḥusayn b. Dāʾūd b. Sakan. *See* Japheth b. David b. Shekhanya

al-Ḥusayn b. Mufarrij, I, 292

al-Ḥusayn b. Ṭahir, I, 292-293

Husband, absence of, III, 155, 184, 189-194, 263, 345; conduct of, III, 156-158; economic power of, III, 180-184; "errand boy" of wife, III, 180; ideal, III, 167; obligations of, III, 118-123, 179-180, 191; runaway, III, 178, 195-205, 302; travel of, III, 144, 155-156, 188, 189-194. *See also* Marriage

ḥushshār (ralliers), II, 370, 385, 389, 608

Ḥusn b. Ḥayyīm II b. Sahlawayh I, III, 136, 439

al-Ḥusn b. Saʿāda, wife of Nathan b. Samuel. *See* Sitt al-Ḥusn b. Saʿāda
Ḥusn b. Saʿdān ha-Kohen, **III**, 495
ḥuṣr (mats), **I**, 437. *See also* Mat
ḥuṣrī (maker or seller of mats), **I**, 416, 437
Huxlley, Thomas Henry, **V**, 28
ḥuzza (underwear, band), **IV**, 415, 465

I

Ibāḍite, **I**, 65
ʿIbillīn, Galilee, **III**, 177
Ibn. *See also* Ben
Ibn ʿAbbūd, mailman, **I**, 271
Ibn ʿAbd Rabbih, **V**, 616
Ibn Abī ʿAqīl, qadi, **I**, 296; **II**, 613
Ibn Abiʾl-Bayān, **II**, 264, 582
Ibn Abī d-Dunyā, **V**, 561
Ibn Abī Qīda, **III**, 289
Ibn Abī Ronda, **III**, 481
Ibn Abī ʿUqba, **III**, 432
Ibn Abī Uṣaybiʿa, **II**, 245, 247, 264, 576, 580, 603; **III**, 460; **V**, 271, 272, 447, 505, 634
Ibn Abū ʿAqīl. *See* Ibn Abī ʿAqīl
Ibn Abū Sahl, **II**, 508
Ibn al-ʿAdl, **II**, 539
Ibn Akhūh, nephew, **II**, 474
Ibn ʿAllān, Abuʾl-Faraj Jacob b. Abraham, **I**, 243, 309, 311, 463; **V**, 207–208, 209, 246, 565
Ibn al-ʿAmmānī. *See* Aaron b. Yeshūʿā
Ibn al-ʿAmmānī family, **IV**, 443
Ibn ʿAmmār, **II**, 356
Ibn al-Amshāṭī ("son of the comb-maker"). *See* Abuʾl-Fakhr Saadya b. Abraham
Ibn Asad, Samuel b. Judah, **I**, 175
Ibn ʿAṭāʾ. *See* Abraham b. ʿAṭāʾ
Ibn ʿAwkal b. Joseph, **II**, 440, 454, 474, 525, 536
Ibn ʿAwkal family, **V**, 239. *See also* Joseph Ibn ʿAwkal
ibn ʿayn sārra ("the son of the man with the gladdening eyes"), by-name, **V**, 575
Ibn Baqara family, **III**, 12–13
Ibn al-Basmalī, a ship, **I**, 312
Ibn al-Baṣrī, **V**, 461
Ibn Baṭṭūṭa, 67; **III**, 185
Ibn al-Būnī, silk merchant, **V**, 549
Ibn Duqmāq, **III**, 11, 428; **IV**, 22, 30, 39, 351, 353, 356, 402
Ibn Ezra, *ṣayrafī*, **II**, 474
Ibn Ezra family, **III**, 290; **V**, 635
Ibn Faḍlān, **II**, 18, 523; **V**, 579
Ibn Faḍlān family, **III**, 429
Ibn al-Furāt. *See* Abraham b. Isaac b. Furāt
Ibn Futayḥ, **I**, 145
Ibn Gabirol. *See* Solomon ibn Gabirol
Ibn Ḥajar al-ʿAsqalānī, **III**, 498
Ibn Ḥallāb the proselyte, **II**, 308
Ibn al-Hamadānī, **III**, 496
Ibn al-Ḥarrānī, Aḥmad, **I**, 192
Ibn Ḥawqal, **II**, 190; **IV**, 54–55, 58
Ibn al-Haytham, **V**, 602
Ibn Ḥayyīm, **II**, 473
Ibn al-Ḥijāziyya, **II**, 341, 602
Ibn Ḥirbish of Damascus, **I**, 445; **II**, 440
Ibn al-Ḥulaybī, **I**, 192
Ibn ʿIdhārī, **III**, 357
Ibn al-Imām of Damascus, **I**, 81
Ibn al-Iskandar, captain, **I**, 302, 309
Ibn Jalāl al-Mulk, **II**, 463, 502
Ibn Jamāhir, **I**, 133, 146; **V**, 266, 580
Ibn Jāmiʿ family, **III**, 6, 426, 43
Ibn Jarwa, **I**, 322
Ibn al-Jāzifīnī, **II**, 568
Ibn Jubayr, **I**, 59, 70, 298, 314, 325; **II**, 610; **IV**, 42, 45; **V**, 636
Ibn Jumayʿ, Saladin's physician, **I**, 122, 253; **II**, 248, 250, 258, 576, 577; **V**, 101, 446–447, 534
Ibn Kaʿb, Jewish convert to Islam, **V**, 563
Ibn al-Kallām, **V**, 633
Ibn Kammūna, **III**, 13
Ibn Khaldūn, **I**, 57, 75, 319, 324; **II**, 64, 176; **IV**, 138; **V**, 256, 565
Ibn Khallāf, a ship, **I**, 312
Ibn al-Khaybarī, **II**, 611
Ibn al-Khāzin family, **IV**, 99
Ibn Killis. *See* Yaʿqūb Ibn Killis
Ibn Lebdī, **I**, 89, 380; **IV**, 321
Ibn al-Maghrebī, **II**, 596
Ibn al-Majjānī. *See* Abū ʿImrān Mūsā Ibn al-Majjānī; Yaḥyā b. Mūsā Ibn al-Majjānī
Ibn al-Malaṭī, **II**, 477
Ibn Mammātī, **II**, 387
Ibn al-Maqdisī, **II**, 308; **III**, 288
ibn al-mara (stepson), **III**, 311. *See also* Stepchildren
Ibn al-Māshiṭa, **V**, 315
Ibn Maṭrūḥ, poet from Upper Egypt, **V**, 563
Ibn Maymūn, **I**, 308
Ibn Migash. *See* Joseph Ibn Migash
Ibn al-Muhandiz, **III**, 333
Ibn al-Mujāwir, Muslim historian, **V**, 523
Ibn al-Muqaddam, **II**, 538
Ibn al-Muqaffaʿ, **V**, 276
Ibn al-Mushnaqa family, **V**, 246
Ibn Muyassar, **I**, 188

Ibn al-Muzaghlil ("The Dazzler"), **II**, 492; V, 524
Ibn al-Nadīm, V, 379
Ibn Naʿīm, a ship, I, 312
Ibn al-Naʿja ("Female Sheep"), family name, V, 590
Ibn al-Naʿnāʿ. *See* Ayyūb b. Tamīm
Ibn Nufayʿ, cantor, **II**, 568, 570
Ibn Nufayʿ family, V, 124–125
Ibn al-Qaṣbī, **IV**, 191; V, 61
Ibn al-Qaṭāʾif. *See* Ḥalfōn b. Manasse Ibn al-Qaṭāʾif
Ibn Qayyōma, V, 588
Ibn al-Qifṭī, V, 447
Ibn Rajāʾ, Muslim *wakīl*, **II**, 295, 590; **IV**, 91, 373
Ibn al-Rayyis, family name, V, 578
Ibn Riḍwān, physician, **IV**, 54; V, 532, 534
Ibn Rushd (Averroes), **II**, 172, 249
Ibn Saʿdān, V, 241
Ibn Sābā, **III**, 484
Ibn Sabra family, **III**, 176, 183–184; V, 227
Ibn Saghīr (not Ṣaghīr), I, 93, 413
Ibn Ṣaghīr family, **II**, 476; **III**, 442
Ibn Saʿīd, Maghrebi Muslim traveler, **IV**, 11, 22, 39, 43, 350
Ibn al-Salamī, **II**, 278
Ibn al-Salār. *See* Ibn al-Sallār
Ibn al-Sallār, Fatimid vizier, I, 269; **II**, 528, 604; **IV**, 15, 450
Ibn Sanāʾ al-Mulk, I, 253, 358; **II**, 298; V, 443–445, 447, 634
Ibn Ṣayrafī, **II**, 610
Ibn Shāʾūl, *shōḥēt*, **II**, 571
Ibn Shaʿyā, family name, **II**, 476, 527; **III**, 9–10, 491; V, 610, 612. *See also* Joseph Ibn Shaʿya
Ibn Shiblūn, I, 311
Ibn Shūʿa, physician to Saladin, **II**, 257; V, 634
Ibn Sibāʿ, **IV**, 421
Ibn Sighmār, **II**, 440, 596; **III**, 6; V, 594. *See also* Isaac b. David, Judah b. Moses I, Labraṭ b. Moses I
Ibn Simʿān ("Simonson"), characteristic name, **II**, 508
Ibn Sīnā (Avicenna), **IV**, 248; V, 407, 452, 622
Ibn al-Ṣiqilliyya, **III**, 468
Ibn al-Sukkarī, **III**, 350–351
Ibn Sunaynāt, the banker, I, 250, 251, 263
Ibn Taghribirdī, **II**, 354
Ibn al-Tāhertī, **II**, 454
Ibn Ṭarsūn, **II**, 473
Ibn Ṭarsūn, cantor, **III**, 217
Ibn al-Tawwazī, **III**, 290
Ibn Thumna, I, 326, 330
Ibn Ṭūlūn, Aḥmad, I, 18
Ibn Yaʿqūb, Ibrāhīm, I, 27
Ibn Yijū family, **III**, 6, 426, 456
Ibn Yūnus, I, 311
Ibn Zabqala family, **IV**, 282
Ibn Zaffān, merchant, **III**, 460
Ibn Zūlāq, **IV**, 59
ibrāʾ (acquittance, yearly assessment), **II**, 359, 434, 600
Ibrahīm, *ḥāvēr*, **II**, 498
Ibrahīm, *parnās*, **II**, 428
Ibrahīm Adham, **IV**, 151
Ibrahīm b. Abiʾl-Ḥayy, **II**, 587
Ibrahīm b. Abū Saʿd, **IV**, 373
Ibrahīm b. Buʾl-Faḍl, I, 366
Ibrahīm b. Faraḥ al-Iskandarānī, I, 304, 439, 485; **IV**, 349; V, 518
Ibrāhīm b. Finḥās b. Yūsuf, **II**, 423
Ibrahīm b. Isḥāq, **II**, 611
Ibrāhīm b. Mūsā, I, 442
Ibrahīm b. Ṣalḥūn, V, 626
Ibrāhīm b. Tashfīn, I, 263
Ibrahīm b. Yūsuf b. Nathan, V, 315
Ibrahīm Ibn al-Mawāzīnī (maker of scales), **II**, 491
Ibrahīm Ibn al-Shāʿir (the Poet), **II**, 429
Ibrahīm II of Tunisia, I, 186
ibrīq, **IV**, 389
ibrīsim, type of silk, I, 60, 103
Ibwān, **II**, 606
Ibyār. *See* Abyār
Ice, imported, I, 115
ʿīd al-fiṭr (feast breaking fast [of Ramadan]), **II**, 591; **IV**, 397
ʿīd al-kabīr (feast of sacrifice), **II**, 425
ʿidl (ship's bale), I, 220, 335, 336. *See also* Bale
Idris, R.H., I, 479; **IV**, 274
ʿīd al-ṣalīb (Feast of the Cross), I, 303, 317, 325
Ifranj, I, 54; **II**, 457, 496, 506. *See also* European; Franks
Ifransa. *See* France
ifrantī, European money, I, 464
Ifrīqiya, **IV**, 7, 438
ifrīz, **IV**, 462
iftidāʾ (ransoming), legal strategy for divorce, **III**, 267. *See also* Divorce
Iftikhār al-Dawla (Pride of the Realm), **IV**, 98
iftiqād (inquiries), V, 109
iggartā (Aram., letter), I, 286
ihlīlaj. *See* Myrobalan
ikhtiyār (request), **II**, 562

ʿilāwa (appendage to package), I, 337
Illness: in adversity, V, 56, 104, 116, 243–244; attitudes toward, V, 103, 107–110; described in correspondence, V, 103–108; diagnosis, V, 105–108, 112–114; God's power over, V, 108–112, 115; infirmities of age, V, 119–120; recovery from, V, 110–111; visits during, V, 26, 110. *See also* Epidemics; Health
Illumination, II, 83, 111, 117, 150, 204, 415, 417, 421, 462, 480, 551, 561
Illustrations, IV, 160. *See also* Miniatures
ʿilm (study), II, 558
iltiqāṭ Andalusī (Spanish "pickups"), I, 454
imāla, I, 398, 462; II, 531, 565, 575
imām, III, 138
ʿimāma. *See* Turban
imlāk (engagement, betrothal), III, 69, 95. *See also* Betrothal; Engagement; *milāk*
Immanuel b. Yehiel, judge, II, 494, 515, 572; III, 72, 133, 453
Impotence, III, 169, 170
"impregnated" = oiled, IV, 163
Impropriety and unpleasantness, in letters, V, 237–239, 296, 411
ʿImrān b. Muhājir, II, 523
al-ʿImrāniyya, V, 65
ʿImrān of Tyre, II, 454
Imruʾl-Qays, I, 283
Inauguration, II, 527
"Incense," slave girl, I, 140
Incense, II, 265
Incense burner (*midkhana*), IV, 137–138, 388
Inconsistency of scribes, II, 236–237, 246
India(n): allegiance to ecumenical and territorial authorities, II, 20–21; David Maimonides in, II, 258; foreigner on wheat distribution list, II, 458; husbands who have deserted wives in, I, 58; II, 301; III, 200; linen as writing material in, II, 232; Malabar coast of, II, 20; IV, 129, 134; manumission of slave girl in, II, 20–21; medicine, II, 253, 268; merchants in (*see* India traders); relative of Abraham Yijū, II, 480; representative of the Aden rabbinical court in, II, 331; route, II, 232; III, 16; IV, 2, 115, 170, 203; trade and traders, I, 6, 7, 16 and *passim*; II, 26, 61, 78, 95, 166, 175, 193, 216, 262, 265, 268, 270, 271, 295, 302, 305, 345, 383, 405, 523, 555; III, 10, 11, 19, 29, 31, 32, 35, 55, 58, 61, 73, 74, 84, 87, 137, 138, 146, 168, 192, 193, 200, 206, 207, 231, 238, 239, 241, 264, 280, 282, 288, 326, 327, 339, 348, 365, 386, 434, 440, 470, 482, 484, 489, 491, 498; IV, 1, 7, 83, 109, 113, 114, 120, 124, 129, 135, 138, 139, 140, 147, 148, 164, 165, 172, 192, 173, 189, 196, 203, 204, 224, 236, 240, 247, 260, 374, 379, 393, 400, 403, 437, 449; V, 18, 50, 67. *See also* Traders and individual names
Indigo (*nīlī*), I, 20, 46, 87, 155, 183, 185, 193, 210, 216, 219, 222, 333, 334, 335, 361; II, 45, 531; IV, 10, 172, 173, 402, 405–406, 410
Individualism, V, 214–216; and conformity, IV, 77
Indonesia, IV, 1
Inequality, social, I, 76
infitāḥ al-baḥr (beginning of shipping season), I, 481
Informal cooperation, I, 163, 164–169, 184. *See also* Partnership; *ṣuḥba*
inharash (bursting of bale and damage to consignment), I, 487
Inheritance, II, 301, 311, 540, 541, 582, 597, 600, 602, 615; III, 46, 130, 139, 143, 186, 236, 238, 247, 251–257, 277-292; of daughters, III, 280–283, 436, 483; Islamic law of, IV, 82; mutual release, III, 257, 287, 289, 333; tax, III, 286. *See also* Succession
Ink, I, 7; II, 233, 574
Innovations condemned, II, 406
Inscriptions, IV, 197, 417
Insecurity and instability of life, III, 182, 310; V, 48, 71, 116, 325, 331
Installments, payment in, I, 96, 152, 208, 260–262, 383, 384, 415
Institut Narodov Azii (Institute of the Peoples of Asia), Leningrad, I, 3; III, 217
Insurance, I, 175; V, 121–122
Intercalation, I, 356; IV, 418
Interest, fixed, I, 256, 384, 464. *See also* Loans on interest
Interfaith relations, II, 273–311, 586-594
Intermarriage: Rabbanite-Karaite, II, 7, 110; III, 107, 136, 149, 169; Muslim-Christian-Jewish, II, 277, 301; III, 158. *See also* Karaites
Inventories, I, 10, 246, 263–266; IV, 106; of synagogue furnishings, II, 83, 149; of estate, III, 283–285
Investment, I, 263–266
ʿiqd. *See* Necklace
iqlāʿāt ("sailings," i.e., groups in convoys), I, 331
iqrār. *See* Acknowledgement of debts

Iran(ians), I, 30; IV, 2, 31, 144; cantors from, II, 222; decay in 10th-13th centuries, II, 204; emigration from, III, 11, 37, 136, 289; IV, 192, 304; immigrant from living in synagogue compound in Egypt, II, 154; influence of on female seclusion, III, 153, 323; Iraq under Persian empire, II, 197; Karaites from, IV, 121; medicine, II, 253; names indicating origin in, I, 400; III, 290, 293; neglected in wheat distribution, II, 463; on bread distribution list, II, 439; on clothing distribution list, II, 444; on poll-tax list, II, 440; prohibition of Jewish public prayer in, II, 160; prosperity of Jewish community in 8th–10th centuries, II, 201; silk industry in, I, 103; as source of Egypt's sugar industry, IV, 247, 253; tax-farming, II, 363; textile industry in, I, 50, 106, 164–165; IV, 109, 306, 402, 414

Iraq(ians), Christian community of, II, 243; court of, II, 601; decline in 10th-13th centuries, II, 204; emigration from, I, 30, 33, 49, 54, 56; II, 205, 441, 467, 520; III, 301; IV, 192, 247, 304; exilarch, II, 17, 25, 28, 29; farming in, III, 322; Gaons, I, 25; II, 14, 401; honorific titles, II, 534; hospitals, II, 264; housing in, IV, 56, 72; immigration to from West, III, 57; Karaites in, I, 65; IV, 121; merchants from, I, 188, 269; II, 21; III, 93; IV, 2, 176; "Mistress of," female name, III, 243; *nāsīs* (rivalry with Palestinian Gaons), II, 30; origin of Hebrew calligraphy in Yeshivas, II, 234, 575; poverty in, II, 11; Rabbanite community in, I, 18; ritual practices of, II, 53, 556; IV, 128; sacred shrines in, II, 20, 90; scarcity of documentary material from, I, 21, 22; seclusion of women in, III, 323; silk industry in, I, 103, 222; spiritual and communal leaders, II, 70; synagogue of (*see* Synagogue of the Babylonians); textile industry in, IV, 121, 184, 463; type of boat from, I, 295; under Persian rule, II, 160; urban autonomy in, IV, 5; yeshivas, I, 51; II, 5, 6, 9, 24, 28, 29, 55, 197, 201, 208, 234 (*see also* Yeshiva)

Iraqian Jewish community in Fustat. *See* Synagogue of the Babylonians

irdabb, measure of wheat, I, 361 and *passim*; II, 479, 490; IV, 235-236, 244, 371, 435

ʿirḍ. *See* Honor

Iron, I, 60, 154; IV, 143, 149

"Iron sheep," term for dowry, III, 182

ʿIsā b. Nestorius, II, 354

Isaac, biblical, III, 27, 62, 233

Isaac b. Abraham Ibn Ezra, poet, II, 302–303, 592; V, 15–16, 453, 454, 459, 507, 638

Isaac b. Asher Sefaradi, II, 455

Isaac b. Barhūn, I, 93; V, 518

Isaac b. Barukh, merchant, V, 454, 457

Isaac b. Benveniste of Narbonne, I, 34, 347; II, 130, 547; V, 33, 514, 609

Isaac b. David Ibn Sighmār, III, 289; IV, 438

Isaac b. Fashshāṭ ("one who boasts"), II, 471; III, 454

Isaac b. Ghālib, cantor, III, 495

Isaac b. Ḥalfōn, V, 624

Isaac b. Jacob al-Maqdisī, II, 472

Isaac (Surūr) b. Jacob b. Aaron, known as al-Jāsūs, III, 202–203, 469

Isaac b. Janūn, V, 572

Isaac b. Khalaf, III, 434

Isaac b. Menaḥēm, judge, II, 514

Isaac b. Moses of Spain, Gaon, I, 53; II, 537, 569, 572; III, 441

Isaac b. Moses, judge of Sunbat, Egypt, III, 284, 490

Isaac b. Nīsān, II, 506

Isaac b. Nissīm Parsī (Fārisī), V, 286–287, 562

Isaac b. PSHʾṬ. *See* Isaac b. Fashshāṭ

Isaac b. Obadiah, V, 507, 637

Isaac b. Samuel, the Spaniard, judge, I, 383; II, 178, 361, 446, 456, 512, 513 514, 537, 545, 567, 570, 572, 606; IV, 458; V, 45, 134, 159, 199, 212, 355, 513, 514, 517, 542, 553, 563, 604

Isaac b. Sāsōn, judge, II, 423, 514, 552; III, 443, 470, 503

Isaac b. Ṣedāqā, IV, 439

Isaac b. al-Sharaf, II, 495

Isaac Derʿa, II, 499

Isaac *ha-melammed* b. Ḥayyīm al-Nafūsī, II, 560

Isaac Ibn Ezra. *See* Isaac b. Abraham Ibn Ezra

Isaac Ibn al-Furāt, II, 243; V, 259

Isaac Ibn Ghiyāth, Spanish poet, III, 475

Isaac Ibn Sīd, V, 588

Isaac Israeli, physician, I, 54, 404; II, 243, 575; IV, 229, 440

Isaac the Jerusalemite, V, 584

Isaac Judaeus. *See* Isaac Israeli

Isaac Luria, III, 33

Isaac Nafūsī, I, 204

Isaac Nīsābūrī, I, 153, 159, 387, 455,

462, 467, 475, 478; II, 587; IV, 375, 413; V, 326–327
Isaac Perdonel, Spanish Jew from Granada, V, 568
Isaac al-Qalaʿī, II, 497
Isaac the Frank, I, 43
ʿiṣāba. *See* Tiara
Isaiah, biblical, III, 9, 43
Isaiah, *mutawallī*, II, 421, 426, 603
Isaiah b. Maṣlīʾaḥ, V, 379
Isaiah al-Fāsī, V, 210–211, 566
Isaiah-Shaʿya family. *See* Ibn Shaʿya
isatis (Gr.-Heb., woad), IV, 172, 405
Isḥāq b. Dāʾūd b. Sighmār. *See* Isaac b. David Ibn Sighmār
Isḥāq b. Eli Majjānī, II, 601
Isḥāq al-Isrāʾīlī. *See* Isaac Israeli
Isḥāq al-Ruhāwī, V, 625
Ishmael, biblical, V, 597
iskāf. *See* Shoemakers
Iskandar(ān)ī (Alexandrian textile), IV, 167
Islam(ic), mentioned *passim*; concept of God, V, 331–332; on death, V, 131, 182; friendship in, V, 275–276; influences on Judaism, V, 23, 360; millennialism, V, 397-398; religious affinities with Judaism, V, 9, 478; scholarship, V, 9; virtues in, V, 53, 198, 199. *See also* Muslims
Islamic law: charity, V, 355; interplay with Jewish law, II, 395–402; and Jewish courts, II, 398–402 (*see also* Courts); V, 384, 430; Jewish influences, V, 19; music, V, 42; procedures, V, 485; Ramadan, V, 223; religious toleration, V, 373; sex, V, 308; taxation, V, 78 (*see also* Poll Tax); veneration of saints, V, 19; wills and inheritance, V, 131–132, 134, 141, 142, 384
Islamic literature, V, 379. *See also* Arabic literature
Ismaʿīl b. Abraham al-Andalūsī, III, 481; V, 536
Ismaʿīl b. Barhūn Tāhertī. *See* Samuel b. Abraham
Ismaʿīl b. Ezra, V, 572
Ismaʿīl b. Faraḥ, I, 481; III, 479, 480; V, 573
Ismaʿīl b. Isḥāq al-Andalūsī, V, 571
Ismaʿīl b. Jacob, I, 453
Ismaʿīl b. Nūḥ, II, 588
Ismāʿīlī sect, I, 30, 31; II, 194, 202, 278, 350; V, 522. *See also* Fatimids
Ismāʿīliyya. *See* Ismāʿīlī sect
Ismaʿīl (Samuel) Tāhertī. *See* Samuel b. Abraham
ʿisqā (Heb., form of partnership), I, 171, 441, 442. *See also* Commenda; Partnerships; *qirāḍ*
isqālā (plank used at lading of a boat), I, 47. *See also* Scala
Israel, ancient, II, 4, 31, 88; IV, 44, 114, 151, 219, 234, 252, 262
Israel b. Joseph b. Bānūqa, IV, 410; V, 537, 584
Israel b. Nathan-Sahlūn, I, 292; III, 462; V, 411
Israel b. Samuel b. Ḥofnī, Gaon, II, 15, 564; V, 579
Israel Museum, Jerusalem, II, 148
Issachar, a proselyte, II, 307
Iṣṭakhrī, IV, 54
Istanbul, Turkey, synagogues in, II, 167
istaghātha ("to call for help"). *See* Prayer, interruption of public
istikhāra ("letting God choose for us"), I, 346, 489; II, 581; V, 331
istiẓhār (precaution), I, 491
Italy, Italian, I, 256, 278; IV, 32, 452; accounting practices, I, 209; Almoravid attack on, I, 308; birthplace of proselyte, II, 308; church crisis in, II, 308; contributions to Jerusalem, II, 171; currency, I, 235; donations to Jerusalem Yeshiva, II, 171; languages, I, 64, 160; Levantine colonies of, I, 33, 192; maritime cities, I, 32, 39, 149, 330; marriage in, III, 131, 440, 441; merchants in/from, I, 70, 211; II, 37; IV, 27, 347; physicians, II, 245; pirates from, I, 308, 327, 332, 347; protagonist of Christendom, I, 29; referred to as Rūm, I, 303; III, 440; responsa sent to, I, 22; shipping to/from, I, 47, 59, 211, 214, 311, 317; II, 37; III, 58; students in Iraqi yeshivas, II, 202; textiles, I, 106; wine, IV, 259;
ithbāt (confirmation by the Jewish court), II, 597
iṭlāq (salary from Muslim ruler), II, 615
ʿitr. *See* Perfume
ʿitra. *See* Genealogy
Iṭrābulsī, I, 20
Ivory (*ʿāj*), IV, 130, 138, 224, 321, 327, 385
ʿIwaḍ ("Substitute"), name for son, V, 520
īwān, IV, 67, 366, 375. See also *līwān*
izār (mantle, shawl), II, 151, 500; IV, 196, 315, 317, 452
ʿizq (Aram.). *See* Finger ring
ʿIzz al-Dawla Ibn Kammūna, III, 13

J

Jabal al-Nafūsa, Libya, III, 262
al-Jabartī, I, 134
jabbān. *See* Cheese maker
Jabbāra, amir of Barqa, I, 308, 327, 328
jābī. *See* Collectors of revenue
Jacob, biblical, II, 111; III, 27, 227; V, 520, 569
Jacob, Ephraim, V, 629
Jacob, the Leonese pilgim, I, 55
Jacob, the Maghrebi, II, 457
Jacob, money assayer, II, 494
Jacob b. Aaron, V, 531
Jacob b. Amram, Nagid, II, 24–25, 352, 525, 604
Jacob Ibn ʿAwkal, V, 239
Jacob b. ʿAyyāsh, III, 471
Jacob b. Bishr, purple maker, II, 424
Jacob b. David, III, 482
Jacob b. Isaac, II, 576
Jacob b. Isaac b. David, the Maghrebi of Hebron, II, 502
Jacob b. Isaiah b. Khalaf, V, 108
Jacob b. Ismaʿīl, I, 453
Jacob b. Joseph ha-Kohen, judge, II, 458, 513; III, 443
Jacob ha-Kohen b. Isaiah, V, 562
Jacob b. Mevassēr, II, 433
Jacob b. Nahum b. Ḥakmūn, V, 584
Jacob b. Nissīm, II, 25; IV, 408; V, 281, 390, 585, 616
Jacob ha-yerūshalmī, *parnās*, II, 539
Jacob of Rūm, III, 471
Jacob Posen, II, 546
Jacob Rōsh Kallā *he-ḥāvēr* b. Joseph Av, II, 563; III, 285, 434, 490; IV, 440; V, 259, 423, 433–434, 627
Jacob b. Salīm, V, 617
Jaʿfar, mason, II, 434
Jaffa, Palestine, I, 214, 275, 316, 320, 326; II, 467, 598; III, 197, 198, 340; IV, 8
jafna (kneading trough), IV, 142, 391
jāh (social position), I, 159, 174; II, 48, 299; III, 44, 430; V, 255–260. *See also* Social rank
jahāz, *jihāz* ("outfit" [for bride], i.e., dowry), III, 124, 453, 454; IV, 297. *See also* Dowry
jahbadh (Per., banker in government service), I, 248–250, 462; II, 379, 504, 610; III, 136. See also *gizbār*
jahbadha, I, 249, 250
jahbadh al-dīwān. See *jahbadh*
jahbadh al-jawālī (government cashier handling poll tax), II, 392
al-Jāḥiẓ, I, 133; IV, 44, 305, 359; V, 255, 613
*jalā*ʾ, *jalwa* (ornamental costume), III, 442
jalājilī. *See* Bell maker
Jalāl al-Dawla, II, 376
Jalāl al-Dīn of Damietta, I, 82
Jalāl al-Dīn Rūmī, Sufi, V, 231, 494
Jalāl al-Mulk, title, II, 463, 502; IV, 11
Jalīla b. Abraham b. Khalfa al-Rashīdī, III, 484
jāliya. *See* Poll tax
al-jāliya al-shāmiyya (poll tax office for Syro-Palestinians), I, 406
jālūt. *See* Head of the Diaspora
jamāʿa (congregation), II, 42, 58, 62, 530, 535, 539, 542, 553, 562. *See also* Local community; *jumla*; *milla*; *ṭāʾifa*
al-jamāʿa al-muqaddasa ("holy congregation"). *See* Local community
jamalūn. *See* Gable roof
Jamīʿ. *See* Sitt al-Jamīʿ
jāmikiyya (salary or stipend from government), II, 604, 615. *See also* Salaries
jān (ornament), IV, 342, 465–466
janāza (burial), I, 1. *See also* Burial; Death; Funerals
Japeth b. David. *See* Japheth b. David
Japheth = Ḥasan ("handsome"), II, 61
Japheth, teacher, II, 559
Japheth Abū ʿAlī b. Toviya ha-Bavlī (Ḥasan b. Ṭayyib al-Baghdādī al-Nīlī), III, 482, 492
Japheth b. Aaron Abuʾl-Ḥasan, II, 536, 537
Japheth b. Abraham, II, 477, 478, 507; III, 262, 485; IV, 287, 354
Japheth b. Abraham b. Sahl. *See* Ḥasan b. Abū Saʿd al-Tustarī
Japheth b. Amram al-Jāzifīnī, cantor, V, 35
Japheth b. David b. Shekhanyā, cantor and court clerk, I, 463; II, 94, 227, 414, 424–425, 434, 438, 542, 553, 569, 570, 597; III, 108, 429, 479, 492, 495, 498; IV, 292, 307, 386; V, 37, 515, 538, 549, 552
Japheth b. Eli, III, 501; V, 363, 607
Japheth b. Jacob, II, 436
Japheth b. Manasse ha-Levi Ibn al-Qaṭāʾif, IV, 407; V, 422, 548, 626
Japheth b. Mawhūb, III, 491
Japheth b. Meshullam Ibn Ḥirbish, III, 287
Japheth b. Nathan Tinnīsī, V, 530
Japheth b. Nethanel, III, 489
Japheth b. Nissīm, II, 532

Japheth b. Shemarya, **I**, 434
Japheth b. Tiqvā, **IV**, 318
Japheth b. Yeshūʿā, **II**, 566; **III**, 431
Japheth b. Zechariah b. Abraham, **III**, 67
Japheth (Abu'l-Ḥasan) ha-Levi b. Eli, **II**, 568
Japheth ha-Levi b. Toviya ha-Bavlī. *See* Japheth Abū ʿAlī b. Toviya ha-Bavlī
al-jārī. *See* Salaries
jarīda (list, usually of the poor), **II**, 476. *See also* Charity; Pious foundations
Jarīr, **IV**, 451, 453
jāriya (girl, maidservant), **I**, 131, 135, 433; **II**, 163. *See also* Slavegirls
jarm (barge), **I**, 295, 322, 473. *See also* Ships
jarra. *See* Containers for wine
Jars: earthenware, **IV**, 142; for storing wheat, **IV**, 235, 435
Jarwī, type of weight, **IV**, 251. *See also* Weights
jary al-qalam ("as the pen runs"), description of textile, **IV**, 455
jashīsh (groats cooked with meat and dates), **I**, 115
jashshāsh (maker of *jashīsh*), **I**, 115, 424; **III**, 489
al-Jāsūs family, **III**, 202
jawālī. See *jāliya*
jawāz. *See* Legal tender
Jawdariyya distict, **II**, 589
jawhar(*ī*) (jewel, dealer in gems), **I**, 438; **IV**, 206, 207. *See also* Gems; *ḥallā*ʾ
Jawjar, Egypt, **III**, 338; **V**, 511
jawza (nutmeg), **I**, 463
al-jawziyya (nougat), sweetmeat made of walnuts, **III**, 442
jaysh aṭ-ṭawāwīs ("the peacock army"), **I**, 283
Jayyān (Jaen), **IV**, 402
jayyid (*ilā ghāya*) (first quality), **I**, 452; **IV**, 381
Jayyida ("First Rate"), f., **III**, 329, 332
jayyid al-qiṭʿa ("of good cut"), a byname, **II**, 448
Jazā'irī (from Greek islands), **IV**, 303
al-Jazfīnī, **V**, 514, 516
al-Jazīra (isle in Nile), **IV**, 288, 295
(Jazīrat) Qawsaniyya, **II**, 606
jazzār. *See* Butcher
Jealousy, **III**, 153; **V**, 235. *See also* Enmity
Jedda, Arabia, **I**, 177, 214; **III**, 135
Jedūthūn, cantor, **II**, 449; **V**, 89, 531
Jekuthiel (I) b. Moses (I) *ha-rōfē* (*al-ḥakīm*), **I**, 446, 447; **II**, 477, 479, 498, 503, 504, 507; **III**, 14–15, 138, 207–208, 261, 266, 296, 327, 456, 470, 484; **V**, 144, 145
Jekuthiel (II) b. Moses (II), **I**, 138
Jenkins, Marilyn, **IV**, 223, 419, 420, 430
Jephthah b. Jacob, judge, **II**, 124–125, 421, 430, 449, 450, 460, 465, 466, 515, 546
Jerba, Tunisia, **II**, 444; **III**, 30, 117; **IV**, 42, 195, 199, 252, 283, 400, 428, 439, 444, 457
Jeremiah, biblical, **IV**, 42; **V**, 19, 509
Jeroboam, biblical, **II**, 87
Jerusalem, **I**, 71, 106, 155, 201, 279, 296, 427; **II**, 186, 303, 559, 562, 599; **III**, 91, 98, 108, 118, 162, 209, 229, 235, 239, 426, 428, 437; **IV**, 47, 128, 158, 192, 349, 363, 373, 374, 390, 413, 426; appointment of public officials in, **I**, 21; **II**, 59, 71; armed forces in, **II**, 370; Ayyubids in, **I**, 36–37; Bedouin attacks, **V**, 58-59; beneficiaries of charity, **II**, 440, 442, 444, 447, 457, 463, 548; burial in, **II**, 413; **III**, 252, 327, 482; **IV**, 89; **V**, 146, 546; cantors in, **III**, 429; charitable foundations for, **II**, 119, 414, 415, 416, 419, 421, 427, 430, 433; city life in, **III**, 47; clothing and jewelry in, **IV**, 193, 215, 428; collections for, **I**, 65; **II**, 501, 542; **III**, 19; confiscation of property in, **I**, 63; **IV**, 28; congregation in Fustat, **III**, 43, 468; copyists in, **II**, 239; Crusaders in, **I**, 35; **II**, 18, 137; **III**, 10, 356; **V**, 49, 54, 58, 372–379, 394, 403–404, 595; destruction of churches and synagogues in, **I**, 18; divorce in, **III**, 260, 261, 262; food, **IV**, 233; foreigners from, in Fustat, **I**, 49; **II**, 157; **IV**, 10; Gaon of, **I**, 18, 60; **II**, 10, 14, 15, 43, 55, 59, 67, 71, 200, 527; **III**, 61, 198; Geniza documents in, **I**, 2, 3, 17; holy places as site for public prayer, **II**, 20; **III**, 337; **IV**, 41–42, 118; housing in, **IV**, 92, 95; incense makers in, **II**, 265; interfaith relations in, **II**, 281, 282, 285, 292, 588, 590; Jewish community of, **II**, 40, 58, 530; Jewish high court of, **I**, 66, 238; **II**, 395-396, 528; **III**, 300, 466; Karaites in, **III**, 26, 50, 51, 74, 75; **IV**, 391; **V**, 361–363, 368–369; letters to/from: business, **IV**, 206, 257, 439; personal, **I**, 426; **II**, 472, 473; **III**, 241, 430, 431, 445; **IV**, 28; mail service, **I**, 284, 286, 287, 288, 289, 291, 293, 294; marriage in, **II**, 554; **III**, 121, 199, 376, 400, 415, 449; **IV**, 152, 226, 380, 391; and Messianism, **V**, 391-395, 401–402,

404, 411, 449; Muslim government in, II, 368; *parnāsīm* from, II, 79, 81, 539; physician from, II, 257; III, 207; pilgrimage to, V, 18, 22, 262, 319, 428; poll tax in, II, 391; poor family in Cairo from, II, 461; prayer in, V, 338; promulgation of ban in, II, 341; III, 284; proselytes in, II, 308, 593; *qāḍīs* in, II, 320; Rabbanite community of, I, 146; II, 110; ruins in, IV, 22, 23; scholars of, I, 58; II, 172; III, 198; scribes from, II, 51, 573; Seljuk conquest of, I, 39; II, 30, 201; IV, 439; V, 30, 70, 84; Spanish merchant in, I, 451; *suftajas* sent to, I, 244, 245; synagogues, II, 97, 146, 155, 158; IV, 32; travelers/immigrants/pilgrims to, I, 55, 57, 61, 63, 158, 240, 323, 338; II, 136, 274, 385, 502; III, 47, 48, 60, 74, 177, 234, 301, 337, 462; IV, 41; value of currency in, I, 360, 378; women in, III, 327, 337, 487, 497; IV, 169; yeshiva, I, 257, 376; II, 24, 25, 29, 30, 47, 78, 94, 200, 215, 234, 537, 595; V, 261–263, 372, 383, 418 (*see also* individual gaons; Yeshiva)
Jerusalem colloquium, 1975, IV, 4
Jerusalem compound, Fustat, I, 413; II, 542
Jets, lustrous (*sabaj*), IV, 206, 216
Jettisoning, I, 319, 320, 323
jeunesse doree, IV, 9, 224, 259
Jew mistaken for Muslim, IV, 195
Jewel. See *jawhar*; Precious stones
Jewel box (*durj, qimaṭra*), IV, 222–223, 322, 329, 344, 429, 467
Jeweler. See *ṣāʾigh*
Jewelry, I, 90, 108, 154, 263, 264, 266; II, 584; IV, 27, 105, 200–222, 450; V, 170–171, 469; cash value of, IV, 186; materials of, IV, 202–208; never in burial outfit, IV, 189; shapes of, IV, 208–211; techniques, IV, 211–213; terms for, IV, 201–207; weight of, IV, 200–201. See also *aʿlāq*
Jewelry House, I, 448; IV, 26, 27, 354, 355, 420
"Jewish quarter," II, 589
Jewish Theological Seminary of America, I, 3, 5
Jews, mentioned *passim*
"Jews," deprecatory usage, II, 541
Jews, described as rich in polemical poem, V, 531
Jews, European, IV, 156, 158
"Jews, the" = "Israel," II, 598
"Jews, the" = "the people," II, 592
jibāya (collection of pledges). *See* Pledges
jibāyat al-jawālī (collection for the poll tax). *See* Poll tax, collection for
jibāyat al-kiswa (collection for clothing). *See* Clothing, collection for
jibāyat al-mujāmaʿa (weekly payments), II, 465
Jibrīn, tax collector, V, 599
jidrān (walls), I, 385
jihāz. See *jahāz*
jilbāb (covering for shipment), I, 485
jinān (gardens), I, 428
jirāb (skin), I, 485
al-Jīsh, Palestine, II, 239, 440, 447, 575
jiwār al-kanīs. *See* Synagogue compound
jīz (chrysalis), I, 455
jīzī, type of silk, I, 455
jizya. *See* Poll tax
Job (Ayyūb), biblical, I, 38; III, 224
Joel, teacher, IV, 349; V, 79–80, 81, 527
Johannes-Obadiah, Norman proselyte, I, 14; II, 186, 287, 305, 308, 309, 311
John Comnenus, I, 39
Jordan valley, IV, 128
Joseph, biblical, I, 56; III, 224, 227; V, 515, 633
Joseph, II, 595
Joseph, Gaon in Palestine, II, 512
Joseph, prison of, II, 285
Joseph, a proselyte, II, 307
Joseph, *shōfēṭ* of Damietta, II, 595
Joseph, son-in-law of Joshia b. Aaron, II, 534
Joseph Abu'l-Riḍā, II, 577
Joseph b. Abraham, *shōfēṭ*, II, 596
Joseph b. Abraham b. Bundār, merchant, V, 195-196, 562
Joseph b. Ăraḥ, IV, 408
Joseph b. Asad, III, 497
Joseph b. ʿAwkal. *See* Joseph Ibn ʿAwkal
Joseph b. Barzel, V, 587
Joseph b. Benjamin, the banker, III, 492
Joseph b. Berachiah. *See* Joseph b. Berechiah
Joseph b. Berechiah, III, 474; V, 209–211, 281–282, 293, 294, 565, 566, 571, 585, 588, 597
Joseph b. Caleb, II, 536
Joseph b. Elazar, V, 538
Joseph b. Eli Kohen (b.) al-Fāsī, III, 503; V, 537
Joseph b. Faraḥ Qābisī, IV, 373
Joseph b. Furqān, rare name, II, 467
Joseph b. Ḥassān al-Mahdawī, I, 364
Joseph b. Ḥātim, II, 445
Joseph b. Ḥāy b. Asad, Nagid, II, 555
Joseph b. ʿImrān, of Sijilmāsa, V, 60
Joseph b. Ismāʿīl al-Būnī, V, 158–160

Joseph b. Jacob of Hebron, Palestine, V, 557
Joseph b. Jacob, cantor, II, 568
Joseph b. Jacob, "Head of the Assembly" (*rōsh kallā*), b. Joseph Ben Isaiah (= Ibn Shaʿya), III, 428
Joseph b. Jacob, *rōsh ha-seder*, II, 564; IV, 276; V, 385
Joseph b. Joseph, the milkman, I, 383
Joseph b. Joshiah, I, 146; III, 30
Joseph b. Judah, III, 161
Joseph b. Khalfa al-Qarawī, I, 413
Joseph b. Kulayb, III, 217
Joseph b. Manasse, II, 428; III, 75
Joseph b. Mevōrākh ha-Kohen, III, 464
Joseph b. Moses the judge, III, 453
Joseph b. Moses Tāhertī, I, 375; III, 42, 430, 476; IV, 413
Joseph b. Mūsā Tāhertī. *See* Joseph b. Moses Tāhertī
Joseph b. Nādīv, cantor, II, 563
Joseph b. Peraḥyā, I, 367
Joseph (II) b. Peraḥyā (II) Yijū, III, 430
Joseph b. Saʿdʾēl, III, 471–472
Joseph b. Saʿīd, IV, 275
Joseph b. Samuel, II, 415
Joseph b. Samuel, III, 474; V, 559
Joseph b. Samuel Ben Naḥūm, IV, 461
Joseph b. Samuel Ibn Asad, III, 9
Joseph b. Samuel Ibn Lukhtūsh (al-Ukhtūsh), III, 58; V, 288–289, 458, 587
Joseph b. Samuel, Nagid of Granada, I, 48; II, 25, 352, 525; V, 552
Joseph b. Shabbethay, II, 591
Joseph b. Shamarya al-Barqī, II, 586, 596; IV, 439
Joseph b. Shemarya. *See* Joseph b. Shamarya al-Barqī
Joseph b. Solomon, *ha-shōfēṭ*, II, 595
Joseph b. Solomon Kohen, I, 137
Joseph ha-Kohen b. Ḥalfōn, V, 628
Joseph ha-Kohen, the Sicilian, b. Moses, I, 407
Joseph ha-Kohen b. Solomon, *muqaddam* of Alexandria, II, 71–72, 537; III, 443; V, 422. *See also* Yeshūʿā b. Joseph ha-Kohen
Joseph ha-Kohen b. Solomon Gaon, II, 168, 414; III, 262
Joseph ha-Levi b. Samuel, judge, II, 611
Joseph ha-Levi b. Samuel b. Saadya, II, 514, 611
Joseph b. Thābit ha-Levi, V, 155
Joseph Ibn Abitur, I, 57, 63; II, 567, 580; III, 465, 477; V, 58, 423, 627
Joseph Ibn ʿAqnīn, V, 629
Joseph Ibn ʿAwkal, I, 144, 158, 163, 165–166, 168, 215, 226, 227, 232, 277, 279, 285, 287, 289, 290, 370–371, 387, 440, 443, 448, 449, 455, 467, 469, 470, 486, 487; II, 61, 62, 191, 276, 295, 402, 472, 560, 590, 591; IV, 26, 156, 355, 420, 438, 442; V, 127, 195, 203, 209–211, 235–236, 239, 241, 256, 281–282, 293, 294, 560, 565, 571, 585, 617, 631. *See also* Ibn ʿAwkal family
Joseph Ibn Migash, I, 279, 406; II, 208–209, 339; V, 61, 457, 636, 637
Joseph Ibn Ṣaddiq, V, 507
Joseph Ibn Shaʿyā, banker, I, 243, 461, 472; III, 9, 290, 331, 428; V, 506. *See also* Ibn Shaʿya family
Joseph Israel, II, 497
Joseph Lebdi, V, 34
Joseph of Maḥalla, II, 566
Joseph al-Rūmī, II, 506
Joseph "the Head of the Pious," IV, 399
Joseph the Scholar (*ha-talmīd*), V, 88
Joshiah, Gaon, I, 286; II, 12, 227, 523, 530, 562, 571
Joshiah b. Aaron, II, 533, 535
Joshua, biblical, II, 4
Joshua b. Abraham (II) Maimonides, Nagid, I, 19; II, 101, 138, 219, 337, 501–502, 526, 529, 530, 534, 549, 551, 605; III, 303; IV, 12, 367; V, 203–204, 295, 561
Joshua b. Hananel b. Abraham al-Amshāṭī, III, 188–189
Joshua b. Dōsā, II, 547; V, 33, 514, 609
Joshua b. Levi, V, 563
Joshua Maimonides. *See* Joshua b. Abraham (II) Maimonides
Josippon, II, 584
jōza (= *zawja*), III, 462
Jubayl, Syria, I, 54; II, 81
jubba. *See* Gown
Judah (I) Asad, III, 9
Judah b. Aaron Ibn al-ʿAmmānī, cantor, II, 221, 529, 539, 548, 560, 569, 576, 596, 597; V, 39, 114, 179, 512
Judah b. Abraham, II, 533
Judah Alluf, V, 570
Judah b. Asher b. Yehiel, V, 289-290
Judah b. Elazar Kohen, II, 533, 603; V, 80–81, 528
Judah b. Ephraim, *ha-shōfēṭ*, II, 566, 595
Judah Ibn Ezra, V, 459
Judah b. Farḥūn, V, 61, 522
Judah b. Ghayyāth. *See* Judah b. Ghiyāth
Judah b. Ghiyāth, poet, V, 454, 637, 638
Judah bar Ilai, Rabbi, V, 581
Judah b. Israel, IV, 376

Judah b. Jacob ha-Kohen, V, 148
Judah b. Joseph Rōsh ha-Seder of Qayrawān, II, 560; V, 190, 507, 572
Judah b. Joseph Janūnī, III, 288
Judah b. Joseph Kohen, "the Great Rav," III, 290, 426, 431, 439
Judah b. Joseph b. Simḥa, V, 604
Judah b. Manasse, IV, 429
Judah b. Moses Ibn Sighmār, I, 48, 158–159, 444; II, 67, 193; III, 17, 56, 439, 462, 463, 473; IV, 239, 355, 435; V, 220–221, 255, 256, 293, 392–393, 443, 516, 519, 540, 577, 617, 629
Judah Ibn Qoraysh, V, 372, 611
Judah b. Saadya, Nagid, I, 249; II, 25, 30, 31, 34, 42, 78, 244, 529, 530, 566, 587; III, 19, 273, 478; IV, 385; V, 84, 347, 529
Judah b. Samuel of Badajoz, Spain, V, 83, 455, 528
Judah b. Samuel b. Judah, III, 9, 428
Judah b. Ṭāhōr, proselyte, II, 594
Judah ha-Kohen b. Ṭōviyāhū, II, 566; V, 506
Judah ha-Levi, poet, I, 301; V, 448–468, 627, 628; biographical details, III, 7; V, 391, 453, 621; called "*muqaddam* of the Jews" by Muslims, II, 69; correspondence, V, 426, 454–455, 462–467; and Ḥalfōn b. Nethanel, V, 196, 241, 273, 280, 287–288, 453–459, 463–467; *Kuzari*, V, 448–449, 456; letters to, V, 83, 241; medical practice, II, 260; IV, 125; V, 450, 456, 457–458, 467; Messianism, V, 449–450; poetry, I, 143, 314, 316, 318; II, 221, 259, 578; III, 7; IV, 200; V, 79, 119, 185, 287, 392, 405, 412–415, 426, 448–452, 546, 573, 586, 621, 638, 641; scholarship, V, 448; visit to Egypt, II, 303, 304, 369, 592; III, 62; IV, 91, 373, 401; V, 32, 80, 119, 148, 280–281, 426, 429, 454–455, 457–461, 469, 506, 572, 591
Judah ha-Levi "The Castilian." *See* Judah b. Samuel of Badajoz, Spain
Judah ha-Nāsī, II, 584; V, 337, 614
Judah al-Ḥarīzī, poet, II, 184; III, 431, 460; IV, 436
Judah Ibn Sighmār. *See* Judah b. Moses Ibn Sighmār
Judaism, mentioned *passim*; divisions within, V, 8, 358–360, 366–371, 379, 437 (*see also* Karaites; Pietism); legal status, V, 353, 360, 367, 398, 400; and other religions, V, 334, 398-399, 430; sense of, for Jews, V, 344, 347–348, 358, 449. *See also* Hebrew; Religion; Scholarship
Judentanzhaus, Rothenburg, Germany, II, 154
Judeo-Persian tombstones, I, 186
Judge(s), I, 64, 66–67, 69, 79, 170, 175; II, 44, 62, 83, 109, 152, 178, 274, 528, 529, 533, 534, 537, 543, 546, 562, 563, 566, 567, 568, 576, 600, 609; III, 30, 58, 137, 186, 288; authority in communal affairs, II, 76, 111, 193; III, 79; beneficiaries of community chest, II, 121, 123, 125, 172, 442, 450, 459, 463; chief, II, 53, 54, 56, 66, 403; III, 29; education, II, 206, 207, 260; elders serving as or assisting, II, 58, 59, 66; and Gaon, II, 17, 20, 22, 29, 71; general description, II, 211–219, 314, 511–515, 594-598; list of, II, 511–515; and local authority, II, 33, 34, 74, 75; III, 209; more than one occupation, II, 260, 269, 293; multiple functions of, II, 89, 224; III, 232; as *muqaddam*, II, 69, 70, 71; plurality, II, 321; principle of heredity, II, 90, 189; III, 2, 3, 4, 14, 240; professional class, II, 172, 260; protector of widows and orphans, II, 36, 187, 425; III, 252, 258, 278, 284, 292, 293, 298; provincial, II, 46, 47, 48, 49, 50; role in betrothal, marriage, and divorce, III, 72, 75, 79, 80, 90, 91, 92, 96, 97, 99, 101, 125, 133, 143, 154, 169–170, 178, 204, 209, 213, 218, 266; as scribes or notaries, II, 229, 237, 321; social rank, II, 42; III, 4, 14; and social services, II, 45, 79, 102, 103, 104, 122, 123, 135, 136, 416, 417, 422, 425, 427, 428, 430, 446, 449, 466, 472, 477, 485; and synagogue, II, 85. *See also* Judiciary, Jewish
Judiciary, Jewish, II, 311–327, 594-598, 607–609. *See also* Judges
Judiciary, Muslim, II, 363–368, 590, 596, 599. *See also* Courts; Qadi
Jug, IV, 147
juhaybidh (little *jahbadh*), I, 249, 462; III, 440. See also *jahbadh*
Jujube, I, 213
jūkāniyya (polo dress), I, 428; II, 131, 132, 444, 448, 449, 456, 459, 500, 547, 556; IV, 154, 155, 199 and *passim*, 320, 323, 324, 327, 329, 330, 331, 396, 397, 409, 453, 454, 455, 456, 459; V, 625
jūkh(a) (woolen cloth), II, 131
jūkhāniyya. See *jūkāniyya*
juʿl (consideration). *See* Bribes

julāb (Per. *gul-āb*). *See* Rose water
juʿl al-dilāla (recompense for broker's work), I, 185, 445
Julep. *See* Rose water
al-jumʿa (weekly salary), II, 463
jumla. *See* Local community
Jurisconsult, II, 92, 325, 584, 615
Jurj (George), a *ghulām*, I, 133
Jurjān, Central Asia, IV, 169, 192, 403
Jurjānī, manufactured in Almeria, IV, 169
al-Jūsh. *See* al-Jīsh
al-Juyūshī, IV, 98

K

Kaʿba, II, 163; V, 534
kab(a)ka. *See* Copper board
Kabbalism, V, 22, 90
Kabīra ("the old one," i.e., mother-in-law), III, 162, 338–339
Kābul, I, 283; II, 583
Kaddish, III, 245
kadhdhān (tuff gravel), IV, 367
kāfūrī (dealer in camphor), I, 438. *See also* Camphor
kāghidh. *See* Paper
kaḥḥāl. *See* Oculist
kaḥaḥāla (f.). *See* Oculist
Kahle, Paul E., I, 5; II, 148
kahramāna. *See* Carpet
kaikji (Turk., boatman), I, 84
kaʿk(ī) (bagel, bagel maker), I, 114, 254, 481; II, 297; V, 532
Kalbashā, I, 118
kale kore (Gr., pretty girl), II, 130; IV, 371
Kalīla wa-Dimna, V, 43
kalla (months of study at the yeshiva), II, 198
kallā (Heb., bride), III, 108
kallām: physician treating wounds, II, 255, 579; male nurse bandaging wounds, V, 634
kalos (Gr., beautiful), I, 192; II, 449
Kalos, a grave digger, II, 449
kamad. *See* Press
kāmil(ī) (complete), a variety of flax. *See* Flax
al-Kāmil, Sultan. *See* al-Malik al-Kāmil
Kāmilī dirhems. *See* Dirhem
kammād. *See* Presser
al-Kāmukhī, III, 13, 251, 351, 429, 481
kāmukhī (preparer of vinegar sauce), I, 115, 424
al-Kanāʾis. See *Raʾs al-kanāʾis*
kand. *See* Sugar
kandūj (locked compartment or cabinet), IV, 75, 369
kandūman (= *kandūj*), IV, 371
kanīs(a) (synagogue), II, 144, 154, 166, 435, 436, 453, 531, 555. *See also* Synagogues
kanīsat al-muʿallima. *See* Synagogue of the woman teacher
kanīs al-muʿallim. *See* Synagogue of the teacher
kanīsiya. See *kanīs(a)*
kānūn. *See* Fire pot
karabos (Gr., seagoing barge), I, 305
Karaite(s), Karaism, I, 399, 446; II, 47, 299, 545; III, 11, 12, 199, 204, 309, 315, 319, 425, 426, 428, 433, 442, 456, 471, 476, 491, 497, 498; IV, 40, 67, 75, 90, 99, 224, 353, 387, 436, V, 530, 568; attitude towards, I, 136, 146, 424; and charity, II, 53, 96, 423, 426, 433, 435, 441, 472, 473, 491; IV, 100; communal authority, II, 16, 23, 27, 526, 613; III, 75, 236–237; communities and congregations, II, 7, 16, 45; IV, 375; counterreformation, V, 379-391, 456; courts, III, 236–237, 289, 446; in Damascus, I, 82; documentation, I, 397; II, 346; IV, 415, 418; V, 371–372; history and doctrines, I, 18, 65; II, 156; III, 210, 470; IV, 351, 442, 452, 453; V, 360–361, 384; in Jerusalem, III, 352; IV, 192, 193, 442; V, 361–363, 368–369; legal status, V, 367, 368–370; marriage, II, 613; III, 53, 74, 101, 135–136, 139, 210, 403, 404, 405, 406, 407, 409, 416, 422, 441, 450, 459, 470; IV, 111, 187, 226, 450; marriage contracts (including betrothals and trousseaus), III, 28, 50, 51, 52, 102, 103, 104, 106, 108, 179, 373, 374, 376, 377, 378, 380, 447, 448, 449, 452; IV, 114, 120, 121, 128, 149, 152, 186, 192, 193, 277, 305, 307, 311–317, 379, 389, 391, 394, 401, 409, 429, 451, 457; marriages with Rabbanites, II, 110; V, 313, 366, 368; III, 26, 57, 107, 149, 158, 208, 392; membership, V, 362, 371; relations with Rabbanites, II, 7, 54, 405, 534; III, 246, 293; scholarship, V, 362–366, 418–419; serving Muslim government, II, 30, 378, 379, 527, 574, 610; IV, 131; on sex, III, 168–169; V, 313; synagogues, II, 149, 166, 167, 555; on tomb veneration, V, 23; writings, I, 55, 114, 397
Karam family, II, 584

Karam, daughter of a cheesemaker, V, 544
karārīs (quires), II, 574. *See also* Paper
karīma (sister, daughter), II, 490; III, 22, 317, 431. *See also* Daughter; Sister
Karīma b. ʿAmmār. *See* Wuḥsha
Karīma b. Joseph, III, 449
Karīmī merchants, I, 149
Karmī, biblical name, V, 630
karnīb (gourd). *See* Dipper
kasād (slump), V, 525
wa-katab (written by) II, 585
katartarioi (Gr., silk spinners), I, 418
kātib (scribe, official), I, 249; II, 172, 229–240, 280, 355, 375, 376, 377, 379, 467, 587, 604, 605, 609, 610; III, 208, 278, 282, 492. *See also* Scribes
kātib al-ʿarab (paymaster of Bedouin levy), II, 379; IV, 358
katifiyya. *See* Shoulder band
Katsh, E. E., V, 629
kattān. *See* Flax; Linen
kattān laythī. *See* Flax
kattān manfūsh (hatchelled flax). *See* Flax
Kaufmann, David, I, 3
kaylaja (vessel attached to grain jar), IV, 390
kaymukht (shagreen leather), IV, 130. *See also* Leather
kaysī (type of cheese), I, 428
Kāzerūn, I, 400
"Keeper of the Curtain," IV, 119, 381
Keepers of compounds, II, 117, 369
kefār (Heb., village or farm), I, 425. *See also* Villages
kellarion (Lat., Gr., cellar), storeroom, IV, 361
Kerchief. See *mandīl*
kesāfīm (Heb., silver pieces), I, 370; *k. levanīm* (white silver pieces), I, 387; *k. sheḥorīm* (black silver pieces), I, 388. *See also* Dirhem; Silver
keshērā (virtuous), III, 166
Ketāma. *See* Berbers
ketubba. *See* Marriage contract
Key, IV, 130
khabbāz(a). *See* Baker
Khabīṣa lane, II, 434
khaddām (servant), term for slave, I, 432. *See also* Slave
khādim (servant). *See* Beadle
Khaḍir, common Jewish name, II, 505
khafāra (protection fee), V, 23
khaff (light baggage), I, 167
khafīr (Bedouin watchman), IV, 35. See also *khifāra*
Khalaf ("Substitute"), as name for son, V, 520
Khalaf (=Abū Ṭayyib b. Nuʿmān), V, 225–6, 569
Khalaf b. Abu'l-Ḥasan al-Damsīsī, I, 364
Khalaf b. Bundar. *See* Khalaf b. Isaac b. Bundar
Khalaf b. Isaac b. Bundār, III, 137; V, 67–68, 231, 519, 570, 626
Khalaf b. Jacob, II, 60, 61, 535
Khalaf b. Maḍmūn, III, 264
Khalaf b. Samuel, I, 365
khalanj. *See* Wood
khalaq (threadbare), IV, 464
khalāṣ (escaping harm at childbirth), III, 226
khalīʿ (cast-off). *See* Second-hand clothes
khalīfa: leader of Rabbanite community, II, 8, 520; representative of the Gaon, II, 317, 596
Khalīj: canal of Alexandria, I, 119, 298, 299; IV, 68, 384; V, 534; canal of Fustat, I, 297; III, 243, 259
khallāl (vinegar maker), I, 124
khallāṭīn (mixers), I, 96
Khallūf, coinage of, I, 373
Khallūf b. Faraḥ Ibn al-Zarbī, IV, 400
Khallūf b. Zakariyya al-Ashqar (the Redhaired), II, 591
khām (raw), said of cloth, IV, 177, 178. *See also* Fulled
khamīra (Per., dough or a conserve flavored with aroma of roses and violets), I, 423
khamīrī (pastrycook), I, 114, 423
khamīs. *See* School fees
khamr. *See* Wine
khamsa ("five"), magic hand, IV, 215, 426
Khān(s), IV, 26
khandaq (trench), place prepared for battle, II, 578, 612
Khandaq quarter, Cairo, III, 328
Kharāb Fazāra, I, 426
kharāba. *See* Ruin
kharaj: landing, I, 483; leaving for the countryside, IV, 9
kharāj (revenue office), II, 385, 609
kharaz. *See* Beads
kharīdī (merchant in unperforated pearls), I, 438. *See also* Pearls
kharīj fi'l-jūda ("exceptional" quality), I, 452
Khārijites, III, 158
kharīṭa (bag). *See* Purses of coins
kharrāṭīn (turners), I, 423. *See also* Carpenters

kharrūba (carob seed), 1/16 of a dirhem. *See* Money of account
kharrāz (shoe maker), **I**, 422. *See* Shoemakers
khashāz (inferior quality), type of silk, **I**, 454. See also *khazāsh*; *khazz*
khaṣr (pearl band with gold beads), **IV**, 216, 427
khāṣṣa (separate account in a shipment), **I**, 183
khāṣṣiyya (designation for something of specific nature or specially prepared), **III**, 166
khāṣṣiyya mubāraka (individual blessing), **III**, 166
khātam. *See* Finger ring
khaṭīb. *See* Preacher
khawkh. *See* Peaches
khawkha (alley, passage), **IV**, 281, 364
Khawlān quarter, Fustat, **IV**, 13, 449
khawlī (gardener), **I**, 425
Khaybar, Jewish women of, **V**, 603
Khaybarī, **II**, 386, 611
Khayrūn, a gardener, **I**, 425
khayyāṭa. *See* Dressmaker
khayzurāna. *See* Baskets
Khazariyya b. Munajjā, **III**, 248, 481
Khāzer river, **V**, 522
khazāsh (inferior quality), said of silk, **I**, 454. See also *khashāz*; *khazz*
khazz (superior quality), said of silk, **I**, 337, 454. See also *khashāz*
khazzaj (inferior quality), said of silk, **I**, 454. See also *khashāz*; *khazz*
khazzān (storekeeper), **I**, 339, 487
Khibā' ("Hidden Treasure"), f., **III**, 138
Khibā' b. Abraham, **III**, 489
khiḍābī (seller of "dyestuff"), **I**, 155. *See also* Dyeing
khidma (government service), **I**, 68; **II**, 355, 541, 604. *See also* Government service; *shērūt*
khidmat al-nās ("Service of the community"), **II**, 541
khidmat yisrāel, **II**, 541
khifāra (*ghifāra*) (protection), **I**, 328, 469; **IV**, 35, 357
khilʿa. *See also* Robe of honor
khilāfī (caliphate-like), **IV**, 139, 145, 389, 392. See also *khusrawānī*
khinzīr (pig), in Syria also the name of a fish, **I**, 477
khinzīra (hub), a type of seagoing barge, **I**, 477
khīṭī (a swift boat), **I**, 295-296, 331, 474
Khiyār, Abu'l-Khayr, banker, **I**, 241, 242
Khiyār, a courier, **I**, 290
khiyār shanbar. *See* Cassia
khizāna (treasury): box containing or serving as amulet, **IV**, 218–219; closet, cupboard, **II**, 101, 552, 584; **III**, 485; **IV**, 66, 131, 377, 386
Khodādād, **I**, 400
khōn [*khān*]-*e-mardom* (Per., "other people's houses"), daughter's family, **III**, 484
Khorāsān (Khurasan), **I**, 60, 81, 103, 400; **II**, 468
Khoshnām, **I**, 400
khubz. *See* Bread
khubz al-balad ("the bread of our place"), profitable, **I**, 457
khuḍarī (greengrocer), **I**, 426
khuddām al-sulṭān (government servants), **II**, 609. *See also* Government service; *khidma*
khuff (boot), **IV**, 399, 400
Khulayf b. ʿUbayd b. ʿAlī b. Khulayf, **III**, 479
Khulla ("Friendship"), f., **III**, 156
Khulla b. Nathan, f., **III**, 465
Khulla b. Shābāt, f., 544
khulṭa (mixing [of investments]), type of partnership, **I**, 170, 179; **II**, 590
khuluq (character), **V**, 187. *See also* Personality
khums (fifth), **II**, 521. See also *ḥōmesh*; *ḥoq*
khūnjā (small tray), **IV**, 145, 392
khurdādī, **IV**, 342, 465
khūristān (wall recess with shelves), **IV**, 66–67, 132, 366, 387
khūṣa (palm leaf), ornament in jewelry, **IV**, 209, 214, 329, 336, 343, 396, 426, 427, 458, 466
khusrawānī ("king-sized"), **IV**, 121, 382, 409. See also *khilāfī*
khuṣṣ (pl. *akhṣāṣ*), light structure, **II**, 425; **IV**, 72, 73, 92, 292, 293, 368
khuṭṭ (district), **II**, 264; **IV**, 13
khuyūṭ (string [of pearls or other ornaments]), **III**, 442
Khuzayr b. Ḥasan, **III**, 499
Kiev, Ukraine, **IV**, 2
Kifā' ("Reward"), f., **III**, 278
al-Kifl, **V**, 508
killa. *See* Canopy
killa[*t khaysh*] (curtain of canvas), **I**, 375; **III**, 444
"Killer," a wife surviving her first two husbands, **III**, 82, 276
al-kīmiyyīn (alchemists), **I**, 411
Kinda tribe, **IV**, 17

King Ferdinand of Spain, V, 568
King(s) of Judah, III, 7
King Saul (biblical), IV, 220
kinnūs (Heb., "entering"), consummation of marriage, III, 441. See also *dukhūl*; Marriage
Kipling, IV, 202
Kirmān, I, 400; IV, 375
al-Kirmānī, Karaite family, IV, 99–100, 375
Kirmānī, Muslim theologian, V, 399
kirā', I, 412
kirnīb (Gr., funnel), II, 584
Kirschner, Robert S., V, 408
kisā. *See* Cloak
Kish, island of, V, 67, 523
Kissing hands and feet, III, 18, 240
al-kiswa (clothing), I, 468; II, 418, 459, 503, 558; III, 471. *See also* Clothing
kīs wāḥid ("one purse"), partnership, I, 170
kitāb: document, letter, I, 291, 463, 469, 470, 471; script with a magic formula, IV, 218
kitābat al-kharāj, II, 609
kitāb al-ṣadaqa (deed of pious endowment), II, 545. *See also* Pious foundations
Kitchen, IV, 68, 72, 136, 141, 142, 143
Kitchenware, IV, 143
Kitmān, slave girl, I, 434
kittōt (Heb., parties), II, 536
kīzān, IV, 394
klimax (Gr.), II, 566
Kneading troughs, IV, 142, 391
kohanim, *kōhanīm* (priests), kohen, I, 135, 357, 436; II, 399, 520, 561, 570, 576; III, 14, 25, 64, 78, 82, 101, 187, 251, 269, 270, 426, 431, 439, 440, 456, 489; IV, 196; V, 266, 379, 402, 620
Kohen. *See* Abu'l-Munā al-Kohen al-ʿAṭṭār
Kohl jar (*mukḥula*), IV, 223–224, 319, 322, 327, 329, 343, 430, 445, 453, 463
Kohl (*kuḥl*), Kohl sticks (*mīl*, *mirwād*), I, 99–100; IV, 223–224, 319, 327, 329, 430, 431, 455, 467; V, 100–101; maker of kohl sticks (*mīlī*), I, 415
koiton (Gr.), IV, 360
kombarion (Gr.), I, 306
kōmer (Heb.). *See* "Monk, The"
Korah, biblical, II, 88
Koran, II, 176; III, 51, 185, 210, 227, 436, 438; V, 161, 215, 299. For individual verses, *see* Index of Scriptural, Rabbinic, and Maimonidean Citations
Korczak, Janusz, III, 305
Kraemer, Joel L., V, 495
Kraus, Paul, V, 399
Krauss, Samuel, IV, 192, 259; V, 165
kṣy. *See* Hood
Kubiak, Wladyslaw, IV, 53
kuchek (Per., small), III, 428. See also *kushik*
Kūfa, Iraq, IV, 43
Kufesque script, II, 583
kuḥlī: blackish-blue, IV, 176; seller of antimony, I, 438. *See also* Kohl
Kujik ("small"), I, 400; III, 11
kūkh murakhkham (cabin paved with marble), IV, 367
kulband, IV, 214, 420, 426
kumba (Phoenician), a type of boat, I, 476
kumm ("sleeve"), vestibule, IV, 65, 366, 387
kummāh (vestibule [Yemenite usage]), IV, 66, 366
kummiyya, IV, 387
kunya (name composed with Abū), I, 357; II, 306, 477, 569, 582; III, 20, 233
al-Kūrānī, nisba of Muslims of Kurdish descent, V, 639
Kurd(s, -ish), I, 31, 37; II, 496
Kurdistan, II, 558
kursī: reading stool, II, 151; IV, 386; stool, chair, II, 584; IV, 130, 392
kuṣbara, *kuzbara*. *See* Coriander
kūshiyyā (Aram.), female Sudanese, I, 433
kuttāb (Bible school), I, 130, II, 176, 182, 185, 187, 194, 561
kutubī. *See* Mailmen
kutub sulṭaniyya bismī. *See* Government papers
kūz (mug for ointments), II, 584. *See also* Cups
kūzī (makers of narrow-necked water jug without a spout), I, 111, 422
kūz zayt. *See* Oil cruse
kyrios (Gr., Lord), II, 147; III, 71

L

laʿb (play), V, 42, 157
Laban (biblical), III, 23
labbah (gala pendant [Yemenite]), IV, 209
labbān *See* Milkman
Labor, more costly than materials, IV, 104
Laborers, II, 440, 441, 478, 479, 491
Labrāṭ (I) b. Moses (I) Ibn Sighmār, III, 6 17, 20, 46, 161, 183, 226, 231, 239,

430, 439, 463, 473; V, 111, 188, 392-393, 516
Labrāṭ (II) b. Moses (II) Ibn Sighmār, III, 6, 7
Labwa ("Lioness") b. Abū Ghālib, III, 218
Laces, IV, 164. *See also* Shoes
Lacquer, I, 155, 185, 190, 197, 200, 222, 335, 438
Lādh. *See* Silk
al-Lādhiqiyya, Syria, I, 212–213, 214, 242, 325, 326; II, 467; III, 81; IV, 411; V, 224
Ladino, I, 19
Lady Gazelle, house of, II, 120, 434
Lady Muqbil, II, 485
Lady Naẓar, d. of ʿAbdallāh, II, 419
laff al-mandīl. See Bracelet
laḥḥām (meat seller), I, 424; III, 489
Laity, lay leaders, II, 16, 24, 50, 56, 69, 76, 83, 86, 103, 161, 169, 195, 207, 216, 219, 224, 314, 319, 322, 403, 405, 417, 461, 464, 498, 542, 548
lājiya (*lawājī*), vessel for wine, IV, 259, 446. *See also* Containers for wine
lakhālikh (aromatic balls), I, 460
lākī (dealer in lacquer), I, 438
Lakkī, shipowner, I, 311
Lālas. See Silk
Lamb, slaughtered privately, IV, 249
Lambert of Hersfeld, II, 370, 608
Lamps, IV, 133; Andalusian, IV, 133-134; brides', IV, 133, 134, 387; Damascene, IV, 134; grillwork, IV, 133; jug, IV, 134; *manāra*, IV, 387, 388; movable parts, IV, 135; oil, IV, 134, 135, 324, 327, 331; silver (*qindīl*), II, 53, 146, 150; IV, 136, 388; taken apart, IV, 135; trousseau, IV, 134, 387; wax candles, IV, 133, 321, 324, 327, 331, 387, 388. *See also* Lantern
Lampstands, IV, 150
lamsat al-ʿibra ("examination of the cadastre"), II, 434
lānas. See Silk
Land of Israel. *See* Palestine
Lane, E.W., I, 296; III, 135; IV, 55, 58, 68, 75, 133, 134, 136, 149, 156, 224, 229
Lane, Frederic C., I, 181
Lane of Azhar the *shōfēṭ*, II, 596
Lane of Ibn Khabīṣa, II, 433, 434
Lane of the Jews, II, 291
Lane of the Lamps, II, 263, 582
Lane of the Poor, II, 435; V, 146, 546
Lane of the Synagogue of the Iraqians, II, 415
Lantern, *miṣbāḥ*, IV, 136, 388. *See also* Lamps
Lapidus, Ira M., IV, 4
Lapis lazuli, I, 154, 203, 210; II, 583-584; IV, 208, 220, 327, 422, 428
laqā'iṭ. See Pincers
laqab. See Honorific titles
"Lashing with shoes," II, 532
Lāsīn. *See* Silk
laṭaf (lit., precious gift, a term for wine), IV, 257, 445, 446. *See also* Wine
Late Antiquity, IV, 5, 47, 48, 66, 151, 186, 229, 372
Late Middle Ages, IV, 5, 22, 41
Latin, I, 52, 64; II, 242, 309, 310, 462, 594; IV, 78, 140, 154, 162, 178, 209; cursive script, II, 235; titles, II, 87
Latticework, wooden, IV, 62
Lavatories, IV, 54
Law: II, 2, 3, 65, 103, 302, 320, 395; customary, II, 327, 345; Islamic, I, 61, 67, 75, 91, 145, 172, 176, 179, 196, 242, 303, 449; II, 115, 119, 289, 304, 337, 347, 395-402, 613; IV, 20, 23, 50, 82, 87, 139, 254; Jewish, I, 145, 146, 176, 177, 196, 368; II, 2, 5, 10, 16, 50, 72, 79, 115, 119, 169, 193, 196, 205, 206, 207, 220-221, 296, 311-345, 395-402, 580; IV, 20, 23, 138, 152, 183, 187, 227, 268; Jewish and Islamic, I, 66–70, 72, 73, 97, 141, 171, 183, 196, 218, 255; Roman, I, 136, 145
Law and practice: Islamic, III, 1, 20, 26, 68, 69, 71, 80, 94, 103, 119, 149–150, 151, 185, 210, 233, 248, 249, 264, 271, 277, 280-281, 290, 301, 329; Jewish, III, 1, 20, 48, 68, 71, 80, 82, 84, 102, 121, 147, 153, 161, 190, 200, 210, 233, 236, 248, 249, 254, 264, 271, 276, 277, 279, 281, 282, 287, 299, 301, 329; Jewish and Islamic—differing, III, 1, 20, 26, 68, 71, 142, 146-147, 210, 279, 301; Jewish and Islamic—similar, III, 1, 80, 147, 155, 168, 190, 211-212, 227, 233, 249, 264, 332; problem of Islamic influence, III, 83, 101, 102, 104, 120, 134, 135, 142, 260, 264, 281, 329
Law of the merchants, II, 328
Laws, interplay of, II, 3, 394–402, 613
Laws of purity, III, 107, 154, 190
lawwāzīn (processors of almonds), I, 115; IV, 246
Layla b. David, wife of Moses b. ʿAdāyā, V, 544
laymūn (lemon, lemon preserve), II, 585
Laythī flax. *See* Flax
laythī qinṭār, I, 227, 361. *See also* Flax

lāzam. *See* Necklace
lazzām (farmer of revenue from agricultural land), **II**, 430. *See also* Farming of revenue
Lead, **I**, 60, 109, 153, 154, 268, 335, 362, 420; **IV**, 184; color, **I**, 419; **IV**, 166, 174
Leah (biblical), **III**, 27
Leap year, **I**, 356, 385
Lease, contract of, **II**, 416, 422, 425, 430
Leather, **I**, 83, 111–112, 154, 334; **IV**, 115, 129, 130, 380 (*see also* Hides; Skins); as writing material, **II**, 232. See also *mizwad*
Lebanon, **I**, xvii, 20, 48, 85, 88, 102, 158, 159, 287, 288, 291, 320; **II**, 442, 467; **III**, 120
lebbe (chest ornament), **IV**, 418
Lebdī. *See* Ibn Lebdī
Lebdī, Abu'l-Barakāt, **III**, 326, 327
Lebdī, Abū Yaᶜqūb Joseph, **III**, 31, 73, 327, 329–330, 348; **IV**, 287, 288, 449
Lebdī family, **IV**, 19, 37, 374; **V**, 543
Legal documents, **III**, 49, 97–108, 160, 238; **V**, 3, 118, 487–488. *See also* Wills
Legal procedures, **V**, 211, 434, 485. *See also* Nagid, duties of
Legal tender (*jawāz*, *naqd*), **I**, 234, 373, 384, 459. *See also* Money
"Legs" (rudders [of the ship]), **I**, 318
lehitparnēs (Heb.), **II**, 571
Lemon, **IV**, 231; green, **IV**, 230
Lemon hen, **IV**, 230, 231, 250
Lemon juice, **I**, 121, 151
lēnas, Indian red silk. *See* Silk
Lengherand, Georges, **I**, 19
Leningrad, **I**, 3, 5, 13; **II**, 18, 21, 343
Lent, **IV**, 258
Lentils, **IV**, 233
Lesbianism, **V**, 316
Le Tourneau, Roger, **I**, 82, 119; **IV**, 3, 234
Letter *l*, long neck of, **III**, 110, 111
Letters, **I**, 22, 304–305; appearance of, **V**, 240–241, 422, 487; between brothers, **III**, 16, 17, 18-19, 56, 226; brother to sister, **III**, 23, 241; business, **III**, 22, 115, 224, 239, 244; conclusions, **V**, 241; of condolence, **III**, 22, 273; of congratulation, **III**, 118, 226; dictation of, **III**, 186, 193, 221, 325; of dignitaries, **III**, 76, 77, 80, 196; exact descriptions, **V**, 108; on holidays, **V**, 17; of husband, **III**, 190, 218–223, 228; of introduction, **I**, 347; mother to son, **III**, 115; occasions for, **V**, 26–27; openings, **V**, 2, 26, 46–47, 76–77, 230–232, 286, 336; of recommendation, **III**, 4, 304; religious phraseology, **V**, 2–3, 48, 51–52, 73, 286, 328–329, 334–336; of suitors, **III**, 59, 60, 75; tailored for recipient, **V**, 62, 218–220, 224–225, 229–240, 246, 296-297; of thanks, **V**, 36; unanswered, **V**, 293-294; of women, **III**, 21–22, 115, 162, 175–176, 193-194, 195, 197, 222, 231, 261, 319, 353–354, 355; writing of, **II**, 180. *See also* Correspondence; News; Personality; and expression of particular feelings
Levant, **I**, 42
Levi, **I**, xviii, 145, 357; **V**, 266
Levi b. Gerson, **V**, 327
Levi ha-Levi b. Abraham, **III**, 449; **V**, 152
Levi ha-Levi *he-ḥāvēr ha-ḥazzān*, **II**, 569
Levirate, **III**, 210–211, 470–471; **IV**, 436
Levites, **II**, 82; **III**, 5–6, 31, 206
Lewin, Benjamin M., **I**, 25
Lewis, Bernard, **IV**, 3; **V**, 505
Lézine, A., **I**, 54, 55
Libations in Temple of Jerusalem, **V**, 603
Libraries, **V**, 4, 80. *See also* Book lists
Libya, **I**, xvii, 31, 32, 43, 276, 327; **II**, 173, 467, 559; **IV**, 2. *See also* Barqa
License, **II**, 577. *See also* Degree
Licenses for stores, **I**, 151, 269, 270
Lichen (*shayba*), **IV**, 260, 446, 447
Lieberman, Saul, **III**, 119
līf (date palm fiber), **I**, 401
Life expectation, **III**, 23
Lighting, **IV**, 132–136. *See also* Illumination; Lamps
Lighting appliances, **IV**, 136. *See also* Lamps
liḥāf. *See* Blanket
Linen, **II**, 520; **IV**, 159, 165–167, 177, 396, 408, 409; Dabīqī linen, **IV**, 110, 112, 113, 119, 121, 165–166, 305–306, 308, 320, 321, 327, 329, 331, 378, 379, 380, 382, 401, 403, 414, 425; Dimyāṭī linen, **IV**, 160 (*see also* Damietta); fine (*sharb*), **III**, 463; **IV**, 117, 166, 306-307, 400; Ṭalī, **IV**, 188, 409, 414; Tinnīsī, **IV**, 113, 166–167 and *passim*, 308, 378, 463 (*see also* Tinnīs); as writing material, **II**, 232
Lingerie, **IV**, 130, 454
"Lion" (Asad), **III**, 9
lippet (Heb.) **II**, 126. See also *adam*
Liquidation, **II**, 473
lisān al-ḥamal (lamb's tongue), **II**, 584
Lisbon, Portugal, **IV**, 61
Lithographs, **IV**, 55

Little Fast, **II**, 129. *See also* Day of Atonement
Little Market of the Jews, **II**, 291; **IV**, 30, 353
Little Market of the Vizier, **IV**, 288, 444
Liturgy, **II**, 72, 177, 220, 449, 537, 615. *See also* Poems, liturgical; Prayer; Synagogue service
Living expenses (*nafaqa*), **I**, 177, 443
"Living room." See *majlis*
Living tradition of the yeshivas, **II**, 203
līwān, **IV**, 67. See also *īwān*
ʿlm (slave girl), **I**, 139, 434. *See also* Slave-girls
Loaf. *See* Bread
Loans, **I**, 97, 246–247, 253–262, 263, 384, 385; **II**, 80, 81, 101, 110, 142, 297, 376, 391, 415, 541, 560, 582, 590, 61; on interest, 170, 247, 254–258, 262, 384. *See also* Credit; Debt; Interest, fixed; Money lenders
loca (Heb., shares in a boat), **I**, 309
Local community, **II**, 40–68, 404, 405, 530–541. See also *jamāʿa*; *jumla*; *milla*; *ṭāʾifa*
Local custom(s), **III**, 66, 90, 91, 129, 148, 154
Lock(s), **I**, 421; **IV**, 61, 131
Locksmiths (*aqfālī*), **I**, 109, 421; **II**, 477
Lodging, cost of, **I**, 349; free, **II**, 124, 132, 430, 433, 434, 546; for visitors, **V**, 31–32
Loggia: *maqʿad*, **IV**, 75, 369; *mustaraqa*, **IV**, 57, 73, 295, 368, 369
Loneliness, **III**, 194, 222
Lopez, Robert S., **I**, 418; **V**, 496
Losses, **I**, 203–204
Louis IX of France, **I**, 37, 40
Louvre, **II**, 551
Love, **III**, 50, 52, 165–171, 198, 219, 222; **V**, 219, 317–318. *See also* Family feeling; Friendship; Sex
Lower class family (-ies), **III**, 88, 97, 98, 99, 121, 123, 135, 140, 187, 189, 191, 195, 271
loxon (Gr., obliquely), **II**, 573
Lucania, Italy, **III**, 21
Lucanica (Lat.), **I**, 115
Lucca, **I**, 40, 43, 65
Lucena, Spain, **I**, 69, 120; **II**, 603; **IV**, 191
"Lucky Fellow," slave, **I**, 138
Ludwig, Emil, **V**, 498
Lukhtūsh, Samuel, **I**, 48
Lukk, **I**, 277
Lunch. *See* Meals
Lunel, **I**, 40
Lupines, **I**, 155; roaster of, **II**, 467
Luxury in clothing and furnishings, **IV**, 151
ʿlyh, **II**, 415

M

Maʿadd (Mustanṣir). *See* Dinar
Maʿālī, common personal name, **II**, 454
Maʿālī, baker, **II**, 443
Maʿālī Ibn Dihqān, **II**, 454; **V**, 581
Maʿālī b. Nuʿmān, **II**, 482, 484
Maʿānī, **II**, 321
Maʿānī bint Karīm al-Aqraʿ, **III**, 487
Maʿānī al-Dajājī, **III**, 206–207
Maʿarra, Syria, **II**, 81, 278, 447, 587
Maʿarrat al-Nuʿmān, Syria, **V**, 513
maʿase (*she-hāyā be-fānēnū*) (Heb., minutes), **II**, 600
maʿāshir (assemblies), **II**, 598
mabqala (vegetable garden), **I**, 119
Mace, **I**, 155, 337
Macedonian, **IV**, 152
Mach, Rudolf, **IV**, 257
madāf, *madhāf* (mixing vessel for perfumes), **IV**, 225–226, 322, 327, 329, 343, 430–431, 455, 466. *See also* Perfumes
madās (shoe), **IV**, 399. *See also* Shoemakers, Shoes
madbagha (tannery), **I**, 366. *See also* Tanner(y)
maddār (worker in clay), **I**, 111, 422
Madder dye, **I**, 344; **IV**, 406
al-Madīna. *See* Palermo, Sicily
madīnī (term for citizen of Palermo), **IV**, 349. *See also* Palermo
Maḍmūn b. Ḥasan. *See* Maḍmūn b. Japheth b. Bundār
Maḍmūn II b. David, Nagid of Aden, **V**, 568, 625
Maḍmūn b. Japheth b. Bundār, representative of merchants in Aden, **II**, 26, 526; **III**, 58, 439; **V**, 35, 52, 66–68, 127, 247, 519, 545, 575, 589
maḍrab (flask), **IV**, 342, 466
madrasa (Muslim house of learning), **II**, 199, 210, 403
Madrid, Spain, **I**, 69
maḍrūb (hammered copper), **I**, 420. *See also* Copper
mafrash (place to hang laundry), **IV**, 74, 369
mafrūz (with geometrical ornaments), **IV**, 380
maftūḥ ("open"), color, **I**, 419. *See also* Colors

maftūl ("twisted"), description of silk yarn, IV, 402. *See also* Silk thread
maghāzilī (maker of spindles), I, 416. *See also* Spindles
maghram (fine), II, 612
Maghreb(ī), I, 122, 383; II, 6, 535; III, 440; IV, 4, 374, 438; Almohad persecutions in, I, 57, 63; II, 293, 300, 480; beneficiaries of charity from, II, 429, 439, 440, 442, 444, 454, 463, 465, 468, 496, 502; III, 63; charitable contributions of, II, 67, 96, 171, 476, 477, 472, 485; communal leaders, II, 70, 76, 463; IV, 45; conversion to Islam in, II, 301; currency, I, 61, 238, 371, 389, 390; family name, V, 519; family life in, I, 48; III, 93, 262; in Egypt, I, 32; II, 154, 167, 460, 480; III, 45, 323; IV, 30; V, 78; material culture, IV, 119, 146, 274, 327, 393, 403, 439, 463; merchants, commerce, I, 21, 133, 149, 153, 157, 159, 184, 192, 201, 214, 220, 223, 233, 236, 242, 245, 268, 380, 384, 455; II, 191; IV, 45, 168, 176, 184, 429; V, 590; pilgrims, I, 34; IV, 41; silver, IV, 148; synagogues in, IV, 128; textiles, IV, 119, 120, 121, 168, 417; travelers from, II, 101, 136, 461, 480; IV, 11. *See also* North Africa
maghsal. *See* Washbasins
Magic, I, 323–324, 346, 489; IV, 221–222
Magnes, J.L., I, 17
maḥabba (love), III, 432, 463. See also *ḥibba*; *ḥīsā*
maḥābis (Indian cotton textile [term not used in this meaning in Egypt]), IV, 171
maḥakka (using a teasel to roughen fabrics), IV, 408. *See also* Fuller, fulling
al-Maḥalla, Egypt, I, 251, 404, 417; II, 42, 187, 238, 239, 530, 536, 555, 559, 566, 591, 593, 614; III, 183, 296, 428, 454, 464, 477, 490; IV, 9, 13, 45, 215, 236, 281, 349, 350, 352, 426, 427, 428, 442, 443, 445; V, 511, 515, 519; beneficiaries of charity, II, 167, 460, 463, 492; charity in, II, 508; communal officials, II, 72, 74, 208, 541; III, 336; communal strife in, II, 158, 193; V, 12, 49; domestic architecture in, IV, 59, 62, 81; economic life, I, 84, 88, 102, 116; II, 46; family life, III, 9, 82, 92, 127, 177, 178, 269, 389, 393, 404, 486; Jewish judges in, II, 214, 533; III, 82, 178, 269, 284; Jewish community of, II, 43, 45, 305, 307; III, 284; IV, 217, 249; letters to/from, II, 605, 611; III, 219–220; Palestinian and Babylonian congregations in, II, 6, 519; pilgrimage to Torah scroll in synagogue, V, 24–25; pillage of, I, 145; V, 524, 538; quarters of, II, 290, 589; IV, 371; refugees from poll-tax in/from, II, 382, 386, 389; silk workers, I, 84, 88, 102, 116, 365; taxes in, II, 359, 384
Maḥallat al-Ymn, II, 606
al-Maḥallī, caravanserai of, I, 349
maḥāris (guards), I, 488
Maḥāsin, II, 124
Maḥāsin, beadle, II, 450, 461
Maḥāsin b. Abi'l-Fakhr, IV, 375
Maḥāsin b. Abi'l-Ḥasan, IV, 375
Maḥāsin al-Kirmānī, IV, 100
maḥbas. See *ḥabs*
maḥḍar (court minutes), II, 600. *See also* Court records
Mahdī, the horse-trainer, I, 328
al-Mahdiyya, Tunisia, I, 20, 48, 49, 68-69, 130, 196, 232, 308, 334, 377, 379, 483; II, 535; III, 66, 118, 235, 247; IV, 44, 45, 181, 245, 261, 355, 381, 397, 410, 440; V, 516; capital city, I, 212; II, 43; IV, 245; caravans leaving from, I, 276, 277; commerce in, I, 32, 44, 212, 256, 268, 271, 272, 290; IV, 7; communal officials, II, 84, 540; III, 176; dinars coined in, I, 234, 235, 236, 237, 238, 377; during Crusades, I, 259; as frontier fortress, IV, 7; Jewish judges of, I, 276; II, 320, 596, 597; III, 6, 17, 46, 56, 161, 183, 239, 289; joint Palestinian and Babylonian congregation of, II, 54, 60, 530, 534; letters to/from: I, 271; II, 41, 54, 60, 530; business, I, 167, 198, 204, 205, 237, 238, 275, 290, 305, 309, 372, 375, 376; II, 191; IV, 264, 355, 435; personal, I, 259, 289, 376; II, 76, 193; III, 56, 57, 161, 482; mail service in, I, 286, 287, 289, 290; merchants in, I, 157, 167, 197, 198, 199, 200, 216, 237, 238, 268, 269, 272, 275, 276, 277, 311, 312, 324; IV, 121, 168, 190, 264; prices in, I, 167, 197, 199, 204, 220, 228, 229, 238, 302, 370, 371, 372, 375, 448; IV, 181; V, 50–51; ship travel to/from, I, 290, 301, 302, 305, 307, 308, 309, 311, 312, 313, 315, 317, 318, 320, 322, 324, 326, 344; III, 66, 280; IV, 190
Maḥfūẓ = Shemarya, II, 574
Maḥfūẓ, beadle, II, 416–417, 418, 419, 430, 449, 459, 540
Maḥfūẓ of Tyre, II, 498
Maḥfūẓa b. Joseph, IV, 369

maḥḥār(ī) (shellfisher), I, 126, 430
maḥlōqeth (Heb., dissension), II, 64
maḥmūda ("the praiseworthy"). *See* Scammony
mahr, III, 32, 120, 142, 439, 457. See also *mōhār*; Marriage gift of husband
Mahra district, Fustat, II, 427, 508; IV, 13, 79, 350
Maḥras quarter, Fustat, IV, 23, 354
maḥras (guardhouse or barracks). See *ḥabs*
mahrūsh (bursting of bale and subsequent damage), I, 487
Maḥrūz of Aden, shipowner, III, 58; V, 240, 573
mā'ida (large tray used as table), IV, 144
Maidservants, I, 129–130; IV, 242, 263, 285, 293, 311, 321, 324, 325, 331, 448, 456. *See also* Domestic help; Slave girls
Mailmen, I, 284, 291, 292, 293, 471; II, 558
Mail service, I, 191, 281-295, 305; V, 501
Maimon, father of Moses Maimonides, IV, 14
Maimonides, Abraham. *See* Abraham Maimonides
Maimonides, Moses. *See* Moses Maimonides
Maintenance. *See* Repairs
majādīl (hewn stones), IV, 376
majāz (passage), IV, 71
majāzir. *See* Slaughterhouses
majd (prestige), III, 473
Majjāna, Tunisia, II, 440
al-Majjānī family, III, 56; V, 207–208
majlis, majālis: as form of address, V, 599; President of the Court, II, 166, 555, 595 (see also *āv*); *m. ḥayrī* (enclosed living room), IV, 69, 367; reception hall, sitting room, seat, IV, 48, 63, 64-69, 71, 75, 109, 118, 119, 133, 304, 365, 366, 369, 370, 377, 379, 454; *m. sūq al-yahūd*, II, 166
majma' (compartmented utensil), IV, 322, 435; V, 97, 533
Majorca, I, 442
makalla' (Ar. "protected"), term for e. harbor of Aden, V, 523
Makārim, oculist, II, 491
Makārim b. Isḥāq b. Makārim, II, 256, 257
Makārim b. Mūsā b. Nufay', V, 575
Makārim b. Salāma, IV, 277
makhāfi, I, 422
makhāzīn. See *makhzan*
Makhlūf ("Substitute"), name for son, V, 520
Makhlūf, messenger of the court, I, 414
Makhlūf, slave, I, 436
Makhlūf b. 'Azarya Bū Majjāna, IV, 438
Makhlūf b. Mūsā al-Nafūsī (Ibn) al-Yatīm, merchant, I, 320; V, 108, 246–254, 255, 575, 584
makhlūq, II, 560
makhlūṭ (type of cheese), I, 429
makhtūma ("bearing a seal"), cloth with an emblem, IV, 199, 323, 324, 327, 455
makhzan (storeroom), I, 339; IV, 75, 352, 369; *m. al-qamḥ* (storeroom of wheat), II, 552; *m. tujjār* (warehouse), I, 187. *See* Storage
al-Makīn ("The Solid"), title, V, 31, 511, 513
Makīn, son of Moses, the judge, IV, 373
al-Makīn, Alexandrian qadi, II, 366, 377, 609,610; III, 286, 490-491
Makīn al-Dawla, honorific title, II, 587, 610, 611
makrūma ("gift of honor"), bribe, II, 608
maks. *See* Customs duties
Malabar coast, India, II, 20
malā'iqī (spoonmaker), I, 421. *See also* Spoons
māl Allāh ("belonging to God"), i.e., community property, II, 99. *See also* Pious foundations
māl al-muslimīn ("belonging to the Muslims"), i.e., community property, II, 99. *See also* Pious foundations
Malatia, Asia Minor, II, 447, 477
malbūs ("worn"), said of clothing, IV, 339, 464. *See also* Clothing
malḥafa. *See* Cloak
Malīḥ, a Christian glassmaker, I, 421
Malīḥa b. Ezekiel al-kohen, IV, 368
Malīj, Egypt, I, 243, 362; II, 592, 606; III, 113; IV, 42, 122, 143, 275; beneficiaries of community chest from, II, 439, 444; bequests in, III, 281, 296, 299, 493, 495; communal officials, I, 260; II, 49, 69, 568, 569, 573, 574; III, 338; V, 507, 536; family life, III, 197, 331, 341, 486; Jewish congregation of, II, 168, 307; Jewish judges in, II, 566; III, 303; letters from, II, 69, 307, 527, 567, 569, 573; III, 197, 213, 338; litigants from, in Fustat court, II, 332, 603; III, 339, 503; marriage documents from, III, 389, 390, 397, 400, 452; IV, 122, 143; pillage of, V, 524; synagogue in, II, 168; travel from/to, I, 280; IV, 264, 265

al-Malik al-ʿĀdil, sultan, **II**, 141, 347, 406, 604; **V**, 491, 493, 555
al-Malik al-Afḍal, Fatimid viceroy, **I**, 34, 35, 45, 297, 312, 347; **II**, 30, 284, 349, 350, 352, 356, 361, 364, 366, 377, 386, 394, 397, 478, 527, 603; **V**, 4, 104, 159, 162, 257
al-Malik al-Amjad, son of Saladin, **II**, 347
al-Malik al-ʿAzīz, Ayyubid sultan, **II**, 346; **V**, 174, 554
al-Malik al-Kāmil, Ayyubid sultan, **I**, 63, 385, 390; **II**, 353, 407, 615; **V**, 477, 493
al-Malik al-Muʿaẓẓam, Ayyubid, **II**, 347
al-Malik al-Nāṣir Dāʾūd, Ayyubid, **II**, 354
Malik Shāh, Seljuk, **II**, 362
Malik al-Umarāʾ, **II**, 361
Mallāl of Tunisia, f., **III**, 357
Malter, Henry, **V**, 380
mamlūk (slave-soldier, servant), **I**, 36; **II**, 548, 608, 612. *See also* Slave(s)
Mamluk(s), **I**, 38, 132, 194, 256, 294, 345, 386, 390, 391; **II**, 23, 40, 62, 251, 608; **III**, 100, 113, 134, 181, 211, 277, 449, 452, 498; **IV**, 30, 37, 46, 55, 64, 67, 111, 133, 147, 205, 207, 219, 372, 420
mamraq (passage), **IV**, 364
mamshūṭ (combed flax). *See* Flax
Mamṣūṣa quarter, Fustat, **II**, 419; **III**, 243; **IV**, 13, 17, 18, 19, 22, 75, 278, 280, 281, 283, 288, 289, 321, 350, 369, 373, 455; **V**, 149, 547. *See also* Maṣṣāṣa
al-Maʾmūn, Abbasid caliph, **V**, 254–255
al-Maʾmūn Ibn al-Baṭāʾiḥī, Fatimid vizier, **I**, 188, 269; **II**, 345; **IV**, 25, 39, 371
(*ʿalā*) *manābir* ("on the pulpits"), i.e., in public, **II**, 551
manāfiḥ (rennets), **I**, 428
Mānak, monk, **IV**, 27
Mānak house, **I**, 246
manāra. *See* Lamps
al-manāra, the Pharos, **I**, 319, 483
al-manāshifī (maker of towels), **II**, 497
Manasse, man in Malīj, **II**, 592
Manasse, Alexandrian schoolmaster, **V**, 82, 528
Manasse, judge of Ṣahrajt, **II**, 596
Manasse b. David of Qayrawān, merchant, **III**, 288
Manasse b. Ibrāhīm Ibn al-Qazzāz, chief secretary of Damascus, **II**, 354; **III**, 10, 56, 57, 438–439, 456
Manasse b. Joseph, judge, **II**, 124, 428, 429, 450, 452, 458, 514, 546, 566; **III**, 443, 445, 489, 502
Manasse al-Ṣadr, chief judge, **II**, 566
Manasse b. Samuel, **III**, 485
Manbij, Syria, **I**, 194; **II**, 51, 75, 606
mandal (magic divination), **II**, 536. See also *yimandilū*
mandīl (*mindīl*) (kerchief), **I**, 46, 402; **II**, 612; **III**, 434; **IV**, 315, 323; *m. kumm* (sleeve kerchief), **IV**, 161, 330, 398, 459; *m. qafaṣ* (*muqaffaṣ*), **IV**, 132, 386; *m. rūmī* (*see* Mantilla)
manfūkh ("puffed up," i.e., hollow), description of bracelets, **IV**, 211, 424
Mangalore, India, **II**, 20–21; **V**, 520
Mangalore document, **II**, 524
mann (two pounds), **I**, 360 and *passim*; **II**, 583. *See also* Weights
Mann, Jacob, **I**, 24–25; **II**, 23, 97, 281, 326; **III**, 6; **V**, 267, 298, 482, 499
manna, *mannī* (grayish, light-colored), **IV**, 166, 174, 320
manqūḍ (unraveled silk), **I**, 104, 455. See also *naqqāḍ*; Silk
manqūsh (covered with stucco work), **IV**, 121
Mansion in Fustat, **IV**, 78–80
al-Manṣūr, Abbasid caliph, **V**, 276
al-Manṣūr, viceroy of Umayyad Spain, **I**, 40
Manṣūr b. Ibrāhīm b. ʿAfīf, physician, **II**, 555
Manṣūr b. Isaac b. Saʿīd b. Fīnḥās (Phinehas), **III**, 93
Manṣūr b. Khalaf of Tyre, **I**, 362
Manṣūr Kohen, **V**, 559
Manṣūr b. Manasse, **II**, 592
Manṣūr b. Mukhtār, **III**, 279
Manṣūr b. Sālim, **IV**, 438
Mantilla (*mandīl rūmī*), **IV**, 167, 191, 401, 455
Mantle (*ghifāra*), **IV**, 116, 182, 196, 197, 397, 411. See also *izār*; *ridāʾ*
Manual work, attitudes toward, **I**, 77
Manuel Comnenus, **I**, 39
Manūf, **I**, 297; **II**, 606
Manūfiyya district, **II**, 591; **III**, 81
Manumission, **I**, 134; **II**, 595; deeds of, 10, 133, 144; of minor slave girl, **II**, 341; **IV**, 456. *See also* Freedmen; Freedwomen; Slave(s); Slavegirl(s)
Manyamūn, **II**, 610
manẓar(a) (belvedere), **IV**, 76, 370
manzil (dwelling), **III**, 461; **IV**, 57, 84, 363, 367. *See also* House(s)
maqʿad. *See* Loggia
maqāma (genre of Arabic poetry), **I**, 324; of Ḥarīrī, **II**, 388
maqāniʿī (scarf makers), **I**, 108; **II**, 483. See also *miqnaʿa*; Veil
al-maqdis. See *bayt al-maqdis* (Jerusalem)

al-Maqrīzī, Egyptian historian, IV, 22, 39, 128; V, 96
al-Maqs, port of Cairo, I, 297, 300, 345; II, 606; IV, 34
maqshūr ("peeled off"), type of silk, I, 104, 418, 455
maqṣūr. *See* Fulled
*maqṭa*ʿ (textiles), I, 90; IV, 7, 320, 382, 409, 446, 454. *See also* Robe
Mār, title for respectable men, V, 521
mara. *See* Widows
Marāgha, I, 400, 460
*ma*ʿ*raqa*. *See* Skullcap
marāwiḥī (fan maker), I, 416; II, 495. *See also* Fans
Marble, IV, 62, 65, 68, 69, 103, 140, 141, 146, 367
Marble-worker, I, 113, 423
Mardūk b. Mūsā, I, 439; IV, 179, 401, 404
marēnū (*we-rabbēnū*), our master (and lord), II, 551; IV, 453
*marfa*ʿ, *mirfa*ʿ (cover with a lid), IV, 147, 315, 393, 394, 463
marfaq (structure), IV, 354
Margoliouth, D.S., I, 283
*ma*ʿ*rifa* ("acquaintance of"), informal designation of a person, I, 251; II, 438
Marijuana, II, 270
maristān. *See* Hospitals
Marital disputes. *See* Marriage: disputes in
Marital strife. *See* Marriage: disputes in
marjānī (coral merchant). *See* Corals
Mār Joseph, poet, V, 16
markab (boat, ship), I, 284, 295, 305, 306, 325, 331, 440, 473, 474, 477–478, 480, 481, 482, 484, 487
markab dujjār = *markab tujjār* (merchantman ship), I, 477
Market(s), I, 193-195; II, 104, 543, 582, 606; IV, 14. *See also* Bazaar; *qaysāriyya*
"Market bread," IV, 238
Market day(s), I, 195; IV, 26
Market of Apples and Dates, IV, 246
Market of the Berbers, II, 263
Market of the Greeks, I, 44; IV, 27, 355
Market of the Jews, Damascus, IV, 286
Market of the Jews. *See* Little Market of the Jews
Market of the Jews, Ramle, II, 291
Market of the Jews, Tiberias, II, 291
Market of the Sellers of seed, IV, 94
Market of the Tanners, IV, 56
Market of the Vizier. *See* Little Market of the Vizier
Market police, II, 247, 584. *See also* Police
Market price, I, 218–220
Market supervision, handbook of, IV, 167, 224, 402, 418
Market supervisor. See *muḥtasib*
Marrākesh, Morocco, I, 277, 340; II, 278; V, 521
Marranos, II, 300, 591
Marriage, III, 47–159; and the authorities, II, 16, 27, 36, 39, 72, 74, 311; III, 80–84; attitudes of women, V, 86; between old people, III, 276; between Rabbanites and Karaites (*see* Intermarriage); of children, III, 76-79; civil, III, 83; consummation, III, 70, 441; court procedure, II, 343; "diplomatic," III, 56–58, 261; disputes in, II, 110, 322; III, 181–184, 200, 212–218; economics of, III, 99, 118–142, 179–184; "exchange," III, 32; impediments to, II, 330; III, 81; jurisdiction of courts, II, 311, 321; metaphor for connection to one's town, IV, 44; nature of, III, 47–65; obligatory for men, III, 48-49; previous, III, 106, 219, 272–273, 311 (*see also* Remarriage); public character of, III, 94; purposes of, III, 47–54; V, 312; sacred and secular aspects, III, 53–55; sex within, V, 218, 312–313; and social esteem, II, 102; V, 256–257; study of sacred law more meritorious than, II, 193; talmudic treatise on, II, 308; to create social ties, III, 56; two contracted by one woman, III, 80; with freedwomen, III, 82. *See also* Betrothal; Dowry; Engagement; Polygyny; Proxy of bride
Marriage contracts and settlements, I, 10, 58, 368, 370, 383, 386–387, 391; II, 47, 50, 235, 276, 580, 591, 598, 600, 603; III, 95–114, 119–120; IV, 9, 310–332, 450; V, 23, 92, 139, 330, 488; artistic aspect, III, 109–113, 448–449; good wishes for congregation inscribed on, II, 41, 530; dealt with outside of regular court sessions, II, 215; docket, III, 113; of emancipated women, I, 145; fees for writing, II, 122, 230, 529; fragmentation of, III, 95–96; Islamic, III, 51–55, 102, 119, 134, 137, 142, 151, 152, 441, 442; V, 337; Jewish (*ketubba*), II, 327; III, 49, 50, 51, 69, 70, 71, 83, 85, 94, 95–114, 126–127, 132, 142, 151, 309; Jewish–Karaite, III, 52, 55, 106, 108, 109, 112,

151, 310, 437, 439, 448, 452; IV, 451; Jewish–Palestinian, III, 52, 55, 106, 107, 264, 425, 438, 452; loss of, III, 114; physical features, III, 107–114; reused for other documents, II, 425, 427, 475; reverse side of, III, 113; signatures on, II, 321; III, 117; special conditions, I, 140; II, 344, 599; III, 82, 84, 91, 105, 106, 132, 142–159, 177, 254, 338; IV, 458 (*see also* Monogyny clause; Polygyny; Slavegirls); special conditions regarding religious observances, II, 155; III, 107, 158 (*see also* Intermarriage); squabbles over, III, 158–159; stipulation concerning wife's earnings, I, 127; writing materials used for, II, 232

Marriage gift(s) of husband, III, 87, 93, 100, 102, 104, 119–123, 180; IV, 314, 318, 451 (see also *mahr*; *mōhār*); and dowries, III, 130–131; V, 141, 151; delayed installment, I, 369; III, 78, 85, 89, 92, 94, 99, 104, 105, 119, 120, 122, 126, 130, 144, 148, 155, 188, 192, 254, 269, 366, 372, 385, 392, 445, 447; IV, 318, 328, 458; delayed installment reduced, III, 250–252, 254, 256; first installment, III, 66–68, 70, 78, 83, 84, 85, 86, 90, 91, 92, 93, 99, 105, 119, 120, 121, 130, 138, 143; IV, 318, 328, 458; first installment deposited with third party, III, 84, 89; forfeit of by wife, III, 186, 267; minimum, III, 119–122, 451–452; Muslim, III, 120, 130, 137; payment in gold, III, 112–121; terms "early" and "late" (installments), III, 120

Marriage House, San Diego, II, 154

Marriage permits: for foreigners and divorcees, III, 81, 82; for taking second wife, III, 208–209

Marriage portion. *See* Dowry

Marriage registers, absence of, III, 80, 98

Marseilles, France, I, 40, 42, 67, 211, 301, 325; II, 221; IV, 1

marsīn. *See* Myrtle pins

martaba (sofa), IV, 108–111, 125, 126 and *passim*, 299–306, 308, 320, 327, 330, 377, 378, 450, 459. See also *maṭraḥ*; *ṭarrāḥa*; *qiṭaʿ*

martak (litharge), IV, 367

martakī (preparer of litharge), I, 421

Martyrdom, Jewish attitudes toward, V, 61

Maʿrūf, III, 185

Mār ʿUqbā, V, 623

Maryūṭ, lake of, II, 234; IV, 7

masannī. *See* Green

Masarra, washer of the dead, V, 549

Masgavyā b. Moses, V, 626

maṣḥaf tōrā, II, 574

mashghūla ("busy" [with child]), i.e. pregnant, III, 475

mashḥānī (masseur), II, 579

Māshīʾaḥ b. Ṣemaḥ, II, 571

māshiṭa. *See* Bride-comber

mashmīʿa (Heb., herald), II, 87, 540

mashqīf (Heb., supervisor), III, 492

mashraqa. *See* Veranda

mashriq ("the east"), referring to Alexandria and Fustat, I, 401

mashshāsh (maker of special type of cheese), I, 428. *See also* Cheese; Cheese maker

mashshāṭ ([flax]-comber), I, 418. *See also* Flax

Maʿshūq ("Beloved"), rare name, II, 465

maskan. *See* Apartment

maskīl (Heb., title usually held by a judge), II, 321

maslaḥa (police station), IV, 351. *See also* Police

maslak (reel), I, 418

Maṣlīaḥ b. Elijah, judge of Palermo, I, 52, 375; II, 338; III, 447

Maṣlīaḥ (Maṣlīʾaḥ) Gaon, I, 260, 380, 485; II, 20, 26, 39, 161, 236, 405, 422, 435, 464, 512, 529, 541; III, 19, 133, 186, 430, 432, 466; IV, 11; V, 124, 200, 236, 294, 564, 576, 577

Masons, I, 80, 86, 90, 95, 96, 97, 113; II, 421, 425, 434

Maṣr. *See* Miṣr

Maṣṣāṣa quarter, II, 264, 425, 508; IV, 353. *See also* Mamṣūṣa

Maṣṣāṣiyyīn, inhabitants of the Maṣṣāṣa quarter, II, 508

Massignon, Louis, I, 229; IV, 3

maṣṭaba. *See* Bench

maṣṭakā. *See* Mastic

Mastaura, Asia Minor, II, 530, 599; III, 98, 452

Mastic gum, I, 154, 268, 337, 467

mastūr(a) (veiled), i.e., of high social rank, III, 438; V, 76, 83, 308. See also *ṣaʿlūk*; Social rank

Masʿūd b. Mawhūb, II, 572

maṭar (Byzantine barrel), I, 465

maṭāridī (maker of hunting spears), I, 416

al-Maṭāridī, I, 326

Maṭariyya (Heliopolis), II, 361, 606

maṭbakh ("place of cooking"), I, 81, 367, 420. *See also* Sugar factory

maṭbakh [*sukkar*]. *See* Sugar factory

maṭbal (Judeo-Ar.). *See* Ritual bath
Matches, sulphur, **IV**, 136
Matching vessels: basin and ewer, **IV**, 139; bucket and dipper, **IV**, 140; bowls, platters, cups, **IV**, 146
Matchmaker, matchmaking **II**, 224, 570; **III**, 55, 73, 75, 90, 141, 212, 260-261
Material culture, **IV**, 266-269
maṭhara (marble plate with a hole), **IV**, 140
mathība, **II**, 17, 315, 561, 595. *See also* Yeshiva
mathībat al-shām. *See* Yeshiva: Palestinian
matjar (government supply center), **I**, 268
maṭmūra: cellar, concealed closet, **IV**, 74-75, 446; "underground prison," **III**, 429
maṭraḥ (mattress), **IV**, 109-110, 115 and *passim*, 304, 333, 377, 379, 380, 460. See also *martaba*
Matriarchs, biblical, on tombstone inscriptions, **V**, 622
Matriarchy, **III**, 12
Mats, **I**, 86, 99-100; **II**, 149, 150, 563; **IV**, 7, 106, 127-129, 409; ʿAbbādānī, **IV**, 128, 339, 464; ʿAzīzī, **IV**, 127; entrance piece, **IV**, 127; "plaited," **IV**, 128, 384; round, **IV**, 128; *samār*, **IV**, 128; traded in pairs, **IV**, 128; as wall hanging, **IV**, 385. See also *ḥuṣr*
mattān. *See* Gifts, anonymous
al-maʿtūq. *See* Freedmen
matzot, **II**, 129
Māʿūn, Transjordan, **II**, 447
maʿūna (police building), **II**, 368, 608. See also *maslaḥa*; Police
Maury, B., **IV**, 56
Mawadda ("Love"), f., **III**, 191
mawadda (love), **III**, 437. *See also* Love
mawāliya battē dīnīm ("My lords, the courts"), form of address of chief judges of Fustat, **II**, 595. *See also* Judges
mawāzīnī (maker of scales), **II**, 491
mawḍiʿ (place [to live in]), **II**, 594; **IV**, 363. *See also* House; Residence
Mawhūb b. Aaron, cantor, **II**, 569; **III**, 479; **IV**, 374
Mawhūb b. Shālōm, cantor, **III**, 469
mawlā ("the attached"), freedman, **I**, 145, 146, 436. *See also* Freedmen
Mawlāt, f., **III**, 117
mawlātī ("my mistress"), i.e., mother or grandmother, **II**, 477
mawridat al-ṣiqāra, Wharf of the Falcons, **IV**, 364
mawt (death), term for plague, **V**, 113. *See also* Epidemics; Plague
mawsim (caravan, fair, business season), **I**, 277, 449, 450, 469; **III**, 503. *See also* Business: season; Caravan(s)
mawwās (maker of razors), **I**, 421
al-mawwāz (banana vendor), **I**, 427
Maxims and proverbs, **I**, 48, 71, 85, 91, 127, 129, 151, 157, 162, 168, 169, 183, 200, 201, 219, 274, 275, 286, 332
mayāzirī (maker of waist cloths), **I**, 254
Mayence (Mainz), Germany, **I**, 64, 65; **II**, 15, 58
Mayer, Leon Arye, **I**, 93
Maymūn, *qā'id*, **I**, 310, 479
maymūn. *See* Amulet
mayzar, **I**, 419
Mazara, Sicily, **I**, 98, 102, 159, 215, 218, 228, 272, 302, 317, 326, 330, 344, 375, 417, 455; **II**, 68, 238; **IV**, 39, 193, 410
Meals, **IV**, 138, 144ff.; evening, **IV**, 229-230, 432; festive, **IV**, 140, 228, 234, 432; morning, **IV**, 229, 432; for partners in a workshop, **I**, 87; **IV**, 432; provided by employers, **I**, 94-96 **IV**, 229-230, 432, 433; two a day, **IV**, 229
Meal carrier, **IV**, 141
Meat, **II**, 546, 571, 588; **IV**, 227, 230, 232, 236, 442; abstinence from, **III**, 353; cooked (not roasted) with light wine, **IV**, 255; cut in kitchen, **IV**, 148; for New Year, **IV**, 231; killing animal a sacramental act, **IV**, 248; price of, **II**, 227; **IV**, 443; yellow = fat, red = lean, **IV**, 249, 443. *See also* Butcher; *qaṣṣāb*
Mecca, Arabia, **I**, 55, 177, 200; **II**, 156, 163; **III**, 153; **IV**, 2, 192, 307, 361
Medical books, **II**, 485
Medical care, **II**, 133
"Medical corps," **II**, 380
Medication, **IV**, 233; **V**, 102, 112. *See* Prescriptions, medical
Medicine, **II**, 265, 270, 271; profession, **II**, 240-261, 422, 429, 575-581 (*see also* Physician); study of, **II**, 247. *See also* Prescriptions, medical
Medina, Arabia, **IV**, 6
Mediterranean Sea (*al-baḥr al-māliḥ*, *baḥr al-rūm*), **I**, 401, 474; names and divisions, **I**, 42-43
Meetinghouse in Ramle, **II**, 166
megillat setārīm (Heb., "secret scroll"), diary kept by Jewish students, **II**, 210, 565
Megilloth. *See* Scrolls
Meḥrez, Gamal, **IV**, 53
Meir b. Baruch, **I**, 68

Meir b. Hamadānī, II, 577; IV, 297, 306
Meir (Mēʾīr) b. Hillel b. Ṣādōq āv, judge, II, 421, 529, 577; III, 30, 502; V, 599
Meir b. Isaac Katzenellenbogen, V, 588
Meir of Rothenburg, III, 184
Meir b. Yākhīn, III, 456
mekhīrūthā ("sale"), betrothal, III, 95. *See also* Betrothal
Meknes, N. Africa, V, 521
melākhā-melūkhā ("A craft is a kingdom"), Hebrew pun found in Geniza, I, 91
melammēd (Heb., teacher), II, 190, 529, 544, 560; III, 445, 485
melekhet ha-melekh (Heb., term used for men in government service), II, 604. See also *ʿamal; khidma*
mellah, Jewish quarter, II, 293
Melodies, II, 159
Melons, I, 121
melūg (Akkadian, wife's personal possessions), III, 182, 465, 483. *See also* Dowry; Husband, economic power of; Marriage, economics of
Memorial lists, I, 12; II, 163, 566; III, 2-6, 240, 425, 426, 456, 477, 478
Memorial service (*tarhīm*), II, 163, 554
Memorizing, II, 174
Memphis, Egypt, V, 20
memunne ("officially appointed") II, 568
Menahem, II, 589
Menahem, physician, II, 579
Menaḥēm b. al-ʿAfīf, II, 497. *See also* Nāṣir b. al-ʿAfīf
Menaḥēm b. Isaac b. Sāsōn, II, 514; III, 209, 255, 483
Mending (*iṣlāḥ*), IV, 182, 412
mene (Aram., a weight), I, 360
Menorah, IV, 199
Menūḥā ha-Kohen b. Joseph, II, 571
meqōnēn. See *muqrī*
Merāyōt ha-Kohen b. Joseph Av ha-yeshiva, IV, 374
Merchants, I, 75, 78, 149-161, 165 and *passim*; II, 2, 21, 26, 32, 37, 42, 45, 55, 61, 67, 98, 108, 110, 113, 134, 154, 172, 174, 175, 177, 178, 179, 180, 191, 192, 193, 195, 198, 205, 229, 258, 277, 279, 287, 294, 295, 307, 337, 340, 345, 349, 363, 378, 379, 395, 440, 442, 445, 458, 464, 472, 475, 476, 477, 478, 512, 520, 523, 530, 539, 572, 578, 580, 583, 592, 604; III, 2, 13, 14, 31, 35, 41, 43, 45, 73, 93, 116, 130, 137, 138, 162, 189, 190, 193, 198, 219, 221, 230, 236, 240, 247, 256, 257, 273, 284, 288, 294, 339
Merchant-bankers, I, 231, 233, 239; II, 214
Mercy. *See* God, mercy of
Mercury, I, 113, 154, 190, 202, 218, 338; II, 607; IV, 406
"Merit of the fathers," III, 15. *See* Social rank
Merx, Adalbert, I, 2; II, 592
meshōrēr (Heb., singer, poet), II, 224, 570, 611
meshōṭeṭē layla (Heb.). *See* Night watchman
meshuḥrār (Heb.). *See* Freedmen
Meshullām, *peqīd ha-sōḥarīm*, I, 446
Meshullam family, III, 154
Meshullām b. Elazar ha-Kohen Kelīl ha-Yōfī ("Perfect Beauty"), V, 617
Meshullām b. Manasse *he-ḥāvēr*, II, 514
Meshullam b. Mevassēr, IV, 359
Meshullām b. Sāsōn *he-ḥāvēr*, III, 460
Mesopotamia, II, 524
mesōs ha-yeshīva, "Delight of the Yeshiva," II, 543. *See also* "Delight of the Yeshiva"
Messenger of the court, II, 82-87
Messiah, messianic, III, 48, 108
Messianic movements, II, 308, 310
Messianism and millennialism: faith in, V, 400-406, 412-415; holidays, V, 394-395; Islamic, V, 397-398, 404; and Jerusalem, V, 391-395, 401-402, 404, 411, 449; personal names, V, 396-397; and resurrection, V, 182, 406-408, 411; Saadya Gaon, V, 390; tenets, V, 402-415
Messina, Sicily, I, 46, 98, 256, 326; II, 157, 167, 238
Metals, I, 108-109, and *passim*
Metalwork, II, 150
methivta (Aram.) = *mathība*, II, 561. *See also* Yeshiva
meturgeman. *See* Broadcaster; Dragoman
meʿulle ("eminent member"), title of dignitary, II, 214, 548, 558, 566, 567; III, 502
meʿuttād (Heb., Gaon designate), II, 15, 566
Mevasser b. Ḥalfōn, III, 443
Mevassēr b. Yeshūʿā, V, 554
al-Mēvīn ("The Understanding"), *parnās*, II, 427, 503
Mevōrākh, Nagid, I, 84, 411, 465; IV, 41, 156
Mevōrākh b. Abraham (Abuʾl-Faḍl) Ibn Sabra, III, 176-177
Mevōrākh b. Amram, III, 137
Mevōrākh b. Mawhūb, III, 491
Mevōrākh b. Nathan b. Samuel, court

clerk and judge, I, 365, 431, 434, 464; II, 343, 427, 458, 483, 493, 502, 514, 532, 552, 570, 572, 582, 585, 597; III, 97, 133, 193, 243, 364-369, 449, 462, 465, 466, 480, 482, 487, 491, 501, 502; IV, 236, 243, 256, 313, 382, 436, 439, 445, 450, 456, 458, 450, 462, 463, 464, 466; V, 110-111, 357, 358, 431, 506, 507, 510, 542, 550, 605
Mevōrākh b. Nathan, son of a schoolteacher, II, 514
Mevōrākh b. Saadya, Nagid, II, 25, 30, 31, 32, 33, 34, 36, 37, 40, 54, 63, 70, 73, 74, 78, 83, 85, 168, 244, 255, 280, 281, 298, 317, 319, 332, 346, 352, 376, 394, 402, 443, 502, 512, 526, 527, 529, 532, 537, 555, 565, 566, 568, 569, 576, 587, 596, 606, 609; III, 19, 76, 132, 148, 241, 247, 258, 273, 286, 296, 298, 302, 332, 356, 357, 430, 448, 477, 478, 490, 492; IV, 385, 463; V, 45, 113, 195, 196-197, 212, 255-256, 258, 261, 373, 394, 419, 423, 512, 519, 529, 538, 542, 562, 578, 579, 590, 591, 609, 617
Mevōrākh b. Sahl, V, 631
Mevōrākh b. Yeshūʿā b. Saʿdʾēl, III, 491
Mevōrākh ha-Kohen b. Joseph (Abuʾl-Ḥusayn al-Mubārak b. Yūsuf b. Yazdād), III, 492
Meyer, Eduard, V, 497
Meyerhof, Max, II, 265, 267
Mez, Adam, IV, 2
mezōnōt (Heb., bread for the poor), II, 98, 449, 459, 466, 498, 503, 529, 544; as alimony, II, 544
mezuzah, as magical protection, III, 226
mīʿād (religious lesson), II, 561
mibkhara. *See* Fumigator
Michael, patriarch of Jacobites, II, 148
mīḍāʾa (basin for ablutions), II, 435. *See also* Ablutions
Middle Arabic, I, xviii, 16, 26
Middle class, I, vii, ix, 74, 75, and *passim*; II, 2, 3, 6, 11, 289, 346, 363; V, 359-360; middle class, III, 122, 129, 137
Middle piece (*wāsiṭa*), IV, 207, 419, 421, 455
midhabba. *See* Flyswatter
midkhana. *See* Incense burner
midrāsh (school of higher studies), II, 199, 202, 203, 204, 205, 562-563, 569; V, 418
(Great) Midrash, II, 27
Midrash(ic), IV, 48-49
Midwife (*qābila*), I, 430; II, 506; III, 175, 232
migdāl (Heb., term for pulpit), II, 147. See also *anbōl*; *al-minbar*
Migrations, I, 30-31, 32, 41, 48-54, 57, 68; IV, 313
miḥakka ("thistle"), teasel, IV, 408. *See also* Fuller, fulling
miḥbas. *See* Necklace; *maḥābis*
miʿjar. *See* Wimple
mijarr (chain), IV, 218. *See also* Chains; Necklace
mijmara. *See* Censer
mijnab. *See* Side piece
Mikāʾīl lane, Fustat, IV, 98, 278, 376
mikhadda. *See* Pillow
mikhadda lil-khadd. *See* Pillow
mikhnaqa (10-11th cy.). *See* Choker
mīl. *See* Kohl stick
Milāḥ, III, 169
milāk, *imlāk* (engagement, betrothal), III, 69, 95. *See also* Betrothal; Engagement
Milan, I, 109
milʿaqa, *malāʿiq*. *See* Spoons
Milasā, Asia Minor, II, 574
Miles, George C., I, 368-387 *passim*, 458
milḥafa (= *malḥafa*). *See* Cloak
mīlī. *See* Kohl stick, maker of
Milk, IV, 252
Milk cure, II, 253, 578
Milkman, I, 150, 383, 428; II, 459, 483; IV, 252
Milk supply, I, 124
milla (local community), II, 530. See also *jamāʿa*; *jumla*; Local community; *ṭāʾifa*
Millenary of Cairo (969-1969), IV, 12
Miller, Larry B., V, 608
Millers, I, 114; II, 590
Mills, IV, 15, 16, 142; hand, IV, 142, 391
Millstones, I, 60, 153, 210
mīnā (enamel-like artifact), IV, 208, 210, 213, 220, 319, 327, 420
mināya (examination [of ritual purity of slaughter]), II, 570. *See also* Ritual slaughter
al-minbar (pulpit), II, 147, 551. See also *anbōl*
minhāg (Heb., custom, rite), II, 226, 227, 571
Miniatures, IV, 161, 163
Minister of finance, II, 348
minnuy (degree granted by Palestinian yeshiva), Talmudic usage, II, 565
Mint, I, 81, 82, 110, 170, 254, 267, 362, 365; II, 106, 354, 358, 370, 375, 454, 477, 480, 605; III, 14, 23, 262; IV, 28. *See also* Money
Minya, Egypt, I, 276; II, 606

Minyat Ashnā, Egypt, I, 256, 404; II, 540, 606; III, 61, 297; IV, 442
Minyat Ghamr, Egypt, I, 384, 386; II, 48-49, 50, 135, 463, 485, 520, 524, 570, 589; III, 70–71, 208–209, 310, 390, 415, 453; IV, 59, 77; V, 508
Minyat al-Qā'id, Egypt, I, 417; IV, 265
Minyat Sammanūd, I, 425
Minyat Sirāj, I, 297
Minyat Ziftā, Egypt, II, 530, 532, 536, 577, 602; III, 338, 464, 492; IV, 296; V, 102; candy production in, I, 126, 425; collection of poll-tax in, I, 63; contract with a widowed mother from, III, 234, 388; contributions to Fustat community from, II, 501; *ḍāmin* of, II, 606; dissolution of industrial partnership in, I, 366; domestic architecture, IV, 363, 369; example of middle-sized community, II, 43–51; excommunication of debtor in, I, 465; honey production, I, 424; house belonging to Jewish community of, IV, 373; interfaith relations in, II, 276, 292, 590; Jewish congregation of, II, 41, 138, 256; Jewish court documents from, I, 204, 366, 382, 463; Jewish judges of, II, 67, 187, 342, 596; V, 44; Jewish physicians of, II, 258; IV, 335, 350; Jewish population of, II, 531; Jewish teachers in, II, 187; Jews from, helping brethren in Fustat, I, 19; letter to A. Maimonides from, II, 560; location, I, 117, 126; marriage contracts from, II, 191; III, 309, 389, 395, 413; merchants in, I, 156, 427; *muqaddams* of, II, 258, 405; *parnāsīm*, II, 539; poll-tax in, II, 382, 499; professional veterinarian in, II, 256; representative of merchants in, I, 190, 446; sale of house in, IV, 275; sesame, I, 427; silk weaving in, I, 417; social services in, II, 106, 138; spiritual leader of Jewish community, IV, 461; sugar production in, IV, 442; synagogue in, II, 145, 436; tannery in, III, 443; trusteeship in, IV, 335
*miqaṭṭ al-sham*ʿ (wick trimmer), IV, 388
miqdāsh (Heb., sanctuary), II, 539, 552; V, 20. *See also* Synagogue
miqnaʿa (women's scarf, i.e., veil), I, 108; II, 37. See also *maqāniʿī*; Veil
miqwā. *See* Ritual bath
Miracles, worked by rabbis or saints, V, 337
mirashsh(*a*). *See* Sprinkler
mirʾātī. *See* Mirrors, maker of
mirḥāḍ. *See* Washroom
Miriam, biblical, V, 590
Miriam, d. of Benayah, II, 184
Miriam, sister of Moses Maimonides, I, 351
mirjānī (coral merchant). *See* Corals
Mirrors, I, 99–100; IV, 130, 222, 319, 322, 323, 327, 429, 458; maker of, I, 416
Mirror script. *See* Script
mirwad. *See* Kohl stick
miṣbāḥ. *See* Lantern
Miscarriage(s), III, 230. *See also* Childbirth
Misgaviyā b. Moses, III, 434; IV, 440
misḥ (haircloth), I, 485
Mishaʾel, I, 256
Mishael b. Isaiah, Maimonides' father-in-law, III, 5
Mishael b. Mufaḍḍal (II) b. Adōnīm, III, 10
Mishael b. Uzziel, II, 612; III, 336
Mishnah, II, 102, 181, 193, 197, 199, 205, 206, 213, 546, 564; IV, 32, 153, 187, 192
mishne (Heb.) = Ar. *nāʾib* (deputy), II, 317, 596; *m. la-melekh* (deputy of the king), II, 351–352; *m. be-Rabbi*, II, 596
mishpāḥā (Heb., [extended] family), III, 2. *See also* Family
mishpāḥōt meyūḥāsōt (Heb., "noble families"), I, 409
mishsh (type of cheese), I, 428. *See also* Cheese
Miska, I, 357
Miskawayh, Muslim historian, V, 276
Miskimin, H., IV, 4
misnad, *masnad* ("support"), bolster for sofa, IV, 108, 377, 379
Miṣr, term for Egypt, IV, 6, 8, 348
Miṣrayim (Heb.), Fustat, IV, 11
Miṣrī, from Fustat, II, 454, 505; "minted in Fustat," gold coin. *See* Dinar
"Miṣr pounds," IV, 179, 409
misṭāḥ (open space), II, 114, 545; IV, 355; for dyeing and tanning, IV, 29
Mistakes in accounts, I, 209
miswāq (on special order, bought at retail), II, 585
miswara (round cushion), IV, 113, 379. *See also* Cushions
mithqāl, I, 360 and *passim*; IV, 418, 419. *See also* Money
Mixed marriage. *See* Intermarriage
miẓalla (hut for Feast of Tabernacles), IV, 77, 370, 376. *See also* Sukkot
miʾzar (waist cloth), I, 254
mizr. *See* Beer

mizwad (leather bag), I, 485. *See also* Leather
Mobility, III, 262–263, 336; of populace, IV, 91–92; of society, II, 64; v. family cohesion, IV, 82
mōdaʿ (secret deposition), II, 341, 342. *See also* Procedure, court
Modesty and meekness, personality traits, V, 528
mōʿēd (Heb., holiday week), II, 472, 506, 507. *See also* Holidays
mōhār (Heb., marriage gift), III, 93, 104, 119. See also *mahr*; Marriage gift of husband
Mollat, Michel, V, 73
Monasteries, II, 144, 205
Monday and Thursday, weekdays when Torah read, II, 57, 108, 109, 110, 157, 193, 194, 342, 343, 463, 475, 491, 545. *See also* Prayer, communal
Monetary compensations instead of clothing, II, 131
Money, I, 60–61, 229–266, 359–360 and App. D; IV, 27–28; distribution to the needy, II, 134–135, 142, 448, 457, 458–459, 461, 462, 463, 465, 499; value of, V, 51, 172. *See also* Dinar; Dirhem; Gold; Money of account; Purses of coins; Silver
Money assayer (*naqqād*), I, 80, 83, 179, 250, 410, 411, 462; II, 483, 494
Money Assayers, The, business address, II, 483
Money changer, I, 80, 234–240, 247, 257, 359; II, 486, 508; IV, 16, 351. See also *ṣayrafī*
Money lenders, I, 247, 257, 258; II, 472; V, 527. *See also* Loans
Money of account: *dānaq* (one-sixth of a *qīrāṭ*), I, 359; II, 476; *ḥabba* (grain or one-third of a *qīrāṭ*), I, 359 and *passim*; II, 387, 482, 611; *kharrūba* ("carob seed," one-sixteenth of a dirhem), I, 360; *qīrāṭ* (one twenty-fourth of a dinar), I, 359; II, 100, 440, 455, 471, 476, 477, 480, 482, 487, 490, 507, 508, 605, 611; IV, 371. *See also* Dinar; Dirhem; Money
Mongols, II, 523; V, 65–66, 522
"Monk, The," minister of finance, II, 281, 348, 425, 426, 588; III, 126, 182; IV, 380; V, 249, 575
Monogamy. *See* Monogyny clause
Monogyny clause, III, 148–150. *See also* Concubinage; Marriage contracts, special conditions; Polygyny; Slavegirls
Monsoon, I, 277
Montpellier, France, I, 40, 65; II, 242
Mordants, IV, 172–173, 405ff. *See also* Dyeing
Mordecai (rare name in West), cantor from Persia, II, 440
mōredet (Heb., "revolting" [against husband]), III, 267. *See also* Divorce; Marriage gift of husband; Wife
Morocco: Almohads in, I, 63; V, 59–62; Almoravids in, I, 41, 65; caravans travelling to/from, I, 276; clothing, IV, 163, 178, 464; coins, I, 360; copy of classical Hebrew thesaurus found in, I, 64; definition, I, xvii, 43; emigrants to Egypt from, III, 124; Gaons from, II, 14, 522; Grand Bazaars of, IV, 31; Ibn Baṭṭūṭa in, I, 67; Ibn Jubayr in, I, 59; Jewish judges of, I, 48; letters to, I, 302; mellahs of, II, 293; merchants in, I, 156, 213; III, 61; IV, 363; Moses Maimonides in, III, 177; oppression of non-Muslims in, IV, 36; overland traffic from, IV, 8; refugees from, II, 46; IV, 229; rugs, IV, 126; scholars in/from, II, 11, 14, 96; silversmiths from, I, 50, 108; teachers from, II, 188, 559; visitors to Egypt from, III, 323. *See also* Maghrib; North Africa
Mortar and pestle (*hāwun wa-yaduh*), IV, 142, 391. See also *hāwinī*
Mortgage(s) of husband's possessions to wife, III, 123, 181, 243, 250, 326. *See also* Marriage gift of husband
Mosaicist (*muzawwiq*), II, 467
Moses, biblical, I, 56; II, 4, 88, 157, 352; IV, 314; V, 525, 536, 537
Moses, Nagid designate. *See* Moses b. Samuel b. Hananya
Moses, physician, II, 541
Moses, man connected with government: prayers for, V, 537
Moses, R., II, 505
Moses, Song of, II, 140, 161
Moses, synagogue of, II, 78
Moses, trustee of the merchants, I, 446
Moses Ben-Asher, V, 372
Moses b. Abraham (II) b. David b. Abraham (I) Maimonides, Nagid, II, 495, 526, 530, 605
Moses b. ʿAdāyā, V, 544
Moses b. Elazar, II, 243, 575
Moses b. Elijah, IV, 408
Moses Ibn Ezra. *See* Moses b. Jacob Ibn Ezra
Moses b. Ghulayb, II, 471, 537; III, 426–427
Moses b. Isaac, III, 436

Moses b. Jacob, I, 293, 461, 472; II, 576; III, 431; IV, 384, 403
Moses (Moshe) b. Jacob Ibn Ezra, V, 448, 585, 587, 627
Moses b. Japheth, *parnās*, III, 467
Moses b. Jekuthiel, III, 436
Moses b. Joshia, III, 30
Moses b. Judah, teacher, II, 560
Moses b. Labraṭ, judge, I, 407
Moses b. Levi ha-Levi, cantor, V, 95
Moses b. Maimon. *See* Moses Maimonides
Moses (Mūsā) Ibn al-Majjānī, merchant, II, 473, 560; V, 207-208, 565, 585, 519
Moses b. Mevōrākh, Nagid, I, 485; II, 25, 30, 47, 244, 512, 526; III, 148, 426, 458; V, 183-184, 558
Moses b. Moses, cantor, I, 431
Moses b. Nathan, banker, V, 77, 527
Moses b. Nethanel ha-Levi, II, 528, 578, 609, 610; IV, 437
Moses b. Paltiel, I, 145
Moses b. Peraḥyā, judge, II, 49, 531, 533, 559; III, 453; V, 557
Moses b. Samuel b. Hananya, I, 139
Moses b. Shahryār, III, 285
Moses b. Ṭōviyāhū ha-Kohen, II, 423
Moses Yerushalmi b. Elijah ha-Levi, V, 509
Moses b. Yeshūʿā, I, 249
Moses ibn al-Maqdisī, II, 599
Moses ha-Kohen (b. Ḥalfōn), II, 162; IV, 437
Moses ha-Levi b. David, clerk, III, 444, 445
Moses ha-Levi, physician, V, 426, 428–429
Moses Kohen, I, 137
Moses Maimonides, I, 97, 183, 253, 295, 406; II, 21, 48, 51, 201, 227, 240, 268, 269, 303, 323, 326, 328, 399, 419, 448, 458, 498, 514, 539, 542, 552, 577; III, 225, 323, 426, 454, 456, 479, 488, 501, 503; IV, 119, 120, 145, 196, 215, 239, 245, 297, 412, 437, 461; V, 271, 506, 508, 510, 522, 532, 541, 547, 550, 561, 582, 622, 629; appeals for charity, II, 46, 95, 499, 549; on astrology, V, 329, 422; on bathing, V, 96; biographical details and family relations, I, 351; II, 172, 244, 248, 258, 612; III, 3, 5, 17, 20, 25, 32, 62, 177, 237, 239, 311, 336, 425, 464, 478; V, 197-198, 393, 477, 539; *Code of Law* (see *Mishneh Torah*); and Dammuh sanctuary, V, 22–23; on death and mourning, IV, 183; V, 131, 161, 173, 234; desire for solitude, V, 26; on disaster, V, 54–55; documents of, I, 122; II, 37, 485; III, 83, 283, 405; on drinking, IV, 254, 255, 258; V, 39, 40, 95; *Epistle on the Sanctification of the Name*, V, 61; on Fustat, V, 310; *Guide for the Perplexed*, I, 64, 68, 184; II, 495, 495; IV, 160; V, 8, 79; head of Jews in Egypt, I, 95; II, 26, 32–33, 39, 116, 352, 524; on health, V, 94–95, 96, 101, 112, 116; and Islamic scholars, V, 430, 443–448; on Karaites, V, 366–367; as legal authority, I, 53, 66; III, 486; letters of, I, 92; III, 161; IV, 36; V, 27, 54–55; letters, petitions, cases, I, 191; II, 89, 134, 163, 254, 421, 422; III, 473, 496, 502; IV, 21, 76, 84, 95, 185; V, 88, 123, 197, 230, 310, 371, 382; livelihood, V, 419; on marriage, III, 65-69, 76, 77, 79, 82, 104, 105, 153, 171, 184, 185, 192, 210-211, 276, 344, 345, 346; on Messianism and resurrection, V, 406, 407–409; *Mishneh Torah*, I, 15; II, 125, 313, 329, 334, 336, 594; III, 306; IV, 128, 160, 187; V, 477, 478, 492; on music, V, 41–42; and Palestinian rite, II, 52; as physician, II, 244, 248, 252, 266, 578; IV, 12, 125, 246, 247, 441; political conflicts, III, 470; V, 491-492; on poetical passages in prayer, II, 160; on poverty, V, 80, 94; on proselytizing, II, 304; queries to and responsa, I, 14, 84, 88, 116, 136, 141, 171, 172, 197, 199, 213, 255, 256, 257, 258, 301, 352, 365, 470; II, 36, 42, 45, 59, 75, 133, 153, 156, 162, 168, 179, 181, 183, 204, 216, 220, 223, 292, 296, 297, 301, 316, 335, 340, 361, 383, 400, 401; III, 65-69, 76, 77, 79, 82, 166, 184, 185, 192, 210-211, 236, 238, 267, 344, 345, 346, 443; IV, 71, 72, 94, 97, 101, 121, 161, 198, 419; on ritual purity, III, 107, 154; on Sabbath prohibitions, V, 13, 17; on sex, V, 316, 323; significance, V, 391; on slavery, I, 142; III, 306; on social concerns, V, 305; "Statute," II, 155; on teaching Bible to women, II, 183, 185, 186; III, 356; *Treatise on Resurrection*, V, 161; on virtue, V, 196, 197-198; on weather, V, 101; on weddings in provincial towns, II, 74
mōshēl (Heb., governor), II, 597
mōshīʿa (Heb., saviour), II, 528
Mosque, II, 144, 149, 163, 164, 165, 185, 204, 284, 554; IV, 3, 31-32, 133, 162, 356; Cathedral (*See* Mosque, Friday); Friday, IV, 31, 154; Ḥujja, IV, 70;

Ministry of, IV, 38; neighborhood, IV, 33, 34. *See also* al-Azhar; Great Mosque
Mosquito net, IV, 117
Mosseri, Jacques, I, 5; II, 145
Mosul, Iraq, I, 36, 111; II, 19, 188, 290, 441, 451, 467, 523, 559; III, 4; IV, 66, 139, 366, 370, 389
Mother(s), II, 244, 477; III, 24, 68, 84, 102, 131; by-named after firstborn, III, 20, 324; family of the, III, 5; taking care of married daughter, III, 217
Mother-in-law, III, 77, 143, 163, 171, 176, 279, 434; V, 515
Mother-of-pearl, IV, 130, 132, 138, 321, 327
Mount of Olives, II, 13, 16, 168, 201, 202, 214, 284, 324, 598; V, 22, 338, 369. *See also* Jerusalem
Mount Sinai, spiritual meaning of, V, 602
Mounts, IV, 261–266, 448
Mourning and "Living with the dead," II, 163, 166, 346, 490; III, 3, 20; IV, 258; V, 28, 155, 156, 165–166, 174, 177–181, 234. *See also* Burial; Death; Funerals
mōzīfīm (Heb., Muslim moneylenders), II, 472
Msaken, I, 349
Msila, Algeria, III, 202; IV, 438
Muʿāfā = Isaac, II, 574
muʿāhid (a Jew from a Christian country), I, 61, 406
muʾākhāt (brotherhood), III, 437
muʾākhī (forming a brotherly relationship), III, 47. See also *rafīq*
muʾakhkhar ("later" [installment of marriage gift]), I, 369. *See also* Marriage gift of husband, delayed installment
al-muʿālij al-ṭabīb (practicing physician), term given in Islamic legal text, II, 575
Muʿallā b. Raḥmūn, III, 501
Muʿallaqa church, II, 147, 148, 291, 384, 550, 589; IV, 30. *See also* Church
muʿallim: master, teacher, I, 96, 164; II, 246, 453, 558, 560; IV, 363; young physician, V, 555
muʿallima (woman teacher), II, 185
muʿāmala (cooperation), I, 169, 441, 442
muʿāmil (accredited customer), I, 231, 246
Muʾammala ("the one hoped for"), II, 457
muʿarraj (waves), description of textile, I, 419
muʿassil. *See* Honey, seller of
Muʿāwiya, caliph, I, 72; III, 339; IV, 17, 351
al-Muʿaẓẓam, Ayyubid, II, 380
muballigh. *See* Broadcaster
muballiṭ (layer of floor tiles), I, 422
Mubārak ("the blessed one"), I, 132, 146
Mubārak, a proselyte, II, 306, 307
Mubārak, *ṣaydanī* (pharmacist), II, 581
Mubārak, son of the female physician, II, 455. *See* Mevōrākh b. Saadya
Mubārak b. Abuʾl-Munā, V, 162–163
Mubāraka, a proselyte, II, 306, 599?
Mubāraka, a slave girl, II, 305, 444
Mubāraka b. Abraham, II, 592
Mubāraka b. Faraḥ ha-Kohen, III, 441
Mubārak b. Isaac, V, 538
Mubārak b. Mundhir b. Sābā, II, 602; III, 484
Mubārak b. Saʿāda. *See* Mevōrākh b. Saadya
al-Mubāriz, amir, II, 428
Mubashshir b. Daʾūd b. Mubashshir, V, 573
muḍāraba (commenda), I, 171 and *passim*; II, 262. *See also* Commenda; *qirāḍ*
muḍarraba (quilted blanket), IV, 316, 380. *See also* Blanket
mudawwin, official, possibly with same function as *ṣāḥib al-dīwān*, II, 610
mudhahhab (with gold threads), IV, 166, 378. *See also* Gold threads
mudhayyal. *See* Hems, ornamental
Muezzin, II, 452
Mufaḍḍal, a scholar and partner in a sugar factory, I, 366
Mufaḍḍal, III, 35
Mufaḍḍal, a supporter of Abraham Maimonides, V, 175, 555
Mufaḍḍal (II) b. Adōnīm, III, 10
Mufaḍḍal b. al-Dimyāṭī al-Kohen, III, 443
Mufaḍḍal I (b. Adōnīm) Ibn Nānū, II, 481–483, 508
Mufaḍḍal Kohen, a tanner, I, 366
Mufaḍḍal of Haifa, a shipowner, I, 311, 476
Mufaddāt, f., III, 85
Mufarraj b. Japheth b. Shuʿayb ha-Durmasqī, II, 553
Mufarrij (a ship), I, 312
mufaṣṣala (intersected with gold beads), IV, 207–208, 424. *See also* Gold
Mufrij b. Mawhūb, III, 491
muftī (scholar authorized to give legal opinion), II, 28, 212, 325, 326, 367, 598; *m. dawlat amīr al-muʾminīn* ("mufti of the realm of the caliph"), II, 406

mughābara fi'l-raḥl ("trying to outdo one another in grabbing the other's possessions"), said of marital disputes, III, 183. *See also* Marriage: disputes in
mughallafa (cases [for shipping]), I, 485. *See also* Packing
mughallif. See Bookbinder
mughlaq, mughallaq (unit that can be locked), IV, 368
mugmār (Heb., aromatic woods burning), IV, 137, 388. *See also* Censer
al-Muhadhdhab, II, 421, 577
muhajjan (description of run-down town), V, 520
muḥallāt (ornamented mirror), IV, 458
Muhammad the Prophet, I, 30, 219; II, 157, 275, 294, 386–387, 579; IV, 151, 431, 432, 467; V, 583, 608
Muḥammad ʿAlī, IV, 416
Muḥammad al-Shāmī, I, 381
Muḥammad b. Ṭāhir, I, 293
muhandis. See Surveyor
muhandiz. See Surveyor
muḥarrar (silk-like), IV, 403. *See also* Silk
muḥimm (affected by fits of fever), II, 448
muhja ("lifeblood"), expression of parental affection, III, 225. *See also* Parents
Muhra ("Filly"), f., II, 119, 545
Muhra house, II, 433, 545
Muḥriz = Shemarya, II, 574
Muḥriz b. Ṭāhōr, II, 494; III, 466
Muḥsin b. Ḥusayn, I, 446; III, 25, 45; V, 355–356
Muḥsin b. Shamʿān, III, 432
muḥtakir (one who leases property), II, 605
muḥtasib (market supervisor), I, 270, 454; II, 355, 369, 371, 587, 608; IV, 40, 238
al-Muʿizz, Fatimid caliph, I, 33, 34, 237; II, 243, 320; III, 357; IV, 352; dirhems of, I, 370
al-Muʿizz b. Bādis of Tunisia, I, 310, 328, 331; II, 24, 286; IV, 438
Muʿizziyya, quarter dinars, I, 459. *See also* Dinar
Mujāhid, ship of, I, 227
mujāmaʿa (weekly salary). *See* Salaries
mujāmala (mutual kindness), I, 441
mujayyirūn. See Stucco-workers
mukallal (studded with pearls), IV, 203, 420. *See also* Pearls
mukammala ("perfect" or "supplemented"), description of jewelry, IV, 425
mukārī. See Muleteer
Mukarram, V, 511
mukawwir (packer), I, 486. *See also* Packing
mukhammas (description of jewelry), IV, 214, 215, 426
mukhfiyāt (type of pottery), I, 111. *See also* Pottery
al-mukhilla ("the woman who behaved improperly"), III, 440
mukhlaf. See Cloak
Mukhtār, a freedman, I, 436
Mukhtār, father of Jabbāra, I, 328
Mukhtār, physician = Ibn Ilyās (Elijah), II, 485
mukḥula. See Kohl jar
mukūs (noncanonical dues and taxes), I, 270. *See also* Customs duties
mulāʾa. See Cloak
mulawwan (fabric of different colors), I, 419; IV, 113, 378, 411
mulayyiṭ (wall plasterer), I, 414, 423
mulāziq (house adjoining a synagogue), II, 152. *See also* House
Mulberry trees, IV, 168
Mule, I, 211, 271, 285; as gift, IV, 262; as status symbol, IV, 264, 266
"Mules," slippers without counter, IV, 163
Muleteer, III, 222; IV, 264–265, 448
mulḥam (cloth of silk warp with woof of another material), I, 418; II, 556; IV, 339, 464
mulḥim (one who weaves a silk warp with woof of another material), I, 104, 418. See also *mulḥam*
Mulūk ("The Queen of the Kings"), f., III, 56
mulūkhiyya (Gr., molokhe). *See* Garden mallow
mumallakati ("my betrothed"), III, 445. *See also* Betrothal; Engagement
mumannī (examiner for ritual killing), II, 570. *See also* Ritual slaughter
mumarrish. See Sprinkler
mumḥe ("expert" or "certified"), often said of cantors, II, 223, 444, 554, 569, 597; III, 488
Munā, a freedwoman, I, 145
Munā, d. of Faraḥ, III, 435
Munā, d. of Samuel b. Nahum and wife of Jekuthiel b. Moses, III, 261, 266; V, 553
Munā the physician, V, 581
munādī (market crier, auctioneer), I, 160, 161, 439; III, 442
Munajjā, I, 365
Munajjā, banker, II, 492
Munajjā b. Ḥātim, II, 482

munajjim(a). *See* Astrologer
munaqqī (cleaner [of slaughtered animals]), **II**, 570. *See also* Ritual slaughter
munāwil (helper), **I**, 94. *See also* Helper
munayyir, **I**, 420
munfalit al-Fayyūm (tax arrears in the Fayyūm district), **II**, 362
Munīr = Mē'ir, rare, **II**, 583
Munjib, a slave, **I**, 436
al-Muntaṣir, Muslim official, **V**, 84, 529
munqaṭiᶜ (confined by illness), i.e., unable to work, **II**, 426, 442, 501; lonely, deserted, **III**, 493
muqaddam (community official), **I**, 465; **II**, 33, 35, 38, 48, 49, 51, 60, 63, 68–75, 76, 79, 82, 85, 89, 90, 122, 161, 208, 257, 258, 308, 314, 405, 426, 467, 528, 529, 534, 535, 537, 538, 572, 593, 595, 600; **III**, 77, 81, 336, 480, 503; judge, **II**, 48, 49, 51, 60, 63. See also *taqaddam*; *taqdima muqaddama*. *See* Bridal trunk
muqaddar (ornamented piece of clothing), **II**, 130, 131, 448, 449, 459, 547; **IV**, 417, 462. See also *muqaddarī*
muqaddarī (maker of *muqaddars*), **II**, 130, 547; **IV**, 387, 462
al-Muqaddasī, **II**, 81, 138, 204, 282, 296; **III**, 323; **IV**, 55, 58, 128, 193, 351, 402
muqaffal ("locked," closed by loops), **IV**, 409
muqaffaṣ. See *mandīl qafaṣ*
muqārib (*kathīr*) (middle quality), **I**, 452
muqarnaṣ. *See* Vault, stalactite
muqashshar (peeled off), waste silk, **I**, 104, 418; **IV**, 402. *See also* Silk
muqashshir (peeler), **I**, 104. See *muqashshar*; Silk
Muqaṭṭam, **IV**, 33
muqāyaḍa (allotment of piece against piece), i.e., divided into equal parts, **II**, 584
muqrī (professional reader of psalms over the dead), **II**, 453. See also *meqōnēn*
murabbaᶜ (hewn stones), **IV**, 376
murabbaᶜa(t) (The Square), **I**, 448; **II**, 532, 582; *m. al-ᶜaṭṭārīn* (Square of the Perfumers), **I**, 448; **II**, 263 (*see also* Square of the Perfumers); *m. al-ṣarf* (*see* Square of the Money Changers)
al-Murābiṭūn. *See* Almoravids
murahhiṭ (writer or singer of liturgical poetry), **II**, 87, 224, 541, 570. *See also* Poetry, liturgical
murājaᶜa ("retaking"), i.e., remarriage, **III**, 487. *See also* Remarriage
Murals, **II**, 150
murattabayn (payments), **I**, 425
murayyash, *murāyash* ("with feathers") i.e., fringes, **IV**, 331, 378, 459. *See also* Fringes; *sakākīn*; Tassels
Murder, **II**, 37; **III**, 80–81
mūrid (supplier of metal to the mint), **I**, 267, 365, 466; **II**, 479, 480, 505
murtadd (renegade), **II**, 591
murtafaq (convenience), i.e., bathroom, **IV**, 367. *See also* Bathroom
murtafiᶜ (first quality), **I**, 452
muruwwa (virtue), **III**, 153, 167, 241; **V**, 191-193
Mūsā, *ṣayrafī*, factotum of Ibn ᶜAwkal, **II**, 474
Mūsā b. Abi'l-Ḥayy, **I**, 228–229, 379, 439, 447, 457; **II**, 445, 587; **III**, 31, 43; **IV**, 355; **V**, 145, 157, 540, 545, 570
Mūsā b. Abi'l-Khayr, **V**, 573
Mūsā b. Bishr, **I**, 363
Mūsā b. Faraj, **V**, 169
Mūsā b. Isaac b. Nissīm *al-ᶜābid* ("Devout," a family name), **V**, 538
Mūsā b. Jekuthiel, the Andalusian, **III**, 207, 208, 470
Mūsā b. Joseph, the Red, **I**, 286
Mūsā b. Khalaf, **III**, 434
Mūsā b. Musallam, silk weaver, **V**, 169, 553
Mūsā b. Yaᶜqūb. *See* Moses b. Jacob
Mūsā Ibn al-Majjānī. *See* Moses Ibn al-Majjānī
Mūsā Tāhertī, **I**, 444
al-Musabbiḥī, **IV**, 240
muṣādara (requisition), i.e., confiscation, **II**, 393, 612
muṣaffī. See *ṣāfī*
Musāfir, *parnās* (b. Wahb?), **II**, 434
Musāfir b. Samuel, **III**, 280, 287, 491
Musāfir b. Simḥā, **III**, 439
Musāfir b. Wahb, **II**, 586, 587; **V**, 603
musāfir ("leaving"), remark in list of beneficiaries, **II**, 457
muṣālaḥa (settlement), **II**, 428, 546, 601
muṣallab (transverse), description of silk threads, **IV**, 402. *See also* Silk threads
musallakh. *See* Deferment
Musallam, a messianic name, **V**, 613. *See also* Meshullām
Musallam b. Barakāt b. Isḥāq, **V**, 378
Musallam the embroiderer, **II**, 499
Musallam b. Mu'ammal, **II**, 454
Musallam Ibn al-Naᶜja, **V**, 590
musallayāt = *muṣallayāt* (prayer carpets), **I**, 419
musāmaḥa (reduction of rent), **II**, 428
Muṣāṣa. *See* Mamṣūṣa

musawwagh (allowance from community chest), **II**, 548
Musaykīn ("little pauper"), nickname, **II**, 506
Museums, **IV**, 133, 137, 145, 201; Coptic tapestries in, **IV**, 121; Islamic Art of Cairo, **IV**, 120, 141; Metropolitan, New York, **IV**, 210; Royal Ontario, **IV**, 118
mushabbak (lattice work). *See* Filigree
mushaliyya (ward of dysentery), **II**, 578
mushammasa ("exposed to the sun"), said of dirhems, **I**, 373
mushāqa (scrap of flax), **I**, 418. *See also* Flax
mushārif. *See* Tax assayers and collectors
mushāṭara (form of partnership), **I**, 124, 428. *See also* Partnership
mushrif (supervisor), **III**, 492. See also *mushārif*
mushtaghil maʿa ("studied with"), **II**, 564
Music (*laʿb*), **II**, 107, 161, 219, 578; **V**, 22, 41–42, 157, 284, 516
Musicians, **II**, 467, 505, 506
Musk, **I**, 153, 154, 219, 337; **IV**, 316, 430, 457; "reddish-brown," **IV**, 176, 182
"Musk," slave girl, **I**, 137, 139, 140, 434, 435
Muslim(s), relations of Jews with, mentioned *passim*; business, **V**, 4; drinking, **V**, 39–40; friendship, **V**, 4, 20, 447–448; living, **V**, 6, 270–272; religious, **V**, 9, 430; scholarly, **V**, 430, 443–448; symbiosis with Jews and Christians, **II**, 589-591. *See also* Islam
(*fiʾl*)-*muslimīn* ("before a Muslim authority"), **II**, 400
muṣmat (plain, unpatterned), description of textile, **I**, 419; **IV**, 117, 333, 424, 460
mustaḥamm (bathroom), **IV**, 367. *See also* Bathroom
al-Mustaʿīn, Abbasid caliph, **IV**, 161
mustakhdam (service room, pantry), **IV**, 71, 368. *See also* Domestic architecture
mustaʿmal (person employed in government workshop), **II**, 483, 612
mustaʿmala (made-to-order), **IV**, 411
mustaʿmil kattān (government agent charged with sale of flax), **I**, 243. *See also* Flax
mustamlī (one who dictates lecturers words to students, broadcaster), **II**, 562
Mustanṣir, Fatimid caliph, **I**, 235, 237, 269, 373; **II**, 16, 72, 351, 377, 512, 606; **III**, 56, 357; **IV**, 130, 448; **V**, 104. *See also* Dinar: Maʿadd
Mustanṣiriyya: dinars (*see* Dinar); description of a bridal trunk, **IV**, 130
mustaqarr (agreed practice), **II**, 571
mustarāḥ (restroom), **IV**, 367. *See also* Bathroom
mustaraqa. *See* Loggia
al-mutaʾakhkhar min al-pesīqā (appendix to the pledges), **II**, 502. *See also* Pledges
al-Muʿtamid, governor, **II**, 604
al-Muʿtamid passage (*khawkha*), **IV**, 281
al-Mutanabbī, poet, **V**, 425, 556
mutaqabbil (term for tax farmer), **II**, 358, 605; *m. al-dabāgha* (tax farmer of taxes on tanning), **II**, 605. *See also* Tax farmers
muṭarrī (seller of flavored waters), **I**, 115, 424
mutasawwiq (purveyor), **II**, 490
al-Muʿtaṣim, Abbasid caliph, **IV**, 145
muʿtaṣimī (tray on which food served, called after Abbasid caliph al-Muʿtasim), **IV**, 145
mutaṭabbib (medical practitioner [not used pejoratively]), **II**, 246, 577
al-Mutawakkil, Abbasid caliph, **II**, 177, 557; **IV**, 194, 195, 416
mutawallī (administrator [of charitable foundations]), **II**, 421, 426, 605, 606, 608, 609; *m. dār al-ḍarb* (director of the mint), **I**, 375; **II**, 605; *m. istiʿmāl* (officer recruiting craftsmen for government textile factories), **I**, 82; *m. al-jawālī* (officer in charge of poll tax), **II**, 606; *m. al-maʿūna* (chief of police), **II**, 608, 609; *m. al-sikka* (director of coinage, i.e., mint), **II**, 605
muṭāyar (textile decorated with figures of birds), **IV**, 378
al-Muṭaylib, **I**, 278, 283, 284
muṭayyab (scented with *ṭīb*), **IV**, 138, 410
Muʿtazz, Abbasid caliph, **I**, 436
Muʿtazz, a freedwoman, **I**, 145
muthallath. *See* "Triple-thread"
muthaqqaba (pierced), said of quarter dinars, **I**, 237, 459
muṭraf (adorned with borders of color different from main piece of cloth), description of a textile, **IV**, 154, 396, 462
Mutton, **II**, 228; **IV**, 231, 249
Mutual services. *See* Informal cooperation
Muwaffaq, a freedman, **I**, 145
al-Muwaffaq, **II**, 495, 577
al-Muwaffaq Nūr al-Dawla, **I**, 283
al-muwaḥḥidūn. *See* Almohads

muwallad ("crossbred" wine), IV, 259
muwallada (girl born in slavery), I, 138. *See also* Slavegirls
muwāqafa = *muwāfaqa* (agreement, i.e., the sum agreed upon), weekly emolument, I, 422
muwashshā (textile embellished by lively colors, gold sewn on garments), IV, 458
muwashshaḥ: form of poetry, II, 594; ornamental stripes, description of textile, IV, 378
muwāyama (daily account or journal), I, 207, 451
al-Muzaghlīl ("the Dazzler"), II, 492
muzanjir = *mujanzir*, I, 420
muzāriᶜ (peasant), I, 410, 418
muzarra. *See* Dressing gown
muzawwiq (painter, mosaicist), I, 113, 423; II, 467. *See also* Painters
muzayyin (decorator). *See* Stucco-worker
al-mūzī (banana grower), I, 427
Myrobalan (*amlaj*, *halaylaj*, *ihlīlaj*), I, 337; II, 267, 268, 464, 583; III, 491; IV, 209, 217
Myrtle pins (*marsīn*, *marasīn*), pins with handles imitating flowers or leaves of myrtles, IV, 209, 423
Myrtles, import of, I, 385; II, 452
Mystical allegory, II, 62
Mysticism, Islamic. *See* Sufism

N

Nabāt, II, 174
nabbādhūn. *See* Wine, winesellers
nabīdh. *See* Wine
Nabīla ("The Noble One"), f., III, 45
nabq. *See* Ziziphus tree
Nadd, slave girl, I, 435
Nadīv b. Isaac, III, 485
nafaqa. *See* Living expenses
nafḍ al-sunnāᶜ, I, 418
naffāṭ (processor or seller of petroleum), I, 85. *See also* Naphtha
Nafīs (al-Dawla), title, II, 376, 609
Nafīsa b. Kathīr, III, 501
naft. *See* Naphtha
Nafūsa, Libya, II, 559
Nagid, I, xvii, 332, 423, 465; II, 55, 56, 59, 90, 155, 164, 183, 190, 239, 307, 493, 537, 540, 544, 563, 565, 566, 613; III, 3, 19, 137, 211, 225, 228, 229, 263, 273, 284, 386, 426, 428, 430, 443, 445, 467, 478; IV, 281; V, 23; administration of community chest, II, 99, 103, 109, 423, 461, 462, 485, 492; and charity, I, 204; II, 107, 109, 227, 486, 487, 488, 494, 495, 500, 502, 506; III, 305; coercive power, II, 35; general description, II, 23–40, 524–530; grievances submitted to, I, 85; II, 153, 561; III, 247, 258, 259, 296, 307; judicial authority, II, 33–34, 310, 323, 331, 403; III, 76, 80, 100, 132, 148, 247, 262, 269; overseeing inheritance, I, 91; pronouncing ban, I, 69; II, 331, 333, 485; ransoming captives, I, 329; relationship to Muslim government, II, 37–40, 374, 391; III, 76, 204; rivals, II, 64, 89, 535; role as peacemaker, I, 85; II, 35–36, 168; scope of authority, II, 62, 64, 70, 76, 223, 316, 546, 568; III, 148, 258, 262; V, 488-491; significance of title, II, 23–27, 244; study of sacred writings, II, 36, 158. *See also* Head of the Jews; *shaykh al-yahūd*
naḥās. *See* Copper
nahb (pillage), III, 81
nahḍa (vigor), V, 119–120, 242
al-Naḥḥāl (Beekeeper), Kohen, II, 453
naḥḥāl. *See* Beekeeper
nāḥiya. *See* Quarter of a city
naḥmilhā yad wāḥida ("We shall shoulder it with united forces"), i.e., payments for communal expenses in equal shares, II, 99
Nahrawāra, Gujerāt, IV, 129, 171, 377
Nahray b. Abū Najm, V, 599
Nahray b. ᶜAllān, V, 540, 575, 576
Nahray b. Nathan, III, 30, 461, 476
Nahray b. Nissīm, I, 159, 278, 285, 293, 294, 309; II, 270, 298, 326, 508, 583; III, 17, 288, 460; IV, 43, 66, 119, 182, 257, 306, 374, 401, 411; V, 523, 536, 537, 573, 586, 591; biographical details and family relations, I, 181, 444; III, 37, 116, 177, 235, 239, 461, 476; IV, 42; V, 111; business activities, I, 153–155, 156, 158, 172, 221, 232, 238, 239, 240, 242, 245, 247–248, 372, 374, 378, 379, 467; II, 294; IV, 26, 168, 170, 179, 181, 206, 241, 384, 399, 400, 404, 405, 407, 410, 412, 414; documents of, I, 195, 372, 378, 387, 388, 389; IV, 355, 381, 399, 400, 404, 407, 410, 412; V, 572; houses in Fustat and elsewhere, I, 61; III, 116; IV, 19, 91, 95, 287; identity as Maghrebī, I, 63; IV, 44; leadership, II, 332, 405, 504; III, 468; V, 127, 273; letters to, I, 8, 232, 238, 304, 318, 378, 440, 462, 473; II, 239, 586; III, 273, 426, 439, 484, 490, 503; IV, 129, 239, 241, 373, 384,

398, 402; V, 32, 46, 108, 111, 240, 309, 327, 411, 418, 508, 539, 540, 541, 562, 564, 571, 596, 602; representative of merchants, I, 189; as scholar and jurisconsult, I, 54, 240; II, 214, 217, 269, 325, 338, 441, 442, 476, 565, 584, 597; V, 209, 280, 419, 443, 572, 578; use of Star of David, I, 337; II, 551; IV, 199, 418; wives, I, 48, 137; III, 30–31, 161, 166, 273; V, 309
Naḥrīr ("Skilled") b. Mawhūb, V, 553
Naḥshōn b. Ṣādōq of Sura, II, 521, 522
(be-)naḥshā ṭāvā (Aram., good omen), III, 448
Nahum b. Faraḥ, III, 435
Nahum b. Joseph Baradānī, III, 300
nā'ib (deputy): judge, I, 118, 280; II, 70, 316, 359, 368, 596, 605, 610 (*see also* Deputy judges); *n. al-nāẓir* (assistant director of finance), I, 466; tax-farmer, I, 118; II, 359, 596, 605
Nā'ila, wife of the caliph Othmān, IV, 154
Naᶜīm b. Benjamin, beadle, II, 416
Najā' b. al-Ḥusayn al-Anṣārī, I, 292-293
Najā' b. Ṭāhir, I, 293
Najera, Spain, II, 95, 542
Najīb, a freedman, I, 436
al-Najīb, *parnās*, II, 459
al-Najīb, sheikh, V, 306-307
Najīb al-Maᶜtūq, II, 505
Nājiya ("The Sacred One"), f., III, 181, 327, 329; V, 542
Nājiya, wife of Japheth b. Abraham, IV, 287
Nājiya bint Sulaymān b. Hiba, III, 434
najjār al-aghlāq (lock carpenter), I, 421
Najm al-Dawla Ibn Kammūna, III, 13
Najmiyya, f., V, 570
"Naked," without proper clothing, IV, 153; V, 524
nakhkh (oblong rugs). *See* Rugs
nakhkhāṣ = *nakhkhās* (slave merchant), I, 452. *See also* Slaves
nākhodā (Per., shipowner), I, 48, 479; II, 489. *See also* Shipowners
nākhudā. See *nākhodā*
nakhwa (high-mindedness), V, 193-194
naᶜma (comfort), synonym for *ᶜāfiya*, V, 518
namaṭ (pl. *anmāṭ*), IV, 124, 125. *See also* Carpets
Names, I, 49, 357–358; II, 413, 429, 431, 433; III, 6–14, 63–64; V, 396-397; absence of Biblical and Hebrew names among women, III, 315; characteristic Jewish, II, 464, 505; common to men and women, III, 318; of children, III, 6–8, 233, 235; of women, III, 314–319, 497-499; ruler's on clothing, IV, 413 (*see also* Tiraz); spelling of, II, 237; transcription of, I, xvii–xviii
Nāmūs, II, 454
Nānū, children's word and family name, II, 490, 508
Nānū-Adōnīm family, III, 10–11
Naomi (biblical), III, 172
Naphtha, I, 85, 154
Napoleon, I, 37; IV, 61
naqāniq (sausage), I, 115
naqd. *See* Legal tender
naqda (currency), I, 465. *See also* Legal tender; Money
naqī (fine flour), I, 423
nāqid (possibly used in same sense as *naqqād*), I, 462
naqliyyīn (vendors of dried fruit), I, 410, 427. *See also* Dried fruit
naqqād. *See* Money assayer
naqqāḍ (unraveler of silk), I, 104, 418. See also *manqūḍ*; Silk
Narbonne, France, I, 40, 65; II, 260; IV, 1
narjisiyya (narcissus-like vessel), IV, 150, 337, 395, 464
al-nās (population, people, public), II, 277, 586
Nasab ("Nobility"), f., III, 278
naṣārā (Christian), II, 586. See also *ᶜārēl*; Christian; *naṣrānī*
nashīlī (preparer of boiled unseasoned meat), I, 424
Nashū, maidservant, V, 542
nashūsh (bushes), IV, 376
nāsī (Heb., "princes" [of the House of David]), title referring to exilarchs, II, 19, 30, 32, 88, 168, 318, 332, 353, 418, 420, 436, 453, 458, 459,492, 508, 523, 527, 528, 529, 530, 548, 565, 595, 596, 603, 615; III, 135, 351, 450. *See also* Head of the Diaspora
nāsikh. *See* Copyists
nāsikha (f.). *See* Copyists
Nāṣir ("helper"), common Jewish name, II, 464, 496, 497
al-Nāṣir, caliph, II, 527
al-Nāṣir, the Ḥammādite, I, 377
Nāṣir b. al-ᶜAfīf, II, 497. *See also* Menaḥēm b. al-ᶜAfīf
Naṣīr al-Dawla b. Ḥamdān, I, 310; II, 347; IV, 447
Naṣīr al-Dīn, II, 386
Nāṣir-i-Khosraw, IV, 54, 55, 58, 91, 95, 373

Nāṣirī *qīrāṭs*, **II**, 487, 488. *See also* Money of account
Nāṣiriyya dirhems. *See* Dirhem
Naṣr, freedman, **I**, 436
Naṣr Allāh, common Jewish name, **II**, 464, 505
naṣrānī (Christian), **II**, 278. See also *ʿārēl*; Christian
nassāja (female weaver), **II**, 459
naʿt (totality of honorary titles possessed by a person), **V**, 530. *See also* Honorific titles
Nathan, Hebrew name meaning "gift," **II**, 24. *See also* ʿAṭāʾ
Nathan b. Abraham Gaon, **II**, 16, 318, 405, 536, 562; **III**, 25, 327, 475–476; **V**, 100
Nathan (II) b. Abraham (II), **II**, 597
Nathan b. Judah, **V**, 515, 556, 591
Nathan b. Nahray, **I**, 473; **III**, 235, 474, 476; **V**, 586
Nathan b. Samuel *he-ḥaver*, court clerk and judge, **I**, 364, 365, 442, 464, 466; **II**, 113, 137, 251, 416, 422, 513, 566, 567, 572, 574; **III**, 99, 133, 137, 169, 215, 221, 274, 297, 334, 385–387, 458, 463, 473, 483, 487, 489, 493, 495, 501–502; **IV**, 22, 289, 311, 313, 322, 328, 352, 353, 369, 429, 450; **V**, 122, 139–140, 147–148, 153, 164, 236, 294, 329–330, 420, 455, 539, 544, 546, 547, 552, 573, 580, 625; wife, **V**, 554
Nathan b. Solomon b. Sāʾir (Yāʾīr), the cantor, **II**, 526, 538
Nathan b. Solomon ha-Kohen, judge, **I**, 363, 425; **II**, 423, 513, 566, 567, 572, 599; **III**, 30, 154, 196, 444, 445, 459, 466, 467, 481, 504; **IV**, 232, 259, 408; **V**, 106, 122, 164, 516, 532
Nathan b. Yehiel, **V**, 596
Nathan b. Yeshūʿā ha-Levi, judge, **II**, 511, 566
Nathan Ephraim, **II**, 497
Nathan ha-Bavli, **II**, 513
Nathan ha-Kohen b. Mevōrākh of Ascalon, **II**, 522–523, 541, 569; **III**, 481
Nathan ha-Kohen b. Solomon. *See* Nathan b. Solomon ha-Kohen
Nathan-Hiba ha-Levi b. Ḥakam b. Joseph Ibn al-Shumaym, **III**, 482
Nathan "the Diadem" (*Nezer*), "Scribe of the Yeshiva." *See* Nathan b. Samuel *he-ḥāvēr*
nathr. See Pearls
naṭif (concoction of certain plant with wine and sugar), **I**, 431
naṭifāniyya (maker of *naṭif*), **I**, 431
Naṭrōnay Gaon, **II**, 522; **V**, 608
nāṭūr = *shōmēr* (guard or supervisor), **II**, 570
Navy, **I**, 313
nawāʾib. See Burial expenses
nawba (repeated performance), i.e., lecture, **II**, 561
nayrūz (New Year Feast), **II**, 425
Naẓar ("Control, Competence"), various women named, **II**, 419; **III**, 136
Naẓar b. Dāʾūd, f., **V**, 539
nāẓir (superintendent), **I**, 59, 313; **II**, 366, 377, 610
nāzīr (Heb., devotee), **II**, 451, 461
nazīra (Heb., holy woman), **II**, 429; **III**, 506
Nazirite(s), **III**, 352–353
nazl. See House, billeting in
naẓẓām (stringer of beads), **I**, 416
Near East(ern), **II**, 2, 197, 285; **IV**, 2, 3, 5, 112, 142, 161, 187, 228, 229, 234, 244. *See also* Middle East(ern)
Necklace, **IV**, 216–217; *ʿiqd*, **IV**, 217; *lāzam*, **IV**, 203, 217, 329, 427, 458; *miḥbas*, **IV**, 203, 207, 210, 216–217; *qilāda*, **IV**, 218, 421, 427, 467. *See also* Choker
Necromancy, **II**, 332
nedāvā (donation), **II**, 498
nēder. See Vows
nedunyā (Heb.-Aram., dowry), **III**, 123, 124, 140, 453. *See also* Dowry
Needlework, **III**, 145, 236, 342; **IV**, 399, 401; **V**, 219, 568
Needy. *See* Poor
neʾemān (Heb.): trustee, **II**, 539, 540; **V**, 32; *n. bēth-din* (trustee of the court), **II**, 80; *n. ha-sōḥarīm* (trustee of the merchants), **I**, 446
negīd ha-gōlā (Heb., "Prince of the Diaspora" = Nagid), **II**, 524, 525; **III**, 108; *n. yisrāʾēl* ("Prince of Israel" = Nagid) **II**, 525. *See also* Nagid
Negro(es), **I**, 131, 135, 137; troops, 31; **II**, 379
Nehemiah, biblical, **V**, 607
Nehemiah b. Kohen Ṣedeq, **II**, 521
Nemoy, Leon, **V**, 360
Neo-Babylonian law, **II**, 519
Nesībīn (Nusaybin), **II**, 523; **III**, 260
Nestorian(s), **III**, 95. *See also* Christians
Nethanel b. Amram, **IV**, 408; **V**, 592
Nethanel b. Ḥalfōn, **II**, 498, 499
Nethanel b. Japheth, **II**, 478
Nethanel b. Joseph, known as Abū Saʿd the Glassmaker, **I**, 363, 364
Nethanel b. Mevōrākh, **V**, 423

Nethanel b. Moses "the Sixth." *See* Nethanel b. Moses ha-Levi, Gaon
Nethanel b. Tiqvā, I, 363
Nethanel b. Moses ha-Levi, Gaon, I, 396; II, 18, 26, 32, 33, 116, 244, 247, 417, 513-514, 521, 524, 528, 550, 602; III, 439; IV, 313; V, 426-432, 443, 444, 491, 542, 628
Nethanel-Hibat Allāh b. Yeshūʿā of Jerusalem, I, 357, 363
Nethanel ha-Levi b. Amram, II, 539; V, 315-316, 592
Nethanel ha-Levi b. Moses. *See* Nethanel b. Moses ha-Levi, Gaon
netīvōt (Heb., "guidelines" [for succession in the yeshiva]), II, 522
Neubauer, Adolf, I, 396
Neumes, Lombardic (musical notation), II, 159, 593
Neustadt, David. *See* Ayalon, David
New Moon day, V, 43, 97-98
News and information, in letters: bad, V, 46-48, 113, 115; importance of, V, 49-50, 53-54
New Testament, II, 7, 41, 176, 196, 312, 363
New Year: Jewish, II, 464, 569; III, 235; IV, 156, 231; V, 350, 351; Muslim: I, 255
New York, library in, II, 18
nēzer (Heb., "Diadem"), title of a judge, I, 414, 442; II, 513; *n. ha-maskīlīm* ("Diadem of the Enlightened"), II, 513
nezīrā (woman teetotaller), V, 43
Nicknames, II, 426, 454, 463, 479, 504, 506. *See also* Family names
niddūy. *See* Excommunication
Niece, marriage with, III, 26, 432-433
Niello (*mujrā* [*bi-*]*sawād*), II, 151; IV, 124, 139, 209, 212-213, 220, 221, 319, 322, 329, 425, 429, 453, 458
Night covers. *See* Blanket
Night watchman (*ṭawwāf*, *meshōṭeṭē layla*), II, 86, 117, 123, 425, 427, 429, 430, 432, 464, 467, 540, 610; III, 61, 92; IV, 35
Nihāwand, I, 400
nīl. *See* Indigo
Nile, I, 7, 20, 27, 244, 284, 295-301, 305, 332; IV, 12, 34, 54, 56, 57, 63, 76, 124, 142, 235, 253, 431, 434
Nile bank house, IV, 58
Nile boat (*sumayriyya*, *ʿushārī*), I, 295, 305, 309, 320, 322, 345
nīlī (indigo merchant), I, 155. *See also* Indigo
Ninth of Av, fast, II, 484, 537, 602; V, 569
niqāʾat al-khawāṣir (cleaning of the thigh of an animal), II, 570
niqāb: face cover, IV, 320, 323, 327, 330, 454 (*see also* Veil); hood attached to burnoose, IV, 463
niqār fiḍḍa, I, 458. *See also* Dirhem
niṣf fiḍḍa. *See* Dirhem
niṣfiyya (half garment, cape), IV, 182
Nīshāpūr (Nīsābūr), I, 400
Nishmat, ancient hymn, II, 551
nishtewān (official letter), II, 522
Nisibis, I, 233; II, 524
Nissīm, common name of N. African Jews, V, 519
Nissīm, recipient of charity, II, 460
Nissīm, Tunisian trader, V, 50-51
Nissīm b. Benāyā, I, 444
Nissīm b. Berachiah, III, 474; V, 565
Nissīm b. Ḥalfōn b. Benāyā, IV, 406, 407
Nissīm b. Isḥāq, V, 280
Nissīm b. Isḥāq Tāhertī, III, 433; V, 599
Nissīm b. Jacob Ibn Shāhīn of Qayrawān, I, 48, 287; II, 203, 210; V, 53, 144, 209, 283, 293, 316, 392, 518, 520, 537, 557, 588, 598, 616
Nissīm b. Nahray b. Nissīm, II, 326, 513; V, 212-213, 540
Nissīm b. Nathan, III, 474
Nissī b. Samuel, II, 538
nissūʾīn (Heb., "taking"), term for consummation of marriage, III, 441. *See also* Marriage, consummation of
Niẓām al-Mulk, Seljuk vizier, II, 362; V, 261, 269, 581
Nizār, Fatimid, II, 350
Nizārī dinars. *See* Dinar
Nizāriyya. *See* Dirhem
Noah (biblical), II, 225; IV, 442
Nō Ammōn (Heb. for Alexandria), III, 67
Nobel, R. Nehemiah, V, 595
Noble families, III, 3, 4, 14, 103, 135-137
Nöldeke, Theodor, V, 598
nomos (Gr., laws), II, 327
Non-paying tenants. *See* Free lodging
Normans, I, 29, 32, 39, 41, 98, 235, 237, 240, 259, 308, 330, 417; II, 68, 192; III, 55, 117, 177
North Africa(n), I, 22, 34, 330 331; II, 89, 120, 124, 193, 239, 275, 298, 339; III, 89, 339; IV, 3, 426; Almohad invasion of, I, 41; Arab conquest of, I, 30; caravan route, III, 298; climate, I, 17;

cloth production in, I, 50; collections for Jerusalem academy, I, 65; family names, IV, 170; Fatimid conquest of, I, 32; Ibn Killis in, I, 34; jewelry, IV, 426; letters from, I, 56, 304; III, 193, 239, 275; mail service, I, 284, 285, 291, 304; Mālikī law in, I, 67; marriage documents from, III, 120, 124; observation points, I, 320; religious character of, IV, 3; responsa sent to, I, 22. *See also* Maghreb
Notables, II, 2, 42, 77, 291, 465, 466, 472, 481, 485, 494, 499, 507, 532, 535, 537, 554, 563, 578
Notary, I, 179, 188, 251, 254, 256, 385, 443; II, 50, 86, 125, 172, 230, 257, 320, 321, 336, 343, 367, 368, 531, 539, 540, 555, 579, 597; IV, 18, 32, 39, 40, 49, 58, 61, 64, 71, 90
Notebooks of judges, I, 9 and *passim*
"Nougat," a girl, III, 76
Nubia(n), I, 135, 136, 137, 434
nufkhatayn ("two protuberances"), description of niello work, II, 552
Nujūm, slave girl, I, 144; V, 547
al-Nuʿmān, family of Muslim judges, II, 320, 596
Numbers, ominous nature of, V, 119
al-Numruqī, the Maker of Saddle Pads, I, 293, 472
Nuptial gift. *See* Marriage gift
nuqāniqā (sausage makers), I, 424
nuqra, pure silver coin. *See* Dirhem
Nūr al-Dīn b. Alkyn, V, 175–176
Nūr al-Dīn Zenjī, I, 36; II, 48, 251, 578
Nursing, III, 233, 255
Nuṣayr b. Thābit, II, 442
nushādir. *See* Sal ammoniac
nushādirī. *See* Sal ammoniac, seller of
nushārī. *See* Sawduster
nūtī (mariner), I, 313, 480
Nutmeg, I, 253, 337, 463
nuwwāb. See *nāʾib*
nuẓẓār. *See* Detectives

O

Oak green (*ubābī*), IV, 407
Oases, Egyptian, V, 575
Oaths, II, 156, 340, 402, 601, 602, 614; IV, 453; imposed on widow, III, 252, 254–255, 256, 257, 284, 285; imposed on wife, III, 67, 91, 105, 190, 223; IV, 318; of partners, I, 172, 178; of repudiation, III, 156
Obadiah, Amīn al-dawla thiqat al-mulk, V, 582
Obadiah, Norman proselyte, II, 593, 594; IV, 416
Obadiah b. Abraham Maimonides, V, 495
Obadiah, great-grandson of Abraham Maimonides, II, 435, 496, 605
Obadiah-ʿAbdallāh b. Meshullām of Tyre, I, 357, 362
Obadiah b. Benayahu, II, 499
Obadiah Bertinoro, V, 509
Obadiah Scroll, II, 593
Obadyah. *See* Obadiah
Obesity disdained, IV, 229
Occupational shifts, I, 79–80
Oculists (*kaḥḥāl*), I, 97; II, 255, 256, 257, 346, 491, 579, 603; III, 10, 13; IV, 16, 463; female (*kaḥaḥāla*), I, 430
Odoriferous woods, I, 44, 155
Officials of the Community, II, 68–92, 117, 121
Oil, I, 76, 83, 120, 165, 195, 200, 223, 334, 361; II, 101, 117, 150, 294, 431, 462; IV, 142, 143; hot, IV, 233, 434; for the house, III, 191; lamp, II, 551; linseed, I, 120, 151, 152; olive, I, 120, 152, 153, 154, 212, 268, 272, 344, 380; II, 480, 492; IV, 252–253, 440; sesame, I, 120, 153 (*see also* Sesame oil)
Oil cruse (*kūz zayt*), IV, 142–143, 444
Oil House, II, 433, 545
Oil-makers, II, 491
Oil press, I, 92; IV, 355. *See also* Perfume
Ointment jars, IV, 226, 431
Ointments, V, 100
Old age, II, 105; IV, 372; V, 116–128, 239–240. *See also* Death
Old Cairo (Fustat), mentioned *passim*
Old Spinnery, The, IV, 13, 79
Old Testament. *See* Bible
"Olive" (*zatūna*), small measurement for wine, IV, 259, 446
Olive green, IV, 182
Oliver(?), a proselyte, II, 305
Omar, caliph, IV, 18
(*hā-*) *ʿōmedīm* (Heb., those in charge of), II, 416, 541, 543
Onions, IV, 230, 233, 245, 434
Onyxes, I, 154
Openwork (*mukharrama*), IV, 423
Ophthalmologist. *See* Oculist
Opium, II, 262, 270
oqonomīn (pl. of Gr. *oikonomos*, manager), II, 541
Orange(s), bitter (*nāranj*), IV, 232, 435; color, IV, 125, 175, 383
Orchards, II, 115, 416, 422, 423, 426, 427, 607; IV, 370

Orders of payment, I, 240–242 and *passim*
Orders to shopkeepers, I, 151
Oria, Italy, II, 199, 242
Ornaments. *See* Jewelry
Ornaments of the Torah scroll, II, 151
Orphanages, Muslim, III, 304
Orphans, I, 265, 373; II, 24, 212, 216, 292, 293, 312, 383, 395, 396, 429, 442, 447, 449, 456, 465, 515, 546, 548, 602, 615; III, 44, 58, 63, 73, 77, 80, 86, 89, 92, 94, 103, 105, 119, 121, 130, 131, 145, 184, 187, 217, 235, 241, 249, 255, 257, 258, 273, 277–282, 289, 291, 292–312, 344, 364, 365, 442, 444, 452, 488-496; IV, 170, 190; arrangements at remarriage, III, 309–311; books for, II, 134, 181; care of, III, 307–308, 312; coming of age, I, 181; III, 299; education of, II, 117, 133, 186, 187, 436, 451, 465, 556; III, 305; girls, I, 379; II, 134, 135, 184, 324, 425, 465, 500, 521, 548; maintenance of, I, 391, 430; II, 38, 104; III, 299–302; marriage of, III, 306–308; misery of, III, 306, 312; property of, I, 296-297, 301; IV, 277; proxy of, III, 295; real estate of, I, 193; III, 298-299; IV, 373; residence of, III, 303–304; special classes for, II, 133; supervision of affairs by courts, I, 255; II, 81, 103; III, 294, 299; working, III, 303, 306
"Orphans whose parents are still alive," III, 302
Otherworldliness, IV, 24
Othman, caliph, IV, 18, 154, 396, 397
Ottoman(s), I, 19; II, 121, 142, 167; III, 113; IV, 31, 46, 55, 415
Outerwear, IV, 152–153, 155, 156, 157; with fringes, mark of rank, IV, 196-198. *See also* Clothing
Overland travel, I, 275–281, and *passim*
Overseas marriages, III, 340
Overseas relations, III, 56, 190
Overseas traders, IV, 41, 45, 184
Overseer, I, 95, 97
Oxford, III, 12
Oxford colloquium, 1965, IV, 4
Oxtongue, II, 583
Oxus river, IV, 420
Oxymel, IV, 248, 261, 442, 447. *See also* Honey and vinegar
Oyster-gatherers, I, 92; II, 62

P

pā (Per., foot), I, 284
Packers, I, 95, 97, 486; II, 452, 467
Packing, I, 332–339, 486
Pad (*barda*ʿ*a*), IV, 115, 304, 316, 321, 380, 452
Pagans, II, 279
Paine, Thomas, V, 205
Painters, I, 84, 411. See also *muzawwiq*
Palermo, Sicily, II, 525, 535, 595; III, 504; IV, 182; attitude toward teachers in, II, 190; coins, I, 232; contact with eastern Mediterranean, I, 42; contributors (to poor) from, II, 476; conversion of Jewish cantor to Islam in, II, 300; council of elders, II, 59; diferent names found in Geniza for, IV, 6, 349, 402, 412; fees paid for commercial documents in, II, 230; interfaith relations in, II, 294, 300; Jewish judges in, I, 52; II, 217, 315, 322; III, 300, 447; Jewish notables rep. community to govt., II, 60; letters from, I, 49, 374, 377; II, 24, 41, 60, 191, 530; III, 246, 442; IV, 39, 184; letters to, I, 304; III, 241; *madīnī* as term for citizen of, IV, 349; marriage of man from, in Egypt, III, 73; prices in, I, 218, 226, 375; IV, 86; rep. of merchants in, I, 374; III, 339, 442; IV, 410; secret police of, II, 371, 608; ships sailing to and from, I, 215, 314, 315, 322, 324, 325, 326; silk exported from, I, 102, 198, 417; IV, 168, 184, 193, 416; tax-farmer (*ṣāḥib al-sūq*) in, I, 194, 448; trade/merchants in, I, 45, 68, 119, 198, 200, 212, 215, 218, 274, 302, 374, 375, 377; II, 294, 322; III, 73, 339, 442; IV, 184, 410, 412; travel for pleasure in, I, 274; III, 241; traveler stranded in, I, 314; trousseau lists from, IV, 117, 130
Palestine, I, 202, 210, 301, 376; II, 84, 536, 588, 595; III, 21, 154, 197, 345, 469; IV, 2, 200, 380; agriculture, I, 119, 121; III, 322; IV, 231; attacks of Genoese fleets on, I, 45, 59; Berbers in, III, 498; cantors from, II, 106, 442; capital city of, IV, 7, 8; cheese industry in, I, 124; climate, I, 17; compared with Babylonia, II, 519; Crusaders in, I, 35, 45, 57, 132, 180, 281; II, 137, 169, 170, 501, 549; earthquake of 1034 in, II, 155; eleventh-century crises in, II, 96; IV, 413; fashion style of, I, 106; IV, 176; food in, IV, 433; Gaons of, II, 14, 26, 30, 31, 55, 200, 226, 341, 405; III, 426; IV, 413; honey and wax industries in, I, 125; immigrants from, in Egypt, I, 64, 85, 117, 121, 159, 265, 281; II, 52, 95, 188, 189, 566; III, 37, 44; IV, 229; immi-

grants from, on Fustat charity lists, I, 57; II, 440, 441, 442, 444, 447, 467; jewelry, IV, 214, 215, 217, 219, 429; Jewish high court, III, 301; Jewish judges in/from, I, 52, 53, 64; II, 47, 20, 513, 549; III, 301, 466; Jewish markets in, II, 291, 342; Karaism, I, 65; II, 7; Ketāmis in, I, 31; legal language used in, II, 598; letters from, I, 118, 132, 210, 288, 333; II, 341; IV, 413; local Jewish communities of, II, 40, 530; mail service, I, 288, 291; III, 436; Maimonides' ancestors in, III, 5; marriages in, I, 49; II, 345; III, 93, 120, 121; IV, 380; *muqaddams* from, II, 69, 70, 73; nagids of, II, 26, 526; Nahray b. Nissim in, I, 240; P. rite, III, 49, 50, 103, 104, 106, 107, 139; P. synagogue in Alex., II, 329; V, 513; P. synagogue or congregation in Fustat, I, 18, 20; II, 10, 28, 52, 55, 291, 534, 597; III, 97, 98, 183, 197, 301, 351; *parnāsīm* in, II, 78; poll tax in, II, 389; promulgation of ban in, III, 284; public charity in, II, 104; Rabbanite communities from, I, 18; Rabbanite-Karaite relations in, II, 7; ransoming of captives in, II, 169, 170, 501; refugees from, II, 95, 188, 189, 447; sale of house in, IV, 16; scholars from, I, 54, 58, 63; script used in, II, 235; III, 466; Seljuks in, I, 35, 103; II, 30, 55, 137; III, 198; ships from, I, 305; silk industry of, I, 102, 103, 104, 430; IV, 192; solicitation of contributions for, II, 502; synagogues in, I, 113; II, 6, 155; IV, 128; trade in, I, 45, 60, 125, 148, 156, 180, 214, 427; III, 300; travel to, I, 56, 67, 314, 320; II, 136, 274; IV, 185; under Byzantine rule, II, 17, 197; under Greek and Roman domination, II, 2, 17; III, 8; wars in, I, 35; II, 11, 188; Westerners settling in, III, 57, 162; Yeshiva of, II, 5, 6, 11, 28, 30, 55, 69, 78, 197, 200, 202, 208, 343, 405, 519, 563; III, 300. *See also* Synagogue of the Palestinians

Palm: branches, II, 452; fiber, I, 154; groves, II, 115, 422; leaf (material for basket), IV, 452. See also *khūṣa*

Palmyra, Syria, II, 6, 204–205, 508, 520, 563, 564; IV, 433

Paltiel, II, 524

Palṭiel b. Shefaṭya, II, 575

"Pamphlets" (Heb. *quṭrās*, *qunṭrās*), II, 593

Pancakes, I, 92

pandocheion (Gr., inn), II, 113

Pantomime, II, 190

Paper, I, 7, 19, 81, 111, 112, 154, 241, 334, 376; II, 232–233; *kāghidh*, IV, 348; red, II, 573. *See also* Papyrus; Parchment; Vellum

"Paper economy," I, 240–250

Papyrus: Antinoopolis, IV, 258, 446; Arabic, I, 5–6, 9, 13; III, 5; V, 524; IV, 25, 53, 76, 164, 254, 258, 261; Hebrew, II, 40, 58, 76, 231. *See also* Paper; Parchment; Vellum

pāqīd (representative of bride [Karaite usage]), III, 103. See also *peqīd ha-sōḥarīm*

Parapet, wooden, IV, 70

Parchment, I, 111, 112, 334, 422; II, 232, 573; maker of, I, 410, 422; II, 447. *See also* Paper; Papyrus; Vellum

Parents, III, 22, 40, 139; blessings of, III, 244; and children, III, 223–250, 473–481; V, 122–126, 141–142, 177; and daughters, III, 228–229; father-son, V, 125–126, 477; mother-daughter, V, 180–181, 185; mother-son, V, 122–123, 222–226. *See also* Children; Family feeling

parnās (welfare official), I, 382; II, 42, 45, 60, 77–81, 83, 89, 94, 100, 101, 102, 103, 108, 111, 113, 115, 117, 123, 127, 128, 129, 130, 132, 218, 262, 388, 414, 415, 416, 417, 418, 419, 422, 423, 424, 426, 427, 428, 431, 433, 434, 442, 444, 445, 448, 449, 455, 456, 458, 459, 464, 465, 475, 488, 501, 503, 504, 535, 539, 543, 568, 609; III, 176, 207, 213, 441, 467; IV, 296; head *parnās*, II, 79, 80, 455

Parsley, IV, 232

Parties and celebrations, V, 27–28, 33–34, 42

Partnership(s), I, 73, 117, 151, 184, 186, 187, 188, 194, 196, 203, 207, 209, 216, 247, 248, 263, 264, 270, 384; II, 185, 192, 230, 432, 436, 471, 477, 478, 485, 494, 545, 571, 578, 580, 581, 582, 583, 599, 606, 615; III, 45, 90, 288, 460; accompanying informal cooperation, I, 167; "according to the gentiles," II, 328; and commercial credit, I, 253; common method of conducting business, I, 72; in drugs and spices, III, 262, 267; family, I, 180–183, 294; III, 40, 41, 42, 225, 436; as form of charity, II, 142; and friendship, V, 273–274, 277; general and commercial, I, 169–179; III, 261; industrial, I, 87–89, 362–367; instead of contracts of employment, I, 11, 163; in mint, II, 358; and organization of shipping, I, 309;

with non-Jews, I, 72, 85, 124; III, 292, 293, 294, 296, 330; V, 4; with/between women, I, 161. *See also* Commenda; Friendship, formal; Informal cooperation; *mushāṭara*
Partridge, eye of (a color), IV, 175, 406
Parts of the body and their covers. *See* Types of clothing
parwanqā (Aram., courier), I, 283, 286
*pāsha*ᶜ (Heb., apostasy), II, 300; V, 516. *See also* Apostasy
Passover, II, 84, 122, 129, 134, 161, 198, 415, 429, 465, 498, 499, 500, 532, 547-548; III, 190; IV, 156, 242, 397, 433, 444, 446; V, 16-17, 350, 351
Pastimes and recreations, V, 12-13, 37-45, 95-96
Pastoral circular, II, 10, 501, 503, 509, 514, 521, 523, 532, 549, 555, 563, 575, 595
Pastry, makers of, II, 492
Patan Patana, Indian slave, I, 133
Patched garment, IV, 323
Paternal: ancestors, III, 5; authority, III, 79; cousin, marriage to, III, 5, 30, 175, 217; family, III, 1-47
Patlagean, Evelyne, V, 73
Patriarch, Christian, I, 311; II, 19, 27, 28, 38, 39, 366, 374, 407, 529; V, 624; Jacobite, II, 148; Jewish, II, 17, 87
"Patriarchs" of Judea, III, 8, 25
Patriarchy, III, 1-47, 282
Patriotism, V, 5-6
Paul, Epistles of, II, 87, 312
Pauty, Edmond, IV, 55
Pawning, IV, 185, 332-333, 413, 417
payk (Per., courier). *See* Mailmen; Mail service
Payment. *See* Collection(s)
payṭān (writer of liturgical poetry), V, 626, 627. See also *piyyuṭ*
*pe*ʾ*ā* (Heb., denomination), II, 534
"Peace," III, 213, 217
Peaches (*khawkh*), I, 121, 469
"Peacock," slave girl, I, 138
Peacock: meaning multi-colored, IV, 191, 203; pendant, IV, 210, 423; pins, IV, 210, 322, 423
"Pearl," designation for deceased relative, V, 591
Pearls, I, 99-100, 154, 155, 202, 241, 416; IV, 202, 203-204, 216, 220, 319, 322, 327, 420, 428, 455; IV, 204, 402; unsorted, IV, 26; *kharīdī* (merchant in unperforated pearls), I, 438. See also *mukallal*
Pears (*kummathrā*), shape in jewelry, IV, 208-209, 319, 343, 422, 466
Pedigree, II, 566, 575. *See also* Genealogy
Pen, cutting of, II, 234
Pendants, forms of, IV, 210-211, 216; with magic formulas, IV, 218-219. *See also* Amulet
Penmanship, II, 228
Pentateuch, II, 205, 238, 557; V, 527. *See also* Bible
Pentecost (Shavuot), II, 54, 415, 465, 497, 501, 608; III, 338-339; IV, 156, 230, 349, 446; V, 16, 23, 350
Pepper, I, 44, 154, 167, 219, 220-222, 267, 337, 376; IV, 232, 260, 355
Peppergray, color, IV, 168
peqīd ha-sōḥarīm. *See* Representative of merchants
*p*ʾ*er* (ornamental headgear, turban), IV, 159. *See also* Turban
perāḥīm (Heb., florins), I, 484
Peraḥyā, R., II, 534
Peraḥyā b. ʿAdāya, IV, 427
Peraḥyā b. Āraḥ, III, 445
Peraḥyā b. Joseph Yijū, III, 43; IV, 382, 429; V, 562
Peraḥyā b. Manasse, III, 430; V, 548
Peraḥyā b. Nissīm, I, 367
perāqīm (Heb., chapters, courses), II, 561, 562. See also *fuṣūl*
Perdinel family, V, 222
Peres, man accompanying ʿAfīf b. Ezra, V, 530
"Perfume," slave girl, I, 138, 139
Perfume, II, 261-272; IV, 138, 316; trade in, 153, 154. See also *madāf*
Perfumed garment, IV, 182
Perfumer(s), I, xvii, 83, 84, 85, 150 and *passim*; II, 49, 102, 261-272, 422, 477, 484, 506, 533, 543, 581-585; IV, 226, 431. *See also* Druggists
Perfumers, Square of the, II, 508, 532
Perfuming, IV, 225-226, 323
Persecutions, II, 289, 299, 591, 593. *See also* Conversion
Persia(n), I, 21, 22, 30, 65, 128, 138, 244, 282-283, 285, 286, 334; II, 521, 523, 599; IV, 16, 66, 73, 78, 123, 145, 152, 192, 207, 219, 225, 227, 432. *See also* Iran(ian)
Persian language, I, 1, 113, 136, 160, 242, 249, 277, 284
Personality: change, V, 188-189; ideal, V, 5, 9, 191-199, 474-475; innate nature, V, 187-188, 228; moodiness, V, 241-243; observation of, V, 190, 215; scholarship, V, 9; and social relations, V, 187, 215-216; terminology, V, 188-191, 194, 196, 215; women, V, 228

and *passim*. *See also* individual attitudes and components
peshārā (Heb., settlement [of a lawsuit]), II, 601
pesīqā (Heb.). *See* Pledges
Pestle. *See* Mortar and pestle
Petaḥyāhū ha-Kohen, V, 294
Petaḥya of Regensburg (Ratisbon), II, 561
petīḥīn (Heb., excommunication), II, 614. *See also* Excommunication
Pharmaceutical products, I, 47, 72, 101, 110, 153, 210
Pharmacist (*ṣaydalānī, ṣaydanī*). *See* Druggist
Pharmacy, I, 87, 364
Pharos of Alexandria, I, 319, 322
Philadelphia, University Museum, III, 201
Philanthropist(s). *See* Charity; Contributions; Pious foundations
"Philosopher, The," nickname, II, 504
Philosophy, not taught, II, 210. *See also* Education
Phineas b. Meshullām, I, 406
Phinehas family, III, 93, 94
Phlebotomist. *See* Bloodletters
Phoenicians, I, 476; II, 366
Physical appearance, V, 309, 476
Physicians, I, 91, 152, 273, 322, 382, 462; II, 46, 86, 168, 188, 189, 193, 269, 289, 372, 485, 528, 530, 532, 533, 540, 541, 552, 555, 566, 575–581, 583, 590, 602, 609, 610; III, 12, 14, 15, 30, 82, 117, 118, 183–184, 189,194, 202, 207, 232, 240, 243, 251, 276, 279, 283, 357, 478, 494, 500; IV, 15, 18; attached to army or navy, I, 73, 252, 379; II, 380, 515; book-dealing, I, 379; III, 331; V, 457; and charity, II, 98, 111, 113, 133, 501, 502, 508; at court, II, 32, 288, 298, 345, 346, 347, 351, 376, 525; III, 5; V, 4, 174, 195, 257, 264, 420, 428–429, 458; as creditor, I, 252, 273, 385; II, 84; education and learning, II, 172, 179, 203, 210, 228, 229; V, 10, 285, 419–420, 450; families of, II, 245; III, 2, 5, 11, 429; fees of, I, 259; II, 256–257; female, I, 127–128; II, 579; III, 64; general description, II, 240–261; as head of Jewish community, II, 243–245; V, 505; as officials of Jewish community, II, 32, 39, 49, 73, 79; letters to, V, 105–106; libraries of, II, 248; IV, 311; office, II, 253; in partnerships, I, 89, 366; prescriptions, II, 254, 266, 272; in the Rīf, IV, 10; social position and prestige, I, 78, 79; II, 2, 42, 166; III, 2; V, 419–420, 428–429; titles of, II, 246; trust in, V, 112, 257
Picker, picking, II, 225, 226
Pietism (-ist), II, 406; IV, 151, 154; V, 8, 23, 292, 346, 478–483, 491-495, 527. *See also* Abraham Maimonides; *ḥasīdīm*
Piety, II, 82, 86, 166, 185, 214, 254, 310
Pigeons, I, 291; II, 85; IV, 143, 250, 339, 443, 464; V, 45
Pilgrim(age), I, 55–56, 281, 323; II, 37, 42, 201, 529; III, 48, 284, 337; V, 18–25, 65, 401–402, 428, 450, 461, 464–465, 467–468. See also *ḥajj*
Pillow, *mikhadda*, IV, 109, 306–307, 316, 321, 327, 330, 379, 380; "for the cheek," for sleep (*mikhadda lil-khadd*), IV, 109, 112 and *passim*, 308, 321, 377, 454
Pillowcases as receptacles, I, 333
Pincers (*hanbāzayn*), II, 609; *laqāʾiṭ* (type of pin), IV, 424
Pine trees, II, 436
Pingree, David, V, 420
Pinḥāsī, family name, II, 574
Pink, IV, 175
Pins (i.e., jewelry), IV, 204, 209, 210, 211, 215–216, 319, 327, 329, 424, 426; sun disks, IV, 204; gold-plated, IV, 204
"Pious, The," title of prominent male donors, II, 99, 542, 566
Pious foundations (*aḥbās al-yahūd, ḥabs, heqdēsh, qōdesh, waqf*), II, 53, 99–103, 108, 112–121, 413–469, 490, 542, 543, 545–546, 548, 572, 588, 590; III, 481; IV, 12, 14, 17, 19, 20, 25, 29, 34, 36, 58, 69, 72, 73, 75, 88, 94, 98; Muslim, IV, 36; Ministry of, IV, 37, 38
Pipe (*barbakh*), II, 584; IV, 214, 426
piqqēd bō (Heb. for *rassam ʿalayh*), house arrest, II, 609
piqqeḥīm (Heb.). *See* Detectives
Piracy, Pirates, I, 306, 327–332, 336; II, 37, 55, 96, 481
Pirenne, Henri, V, 496
Pisa, Italy, I, 32, 40, 44, 310; II, 528; IV, 1
pishʿūth. *See* Apostasy
piṣṣūy (Heb., acquittance), release from further obligation, II, 600
Pistachios I, 121; IV, 441
Pitch, I, 154
pitrōn (interpretation of the biblical text), II, 567; V, 505
pittāqē (Gr. *pittakion*) *ha-mas* (arrest warrants for non-payment of poll tax), II, 612. *See also* Poll tax

piyyūṭ (Heb.) *See* Poetry, liturgical
Placards, IV, 122-123
Plague, II, 141, 276; V, 113, 114, 537. *See also* Epidemics
Plain, without patterns (*musmaṭ*), IV, 117
Plain-clothesmen, II, 371
Platearius family, Salerno, II, 246
Plated (*maṭlī*), IV, 211, 424
Platters, IV, 145, 146, 147
Playing cards, IV, 161
"Pleasure," slave girl, I, 137, 139
Pledges (*pesīqā*), II, 106, 107, 108, 122, 142, 432, 440, 455, 465, 475, 476, 485, 487, 488, 496, 499, 502, 503, 506, 521, 544, 569; for community officials (*pesīqat ṣedāqā*), II, 106, 109, 122, 123, 136, 432, 440, 455, 465, 485, 500, 502, 503, 521, 544, 569; for Passover (*pesīqat pesaḥ*), II, 465
Plenary deliberations, II, 57
Poet, family name, II, 429
Poetry, Poets, II, 219, 238, 574, 580, 604; III, 20, 431; IV, 188, 195, 227, 253, 255, 266; drinking, V, 39; elegies, V, 178-179, 183-185; exchanged between friends, V, 16, 285-287; friendship in, V, 294; Hebrew, II, 259, 260, 354, 512, 611; in honor of special events, V, 27, 34, 111, 285; importance of, V, 423-426; in letters, V, 422; liturgical (*piyyūṭ*), I, 87, 176, 406, 499, 534, 553, 569; II, 159, 160, 161, 221, 557, 568; III, 221-222, 358; V, 285, 381-383, 424, 451-452 (*see also* Liturgy); praising a benefactor, V, 79; Spanish Hebrew, V, 391, 405, 425-426, 468 (*see also* individual poets); of thanks, V, 35; women (absence of), III, 358, 507; V, 468-470
Police, II, 35, 86, 361-362, 368-373, 379, 428, 492, 528, 548, 607-609; IV, 13, 39, 351; V, 593. *See also* Market police; Secret police
Political turmoil (including pillage, invasion, and civil war), V, 524; Alexandria, V, 50-51, 56-57, 104, 422-423; attitudes toward, V, 49, 54-56, 58, 69, 70, 72, 248; Egypt, V, 210-211, 220; information about, in letters, V, 46-47, 49-50, 54, 62; and religious conflict, V, 368-369, 398-399, 403, 450; and trade, V, 67-70; Tunisia, V, 46-47, 209-211. *See also* Adversity
Poll tax (*jāliya*), I, 62, 97, 182, 257, 300, 382, 488; II, 38, 46, 60, 67, 73, 88, 92, 95, 98, 106, 121, 132, 137, 188, 189, 191, 227, 238, 280, 288, 360, 367, 372, 380-393, 423, 426, 440, 453, 454, 455, 460, 461, 463, 464, 466, 467, 473, 474, 476, 486, 492, 495, 499, 502, 505, 529, 544, 546, 547, 559, 563, 605, 610-612; III, 121, 191, 218, 233, 286, 345; IV, 39, 276, 443; V, 78-79, 80, 89-90, 91-92, 122, 400-401, 531
Polygamy. *See* Polygyny
Polygyny, I, 73, 134; II, 348, 357; III, 147-150, 175, 178, 182, 188, 205-211, 319, 458, 460; V, 313-314. *See also* Marriage; Marriage contracts, special conditions; Monogyny clause
Pomegranate(s), I, 151; IV, 441; as color, IV, 117, 175, 307, 320, 323, 327, 331; as name of trinkets, I, 154; as ornament on Torah scroll, IV, 209, 422, 425
Pompei, IV, 121
Poor, II, 37, 45, 67, 80, 88, 89, 92-143, 171, 185, 216, 284, 292, 306, 381-392, 413, 418, 419, 423, 427, 428, 429, 430, 432, 435, 436, 438-469, 473, 476, 478, 492, 501, 504, 505, 506, 515, 529, 543, 544, 578, 580, 590; V, 76. *See also* Poverty
Poor, house for the, II, 590
Population: composition and character of, IV, 8; decline in, IV, 25; figures, II, 139-143; movements (*see* Migration)
Porcelain (*ghaḍār*), I, 421; IV, 145, 146, 392-393; maker of (*ghaḍāʾirī*), I, 111, 422
Porters, I, 84; II, 459-467
Portico (*saqīfa*), IV, 27, 30, 60, 277, 355, 356
Portugal, IV, 411
Posen, Jacob, II, 546
pōshēaʿ (renegade). *See* Apostasy; Conversion
Postal agencies. *See* Mail service
Potions (i.e., wine and soft drinks), II, 45, 67, 100, 261-272, II, 426, 492, 531, 581, 585; IV, 147-148; preparers or sellers of, I, 151; II, 46, 253, 261, 263, 264, 271, 272, 539, 581-585; III, 489; IV, 254, 261, 447. *See also* Beer; Drinking; *fuqqāʿ*; Wine
Potter (*qaddār*), I, 110, 422; II, 63, 536; IV, 19
Pottery, I, 92, 110-111, 334; IV, 106; fine (*ghaḍār*), IV, 145-146, 148
Poultry, II, 46
Pound (*raṭl*), types of, I, 360-361 and *passim*
Poverty, III, 15, 31, 42, 43, 65, 68, 92, 109, 116, 132, 186, 259, 276, 345; atti-

tudes toward, V, 75-76, 91-94, 354, 530; extent of, V, 73-75, 80, 91-92. *See also* Charity; Fine(s) paid to the poor; Poor
Power of attorney, **II**, 230, 462, 599, 608; V, 118
Prayer, **II**, 2, 19-20, 155-165, 201, 523; **III**, 355; **IV**, 138, 154; communal, **II**, 54, 164-167, 351, 480; during day, V, 342, 416; for beloved person, **IV**, 157; for the dead, **II**, 163; intercessional, V, 338-340; interruption of public, **II**, 323-325, 597; pietistic, V, 479, 480, 494; for powerful, V, 298-299, 340; in Qurʾān, V, 215; for rain, V, 531; for recovery from illness, V, 109; for the ruler, **II**, 164; for traveler, **I**, 346; private place of, **II**, 21, 50, 166, 480, 500, 555. *See also* Poems, liturgical; *qerōvōt*; *qiddūsh*; Services, religious
Prayer book, **II**, 520, 608; **IV**, 416; V, 540
Prayer carpet (*muṣallā*), **IV**, 123, 125, 383, 411
Prayer mantle, **IV**, 152, 153, 196-198
Prayer shawl. *See* Prayer mantle
Preacher(-ers, -ing), **II**, 16, 85, 164, 211-219; guest, **II**, 54, 62, 85, 158, 194, 534, 553, 567, 568; itinerant, **II**, 217-219; Muslim (*khaṭīb*), **II**, 485, 567
Precious stones, **I**, 154, 155, 195; **IV**, 204-207, 420. See also *jawhar*
Pregnancy, **III**, 22, 197, 230-231
Prescription(s), **II**, 254, 266, 267, 272, 343, 426, 578-579, 581, 583; **IV**, 422. *See also* Druggist; Pharmaceutical products
Presents. *See* Gifts
"President of the Congregations," **II**, 563
President of the High Court (*āv*), **II**, 13, 15, 28, 34, 168, 198, 313, 511, 512, 528, 562, 573, 577, 595, 597
Press: for clothing (*kamad*), **IV**, 178, 183; for oil and wine, **IV**, 15
Presser, pressing (*kammād*), V, 178, 408, 412
Price lists, **I**, 201, 218
Prices, **I**, 94-98, 139, 217-219 and *passim*; approximate in trousseaus, **IV**, 106; stability, **III**, 140
"(The) Pride," honorific title, **II**, 568
"Pride of the Community," honorific title, **III**, 240
"Pride of the Physicians," honorific title, **III**, 500
Primogeniture. *See* Son, firstborn
Prince of the Diaspora, **II**, 525. See also *negīd ha-gōlā*
Princeton conference, 1970, **IV**, 4
Princeton Theological Seminary, **I**, 6
Prisons, **II**, 35, 92, 372-373, 455, 472, 482, 486, 611
Privacy, V, 31, 33, 172-173
Procedure, court, **II**, 334-345
Processions, synagogue, **II**, 151
Procreation as religious duty, **III**, 49, 54, 224, 276
"Prodigality," slave girl, **I**, 139
Professional class, **II**, 568-585
Profits, **I**, 87, 202-204, 247
Promissory notes, **I**, 242, 245-247, 461; **II**, 435, 458; **III**, 450. *See also* Bill of exchange
Property rights, **IV**, 23
Prophets, **II**, 10, 238
Proselytes, **I**, 301; **II**, 79, 129, 153, 299-311, 444, 445, 455, 591-594, 599. *See also* Conversion; *gēr*
prostatīn (Gr., *prostatai*), leaders, **II**, 541
Prostitution, **I**, 350; **III**, 263; V, 322
Protestant (-s, -ism), **III**, 158
Proxy of bride, **III**, 72, 103, 142, 335; brother, **III**, 93, 336; father, **III**, 57, 88, 89, 91; mother's brother, **III**, 67, 91. *See also* Marriage
Prunes, **I**, 121
Psalms, **II**, 522
Ptolemaens, **III**, 8
Public appeals. *See* Appeals
Public lecturers, **II**, 562
Pulpit, **II**, 146-147. See also *anbōl*; *bēmā*; *migdāl*; *minbar*
Pumbedita, yeshiva of, **II**, 5
Purdah. *See* Women, seclusion of
Purim, **I**, 448; **II**, 101, 168, 532, 550; **III**, 143; **IV**, 433; V, 350, 352, 369, 395, 604
Purple cloth, **I**, 202, 207, 339, 364
Purple dye(r) (*arjawān*[*ī*]), **I**, 85, 86, 107; **II**, 297; **IV**, 171, 172, 404, 405
Purplish-brown of basil flower, color, **IV**, 175
Purses of coins, sealed (*kharīṭa*), **I**, 231, 375; **IV**, 28

Q

qāʿa: main, ground floor, **I**, 187, 382, 446; **II**, 420; **III**, 485; **IV**, 16, 23, 56, 63-64, 67, 68, 73, 362, 365; uses of, **IV**, 69-70, 278, 292, 295, 367, 368; store, **I**, 439; *q. ḥarīr* (company running a silk workshop), **IV**, 70; *q. al-sharāb* (tavern), **II**, 492. *See also* Houses
Qabīl, **II**, 606
qābila. *See* Midwife

qabw. *See* Vault
qadaḥ (tumbler), IV, 148
qadaḥ. *See* Copper: basin
qaddam (to appoint to a communal post), II, 70. See also *muqaddam*
qaddār. *See* Potter
qaddēsh (formal conclusion of a marriage), III, 441. *See also* Marriage
Qadi (judge), I, 117, 187, 188, 190, 192, 195, 218, 261, 267, 296, 310, 312, 380, 446; II, 29, 34, 67, 68, 86, 103, 172, 216, 229, 250, 279, 292, 294, 298, 304, 312, 316, 317, 319, 341, 356, 357, 363–373, 587, 596, 602, 607, 608, 609, 611, 613; IV, 27, 31, 36, 281; V, 624. *See also* Authorities, Muslim
qaḍīb ("bar"), thin stripe decorating textile. See *quḍbān*
qafaṣ. *See* Baskets
qaffāṣ. *See* Basketmaker
qāfila. *See* Caravan
qafīz (measurement for cereals), IV, 242–243, 439
al-Qafsī (from Qafsa, Tunisia), IV, 359
qāhāl (congregation). *See* Local community
(ha)-qāhāl ha-qādōsh (Heb., congregation), II, 530. *See also* Local community
al-Qāhiriyyīn, list of indigent families from Cairo, II, 461. *See also* Charity
qahramāna (*kahramāna*). *See* Carpet
qāʾid (commander, governor). *See* Governor
qāʾimat al-nedāvā (Heb., list of donations), II, 498. *See also* Donations
Qalʿa, Citadel, IV, 33
Qalahā, Egypt, II, 539; III, 207–208, 470
Qalʿat Jabar (on Euphrates), IV, 398
Qalʿat Ḥammād, Algeria, I, 50; II, 444, 533, 559
qālī (fryer), I, 115
qalīnā. See *kale kore*
qalī qurī. See *kale kore*
al-Qalqashandī, II, 219, 526, 568; IV, 43
Qālūṣ, bourse, I, 193-194, 195, 224, 227, 448; IV, 29, 355
Qalyūb, Egypt, I, 350, 380, 497; II, 420; III, 55; IV, 8; V, 532; cheese imported to, IV, 251; convert to Islam from, II, 591; III, 81; domestic architecture, IV, 76, 370; gardens of, V, 95; Jewish elders of, II, 58, 187, 530; marriage documents from, III, 99, 371, 389, 390, 410; *muqaddam* of, III, 81; Nile river traffic from, I, 297, 299; one man acting as cantor, teacher, notary, slaughterer in, II, 533, 572; physician from, II, 257; III, 30; silk production in, I, 417; II, 359, 606; tax-farming in, II, 359, 606; teachers in, II, 187, 381, 559
qamḥ. *See* Wheat
qamīṣ (robe [not shirt]), IV, 154, 396. *See also* Robe
qammāḥ (wheat merchant), II, 476. *See also* Wheat
al-Qamra (Alexandria), III, 479; IV, 350, 446
qanā (Judeo-Ar., to acquire a right), concerning symbolic purchase, II, 329. *See also* Symbolic purchase
qand. *See* Sugar
qandiyya (producers of candy sugar), I, 126. *See also* Sugar
qanīnū ("we made the symbolic purchase"), II, 599, 600. *See also* Symbolic purchase
qānūn. *See* Register
al-qānūn wal-mustaqarr ("the law and agreed practice"), II, 570
qarawiyya. *See* Dirhem
qārib (barge), I, 305–306, 307, 320, 322, 325, 326, 476, 480; IV, 411. *See also* Ships
Qarqashandī, IV, 359
Qarqīsiya (on the Euphrates), III, 57, 439
qarrāba ("box"), type of ship, I, 477; container, IV, 394
Qarsantī, common family name, II, 497
qarya. *See* Villages
Qasamūna b. Ismāʿīl, III, 507
qaṣdīr. *See* Tinner
qashāshī. See *qashshāsh*
qāshsh. *See* Second-hand clothes, dealer in
qashsha (things left when household dissolved), IV, 297
qashshāsh. *See* Second-hand clothes, dealer in
qashwa. *See* Baskets
Qāsim, the silk-weaver, II, 440
Qāsimī, Jamāl, I, 99
Qāsimī, Muhammad Saʿīd, I, 99
Qasmūna, d. of Samuel ha-Nagid, V, 469
qaṣr: castle, I, 119; rustic building, III, 500
qaṣr: hall, II, 434; isolated structure, IV, 76, 292, 370. *See also* Domestic architecture; Houses
qaṣṣāb (meat carver), I, 424. *See also* Butcher
qaṣṣār (Aram.). *See* Fuller
qāt (stimulating plant), V, 515

qaṭᶜ ("cuts" [of paper]), **II**, 232; "cutting up" (*see* Tailoring)
Qaṭāʾiᶜ suburb, **IV**, 54
qaṭāᶜi. *See* Warships
qaṭāʾif. *See* Sweetmeats
qaṭāra. *See* Sugar
qaṭārish (floss silk). *See* Silk
qaṭarmīz, -āt (glass jar, bottle), **I**, 428, 486
qaṭawī (color of sandgrouse), **IV**, 403
qāṭin (permanent resident), **II**, 385; **IV**, 39, 44
qaṭṭān. *See* Cotton
qāvūᶜa (tenure), **II**, 431, 567
qawwāra, quwāra (round piece), a textile, **IV**, 384, 392, 463
Qayrawān(ese), **I**, 8, 58, 100, 200, 237, 286, 421, 427, 444, 483; **III**, 261, 339, 489; **IV**, 45, 127, 396; Andalūsī brothers of, **III**, 14; apprentice with Tustaris in Fustat, **II**, 560; artisans in, **I**, 84; bazaar of, **IV**, 8; Berachiah brothers of, **III**, 19, 56, 474; caravan routes through, **I**, 212, 213, 277, 278, 279, 281; case of endogamy in, **III**, 26; center of Mediterranean trade, **I**, 32; cloth, **IV**, 168, 169; contributors from, **II**, 475; court records, **II**, 595, 602; currency in, **I**, 235, 370, 375; documents pertaining to marriage from, **III**, 378, 433; dyeing materials imported to, **IV**, 172; export of Hebrew books from, **III**, 300; fashion, **III**, 167; **IV**, 180, 191, 410; flourish of Jewish learning in, **II**, 203–204; food, **IV**, 241, 252, 439; head of Jewish community in, **I**, 145; Hilālian invasion of, **I**, 377; houses in, **IV**, 19, 56, 86, 287, 353, 362, 363; institution of "elders" in, **II**, 58, 403; international commuting from, **I**, 42; Jewish market in, **II**, 291, 590; Jewish-Muslim partnership in, **I**, 173; Jewish physicians from, **II**, 243; Jewish quarter in, **I**, 71; **II**, 290, 589; Judah Ibn Sighmār of, **I**, 159; **III**, 56; legal practice (concerning marriage), **III**, 72, 88, 98, 138, 142, 212, 442; letters from, **I**, 20, 78, 84, 145, 162, 163, 165, 198, 220, 243, 265, 281, 287, 290, 377; **II**, 434; **III**, 12–13, 14, 167, 247, 319, 437, 481, 484; **IV**, 163; **V**, 110; letters to, **II**, 41, 530; **III**, 22; mail service to/from, **I**, 285, 287, 290, 291; man sues stepmother in, **III**, 256; merchants in/from, **I**, 44, 60, 68, 84, 91, 157, 165, 168, 169, 182, 193, 198, 201, 210, 216, 232, 253, 258, 265, 277, 338, 374; **II**, 402, 440, 563; **III**, 12–13, 41, 288; **IV**, 7; Muslim marriage custom in, **III**, 212, 454; Nagids, **II**, 25, 563; Nahray b. Nissim of, **I**, 54, 61, 158, 189, 372, 373; **IV**, 44; names of women in, **III**, 498; Nissim b. Jacob Ibn Shāhīn of, **I**, 48; **II**, 203; pillage of, **V**, 46, 53, 129, 518, 520, 588; price lists from, **I**, 219, 228, 371; **IV**, 241; qadi of, **I**, 312; R. Hananel of, **I**, 52; refusal to acknowledge suzerainty of Fatimid caliph, **II**, 165; replaced by al-Mahdiyya as capital, **II**, 43, 320; representative of merchants in, **I**, 126; responsa sent to, **I**, 53; **II**, 15, 208, 564, 565; sack of, **II**, 43; **III**, 226; scholars of, rebuked by Gaon, **II**, 521; sea voyage from, **I**, 326; sieges of, **II**, 588; silk sold in, **I**, 417; standard of education in, **II**, 173; Taherti family of, **I**, 182, 372, 373, 375; **III**, 6, 118, 294, 433, 474; **V**, 130; textiles sent to, **I**, 268; ties to Babylonian yeshivas, **II**, 9, 11, 14, 203–204; wife emigrating to Egypt with husband from, **III**, 202; wills from, **III**, 238, 281; yeshiva alumni in, **II**, 199
Qayrawanese costume (robe, veil, wimple and cloak), **IV**, 191
qaysāriyya (market hall), **I**, 191, 194, 365; **IV**, 29, 58, 355, 364
qayyim(a) (superintendant [of church or synagogue]), **II**, 77, 540, 548
qazdīrī. *See* Tinner
qazz. *See* Silk
qazzāz. *See* Silk weaver
qehillā (congregation). *See* Local community
Qentōrīm (Lat. *centuriones*). *See* Communal officials
qerōvōt (section of prayer), **II**, 537. *See also* Prayer
qiddūsh (Heb., "sanctification"), part of prayer service, **II**, 550–551
qiddūshīn (Heb., "consecration"), betrothal, **III**, 69, 70–71, 95. *See also* Betrothal
qidr. *See* Caldron
qifāq (Per. *qifk*, cups), **II**, 585
Qifṭ, **I**, 299; **IV**, 359
qiḥf (drinking vessel, shallow bowl), **IV**, 148, 208, 322, 323
qilāda. *See* Necklace
qild (caravan), **I**, 468
qillat al-ᶜaql ("smallness of mind"), hypersensitivity, **I**, 451
qimᶜ (candle snuffer), **IV**, 388
qimāṭ ("bandage," "swaddle"), variety of flax. *See* Flax

qināᶜ. *See* Veil
qindīl. *See* Lamps
qinna (galbanum), III, 491
qinnīna (flasks), II, 584
qinṭār (100 pounds), weight, I, 360 and *passim*. See also *laythī qinṭār*
qinyān. *See* Symbolic purchase
qinyān aggāv ("transfer adjunct"), symbolic act conveying intangible rights, II, 329
qirāḍ (commenda), I, 171, 183, 384; *q. betōrat ᶜisqā* (commenda in form of an *ᶜisqā*, Jewish partnership), I, 171, 441 (see also *ᶜisqā*); *q. al-gōyīm* (mutual loan according to Muslim law), term for commenda, I, 171. *See also* Commenda; *muḍāraba*
qīrāṭ (one twenty-fourth of a dinar). *See* Money of account
qirba (skin for oil and wine), I, 485
qirmizīnī. *See* Crimson
qirmiz shadhūnī. *See* Crimson
Qirqisānī, Karaite scholar, V, 363, 364, 608
qirtās (*qirṭās* [paper container used to transport small quantities]), I, 334; *q. darāhim* (paper containing silver pieces), II, 569; *q. al-taḥyīj* (popular medicine making women stout), I, 364
[*bil*]-*qism wal-rizq* ("with apportionment and livelihood"), phrase used in business letters granting seller half share in the profit and living expenses, I, 185, 445
qiṭᶜa (decorative piece), IV, 462; (pl. *qiṭaᶜ*), pieces of the *martaba*, IV, 108–113 and *passim*. See also *martaba*; *ṭarrāḥa*
qiṭirmiz (short-necked bottles), II, 584
qīṭōn (Gr. *koiton*, bedroom), IV, 372
qōdesh (Heb). *See* Pious foundations
Quality, designations of, I, 337, 452, 454, 456
Quarry, female name, I, 433
Quarter dinar. See *rubāᶜī*
Quarter of a city (*ḥāra*, *nāḥiya*) ,II, 589, 608; IV, 5, 13, 35, 46, 57, 350. See also *ḥāmi ʾl-ḥāra*; *ṣāḥib al-rubᶜ*; Streets and quarters in Cairo; Streets and quarters in Fustat
Qubba mosque, I, 265; IV, 281
quḍāᶜ (stomach trouble), II, 255
quḍāᶜī (healer of stomach trouble), II, 255, 579
quḍbān (bars, a thin stripe), decoration of textile, IV, 411
Queen Isabella of Spain, V, 568
"Queen of the Lovers," slave girl, I, 139. *See also* ᶜUsshāq
Queries submitted to scholars, II, 9, 10, 13, 535, 537, 564, 567, 590, 591, 611, 615
quffa. *See* Baskets
Qūjandima, Egypt, III, 388, 395, 437, 448, 452; IV, 380
qulla (earthen vessel), I, 485
Qulzum, I, 215
qumāsh (household effects), I, 452; IV, 297
Qūmis, I, 400
qumqum (sprinkler for sprinkling rose water), II, 585, 590; IV, 149
qunbār (pronounced *qumbār*, ship), I, 306, 331, 476, 480
qunn (chicken coop), I, 125, 429
qunnī (keeper of a poultry yard), I, 429
quppā shel ṣedāqā (Heb., bread basket [of the community]), II, 104, 105, 110, 492, 543, 544. *See also* Charity
Qurʾān. *See* Koran
Qurqūbī, a costly textile, I, 103; IV, 121, 196, 197, 308, 381, 382, 417, 454
Qurra ("Delight of the Eyes") b. Solomon, f., III, 280
Qurrat al-ᶜAyn Sitt al-Milāḥ, f., V, 553
Qurṭub. *See* Cordova
qurṭum. *See* Safflower
Qūṣ, Upper Egypt, III, 263; IV, 385; V, 535; beneficiaries of community chest from, II, 460, 468; bigamist in, II, 333; III, 209; contributors from, II, 496; document concerning inheritance from, III, 278; family of an *ᶜarīf* in, I, 84; French monograph on, IV, 348; general character of, II, 43; hospitality in, V, 31-32; Jewish population of, II, 45, 77; letters from, II, 77, 258, 613; mail service, I, 287, 288, 290; marriage documents from, III, 390, 413; merchants in, I, 387; II, 307, 442; IV, 240; Nile river traffic from, I, 295, 298, 299; physicians in, II, 258; III, 278; IV, 44, 350; proselyte in, II, 307, 310, 593; qadi in, II, 364
qushāshī. *See* Second-hand clothes, dealer in
quṭāra. *See* Sugar
quṭn. *See* Cotton
quṭn muzbid ("foaming" or "cream-colored" cotton), I, 419. *See also* Cotton
quṭrās, *qunṭrās* (L. *commentarius*). *See* "Pamphlets"
quwāra (round piece of fabric). See *qawwāra*

Quzmān, House of (quarter in Damascus), IV, 19, 57

R

*rab*ᶜ (area, residence), II, 153; IV, 13, 14
rabbān (master), reference to Moses Maimonides, II, 326. *See* Moses Maimonides
Rabbānā Abraham. *See* Abraham b. Sahlān
Rabbāna Ḥiyya, IV, 255, 445
Rabbanites, I, 17–18, 114, 146, 397, 446, 460; II, 8, 16, 17, 23, 27, 29, 53, 54, 57, 66, 96, 98, 110, 140, 166, 299, 306, 346, 405, 415, 426, 433, 472, 473, 486, 545; III, 11, 26, 50, 51, 52, 57, 75, 102, 107, 108, 125, 149, 158, 169, 179, 210, 289, 293, 468; IV, 317–321, 442, 451, 452; V, 362, 371–372. *See also* Karaites
rabbēnū ("our master"), II, 211, 490, 551; III, 235, 473; *r. ha-me*ᶜ*ulle* ("our master, the eminent"), II, 214
rabbī ("master"), designation of a prominent scholar, II, 211, 497, 505, 565
Rabbinic court of Fustat, V, 25, 49. *See also* Legal procedures; Nagid
rabīb(a) (foster child, stepdaughter), II, 540; III, 311, 496
Rachel (biblical), III, 27
Racks for clothes (*minṣab, mishjab*), IV, 183, 412
radda. *See* Scarf
al-Rāḍī, Abbasid caliph, IV, 212
Raḍī b. ᶜAbd al-ᶜAzīz, I, 367
al-Raḍi Barābik, II, 505
Raḍī b. Elijah, physician, III, 480
Rāḍī Kohen, I, 366
Radishes, IV, 232, 245
Rafaḥ, Palestine, II, 365, 595
Rafāʾīl b. Abī Rūna, III, 488
raffā (darner, mender of clothes), II, 474
*rafī*ᶜ (first quality), I, 452; IV, 381
Rafīᶜa ("Sublime"), f., III, 243
rafīq (travel companion), I, 347–348, 349, 489; II, 462; III, 47; V, 274, 277
raghbal. See *gharbal al-turāb*
raghīf ("kneaded into a mass"), term for bread, IV, 439. *See also* Bread
Raḥamān, religious poem beginning with this word, II, 499. *See also* Poetry, liturgical
Raḥamīm b. Amram, I, 407
Raḥamīm b. Nissīm, III, 482
rahaṭ (type of liturgical poetry), II, 541; III, 505. *See also* Poetry, liturgical
al-rāhib. *See* "Monk, The"
Rahdāniyya, I, 104
Rahj, slave girl, I, 434
raḥl (luggage), term for dowry, III, 124, 444, 453; IV, 297, 344, 467. *See also* Dowry
raḥmānā, "The All-Merciful" (Talmudic), III, 448
Raḥmūn, II, 454
rahn (security), i.e., collateral, I, 463. *See also* Collateral(s)
rāʾiḍ (horse trainer), I, 416, 484
raʾīs: captain, chief, I, 480; II, 246, 459, 537, 565, 578 (see also *rayyis*); *r. al-yahūd*. *See* Head of the Jews
Raisins, I, 195, 213; II, 430, 450; IV, 247, 257, 439, 441, 446; black, IV, 247, 441; imported, IV, 247; seller of, IV, 16
rājil (policeman on foot), V, 593. *See also* Police
al-rajjāla (footmen), II, 608, 609. See also *raqqāṣīn*
rakhkhām. *See* Marble-worker
rakkāḍ (runner), travelling merchant, I, 156
"Ralliers" (poll tax officials). See *ḥushshār*
Ramaḍān (Ramadan), Muslim fasting month, IV, 156, 397; V, 40, 223
Ramle, Palestine, attacks on funeral processions of non-Muslims in, II, 285; bankers in, I, 245; Bedouin pillage of, III, 43; V, 58; beneficiaries of community chest from, II, 439, 441, 454; cantor from, II, 61; capital of Palestine, IV, 8, 193; cases of trouble between husband and wife, III, 197, 198, 199; charitable use of revenues from, II, 97, 415; clothing in, IV, 193; commerce in, I, 178, 188; IV, 8; complaint of Rabbanite Jews about governor of, II, 16; deputy of Palestinian gaon in, II, 318, 596; earthquake, II, 155, 421; V, 62–65, 326; elders of Jewish community, II, 58, 62, 318, 536; emigrants from Iran and Iraq in, IV, 304; foundation of, IV, 7; hospital, II, 243, 251, 347; Jewish court records from, II, 601; Jewish high court in, II, 200, 562; III, 301; IV, 22; Jewish judges in, II, 314, 316, 512, 562; joint Jewish congregations of, II, 54; Karaite court of, III, 446; large house in, IV, 366; letters from, II, 78, 157, 165, 168, 415, 534, 536, 562, 606; III, 137, 197, 456, 460, 468; IV, 22, 400, 442; loan made to refugee from Seljuks in, I, 260; mail service to/from, I, 285, 286, 288, 291,

293; market of Jews in, II, 166, 291, 543, 590; marriage documents from, III, 148, 375, 388, 391, 395, 409, 438, 446, 447, 452; meetinghouse, II, 165, 166, 543; Muslim government of, II, 368; oil dealer from, I, 110, 427; overrun by Seljuks, III, 198; physicians in, II, 245, 254, 347, 577; pilgrims in, II, 168, 371; IV, 45; price of house in, IV, 279; *qaddārs* sent to, I, 111; Rabbanite community of, II, 16, 53, 534; IV, 442; ransom of captives in, I, 327; representative of merchants in, I, 191, 192, 209; III, 280, 432; ritual bath, II, 155, 552; size of Jewish community, II, 43; synagogues of, II, 6, 42, 53, 155, 168, 421, 520, 542, 552; "Ṭabari" upholstery from, I, 50; IV, 110, 304, 306, 452; travel to/from, I, 275, 320, 326; use of title "Nagid" in, II, 530; Yaʿqub ibn Killis in, I, 33
rammāḥ (maker of lances), I, 416
Ransom. *See* Captives, ransom of; Books, ransom of
"Ransoming" as metaphor for being refugee, V, 548
Rape, during Crusades, V, 375, 521
Raqqa on the Euphrates, II, 71, 442; III, 227
raqīqī. See *ruqūqī*
raqqām(a) (embroiderer [rare]), II, 467; III, 503; female, I, 430. *See also* Embroiderer
raqqāq. *See* Parchment, maker of
raqqāṣ (runner, errand boy): unskilled laborer, I, 94, 96; II, 35; policeman, II, 370, 378, 379, 424, 428, 608, 610; *r. raghbal al-turāb* (workman sifting earth), II, 424
raqqāṣīn (runner or errand boy), unskilled laborer, II, 608; auxiliary police, II, 35, 370; *r. al-wālī* (state police), II, 528. See also *rajjāla*
rāṣ (Heb., runner), I, 284. *See also* Mailmen; Mail service
raṣāṣī (lead), color. *See* Lead
rāshē perāqīm (Heb., public lecturers), II, 562; *r. sīʿā* (group leaders), II, 562
Rashīd, III, 70–71
Rāshida, granddaughter of a cheesemaker, V, 544
Rashīd b. Mufaḍḍal, II, 606
al-Rashīd al-Samawal, I, 463; II, 553; IV, 288
Rashīda, f., III, 70
ra'ʾs al-jālūt. *See* Head of the Diaspora
Ra'ʾs al-kanāʾis ("Cape of the Churches"), harbor in North Africa, I, 326, 331
ra'ʾs al-kull. See *Rōsh Kallā*
ra'ʾs al-mathība (head of the academy). *See* Gaon
rassam (legal term indicating house arrest), II, 372, 609; V, 535. See also *tarsīm*
raṣṣāṣ (worker and/or dealer in lead), I, 420. *See also* Lead
rasūl ([special] messenger), I, 283, 284; II, 599, 608. See also *shālīʾaḥ*
Rāṣūy, notable, II, 429, 465, 486, 488, 491, 500, 602
Rate of exchange. *See* Exchange
Rathjens, Carl, IV, 71
raṭl. *See* Pound
rāv (master), designation of prominent scholar, teacher, or jurisconsult, I, 130; II, 209, 211, 292, 325, 326, 417, 458, 492, 508, 513, 515, 535, 598; III, 447; *r. rōsh* (grand mufti), II, 28 (see also *muftī*)
Rav Huna, IV, 234
rāwandī (dealer in [Chinese] rhubarb), I, 438. *See also* Rhubarb
rawshan (Persian). *See* Bay window
ray, raʾy (opinion, consensus), II, 535, 542
(*ʿan*) *raʾy al-jamāʿa* = *ʿal daʿat ha-qāhāl* ("with the consent of the community"), said on order of payment from public fund, II, 542
al-Rāya quarter, Fustat, IV, 13, 58, 286, 352, 364; V, 547
Rayḥān ("Basil"), slave, I, 147; II, 387
Raymond, André, I, 99; IV, 3; V, 96
Raymond III of Tiberias, I, 58
rayyis: honorary title for physician, II, 246; IV, 453; V, 640; judge, II, 537; various meanings of, V, 587
rayyis (al-Yahūd). See *Raʾīs al-Yahūd*
Rayyisa, f., III, 22, 242; IV, 317; V, 179–181, 556
Rayyisa b. Joseph Bīmī, II, 611
Rayyisa b. Manṣūr, III, 497
al-Rāzī, II, 249
razzāz (rice merchant), I, 119
Reading, silent, II, 182
Real estate, source of income for orphans, IV, 92
Real estate, transfer of, IV, 89
Real estate broker, IV, 90, 373
Ream, I, 336
Rebekah (biblical), III, 23, 27, 62, 163, 165, 166
Rebekah d. of Abraham, wife of Abu'l-Majd b. Yākhīn, III, 71–72; V, 515

Record book, II, 520
Record of public meeting, II, 614
Red, IV, 117, 125, 126, 163, 175
"Reddening" of coins, I, 378. *See also* Dinar
Red gold. *See* Gold
Red Sea, I, 7, 42, 319; IV, 2, 403
Reeds, fine (*sāmān*), IV, 115, 128, 324, 333, 380, 384, 455, 461
Refugees, II, 46, 188, 189, 441, 462, 480; III, 56; V, 29–30, 83–84, 233, 290, 372–373
Register (*qānūn*), IV, 39, 358
Rehoboam, biblical, V, 583
Releases (renouncements of claims), I, 11, 179, 249; bills of, III, 45
"Relief after Hardship" stories, V, 53
Religion, IV, 141, 143, 145, 151, 154, 155, 156, 165, 168, 170, 228, 248–249, 251, 252, 253, 258, 261, 265; V, 8–9, 191-192, 202, 323–324, 336–338, 341–343, 347, 348, 469–474, 502, 508. *See also* God; Islam; Judaism; Karaites; Scholarship; and other individual religious topics
Religious education. *See* Education
Remarriage(s), III, 102, 109, 120, 264, 271–277, 374, 376, 377, 378, 382, 383, 384, 387, 393, 481–488; for children's sake, III, 275; impediments to, III, 275–276; with one's divorcee, III, 99, 120, 133, 181, 210, 271, 391-393, 451. *See also* Marriages, previous
Rents, II, 100, 115, 122, 132, 284, 293, 414–437, 464, 536, 546, 605; III, 174, 191, 192; IV, 13, 23, 37, 91–97; of communal buildings, IV, 291-296; of premises belonging to wife's family, III, 92, 144, 151, 196; prepayment of, II, 115, 422, 428, 432, 545
Repair of houses. *See* Houses, repair of
Representative of the merchants (*wakīl al-tujjār*), I, 79, 158, 159, 178, 186-192, 342, 445, 446, 447; II, 37, 42, 162, 258, 295, 336, 366, 372, 423, 454, 477, 498, 525, 530, 607; III, 11, 37, 58, 138, 207, 208, 238, 264, 280, 282, 289, 339, 412, 428, 432, 442, 467, 489; IV, 352; V, 30, 208
Repudiation. *See* Divorce
Reputation, social, V, 200–203, 302–305, 307. *See also* Shame; Social rank
Rescript of ruler, II, 65, 384, 405, 536
rēsh bē rabbānān = *bē rabbānān* (Head of the School), II, 595
Rēsh Gālūthā. *See* Head of the Diaspora
reshūth ("taking permission"), expression of loyalty to an authority, II, 20–22, 524, 571, 614
Residence, III, 36, 39, 243, 244 (*see also* Extended family, joint domicile of); of couple, III, 67, 69, 70, 71, 84–85, 90, 91, 94, 104, 106, 119, 121, 143, 150–153, 164, 171, 174, 177, 191, 216, 272, 326; choice of husband, III, 143, 152; choice of wife, III, 152, 173–174; in house belonging to wife, III, 151; with husband's family, III, 143, 150–153 and *passim*, 458–459; with wife's parents, III, 90, 144, 150–151, 154–155, 196
Responsa, I, 13–14, 20, 22, 25, 258, 398; II, 4, 13, 14, 198, 203, 206, 208, 209, 210, 216, 521, 564, 567, 600. *See* Abraham Maimonides, queries and responsa; Index of Scriptural, Rabbinic, and Maimonidean Citations, s.v. Abraham Maimonides, Moses Maimonides
Rest room. *See* Toilet
Restrictions on non-Muslims. *See* Discrimination
Resurrection, V, 129, 130, 161, 182–185, 245, 406–409, 411
Retailers, I, 150–152
Retired officials, II, 124
Reuther, Oscar, IV, 55, 56
(*hā-*) *re'ūyā le-qiyyūm ha-miṣvōt* (Heb., "girl able to fulfill religious duties"), phrase in Karaite marriage contracts indicating girl who has come of age, III, 102, 447
Revault, J., IV, 56
Revenue, sources of, II, 543–545
Reverence: towards in-laws, III, 156, 215; towards parents, III, 240–242. *See also* Family feeling; Parents
Rhodes, I, 214
Rhodian sea law, I, 313, 332
Rhubarb (Chinese), I, 155
ribā (fixed interest). *See* Interest, fixed; Loans, on interest
ribaʿ (pious foundations), IV, 351. *See also* Pious foundations
rībās, a medicine, II, 268, 584
ribbīth (Heb.). *See* Interest, fixed; Loans, on interest
Ribbons (*sakākīn*, "knives"), IV, 336, 462
Ribes, a plant, II, 268
ribḥ (profit), I, 450. *See also* Profits
Rice, I, 119, 195, 211, 426; II, 546
Rice, D.S., II, 150; IV, 134
Richards, D.S., IV, 53
Richard the Lion-Hearted, IV, 161
Richardson, Bessie Ellen, V, 118

*ridā*ʾ (coat, mantle), II, 500, 501; IV, 116, 157, 380, 397, 451. *See also* Mantle
Riḍā, slave girl, I, 434
Riding beasts. *See* Mounts
Riḍwān, vizier, II, 528
RIF (R. Isaac of Fez), II, 338
Rīf, Egyptian countryside, allegiance to Jewish leadership in Fustat, II, 29; average size of Jewish community in, II, 45, 531; censures by religious leaders addressed to, II, 168; collections in, I, 381; II, 137, 481, 482, 532, 539, 549; III, 306; commercial travel to, III, 189; court settlement between husband and wife from, III, 214–215; exodus to major cities from, IV, 10; food, IV, 444; foreigners in, I, 54, 116; II, 95, 542; individuals from, II, 270; IV, 26; letters from, I, 54; II, 29, 270, 527, 596; IV, 245; marriage documents from, III, 99; merchants in, I, 156, 173, 175, 178, 197, 203, 214; *muqaddams* in, II, 73, 74, 384; Muslim government in, II, 359, 368, 377, 384; relief from payment of poll-tax sought in, II, 389, 527, 542; scribe in, II, 51; silk industry in, I, 102; term used in Palestine, I, 118; IV, 349; wife refuses to move to Fustat from, III, 464; wife runs away from, III, 178; IV, 9
rifqa (small group of fellow travellers), I, 277, 469. See also *rafīq*
Rīḥā, Syria, IV, 390
rijāl shuyūkh (respectable elders), II, 62
Rims of bracelets (*fumm*, pl. *afmām)*, IV, 208
Ring(s), III, 67, 70, 74, 86, 87, 88, 89, 90, 92, 95, 154 (*see also* Finger ring); IV, 322; as deposit, III, 367, 370, 379, 380, 383, 389; silver, II, 498; Shīrāzī, III, 67
"Ring of pledge," III, 93. *See also* Betrothal
*riqā*ʿ (Ar.) *bēth dīn* (Heb.) (orders of payment issued by the court), III, 299
*riqā*ʿ *al-jāliya* (warrants of arrest for nonpayment of poll tax), II, 612
*riqā*ʿ *ṣayārif*. *See* Promissory notes
riqq. *See* Parchment
risāla (shipment), I, 183, 184
Ritual, religious, II, 55, 72, 207, 529, 532, 534, 536
Ritual bath (*miqwā, maṭbal*), II, 154–155, 552. *See also* Ablutions
Ritual slaughter, I, 381, 382; II, 529, 543, 570, 571, 588; prohibition of, II, 282. *See also* Slaughterhouses
Ritual slaughterer, I, 424; II, 17, 50, 85, 89, 90, 121, 122, 225–228, 570, 571–572, 614. *See also* Slaughterhouses
River traffic, I, 295–301. *See also* Nile
riwāq (Per., arcade), IV, 73
rizma (bundle), I, 336, 337, 418, 426, 486; IV, 403
rizq al-baḥr (overseas business), I, 256. *See also* Loans
Roads, safety of, IV, 240
Robbery, II, 37
Robe (*thawb, maqṭa*ʿ*, farkha, shuqqa*), II, 131, 444, 547; IV, 154, 157, 180–182, 397, 401, 407, 409, 410, 455. See also *sādīn miṣrī*
Robe of honor (*khil*ʿ*a*), I, 468; II, 24, 25, 351; III, 91; IV, 11, 184, 320, 322, 324, 329, 458–459. *See also* Gala costume
Roberts, David, IV, 55
Rōḍa, IV, 19, 280
rōfē (Heb.), II, 246, 566, 576, 577. *See also* Physicians
Romania (European Byzantium), I, 49
Romaniotes, II, 167
Rome, Roman, ancestor worship, III, 15; anti-Semitism in Roman times, II, 279; attitude towards teachers, II, 190; basilica, II, 166; city organization, IV, 3; classical Hebrew thesaurus written in, I, 64; clothing, IV, 116, 157, 159, 216, 408; *coloni*, I, 117; craftsmen, I, 85, 97; enmity towards Persian empire, IV, 192; food, IV, 244, 260, 432; fortress in Fustat, II, 290; home furnishings, IV, 114, 117, 118; impoverishment of Near Eastern Jews by, IV, 152; influence on Jewish communal organization, I, 73; II, 2, 35, 68, 89, 312, 325; jewelry, IV, 202, 212, 216; Jewish law in Roman times, II, 65; Jewish settlements in Egypt under, I, 20; law, I, 136; II, 17, 42, 329, 335; money-handling system, I, 231; naming practices, III, 8; North Africa under, I, 30; situation of provincial capitals, IV, 7; slaves, I, 131, 134; tax-farming, II, 363; use of leather, I, 111; yeshivas in Roman times, II, 13, 17
Ronall, J. O., I, 458
Roofs, IV, 74ff. *See also* Domestic architecture; Houses
Rope of well, II, 393
Rosary (*subḥa*), IV, 218
Rose marmalade (*ward murrabbā*), I, 185 (see also *ward*); as color, IV, 409
Rose oil, I, 151, 179; II, 267, 269, 585
Rose water, II, 262, 271, 422, 584; IV, 149, 233, 261, 434

Rosenblatt, Samuel, V, 475, 476
Rosenthal, Franz, II, 255; V, 44, 299, 415, 444, 633
Rosenzweig, Franz, V, 597
Rosetta, Egypt, I, 20, 110, 207, 213, 246, 295, 298, 323, 340, 341, 342, 474; II, 270, 608; IV, 55, 59, 240, 438
rōsh ha-dayyānīm (Heb., "Head of the Judges"), title, II, 514
rōsh ha-gōlā (Heb.). *See* Head of the Diaspora
rōsh kallā ("Heb., "Head of the Assembly"), title conferred by yeshiva, II, 472; III, 428, 472
rōsh ha-keneset (Heb.). *See* Head of the synagogue
rōsh ha-medabberīm (Heb., main speaker), II, 563
rōsh ha-qāhāl (Heb.). *See* Head of the congregations
rōsh ha-qehillōt (Heb.). *See* Head of the congregations
rōsh ha-seder (Heb., "Head of the Row"), title of scholars, II, 198-199, 526, 560, 562, 564
Rōsh ha-Seder b. Joseph of Qayrawān, V, 570
Rostovtzeff, Michael I., V, 497
Rote, learning by, II, 209
Rouen, I, 27; IV, 1
Round sums, goods ordered in, I, 210; of gold, I, 232, 265
Rozbih, I, 400
rubᶜ. See *rabᶜ*
rubᶜ al-kanīs (synagogue compound), II, 153
rubāᶜī (quarter dinar). *See* Dinar
rubāᶜiyya (Sicilian quarter dinar). *See* Dinar
rubb sūs sharāb (liquorice jam), II, 584. See also *sharāb*
Rubbish removal, II, 117, 422, 430, 431; IV, 354
Rubies (*balas, balakhsh, yāqūt*), IV, 205-206, 420
Ruby (color), IV, 175
Rugs: *busuṭ*, sing. *bisāṭ*, IV, 126, 298, 459; *nakhkh* (oblong rugs), I, 334, 485. *See also* Carpet
Ruins, II, 115, 120, 421; IV, 17, 19, 20, 21-24, 23, 100
Rulers, Muslim, II, 345-354. *See also* Caliph; Sultan
Rūm(ī) (Byzantine, European), II, 25, 440, 463; beneficiaries of community chest from, I, 56, 57; II, 127, 130, 140, 429, 441, 442, 443, 445, 454, 462, 467, 506; cheese, IV, 443; Christian merchants from, IV, 402; clothing, IV, 167, 315, 403, 415, 436, 452, 453; converts to Judaism from, II, 304; definition, I, 43; III, 440; emigrants to Egypt from, I, 49, 51, 54, 56, 57; II, 79, 127; IV, 14; home furnishings, IV, 106, 303, 377; impact on Mediterranean trade, I, 44, 45, 148; in Ottoman times, II, 167; *parnāsīm* in Fustat, II, 79; refugees from the Crusades, II, 130; relations with Muslim East and West, I, 44; ships, I, 313, 318; silk, I, 154; wine, IV, 259
al-Rumayla, I, 300
Rūmiyya, type of clothing, IV, 191, 323, 324
Runciman, Steven, IV, 19
"Runner" (errand boy), I, 94. See also *rakkāḍ; raqqāṣ; raqqāṣīn; rāṣ*
Runners, IV, 125-126, 383, 411; clothing, IV, 182
ruqᶜa (order [of payment]). *See* Promissory notes
ruqaᶜī (banker), II, 456, 457. *See also* Bankers
ruqᶜat dalāla. *See* Promissory notes
ruqūqī. *See* Parchment, maker of
ruṣṣat al-aḥmāl (setting up or arrangement of bales in good order), I, 487
Russia, IV, 144
rusūm: ceremonial, II, 594; salaries, II, 451
Ruth, biblical, III, 27, 50, 172; V, 531
rūz-nāma (Per., journal), a government account book, I, 208, 249, 451
ruzz. *See* Rice

S

Ṣā (Saʾis), Egypt, III, 388
ṣāᶜ (measure of barley), IV, 243
Saᶜāda, a ship, I, 312
Saᶜāda, slave nurse (*dāda*) for children, I, 434; III, 353-354
Saadya, II, 528
Saadya, cantor, II, 455
Saadya Gaon: on benedictions, V, 341-342, 352; biographical details, I, 53, 54; II, 522; V, 155, 379-380, 382-384, 391, 418, 615; condemnation of withdrawal from world, V, 362, 607; on love, III, 52; V, 317-318, 593; on messianism, V, 391, 397, 402, 403, 406-407; on resurrection, V, 161, 402, 411; writings and letters, I, 444, 491; II, 10,

158, 205, 220, 534; III, 6, 19, 88, 126, 454; IV, 416; V, 26, 298, 325, 341-342, 352, 362, 363, 379-390, 397, 419, 424, 425, 544, 614, 627
Saadya b. Benjamin Khaybarī, II, 611
Saᶜadya b. Ephraim, III, 502
Saadya b. Israel, II, 553
Saadya b. Judah, V, 150
Saadya b. Ṣedāqā, II, 532
Saadya (II) b. Solomon (I) Ben Ṣaghīr, III, 428
Saᶜadyāhū ha-meᶜulle ba-ḥavūrā, II, 566
ṣaᶜālīk. See *ṣaᶜlūk*
ṣabagh (term for henna or *ᶜūd*). *See* Henna
sābāṭ (structure similar to roofed passage), IV, 30
Ṣabaṭ Ibn Ayyūb, IV, 30, 356
sabbāk (metal caster in mint), I, 420; II, 483. *See also* Mint
ṣabbān. *See* Soapmaker
Sabbath, I, 376, 350, 357; II, 168, 173, 193, 194, 218, 221, 222, 224, 274, 286, 292, 296, 297, 309, 310, 373, 393, 455, 504, 537, 568, 579, 586, 594, 613; III, 80, 92, 115, 117, 163, 201, 221, 222, 335, 343, 463; IV, 21, 137, 265, 396; charity, II, 105, 129, 464, 466, 496; clothing, II, 111; IV, 155-158, 397; and death, II, 383; V, 148, 155; food, I, 72; IV, 141, 227, 230, 233, 249, 432; among Karaites, V, 366; marital relations, II, 168, 196; V, 312-313, 323; recreation, V, 12-13, 344-345; religious services and practices, II, 57, 158, 159, 219, 220, 232, 236; V, 11-12, 343; rest, I, 86, 136, 280-281, 285, 298, 299, 311, 469; significance, II, 283; V, 343-344, 349; and socializing, V, 11-14
ṣabī (boy, young man, freedman, slave), I, 93, 161, 164; II, 62, 440, 467, 599; helper in workshop, I, 94. See also *ṣibyān*; *ghulām*
sabīka (cast copper), I, 420. *See also* Copper
(*ᶜala*) *sabīl al-taqdima* (prepayment of rent). *See* Rent, prepayment
Sābiq al-Kohen b. Maḥfūẓ, V, 539
Sābiq b. Mawhūb, II, 572
ṣabiyya (girl), meaning wife, III, 162. *See also* Wife
sabk (foundings [of coins]), I, 373. *See also* Dirhem
ṣabr (patience), V, 53
sabt. *See* Sabbath
ṣābūn. *See* Soap
Sachet, IV, 131, 183, 337, 463
Sachkultur (material civilization), note on, IV, 270
Sacrifice of Isaac, night of, II, 221
saᶜd (good fortune), II, 374
Saᶜd al-Bāniyāsī, II, 440
Saᶜd al-Dīn, V, 582
Saᶜd al-Mulk ("A Blessing for the Government"), title, II, 356; III, 358
Ṣaᶜda, Yemen, II, 21; IV, 455; V, 514
Saᶜdān, cantor, II, 455
Saᶜdān b. Thābit Baghdādī, V, 243, 574
ṣadāqa (friendship), term for informal business cooperation, I, 169. *See also* Friendship, formal; Informal cooperation
ṣadaqa (charity, pious foundation), II, 138, 442, 545; III, 243, 489; IV, 88
Ṣadaqa al-ᶜAṭṭār, banker, II, 507
Ṣadaqa b. Ḥakmūn, III, 474; V, 559
Ṣadaqa b. Jarīr, IV, 314
sādatuna ʾl-mathāʾib (our lords, [the heads] of the academies), II, 595
ṣaddeqet (pious), III, 166
Saddler, I, 422
Saddles, saddling, IV, 264, 265, 448
Sadducees, V, 359
sādhaj(*a*) (plain, of one color or material), said of clothing and jewelry, IV, 208, 211, 424, 462, 466
al-Sadīd, honorific title, II, 508, 577, 605, 609
Sadīd al-Dawla Abū Saᶜd, V, 582
sādīn miṣrī (Heb., Egyptian robe), III, 445. *See also* Robe
ṣadr: different meanings of, IV, 107, 120; service tray, IV, 145, 327, 392, 395; textile covering wall opposite entrance, IV, 126, 320, 354; wall opposite entrance, IV, 65, 111
al-Ṣadr, chief judge, II, 566
Ṣadr al-Dīn, qadi, I, 188
safāsif ("poor stuff"), people of low social standing, II, 536. *See also* Social rank
safaṭ (cases of wood), I, 486; IV, 386
Safed, Palestine, II, 502; V, 18, 508, 529, 530
ṣaffayn ("Two Rows," Colonnade), area in Fustat, I, 194; II, 474; IV, 28-29
Safflower, I, 120, 427; II, 442; III, 77; IV, 175, 230, 440
Saffron (*zaᶜfarān*), I, 153, 154, 155, 168, 200, 334; II, 78, 509; III, 77, 442; IV, 173, 175, 233, 260, 380, 386, 406, 429. See also *zaᶜfarānī*
Ṣaffūriyya, Palestine, III, 501
ṣāfī (uniform in color), IV, 177, 182, 411

Ṣāfī, slave, **I**, 133, 139; **IV**, 445
Ṣāfī b. Naḥrīr, V, 169
safqa (transaction), **I**, 196
safsārī, **IV**, 412
safūfī (preparer of medical powders), **II**, 261, 581. *See also* Pharmacist
ṣāgha. *See* Goldsmith
ṣaghīra ("the little one"), term for wife, **III**, 162. *See also* Wife
al-sāgūl ("the Cherished"), **II**, 475
sāḥa (site, open space), **I**, 385; **IV**, 364. See also *ṭaḥṭāḥa*
saḥābī (white), **IV**, 173, 174
Sahara, **I**, 41
ṣaḥḥ (in order, paid), term used in account, **II**, 467
ṣāḥib: companion, **I**, 169, 441; **II**, 275, 454, 467, 604; employee, **II**, 454, 467; meanings of, **V**, 583; *ṣ. barīd* (postmaster), **I**, 283; *ṣ. dār al-ḍarb* (director of the mint), **II**, 605; *ṣ. dār al-ṭirāz* (director of government workshop for gala robes), **I**, 82; **II**, 376; *ṣ. dār al-wakāla* ("proprietor of agency house"), i.e., representative of the merchants, **I**, 187, 446; **II**, 609 (*see also* Representative of the merchants); *ṣ. al-dīwān* (finance director), **II**, 378; **IV**, 24; *ṣ. al-jāliya* (government cashier handling payments of poll tax), **II**, 612; *ṣ. khabar* (chief of secret police), **II**, 608; *ṣ. al-māl* (investor), **I**, 175; *ṣ. al-mawārīth* (Muslim judge in charge of estates), **I**, 380; *ṣ. al-rubᶜ* (supervisor of the quarter), **II**, 369, 608; **IV**, 14, 35, 40, 351 [*rabᶜ*] (see also *ḥāmi 'l-ḥāra*; Quarter of a city); *ṣ. al-shurṭa* (head of the police), **II**, 368, 607; *ṣ. al-sūq* (master of the market, tax farmer), **I**, 194, 483; *ṣ. al-ṭarīq* (guard), **IV**, 351; *ṣ. al-tartīb*, title of a judge, **II**, 607
Sahlān IV b. Abraham III b. Sahlān III, **I**, 48; **II**, 435, 504, 511, 554, 566; **III**, 6, 7, 118, 137–138, 472; **IV**, 265, 312, 450; **V**, 558, 579
Sahlawayh b. Ḥayyīm, **III**, 56, 136, 438
Sahlawayh II b. Mulūk, **III**, 439
Sahl b. Ḥātim, **V**, 569
Sahl b. Israel b. Jacob Tustarī, **III**, 136
Sahl b. Maṣlīʾaḥ, **III**, 26; **V**, 361, 607, 608
ṣaḥn (open court), **IV**, 366
Ṣahrajt, Egypt, **I**, 249, 474; **II**, 40, 50, 218, 233, 239, 438, 441, 526, 527, 530, 533, 534, 573, 596, 607; **III**, 39, 83, 212, 282, 339, 388, 435, 503; **IV**, 265, 275, 361
Saida, Lebanon, **III**, 201
Saᶜīd b. Isaac, **II**, 471
Saᶜīd b. Marḥab, **V**, 595
Saᶜīd b. Muᶜammar, **III**, 197
Saᶜīd b. Munajjā. *See* ᶜUllā ha-Levi b. Joseph
al-Saᶜīd b. Nīsān, **II**, 500
ṣāʾigh (gold or silversmith, jeweler), **I**, 108, 420; **IV**, 207. *See also* Goldsmith; Silversmith
Sailors, **I**, 157, 313, 342
St. Augustine, **I**, 41
St. Michael's church, **II**, 148, 284, 291
St. Sergius (Bū Sargā) church, **IV**, 16, 29
Saᶜīr = Sheʾērīt (H), **II**, 538
sakākīn ("knives"): ribbons, **IV**, 336, 462; unravelled ends of fabric, **I**, 419 (*see also* Fringes; *murayyash*; Tassels)
sakākīnī (cutler), **I**, 421
Sakan = Shekhanya, grandfather of Japheth b. David, **II**, 569
sākin (resident), **II**, 537
ṣakka (Per., note), **I**, 245. *See also* Bill of exchange
salᶜ (goods, commodities), **I**, 452
Saladin, **I**, 36–38, 59, 61, 63, 270, 271, 345, 424; **II**, 48, 105, 137, 251, 257, 264, 289, 342, 353, 357, 387, 398, 405, 578, 603; **III**, 127, 278; **IV**, 205, 356; **V**, 537, 556, 634
salaf (loan, advance), **I**, 247, 463, 464. *See also* Loans
Salāma, a freedman, **I**, 436
Salāma, d. of Furayj b. Suhayl, **III**, 482
Salāma, brother-in-law of Judah Ibn Sighmār, **V**, 568
Salāma b. Joseph, **IV**, 369
sālār (Per., chieftain), **III**, 442
Salamiyya, Syria, **II**, 278
Sal ammoniac (*nushādir*), **I**, 79, 228–229, 334, 337; seller of, **I**, 410; **II**, 506
Salaries, **II**, 108, 117, 121–126, 186, 357, 358, 436, 441, 453, 461, 462, 463, 559, 605. See also *jāmikiyya*; *al-jumᶜa*; School fees
Salé, Morocco, **V**, 75
Salerno, Italy, **I**, 40, 211; **II**, 25, 242, 247; **III**, 21
Sales tax, **I**, 140, 271, 342
Saleswoman, **III**, 145
ṣalīb(iyya), winds blowing at time of the Feast of the Cross, **I**, 317, 482
ṣāliḥ (first quality), **I**, 452
Ṣāliḥ b. Bahlūl, **V**, 541
Ṣāliḥ b. Barhūn Tāhertī, **III**, 463, 469; **V**, 604
Ṣāliḥ b. Dāʾūd, **V**, 108
Sālim, the beadle, **I**, 261; **II**, 432, 456, 459
Sālim, the porter, **II**, 459

Sālim al-Ḥalabī, V, 135
Sālim b. Hārūn, III, 304
Sālim *al-khādim,* II, 540
salla. See Baskets
Salma, daughter of Nathan, III, 215
Salmān, Egypt, I, 468
Salmān al-Levi b. Solomon, V, 542
Salmūn, Egypt, II, 610
Salonica. *See* Salonika
Salonika, I, 52, 58, 214; II, 167; III, 440; IV, 103; V, 438, 442–443
Salqaṭa, I, 322
"Salt," slave girl, I, 137
Saltykov-Shchedrin Library. *See* Leningrad
ṣaʿlūk (beggar, poor), i.e., destitute, I, 410; II, 435; V, 76; said of merchant with little cash, V, 526. See also *mastūr*; Poor; Social rank
salwā lil-marʾa (cheering money for the wife), III, 167
Salyāṭa (Salqaṭa?), I, 483
samāḥa (favor) or small discount (*ḥaṭāṭ*), I, 196, 197, 445, 449. *See also* Discount
sāmān (fine reed). *See* Reeds
samār (rush used for mats), IV, 128
Samaritans, I, 424; II, 7, 8, 16, 23, 27, 520, 526, 602; III, 158
Samarkand, Central Asia. *See* Samarqand
Samarqand, I, 400; IV, 1
Samawʾal al-Maghribī. *See* Samuel the Maghrebī
Sambari, II, 534
Samḥūn the Sicilian, V, 203
ṣāmit (solid), said of jewelry, IV, 211, 424
sammāna (seller of melted butter), II, 413
Sammanūd, Egypt, I, 404, 417, 474; II, 506, 566, 596; III, 221, 483
sammāq. See Sumac
Samrā ("Dark Brown"), f., III, 327
samsara (brokerage), I, 185, 439, 445, 449. See also *simsār*
Samuel (biblical), II, 4
Samuel, Heb. equivalent of Ismaʿīl, V, 632
Samuel, a cantor, V, 580
Samuel, French rav, II, 492
Samuel b. Aaron, V, 573
Samuel al-Amshāṭī, IV, 413
Samuel b. Abraham, II, 538; V, 190, 538, 604
Samuel b. Avṭalyōn, judge, II, 438, 455, 472, 511, 539; III, 294, 492; V, 509, 513
Samuel (Ismaʿīl) b. Barhūn Tāhertī, III, 294
Samuel b. Daniel b. Azarya, V, 578
Samuel b. Eli, Gaon, I, 278; II, 13, 90, 184, 198, 213, 303, 522, 541, 564, 575; III, 13, 153, 459
Samuel b. Ḥalfōn, physician, V, 378
Samuel b. Hananel, II, 515
Samuel b. Hananiah. *See* Samuel b. Hananyah, Nagid
Samuel b. Hananya(h), Nagid, I, 139, 280, 465; II, 26, 32, 100, 113, 115, 142, 168, 244, 280, 352, 376, 386, 485, 502, 506, 513, 528, 531, 541, 576, 595, 596; III, 5, 21, 81, 137, 275, 289, 296, 426, 448, 505; IV, 233, 277, 313, 326, 457; V, 239, 455, 469, 546, 579, 590, 629, 635, 639
Samuel b. Ḥofnī, Gaon, II, 15, 424, 519, 564; III, 261, 430; V, 385–386, 390, 419, 565, 615
Samuel b. Isaac Ibn al-Fakhkhār, V, 587
Samuel b. Jacob (Ismaʿīl b. Yaʿqūb) al-Andalusī, II, 560
Samuel b. Jacob Ibn Jāmiʿ, III, 431
Samuel b. Japheth. *See* al-Rashīd al-Samawal
Samuel b. Joseph Yijū, III, 43
Samuel b. Judah. *See* Abuʾl-Maʿālī b. Judah, known as Ben Asad
Samuel b. Judah Ibn Asad. *See* Abuʾl-Maʿālī b. Judah
Samuel b. Moses, II, 566
Samuel b. Nahum, II, 504; III, 484; V, 553
Samuel b. Nathan *he-ḥāvēr,* III, 489
Samuel b. Nethanel, II, 538; IV, 351
Samuel b. Saʿadya ha-Levi, judge, I, 381, 409; II, 124, 268–269, 417, 427, 432, 433, 449, 459, 485, 504, 514, 546, 552, 572, 584, 585; III, 324, 443, 445, 458, 478, 488, 489; V, 431, 445, 629, 634
Samuel b. Shela, II, 553
Samuel b. Solomon, II, 452, 553
Samuel b. Ṭalyūn. *See* Samuel b. Avṭalyōn
Samuel ha-Kohen, II, 496
Samuel ha-Kohen b. Moses b. Ṣemaḥ, I, 362
Samuel ha-Kohen b. Wahb, III, 439
Samuel (Ismaʿīl) ha-Levi b. Abraham, III, 293
Samuel ha-Levi b. Japheth al-Bathanūnī, IV, 359
Samuel *ha-mēvīn,* cantor, II, 504
Samuel ha-Nagid, poet, I, 48, 52; II, 25, 173, 525; IV, 318, 418; V, 119, 128, 178–179, 204, 390-391, 423, 470, 557, 617, 627

Samuel Ibn Nagrela. *See* Samuel ha-Nagid
Samuel Ibn Lukhtūsh, III, 57; V, 453, 457, 637
Samuel of Granada. *See* Samuel ha-Nagid
Samuel Tāhertī. *See* Isma'īl Tāhertī
Samuel Ibn al-Ukhtūsh. *See* Samuel Ibn Lukhtūsh
Samuel the Maghrebi, convert to Islam, I, 49; II, 159, 184, 226, 302, 303; III, 355; V, 602, 639
sāmūkh (Heb., licensed [in the yeshiva]), II, 565
San'a, Yemen, II, 22, 316; III, 36, 104; IV, 71, 150, 408; V, 25
ṣanādiqīn. *See* Chestmakers
ṣanānīrī (maker of hooks), I, 421
sanbūsaqa (triangle candle holder), II, 150
Sandafā, II, 605
ṣandal. *See* Sandalwood
Ṣandal, slave, I, 144
Sandal, color, IV, 182
Sandalwood, I, 175, 223, 226; II, 581
Sanders, Paula, IV, 59, 128, 370, 425, 435; V, 632
ṣandūq. *See* Chests
Ṣanhāja, I, 41
Sanhedrin, II, 196, 197
Sanhūr, Egypt, I, 438; II, 602, 606; III, 269; IV, 448
ṣāni' (artisan), I, 93, 410, 414, 415, 418; II, 478. *See also* Artisans; Laborers; Weavers
ṣanī'a (client), V, 81
Sanitation, IV, 33–40, 54
Saniyyu 'l-Dawla wa-Amīnuha, II, 356, 587
ṣanja (weight), I, 254
Sanskrit, IV, 172, 173
Saphir, Jacob, I, 395; II, 145, 147; V, 620
Saqāliba quarter, Cairo, IV, 283
saqīfa. *See* Portico
Saqīfat sha'īra, a location, IV, 280
sāqiya, family name (exact meaning unknown), I, 129, 431
Ṣaqlābī, of Slavic origin, I, 31, 400; II, 440; material, IV, 116, 380
sār ("prince"), Heb. title, I, 76; *s. ha-midrāsh* ("Prince of the midrash), II, 563; *s. ha-sārīm* ("Prince of Princes"), V, 629
ṣārā (Heb., rival wife), III, 209
Sarah (biblical), III, 62, 210
Sarah b. Israel b. Sahl, III, 28
ṣarāwīl (*ṣ* = *s*), pants, IV, 399
Sardinia, I, 325
Sardis, synagogue of, II, 144, 145
ṣarf. *See* Exchange rate
ṣarf al-fiḍḍa (change into silver money), I, 240. *See also* Exchange rate
sarīr. *See* Bedstead
al-Sāriya (*maḥras*), IV, 34
Sariyy b. Ḥayyim, III, 443
sarjī. *See* Saddler
Sarqanā, IV, 402
sarrāj. *See* Saddler
Sar Shalom (ha-Levi) Gaon b. Moses, II, 26, 32, 33, 122, 352, 528, 546, 571, 572, 573; III, 81, 111, 133, 252, 336, 482, 502; V, 110, 491, 492, 512, 547, 564, 572, 581
Sarūj(ī), IV, 24
Sarwa ("Cypress"), f., III, 45, 50; IV, 314, 315, 316–317, 375
sās (flock or oakum), IV, 376
sa'sam. *See* Wood, ebony
Sāsōn b. Japheth, III, 502
Sāsōn b. Meshullām, II, 514; III, 460; V, 538, 556
Sassanian, Sassanid, IV, 109, 125, 184, 197, 305, 413
Satan, V, 337, 590. *See also* Hell
ṣaṭl. *See* Bucket
sāṭūr (knife for cutting meat), IV, 297
Saturday. *See* Sabbath
Saudi Arabia, II, 144; IV, 149
Saul (biblical), II, 4
Sauvaget, IV, 3
Sawāda, II, 439
"Sawduster," I, 100, 416
sawm (market price [Spain]), I, 453
ṣawwāf (wool maker or seller), I, 448
Sawyers, I, 90, 97, 113; II, 424
ṣayārifī (banker), I, 400. See also *ṣayrafī*; Bankers
Ṣayd ("Quarry"), slave girl, I, 136
ṣaydalānī (dealer in sweet-smelling wood), II, 581
ṣaydalānī. *See* Pharmacist
ṣaydanī. See *ṣaydalānī*
sayf (sword), I, 475; II, 606; III, 468
Sayf al-Islām, II, 256
ṣayrafī (banker), I, 234, 246, 247, 248, 376, 410, 462; II, 375, 392, 474, 484, 490, 494, 508, 582, 609, 612; III, 492, 505. *See also* Bankers; Money changer
Ṣayyādīn street, Fustat. *See* Fishermen
Sayyida, f., V, 145–147
Sayyid al-Ahl b. Hiba, pharmacist, I, 364
sayyida(tī) [*al-ukht*] ("my mistress"), form of address, III, 431
Sayyidat al-Mulk, sister of caliph al-Ḥākim, III, 357

Sayyid al-kull b. Abū Yaʿqūb, cantor, V, 564
sayyidī ("my lord"), form of address, I, 413; II, 442
scala (Ital., ship's plank), I, 47
Scammony, I, 184, 200; II, 267, 584
Scanlon, George T., I, 110; IV, 13, 36, 53, 54
Scarf, IV, 197, 320; V, 549
Scarfmakers, house of, II, 432
Schechter, Solomon, I, 3–4, 5, 8, 9, 24
Scheiber, Alexander, I, 4; II, 306
Schirmann, J., I, 4; V, 287, 320
Scholars, scholarship, II, 42, 65, 79, 83, 197, 226, 228, 229, 291, 522, 523, 534, 548, 557, 595, 598, 615; III, 13, 31, 189, 198, 204, 218, 219; as entertainment, V, 37–38; and charitable foundations, II, 423, 441, 442, 454, 462, 463, 464, 476, 478, 495, 498, 499; financial support, I, 92; II, 85, 121, 123, 546; V, 9–10, 363, 417–419, 431–433; and friendship, V, 283–285; importance, V, 9, 267, 415–417, 431, 442–443, 474–475, 502; international character, I, 51–54; II, 94, 95, 172; V, 438–439, 442–443, 464–465; Islamic, V, 9, 443; Karaites, V, 362–364; and marriage, III, 56, 58, 59, 88, 137, 154, 168, 173; methods and education, II, 158, 160, 179, 205, 211–219, 561; V, 384–385, 419, 429–430; pietistic, V, 479–480; prestige of, II, 77; III, 7, 14; V, 415-496; relationship to local and ecumenical authority, II, 23, 70, 74, 75, 76, 521; scientific, V, 10, 285, 419–420; secular and religious combined, II, 260–261; titles related to, II, 189; V, 266–268. *See also* Theology; Yeshivas
Scholasticism, II, 206
Schoolboys, II, 153, 173–183, 453; clothing of, II, 181, 182
School fees, II, 124, 133, 174, 187, 188, 419, 463, 465, 495, 544, 559
Schoolmaster, II, 433, 544, 572; III, 64, 165, 241, 281, 345
Schools. *See* Education
Schrire-Steiger, Carmel, V, 538
Sciacca, I, 330
Sciences, secular, II, 197, 241, 243. *See also* Greek science
"Scribe of the yeshiva," title, II, 15, 513
Scribes, I, 51, 79, 162; II, 42, 50, 69, 72, 73, 85, 89, 125, 127, 189, 198, 228–240, 429, 444, 446, 457, 463, 514, 540, 550, 560, 572–574, 576, 597, 605; III, 13, 14, 87, 138, 201, 226 (see also *kātib*); remuneration of, II, 237–239. *See also* Copyists
Script: Arabic, I, xviii, 14, 16, 241, 294, 336, 374; II, 174, 177, 179, 180, 182, 193, 229, 232, 235, 253, 254, 266, 346; cursive, II, 557; Cyrillic (Russian), I, 15; decorative on *ketubba*, III, 111–113; Hebrew, I, xviii, 2, 13, 14, 15, 16, 209, 241, 271, 286, 288, 294, 336, 374; Latin, I, 16; mirror, I, 218; of Geniza documents, I, 14, 19; on clothing, IV, 181, 182, 198; Spanish-Jewish, I, 19 (*see also* Ladino); Syriac, I, 15, 218. *See also* Calligraphy; Writing, art of
Scripture. *See* Bible
Scripture lections. *See* Bible, reading of
Scrolls (*megilloth*), I, 14
Seafaring, I, 27, 273ff.
"Sea loan," I, 256. *See also* Loans
Seal ring (*khātam*). *See* Finger ring
Seat (*takht*), IV, 131, 307, 378, 379, 386
Seating, IV, 107–117, 298-299, 307–309, 377
Sea vessels, I, 305–308. *See also* Ships
"Sea wool," I, 106; IV, 182
Secession from congregation, II, 65. *See also* Local community
Seclusion of women, III, 153ff., 358. See also *ḥarīm*; Women
Second-hand clothes (*khalīʿ*, "cast-off"), I, 150; IV, 184–185, 400, 413. *See also* Clothing
Second-hand clothes, dealer in (*qashshāsh*, *qāshsh*, *qushāshī*), I, 437–438, 448; II, 448; IV, 184, 298
Second marriage. *See* Remarriage
Second Temple, V, 620
Second wife. *See* Wife
Secret deposition, II, 341–342
Secret door (*bāb al-nisāʾ*, *bāb al-sirr*), women's entrance, II, 144, 152, 293, 429; IV, 60–61, 364, 368. *See also* Women, gallery
Secret Gate. *See* Secret door
Secret police, I, 271; II, 279, 304, 608, 610. *See also* Police
Security, IV, 6, 25, 33–40
ṣedāqā (Heb., charity), II, 138, 500, 543, 549, 555. *See also* Charity; Pious foundations
Ṣedāqā = Ṣadōq, II, 576
Ṣedāqā, the Translator, II, 478
Ṣedāqā, man of Tripoli, V, 121
Ṣedāqā b. Abraham Ibn Warda, III, 435
Ṣedāqā b. Bunān, I, 364
Ṣedāqā b. Jonah, I, 446
Ṣedāqā b. Muvḥār, I, 363

Ṣedāqā b. Nufayʿ, II, 501; III, 59, 484
Ṣedāqā ha-Levi b. Moses, V, 597
Ṣedāqā ha-Levi b. Solomon, cantor, II, 569; V, 540
Ṣedāqā ha-meshōrēr b. Ṣemaḥ, III, 465; V, 543
Ṣedāqā al-Ramlī, III, 154
Seeds, I, 155
sēfer tōrā. *See* Torah scroll
Segan (ha-kōhanīm), II, 561
sekhar baṭṭālā (Heb., compensation for loss of time), II, 546, 565
Selah, as ending to letter, V, 528
Seleucia. *See* Silifke
Seleucid Era. *See* Era of the Documents
Seleucids, III, 8
Self-respect, importance of, V, 76
Seljuks, I, 22, 35, 39, 58, 261, 380; II, 30, 55, 137, 201, 286, 441, 501, 585, 604; III, 198, 201, 239; IV, 24, 41, 416, 439
Seller of potions. *See* Potions, preparers or sellers of
Ṣemaḥ b. David, and wife, V, 146, 147
Ṣemaḥ b. Japheth. *See* Abū Manṣūr Ṣemaḥ
semīkhūth (Babylonian degree), II, 565
Semi-precious stones (*faṣṣ*, pl. *fuṣūṣ*), IV, 205–206, 420
"Semites," "Semitic," II, 282–283
sena (senna), II, 583
Senegal. *See* Ṣanhāja
Senna, II, 267, 583
Sensitivity to others, V, 62, 218–220, 224–225, 229–240, 246, 296-297
ṣenūʿā (Heb., chaste), III, 166
Senyōn, perhaps an Arabism for Senior, I, 402
Sepharadim, in Istanbul, II, 167
ṣērafī. *See* Bankers; *ṣayrafī*
Serjeant, R.B., IV, 4, 192, 199
Sermons, II, 158, 216, 217, 553
Services, religious: daily, V, 11; liturgy, V, 382, 417, 424 (*see also* Poems, liturgical); memorial, V, 115, 186; Sabbath, V, 11–12, 343; visiting preachers, V, 32–33, 57. *See also* Prayer; Synagogue
Sesame, female nickname, II, 463
Sesame, I, 120, 155; II, 531; as color, IV, 409, 465
Sesame oil, IV, 230, 231, 232, 246, 252, 427, 440
Set (*dast*), IV, 146–147, 390
"Settlement [of a lawsuit]" (Heb. *peshārā*), II, 601
Settlements outside the court, II, 335
Seven, as a communal board, II, 59, 79, 535, 537
(The) Seventh, a title, II, 586
Severus Ibn al-Muqaffaʿ, IV, 183
Seville, Spain, I, 41, 42, 69, 212, 213, 306, 315, 316, 318, 321, 325, 326, 331, 338; II, 10, 588; IV, 1, 403
Sewage. *See* Drainpipes
Sexes, separation of, V, 22, 98, 143, 163, 310–311, 409, 439. *See also* Women
Sexual activity and mores: adultery and fornication, V, 314–316; class differences, V, 308–309; homosexuality, V, 21, 202, 311–312, 316, 319–320; Islamic society, V, 308–312, 317–318, 321; marital, V, 218, 312–313; offenses, II, 330; phraseology, V, 309; polygamy, V, 313–314; religious differences, V, 310–311
Sexual deviation, and personal honor, V, 202–203. *See also* Homosexuality
Sfax, Tunisia, I, 68, 205, 212, 220, 272, 289, 302, 307–308, 310, 318, 340, 342, 343, 344, 388; II, 68, 608; IV, 404; V, 507
shaʿʿāb (tinker), I, 421
Shabbat, a name, II, 454
Shabbāt b. Elazar, scribe, II, 534
Shabbat *ha-shōfēṭ*, II, 595
Shabbetay b. Abraham, judge, II, 44, 48, 67, 531, 532, 533; IV, 461
Shabbetay Donnolo, II, 242
Shabbethay Qalaʿī, II, 497
Shābūr, Egypt, I, 297
shadāʾid (hardships), II, 612
shaddād. *See* Packer
shādhirwān (cooling device), IV, 65
Shadhūna, IV, 169, 193, 403
Shadow plays, V, 21, 43–44
al-Shāfiʿī, II, 562; V, 613
Shāfiʿīs (school of law), II, 201, 381
shafrīr (beauty, adornment), II, 530
Shafrīr Miṣrayim (Old Cairo), II, 530
Shagreen, IV, 130, 132, 385
shahd (honeycomb), I, 429. *See also* Honey
shah-bender (Per., provost of the merchants of Cairo), I, 192
shāhid (notary), II, 321
Shāhīn, I, 400
Shāhinshāh (King of Kings), title for ruler, II, 350
Shahryār, I, 400
shaḥtūra (small boat), I, 325
shāʿir (poet), II, 224, 429, 491, 500. *See also* Poetry, Poets
al-Shāʿir (the Poet), family name, II, 491, 500

shajarat Allāh ("God's tree"), deodar, **II**, 584
shāka (a boat used to transport flax), **I**, 474
shakāra (bag, bale), **I**, 336. See also *shikāra*
Shaked, S., **I**, 6, 24
shākha. See *shāka*
shakhṣ (one piece in a consignment), **I**, 487
shakhtūr (type of seagoing barge), **I**, 477
shālīaḥ (Heb., [special] messenger), **I**, 288, 446; **II**, 464, 542, 599. See also *rasūl*
shālōm (Heb., communal peace), **II**, 64, 594; **III**, 354. *See also* Peace
Shālōm Ṣughayyir (Heb., Very Small), name, **II**, 497
shām (Palestine or Damascus), **II**, 589; **III**, 197. *See also* Palestine; Syria
shamᶜa. *See* Candle
Shamᶜān (Simᶜān), **I**, 446
Shamᶜān's sister's son, **III**, 25
shamārī. *See* Fennel
Shame, **V**, 76, 199–200, 249, 304–305. *See also* Family honor
shāmī (from Palestine or Damascus), **II**, 448, 463, 475, 559; Damascene (paper), **I**, 410
shāmiyya musaṭṭara, Syrian coins whose legends are arranged in parallel lines, **I**, 460
shammāᶜ. *See* Wax, waxmakers
shammās (deacon of church), **II**, 82, 434
shammāsh (Heb.). *See* Beadle
Shams, f., **II**, 245
Shams, a man's name, **II**, 496
Shams al-Dīn Alkyn, **V**, 175, 555
*Shams al-ḥukamā*ʾ ("The Sun of the Doctors"), title for physician, **II**, 577
shamshak (term for slipper), **IV**, 400
Shamṭūniyya, **V**, 30, 113
Shamūn, name, **V**, 591
sharāb (medicine, soft drinks, potions). *See* Potions; *s. sādhij* (plain [unflavored] potion), **II**, 585; *s. ward* (*see* Sherbet); *rubb sūs sharāb* (liquorice jam), **II**, 584
sharābī. *See* Potions, preparers or sellers of
sharābiyya (vessel for wine or soft drinks), **IV**, 147, 148, 321, 393, 394
Sharaf al-Dawla, **II**, 495
Shaᶜrānī ("Hairy"), family name, **II**, 467
al-Shaᶜrānī, **IV**, 43, 46, 359; **V**, 471
sharb (fine linen). *See* Linen
Sharbīn, **II**, 606
sharīf (Muslim notable), **II**, 120, 545
Sharqiyya province, Egypt, **II**, 295, 468
sharrāba, shurrāba. *See* Tassel
Sharyānī, **I**, 311
shāshiya (long piece of fine material), **IV**, 196, 416, 417
shaṭranjī. *See* Chessplayer
Shaṭṭanawf, **I**, 297, 417
Shavuot. *See* Pentecost
shāvūy (Heb., captive), **II**, 490. *See also* Captives; Prisoners
Shāwar, Fatimid vizier, **IV**, 12, 103
Shawdar(ī), **IV**, 169
Shawl, **IV**, 152, 392. *See also* Prayer mantle
*shawwā*ʾ (roaster), **I**, 115, 424
shay (goods, commodities), **I**, 452
Shaᶜyā, abbrev. of Ibn Shaᶜya, **III**, 9, 10. *See also* Ibn Shaᶜya
shaykh. *See* Elder
al-shaykh ha-baḥūr ("the elder, the young man"), **II**, 61
shaykh al-yahūd (elder [i.e. head] of Jews), **II**, 77; **III**, 24. *See also* Head of the Jews
Shaᶜyūn b. Isaac, **II**, 471
Sheep(breeding), **I**, 76, 105
Sheʾērīth b. Japheth ha-Kohen, **III**, 492
Sheʾērīth b. Yākhīn ha-Kohen, **IV**, 461
shekel (Heb.), **I**, 360
Shela b. Amram al-Qirqīsānī, **III**, 439
Shelah b. Ayyash, **V**, 212–214, 566
Shēlā b. Elazar, **III**, 489
Shela b. Mevassēr, judge, **II**, 587, 595; **III**, 481; **IV**, 374
Shelah, known as Faḍāʾil, **I**, 365
Shela ha-Levi *ha-talmīd*, cantor, **II**, 569
Shelah al-Makīn, **I**, 367
Shelah b. Zadok b. Maṣliaḥ, **V**, 378–379
Shellfish (source of purple), **IV**, 171–172
Shemarya = Maḍmūn ("Protected by God"), **II**, 26; **V**, 598
Shemarya b. David, Nagid, **II**, 26, 526
Shemarya b. Elhanan, **II**, 28, 202, 308, 511, 526, 537, 542, 596, 598, 600; **III**, 471; **V**, 418
Shemarya b. Ḥalfōn, **III**, 481
Shemaryah b. Solomon Ibn Maḥāra, **III**, 492
Shemaryah ha-Kohen b. Manasse, known as Abu'l-Wafā b. al-Nāqid, **I**, 36
Shemaᶜya, Gaon, **II**, 512
shēmōth (writings bearing, or supposed to bear, the name of God), **I**, 2
Shem Tov ("Good Name") *al-ḥāmī*, **II**, 608; **V**, 536
Shepherd, Dorothy G., **I**, 455
Sherbet (*sharāb ward*), **II**, 584. *See also* Potions

Sherira Gaon, **II**, 15, 203, 204, 209, 563, 564, 596, 600; **III**, 430, 450; **V**, 262, 390, 585, 616
shērūt (service), **II**, 541. See also *khidma*
sheṭār (Heb., document), **I**, 251; **II**, 344; **III**, 458, 483; *s. avīzārya* (Aram., acquittance), **II**, 600; *s. yeziftā* (Jewish loan), **I**, 464. *See also* Loans
shevūyīm. *See* Captives; Prisoners
Shibām, South Arabia, **IV**, 55, 362
shiddēkh (*we-qiddēsh, we-ērēs*) (engagement and betrothal), **III**, 441. *See also* Betrothal; Engagement
shiddūkhīn (Heb., engagement), **III**, 69, 444. *See also* Betrothal; Engagement
Shiʿite, **II**, 569; **III**, 158; **V**, 399. *See also* Fatimids; Ismailis
shikāra (bag, bale), **I**, 81, 336, 426
Shiloah spring, Jerusalem, **II**, 282, 588
Shiloh b. Mevassēr, **V**, 557
shimmūsh (personal contact [with scholars]), **II**, 563, 597; *sh. (bēth dīn)* (minutes), **II**, 600
shīnī (war galley), **I**, 477
Shīnīz, **I**, 400
Shipment (*risāla*), **I**, 183
Shipowners, **I**, 156, 309–312 and *passim*
Ships, **I**, 268, 295–338 and *passim*. See also *markab*; Sea vessels
al-Shīr (Heb., the Song [of Moses]), **II**, 553
shīrajī = *shīrājī* (maker of sesame oil), **I**, 427. *See also* Sesame oil
shirka (partnership), **I**, 170, 443. *See also* Partnerships
shiwār. See *shuwār*
Shoemakers, Shoes, **I**, 111, 153, 154, 210, 422; **II**, 287; **IV**, 153, 162–164, 399, 400, 411. See also *khuff*; *madās*
shōfār (ceremonial trumpet), **II**, 340
shōfēṭ (Heb., judge), **II**, 22, 315–316, 319, 533, 566, 568, 595, 596, 599; **III**, 445; *sh. ha-shōfeṭīm* (Muslim chief justice), **II**, 599. *See also* Judges
shōḥad (Heb., bribe), **I**, 488; **II**, 607. *See also* Bribes
shohet (Heb.). *See* Ritual slaughterer
shōmēr (Heb., guard, supervisor), **I**, 363; **II**, 131, 442, 444, 448, 459, 570, 571
Shop. *See* Store
Shopkeeper, **III**, 146
shōshevīn (Heb., best man), **III**, 117, 450
Shoulder bands (*katifiyya, kitfiyya*), **IV**, 207, 217–218, 322, 342, 427, 466, 467
Shrines. *See* Pilgrimage
Shrouds. *See* Burial outfit
Shūʿa, abbrev. of Yeshūʿā (= Ar. Furqān), **V**, 619
shubbān (youth), **II**, 62, 536. *See also* Young men
Shubrā, Egypt, **II**, 222
shūḥāt (fir trees), **II**, 434
shulḥānī (Heb., "the man with the table"), banker, **I**, 248; **III**, 492
shunūf (a type of earring), **IV**, 215, 426
shuqqa: bolt of cloth, **II**, 131, 448; type of clothing, **II**, 448; **IV**, 178, 179, 409, 410, 415. *See also* Robe
shūra (travel outfit, trousseau), **III**, 453; **IV**, 297. *See also* Dowry; Trousseau lists
shurṭa (police, prison), **II**, 368, 379, 607, 609. *See also* Police
shūthāfūth = *shuttāfūth* (Heb., partnership), **I**, 170, 441, 442. *See also* Partnership
shuwār, shiwār ("travel equipment"), term for dowry, **III**, 124, 453; **IV**, 297. *See also* Dowry
Shuwayʿ family, **II**, 16
Shuwayk ("Little Thorn"), nickname, **II**, 506
al-shuyūkh al-mashhūrīn ("noted elders"), **II**, 60. See also *zuʿamāʾ*
shuyūkh al-milla (leading men of the community), **III**, 45
Sibāʿ of Ramle, **I**, 178
ṣibbūr (Heb., community chest), **II**, 108, 122 (*see also* Pious foundations); (*Ṣ*), ten persons, **IV**, 316, 453
ṣibyān (young men, boys), **I**, 414; **II**, 61, 62, 560, 608 (see also *baḥūr*; Young men); *ṣ. al-ḥisba* (market police), **II**, 584 (*see also* Market police)
Sicily, Sicilian, **II**, 136, 357, 539; **III**, 45, 148; **IV**, 163, 168, 180; Arabic vernacular of, **I**, 15; beneficiaries of community chest from, **II**, 440, 442, 467; canopy from, **IV**, 381; cheese from, **IV**, 251, 252, 443; clothing from, **IV**, 157, 397, 398, 452; collection for Jerusalem in, **II**, 96, 472; currency, **IV**, 453; firāshes from, **IV**, 379, 380; hardwood from, **IV**, 144; how referred to in Geniza, **IV**, 6; influence of Spanish Jew with Muslim authorities in, **II**, 60, 61; Jewish merchants robbed in, **II**, 37; letters from, **II**, 67, 192, 301, 536; **IV**, 39; merchants from/in, **II**, 67, 395; **IV**, 251, 280; orphan in, **III**, 300; Palermo cantor converts to Islam, **II**, 301; payment of poll-tax in, **IV**, 39; purchase of house in, **IV**, 282; refugees in, **III**, 56; spelling of name, **V**, 527; syna-

gogues in, II, 167; teachers from, in Egypt, II, 188, 559; textiles from, IV, 114, 169, 181, 379, 410; travel from/ to, II, 192; III, 16, 190; IV, 2, 280
Sick, care for the, II, 109, 134, 216. *See also* Illness
Side, Asia Minor, II, 147
"Sidepiece" (*mijnab*) in carpets, hangings, seats, IV, 120, 126, 127, 320, 381, 382, 384, 454
Sīdī ("Grandpa"), III, 7
sidillā (settee), IV, 68, 362
Sidriyya, Gate, I, 340
Sieves, I, 99–100; IV, 142. See also *gharābiliyya*
Siglaton, a textile, I, 419; II, 111, 151, 545, 551; IV, 116, 121, 124, 131, 177, 305, 323, 324, 327, 330, 381, 382, 384, 386, 407, 454, 455, 459, 461, 463
siglāṭūn. *See* Siglaton
Signet rings worn by men, IV, 206
ṣihr (son-in-law), II, 90, 592; III, 439
Sijilmāsa, Morocco, I, 48, 49, 56, 192, 195, 212, 213, 244, 279; II, 9, 208, 300, 302, 314, 316, 402, 403, 595; III, 137; IV, 1, 419; V, 508
Sijilmāsī, family name, II, 497
sikanjabīn rummānī (syrup of honey and vinegar, flavored with pomegranates), II, 584
Silifke (Seleucia), I, 22, 58, 214; IV, 86, 284
Silk, I, 76, 210, 263, 333, 412, 425, 450; IV, 183, 184, 187, 193, 396, 402, 403, 410, 445, 454, 459, 465; *catarzo* (Ital.) = *qaṭārish* (floss silk); Constantinople, I, 417; dyers, I, 50, 100, 116, 128, 366; II, 35, 67, 536; floss silk (*qaṭārish*), I, 104, 455; Gabes, IV, 168; industry, I, 87, 88, 90, 101–104, 417; IV, 167–170, 305; *khazāsh*, IV, 168; *khazz*, IV, 168, 315, 402; *lādh*, IV, 315, 330, 452; *lālas*, IV, 327, 331; *lānas*, *lēnas* (Indian red silk), I, 454; Lāsīn, I, 191, 417, 454; IV, 168, 402; local varieties, IV, 169; Maghrebi, IV, 120, 121; mixed with linen, IV, 166, 403 (*see also* Dabīqī); partnerships in, I, 178, 203, 207; prices, I, 222–224, 245, 267, 343, 372, 381; *qazz* (black and red silk [inferior quality]), I, 454; IV, 382, 403; qual-ity of, I, 454–455; textiles, IV, 18, 159, 165, 167–170, 299–301, 379, 386; threads, IV, 168, 402; trade in, I, 46, 153, 154, 193, 195, 197, 198, 200, 208, 217, 220, 222–224, 268, 303, 313, 334, 337; II, 45, 78, 465; IV, 305; weavers (*qazzāz*), weaving, I, 51, 71, 78, 79, 86, 93, 96, 104, 128, 255, 264, 365, 384, 410; II, 35, 46, 84, 134, 297, 301, 383, 440, 540, 548; IV, 282, 367, 438; worker (*ḥarīrī*), I, 79, 104, 417, 84, 116; II, 61, 427; IV, 278
Silone, Ignazio, IV, 247
silsila. *See* Chains
Silver, I, 78, 99–100, 154, 155, 200, 216, 233, 235, 267, 301; II, 471, 482, 487, 498, 501, 569; IV, 137, 138, 139, 141, 145, 146, 147, 148, 149, 174, 202–203 and *passim*, 429 (*see also* Dinar; *ḥajar fiḍḍa*; *ḥajar nuqra*; *kesāfīm*; Money); censers, IV, 137; cups, IV, 148; describing color white, IV, 174; ornaments, II, 115, 146, 150–151; value of, V, 170; *ṣiniyya*, IV, 144, 145
Silversmith(ing), I, 85, 87, 100, 108, 365, 366; II, 46, 191, 532, 552; IV, 208, 422, 424; V, 76, 527
Simʿān. *See* Shamʿān
Sīmān Tōv (Heb., "good augury"), name, II, 497
Simeon, patriarch of Judea, III, 8
Simḥā, R., II, 578
Simḥā b. Isaac b. Simḥā Nīsabūrī, V, 584
Simḥa Kohen b. Solomon, IV, 436; V, 105
Simḥa ha-Levi, IV, 375
Simḥa a gravedigger, II, 456; V, 549
simsār (agent), I, 160, 252, 385, 439. See also *samsara*
sinʾā (*sinʾat ha-gōyīm*), II, 587
al-Ṣināʿa, arsenal of Fustat, I, 189, 340–341; II, 606; IV, 27, 34
ṣināʿat al-ʿiṭr (art of perfumery), II, 262
Sinai Desert, I, 276, 278, 294
Sinān, I, 400
Singers, II, 507
Single. *See* Unmarried
ṣīnī (fine earthenware, porcelain), IV, 145, 322. *See also* Porcelain
ṣiniyya (tray), collection, II, 499; III, 116; IV, 144–145, 392
Sinnārī mansion, IV, 61, 364
Sinop(e), Asia Minor, II, 497
Sinoplī, common family name, II, 497
sinʾūth (Heb., "hatred," anti-Semitism), II, 278, 279, 280, 587
Siponto, I, 53
Ṣiqillīya. *See* Sicily
siʿr (price [of the unit sold]), I, 218, 239, 370, 371, 374, 377, 378, 380, 453, 454
Ṣīra, V, 523
Ṣiraqūsī, native of Syracuse, Sicily, V, 569

sirāj. *See* Lamp, oil
Sīrāf, I, 400
Sirāqaws, near Cairo, II, 464
Sirb, a freedwoman, II, 132
Sīrjān, I, 400
sirāj, IV, 387, 388. *See also* Lamps
ṣīr maṭḥūn (minced fish pickles), I, 429
sirwāl (breeches), IV, 162
ṣīṣīth (prayer shawl), IV, 156, 157. *See also* Prayer mantle
Sister(s), III, 32, 47, 174, 177, 308; and brothers, II, 399. See also *karīma*
Sister-in-law, III, 173
Sister's son, III, 24–26, 74, 200
sitr. *See* Curtain
sitt ("mistress"), III, 316, 431, 506. *See also* under individual names
Sitt al-Ahl, wife of Abū Naṣr, V, 152–155, 166, 171, 547, 554
Sitt al-Ahl ("Mistress of the Family"), III, 31, 59, 73, 74, 156; IV, 449
Sitt al-Ahl b. Ibrahīm, III, 504
Sittān b. Abū Naṣr, III, 489
Sitt Baghdad, IV, 430
Sitt al-Banāt ("Queen of the Girls"), II, 560
Sitt al-Bayt ("Lady of the House"), I, 145; III, 229
Sitt al-Bayt b. Jacob, III, 467
Sitt al-Bayt b. Joseph, III, 469
Sitt al-Dalāl ("Lady Bold"), III, 144
Sitt al-Dār ("Mistress of the House"), III, 29, 78, 181, 188
Sitt al-Dār b. Isaac, II, 532
Sitt al-Dār b. Joseph, III, 483
Sitt al-Dār b. Solomon, III, 188
Sitt al-Fakhr ("Glory"), III, 154; V, 41
Sitt al-Fakhr b. Japheth b. Abraham, III, 262
Sitt al-Fakhr b. Tovia, III, 467
Sitt al-Furs, IV, 430
Sitt Ghalb ("Lady Overcoming"), III, 231
Sitt Ghazāl ("Gazelle"), II, 431
Sitt Ghazāl, d. of Wuḥsha, III, 347–348
Sitt al-Ghazāl, wife of Elijah b. Zechariah, V, 515
Sitt al-Ḥasab, I, 433; III, 386; IV, 325–326, 328, 456, 457
Sitt Ḥidhq ("Efficiency"), III, 181
Sitt al-Ḥusn ("Beauty"), III, 80, 92, 310
Sitt al-Ḥusn b. Saʿāda (Saadya), III, 487; V, 147–149, 171, 546, 547
Sitt al-Jamīʿ ("Ruler over Everyone"), III, 92, 316
Sitt al-Kamāl ("Lady Perfection"), II, 478
Sitt al-Khāṣṣa ("Mistress of the Elite"), III, 84
Sitt al-Khāṣṣa b. al-shaykh al-ʿAfīf Abi ʾl-Maʿālī Mevōrākh b. Yaḥyā, III, 443
Sitt al-Khāṣṣ b. Joseph Lebdī, IV, 317–319
Sitt al-Khawāt b. Ṣedāqā, III, 435
Sitt al-Kull ("Ruler over All"), III, 182, 266, 316
Sitt al-Kull, wife of Abuʾl-Ḥusayn Moses b. Solomon, V, 544
Sitt al-Kuttāb ("Queen of the Clerks"), II, 355, 604; III, 291
Sitt Masʿūd, mother-in-law of Abuʾl-Majd b. Yākhīn, V, 515
Sitt al-Milāḥ ("Fairest of the Fair"), d. of Ephraim ha-Levi, III, 328
Sitt al-Nabaʾ ("Excellence"), II, 428; III, 328, 333
Sitt al-Nasab ("Lady of Noble Birth"), III, 173–174
Sitt al-Nasab, wife of Tiqwa b. Amram, V, 567
Sitt al-Naẓar, d. of Ḥalfōn, II, 427
Sitt al-Qawdaf ("Lady Slim"), II, 423
Sitt Rayḥān, wife of the physician Joseph, V, 577
Sitt al-Riyāḍ ("Lady Gardens"), II, 433
Sitt al-Riyāsa, IV, 328
Sitt al-Rūm, slave girl, I, 138
Sitt al-Sāda, III, 449; IV, 286, 317, 319, 375; V, 568
Sitt Ṣāfī, blind woman, II, 458
Sitt Ṣalaf ("Inaccessible"), II, 432; III, 457
Sitt al-Sirr, d. of Wuḥsha, III, 354
Sitt al-Suʿadā ("Mistress of the Happy Ones"), III, 124
Sitt al-Sumr, slave girl, I, 433; V, 547, 605
Sitt al-Thanāʾ ("Praise"), III, 280
Sitt al-Turaf ("Cherished Gifts"), d. of Elazar, III, 67
Sittūna ("Little Lady") b. Faraḥ, III, 435
Sittūna b. Ḥayyīm al-Raḥbī, III, 203
Sittūna b. Japheth, III, 500
Sittūna b. Sulaymān b. Hiba, III, 434
Sitt al-Yumn ("Good Luck"), III, 60, 117
siyyūm (Heb., festive conclusion of yearly reading of Pentateuch), II, 506
Size of Jewish community, II, 44, 139–141
Skins, I, 334
Skoss, Solomon L., V, 381
Skullcap (*maʿraqa*), IV, 154, 320, 323, 327, 330, 396, 413, 456
Sky blue, IV, 117, 193, 327
Slander and rumor, V, 300–303. *See also* Enmity; Reputation

Slaughterhouses, II, 100, 104, 114, 123, 125, 225, 291, 536, 543; IV, 30. *See also* Ritual slaughter; Ritual slaughterer

Slave(s), I, 48, 78, 130–147, 164, 196, 204, 211, 270, 338, 345; II, 189, 257, 305, 311, 349, 402, 590; III, 457, 458, 464. *See also* Freedmen; *ghulām*; *khaddām*; *mamlūk*

Slavegirl(s), I, 131–147, 239, 264, 386; II, 416, 449, 473, 560, 602; III, 24, 67, 82, 106, 143, 144, 147–148, 170, 175, 183, 194, 306, 330–331; V, 42, 213–214, 321–322, 486–487 (see also *jāriya*); manumission, V, 143, 148–150 (*see also* Freedwomen). *See also* Concubinage

Slavs. *See* Ṣaqlabī

Sleeve kerchief. See *mandīl*

Sleeves, I, 205–206; IV, 161–162, 181, 399, 452

Slip. See *ghilāla*

Slippers (*tāsūmā*), IV, 163, 399, 400

"Small," family name, III, 11–12, 289

Smallpox, V, 107

Smith, Adam, I, 131

Smithson, James, III, 285

Snuffer (*qimʿ*), IV, 135, 388

Snyh, II, 606

Soap, I, 154, 165, 184, 267, 302, 344, 437; IV, 140, 183

Soapmaker, I, 437; II, 467

Sobriquets, I, 358

Social life, in general: importance of, V, 25–26; parties and get-togethers, V, 27–28; and personality, V, 187, 215–216; reputation, V, 200–203, 302–305, 307. *See also* Enmity; Family feeling; Friendship; Sex; and other social relations

Social rank: changes in, V, 257–258; class divisions, V, 80, 254–255; high rank, V, 255–260; importance, V, 255–256, 260; traditional phrases, V, 2, 255, 256. See also *jāh*; *mastūr*; *safāsif*; *ṣaʿlūk*

Social safeguards for wife, III, 142–159, 191. *See also* Marriage contracts, special conditions

Social service officers. See *parnās*

Social services: Jewish, II, 3, 91–143, 216, 442, 542–550; Islamic, II, 94. *See also* Charity; Community chest; Pious foundations

Social status, III, 15, 44

Socks (*jawārib*), IV, 182

Sofa. See *martaba*; *ṭarrāḥa*; *qiṭaʿ*

sōfēr (Heb., scribe), II, 229, 230, 531; *s. bēt-dīn* (court clerk), II, 574; *s. ha-malkhūth*, II, 603

Soft drinks. *See* Potions

Soghdian, I, 283

Soldiers, II, 608

Soliciting funds, II, 11, 52, 73, 79, 96, 107, 542, 544

Solitaire (*farīda*), IV, 207, 421, 465

Solomon, biblical, II, 31; V, 583

Solomon, teacher, II, 559

Solomon, son of the judge Elijah. *See* Solomon b. Elijah

Solomon b. Abraham, I, 362

Solomon b. Abū Zikrī Judah Sijilmāsī, III, 282; IV, 18, 189, 196, 415, 416; V, 59–62, 106–107, 545

Solomon b. ʿAzzūn, IV, 443

Solomon b. Elijah b. Zechariah, teacher and scribe, I, 366; II, 94, 101, 104, 381, 430, 450, 451, 452, 461, 463, 487, 493, 495, 499, 505, 509, 542, 543, 559, 560, 570, 571, 575, 597; III, 30, 60, 116, 170, 186, 263, 426, 435, 444, 450, 462, 471, 473, 480, 482, 484, 486, 487, 491, 500; IV, 231, 234, 255, 259, 349, 360, 433, 465; V, 13–14, 26, 394, 396, 418, 505, 506, 515, 543, 572, 577, 590, 597, 642

Solomon b. Ḥayyīm "the Seventh," I, 460; II, 262, 415; III, 482

Solomon b. Japheth, V, 567

Solomon b. Jesse (Yīshay), II, 19, 492, 493, 530; V, 65, 103, 506, 513, 522, 524, 535, 582, 589

Solomon b. Joseph, judge, I, 407; II, 351, 512; III, 442

Solomon b. Joseph, Nagid, II, 530; III, 211

Solomon b. Judah, Gaon, I, 53; II, 14, 15, 16, 56, 58, 71, 72, 88, 104 125, 161, 166, 200, 213, 236, 243, 313, 318, 319, 341, 405, 512, 515, 521, 524, 527, 535, 536, 543, 545, 546, 553, 562, 582, 594, 596; III, 198, 199, 245, 468; IV, 413, 461; V, 62–65, 120, 159, 259–260, 298, 326, 368–369, 339, 412, 433, 509, 558, 579, 597, 610, 618, 620, 622, 630, 631

Solomon ha-Kohen Gaon, V, 259

Solomon b. Mevassēr b. Sahl, III, 28

Solomon II b Moses b. Solomon I, III, 6

Solomon b. Musāfir, III, 489

Solomon b. Mūsā al-Mahdāwī, IV, 382

Solomon b. Nathan, judge, IV, 251; V, 155

Solomon b. Nathanel, III, 268

Solomon b. Nissīm, V, 152

Solomon b. PSh'Ṭ (Fashshāṭ, one who boasts), **II**, 471
Solomon b. Saadya *ha-shōfēṭ*, **II**, 595
Solomon b. Saadya Ben Ṣaghīr. *See* Solomon b. Saadya Ibn Ṣaghīr
Solomon b. Saadya Ibn Ṣaghīr, **II**, 239; **III**, 428
Solomon II b. Saadya II b. Solomon I b. Saadya I Ben Ṣaghīr, **III**, 11
Solomon b. Samuel b. Saadya ha-Levi, **II**, 229, 572
Solomon b. Yeshūʿā, **II**, 589
Solomon b. Yīshay. *See* Solomon b. Jesse
Solomon *he-ḥāsīd*. *See* Abraham the Pious
Solomon ha-Kohen b. Sār Shālōm, **III**, 446
Solomon Ibn Gabirol, poet, **II**, 221, 238; **III**, 207; **V**, 287, 405, 409, 421–422, 423–424, 426, 562, 586
Solomon of Fez. *See* Solomon b. Judah
Solomon's ring (*khawātīm sulaymān*), **IV**, 211, 215, 426. *See also* Solomon's seal
Solomon's seal, as ornament, **IV**, 134
sōmēkh (Heb., assistant cantor), **II**, 224, 501
Son(s), **III**, 201–202, 224–226; education of, **III**, 234–235; executor and guardian, **III**, 283, 298; in control of family purse, **III**, 282; named after father, **III**, 8; support of father, **III**, 225; firstborn, **III**, 279–280; as substitute, **II**, 216
sōnē (Heb., "anti-Semite"), **II**, 278, 586
sōneʾē yisrāʾēl (Heb., haters of Israel), **II**, 586
Song School, **II**, 175, 560
"Son of the Mule," nickname, **II**, 504
"Sons of the Torah." See *benē torah*
Sophocles, **III**, 21, 172
ṣorkhē (*ha-heqdēsh, ha-qāhāl*), **II**, 416, 543
Sororate, **III**, 211–212
Soup, **IV**, 148, 232
Sourdel, Dominique, **I**, 283
South Arabia, **I**, 7, 133; **IV**, 2, 55, 73
Spaciousness, **IV**, 108
Spain, Spanish, **I**, 27, 120, 190, 214, 244, 258–259, 277, 444; **II**, 28, 230, 308, 563, 572; **III**, 20; Almohad persecutions in, **II**, 300; amount of Geniza documents from, **I**, 21; assimilation of Jews in, **V**, 390; beneficiaries of community chest from, **II**, 440, 447, 542; calligraphic style, **II**, 180, 611; cantors in/from, **II**, 90, 136, 222; Christianity in, **I**, 29; clothing, **I**, 50, 416; **IV**, 169, 175, 178, 181, 185, 198, 199, 410, 411, 464; collection on behalf of Jerusalem academy in, **I**, 65; condemnation of al-Ghazzali in, **I**, 65; contributions to Baghdad academies, **II**, 171; correspondence with Gaons, **II**, 9, 10, 11, 171, 564; decisions of Jerusalem and Baghdad courts sought by, **I**, 66; definition of, **I**, xvii; domestic architecture, **IV**, 361; excommunication in, **I**, 69; **II**, 302; family names from, **I**, 20; **II**, 560; family ties with Egypt, **I**, 48; Gaons from, **I**, 53; **II**, 14, 522; handbook for market supervision from, **I**, 83, 97, 117, 234; Ḥisday Ibn Shaprūṭ of, **I**, 191; history of, **I**, 40; home furnishings in, **IV**, 109, 126, 133, 134, 324, 379, 389, 459; immigrants to Egypt from, **I**, 49, 54, 56, 57, 63; **II**, 70, 188, 440, 446, 512, 542, 559, 591; **III**, 60, 130; **IV**, 26; jewelry, **IV**, 420; Jewish scholars in/from, **I**, 64, 126; **II**, 14, 208, 216, 446, 512, 513; **IV**, 198; **V**, 287, 587; Judah ha-Levi of, **II**, 245, 260, 303, 304, 578; **IV**, 185; languages of, **I**, 15, 19, 476; **II**, 167, 180; legal tender, **I**, 234, 235, 360, 370; letters from, **I**, 304, 376; **II**, 180, 611; literary style, **V**, 233, 425; local communities, **II**, 530; mail service, **I**, 284, 289, 291; marriage documents from, **III**, 459; marriage practice for third marriages, **III**, 276; merchants from/to, **I**, 44, 61, 64, 68, 69, 148, 156, 157, 167, 182, 191, 200, 210, 213, 215, 338, 451; **II**, 60, 322, 323; **III**, 61, 439; Moses Maimonides in, **III**, 177, 276, 454; **IV**, 198; *muqaddams*, **II**, 69, 70; Nagids, **II**, 25; ownership and operation of vineyards, **I**, 123; paper production, **I**, 81; partnerships with Muslims in, **I**, 428; pilgrims from, **I**, 55; poets, **V**, 287, 390-391, 425–426, 453, 468, 587; pottery, **I**, 111; price lists from, **I**, 218, 453; proselytizing in, **II**, 305; ransoms, **II**, 95, 542; **V**, 462–463; representative of merchants in, **I**, 191; responsa sent to, **I**, 22; runaway husband in, **III**, 203; sea travel to/from, **I**, 32, 42, 43, 59, 213, 227, 301, 302, 304, 308, 310, 312, 314, 317, 318, 319, 320, 330, 351; **III**, 280; **IV**, 2; silk production, **I**, 102, 193, 222, 417; **IV**, 114, 168, 169, 379; synagogues, **IV**, 128; Taherti brothers in, **I**, 182; title "*ṣāḥib al-shurṭa*" in, **II**, 368; Tujīb clan in, **IV**, 18
"Speeding up," prompt payment or prepayment, **I**, 199; **II**, 545. *See also* Rent, prepayment of

Spengler, Oswald, V, 496
Speyer, Germany, II, 58
Spices (*ḥāja*), I, 154, 214; II, 12, 261-272; IV, 26, 227, 232, 248, 253, 434
Spiegel, Shalom, I, 4
Spikes for cups, IV, 144
Spindles, I, 99-100, 416; V, 37, 515
Spinnery, II, 545
Spinning, I, 100, 127, 128; III, 132, 145, 191, 236
Spinsters. *See* Unmarried women
Spiritual leader, II, 4, 57, 113, 123, 193, 204, 206, 215-217
Spiritual perfection at forty, III, 62
"Splendor of the Yeshiva" (*Hōd*), II, 525
Spools of gold (*bakara*), IV, 217, 322, 427
Spoons (*milʿaqa, malāʾiq*), ornament in jewelry, IV, 107, 424
Spraying. *See* Sprinkler
Spreading the risk (in investments), I, 155, 203, 263-264
Sprinkler (*mumarrish*), IV, 178, 408; of rosewater on guests (*mirashsh[a], qumqum*), II, 585; IV, 149, 224, 394
Square of the Money Changers, I, 194, 448; IV, 28
Square of the Perfumers, I, 194; II, 263, 264; IV, 15, 240
Stables, IV, 60, 75-76, 263, 370, 448
Stairs, staircases, IV, 62-63, 70, 72, 73, 74, 369
Standard prices, I, 222, 229
Standardization of consumption and prices, IV, 244, 256-257, 303
Star of David, I, 337; III, 113; IV, 199
Starch(er) (*nashā, nashshā*), I, 154; IV, 174, 183, 412
Statutes, II, 21, 42, 54, 60, 65-66, 155, 536
Steinschneider, M., V, 397
"Steadiness," slave girl, I, 138
Stepchildren, III, 251, 253, 256, 259, 311. See also *ibn al-mara*
Stepfather, III, 309
Stepmother, III, 232, 256, 280
Stern, S. M., I, 82; IV, 4; V, 399, 517, 637
Stillman, Norman, IV, 194, 297
Stillman, Yedida, IV, 214
Stockings, I, 210
stolos (Gr., fleet), I, 307
Stomach trouble, IV, 250
Stone, IV, 73, 143, 369; flint, IV, 136; hewn, IV, 376; jars (for wheat), IV, 141, 235
Stonecutter (*ḥajjār*), I, 113, 422
Stool for a table, IV, 144
Storage, I, 187, 338-339. See also *makhzan*
(The) Store Guide, II, 582
Storerooms. See *makhzan*
Stores, IV, 15, 58; twin, IV, 16, 19; two, IV, 17
Storytelling, V, 43-44, 284
Stove, IV, 136
Strasbourg, France, II, 591
Strauss-Ashtor, E. *See* Ashtor, E.
Streets, upkeep, IV, 40
Streets and quarters in Cairo. *See* Khandaq; Ṣaqāliba; Zuwayla
Streets and Quarters in Fustat (includes districts, neighborhoods). *See* Alchemists; Banāna; Banū Wāʾil; Bottlemakers; Coppersmiths; Dār al-Fāʾizī; *darb*; Dyers; Fisherman; Fortress of the Greeks; Furriers; Ḥarrānī; Ḥudayjī; Khawlān; Lane of . . . ; Mahra; Maḥras; Mamṣūṣa; Market of . . . ; Maṣṣāṣa; Mikāʾīl; Quarter of a city; al-Rāya; Surayya; Tujīb; Turners; Waʿlān; Waxmakers; Winesellers
Strings for the hair (*khuyūṭ*), IV, 214, 426
Stripes, IV, 113, 161, 181, 182, 306, 309, 323, 378, 411, 465
Stucco, IV, 69, 99, 121, 433
Stucco-workers, I, 96, 113, 423
Students, II, 197
Students of the Torah. See *benē torah*
Study. *See* Scholarship
Suarez, Felix, V, 186
(Mr.) Ṣubḥ, II, 426
subḥa. *See* Rosary
al-Subkī, IV, 43
"Sublime Port," II, 523
"Substitution," as name of son replacing child who died, V, 520. *See also* ʿIwad; Khalaf; Makhlūf
Suburbs, IV, 54
"Success," slave girl, I, 136, 139, 142
Succession, III, 277-280, 290. *See also* Heirs; Inheritance; Orphans
Sudan(ese), I, 135, 136, 137, 235, 244; II, 268
ṣuffa. *See* Bench
Sufism, II, 253, 277; V, 276, 430, 471-474, 478, 479, 480
sufl (ground floor), IV, 63, 295
ṣufr. *See* Copper
sufra (cover for the table), IV, 144, 392
suftaja. *See* Bill of exchange
Sugar, I, 125-126, 154, 185, 190, 195, 197, 216, 220, 263, 264, 337, 428; IV, 15, 246, 441, 442; V, 615; cane, IV, 247-248; molasses (*qaṭāra, quṭāra*), I,

252, 463; raw (*kand, qand*), I, 252, 366; II, 45
Sugar factories and industry, I, 81, 87, 89, 252, 366, 367; II, 45, 98, 258, 494, 531, 580; III, 14; IV, 247–248, 253, 287, 373. See also *maṭbakh*
Sugar maker (*sukkarī*), I, 126, 152; II, 474, 494; III, 14. *See also* Sugar merchant
Sugar merchant, IV, 19, 441
al-ṣughayyira ("the little one"), wife, III, 162
ṣuḥba: formal friendship, I, 169, 440; V, 275, 277, 279 (*see also* Informal cooperation; Partnership); small company of travellers, I, 277, 469
ṣuhūn (plates), IV, 386, 393
Suicide, V, 244–246. *See also* Death
sukhar (corvées), II, 612
sukka (hut for Feast of Tabernacles), II, 152, 154, 168
sukkān (rudder), I, 475; III, 468
sukkarī. *See* Sugar maker
Sukkot, II, 452, 506, 598; IV, 370, 384, 437, 461; V, 16, 17, 350, 351, 531
sukn (residence), II, 152, 420; IV, 15, 57, 286, 288, 363, 367
sulāla (lineage, race, stock), family, III, 436
al-Sulamī, Muslim mystic, V, 479
Sulayman b. Abū Zikrī Judah Kohen. *See* Solomon b. Abū Zikrī Judah Sijilmāsī
Sulaymān II b. ʿAlī b. Sulaymān I, III, 6
Sulaymān b. Hānī, II, 463; III, 464
Sulaymān ha-Levi, collector, II, 451
Sulaymān b. Samḥūn Ibn al-Sahl, V, 566
sulfa (the whole freight), I, 488
Sulfur, I, 154
ṣulḥa (peace settlement), II, 36; III, 291; IV, 372; V, 39
Sullamī, pietist and maker of ladders, II, 566
Sultan, II, 160, 287, 288, 603, 604, 615
sulṭān (government at large), IV, 38, 40; *s. wa-sibyān* (government and officials), I, 414; II, 608
Sumac, I, 154, 213; IV, 440, 441; dyer with, I, 107, 420
Sumāna ("Quail"), female name, II, 413, 545
Sumāna, House of, II, 545
sumayriyya. *See* Nile boat
Sumbāṭ, IV, 442, 445
Sumerian language, I, 161
Summons to court, II, 332
Sumr, d. of Moses, V, 357–358
sumsumī (sesamist), I, 427, 438. *See also* Sesame
ṣunayjāt kibār naḥās ("large little copper scales"), II, 584
Sunbāṭ, Egypt, I, 77, 105, 381, 404, 406, 455; II, 108, 170, 216, 231, 511, 529, 537, 538, 540, 544, 569, 572, 608; III, 284, 389, 392, 495; V, 101
Sunday, III, 169
Sun disk (*shamsa*), pendant, IV, 204, 210, 213, 423, 426
ṣundūq (chest, trunk), III, 454; IV, 130, 378, 379, 385, 387. *See also* Chests
Sunni(te), II, 27; III, 158
Superintendant of the markets. See *muḥtasib*
Superintendant of port, I, 59, 313; II, 366. See also *nāẓir*
Supervisor of guardians, III, 292-293. *See also* Orphans
ṣuqʿ (block, area), IV, 13, 14, 354
sūq al-dhibāḥa (market where animals butchered), II, 543. *See also* Slaughterhouses
sūq al-kattānīn (bazaar of the flax merchants), I, 448. *See also* Flax
sūq al-ṣarf (money changers' bazaar), I, 238. See also *dār al-ṣarf*
Sūq Sandafā, II, 606
Sūq Wardān. *See* Wardān Market
sūq al-yahūd (The Jewish Market), II, 543
Sura, Yeshiva of, II, 5, 15. *See also* Yeshiva
surādiq (canopy), IV, 381
Surayyā, The, II, 483
Surayya lane, quarter, Fustat, IV, 277, 281
Surgeon, II, 252, 255. *See also* Physicians
Surnames. *See* Family names
ṣurra (bag, purse), bale in Indian trade, I, 375, 388, 486
Surūr ("Happiness"), II, 474
Surūr, a courier, I, 291
Surūr, beadle, II, 464
Surūr b. Ḥayyim Ben Sabra (Sabrī), V, 538
Surūra b. Solomon b. Rabīʿ, III, 469
Surūra al-Jāsūs, III, 202–203
Surūr al-Jāsūs. *See* Isaac b. Jacob b. Aaron
Surūr the Khurasānī, II, 468
Surūr - Simḥa - Shād (Per.), II, 468
Surveyor (*muhandis, muhandiz*), IV, 38-39
Sūsa, Tunisia, I, 119, 198, 212, 308, 349, 350, 376; III, 17; IV, 168, 178, 180, 181, 402, 410, 464; V, 518
sūsanjird (embroidered Iranian material), IV, 306–307, 308, 320, 327, 378
Sutayt b. Nadīv, III, 483

Sutayt, wife of Ṣemaḥ b. David, **V**, 145–147
sutūr (sing. *sitr*). *See* Curtains
Suwākin, on Red Sea Coast, **IV**, 403
Suwayd, elder, **II**, 553
Suwaydiyya, Syria, **I**, 38, 212–213, 427; **IV**, 441
Swearing, **V**, 204, 211. *See also* Oaths
Sweetmeats, **I**, 115; **IV**, 243, 246, 441
Swimming, **V**, 12–13, 95
Sycamore, fruit tree, **I**, 121; **II**, 436, 561
Symbolic purchase (*qinyān*), **II**, 42, 329, 330, 334; **III**, 66, 67, 70, 85, 192, 215, 308
Symmetry, sense of, **IV**, 111
Synagogues, **II**, 82, 114, 115, 143–170, 183, 185, 284, 414, 435, 436, 457, 462, 480, 492, 520, 523, 550–552, 588, 601; **III**, 188, 351; **IV**, 15, 21, 29, 36, 137, 162; as address, **II**, 153; adjacent to stores and shops, **IV**, 17, 20; architecture, **II**, 143–149; **IV**, 66, 74, 77; charitable functions, **V**, 92–93, 265; compound, **II**, 84, 145, 152–155, 424, 432, 542, 551; furnishings, **II**, 55, 149–152, 426, 588; **IV**, 124, 126, 128; "great" (*see* Synagogue of the Palestinians); guests, **II**, 161–162; illumination, **II**, 561; **IV**, 133; Karaite, **IV**, 19 (*see also* Karaites); large, main (*see* Synagogue of the Palestinians); library, **II**, 111, 426; multiple functions of, **II**, 155–170; **IV**, 32–33; not for funerals or weddings, **II**, 163; school building, **II**, 557; service, **I**, 98; **III**, 2, 3, 20, 36, 60, 88, 189, 217, 236, 343, 351, 369 (*see also* Prayer; Services, religious); singers, **III**, 460, 465; small (*see* Synagogue of the Babylonians); street of, **II**, 435; tourist attraction, **V**, 20; women in, **V**, 311. See also *kanīs(a)*
"Synagogue boys," **II**, 153
"Synagogue children," **II**, 558
Synagogue Lane, **II**, 434
Synagogue of Dura-Europos, **IV**, 121
Synagogue of Moses. *See* Dammuh
Synagogue of the Babylonians, **I**, 21, 431, 463; **II**, 6, 8, 52, 57, 83, 84, 85, 104, 110, 129, 144, 148, 149, 153, 168, 279, 284, 291, 342, 413, 414, 415, 419, 422, 425, 435, 442, 455, 464, 471, 504, 520, 533, 534, 551, 553, 555, 566, 575, 596; **III**, 6, 137, 294, 351; **IV**, 46, 99, 118, 124, 177, 312, 364, 381, 383, 415; **V**, 383–384
Synagogue of the Iraqians. *See* Synagogue of the Babylonians
Synagogue of the Jerusalemites. *See* Synagogue of the Palestinians
Synagogue of the Palestinians (Geniza synagogue), **I**, 18, 20, 21, 95, 122, 173, 181, 233–234, 293, 431; **II**, 6, 8, 10, 29, 32, 52, 55, 56, 57, 83, 85, 104, 110, 112, 144, 145, 146, 147, 148, 149, 150, 153, 157, 158, 161, 239, 279, 291, 329, 413, 415, 417, 420, 425, 429, 431, 433, 435, 438, 442, 452, 504, 520, 533, 540, 551, 555, 556, 566, 597; **IV**, 33, 36, 40, 102, 118, 124, 127, 364, 381
Synagogue of the teacher, **II**, 453
Synagogue of the woman teacher, **III**, 355
Syracuse, Sicily, **I**, 46, 102, 111; **II**, 40, 58, 340, 530, 602; **IV**, 168, 193, 402, 416
Syria(-ns), **II**, 383, 386, 611; **III**, 246; **IV**, 2, 231, 429; Ayyubids in, **I**, 266; bankers from, **II**, 81; beneficiaries of community chest from, **II**, 441, 447, 467; calligraphic style, **II**, 180, 235; cities, **IV**, 5, 6; commodities exported from, **I**, 154, 202, 214, 334, 381; **IV**, 140, 170; Crusaders in, **I**, 35, 56, 57, 103, 180; definition of, **I**, xvii; domestic architecture, **IV**, 65, 73; elders sent to, **II**, 535; Fatimids in, **I**, 33, 266; **III**, 10, 56; Geniza material from, **I**, 20; Geniza of Aleppo in, **I**, 17; "head of the congregation" in, **II**, 75; hospitals, **II**, 264; in early Islamic times, **I**, 30; in Egypt, **I**, 54; **II**, 188, 269, 385, 441, 447, 467, 559; Karaism in, **I**, 65; Ketāmi conquest of, **I**, 31; letters from, **I**, 56; **IV**, 170; mail service, **I**, 287, 288, 291; Mamluk rule of, **I**, 38; marriage documents from, **III**, 120; **IV**, 217; marriages with Egyptians, **I**, 48; merchants in/from, **I**, 148, 156, 159, 176, 178, 188, 211, 214, 220, 269, 287; **IV**, 176; *muqaddams* in, **II**, 71, 537; Nagids in, **II**, 26; origins of Rabbanite communities in, **I**, 18; *parnāsīm* from, **II**, 81; prices in, **I**, 201; representative of merchants from, **I**, 188, 192; Seljuks in, **I**, 35; **II**, 55; silk production in, **I**, 102, 103, 154, 222; **II**, 35; tax-farmer in, **I**, 194; **II**, 75; trade with Egypt, **I**, 176; under Seleucids, **III**, 8
Syriac, **I**, 15; **II**, 176
Syro-Palestine (-ian), **II**, 454, 520, 526
Syrta, **I**, 212

T

ta'akhkhar ʿalayhim (balance to debit of the community), **II**, 464
ta'akhkhar lahum (balance in favor of the community), **II**, 464

taʿālīq ("what is hung up"), draperies, IV, 298. *See also* Curtains; *busuṭ*
ṭaʿanat shemmā (Heb., claim founded on surmise), III, 146
ṭabaqa (floor, story, apartment), II, 152, 420; III, 459; IV, 57, 58-59, 70, 84, 295, 363, 373
al-ṭabaqa al-ʿaliyya (the uppermost story of a building, upper class), I, 76
Ṭabari(stān), I, 50, 103, 116; II, 283; IV, 109 ff., 128, 304–305, 308, 316, 320, 327, 331, 377, 378, 379, 452, 454
ṭabbākh (meat cook), I, 115, 424; *ṭ. sharāb* (cooker of potions), II, 581
tabbār (merchant in gold nuggets), I, 438
ṭabīb (physician), I, 463; II, 246, 575, 609; *ṭ. al-murabbaʿa*, II, 582; *ṭabība* (woman doctor), I, 128. *See also* Physicians
Tables, IV, 144, 147; absence of, IV, 107, 108; manners at, IV, 229, 432
taʿdiya ("passing out of sight"), said of ship reaching high seas, I, 319
tadhkira (memo), II, 601
ṭafālī (manufacturer of fuller's earth), II, 540. *See also* Fuller's earth
ṭafl. *See* Fuller's earth
tafriqa(t) (distribution), II, 459; *t. al-maqādisa* (collection for community in Jerusalem), II, 96. *See also* Money, distribution of
tafṣīl (cutting up), IV, 178, 182. *See also* Tailoring
tafṣīla (tailored piece), IV, 409, 465
taghlīq al-ḥisāb (closing of the account), I, 451; *t. al-jawālī* (poll tax), I, 451
Ṭaḥāwī, IV, 50
taḥāwiq (popular medicine making women stout), I, 364
Tāhert, I, 20, 181
Tāhertī family, I, 20, 181–182, 216, 233, 350, 370, 378, 443, 444, 468; III, 6, 14, 56, 430, 433, 463, 474; V, 130, 206, 231, 239–240
ṭaḥīna (sesame-meal paste), IV, 245, 440
Ṭāhir, *ghulām*, I, 133
Ṭāhir, shipowner, I, 366, 478
Ṭāhir, beadle, II, 450, 460, 461, 546; III, 456
Ṭāhōr b. Nāmēr, III, 268; V, 626
taḥṭāḥa (open space), II, 475. See also *sāḥa*
ṭāḥūna (hand mill), IV, 391
ṭāʾifa (local community), II, 530. See also *jamāʿa*; *jumla*; Local community; *milla*
ṭāʾifatayn ("the two denominations"), i.e., Rabbanites and Karaites, II, 53
Tailor(ing) (*khayyāṭ, khayyāṭa*), I, 51, 83, 85, 87, 91, 92, 363; II, 98; IV, 177–183, 412
Tāj ("Crown"), model codex of bible, II, 220
tajammul (adornments on clothing), IV, 397; V, 528
taʿjīl (speeding up). *See* Rent, prepayment of
tājir (prominent merchant), I, 149–150, 155, 204, 239, 437, 438, 467; II, 575, 578; III, 10; IV, 15
tājir al-nīl (indigo merchant), I, 438
Tāj al-riyāsa ("The Crown of the Leadership"), title, IV, 11
tajsīs (stucco work in bathhouse), V, 99, 533. *See also* Stucco
takht. *See* Seat
taklīl (adornment with pearls), IV, 203
ṭalab ("asking" [the father for woman's hand]), III, 441
Ṭalāʾiʿ Ibn Ruzzīk, V, 162
Ṭālaqān, Iran, I, 49, 50
Ṭalḥa b. Ṭāhir, I, 81
Ṭalḥī paper, I, 81, 376. *See also* Paper
Ṭalī. *See* Linen
taʿlīm (teaching), II, 556, 560; III, 353
ṭallaq (to repudiate), III, 485. *See also* Divorce
ṭallīth. *See* Prayer mantle
talmīʿ (glitter), said of textile, I, 419
talmīd (Heb., abbreviation of *t. ḥakhāmīm*, "disciple of the sages"), scholar, II, 189, 214, 415, 563, 565, 567, 569; III, 500. *See also* Scholar
Talmud(ic), I, 53, 154, 170, 259, 266, 283, 428, 476; II, 41, 57, 59, 67, 75, 76, 82, 138, 142, 143, 146, 147, 152, 159, 161, 163, 174–175, 222, 228, 265, 278, 312, 345, 363, 403, 501, 521, 564, 600; III, 7, 9, 25, 26, 28, 53, 54, 58, 59, 62, 76, 105, 107, 119, 120, 123, 126, 132, 134, 140, 146, 153, 158, 159, 168, 185, 199, 224, 228, 264, 265–266, 276, 292, 302, 322, 323, 354; IV, 46, 47, 87, 138, 153, 156, 159, 163, 164, 176, 187, 204, 205, 225, 229, 234, 247, 254, 259, 260; cantillation, II, 562; Karaites and, II, 7; V, 365, 372; prestige of, V, 442–443; study of, II, 184, 193, 197, 198, 199, 205, 206, 208, 209, 225, 248; V, 385, 419
talyīṭ (plastering), I, 414
Tam, Jacob, medieval scholar, V, 615
tamar hindī. *See* Tamarind
Tamarind, I, 200; IV, 261, 447
ṭamāwiyā. *See* Containers for wine

ṭamāya. *See* Containers for wine
Tambourines (*dufūf*), **IV**, 424
Tamīm b. Joseph, **IV**, 370
Tamīm b. Muʿizz, ruler of Tunisia, **I**, 376, 377
Tamīm b. Najāʾ, **I**, 292-293
Tanān, village in Qalyūbiyya district, **III**, 579
Tanḥūm b. Jacob, **III**, 430
tannāʾīm (repetitors), lowest grade of teachers in yeshiva, **II**, 199–200
Tanner(y) (*burseqī*, [Heb. derived from Gr.], *madbagha*), **I**, 366; **II**, 46, 265, 307, 430, 532, 583, 605, 608
Tanning, **I**, 75, 87, 111–112, 154, 366. See also Dyeing; *misṭāḥ*
tannūr (cuff made of silver), **IV**, 319, 453
tannūrī (maker of ovens), **I**, 423
Tapestry, **IV**, 120, 122
ṭāqa (Per.). *See* Window
taqaddam: to be appointed as head, **II**, 69, 537; to make an appeal, **II**, 594. See also *muqaddam*; *taqdima*
ṭāqat al-anbōl (niche in synagogue platform for Torah scroll), **II**, 147
ṭāqat zujāj (glass window). *See* Window
taqdima (office of *muqaddam*), leadership, **II**, 49. See also *muqaddam*
taqdīs (betrothal), **III**, 453. *See also* Betrothal
taqiyya (dissimulation), **V**, 622
taqqan (Judeo-Ar., to make a *taqqānā*, statute), **II**, 66, 536. *See also* Statutes
taqqānā (Heb., statutes), **II**, 65, 66, 522. *See also* Statutes
taqsīm (partition), dissolution of partnership, **I**, 367
taqsīṭ (installment in payment of debt), **I**, 261, 489. *See also* Credit; Loans
taqṭīʿ. See *qaṭʿ*
taqwīm (assessment of bride's outfit), **III**, 86, 124–126, 129, 137, 444; **IV**, 420. *See also* Trousseau lists
tarammal (to live as a widow), **III**, 481, 484. *See also* Widows
tarbiya (education), **II**, 558, 559, 560; **III**, 432. *See also* Education
Tare, **I**, 335, 342
Targūm, **II**, 158, 175, 177
ṭarḥ (tare), **I**, 335, 455
tarḥa (mold), **I**, 367
tarḥīm. *See* Memorial service
ṭarī (fresh), coins of full weight, unimpaired by wear, **I**, 146, 237, 263, 264, 359, 459. *See also* Dinar; Dirhem; Money
ṭārīʾ (newcomer), **II**, 385
tarida (Heb., cross between sailing ship and galley), **I**, 307
Ṭarīf b. Manasse, **II**, 592
ṭārma: small cabin on Nile boat, **I**, 295, 473, 481; wooden structure on top of *ṭabaqa*, **IV**, 72, 295, 372
tarrābīn (mortar mixer), **I**, 96
ṭarrāḥa (sofa, daybed), **IV**, 110–111, 115 ff., 128, 304, 305, 308, 320, 327, 330, 331, 377, 380, 384, 450, 459, 461. See also *martaba*; *qiṭaʿ*
tarsīm (dues for guardsmen), **I**, 243; **II**, 372. See also *rassam*
Tarsus, Asia Minor, **I**, 67, 214, 323; **II**, 214
Tartar (*ṭārṭār*), **IV**, 405
tartīb, as part of title (unusual usage), **II**, 607
ṭāsa (drinking vessel), **IV**, 147, 386, 393; **V**, 97, 533
tasallam ("received"), **II**, 444, 456, 487
Tāshfīn, Almoravid leader, **V**, 59
tasmiya (pledge), **II**, 544. *See also* Pledges
tasqīʿ, *taṣqīʿ*. *See* Cadastre
Tassels, **IV**, 113, 152, 196, 343, 466
ṭast. *See* Basin
tastaynaq. *See* Bracelet
tāsūma. *See* Slippers
Tatars. *See* Mongols
Taṭay, Egypt, **I**, 436; **II**, 151, 567, 570; **III**, 262; **V**, 24, 511
ṭāʾūsī ("like a peacock"), irridescent, **I**, 419
Taverns (*qāʿat al-sharāb*), **II**, 98, 492, 493; **V**, 40
tawallī wa-naẓar (office of administration and overseeing), **II**, 546
Tawfīq ("Success"), slave girl, **I**, 434
Tawfīq al-Ḥakīm, modern Egyptian writer, **II**, 74
al-Tawḥīdī, **V**, 583
tawkīl (cost of a lawsuit), **I**, 243; **II**, 608
al-tawqīʿ al-ʿālī (rescript from caliph's court), **II**, 364, 606
tawqīʿ mukammal (properly ratified rescript), **II**, 611
tawqīʿ qāḍi ʾl-quḍāt (signed instructions of chief judge of Cairo), **II**, 364
ṭawwāf. *See* Night watchman
tawwān (fishermonger specializing in tuna), **I**, 126, 430
Tawwaz, **I**, 400
Tax assayers and collectors, **I**, 117; **II**, 48, 222, 532, 357, 358, 361, 366, 377, 378, 379, 605, 608, 610
Taxes, **II**, 104, 358–363, 473, 546, 580, 587, 609; **IV**, 289; **V**, 78-79, 524

Tax farmers, farming, I, 73, 161, 162, 170, 178, 180, 189, 191, 194, 260, 263, 265, 269, 270, 272, 379; II, 35, 38, 46, 67, 75, 354, 358–363, 532, 540, 604–607
ṭayfur. *See* Bowls
Taylor, Dr. Charles, I, 4
Taylor-Schechter Collection, Cambridge, I, 4, 8, 13; III, 96
ṭayyib (first quality), I, 452, 456
Ṭāzān, name, III, 248
tazkiya (certificate of good conduct), II, 250, 577
Tea, II, 585
Teachers, II, 32, 42, 49, 50, 51, 70, 73, 89, 92, 100, 106, 107, 117, 121, 122, 125, 136, 152, 153, 172, 182, 183, 185–190, 211, 212, 218, 228, 229, 237, 281, 381, 419, 428, 430, 434, 441, 442, 451, 453, 463, 467, 515, 533, 534, 543, 544, 546, 548, 556, 558–560, 577
Teaching methods, elementary schools, II, 178–185; higher studies, II, 209–210, 247–250
Teak, IV, 114, 131
Teasel, IV, 178
tekel (Aram.), I, 360
Temple of Jerusalem, II, 2, 7, 12, 82, 95, 99, 109, 143, 144, 155–156, 203, 225, 265, 285, 524
Tenants, II, 100, 114, 115, 116, 132, 536; restrictions imposed on, IV, 96–97
Ten Commandments, II, 340
Ten persons as public body, II, 32, 58, 59, 194, 535, 601
tersā(wiyya) (Per., Christian), I, 136
tēvā (Heb., reading desk), II, 151
Textiles, I, 60, 72, 100, 101–108, 150, 153, 155, 163, 164, 236, 268, 333; III, 45, 53, 78, 115, 150. *See also* Cotton; Linen; Silk
'ṭfhn', a location in Egypt, II, 606
thabat (roll of names), II, 476; *t. jarīdat al-ʿaniyyīm* (record of the list of the poor), II, 456
Thābit Ibn al-Munajjim, II, 464
thaghr (frontier seaport), I, 376
thallāj (ice man), I, 115
thaman (the total proceeds of one sale), I, 218, 374, 453
Thāmira ("Fertile"), f., III, 280
Thanksgiving after travel, I, 352
thaqqāb al-lūlū (perforator of pearls), I, 416. *See also* Pearls
thawb. *See* Robe
Theaters, puppet, V, 43–44
Thebes, Greece, I, 52
Theology, II, 210, 242, 248; V, 430, 443. *See also* God; Religion; Scholarship
al-Thiqa ("the Trusted"), title, II, 612; IV, 437
Thiqat al-Dawla, II, 607
Thiqat al-Mulk. *See* Trusted Servant of the State
Thompson, Dorothy, IV, 199
Thousand and One Nights. See *Arabian Nights*
Thread (*ghazl*), IV, 408
Threads, Bazaar of, II, 612
Three, as witnesses or committee, II, 59, 433, 548, 600
Thrupp, Sylvia, IV, 4
thumn (measure of cereal in Tunisia), IV, 241
Thurible, IV, 137
Thursday, II, 188. *See also* Monday
Thursday night, III, 168
Thyme, I, 47; II, 583; IV, 245
Tiara (*ʿiṣāba*), IV, 213–214, 322, 327, 342, 401, 425, 466
ṭīb. *See* Perfume; Aloe; Wood
Ṭībān Ben Nahum, II, 504
al-Ṭibb, members of medical profession, III, 502
Tiberias, Palestine, I, 49; II, 97, 167, 168, 440, 441, 442, 444, 467, 530, 542, 559, 589, 598; III, 63, 81; IV, 45, 155
tibr (gold bullion), I, 232. *See also* Gold
Tierney, Brian, V, 74
ṭifla (baby), term for wife, III, 162
Tiflis, Georgia, I, 49; II, 439, 440
tillīs (sack of wheat), I, 333; II, 478; IV, 240, 438. *See also* Wheat
tilmīdh (pupil), I, 93; II, 560
Timber, I, 211; II, 431, 435; IV, 108
"Time," agent of fortune, V, 48, 49, 294, 329–330
Tin, I, 154, 335, 337, 339; II, 583
Tinner, I, 109, 420
Tinnīs, I, 314; IV, 43; attitude toward hospitality in, V, 30; ban on *ḥāvēr* of, II, 332; books sent to, II, 194, 520, 561; III, 31; and charity, II, 438, 534; Christians in, II, 394; divorce in, III, 501; famine, I, 47; Jewish congregations, II, 520; letters from, I, 301; II, 254; IV, 176, 84, 396; linen industry, I, 98, 156; II, 194, 520; IV, 167, 176, 191, 307, 396, 401; mail service, I, 291, 293, 294; marriage documents from, III, 98, 374, 410, 446; merchants, I, 156, 178, 223; II, 520; III, 446; overland travel to, I, 301; physicians in, II, 254; pottery, I, 111; repre-

sentative of merchants in, I, 245; seaport, I, 178, 213, 223, 296, 316, 320, 326; scribe, II, 355, 604
Tinnīsī linen. *See* Linen
"Tinnīsī Rūmī mantilla," IV, 167, 401
tiqqūn (statute), III, 466. *See also* Statutes; *taqqan*; *taqqānā*
Tiqwā b. Amram (Abu'l-Munā), V, 212–214, 566, 567
ṭirāz (workshop for textiles), I, 82; IV, 455. *See also* Needlework
Titles. *See* Honorific titles
Tlemcen (Tilimsān), I, 64, 452; II, 603; III, 239; IV, 405
Tobruk, I, 212, 279, 319, 324, 326, 327
Toilet, IV, 62, 69; V, 533
Toledo, Spain, I, 57, 69, 244; II, 135; III, 19, 239, 241
Toll houses, I, 194-195
Tombs, V, 144–145, 165–166
Tombstones, destruction of, II, 285
Tomiche, Nada, I, 418
Torah scroll (*sēfer tōrā*), II, 52, 53, 146, 151, 156, 167, 436, 519–520, 532, 550, 564, 567, 602; III, 7, 8, 19, 20, 54, 58, 62, 224, 247, 322; as object of veneration, V, 24, 373. *See also* Bible
Tortoiseshell, I, 154; IV, 130, 327, 385
Tortosa, Spain, III, 111
Torture, II, 373, 609; III, 23
Tovia b. Eli, III, 30; IV, 259
Tovia b. Eli, V, 562
Ṭōvia b. Eli b. Khalaf, III, 460
Ṭōviyāhū b. Judah, II, 566; V, 603
Ṭōviyāhū ha-Kohen b. Eli ha-Meʿulle, III, 558; IV, 408; V, 106, 516
Towns, provincial, IV, 35; small, IV, 10, 43, 47
Toynbee, Arnold, V, 496
Trademarks, I, 49
Trade names, IV, 306
Trade routes, I, 211–214, 278, 318
Traders, II, 477, 555, 590; V, 16, 18, 50–51, 54, 322–323. *See also* Business; individual traders and merchants
Tragacanth gum, I, 213
Translucent (*zujājī*), description of textile, IV, 174, 315
Transport, I, 156–160, 166–167, 322–346; of grain, IV, 242
Trapani, Sicily, I, 256, 301; II, 305
Travel companion. See *rafīq*
Travel(ers), I, 27, 156–160, 273–281 and *passim*; II, 114, 134, 135, 153, 154, 222, 223, 301, 383, 384, 402, 455, 462, 479, 487, 502, 506, 557, 586, 589, 594, 611; IV, 414
Traveling in stages, IV, 265
Trays, IV, 144–145; small (*khūnjāt*), IV, 424
Treasury, I, 231
Trent, Council of, III, 55
Triangles, IV, 133
Tribes, Jewish, V, 266
Trinkets. *See* Beads
"Triple-thread" (*muthallath*), IV, 114, 379
Tripoli, Lebanon, agriculture, I, 119; beneficiaries of community chest from, II, 447; IV, 155; Crusader conquest of, I, 45; III, 114, 379; dinars, I, 207, 239; hospitality in, V, 30; Judah b. Moses Ibn Sighmār in, I, 159; mail service, I, 293; merchants in/from, I, 191; III, 301; IV, 46; physicians, II, 245; pirates from, II, 37; qadi of, I, 310; II, 366; representative of merchants in, I, 190; on trade route, I, 212; travel to/from, I, 275, 276, 321, 323, 325, 326, 330; V, 529
Tripoli(tania), Libya, I, 20, 43, 232; III, 150, 262, 494; Almohad conquest of, I, 41; beneficiaries of community chest from, II, 444; cantor from, I, 439; famine in, IV, 242; felt production, I, 50; home furnishings in, IV, 129; immigrants to Egypt from, II, 188; IV, 45, 179; invasion of Tunisia, I, 331; III, 66; Jewish court of, II, 395-396; III, 300; letters from, I, 55, 245, 287; IV, 129, 404; mail service, I, 287; marriage in, III, 373; merchants in/from, I, 68, 245; III, 300; IV, 404; Norman invasion of, IV, 457; physicians, II, 256, 576; pilgrims in, I, 55; ruled by Bedouin factions, I, 439; teachers from, II, 188; on trade routes, I, 212; travel to/from, I, 278, 301, 306, 315, 316, 317, 318, 321, 322, 323, 325, 326, 477
Trousers. *See* Underpants
Trousseau lists, II, 84, 131, 236, 428, 585; IV, 105ff. and *passim*; translated, IV, 310–333. *See also* Dowry
Truffles, IV, 245, 440
Trunks, IV, 129–131. *See also* Chests; *ṣundūq*
Trusted Servant of the State (*thiqat al-mulk*), title, II, 48, 355, 356, 357, 589; IV, 439 V, 80–81, 270, 527
Trustees, II, 80, 539 (see also *haymana*; *hēmān*); of the courts, II, 17, 77–82
Trustworthiness of wife, III, 67, 105, 143, 144–147, 154, 182, 251, 256
ṭūb (brick), I, 113

al-ṭubayba ("the little [or beloved] doctor"), I, 128
"Tube" (*qaṣaba*), stones of longish shape, IV, 206, 421
Tubes, gold (*qawādīs*), IV, 322, 455
Tuesday and Friday, days of bread distribution, II, 105, 127, 443, 444, 450, 490
ṭufāl. *See* Fuller's earth
tuffāḥī (appleman), I, 427
tuffāḥiyye (fruiterer), I, 428
tuḥfa (present), II, 546. *See also* Gifts
Tuition, private II, 187
Tujīb quarter, Fustat, II, 419, 434, 448; IV, 13, 17, 18, 19, 25, 30, 281, 352
Tujjār ("Queen of the Merchants"), a widow, IV, 276
Tumblers, IV, 146, 148
Tūna, Egypt, IV, 167, 401
ṭunfusa (carpet), IV, 123–124, 383, 460. *See also* Carpet
Tunis, city of, I, 212, 256, 319, 324, 325, 333; II, 577
Tunisia, I, xvii, mentioned *passim*; II, 24, 88, 110, 192, 545, 558, 576, 597; III, 20, 246; IV, 2, 39; bedouin invasions of, II, 55, 283; V, 46–47; bishop of, II, 8; book production, II, 239; calligraphic style, II, 180, 235; cantor in, II, 90; cases of marital strife in, III, 176, 183, 469; cities, II, 43; civil strife in, V, 209–211; clothing, IV, 163, 169, 180, 181, 206, 398, 409, 415; correspondence with Baghdad Gaons, II, 14, 203, 235; court records from, II, 601; domestic architecture, IV, 56; flourish of Jewish learning in, II, 203, 235; food, IV, 241, 242, 245, 252, 439; home furnishing in, IV, 126, 383; immigrants to Egypt from, II, 78, 153, 188, 191, 536, 559, 565, 567; III, 13, 43, 57, 124, 177, 202; interfaith relations in, II, 298; Jewish authorities in, II, 25, 27, 39, 525, 613; Jewish physicians in, II, 243; kohl containers from, IV, 453; letters from, II, 191; III, 22, 117, 167, 497; IV, 206, 245; marriage documents from, III, 441, 459; merchants from/in, II, 37, 275, 294, 295, 397; III, 294; IV, 26; *mudawwin* in, II, 610; Muslim *faqīhs* in, II, 607; Nahray b. Nissim married to girl from, III, 273; Norman invasion of, III, 55; prominence of women in Zirid times, III, 357; "*rāvs*" from, II, 212; shipwreck documented in, III, 280; silver imported to, IV, 145; soap exported from, IV, 140; Taherti brothers of, II, 475; III, 463; IV, 384; yeshiva's representative in, II, 11
tunnī (fishmonger of tuna), I, 126, 430
tunn tamlīḥī (salted tuna fish), I, 429
turāb: clay, I, 96; garbage removal, IV, 357
Turayk ("Little Turk"), f., III, 45, 238; V, 604
Turayk, d. of Abraham Ibn Qurdūsī, V, 355–356
ṭurāt ("newcomers"), foreigners, I, 488
Turban (*biqyār*, *ʿimāma*), I, 105, 419; II, 182; IV, 159, 163, 164, 174, 179, 185, 397, 398, 401, 403, 404, 408, 417, 458, 464
Turcomans, Seljuk, II, 351
Tureen, IV, 145
Turfa ("Precious Gift"), III, 109
Turfa b. Ṭoviah, III, 501
turgeman. *See* Dragoman
Turk(-s, -ish), I, 30, 31, 35, 36, 39, 83, 132; II, 23, 150, 167, 379; III, 198, 259
turmusānī (distributor of lupines), I, 438
Turner, Eric, V, 499
Turners, I, 83, 113; II, 148; Street of, IV, 277
Turquoise, I, 154
"Turquoise," slave girl, I, 140
Ṭūs, I, 400
Tustar, Iran, I, 50, 400; IV, 402; V, 609
Tustarī: family, I, 78, 103, 164–165, 183, 244, 406, 443; II, 7, 346, 453, 472, 527, 560; III, 37, 289, 331, 455; IV, 28, 119, 168, 169, 181, 381; V, 231, 239, 367, 392, 572, 585, 609; fabric, IV, 454
"The Two Sultans," rulers of forts of Aden, V, 525
Tyre, Lebanon, I, 233, 268; III, 197, 207; artisans from, I, 49, 89, 411; II, 456; beneficiaries from, II, 441, 454, 456, 459, 467; bequest to community chest of, II, 110, 544, 545; communal strife in, V, 204; contract concerning living arrangements in house in, IV, 84, 372; contributors from, II, 498; Crusaders in, I, 37; II, 277; III, 190, 191, 201, 202, 339; IV, 45, 232; domestic architecture in, IV, 73, 75, 363, 369; father donates property to his two sons in, III, 243; frontier fortress, 7; general character, II, 43; glass industry in, I, 109, 110; II, 456; head of Jewish community, II, 214, 566; home furnishings in, IV, 123, 128, 142, 306, 380, 384, 392; Iraqi emigrants in, III, 301; jewelry, IV, 215, 221, 426; Jewish court

of, II, 413, 567; III, 57, 280; V, 530; joint Jewish congregations of, II, 54, 534; letters from, I, 54, 200, 275, 291, 293, 332; II, 41, 54, 110, 277, 530, 534; III, 240; mail service, I, 284, 287, 291, 293, 294, 295; marriage documents from, III, 57, 98, 136, 151, 375, 377, 393, 396, 398, 406, 407, 416, 425, 438, 439, 448, 452, 456; IV, 123, 142, 221, 363, 380; merchants in/from, I, 69, 200, 242, 275, 287; III, 289, 339; IV, 236; Muslim judges in/from, I, 296, 310; II, 366; Muslim returning to, IV, 45; palace in, II, 354; Palestinian academy in, II, 30, 47, 201; part of commercial sea route, I, 60, 81, 212, 214, 318; II, 575; III, 57, 190; IV, 7, 8; pilgrims from, II, 168; representative of merchants in, I, 190; scribe in, III, 201; Seljuks in, III, 198, 201; *suftaja* in, I, 245; synagogue in, II, 157; tax-farmers in/from I, 194; II, 35

U

ubābī (oak green), IV, 407
ʿUbayd, uncommon Jewish name, II, 499
ʿUbaydī robes, IV, 182
Ubulla, I, 474
ʿūd. See Wood, aromatic
ʿūd kibrīt (sulphur chip), III, 463
al-ʿudda (the equipment), I, 474
ʿuddat al-zayyātīn (oil-maker's equipment), I, 427
ʿūdī: dealer in *ʿūd*, I, 438; II, 503; splinter, I, 482
Udovitch, A. L., I, 441, 445; IV, 4, 195, 433, 439, 444; V, 534, 577
ʿudūl. See Notary
ʿUkbara, Iraq, II, 440, 441
ʿulamāʾ (Muslim religious scholars), III, 138
ʿUllā b. Joseph, I, 174, 184, 186, 260, 462; II, 78, 81, 444; III, 295; V, 159, 204
ʿullāba (container made of tin or lead), I, 335, 486
ʿulqa (impediment [to marriage]), III, 443
ʿulūw (stories atop stores used as domiciles), IV, 15, 19, 280. See also *ʿalw*
ʿumāla (commission), I, 169, 184–185
ʿUmar b. Yūsuf, I, 292
Umayyads, I, 40, 106, 283, 370; IV, 451
umma (nation), II, 274, 280
Umm Abu ʾl-Faraj, III, 497
Umm ʿAzīza, III, 429
Umm Baqā, III, 475
Umm Ḥayyūn, rare name, II, 462
Umm Kifaʾ, rare name, II, 462
Umm Maʿānī, II, 449
Umm Malāl, I, 310
Umm Sitt al-Nās, III, 175
Umm Thanā ("Praise"), d. of judge in al-Maḥalla, III, 219–220
Umm al-ʿUluww, I, 310
Underpants, IV, 161
Unemployment, I, 86
United States, II, 11, 226, 229, 289; III, 49, 245, 260, 272, 356
University Library, Cambridge, I, 3, 5, 7, 13, 24; II, 297
University Museum, Philadelphia, I, 5
Unmarried men, III, 61–62, 64–65, 159. *See also* Marriage
Unmarried women, III, 49, 62–65, 173, 340. *See also* Marriage; Women
Unna, Dr. Isaac, rabbi in Karlsruhe, Germany, V, 532
Unna, Moses, V, 532
ʿunnāb (jujube), V, 543
Unskilled labor, I, 574
Upper arm (symbol of strength), IV, 161–162, 399
Upper class, I, 76–77
Upper Egypt, I, 7, 20, 45, 175, 214, 278, 297, 333, 364; IV, 437
Upper garment, IV, 152, 153, 159
ūqiya (ounce), I, 360
ʿuqūba (corporal punishment), II, 381
Urbanism, Islamic. *See* City
ʿurbūn (prepayment in full), I, 199. *See also* Rent, prepayment of
Urmiya, I, 400
Urraca, Doña of Toledo, V, 462
al-usayd ("the little lion"), nickname, III, 440
Usayd b. Abraham, III, 436
ʿushārī. See Nile boat
al-ʿushāriyyāt al-saʿīda (royal river boats), I, 474
Ushmūn, I, 283. *See also* Ashmūnayn
ushnān (soda ash), IV, 140, 183, 315, 321, 324, 390
ushnāna (box for soda ash), IV, 140, 141, 327
ʿUshshāq, slave girl, I, 434
ustādh (personal mentor), II, 250; III, 488
ustukhūdus (Gr. *stoikhas, stoikhodos*), Lavandula stoechas, II, 583
usṭūl (warship), I, 307–308, 463, 478, 480, 482; II, 380

uṣūl (foundations [of a house]), IV, 354. See also *marfaq*
Utensils, II, 584
utrujj (citrus medica), I, 121
Uzziel, servant of teacher Solomon, II, 559
Uzziel b. Ṭāhōr *ha-nāzīr*, III, 502

V

Vacations, II, 182, 188
Vajda, G., V, 387
Valensi, Lucette, IV, 195, 418
Validation by court, II, 336, 337, 601
Vase, IV, 316, 324
Vashti (biblical), III, 170–171
Vault (*qabw*), IV, 70, 368
Vegetables, I, 119; IV, 148, 234, 245
Veil (*qināʿ*, *khimār*), IV, 315, 317, 320, 327, 451, 452. See also *ḥibrāʾ*; *miqnaʿa*
Veiled interest at repurchase of house, IV, 87–88
Vellum, II, 232, 238. *See also* Paper; Papyrus; Parchment
Venice, Venetians, I, 29, 40, 46, 54, 181, 282, 301, 303-304, 313; II, 79; IV, 1, 168, 402
Ventilation shaft. *See* "Wind catcher"
Veranda (*mashraqa*), IV, 73–74, 369, 435
veredarius (Lat., courier), I, 282
Veterinarian, I, 421; II, 46, 256, 415, 532
Vienna, National Library, I, 5
Vigils, II, 569
Villages, I, 117–118, 224, 425
Vinegar (*khall*), I, 124; IV, 260, 441. *See also* Honey and vinegar
Vinegar house, II, 545
Vineyard, I, 428; II, 430
Violence, within Jewish community, V, 41, 305-306. *See also* Banditry; Political turmoil
Violet (color), IV, 182
Virgins, III, 100–101, 102, 169, 274; divorced after betrothal, III, 101; recognized by hairdress, V, 521
Virtue, concepts of, V, 5, 9, 53, 191-199, 474–475
Visiting and hospitality: customary behavior, V, 30–37; during illness, V, 26, 110; importance of, V, 28-29; refugees, V, 29–30; on Sabbath, V, 12, 13–14; spouse's family, III, 152, 337. *See also* Charity
Vitriol, I, 154
Vizier, II, 528, 604, 606, 610
Vocational training, II, 191-192, 560-561
von Grunebaum, Gustave, IV, 44
von Maltzan, III, 135
Votes, taking, II, 57
Vows, II, 12, 65, 106, 544; III, 193, 201-202; V, 43, 110, 470

W

wabāʾ. *See* Plague
wadāʿa (courtesy, kindness), II, 584
wadīʿa (deposit, on commission), II, 584
Wages, I, 89, 94–98, 162–164
Wailing, II, 433
Wailing women, I, 129; II, 285; V, 153, 163
Waistband (*zunnār*), IV, 330, 398
wajh (front of a house), IV, 60
wājib (dues), I, 270, 489; *w. mushtarā* (purchase tax), I, 271
wakāla. *See* Caravanserai; *dār al-wakāla*
wakham (sickness), V, 113. *See also* Illness
wakhsh (poor quality), I, 452
wakīl: agent, representative, III, 103, 295; administrator of the *qōdesh*, II, 423; employee, II, 454; warehouse, II, 607 (see also *dār al-wakāla*). *See also* Proxy of bride; Representative of the merchants
wakīla (female agent), I, 129
wakīl al-tujjār. *See* Representative of the merchants
Wakin, Jeanette A., IV, 50
waks (loss), difference between Egyptian dinar and foreign currency, I, 239, 460
walāʾ (jurisdiction), III, 445
Walāʾ, slave girl, I, 435
Waʿlān quarter, Fustat, IV, 13
wālī: governor or chief of police, II, 250, 355, 358, 368, 369, 370, 371, 528, 608; IV, 40, 435; male guardian, III, 71, 103; V, 520
Walī al-Dawla ("The Confident of the Governent"), II, 500
wālidī ("my father"), III, 249, 432
Walking, for pleasure, V, 12, 344–346
Wallāda, poetess, IV, 399
Walls, IV, 60
Walnuts, I, 121, 213
Waltzing, J.T., I, 99
"Wandering scholars," II, 201-202, 218. *See also* Scholars
waqf. *See* Pious foundations
waraq: silver coin, I, 230, 241, 381, 382, 384, 387, 388; II, 414, 465, 481, 490, 494, 505, 508; III, 285, 490; silver of low value, II, 465, 490. *See also* Dirhem; Money; Silver
waraq[*a*] (sheet [of paper, parchment]),

II, 574; *w. dimashqī* (Damascene paper), I, 410; IV, 349. *See also* Paper; Parchment
ward (rose-preserve), II, 584, 585. *See also* Potions; Rose marmalade; Sherbet
Wardān Market, II, 263, 582
Warehouse. See *makhzan*; *wakīl*
Warfare, V, 10, 55–56. *See also* Political turmoil
Wargla, I, 55, 65, 279
warrāq (bookseller), II, 597; IV, 358
Warships, I, 296, 307–308, 318, 330, 477–478
wasaṭ (middle quality), I, 452
Washbasins (*maghsal*), IV, 139, 315, 324, 331, 333, 390, 460
"Washed" (*ghasīl*), worn-out clothes, IV, 183, 184, 412
Washers of the dead, I, 129; III, 40; V, 165
Washing utensils, IV, 138–141
Washroom (*mirḥāḍ*, *bayt al-mā'*), IV, 67, 367. *See also* Toilet
waṣīf (servant), I, 131, 132
waṣīfa (female servant), I, 131, 135, 433
Wāsiṭ, Iraq, I, 68; III, 13; IV, 121
al-wāsiṭa (middleman), I, 160
waṣiyy (executor, guardian), II, 336. See also *wakīl*
waṭā (sleeping carpet), IV, 462. *See also* Carpet
waṭan: homeland, II, 274; hometown, IV, 41ff.; V, 6
Water, IV, 142, 147; for drinking, IV, 434
Water carrier, I, 95; II, 457, 463; IV, 11, 63, 232, 350
Water jugs, IV, 63, 142
al-Wāthīq, administrator of shrine at Dammuh, V, 27
Wax, Waxmakers, I, 60, 76, 120, 125, 153, 154, 208, 219, 223, 268, 337, 344, 448; II, 492, 529; IV, 16, 175; Street of, IV, 15, 286. *See also* Candles
wayba (measure of wheat [fifteen liters, four gallons]), I, 361, 371; II, 129, 357, 423, 444, 445, 448, 457, 462, 479, 483, 484, 490; IV, 235. *See also* Wheat
wazan (payment), I, 458
wazn (weight), I, 465. *See also* Weights
wazzān (weigher), II, 479. *See also* Weights
Weaning, III, 194, 233–234
Weather, sensitivity to,V, 101–102
Weaver, weaving, I, 75, 85, 87, 90, 92, 362, 363, 416; II, 297; III, 145; IV, 177, 408, 412. *See also* Silk weaving
Wecelinus, Slovenian cleric convert, II, 593
Wedding(s), II, 125, 250, 555; III, 17, 20, 27, 54, 58, 66, 67, 70, 78, 85, 89, 114–118; 159, 220; banquet, II, 20; III, 116; celebrations restrained, V, 27; ceremony, III, 54–55, 116–117; IV, 314; collections at, II, 107, 492, 495, 506, 544; date, III, 84, 86, 87, 90, 92, 114–115, 125; expenses, II, 499; III, 71, 77, 91, 106, 116, 120; female professions associated with, I, 127 (*see also* Bride-comber); location of, II, 154, 163, 166; poem, III, 54, 117; postponement of, III, 114; witnesses at, IV, 317
Weekly lection, II, 152, 567. *See also* Bible, reading of; Haftara
Weights, I, 360–361; II, 588; Jarwī, IV, 251
Weiss, Gershon, IV, 50
Welfare officials. See *parnās*
Well, II, 292; IV, 68, 140
Wellhausen, Julius, V, 497
Well-to-do families, III, 84, 85, 89, 91, 97, 99, 122, 125, 129, 132, 138, 167, 173, 237, 240, 259, 274, 348
Wertheimer, Rabbi Solomon A., I, 2, 3, 396
West, Muslim. *See* Maghreb
Westerners (Jews of Palestine), II, 6
Western Europe, III, 356
Westminster College, Cambridge, I, 5
Wet nurse, I, 127, 430; II, 282, 588
Wheat (*qamḥ*), I, 114, 117, 118, 119, 123, 211, 255, 257, 337, 371, 378; II, 154, 174, 188, 393, 451, 467, 539, 547–548, 552; III, 191, 192, 194, 205, 234, 251, 324; IV, 7, 141, 142, 230, 234–244, 261, 371, 435; distribution of, II, 97, 101, 108, 109, 123, 128–130, 134, 135, 142, 423, 442, 444, 448, 457, 458, 462, 490, 498; IV, 235, 435, 438; donation and collection of, II, 477, 478, 479, 483; storage of, IV, 235, 435. See also *irdabb*; *tillīs*
White ("cloud," pale, "pearl," silvery-white, "snow"), color, IV, 117, 166, 173–174, 177, 182
White, Lynn, V, 420
"Whitened" (tinned), IV, 147
"Whitening" (*bayāḍ*), IV, 408
Wholesalers, I, 150–152
widn (handle), IV, 390
Widowers, III, 60, 70–71, 78, 138, 234, 250, 259, 308
Widows, II, 36, 103, 395, 396, 493, 527,

529, 545, 568, 602, 613; III, 1, 22, 46, 63, 70, 74, 101, 120, 123, 127, 131, 210, 238–239, 247, 250–260, 274, 290, 366, 373, 374, 375, 379, 380, 382, 386, 387, 389, 390, 448, 451, 471, 481–488; charity for, II, 38, 124, 216, 459, 501; dues withheld by heirs, III, 257; from second marriage, III, 259; grass (*ʿagūnā*), II, 591; III, 204, 264, 469; living with married children, III, 227, 258; V, 123; remarrying, III, 274–275; lodgings, III, 259

Wife: appealing to community, III, 186, 195, 217; "baby," III, 160–163; beating and cursing, III, 157, 174, 175, 184–189, 195, 216; beauty of, III, 166–167; buying freedom by renouncing marriage gift, III, 186, 267; children preceding in greetings, III, 229; companion of husband, III, 165, 205; conduct of, III, 156–157; "dear to the family and the town," III, 183; deathbed gift to, III, 251; divorcing husband, II, 301; III, 83, 265, 267; earnings of, III, 106, 132–135, 141, 145, 174, 191, 192; economic role of, III, 132–135, 332; executor and guardian, III, 253–254, 331; following husband to new locality, II, 68, 359; household chores, III, 185, 250, 341; ideal, III, 163, 166, 170–173; like prisoners of war, III, 153; loans to husband, III, 181, 251; "lonely stranger," III, 171–172; mistress of the house, III, 160, 164; not heir of husband, III, 252–253, 278; possessions of, III, 179–183, 186; problems with in-laws, III, 171–179; problems with parents, III, 178–179; proxy of, III, 214; reference in letters to, III, 160–162, 229; refusing to follow husband to another locality, III, 177–178, 188, 198, 202; second, III, 67, 106, 143, 144, 147–150, 206–211, 251, 346; suspected of infidelity, III, 176; transactions of, III, 181; visiting her family, III, 217. *See also* Trustworthiness of wife

"Wild Rose," slave girl, I, 139

Wills, I, 10, 263–266; II, 12, 36, 100, 110, 111, 423, 426, 436, 545, 560, 577, 580, 600; III, 42, 163, 238, 251, 411, 412; attitudes toward, V, 131–132, 140–143; and business concerns, V, 136–138, 144–145; and care of elderly, V, 121–122; and charity, III, 349; V, 142–143, 145–147; circumstances, V, 132–135; ethical, V, 143, 289; examples, V, 137, 144–155; executors, V, 138; female inheritance, V, 133; honoring dead person's, III, 79, 296; intestate deaths, V, 120–121, 131; Islamic law, V, 131–132, 134, 141, 142, 384; personal expression in, V, 3; by women, II, 545; III, 232; IV, 418; V, 134, 143, 145–149, 152, 163, 227-228. *See also* Death; Estates

Wimple (*miʿjar*), IV, 158, 164, 176, 191, 320, 323, 329, 330, 333, 398, 401, 407, 415, 425, 451, 456, 459

Wind catcher, IV, 65, 78, 365, 366; V, 101, 534

Window (*ṭāqa*), II, 145, 550; IV, 61-62, 117-118, 365, 382

Window panes, II, 430

Wine, Winesellers (*nabīdh, nabbādhūn*), I, 46, 76, 87, 92, 122–124, 152, 167, 170, 182, 197, 198, 208, 210, 223, 264, 361, 364; II, 174, 267, 270, 277, 323, 393, 414, 430, 450, 461, 500, 578, 581; IV, 18, 224, 253-261, 445, 446; V, 38-30, 505, 515; Street of, IV, 18, 254, 288, 444. *See also* Drinking; Potions

Wine, color, IV, 125, 174, 383

Winter, IV, 117, 182

wiqāya. See Cloak

Wirth, Eugen, IV, 2, 15, 270

wishāḥ (belt with precious or semi-precious stones), IV, 378

Wissa Wassef, Ceres, IV, 234

Witnesses, II, 601; III, 80, 81, 82, 83, 94, 103, 107, 237, 374. *See also* Notary

Woad. See *isatis*

Women, II, 130, 223, 280, 287, 352, 546; ancient, III, 319–322; attitudes toward, II, 190; V, 592; bathhouse visits, II, 155; V, 43, 97–98; beneficiaries of charity, II, 132, 136, 170, 418, 420, 430, 435, 438, 439, 441, 442, 444, 446, 448, 449, 456, 458, 459, 460, 462, 464, 466; V, 227; business activities, III, 346–352; V, 25; caretakers of synagogues, II, 85; charitable activities/donations, II, 99, 105, 107, 113, 129, 137, 252, 413, 416, 429, 432, 433, 479, 485, 493, 500, 501, 544; chastity, V, 200; convert to Judaism, II, 309; drinking by, V, 42–43; economic activities, I, 256; III, 324–336; education, II, 183–185; III, 321–322, 353, 356; V, 468; entrance of (*see* Secret door); excommunicated, II, 331; gallery, II, 144, 324; hair, III, 272; illiterate, III, 109, 354, 355; in court, III, 332–336; independent, III, 344–345; influence

on matchmaking, III, 28, 55, 72; inheritance by, II, 436, 582; III, 277, 280–281; V, 133, 141, 170–171; Karaites, II, 544; V, 361; of Khaybar, V, 603; letters to and from, I, 12, 286 and *passim*; II, 144, 550, 558, 567, 589, 602; V, 84–86, 179–181, 214–228, 229, 470, 472–474; living quarters, I, 71; as members of congregation, II, 41–42, 111, 169, 323; Muslim, agents of tax farmer, II, 362; never listed in genealogies, III, 5, 318; oaths of, II, 340; pastimes of, III, 342–344; pietist, III, 353; as pilgrims, III, 337; poetry by, V, 468–470; poverty among, V, 75; professions, I, 127–130 and *passim*; proprietors of real estate, II, 532; III, 37, 85, 91, 94, 150, 181, 192, 281, 282, 326–329; providing or receiving loans, III, 330; proxy for court action, III, 335–336; ransom of captive (*see* Captives, ransom of; Women, charity appeals for); reasons for discrimination, III, 283; religious life, II, 153; III, 352–356; V, 361, 469–474; seclusion, II, 292; IV, 21; V, 310–311 (see also *ḥarīm*; Sexes, separation of); separate sphere, III, 312, 354–359; slave (*see* Slavegirls); social life of, V, 25, 43, 97–98, 470; teachers, II, 183–185, 186, 558; III, 344–346, 355–356; and textile industry, I, 128; II, 45, 67, 360; V, 88, 530; travel of, I, 322; III, 202, 336–341; violation of, I, 328, 329; as visionaries, II, 350; III, 352; and visitors, V, 36–37; vows by, V, 43, 470; wills by (*see* Wills, by women); working, III, 132–135, 145, 181, 187, 233, 255, 324. *See also* Unmarried women; Widows
Wood, I, 46; IV, 138, 149, 369; aromatic, I, 401; IV, 137, 138, 176, 389; ebony, IV, 113, 137, 379; for fuel, III, 191; IV, 440; hardwood or heartwood, IV, 113, 142, 144, 146, 223, 393; panels, III, 20, 189
Woodwork, II, 147, 149
Wool, I, 76, 83, 105, 153, 155, 200, 344, 448; IV, 126, 151, 165, 171–172, 305, 404
Wool Hall (*qaysāriyyat al-ṣūf*), IV, 16, 352
Working hours, I, 97
Workmen. *See* Laborers
Workshop (*maʿmal*), IV, 16, 70
Wormann, Ernest J., I, 4; III, 260
Worms, Germany, II, 58
Worship, House of. *See* Synagogue
Wrap (*malḥafa*), V, 116. *See also* Cloak
Wristband. *See* Bracelet
Writing, art of, II, 44, 178, 228–240; III, 355; cases, I, 99–100; materials, II, 574; spelling, II, 237
Wuḥsha (Karīma b. ʿAmmār), businesswoman, II, 110; III, 274, 330, 346–352, 464, 499, 504, 505; IV, 101, 126, 188–189, 215, 305, 377, 388, 414, 418, 428, 452; V, 171, 226–227, 527, 554, 569, 624
wundarzt. See *kallām*
Wusayd b. ʿUqayb ("Little Lion, son of Young Eagle"), V, 552

Y

Yabqā, a pirate, I, 328
Yahuda, A.S., I, 281
yahudī (Jew), I, 295
Yaḥyā (= Heb. Ḥayyīm or Ḥiyyā, "life"), II, 78
Yaḥyā, I, 174, 184, 186
Yaḥyā, son of the Tiberian, II, 455
Yaḥyā b. ʿAzīz, I, 310
Yaḥyā b. Mūsā Ibn al-Majjānī, I, 374, 453, 468; II, 440; V, 207–208, 244, 518, 565, 598
Yaḥyā ha-Kohen b. Samuel al-Baghdādī, III, 288
Yaḥyā of Fez, II, 478
Yaḥyā-Yiḥyē, I, 357
Yāʿīr (Zuhayr) b. Abraham, V, 542
Yaʿīsh II b. Abraham b. Yaʿīsh I, III, 6
Yaʿīsh-Yaḥyā b. Abraham, III, 470
Yakhīn, poet, II, 386
Yakhīn *ha-meshōrēr*, II, 611
Yakhīn senior, cantor, II, 507
yam (Heb., sea), term for Nile, I, 474
Yamāma, Arabia, II, 11
Yanūnash, I, 272
Yaʿqūb (Jacob), collector of rent, II, 431, 445
Yaʿqūb b. Abuʾl-ʿAynayn, V, 175
Yaʿqūb b. Ismaʿīl Ibn Ukht Ibn Abī ʿUqba, III, 432
Yaʿqūb b. R. Mufliḥ b. R. Benjamin, IV, 197
Yaʿqūb Ibn Killis, Fatimid vizier, I, 33, 34, 39; II, 202, 281, 290, 301, 377; III, 37; IV, 19, 304
Yāqūt, Arab geographer, IV, 44
Yarns, IV, 165, 408
yāwān (Heb., Greece), I, 433
Yazdād, I, 400
Yearning, expressed in letters, V, 230–232
Yedaya of Narbonne, I, 55

Yedūthūn, cantor. *See* Jedūthūn
Yedūthūn, physician, II, 578; V, 285–286
yeḥayyē ("may [God] keep [him] alive), II, 568
yeḥīd ha-dōr (Heb., "the unique"), title, I, 406
Yehiel, II, 567
Yehiel, R., II, 546
Yehiel b. Abraham, poet, V, 596
Yehiel, chief judge, II, 485, 488
Yehiel b. Eliakim of Aleppo, judge, I, 366; II, 217, 486, 509, 515, 572; III, 303, 471, 488
Yehiel b. Isaac, III, 462; V, 557
Yehōsēf b. Nathan, II, 514; V, 506, 574
Yehōsēf b. Samuel ha-Nagid. *See* Joseph b. Samuel ha-Nagid
Yehuda Halevi. *See* Judah ha-Levi
Yehuda b. Ilʿay, IV, 153–154
Yehudā b. Ismaʿīl, merchant, V, 392
Yehuda ha-Nasi. *See* Judah ha-Nāsī
Yehuday Gaon, III, 185
Yekuthiel b. Moses. *See* Jekuthiel (I) b. Moses (I) *ha-rōfē*
Yekuthiel of Spain, III, 207
Yellow, IV, 18, 117, 125, 163, 174, 175, 406; badge of non-Muslims, IV, 194–195, 406; symbol of treachery, IV, 175
Yemen(ites), I, 42, 141; II, 295, 379, 452, 590; III, 47, 238, 262; IV, 45, 124, 383; Arabic of, I, 16; II, 180; III, 464; bedding, IV, 114, 116; clothing, I, 71; IV, 162, 191, 196, 197, 216, 403, 462; commodities exported from, I, 45, 401; IV, 114; community chest in, II, 542; connections with Iraqi yeshivot, II, 11, 21, 22, 76, 521; connections with other Jewish communities, II, 21, 216; craftsmen from/in, I, 57, 92, 93, 109, 420; II, 179; IV, 32, 202, 208; denoting all of India trade route, I, 180; III, 484; domestic architecture, IV, 66, 368, 370; donors from, II, 477, 521; economy, I, 114; education, II, 175, 179, 181, 184, 187, 199, 208, 228, 557, 561; in Egypt, I, 57; II, 208; exilarchs in, II, 19; food, IV, 227, 228, 249; head of the congregations in, II, 76; head of the Jews in, III, 58; isolation of Jewish communities in, I, 71; II, 226; IV, 418; jewelry, IV, 202, 203, 208, 209, 210, 216, 423; Jewish emigration to, II, 300; Jewish popular literature, II, 386; Jews in arms industry, I, 109; lack of physicians in, II, 241; letter to Maimonides from, I, 470; II, 216; letters from, III, 246; IV, 42; marriage in, III, 101, 149, 179, 211, 275, 447; merchants in/from, I, 7, 57, 105, 205, 214, 264; III, 192, 253, 258, 330, 482; IV, 203, 224, 423; Muslim folktales from, III, 144; Nagids in, II, 26, 27, 88; III, 456; oppression of non-Muslims in, IV, 36, 37; orphans in, III, 305; prices in, I, 201; prisons, II, 373; proverbs, I, 114, 129; III, 21, 179, 244, 431; Sabbath customs in, V, 506; *shōfēṭs*, II, 316; scholars from/in, I, 57, 92; II, 27, 208; synagogues, II, 97, 158, 551; IV, 32; responsa sent to, II, 567; recognition of Ibn Migash in, I, 279; women, I, 114, 127, 430; II, 184; III, 21, 149, 179, 315, 341, 355, 431; "wedding houses" in, II, 154; travelers from, I, 274; II, 480; III, 246; textiles, IV, 463
yerīʿōt (sheets [of paper, parchment]), II, 573. *See also* Paper; Parchment
Yeshaʿayāhū Rōsh ha-Seder, Isaiah, V, 482
Yeshiva, I, 51, 60, 65, 158, 181, 244, 444; II, 5–22, 24, 28, 30, 54, 56, 76, 136, 195–210, 234, 313, 316, 403, 521, 522, 523, 533, 537, 561, 566, 595 (see also *mathība*); Babylonian, II, 511, 513, 564, 571, 614; III, 261; V, 514; Palestinian, II, 511, 512, 513, 522, 563, 573, 595, 614; III, 148; V, 261–263, 372, 383, 418; term explained, II, 196; titles, V, 261–264, 267, 513; importance, V, 360, 365. *See also* Gaon; Head of Yeshiva
yeshūʿā (Heb., salvation), III, 442
Yeshūʿā, R., II, 420, 450, 492
Yeshūʿā b. Aaron, physician, II, 576
Yeshūʿā b. Abraham, teacher, II, 544
Yeshūʿā b. Elazar b. Judah b. Japheth ha-Levi, III, 479; IV, 367
Yeshūʿā b. Ismaʿīl (Samuel), Tunisian merchant, V, 32, 144–145, 208–209, 246, 280, 327, 336, 540, 545, 565, 571
Yeshūʿā b. Jacob, II, 582
Yeshūʿā b. Japheth, Abu ʾl-Faraj b. Abu ʾl-Ḥusayn, I, 364
Yeshūʿā b. Joseph, Nagid, II, 530, 595; III, 211
Yeshūʿā b. Joseph ha-Kohen, II, 72, 454, 527, 535, 548; III, 443; V, 422–423, 609. *See also* Joseph ha-Kohen b. Solomon
Yeshūʿā b. Joshiahu b. Shemaʿya Gaon, II, 584
Yeshūʿā b. Merāyōt, V, 150
Yeshūʿā b. Nissīm, II, 611

Yeshūʿā b. Saʿadyāhū, IV, 375
Yeshūʿā b. Samuel (Ismaʿīl al-Makhmūrī), I, 465; IV, 384
Yeshūʿā b. Sedāqā, III, 292
Yeshūʿā Dukhān, I, 367
Yeshūʿā ha-Kohen b. Ghālib, III, 471
Yeshūʿā ha-Levi b. Ṣedāqā, al-Ramlī, III, 154, 460
Yeshūʿā ha-Levi b. Solomon, II, 553
Yeshūʿā *he-ḥāvēr* b. rabbi Nathan, *gūr aryē*, III, 476
Yeshūʿā *he-ḥāvēr ha-meʿulle*, II, 566
Yeshūʿā Mēʾīr, II, 497
(*la-*)*yeṣīrā*. *See* Era of the Creation
al-Yesōd, notable, II, 432
Yiḥye b. Hillel, II, 557
yikhūs (Heb., noble descent), III, 5
yimandilū ("they exhibited the letter"), referring to divination, II, 536
yiqaddis (to sanctify), II, 550
Yohanan, Rabbi, IV, 152, 432
yōṣerōt (Heb., poems), II, 569, 580
"Young man," slave or employee, I, 93, 132, 144, 161-164
Young men, II, 42, 61, 62, 80, 285, 370, 536, 608
yughayyir (to proselytize), II, 594
Yuḥanna, II, 590
Yūnus (*ḥabs*), IV, 34
Yūshaʿ b. Nathan, I, 453
Yūsuf al-ʿAjamī al-Kurānī, V, 471-472, 639
Yūsuf al-Baṣīr, Karaite theologian, V, 606
Yūsuf b. Shuʿayb Ibn al-Naghira, III, 429; V, 598
yūsufī cloth, II, 123, 449, 546
yuṭʿim al-aṭrāf (incompetent in ritual matters), II, 614

Z

zabdiyya, zubdiyya (deep bowl), IV, 145, 146, 386, 392, 393, 429, 455
Zachariah b. Tammām. *See* Zakariyyā b. Tammām
Zadok b. Samuel, physician of Ibn al-ʿAmmānī family, IV, 443; V, 556
zaʿfarān. *See* Saffron
zaʿfarānī: dyer with saffron, I, 107, 420; seller of saffron, I, 438
Zaffān ("Buffoon") family, III, 157; V, 517
Ẓāfira ("Victoria") b. Japheth, III, 216-217; IV, 275
zaghghāb (downer), I, 416
al-Ẓāhir, Fatimid caliph, II, 16, 522
zāhūv (Heb., gold piece), I, 370. *See also* Dinar; Gold
zāʾid (addition), I, 239, 460
zajjāj. *See* Glassmaker
Zakariyyāʾ, sons of, I, 444
Zakariyyā b. Tammām, I, 49; III, 439
zakāt (alms), II, 606
Zakī, II, 493
Zakkār b. ʿAmmār, Nagid and representative of merchants in Sicily, II, 25, 525; III, 503; V, 242
Zakkay b. Moses, judge, II, 533, 574
Zakkūr, Christian shipowner, I, 479
zalabānī (preparer of pancakes), I, 115, 424
zanājil. *See* Canister makers
zanfalīja (slip cover for a book), IV, 387
zanjabīlī. *See* Ginger
zanjala, zinjila. *See* Canister
zāqēn (Heb., elder), II, 60; III, 427. *See also* Elder
zarbiyya (rug), IV, 126, 384. *See also* Carpet
zareba (cattle pen), I, 124; IV, 18, 19
ẓarf (large container), I, 334, 486
zarība. See *zareba*
zarrāqāt (fountains), IV, 367. *See also* Fountain
Zarzīs, Tunisia, IV, 418
zaʾuq. *See* Mercury
Zawīla quarter, Cairo. *See* Zuwayla
Zawīlat al-Mahdiyya, Tunisia, I, 416; II, 58, 236, 323, 597, 601; III, 176; V, 98
Zaydis, IV, 403
Zaylūsh, Palestine, II, 477
Zayn, *parnās*, II, 449
Zayn b. Abu ʾl-Khayr, merchant, II, 592
Zayn al-Dār, f., III, 194
Zayn al-Dār b. ʿAllān b. Ḥassūn, V, 568
Zayn al-Dīn, jurist, V, 175
Zayn al-Kuttāb, II, 355
zayt bizr (seed oil), linseed oil, I, 426
zayt ḥarr (hot oil), linseed oil, I, 426
zaytūnī mujallā (gloss of "satin"), description of textile, I, 419, 455
zayyāt (dealer in olive oil), I, 120, 152; II, 453. *See also* Olive
al-Zayyiq, rare name, II, 441
Zechariah b. Ḥayyīm, V, 583
Zeganzāl (Zgnzāl), court clerk, V, 599
zehāvī (Heb., "gold man"), I, 108
zekhūth (Heb., religious merit), III, 435
zeqēn. See *zāqēn*
Zeresh (biblical), II, 74; III, 171
zibbūrīt (Heb., ancient term for dinars "of the worst sort"), III, 482
zifāf. *See* Bridal procession

zikhrōn ʿēdūth (Heb., record of witness), minutes, **II**, 600
Zikrī b. Ḥalfōn, **III**, 297
Zikrī b. Musallam Ibn al-Naʿja, physician, **V**, 301–302
zimiya (Heb.). *See* Fines
zinād (flintstone), **IV**, 297
zinbīl (type of basket), **I**, 486. *See also* Baskets
zinjār (verdigris), **I**, 420
ziqnē yōsher, ha-zeqēnīm ha-yeshārīm (*ha-keshōrīm*) (trustworthy elders), **II**, 543
ziqq (skin, bag), **I**, 215, 453, 485
zīr (jar), **I**, 485; **IV**, 390, 391, 393, 435
ẓiʾra = *ẓiʾr*. *See* Wet nurse
Zirids, **I**, 269, 373, 375, 390; **II**, 25; **III**, 357
Zirkiyoff, Ephraim Hay, **V**, 517
ziyāra (visit of pilgirmage), **V**, 20. *See also* Pilgrimage
Ziziphus trees, **I**, 427; **IV**, 77
Zoar (biblical). *See* Zughar
Zodiac, as ornament, **IV**, 124, 129
Zoning, **IV**, 15–21
Zoroastriansim, **V**, 334, 598
zuʿamāʾ (leaders), **II**, 60, 535; *z. al-yahūd* (leaders of the Jews), **II**, 535
zubda (butter), **I**, 124
zubdī (butter maker), **I**, 429
Zucker, Moshe, **I**, 4
Zughar, Palestine, **IV**, 45, 360
zuhdī dancing, **V**, 202
Zuhr ("Flower," maidservant), **IV**, 321
zunnār. *See* Waistband
Zunz, Leopold, **V**, 557
zuqāq al-baṭṭāṭīn. *See* Bottlemakers
Zurʿa, a shipowner, **I**, 312
zurumbāq (type of jewelry), **IV**, 355
Zūṭā ("Mr. Small"), **IV**, 453
Zurʿa(h) ha-Levi b. Abraham, **II**, 600; **III**, 484
Zuṭṭā, **II**, 32, 39, 67, 244
Zuṭṭā, the imposter, **II**, 527, 543
Zuwayla quarter, Cairo, **III**, 38, 347; **IV**, 80, 101, 283, 331
zūz (silver piece), **I**, 368, 370, 386; **III**, 119, 121. *See also* Dirhem; Silver

Index of Geniza Texts

References will be found in the Appendices and Notes of the five volumes. Volume I contains chapters i–iv; volume II, chapters v–vii; volume III, chapter viii; volume IV, chapter ix; volume V, chapter x. References are given by chapter, section, subsection, and note number. Sections or subsections of a chapter are separated by semicolons; chapters are separated by periods. References to appendices precede those to notes, following the order established in the volumes. Lower case plain roman numerals indicate chapters; upper case bold roman numerals indicate volumes. For references to the *Responsa* of Abraham and Moses Maimonides, see the Index of Scriptural, Rabbinic, and Maimonidean Citations.

Abraham Maimuni, *Responsa* *see* Index of Scriptural, Rabbinic, and Maimonidean Citations
AIU: Alliance Israelite Universelle, Paris

AIU VII A 17	v, B, 1, n. 76; v, B, 2, n. 89. viii, C, 2, n. 127. ix, A, 1, n. 207
23	vii, C, 1, c, nn. 26, 35
C 16	ii, 5, n. 18
123	ii, 5, n. 18
D 4	v, B, 2, n. 20
4*c*	viii, A, 1, n. 23; viii, C, 4, n. 77; viii, D, n. 106
7	viii, D, n. 62. **IV**, App. A, VII. ix, A, 3, n. 8
E 21	ii, 5, n. 72. v, D, 2, n. 1. vii, A, 2, n. 40
93	**I**, App. D, sec. 42. iii, F, n. 11
145	**II**, App. D, sec. 31
*3	**II**, App. C, sec. 82a
Shaked 298	vii, D, 2, n. 14
MS AJ (Private)	viii, A, 2, n. 77; viii, B, 5, n. 90; viii, C, 1, n. 13

Antonin: Antonin Collection, Leningrad

Antonin 164	**III**, App. pt. II, no. 344
460	**III**, App. pt. II, no. 46. viii, B, 4, n. 55
521	vi, 2, n. 31
634	**III**, App. pt. I, gr. 5; **III**, App. pt. II, no. 34. viii, B, 4, n. 14
635	**III**, App. pt. II, no. 60. viii, B, 1, n. 19; viii, B, 3, n. 13. ix, A, 4, n. 104; ix, A, 5, nn. 69, 73
637	vii, B, 2, n. 3. viii, B, 5, n. 88
904	i, 2, n. 84. iv, 2, n. 15; iv, 8, n. 32. viii, B, 1, n. 34
1064	**IV**, App. A, II. ix, A, 3, n. 126
1105	iv, 8, n. 25. vi, 2, n. 27
1154	v, D, 2, n. 26. x, D, n. 79
MS Bibl. Nat., Paris 2325, f. 163*a*	ix, A, 3, n. 118

BM: British Museum (now: British Library), London

BM Or 2538, f. 88	viii, B, 3, n. 11
2598, f. 162	v, B, 2, n. 122

3179, I, f. 82*a*	x, B, 3, n. 1
5338 II	v, A, 1, n. 35
5524, fs. 1–8	viii, C, 3, n. 64
f. 6	viii, C, 3, n. 121; viii, D, n. 96
f. 7	viii, C, 3, n. 121; viii, D, n. 96
5529	viii, A, 1, n. 46
5532	viii, B, 1, n. 8
5536 I	viii, C, 1, n. 223
II	**III**, App. pt. I, gr. 1; **III**, App. pt. II, no. 337. viii, B, 2, n. 15; viii, B, 4, n. 81; viii, D, n. 14
III, nos. 8–9	v, A, 1, n. 30
5542, f. 5	viii, A, 2, n. 64
f. 6	ii, 5, n. 86. iii, C, n. 12. viii, A, 2, n. 56; viii, A, 3, n. 54. x, C, 3, n. 38
f. 8	**II**, App. B, sec. 62
f. 9	ii, 4, n. 4
f. 10*v*	viii, C, 1, n. 155
f. 11	viii, C, 4, n. 40
f. 13	x, B, 1, n. 95 (*see also* f. 24)
f. 15	i, 3, n. 9. iii, B, 3, n. 5. iv, 8, nn. 21, 46; iv, 10, n. 36
f. 19	viii, A, 1, n. 86. ix, B, n. 64
f. 20	viii, B, 3, n. 98
f. 23 (now f. 14)	**II**, App. B, sec. 98. x, B, 1, n. 45
f. 24	x, B, 1, nn. 91, 95 (*see also* f. 13)
f. 27	i, 2, n. 29. iii, D, n. 5
f. 33	viii, C, 4, n. 142
f. 34	**II**, App. C, sec. 81
5544	ix, A, 1, n. 3
5544, f. 1	i, 3, n. 20. v, C, 1, n. 9
f. 2	v, C, 5, n. 2
f. 8	x, B, 3, n. 42
f. 9	vii, A, 2, n. 8
5549, f. 5*v*	iii, G, n. 2. **II**, App. C, sec. 23
f. 6	**II**, App. A, sec. 149
f. 7	**II**, App. B, sec. 90
f. 8	**II**, App. B, sec. 58
5551 (Glass 1151)	**III**, App. pt. II, no. 278. viii, C, 3, n. 45
5552 B	x, C, 4, n. 121
5554 B, f. 20	viii, C, 1, n. 39; viii, D, n. 216
5560 A	v, A, 1, n. 3
5561 B, f. 2	**III**, App. pt. I, gr. 1; **III**, App. pt. II, no. 128. ix, B, n. 426
f. 3	**III**, App. pt. I, gr. 1; **III**, App. pt. II, no. 51. **IV**, App. C, 2. ix, B, n. 440
5563 D	iii, B, 2, n. 32
5566 A I	**III**, App. pt. II, no. 265. viii, C, 1, n. 207
5566 B, f. 6*a*	*see* f. 7
f. 7	**II**, App. A, sec. 12. v, A, 1, n. 3. ix, A, 1, n. 96
f. 15	vi, 12, n. 86
f. 20	ix, B, n. 265
f. 26	ix, C, 1, n. 154
f. 29	**II**, App. A, sec. 163
f. 30	x, D, n. 66
f. 32	ix, A, 4, n. 91
f. 33	**II**, App. A, sec. 44
f. 33*v*	**II**, App. C, sec. 38
5566 C, f. 1	**II**, App. B, sec. 73
f. 2	**II**, App. B, sec. 79

f. 9 i, 2, n. 32. ii, 4, nn. 2, 100. x, B, 3, n. 72
fs. 9–10 **II**, App. B, sec. 32. vi, 10, n. 36; vi, 12, n. 51
10 col. II x, A, 2, n. 413
f. 10 ii, 6, nn. 17, 25. iii, A, 1, n. 5
f. 11 ii, 3, n. 9
fs. 11–12 **II**, App. C, sec. 50
f. 12 ii, 3, n. 9
5566 D, f. 6 viii, A, 3, n. 1
f. 10 **II**, App. B, sec. 56
f. 11 viii, A, 3, n. 66
f. 16 iii, A, 1, n. 9
f. 22 viii, B, 2, n. 5
f. 24 ii, 4, n. 99. x, A, 1, n. 115
10126 **I**, App. D, sec. 65. iii, F, n. 164. vii, D, 1, n. 30. **IV**, App. A, II. ix, A, n.24
10126, f. 19 vii, C, 1, c, n. 15
10578, fs. 1–2 **II**, App. C, sec. 130
10587 iii, F, n. 165
10588 ii, 3, n. 29. iii, A, 1, n. 1
10589, f. 16 **II**, App. B, sec. 18
10599*v* viii, C, 1, n. 45. ix, C, 1, n. 38
10652 ii, 7, n. 21. x, D, n. 315
10653, f. 5 ii, 7, n. 54
10656, f. 17 ii, 5, n. 83
12186 viii, B, 1, n. 56; viii, C, 3, n. 145
Bodl.: Bodleian Library, Oxford
Bodl. MS Heb.
(In parentheses is the number of the MS in the printed *Catalogue of the Hebrew Manuscripts in the Bodleian Library*, ed. A. Neubauer and A. E. Cowley, Oxford, 1906, with the number of the unit if it is not identical with the folio of the shelf mark. Some manuscripts are not listed in the *Catalogue*.)
a2 (2805), f. 2 **III**, App. pt. I, gr. 4; **III**, App. pt. II, no. 184. viii, B, 3, n. 92
f. 3 iii, C, n. 15; iii, F, n. 21. vii, B, 1, n. 48; vii, B, 2, n. 4. viii, A, 3, n. 59; viii, D, n. 11
f. 4 vi, 10, n. 44. vii, B, 1, n. 6. **III**, App. pt. I, gr. 4; **III**, App. pt. II, no. 44. **IV**, App. C, 3. ix, A, 4, n. 193
f. 5 viii, B, 3, n. 82
f. 6 **III**, App. pt. I, gr. 5; **III**, App. pt. II, no. 358. viii, D, n. 14. **IV**, App. C, 2. ix, B, n. 124
f. 7 viii, C, nn. 22, 99. ix, A, 3, n. 114
f. 9 ii, 2, n. 24. iii, F, n. 211. v, B, 2, nn. 84, 91. vii, D, 1, n. 15. **III**, App. pt. II, no. 257. viii, C, 1, n. 107; viii, C, 3, nn. 6, 30; viii, D, 4, n. 25. x, A, 3, nn. 37, 121
f. 10 viii, C, 4, n. 174
f. 11 iii, B, 4, n. 8; iii, D, nn. 25, 26, 53, 70. iv, 10, nn. 13, 19
f. 13 ii, 5, n. 53
f. 15 vii, B, 1, n. 3; vii, B, 3, n. 2
f. 16 x, D, n. 39
f. 17 i, 2, nn. 46, 84. iv, 3, n. 61; iv, 4, n. 5; iv, 6, n. 26; iv, 8, nn. 32, 42; iv, 9, n. 29. v, A, 2, n. 9. vi, 5, n. 7
f. 18 i, 2, n. 20. iii, B, 2, n. 10. iv, 10, n. 28
f. 19 ii, 7, n. 12. iii, B, 1, nn. 9, 14; iii, G, n. 28. iv, 7, n. 16; iv, 10, n. 17
f. 20 iii, B, 1, n. 12; iii, E, n. 61; iii, F, n. 29. iv, 7, n. 12; iv, 10, n. 26. ix, B, n. 224
f. 21*v* x, B, 1, n. 16; x, B, 4, n. 37
f. 22 vii, A, 2, n. 12; vii, C, 1, b, n. 20

f. 23 vii, B, 1, n. 6. viii, B, 5, n. 32; viii, C, 4, n. 24. ix, A, 1, n. 93

a3 (2873), f. 2 ii, 5, n. 86. iii, D, n. 63; iii, F, n. 193. iv, 1, n. 1. v, A, 2, nn. 51, 53, 62; v, B, 2, nn. 8, 25; v, C, 4, n. 47. vi, 10, n. 5

f. 3 vi, 12, n. 26. vii, B, 3, n. 40

f. 5 iii, E, n. 55. vii, B, 1, n. 12. viii, A, 1, n. 39; viii, B, 2, n. 52; viii, C, 4, nn. 91, 99

f. 6 v, A, 2, n. 47. vii, B, 1, n. 8; vii, C, 1, b, n. 3. viii, C, 4, nn. 99, 122. x, B, 3, n. 80; x, D, n. 73

f. 7 **I**, App. C, sec. 8. ii, 2, n. 8

f. 8 **I**, App. C, sec. 9. ii, 3, n. 13. iii, B, 2, n. 51; iii, F, n. 184. **IV**, App. A, I. ix, A, 3, n. 18. x, C, 2, nn. 8, 28

f. 9 iii, B, 4, n. 4. iv, 8, n. 74; iv, 11, n. 19. vii, D, 1, n. 1

f. 12 viii, B, 3, n. 6

f. 13 ii, 7, n. 8. iii, B, 1, n. 8; iii, B, 4, n. 2; iii, D, nn. 23, 27, 30, 36, 49, 72, 83, 84; iii, E, nn. 13, 52. iv, 3, n. 32; iv, 6, nn. 10, 13; iv, 7, nn. 11, 29; iv, 8, n. 6; iv, 10, nn. 2, 30. ix, B, n. 224. x, B, 1, n. 14

f. 15 v, B, 1, n. 54. x, B, 2, n. 86; x, D, n. 325

f. 16 **I**, App. C, sec. 26. viii, A, 3, n. 34. x, B, 3, n. 62

f. 16*v* vii, D, 2, n. 14

f. 17 v, A, 2, n. 35. vi, 12, n. 12. vii, C, 1, a, nn. 9, 29. x, B, 2, n. 108; x, B, 3, nn. 18, 47; x, B, 4, n. 59; x, C, 1, n. 40

f. 19 iv, 10, n. 16. ix, A, 5, n. 51; ix, B, n. 99

f. 20 viii, C, 4, n. 61

f. 21 v, B, 1, n. 1. vi, 7, n. 18

f. 22 vii, C, 1, b, n. 8

f. 23 iii, D, nn. 44, 48; iii, E, n. 22. iv, 8, n. 27; iv, 9, n. 23

f. 24 v, A, 1, n. 49. vii, C, 1, d, n. 7. x, A, 2, nn. 86, 87; x, A, 3, n. 64

f. 26 ii, 4, n. 55. iii, A, 2, n. 3; iii, E, n. 31. iv, 6, n. 14; iv, 8, n. 24; iv, 9, n. 5; iv, 10, n. 27. **II**, App. C, sec. 7. v, A, 2, nn. 3, 8. vii, B, 1, n. 54; vii, B, 3, nn. 14, 25; vii, D, 1, n. 22

f. 28 v, B, 1, n. 73; x, D, n. 42

f. 29 **I**, App. D, sec. 47. iii, D, n. 5; iii, F, n. 94. vi, 12, n. 95. vii, C, 1, d, n. 33

f. 32*v* **III**, App. pt. II, no. 20. viii, B, 1, n. 6; viii, B, 3, n. 6; viii, B, 4, n. 18; viii, B, 5, n. 41. **IV**, App. A, III

f. 35 i, 3, n. 16. vii, A, 2, n. 9. ix, A, 1, n. 143; ix, A, 2, nn. 37, 51

f. 37 **II**, App. A, sec. 2. v, A, 1, n. 3; v, B, 1, n. 5; v, B, 2, n. 61. x, C, 5, n. 22

f. 38 i, 2, n. 30. **III**, App. pt. II, no. 61. viii, B, 1, n. 7. x, A, 3, n. 305

f. 39 **III**, App. pt. I, gr. 4; **III**, App. pt. II, no. 152. viii, B, 3, n. 84. ix, A, 4, nn. 5, 42, 64, 217; ix, A, 5, n. 14; ix, B, nn. 385, 526

f. 40 **III**, App. pt. I, gr. 5; **III**, App. pt. II, no. 82. viii, B, 3, nn. 36, 64; viii, B, 5, n. 9; viii, C, 1, nn. 112, 131. ix, A, 4, nn. 7, 44, 49, 51; ix, A, 5, n. 10; ix, B, n. 536

f. 40*v* **III**, App. pt. I, gr. 5. viii, B, 5, n. 65; viii, D, n. 4

f. 42 v, C, 2, n. 35. vii, D, 1, n. 32. **III**, App. pt. I, gr. 5; **III**, App. pt. II, no. 159. viii, B, 1, n. 8; viii, B, 3, n. 67; viii, B, 5, n. 45; viii, C, 4, n. 160. **IV**, App. C, 2. ix, A, 4, nn. 15, 81, 93; ix, A, 5, n. 46; ix, B, nn. 455, 457, 534. **IV**, App. D, n. 263

f. 43 **III**, App. pt. II, no. 148. **IV**, App. C, 2. ix, A, 4, nn. 9, 26, 38, 167, 178, 190

f. 44 **III**, App. pt. II, no. 350

f. 45	**III**, App. pt. I, gr. 4; **III**, App. pt. II, no. 331. viii, B, 3, n. 49; viii, B, 4, n. 60
f. 46	**I**, App. D, sec. 91. viii, B, 3, n. 84; viii, B, 4, n. 84; viii, B, 5, n. 89
b3 (2806), f. 1	iii, B, 3, n. 16
f. 4	vii, C, 1, b, n. 2. viii, B, 2, n. 43
f. 5	**II**, App. C, sec. 133
f. 6	ii, 5, n. 71. v, A, 2, n. 18. viii, C, 4, n. 86. **IV**, App. A, III. ix, A, 1, n. 44; ix, A, 3, n. 24. x, D, n. 358
(2806, no. 7), fs. 7–8	viii, D, n. 5. **IV**, App. A, I
(2806, no. 8), f. 9	**III**, App. pt II, no. 53. viii, B, 5, n. 52
(2806, no. 10), f. 11	**III**, App. pt. II, no. 332
(2806, no. 11), f. 12	**III**, App. pt. II, no. 339. ix, A, 4, n. 36
(2806, no. 15), f. 16	ii, 5, n. 52. iv, 3, n. 44. v, B, 2, n. 56. vii, A, 1, n. 32. x, B, 3, n. 7
(2806, no. 16), f. 17	i, 2, n. 46. x, A, 2, n. 292
f. 19	iii, D, n. 61; iii, E, n. 53. iv, 8, n. 77. ix, A, 4, n. 65; ix, B, nn. 134, 136, 223
f. 20	iii, D, n. 53. ix, A, 1, n. 125; ix, A, 4, n. 133; ix, B, nn. 223, 399
(2806, no. 19), f. 21	iii, F, n. 48
(2806, no. 20), f. 22	ii, 4, n. 87. iii, E, nn. 36, 57
(2806, no. 21), f. 23	ii, 2, n. 46. iv, 8, n. 31
(2806, no. 24), f. 26	i, 2, n. 24. iii, C, n. 10. vi, 2, n. 10; vi, 4, n. 25
(2806, no. 26), f. 28	**III**, App. pt. I, gr. 4; **III**, App. pt II, no. 58
(2806, no. 30), f. 32	x, A, 2, n. 273
b11 (2874), f. 1	vi, 12, n. 11
f. 2	iii, F, nn. 105, 111
f. 3	**III**, App. pt. I, gr. 5. viii, C, 1, n. 113
f. 5	ii, 3, n. 24; ii, 4, nn. 12, 87; ii, 5, n. 36. iii, D, n. 83. **II**, App. A, sec. 5. vii, C, 1, c, n. 37. ix, A, 1, n. 55; ix, A, 4, n. 125
f. 7	i, 1, n. 10; i, 2, n. 91; i, 3, n. 26. vii, C, 1, a, n. 21. ix, A, 1, n. 205. x, A, 2, n. 317; x, C, 4, n. 75
f. 8	iii, B, 2, n. 45; iii, C, n. 12. viii, A, 2, n. 57
f. 9	iii, F, n. 115. v, A, 2, n. 54; v, B, 1, nn. 1, 6, 61, 98
f. 10	ii, 5, n. 21
f. 11	ii, 5, n. 64
f. 12	viii, C, 3, n. 45
f. 13	v, A, 1, n. 5
f. 14	iv, 12, n. 44. viii, C, 3, nn. 98, 113. ix, A, 2, n. 154
f. 15	iv, 6, nn. 13, 22. x, B, 2, n. 44
(2874, no. 21), f. 22	iv, 2, n. 3
(2874, no. 22), f. 23	v, B, 1, nn. 16, 19; v, C, 2, n. 8

(2874, no. 33), f. 34	**III**, App. pt. II, no. 207
(2874, no. 34), f. 35	**IV**, App. A, II
f. 36	**II**, App. D, sec. 18. v, C, 2, n. 32. vii, D, 1, n. 26. viii, A, 1, n. 39
b12 (2875), f. 1	**III**, App. pt. I, grs. 7 and 8; **III**, App. pt. II, no. 11
f. 2	vi, 13, n. 15. viii, D, n. 101
f. 3	**III**, App. pt. II, no. 172. viii, B, 4, nn. 66, 88
f. 4	ix, A, 2, nn. 59, 77
f. 5	**III**, App. pt. II, no. 282
f. 6	viii, A, 3, n. 14. ix, A, 1, n. 70; ix, A, 3, n. 88
f. 7	viii, C, 1, n. 236
f. 8	ii, 5, n. 71. iii, F, n. 156
fs. 9, 29	vii, A, 2, n. 5
f. 10	viii, A, 2, n. 78, no. 11; viii, C, 1, n. 223
f. 11	**III**, App. pt. II, no. 110. viii, B, 4, n. 47; viii, B, 5, n. 37; viii, D, n. 19
f. 12	**III**, App. pt. II, no. 333
f. 13*b*	vi, 9, n. 15
f. 14	**III**, App. pt. II, no. 5. viii, B, 4, n. 16
f. 15	viii, B, 4, n. 60
f. 18	**III**, App. pt. I, grs. 5 and 8; **III**, App. pt. II, no. 241
f. 19	**III**, App. pt. I, gr. 5; **III**, App. pt. II, no. 330. viii, B, 4, n. 78
f. 20	ii, 7, nn. 34, 64
f. 22	**III**, App. pt. II, no. 304. viii, B, 3, n. 84
f. 26	**III**, App. pt. I, gr. 8; **III**, App. pt. II, no. 62. viii, B, 3, nn. 76, 84; viii, B, 4, n. 60 (*see* Merx, *Paleographie hebraique*, pp. 39–44)
f. 28	**III**, App. pt. II, no. 312. viii, D, n. 156
f. 29 (*see* f. 6)	viii, A, 3, n. 14. ix, A, 1, n. 70; ix, A, 3, n. 88
f. 30	viii, C, 4, n. 28
f. 31	**III**, App. pt. II, no. 204. viii, B, 4, n. 18. ix, A, 2, n. 35
f. 32	ii, 7, n. 14. v, A, 2, n. 48
b13 (2834), f. 20	vii, C, 1, b, n. 4
(2834, no. 19), f. 34	viii, C, 3, n. 156
f. 38	viii, C, 4, n. 14
(2834, no. 20), f. 39	ii, 7, n. 50
(2834, no. 22), f. 41	v, A, 2, n. 37; v, B, 1, nn. 13, 101; v, D, 1, n. 9
(2834, no. 23), f. 42	vii, B, 1, nn. 44, 53
(2834, no. 25), f. 44	v, B, 1, n. 6
(2834, no. 27), f. 46	iii, B, 3, n. 3. viii, C, 3, nn. 56, 156; viii, C, 4, n. 97. **IV**, App. C, 1. x, A, 3, n. 52
(2834, no. 28), f. 47	**III**, App. pt. II, no. 353
(2834, no. 29), f. 48	**III**, App. pt. I, gr. 5. viii, B, 5, n. 25
(2834, no. 30), f. 49	**I**, App. D, sec. 26. ii, 5, n. 23. iv, 3, nn. 19, 39; iv, 5, n. 20; iv, 6, n. 18. viii, A, 2, nn. 8, 74; viii, B, 1, n. 36
(2834, no. 31), f. 50	ii, 7, n. 8. ix, C, 2, n. 38

(2834, no. 33), f. 52 viii, B, 1, n. 61. x, A, 1, n. 132; x, A, 2, n. 369
(2834, no. 35), f. 54 viii, A, 3, n. 51
(2834, no. 36), f. 55 **II**, App. C, sec. 68. x, B, 2, n. 132
b18, f. 21 vii, D, 2, n. 5
c13 (2807), f. 1 iii, D, n. 24. x, B, 1, n. 83
(2807, no. 5), fs. 6–8 **II**, App. C, sec. 59
(2807, no. 9), f. 12 vii, A, 2, n. 8
(2807, no. 13), f. 16 viii, B, 3, n. 13
(2807, no. 16), f. 20 vi, 9, n. 31; vi, 11, n. 33. vii, B, 1, n. 66
(2807, no. 17d), f. 22 v, B, 2, n. 85. ix, A, 2, n. 78
(2807, no. 18), f. 23 v, B, 1, n. 140
(2807, no. 20), f. 25 viii, B, 3, n. 57
(2807, no. 20), f. 26 viii, B, 3, n. 57
c18 (2634), f. 11 vi, 13, n. 53
(2634, no. 15), f. 38 ii, 7, n. 95
c27 (2835), f. 82 iii, A, 2, n. 9; iii, E, nn. 6, 50, 61. iv, 8, n. 36
c28 (2876), f. 1 ii, 7, n. 64. ix, A, 1, n. 220
f. 2 v, D, 2, n. 36
f. 5 v, B, 1, nn. 63, 67
f. 6 i, 2, n. 70. iv, 7, n. 11. **II**, App. B, sec. 12. v, B, 2, n. 86. vi, 9, n. 4; vi, 10, nn. 2, 50. viii, A, 1, n. 82
f. 7 **II**, App. D, sec. 17. viii, C, 1, n. 133
f. 10 v, A, 1, n. 53; v, B, 1, n. 60; v, B, 2, n. 7
f. 11 i, 2, nn. 9, 25; i, 3, n. 14. iii, A, 1, n. 35; iii, B, 2, n. 43; iii, D, n. 53
f. 14 viii, C, 1, n. 207; viii, C, 3, n. 159; viii, C, 4, n. 175
f. 15 vi, 10, n. 25
f. 16*v* x, B, 2, n. 70
f. 20 iii, F, n. 86. iv, 3, n. 76. vi, 11, n. 56. viii, C, 4, n. 107
f. 22 x, B, 4, n. 35
f. 23 vi, 11, nn. 8, 52
f. 24 **II**, App. B, sec. 54. x, B, 1, n. 28
f. 26 vii, C, 1, a, n. 32
f. 28 vi, 8, n. 3; vi, 10, n. 38
f. 29 iii, F, n. 145
f. 30 **II**, App. D, sec. 8. v, B, 1, n. 70. vi, 9, n. 15; vi, 10, n. 3
f. 31 iv, 8, n. 51. vii, A, 3, n. 18; vii, C, 1, d, n. 2. x, B, 2, n. 122
f. 32 **I**, App. C, sec. 2
f. 33 iii, B, 4, n. 7; iii, E, n. 48. iv, 2, n. 10; iv, 3, n. 30
f. 34 vii, A, 1, n. 20. ix, B, n. 398
f. 35 vii, C, 1, d, n. 25
f. 36 iv, 3, n. 41. vii, C, 1, c, n. 3
f. 37 vii, B, 1, n. 46. ix, A, 3, n. 7
f. 38 v, B, 2, n. 34. vii, C, 1, b, n. 30

f. 41 viii, C, 1, n. 196. ix, A, 1, n. 93; ix, A, 2, n. 35
f. 43 iv, 3, n. 66. vii, C, 1, d, n. 20
f. 44 vi, 13, n. 15
f. 45 x, D, n. 298
f. 46 x, D, n. 298
f. 47 ii, 1, n. 10; ii, 2, nn. 14, 33; ii, 3, n. 6; ii, 5, nn. 27, 71. iii, A, 1, n. 19; iii, F, n. 123. iv, 7, n. 17. **II**, App. C, sec. 46
f. 48 viii, C, 1, n. 198
f. 49 vii, B, 1, n. 7; vii, B, 3, n. 2
f. 50 iii, D, nn. 33, 66. iv, 8, n. 74
f. 52 **I**, App. D, sec. 29. iv, 6, n. 7; iv, 8, n. 35. vi, 4, nn. 1, 20; vi, 12, n. 70. viii, A, 2, n. 80; viii, A, 3, n. 47. x, A, 1, n. 159; x, A, 2, n. 396; x, A, 3, n. 162
f. 54 ii, 7, n. 100. iii, C, nn. 4, 20. **II**, App. D, sec. 23. **III**, App. pt. II, no. 287
f. 55 iii, D, n. 14. iv, 11, n. 4
f. 56 iv, 5, n. 15
f. 57 **I**, App. D, sec. 46
f. 58 viii, C, 2, n. 34. x, A, 1, n. 77
f. 59 v, D, 2, n. 10. vii, C, 1, a, n. 19
f. 60 iv, 6, n. 20; iv, 9, n. 27. v, A, 2, n. 72. viii, B, 1, n. 42; viii, B, 3, n. 100
f. 61 ii, 1, n. 13; ii, 4, n. 2. iii, E, n. 60. iv, 10, n. 30. viii, C, 4, n. 107
f. 64 vii, B, 1, n. 72. viii, A, 2, n. 79; viii, C, 1, n. 65. ix, A, 1, n. 234
f. 65 iv, 12, n. 5. v, A, 1, n. 44; v, B, 2, n. 111. vii, C, 2, n. 16
f. 67 vi, 12, n. 11. x, B, 3, n. 47; x, C, 2, n. 2
f. 68 v, B, 1, n. 40. vii, B, 3, n. 42. x, B, 1, n. 83
f. 69 ii, 4, n. 14. v, B, 1, n. 37. vii, C, 1, b, n. 29. **III**, App. pt. I, gr. 7. viii, B, 4, n. 27
c50, f. 14 **II**, App. A, sec. 147. ix, A, 3, n. 130
f. 16 **II**, App. C, sec. 115
f. 19 iv, 8, n. 4
f. 20 viii, C, 2, nn. 19, 68
f. 24 x, A, 1, n. 134
c56, f. 10 **II**, App. A, sec. 141
d23 (2752) x, D, n. 295
d37 (2603), f. 1 vi, 2, n. 29
d44 (2624), f. 3 vi, 2, n. 29
d47 (2699, no. 25), f. 62 iv, 4, n. 32; iv, 7, n. 29; iv, 10, n. 30
d48 (2760), f. 31 viii, B, 4, n. 46
d61 (2859, no. 3a), f. 9 **I**, App. D, sec. 62. v, C, 4, n. 46
d65 (2877), f. 1 **III**, App. pt. II, no. 106. ix, B, n. 385
f. 4 v, B, 1, nn. 139, 145. x, B, 1, n. 127; x, B, 4, n. 18
f. 8 **III**, App. pt. II, no. 141
f. 9 iii, B, 3, n. 7. iv, 2, nn. 13, 17. viii, A, 2, nn. 19, 20; viii, B, 1, n. 34. x, B, 1, nn. 7, 124
f. 10 iv, 3, nn. 20, 31
f. 11 **III**, App. pt. II, no. 185
f. 13 ix, A, 3, n. 27
f. 15 iii, E, n. 41. **III**, App. pt. II, no. 31. viii, B, 4, nn. 15, 20
f. 16 **III**, App. pt. II, no. 3
f. 17 i, 2, n. 44. iii, B, 1, n. 11; iii, E, nn. 45, 52, 61; iii, G, n. 33. iv, 6, n. 11; iv, 7, n. 8; iv, 8, n. 71; iv, 10, nn. 20, 21; iv, 11, nn. 11, 18. x, A, 2, n. 351

f. 18 **I**, App. D, sec. 92. i, 2, n. 37. ix, A, 1, n. 131
f. 20 **III**, App. pt. II, no. 315
f. 21 **IV**, App. A, III
f. 25 **II**, App. D, sec. 13
f. 26 **III**, App. pt. I, gr. 4; **III**, App. pt. II, no. 58. viii, B, 3, nn. 3, 5; viii, B, 4, n. 71
f. 27 i, 2, n. 30
f. 30 **III**, App. pt. I, gr. 3; **III**, App. pt. II, no. 164. viii, B, 3, n. 29; viii, D, n. 9. ix, A, 4, nn. 88, 214; ix, A, 5, n. 27; ix, B, nn. 278, 480
f. 44 **IV**, App. A, VII
d66 (2878), f. 3 iii, G, n. 29. vii, C, 1, c, n. 42. **IV**, App. A, II. ix, A, 2, n. 38
f. 4 *see* TS 10 J 26, f. 1
f. 5 iii, A, 1, n. 35; iii, B, 2, n. 43. ix, B, n. 114. x, B, 4, n. 29
f. 6 vi, 2, n. 1. vii, C, 1, c, n. 47. ix, A, 2, n. 70
f. 7 **II**, App. D, sec. 12. vi, 10, n. 34
f. 8 ii, 4, n. 14. v, A, 1, n. 5. vi, 11, n. 42. vii, B, 1, n. 19; vii, C, 1, b, n. 38
f. 10 x, A, 2, n. 110
f. 11 iii, F, n. 124. v, B, 2, n. 58
f. 15 ii, 1, n. 18; ii, 7, n. 8. iv, 6, n. 16; iv, 7, nn. 3, 15
f. 17 vii, C, 1, b, n. 42
f. 19 v, B, 2, n. 115. vi, 10, n. 48
f. 21 iv, 1, n. 5; iv, 12, n. 38. viii, C, 2, n. 164. ix, B, n. 37. x, A, 1, n. 150; x, B, 2, nn. 19, 65
f. 22 **III**, App. pt. I, gr. 7. ix, B, n. 123
f. 29 i, 2, n. 72. v, B, 1, n. 99; v, B, 2, n. 19. vi, 4, n. 21. vii, A, 2, n. 6
f. 32 viii, C, 4, n. 122
f. 41 iii, D, n. 17; iii, F, n. 9. iv, 2, n. 22
f. 42 ii, 4, n. 27. iv, 5, n. 14. ix, B, n. 224
f. 45*v* viii, D, n. 53
f. 46 **II**, App. D, sec. 15. vii, B, 1, n. 71
f. 47 ii, 4, n. 44. **III**, App. pt. I, gr. 6; **III**, App. pt. II, no. 178. viii, B, 2, nn. 3, 15, 17, 58; viii, B, 4, nn. 39, 43, 103; viii, B, 5, n. 15. ix, A, 4, n. 2
fs. 47–48 vi, 13, n. 16. **IV**, App. C, 2, 3. ix, A, 1, n. 89; ix, A, 4, nn. 8, 53, 56, 82, 163, 166, 188, 196, 208, 219; ix, A, 5, nn. 4, 27; ix, B, n. 59; ix, D, n. 35
f. 48 **III**, App. pt. I, gr. 6; **III**, App. pt. II, no. 178. viii, B, 2, nn. 15, 58; viii, B, 4, nn. 39, 43, 103
f. 52 ii, 4, n. 15. iii, B, 1, n. 5; iii, D, n. 40. iv, 8, n. 52. ix, B, n. 166. x, A, 2, n. 255
f. 54 ii, 2, n. 12. iii, A, 2, n. 4. iv, 8, n. 75
f. 57 iv, 2, nn. 5, 7, 34; iv, 3, n. 10. viii, C, 2, n. 159. x, A, 3, n. 260; x, B, 1, nn. 3, 18; x, B, 2, n. 83; x, B, 4, n. 164
f. 58 ii, 5, n. 86. v, A, 1, n. 2. vi, 6, n. 10. viii, A, 2, n. 80
f. 59, sec. 3 **II**, App. B, sec. 97
f. 62 **II**, App. B, sec. 15. vi, 4, n. 6
f. 63 vi, 9, n. 21. vii, C, 1, b, n. 24. ix, C, 1, n. 64
f. 76 iii, D, n. 65
f. 77 iii, D, n. 4. **III**, App. pt. II, no. 358. **IV**, App. C, 2. **IV**, App. D, nn. 114, 119. ix, A, 4, n. 219
f. 78 ii, 7, n. 11. viii, A, 1, n. 42. x, C, 3, n. 42
f. 79 v, A, 2, n. 42
f. 81 ii, 2, n. 12
f. 83 viii, C, 4, n. 11
f. 84 **I**, Introduction, n. 31. ii, 5, n. 55

f. 85 v, B, 2, n. 26. x, D, n. 312
f. 88 **II**, App. A, sec. 14. v, B, 1, n. 80. ix, A, 3, nn. 31, 108
f. 91 ii, 2, n. 38. viii, C, 2, n. 12. ix, B, nn. 220, 394
f. 92 iii, F, n. 123. viii, D, n. 64. **IV**, App. A, IV. x, B, 3, n. 63
f. 93 ii, 4, n. 3. ix, A, 4, n. 139
f. 99 iii, F, n. 196. **IV**, App. A, VII. ix, A, 1, n. 84; ix, A, 2, n. 55
f. 109 **IV**, App. A, IV. ix, A, 3, n. 37
fs. 110v–111 **IV**, App. A, I. ix, A, 3, n. 20; ix, A, 5, nn. 5, 21
f. 111*v* ix, A, 5, n. 30
f. 119 iii, B, 4, n. 5. **II**, App. C, sec. 66. vi, 4, n. 27
f. 121 viii, C, 2, n. 100; viii, C, 4, n. 17
f. 121*v* **III**, App. pt. I, gr. 4; **III**, App. pt. II, no. 101. viii, B, 2, n. 69. ix, B, n. 449
f. 125 v, C, 2, n. 8
f. 133 vii, B, 1, nn. 23, 32; vii, D, 1, n. 21
f. 133*v*, item *b* viii, B, 2, n. 42
f. 135 vii, C, 2, n. 42
f. 136 **II**, App. C, sec. 46. **IV**, App. A, V. ix, A, 3, n. 24
f. 137 ix, A, 3, nn. 54, 70. x, B, 2, n. 144
f. 141 vi, 12, nn. 62, 68. x, A, 2, n. 327
d68 (2836), f. 28*v* x, A, 3, n. 315
(2836, no. 21), f. 99 vii, D, 1, n. 37
(2836, no. 22), f. 100 **II**, App. A, sec. 21. ix, A, 2, nn. 95, 112; ix, 3, n. 111
(2836, no. 23), f. 101 **II**, App. A, sec. 109
(2836, no. 28), f. 106 vii, B, 3, n. 18. viii, B, 2, n. 76
(2836, no. 29), f. 107 **II**, App. B, sec. 95
(2836, no. 30), f. 108 iii, F, n. 27
d70 (2902) viii, C, 1, n. 211
d74, f. 35 viii, B, 4, n. 48
f. 37 v, B, 2, n. 121. x, A, 2, n. 424
f. 39 viii, C, 4, n. 23
f. 40 v, B, 2, n. 116
f. 41 iv, 5, n. 4; iv, 6, n. 7; iv, 8, n. 80
f. 42 i, 2, n. 72. vii, C, 1, b, n. 32
f. 44 ii, 2, n. 8
f. 47 ii, 2, n. 17. vii, C, 1, c, n. 26; vii, C, 2, n. 55
d75, f. 11 vii, B, 3, n. 18
f. 13 v, A, 2, nn. 15, 37. vi, 9, n. 17. ix, B, n. 333. x, B, 1, n. 67
f. 14 ix, B, n. 266
f. 19 x, A, 2, n. 432; x, A, 3, n. 88
f. 20 vii, A, 1, n. 43. **IV**, App. C, 2. ix, A, 4, n. 132
d76, f. 59 v, A, 2, n. 11
f. 60 viii, A, 3, n. 65. ix, A, 1, n. 111
f. 62 vi, 10, n. 25
f. 65 viii, D, n. 124
d79, f. 34*v* vii, D, 2, n. 4
f. 35 **II**, App. C, sec. 21. ix, B, n. 211
f. 36 v, B, 1, n. 3. vii, B, 3, n. 37
f. 42 **III**, App. pt. I, gr. 5
d98, f. 58 viii, C, 3, n. 130
e39 (2712, no. 23), ff. 125–136 v, B, 1, n. 70. vi, 11, n. 55

e44 (2668, no. 19), f. 81*v*	vi, 8, n. 10
(2668, no. 25), fs. 98–99*v*	viii, D, n. 98
e74 (2862)	vi, 11, n. 16
f. 7	x, D, n. 300
(2862, no. 20), f. 58	viii, D, n. 211
e94, f. 18	viii, B, 2, n. 43
f. 19	ii, 2, n. 52. viii, D, nn. 70, 90
fs. 19 and 25	**IV**, App. A, III
f. 21	**II**, App. C, sec. 15. viii, A, 2, n. 66. x, B, 3, n. 72
f. 22	**II**, App. C, sec. 80
f. 25	viii, D, n. 71
f. 27	**II**, App. B, sec. 103. x, A, 2, n. 218
f. 28	vi, 12, n. 47. vii, B, 2, n. 23. ix, B, n. 369
e98, f. 59	viii, B, 3, n. 22
f. 60	**III**, App. pt. I, gr. 8. ix, B, n. 497. x, C, 4, n. 81
f. 63	**I**, App. C, sec. 11. v, B, 2, n. 33. **IV**, App. A, VII. ix, A, 1, n. 92. x, A, 2, n. 282
f. 63*v*, item 1	viii, C, 4, n. 169. ix, A, 1, n. 57
f. 63*v*, item 2	viii, A, 1, n. 64
f. 64	ii, 4, nn. 15, 26. iii, A, 2, n. 5; iii, B, 2, n. 37; iii, B, 4, n. 7; iii, D, nn. 12, 74, 82; iii, E, nn. 6, 57, 78. iv, 6, n. 3; iv, 10, n. 28; iv, 12, n. 38. ix, B, nn. 230, 248
fs. 64–65	iii, D, nn. 74, 82. vi, 13, n. 58
f. 65	iii, D, n. 12. iv, 10, nn. 2, 9; iv, 12, n. 22
f. 67	v, B, 2, n. 9. vi, 9, n. 2
f. 68	ii, 4, n. 100
f. 69	vi, 10, n. 25. ix, B, n. 43
f. 74	ix, B, n. 29
f. 76	v, B, 2, nn. 104, 114
e100, f. 59	ix, B, nn. 495, 533
e101, f. 13	vi, 12, n. 92
f. 14	x, B, 4, n. 166
f. 15	viii, A, 3, n. 64. x, B, 4, n. 166
f. 16	ix, C, 2, n. 14
e108, f. 70	vii, C, 1, a, n. 42. viii, B, 1, n. 33
f22 (2728), fs. 25*v*–52*v*	vi, 12, n. 94
f. 39*v*	vii, C, 1, b, n. 15
(2728, no. 5), f. 43	**II**, App. A, sec. 164. ix, A, 1, n. 166
f. 47	**II**, App. A, sec. 165
f27 (2642)	ii, 5, nn. 32, 54. vii, B, 3, n. 55
f34, f. 40*v*	v, A, 1, n. 10
f56 (2821), f. 12*v*	ii, 7, n. 5. viii, A, 2, n. 50
(2821, no. 16), f. 13*v*	vii, A, 1, n. 54
f. 14*v*	**III**, App. pt. II, no. 354
(2821, no. 1 *h*), fs. 14*v*, 18*v*	**III**, App. pt. I, gr. 1; **III**, App. pt. II, no. 354
f. 15	vii, C, 1, a, n. 2
(2821, no. 16), f. 17	v, A, 1, n. 41
f. 18	vii, C, 1, a, n. 22. viii, A, 1, n. 77
f. 18*v*	**III**, App. pt. II, no. 354
f. 19	vii, C, 2, n. 22
f. 42	ii, 7, n. 59

f. 43	**II**, App. A, secs. 25, 26, 37. v, D, 1, n. 8. vii, A, 2, n. 9. ix, A, 2, n. 76; ix, A, 3, n. 57
f. 45	ii, 4, n. 100. iii, F, n. 138. vi, 12, n. 73. vii, C, 2, n. 26. x, A, 3, n. 65; x, D, n. 147
f. 45*a*	viii, A, 2, n. 80
f. 45*v*	viii, C, 4, n. 8; viii, D, n. 12
f. 46	ii, 4, n. 100
f. 46*a*	ii, 7, n. 41
f. 46*v*	**III**, App. pt. I, gr. 2; **III**, App. pt. II, no. 343. viii, B, 2, n. 64; viii, B, 5, n. 69; viii, C, 4, n. 8; viii, D, n. 12
f. 47	**III**, App. pt. I, gr. 2; **III**, App. pt. II, no. 362. **IV**, App. C, 2. ix, A, 4, n. 196; ix, A, 5, n. 70; ix, B, nn. 125, 439, 440, 552
f. 48	**II**, App. A, sec. 38. **IV**, App. C, 2. ix, A, 3, n. 32; ix, A, 4, n. 17; ix, A, 5, nn. 5, 28, 31, 63, 70; ix, B, nn. 124, 179, 424, 447, 465, 525, 539. **IV**, App. D, n. 220
f. 48*a*, item II–48*b*	**III**, App. pt. I, grs. 2 and 7; **III**, App. pt. II, no. 137
f. 49	ii, 6, n. 13. v, B, 2, nn. 91, 121, 123. ix, A, 4, n. 208
f. 50*v*	ix, A, 2, n. 105; ix, A, 4, n. 3
f. 51	**III**, App. pt. I, gr. 2; **III**, App. pt. II, no. 65. viii, A, 2, n. 78; viii, B, 2, n. 66. **IV**, App. D, n. 135
f. 52	**II**, App. A, sec. 167. **II**, App. C, sec. 116
f. 52*b*	v, A, 2, n. 48
f. 52*v*	x, B, 3, n. 73
f. 53	ii, 7, n. 100. ix, B, nn. 125, 438
f. 53*a*	**III**, App. pt. I, gr. 2; **III**, App. pt. II, no. 130. ix, A, 5, n. 44; ix, B, n. 477
f. 53*b*	**III**, App. pt. I, gr. 2; **III**, App. pt. II, no. 123. ix, A, 5, n. 79
f. 53*b*–54*a*	**III**, App. pt. I, gr. 2; **III**, App. pt. II, no. 124
f. 54, item I	**III**, App. pt. I, gr. 2; **III**, App. pt. II, no. 249
f. 54*v*	vi, 12, n. 88. viii, D, n. 15
f. 54*v*, item II	**III**, App. pt. I, gr. 2; **III**, App. pt. II, no. 250
f. 55	viii, B, 4, n. 82. ix, B, nn. 124, 418, 532
f. 55*a*, item I	**III**, App. pt. I, gr. 2; **III**, App. pt. II, no. 78
f. 55*a* II-*b*	**III**, App. pt. I, gr. 2; **III**, App. pt. II, no. 270
f. 55*v*	ix, B, n. 124
f. 55*b*, item II	**III**, App. pt. I, gr. 2; **III**, App. pt. II, no. 256
f. 55*b*, item III–56*a*	**III**, App. pt. I, gr. 2; **III**, App. pt. II, no. 79
f. 56	ix, A, 1, n. 150; ix, B, nn. 125, 418
f. 56*a*, item II	**III**, App. pt. I, gr. 2; **III**, App. pt. II, no. 80
f. 56*a*, item III	**III**, App. pt. I, gr. 2; **III**, App. pt. II, no. 25
f. 56*v*	ix, B, nn. 124, 500
f. 56*b*, item I	**III**, App. pt. I, gr. 2; **III**, App. pt. II, no. 114
f. 56*v* II	**III**, App. pt. I, gr. 2; **III**, App. pt. II, no. 342. viii, B, 4, n. 55
f. 57	**III**, App. pt. I, gr. 2; **III**, App. pt. II, no. 77. viii, B, 2, nn. 3, 82; viii, B, 3, n. 84; viii, B, 5, n. 15
f. 58	viii, B, 2, n. 82
fs. 59–61	**II**, App. A, sec. 35. v, C, 4, n. 41
f. 59*v*	ix, A, 1, n. 107
f. 61	ix, A, 1, n. 172; ix, A, 2, n. 117
f. 62	ii, 6, n. 16
(2821, no. 35), f. 122	vi, 12, n. 32
(2821, no. 38), f. 126	iv, 1, n. 1. vi, 12, n. 67. x, D, n. 331
(2821, no. 40), fs. 129–130	**II**, App. A, sec. 128. v, B, 1, n. 83. vi, 9, n. 16. vii, A, 1, n. 34
f. 130	viii, C, 1, n. 114

f61 (2855, no. 8),
f. 46 viii, A, 1, n. 17
(2855, no. 11),
f. 49 vi, 11, n. 57
f. 60 **II**, App. A, sec. 34
f102, f. 29 ix, C, 1, n. 155
f. 43 vi, 12, n. 92
f. 52 v, D, 2, n. 15. vii, C, 1, c, n. 32. viii, A, 2, n. 11; viii, D, n. 122. ix, C, 1, n. 149
f103, f. 39 iv, 7, n. 22; iv, 12, n. 41
f. 40 x, A, 3, nn. 155, 197, 203
f. 41 **II**, App. B, sec. 68
MS B. Chapira, private MS iii, D, n. 56
Christ College, Cambridge, no. IX x, B, 1, n. 54
Abrahams Coll. 10 ii, 5, n. 66
CUL: Cambridge University Library Collection (historically cited by Goitein as ULC). *See* ULC
DK: David Kaufmann Collection, Budapest
DK I i, 2, n. 27. iii, D, nn. 2, 25, 35; iii, f, n. 79. iv, 3, n. 56; iv, 10, n. 3. ix, B, nn. 148, 166. x, C, 1, n. 48
II viii, A, 2, nn. 35, 55
III viii, C, 4, n. 152
VI ii, 2, n. 2. iv, 10, n. 3; iv, 12, n. 18. vii, A, 2, n. 30; vii, C, 1, d, n. 21. ix, A, 1, n. 19
VII iv, 3, n. 66. viii, C, 3, n. 16
VIII i, 2, n. 41. iii, A, 1, n. 6. vi, 13, n. 59
IX vii, B, 1, n. 72
X ii, 7, n. 85. iv, 12, n. 36. viii, A, 3, n. 28; viii, C, 1, n. 163; viii, C, 2, nn. 67, 116
XI iii, F, n. 107. iv, 8, nn. 13, 17, 56. x, C, 1, n. 17
XII ii, 4, n. 41. iii, D, n. 49
XIII iv, 1, n. 6; iv, 3, n. 33; iv, 12, n. 14. viii, C, 1, nn. 36, 83; viii, C, 2, nn. 41, 121, 152; viii, C, 3, n. 150. x, A, 1, n. 166; x, A, 2, nn. 264, 267; x, C, 5, n. 97
XV i, 2, n. 18. ii, 4, n. 12. iii, B, 3, n. 10. iv, 3, n. 29; iv, 10, nn. 34, 35. viii, A, 1, n. 82; viii, A, 2, n. 66. ix, C, 1, n. 118. x, A, 3, n. 45
XVII x, B, 2, n. 99
XIX ii, 5, n. 29; ii, 7, n. 44. iv, 2, n. 4; iv, 4, nn. 1, 19; iv, 12, n. 29. **II**, App. C, sec. 18. viii, C, 2, n. 26
XX ii, 4, n. 68. vi, 13, n. 45. ix, A, 4, n. 182; ix, A, 5, n. 31
XXI ii, 3, n. 23. **II**, App. A, sec. 41. vii, C, 2, n. 27. x, A, 1, n. 64
XXV ii, 7, n. 21. x, D, n. 315
XXVI vii, A, 1, n. 14; vii, D, 1, n. 6. ix, A, 1, n. 106
XXVIII i, 2, n. 85; i, 3, n. 8. ii, 4, n. 32. iii, D, n. 41. viii, C, 2, n. 117. x, A, 3, n. 171
XXIX vi, 2, nn. 35, 40. vii, C, 1, b, n. 39
XXX vii, C, 2, n. 8
XXXI vii, C, 1, b, n. 24
DK 1 iii, D, n. 49; iii, F, n. 79. iv, 3, n. 73. **II**, App. C, sec. 5
2 viii, C, 2, n. 165
3 **I**, App. D, sec. 41. iii, D, n. 29; iii, G, n. 4. iv, 4, n. 18. viii, A, 2, n. 79. x, B, 2, n. 111
4 iv, 4, n. 37
13 ii, 2, n. 12. iii, B, 1, n. 4; iii, B, 3, nn. 7, 9; iii, D, n. 29; iii, E, nn. 20, 58; iii, F, n. 11. iv, 2, n. 28; iv, 8, n. 32. x, B, 1, n. 55

14 ii, 4, n. 37. iii, D, n. 43; iii, F, n. 32. iv, 1, n. 8. viii, C, 3, n. 16. ix, A, 1, n. 128
15*v* x, A, 2, n. 371
16 vi, 10, n. 11
18 ix, A, 1, nn. 137, 204. x, A, 2, n. 270; x, B, 2, nn. 80, 102
22 ii, 4, n. 73. iv, 5, n. 20; iv, 8, n. 26. x, B, 1, n. 4; x, C, 1, n. 37
75 x, A, 2, n. 249
120 x, B, 3, n. 26; x, B, 4, n. 133
121 vi, 4, n. 13. x, A, 1, n. 6
123 iv, 3, n. 81. viii, B, 4, n. 96
129 iii, F, n. 51. vii, C, 1, a, n. 12
164 vi, 12, n. 103
170*b* viii, A, 1, n. 86
245 (recent) ii, 5, n. 6. vii, C, 1, a, n. 8; vii, C, 1, b, n. 13; vii, C, 1, c, n. 6. ix, A, 2, n. 103
278*d* x, A, 2, n. 338
Obadiah Scroll vii, A, 1, n. 53; vii, A, 3, n. 45
Dropsie: Dropsie College (now: Annenberg Institute), Philadelphia
Dropsie 331 **I**, Introduction, n. 43. viii, B, 3, n. 44
332 iii, B, 3, n. 5. viii, A, 1, n. 26; viii, A, 2, n. 17
333 **III**, App. pt. II, no. 100. viii, B, 3, n. 76. **IV**, App. A, IV. ix, A, 5, nn. 21, 32, 41; ix, B, n. 508
335 v, B, 1, n. 59. **III**, App. pt. I, gr. 7. viii, A, 3, n. 26; viii, C, 4, n. 30. **IV**, App. A, I. ix, A, 2, n. 9
336 **II**, App. C, sec. 175. **II**, App. D, sec. 4
337 vii, B, n. 23
338 viii, D, n. 23
339 v, B, 1, n. 42. **III**, App. pt. II, no. 45
340 viii, A, 3, n. 67. ix, A, 2, n. 157
341 ii, 7, n. 38. vii, B, 1, n. 23
344 ii, 4, n. 24. iii, D, n. 2. v, B, 1, n. 121
346 viii, A, 1, n. 39
347 **II**, App. D, sec. 29
351 vii, B, 3, n. 16; vii, C, 1, b, n. 31
354 v, A, 1, n. 38
354*v* vi, 6, n. 7
358 **II**, App. C, sec. 54. vii, C, 1, c, n. 40; vii, C, 2, n. 37
363 ix, B, n. 88
379 vii, C, 1, c, n. 50; vii, C, 2, n. 49
382 ix, B, n. 487
383 iv, 8, n. 18
385 ix, B, n. 150
386 v, C, 2, n. 11. vi, 4, n. 20. viii, B, 1, n. 3; viii, C, 2, n. 52. ix, A, 1, n. 111. x, A, 1, n. 35
388 iii, F, n. 139
389 i, 2, nn. 28, 44. ii, 7, n. 11. iii, A, 1, n. 33; iii, B, 1, nn. 13, 17; iii, B, 2, n. 50; iii, D, nn. 13, 29, 39, 40, 48; iii, E, nn. 45, 52, 73; iii, F, nn. 16, 90; iii, G, nn. 30, 32. iv, 5, n. 7; iv, 6, nn. 3, 17; iv, 8, n. 16; iv, 9, nn. 18, 20; iv, 10, nn. 30, 31; iv, 11, nn. 16, 19; iv, 12, n. 32. v, B, 1, n. 150. vi, 5, n. 8; vi, 11, n. 11. vii, A, 2, n. 15; vii, C, 1, d, n. 23. viii, C, 1, n. 22. **IV**, App. A, VI. ix, B, n. 224. x, B, 2, n. 47; x, B, 4, nn. 29, 102; x, C, 1, n. 20
392 **II**, App. A, sec. 11a. v, B, 1, n. 104. vi, 4, n. 6; vi, 10, nn. 24, 25. vii, C, 2, n. 47
393 v, C, 4, n. 29. vii, C, 2, n. 23. x, A, 1, n. 114; x, C, 4, n. 38

394 vi, 4, n. 27. x, A, 1, nn. 36, 81
395 **I**, App. D, n. 16. ii, 4, n. 115; ii, 5, nn. 9, 57. iii, A, 1, n. 14; iii, F, n. 107. iv, 11, n. 22. vi, 13, n. 20. vii, C, 1, b, n. 14. ix, C, 1, n. 68
397 iii, A, 1, n. 34. iv, 3, n. 66
398 vii, C, 1, c, n. 40; vii, C, 1, d, n. 31; vii, C, 2, nn. 12, 37. viii, A, 2, n. 79; viii, C, 1, n. 26; viii, C, 3, n. 89
399 iii, F, n. 71
400 ii, 4, n. 24; ii, 6, n. 11; ii, 7, n. 80. viii, C, 2, n. 161
402 vi, 11, n. 43. ix, A, 4, nn. 61, 106, 147, 187; ix, A, 5, nn. 15, 19, 23, 26, 37, 72; ix, B, nn. 29, 499
410 4, n. 17. vii, C, 2, n. 40. ix, C, 1, n. 174. x, B, 2, n. 94
411 iii, F, n. 85. iv, 3, nn. 14, 81. viii, A, 2, n. 29
414 iii, B, 1, nn. 17, 20. x, B, 2, n. 47; x, B, 4, n. 102
461 viii, A, 1, nn. 3, 10
464 **II**, App. C, sec. 134
465 **II**, App. B, sec. 106
466 **II**, App. C, sec. 135
467 **II**, App. C, sec. 136
468 **II**, App. B, sec. 107
472 ix, B, nn. 100, 539; ix, C, 1, n. 131

ENA: E. N. Adler Collection, Jewish Theological Seminary of America, New York (*see also* JTS)
ENA 136*a* viii, D, n. 45
151 (2557), now in NS 1 ii, 3, n. 38. iv, 6, n. 5; iv, 8, n. 80. v, D, 2, n. 6. vi, 11, n. 48
154 (2558), now in NS 1 i, 2, n. 81. iii, A, 1, n. 32. viii, C, 3, n. 127. ix, A, 1, n. 54. x, B, 2, n. 155
159 (2558), now in NS 1 x, A, 3, n. 73
190 (2559) viii, B, 2, n. 47
191 (2559) v, B, 2, nn. 68, 76, 121. vi, 7, n. 26
223, p. 3 iii, F, n. 167
1215 **II**, App. D, sec. 23
1822, f. 2 ii, 5, n. 38
f. 4 viii, B, 2, n. 83
f. 5 iii, D, n. 14
f. 7 iv, 4, n. 15
f. 8 viii, C, 1, n. 214
f. 10 **III**, App. pt. I, gr. 1. **IV**, App. C, 2. ix, A, 4, nn. 12, 176; ix, A, 5, n. 70
f. 17 **III**, App. pt. II, no. 283. viii, C, 3, n. 7. x, A, 3, n. 62
f. 23 viii, B, 2, n. 25
f. 24 vi, 13, n. 57
f. 44 x, B, 1, n. 101
fs. 44–45 vii, B, 1, n. 38. x, C, 1, n. 19
f. 45 x, D, n. 13
f. 46 ix, A, 4, nn. 107, 148, 183, 186; ix, A, 5, nn. 10, 17, 18, 20, 23, 24, 26, 27, 30, 32, 35, 56, 64, 81; ix, B, n. 446. x, A, 3, n. 255
f. 47 ix, A, 1, n. 22. x, A, 2, n. 124; x, B, 4, n. 30
f. 48 viii, C, 1, n. 223
f. 49*v* viii, A, 2, n. 63
f. 50 viii, C, 4, n. 127
f. 51 x, B, 4, n. 167
f. 52 v, C, 2, n. 16

f. 53 vi, 10, n. 12. ix, B, n. 22
f. 55 iv, 3, n. 87
f. 57 **IV**, App. D, n. 226. ix, A, 5, nn. 40, 79; ix, B, nn. 147, 337, 531, 546
f. 59 ix, C, 2, n. 15
f. 60 viii, B, 5, n. 12
f. 64 ix, A, 1, n. 65
f. 65 v, C, 1, n. 29
f. 68 **II**, App. A, sec. 161. **IV**, App. B
f. 69 iv, 4, n. 34
f. 71 viii, C, 2, n. 150
f. 76 **II**, App. C, sec. 100
f. 84 viii, B, 3, n. 71
f. 92 ix, C, 1, n. 152
2156*v* vi, 12, n. 2
2348, f. 1 vii, B, 1, n. 58
f. 1*v* **II**, App. C, sec. 121. vii, C, 2, n. 25
fs. 2–5 **II**, App. C, sec. 129
2556, f. 1 **III**, App. pt. I, gr. 7. x, B, 1, n. 124
f. 1v ii, 6, n. 17. x, A, 1, n. 164
2558, f. 1 vi, 13, n. 14
f. 2 iii, F, n. 139. ix, A, 2, n. 60
f. 3 **I**, App. D, n. 27. vi, 4, n. 28. **IV**, App. A, III. ix, A, 1, n. 43; ix, A, 3, n. 3
f. 4 ii, 4, n. 25. **IV**, App. A, III. ix, A, 1, nn. 81, 150, 167; ix, A, 2, nn. 72, 162
2559, f. 178 x, C, 1, n. 8
2560, f. 1 viii, C, 4, n. 175
f. 2 viii, B, 4, n. 83
f. 32 v, C, 1, n. 16. x, B, 4, n. 127
2591, f. 1 **II**, App. C, sec. 124
f. 4 **II**, App. C, sec. 130
f. 6*v* **II**, App. C, sec. 128
f. 7 viii, C, 3, n. 46
fs. 8, 11 **II**, App. C, sec. 126
f. 9 **II**, App. C, sec. 125
f. 11 *see* 2591, f. 8
f. 12 ix, A, 4, n. 80; ix, B, nn. 91, 123
f. 13 ix, A, 4, n. 158
fs. 14, 15 **II**, App. A, sec. 172
f. 18 **II**, App. B, sec. 102
f. 21*c* **II**, App. B, sec. 101
2592 vi, 9, n. 11
2592, f. 3 x, A, 1, n. 103
f. 24 viii, A, 1, n. 10
2700, f. 32*a* ix, A, 4, n. 199
f. 33*b* ix, A, 4, n. 167; ix, B, nn. 439, 542, 544
2713, f. 26 **II**, App. B, sec. 2b
2727, f. 4 viii, C, 2, nn. 47, 64
f. 5 viii, B, 4, n. 85; viii, B, 5, n. 34. ix, A, 4, nn. 47, 192; ix, A, 5, nn. 58, 59; ix, B, nn. 120, 539
f. 6*b* x, B, 2, n. 110
f. 7*a* **II**, App. A, sec. 151
f. 7B x, A, 2, n. 222
f. 8A **III**, App. pt. II, no. 121. viii, C, 1, n. 85; viii, D, n. 161. **IV**, App. C, 2. **IV**, App. D, n. 46. ix, A, 4, nn. 85, 97, 132, 207, 217; ix, A, 5, nn. 42, 82; ix, B, nn. 361, 470, 505, 534

f. 9A x, A, 1, n. 102
f. 11A **III**, App. pt. II, no. 139. viii, C, 3, n. 29
f. 11B **II**, App. C, sec. 12
f. 11E x, D, n. 16
f. 14, item II **III**, App. pt. II, no. 87. viii, B, 5, n. 45; viii, C, 4, n. 178
f. 15*c* viii, C, 3, n. 54
f. 15E **II**, App. C, sec. 37
f. 18*bv* **III**, App. pt. I, gr. 5; **III**, App. pt. II, no. 156. viii, B, 5, n. 76
f. 18*dv* **III**, App. pt. I, grs. 8, 25
f. 22 **II**, App. C, sec. 53
f. 23A iii, B, 2, nn. 3, 29
f. 23B iii, A, 1, n. 12
f. 28 ii, 7, n. 6
f. 31 iii, F, n. 166. x, A, 1, n. 163
f. 37*v* ii, 7, n. 89
f. 38 iii, E, n. 29. iv, 7, n. 14; iv, 8, n. 14
f. 43 iii, A, 1, n. 42
f. 48 vi, 13, nn. 18, 52
f. 54 **II**, App. B, sec. 82
f. 55 ii, 7, n. 50
2728, f. 2 v, C, 2, n. 34; v, D, 2, n. 52. viii, D, n. 24
f. 5*v* viii, C, 3, n. 34
f. 9 **II**, App. D, sec. 26
2730 vii, A, 1, n. 58
2730, f. 1 x, A, 1, n. 105
2736 **II**, App. B, sec. 39
2736, f. 20 v, B, 1, n. 117; v, D, 2, n. 52. x, A, 2, n. 339
2738, f. 2 **II**, App. A, sec. 3
f. 7 iv, 5, n. 13
f. 20 x, C, 1, n. 38
f. 22 x, A, 1, n. 145
f. 23 ix, D, n. 8. x, A, 1, n. 27
f. 32 iii, A, 2, n. 6. viii, A, 2, n. 38
f. 33 **III**, App. pt. I, gr. 4; **III**, App. pt. II, no. 153. viii, C, 1, n. 234. **IV**, App. C, 2. **IV**, App. D, n. 83. ix, A, 4, nn. 5, 45, 61, 64, 79, 89, 178, 205, 206, 217; ix, A, 5, nn. 3, 9; ix, B, n. 536
2739, f. 13 viii, C, 4, n. 63
f. 14 vi, 10, n. 41
f. 16 viii, C, 1, nn. 1, 51. x, B, 2, n. 7
2743, f. 2 v, B, 2, n. 99. vii, C, 1, b, n. 35. **III**, App. pt. II, no. 181. **IV**, App. C, 2. ix, B, nn. 491, 510
f. 4 v, A, 2, n. 75. ix, A, 3, n. 59
2744 i, 3, n. 36
2747, f. 1 **IV**, App. C, 2. ix, A, 4, n. 34; ix, B, nn. 417, 443
f. 2 **III**, App. pt. II, no. 177. ix, A, 4, n. 97
f. 5 iii, E, n. 13
f. 19*v* viii, C, 4, n. 85
f. 29 ix, A, 4, n. 92
2748 x, A, 2, n. 419
2763, f. 20 **II**, App. B, sec. 92
2779, f. 3 **III**, App. pt. II, no. 339. viii, B, 2, n. 7. ix, B, nn. 472, 487
2804 iv, 9, n. 7. viii, D, n. 133
2804, f. 1 v, B, 1, n. 105. vii, B, 1, n. 7
f. 4 x, A, 2, n. 403
f. 7 v, B, 1, n. 7. ix, C, 1, n. 56
f. 20 (was f. 1) x, C, 5, n. 53

2804 (loose leaf)	v, C, 1, n. 18 (*see* Jacob Mann, *The Jews in Egypt and in Palestine under the Fatimid Caliphs*, vol. II, Oxford, 1922, p. 179)
2805, f. 4B	ix, C, 1, n. 160
f. 5*bv*	ix, B, n. 289
f. 6	x, A, 2, n. 286
f. 6A	ix, B, n. 337
f. 9	vii, A, 1, n. 1. ix, C, 1, n. 123. x, A, 2, n. 298
f. 11A	ix, C, 1, n. 121
f. 11*b*	**II**, App. C, f. 123
f. 12	x, A, 1, n. 110; x, C, 1, nn. 16, 18
f. 13	vii, A, 1, n. 1. ix, C, 1, n. 123
f. 15	viii, C, 4, n. 14
f. 16B	x, A, 2, n. 261
2806, f. 9*v*	vi, 9, n. 13
f. 11	*see* ENA 2727, f. 18*bv*
f. 12	iii, A, 1, n. 5
2808, f. 9	vi, 12, n. 63
f. 12	viii, C, 3, n. 44
f. 13	**III**, App. pt. II, no. 171. **IV**, App. C, 2. ix, A, 4, nn. 20, 49, 205, 219; ix, B, nn. 488, 515
f. 15*a*	viii, C, 2, n. 174; viii, C, 3, n. 126
f. 16	ix, C, 1, n. 162; ix, D, n. 9. x, A, 1, n. 17
f. 17*v*	x, C, 1, n. 46
f. 22	vi, 13, n. 1. ix, C, 2, n. 47
f. 36	viii, C, 3, n. 86
f. 49	ix, C, 2, n. 34
f. 63	**II**, App. A, sec. 169
f. 66	**II**, App. A, sec. 171
2875, f. 35	ix, B, n. 127
2935, f. 14	vii, C, 1, d, n. 10
f. 16	vi, 3, n. 10. viii, C, 2, n. 77
f. 17	vi, 3, n. 10. viii, C, 2, n. 77
2957, f. 32	ix, B, nn. 416, 429, 438, 448, 488, 500
2958, f. 2	viii, C, 1, n. 232
ENA 3030, f. 6*v*	ix, A, 5, n. 56
f. 7	**III**, App. pt. II, no. 290. ix, B, nn. 122, 421, 482. x, A, 3, n. 75
3124, f. 13	**II**, App. A, sec. 160. viii, D, n. 191
3150, f. 7*v*	**II**, App. C, sec. 54
f. 8	viii, D, n. 70
3616, f. 9	ix, B, n. 101; ix, C, 1, n. 165
3626, f. 6	**III**, App. pt. I, gr. 1; **III**, App. pt. II, no. 129
3652, f. 8	ix, A, 4, nn. 174, 191; ix, B, n. 311
3697, f. 3	viii, A, 3, n. 66
3738, f. 11*v*	**II**, App. C, sec. 120
3755, f. 6	viii, B, 4, nn. 44, 47, 49; viii, B, 5, n. 27
3765, f. 8	v, A, 2, nn. 3, 13. vi, 9, n. 24. x, A, 3, n. 217
f. 10	x, A, 1, n. 163; x, B, 4, n. 50; x, B, 5, nn. 25, 47
3787, f. 10	viii, C, 1, n. 184. x, C, 4, n. 59
3788, f. 6	ix, B, n. 254
3793, f. 1	v, B, 2, n. 63. viii, C, 2, n. 99
f. 2	x, B, 1, n. 59
3795, f. 8	v, B, 2, n. 92. viii, D, nn. 54, 56. x, A, 3, nn. 66, 68; x, C, 3, n. 27
3824, f. 1	**II**, App. A, sec. 156
3846, fs. 6–7	**II**, App. C, sec. 119

3971, f. 5	ix, C, 1, n. 177
fs. 13–24, 31, 33, 34	vi, 13, n. 65
4009, f. 8	vi, 4, n. 20
4009?	vi, 10, n. 42
4009, loose leaf	vi, 10, n. 29. x, A, 2, n. 265
4010, f. 1	v, B, 2, nn. 71, 87; v, C, 2, n. 10; v, C, 4, n. 1. vi, 2, n. 33. vii, B, 1, n. 67. ix, A, 4, nn. 73, 140; ix, B, n. 332
f. 1*v*	ix, B, n. 536
f. 2	iii, B, 2, nn. 2, 5, 16, 36, 38, 51
f. 14	viii, C, 4, n. 157
f. 15	vii, C, 1, a, n. 21; vii, C, 1, c, n. 46
f. 19	viii, C, 1, n. 199. ix, A, 3, n. 79
f. 25*v*	ix, C, 1, n. 111
f. 26	viii, C, 2, n. 169
f. 28	viii, B, 5, n. 23
f. 31	viii, C, 4, n. 19
f. 32	x, C, 4, n. 52
f. 36	viii, A, Introduction, n. 1; viii, B, 1, n. 19
f. 39	ix, B, nn. 32, 47
f. 41	x, A, 3, n. 221
f. 42	viii, C, 4, n. 90
f. 43	**III**, App. pt. II, no. 244. viii, C, 1, n. 104
fs. 43*v*–44	viii, C, 1, nn. 104, 234
4011	v, B, 2, n. 44
f. 5	viii, C, 3, n. 43
f. 5 top	**III**, App. pt. II, no. 346
f. 11	viii, C, 1, n. 223
f. 17	v, B, 2, n. 65. viii, A, Introduction, n. 2; viii, B, 2, n. 25; viii, C, 3, n. 132
f. 18	viii, B, 2, nn. 2, 17
f. 19	vii, A, 2, n. 38
f. 22	viii, C, 4, n. 90
f. 25	**II**, App. B, sec. 57c
f. 26	x, D, n. 78
f. 28	**II**, App. A, sec. 112
f. 29*v*	ix, A, 1, n. 61
f. 32	ix, A, 1, n. 108
f. 33	vii, D, 1, n. 30
f. 34	v, B, 1, n. 51. viii, C, 1, n. 91
f. 35	viii, B, 2, n. 44
f. 35*v*	**II**, App. A, sec. 135
f. 41	ii, 1, n. 11
f. 42*v*	**II**, App. A, sec. 130
f. 43	iii, F, n. 201
f. 44	**II**, App. A, sec. 132
f. 48	ii, 7, n. 39
f. 50	iii, F, n. 192
f. 51	x, A, 3, n. 38
f. 52	ii, 5, n. 71. iv, 10, n. 37
f. 55	vii, B, 1, n. 43. viii, C, 3, n. 45
f. 56	viii, C, 2, n. 143
f. 56 (was f. 57)	vii, B, 1, n. 3
f. 57 (now f. 56)	**I**, App. C, sec. 7. iii, B, 3, n. 5; iii, F, n. 125
f. 57*v*	vii, D, 1, n. 28
f. 62	ii, 7, n. 48
f. 62*v*	**II**, App. A, sec. 138. viii, D, n. 95

f. 63	ii, 7, nn. 41, 64
f. 65	v, B, 1, n. 19
f. 67	viii, B, 4, n. 47; viii, C, 3, n. 14
f. 69	ii, 3, n. 16
f. 72*d*	viii, C, 4, n. 10
f. 73	x, A, 3, n. 208
4020	iii, F, n. 86
4020, f. 1	vi, 4, nn. 4, 12, 20. viii, A, 3, n. 46
f. 2	vii, B, 1, n. 71. viii, C, 4, n. 61
f. 3	viii, B, 4, nn. 40, 60; viii, B, 5, n. 83. ix, A, 4, nn. 57, 92
f. 5	v, B, 1, n. 88
f. 6	v, D, 1, n. 17. vii, A, 2, n. 39; vii, C, 1, a, n. 43. ix, A, 2, n. 100
f. 8	vi, 13, n. 53. x, B, 2, n. 140
f. 11	ii, 7, n. 61
f. 13	viii, C, 2, n. 60
f. 16	**II**, App. B, sec. 27
f. 18	viii, C, 2, n. 118
f. 20	ii, 4, n. 31. iii, E, nn. 39, 79. iv, 10, n. 17
f. 24	viii, A, 2, n. 80; viii, C, 1, n. 28
f. 26	iii, C, n. 6
f. 28*v*	viii, C, 4, n. 14
f. 30	ii, 5, nn. 1, 2, 20. iv, 2, n. 8. vii, C, 1, d, n. 18; vii, C, 2, n. 35. viii, A, 2, n. 43
f. 32	x, C, 5, n. 53
f. 33	viii, B, 3, n. 102
f. 34	v, C, 2, n. 13. vii, B, 3, n. 37
f. 36	ix, B, n. 536
f. 37	**III**, App. pt. I, gr. 4; **III**, App. pt. II, no. 327
f. 42	x, A, 2, n. 57
f. 43	ix, A, 1, nn. 63, 136. x, B, 3, n. 11
f. 47	ii, 7, nn. 49, 72, 78. vii, B, 3, n. 37. **III**, App. pt. II, no. 297. viii, B, 3, n. 1; viii, B, 4, n. 103; viii, C, 3, nn. 73, 99, 107
f. 49	viii, C, 1, n. 58. x, B, 3, n. 55
f. 51	viii, C, 2, n. 113
f. 52	viii, A, 3, n. 66
f. 52*v*	viii, D, nn. 5, 63, 89, 164. ix, A, 3, n. 37. **IV**, App. A, V
f. 53	**IV**, App. A, V
f. 54	**IV**, App. A, IV
f. 57	viii, B, 3, n. 3
f. 60	viii, C, 4, n. 34. ix, C, 1, n. 163
4025	vi, 3, n. 7
4096*a*	x, C, 5, n. 38
4100, f. 8	**III**, App. pt. II, no. 151. ix, C, 2, n. 25
f. 8A	x, A, 1, n. 136
f. 8B	ix, A, 4, nn. 64, 174, 205, 217; ix, B, n. 472
f. 9A*v*	ix, A, 4, n. 119
f. 12	x, A, 2, n. 294
f. 21A	viii, C, 4, n. 108
f. 21B	x, A, 1, n. 15
f. 23	viii, C, 3, n. 68
4101, f. 16B	viii, C, 2, n. 54
ENA NS 1, f. 13 (was laminated 49)	ix, A, 4, n. 37
f. 62*a*	x, B, 2, n. 38
f. 89*a*	viii, B, 2, n. 33
NS 2, f. 5*v*	x, B, 2, n. 119; x, C, 3, n. 18

f. 8*v* ix, C, 1, n. 52
f. 21 x, C, 4, n. 58
NS 2, I, f. 5 x, C, 5, n. 15
NS 2, I, f. 9 viii, C, 2, n. 58
f. 11 viii, C, 2, n. 129; viii, D, n. 123
f. 12*v* viii, C, 2, n. 4
f. 13 ix, B, n. 128. x, A, 2, n. 29
f. 16 viii, C, 1, n. 15; viii, C, 2, n. 19. x, C, 3, n. 18; x, C, 5, n. 15
f. 17 viii, D, n. 204. x, A, 2, nn. 112, 126
f. 20 viii, B, 5, n. 91; viii, C, 1, n. 93. ix, A, 1, n. 60
f. 21 viii, C, 2, n. 59
f. 25 ix, A, 4, nn. 37, 158; ix, B, nn. 143, 366, 425, 516
f. 27 viii, B, 1, n. 58; viii, C, 4, n. 63
f. 31 viii, C, 3, n. 32
f. 37 x, A, 2, n. 111
f. 40*v* ix, C, 1, n. 104
f. 41 viii, C, 1, n. 243; viii, C, 2, n. 90
f. 45 viii, D, n. 52. ix, A, 4, n. 197; ix, A, 5, n. 11
NS 3 (vellum), f. 3 viii, B, 3, n. 76
f. 5 **III**, App. pt. I, gr. 1; **III**, App. pt. II, no. 324
f. 8 **III**, App. pt. II, no. 26
f. 18 ix, B, nn. 442, 464
f. 19*a* **III**, App. pt. II, no. 216
f. 24 **III**, App. pt. I, gr. 4; **III**, App. pt. II, no. 58. **IV**, App. C, 2, 3. ix, A, 4, nn. 23, 216; ix, B, n. 534. **IV**, App. D, n. 267
f. 26 ix, A, 5, n. 42; ix, B, nn. 530, 539
NS 4, f. 13 viii, B, 4, n. 97
NS 7, I, f. 20 **III**, App. II, no. 226. ix, B, n. 124
f. 20*a* ix, B, n. 554
f. 24*v* viii, C, 1, n. 223
f. 25 viii, C, 4, nn. 84, 85
NS 7, II, f. 43 viii, C, 3, n. 136
f. 76 x, D, n. 52
NS 16, f. 6 **III**, App. pt. II, no. 245. viii, B, 4, n. 10
f. 11 x, A, 3, n. 36
f. 30 viii, C, 1, nn. 75, 137
f. 32, margin ix, B, n. 411
NS 17, f. 10 viii, B, 5, n. 22
f. 12 **III**, App. II, no. 42. **IV**, App. C, 3; ix, A, 4, n. 36
f. 12*a* ix, A, 4, n. 164
f. 16 viii, C, 3, n. 30
f. 18 viii, C, 4, n. 25
f. 21 viii, C, 2, n. 100; viii, C, 3, n. 6. x, A, 2, n. 388; x, A, 3, n. 59; x, C, 5, n. 53
f. 22 viii, C, 4, n. 17; viii, D, nn. 4, 23
f. 24 **III**, App. pt. I, gr. 4; **III**, App. pt. II, no. 173. viii, D, n. 7
f. 28*a* **III**, App. pt. I, gr. 8. viii, C, 1, n. 206; viii, D, n. 26
f. 31*a* margin viii, B, 4, n. 89
f. 31*b*, col. I viii, C, 2, n. 53, 175
f. 31*b*, col. II, item 2 **III**, App. pt. I, gr. 8; **III**, App. pt. II
f. 31*v* **III**, App. pt. II, no. 70. ix, A, 4, n. 57
NS 18, f. 4*a* viii, C, 4, n. 81
f. 6 ix, C, 1, n. 181
f. 7 viii, C, 2, n. 18. x, B, 1, n. 6
f. 21 **III**, App. pt. II, no. 27
f. 23 viii, C, 3, n. 45

f. 24	ix, B, n. 129. x, A, 2, n. 4
f. 25	viii, C, 3, nn. 37, 156
f. 27	viii, B, 5, n. 20
f. 29	**III**, App. pt. II, no. 32. ix, B, n. 423
f. 30	x, A, 2, n. 302
f. 31	x, A, 2, n. 14
f. 34	**III**, App. pt. II, no. 322. ix, A, 4, n. 191; ix, B, n. 84
f. 35	viii, C, 2, nn. 51, 107. x, C, 1, n. 41; x, C, 5, n. 7
f. 37	**III**, App. pt. II, no. 206. x, C, 5, n. 53
NS 19, f. 10	ix, A, 2, n. 115; ix, C, 1, n. 102. **IV**, App. D, n. 201. x, A, 3, n. 195
f. 31	ix, C, 1, nn. 77, 128; ix, C, 2, n. 17. x, A, 1, n. 22
f. 131	viii, C, 1, n. 156
NS 21, f. 6	viii, B, 5, n. 87
f. 14	x, B, 4, n. 36
f. 18	viii, C, 4, n. 56
NS 22, f. 1	ix, A, 1, n. 235. x, A, 2, n. 6
f. 2	ix, A, 1, n. 163
f. 7	x, A, 2, n. 220
f. 9	x, A, 2, n. 354
f. 17	ix, B, n. 207
f. 20	**IV**, App. C. x, A, 2, nn. 10, 128
f. 25*v*	ix, A, 4, n. 119
f. 26	ix, C, 1, n. 111
f. 27	viii, A, 2, n. 79; viii, C, 2, n. 25
NS 31, f. 21	ix, B, n. 87
uncatalogued 40	ii, 2, n. 2. vi, 12, n. 107
uncatalogued 89	ii, 7, n. 112. **II**, App. B, sec. 44. vi, 4, nn. 9, 11. vii, D, 1, n. 42. viii, C, 1, n. 129
uncatalogued 98	**II**, App. C, sec. 94. v, D, 2, n. 60. x, B, 2, n. 38
uncatalogued 109	vii, B, 1, n. 25; vii, D, 2, n. 3
uncatalogued 112	v, B, 1, n. 139. vii, B, 3, n. 43; vii, C, 1, c, n. 42
unnumbered fragment	ii, 3, n. 26
frag.	v, B, 1, n. 78 (*see* Jacob Mann, *Texts and Studies in Jewish History and Literature*, vol. I, Cincinnati, 1931, p. 455, n. 17)
MS *30 Shaked	v, A, 1, n. 59 (*see* Shaul Shaked, *A Tentative Bibliography of Geniza Documents*. Paris and The Hague, 1964)
unidentified MS	v, C, 4, n. 16

Firkovitch: Firkovitch Collection, Leningrad

Firkovitch II, fs. 210–211	v, D, 2, n. 3
f. 1071	viii, D, n. 7
f. 1367	**II**, App. A, sec. 173. ix, A, 1, n. 201
f. 1412	**II**, App. A, sec. 174
f. 1415	**II**, App. B, sec. 105
II, 1700	vii, B, 3, n. 53
II, 1700, f. 1	viii, A, 1, n. 55
f. 2	iii, F, n. 184. vii, A, 2, n. 10
f. 3	**III**, App. pt. I, gr. 1. viii, C, 3, n. 156; viii, C, 4, n. 29; viii, D, n. 212
f. 5	**III**, App. pt. I, gr. 1. viii, C, 4, n. 29
f. 6	vi, 13, n. 17
fs. 8–9	viii, D, n. 75
f. 8*b*	**IV**, App. A, VI. ix, A, 3, n. 124
f. 10	viii, B, 2, n. 1

f. 10*a* **III**, App. pt. I; **III**, App. pt. II, no. 28. viii, A, 2, n. 78; viii, B, 4, n. 16
f. 10*b* viii, B, 2, n. 16
f. 12 iii, B, 2, n. 24
f. 13 iii, B, 2, n. 42; iii, E, n. 61
f. 13, item *c* vii, C, 1, b, n. 41
f. 13*v* **III**, App. pt. I, gr. 1; **III**, App. pt. II, no. 157. viii, B, 3, n. 24
f. 14 ii, 7, nn. 63, 65
f. 14*b* **III**, App. pt. I, gr. 1
f. 15*a* **III**, App. pt. I, gr. 1. viii, B, 2, n. 16; viii, B, 4, n. 67. x, D, n. 151
f. 16 iii, F, n. 200
f. 16*a* **III**, App. pt. I, gr. 1; **III**, App. pt. II, nos. 15 and 30. viii, B, 4, n. 16. ix, C, 2, n. 17
f. 17*b* viii, B, 5, nn. 54, 73
f. 18*a* **III**, App. pt. I, gr. 1. viii, C, 4, n. 29. **IV**, App. A, VII. ix, A, 1, n. 86; ix, C, 2, n. 3
f. 18*b* viii, B, 2, n. 15
f. 19*b* viii, C, 3, n. 12
f. 20 iii, F, n. 153. viii, D, n. 75 (correction)
f. 21 ii, 7, n. 68. vi, 12, n. 63. ix, A, 3, n. 98
f. 22 viii, A, 3, n. 15
f. 22*a* ii, 6, n. 15. ix, A, 1, n. 100
fs. 22*b*–23*a* ix, A, 2, n. 59; ix, A, 3, n. 113
f. 24 viii, A, 3, n. 19; viii, B, 3, n. 24. ix, B, n. 451
fs. 24–25 **III**, App. pt. I, gr. 1; **III**, App. pt. II, no. 186. viii, A, 3, n. 19; viii, B, 3, n. 37. **IV**, App. C, 1, 2, 3, 4. ix, A, 4, nn. 15, 219; ix, A, 5, n. 2; ix, B, nn. 439, 536
fs. 25*b*–26 **III**, App. pt. I, gr. 1; **III**, App. pt. II, no. 187. viii, B, 3, n. 37; viii, B, 4, n. 67; viii, B, 5, n. 46. **IV**, App. C, 2. ix, A, 1, n. 38; ix, A, 4, nn. 56, 83, 208; ix, B, nn. 418, 451, 484, 492, 535, 545, 546, 552. **IV**, App. D, nn. 92, 159
f. 27 **III**, App. pt. I, gr. 1; **III**, App. pt. II, no. 160. viii, A, 2, n. 78; viii, B, 1, n. 32; viii, B, 3, n. 37; viii, B, 4, n. 101. ix, B, nn. 124, 379, 429, 436, 440, 446, 447, 451, 531, 539. **IV**, App. D, n. 142
f. 28 **III**, App. pt. I, gr. 1. viii, C, 4, n. 29
II, 1701 x, B, 5, n. 22
MS Frankfurt vii, C, 1, c, n. 40
MS Friedenberg viii, A, 1, n. 41; viii, A, 3, n. 45; viii, D, n. 47. x, C, 3, nn. 44, 56
MS (Richard) Gottheil v, B, 2, n. 46
Gottheil-Worrell: Gottheil-Worrell, *Fragments from the Cairo Geniza in the Freer Collection*
Gottheil-Worrell
I viii, A, 2, n. 61
II v, B, 1, nn. 46, 47. vii, D, 2, n. 10
III vi, 12, n. 69. vii, A, 1, n. 31
V viii, C, 1, n, 179
VII iii, B, 2, n. 31; iii, C, n. 3. vi, 11, n. 45. vii, B, 2, n. 42. viii, A, 1, n. 39
VIII, p. 40 viii, D, n. 11. ix, A, 1, n. 47
VIII, p. 41 **II**, App. D, sec. 32. vii, D, 1, n. 4. x, B, 5, n. 19
IX ii, 4, n. 56; ii, 7, n. 7. viii, A, 2, n. 4
p. 55 x, B, 2, n. 120
XII iv, 4, n. 8. ix, A, 2, n. 164
XIII, p. 66 ix, A, 4, n. 103

XIII, p. 70 ii, 4, n. 53; ii, 5, n. 71. iii, D, n. 12. **II**, App. C, sec. 7. vii, A, 3, n. 31; vii, C, 1, c, n. 26
XIV ii, 3, n. 21; ii, 4, n. 51; ii, 5, n. 30. iv, 10, n. 26
XVI ii, 4, n. 94. iii, F, n. 151
XXI vii, A, 3, n. 19. x, A, 1, n. 32
XXII iii, E, n. 61
XXVII ii, 5, n. 8. iii, A, 1, n. 19; iii, F, n. 44. iv, 3, n. 72. ix, A, 2, n. 43; ix, A, 3, n. 68. x, A, 1, n. 14; x, A, 2, n. 274
p. 119 and
p. 123 x, B, 2, n. 125
XXVIII, p. 131 ix, A, 3, n. 53
XXXI–XXXII iv, 12, n. 6
XXXII v, D, 2, n. 7
XXXIII, p. 152 i, 2, n. 66. ix, B, n. 166
XXXIV viii, C, 2, n. 80
XXXIV, p. 157 ix, A, 1, n. 208
XXXV iii, B, 1, n. 21
XXXVI ii, 3, n. 8. iii, D, n. 55; iii, F, nn. 33, 118; iii, G, n. 27. iv, 10, n. 26; iv, 11, n. 1; iv, 12, n. 22. vii, C, 1, b, n. 16; vii, C, 1, c, n. 42
XXXVII, p. 121 x, A, 2, n. 274
XXXVII, p. 122 ix, C, 1, n. 151
XL v, D, 2, n. 56. viii, B, 5, n. 52
XLIII vi, 7, n. 12. vii, B, 1, n. 21
XLV, p. 218 viii, C, 1, nn. 130, 237
XLV, pp. 220–222 **III**, App. pt. I, gr. 6; **III**, App. pt. II, no. 362
XLV, pp. 222–225 ii, 7, n. 57
XLVII iv, 12, n. 16
L ii, 5, n. 74
Gottheil-Worrell viii, B, 4, n. 88
Gottheil, Private MS
MS Gottheil **II**, App. A, sec. 110
B. Halper, *Descriptive Catalogue of Genizah Fragments in Philadelphia*
B. Halper, 175, no. 331 *see* Dropsie 331
Harkavy 60.9 (Private MS) viii, D, n. 7
MS Harkavy ix, A, 1, n. 239
HUC: Hebrew Union College, Cincinnati
HUC, Geniza 2 v, A, 1, n. 18
4 v, D, 2, n. 21. vi, 13, n. 54. viii, A, 1, n. 4
15 ix, A, 4, nn. 39, 187, 204; ix, A, 5, nn. 20, 33, 35, 43, 64, 79
24 ii, 2, n. 49. **II**, App. C, sec. 32. vi, 12, n. 77
INA: Institut Narodov Azii, Leningrad
INA D 55, f. 2 viii, C, 1, n. 238
f. 3 viii, C, 1, n. 164. ix, C, 1, nn. 35, 77, 119. x, B, 1, n. 92; x, C, 2, n. 32
f. 4 vi, 10, n. 8; vi, 13, n. 24. x, A, 3, n. 142
f. 6 iii, F, n. 175
f. 8 iii, B, 2, n. 17. viii, A, 3, n. 33. x, A, 3, n. 219; x, C, 2, n. 28
f. 9 viii, C, 2, n. 61
f. 10 v, A, 1, n. 54
f. 13 iv, 2, n. 6. vi, 4, n. 25. vii, A, 2, n. 19; vii, B, 3, n. 30. viii, A, 2, n. 7. x, A, 2, n. 360
f. 14 iii, B, 1, n. 19; iii, B, 2, n. 50. iv, 5, n. 20; iv, 10, n. 8. v, B, 1, n. 148. ix, A, 1, n. 198
JNUL: Jewish National and University Library, Jerusalem
JNUL 1 iii, E, n. 22; iii, F, n. 67. vii, D, 1, n. 32
2 ii, 4, n. 4. iii, D, nn. 20, 31; iii, E, nn. 45, 46; iii, F, n. 50. iv, 3, n. 83. **IV**, App. C, 2. x, B, 3, n. 59

3	i, 2, n. 67. vii, D, 1, n. 30. **IV**, App. A, IV. ix, A, 3, nn. 24, 76
4	viii, D, n. 188
4°577, 10	ix, A, 1, n. 33
4°577, no. 83	x, A, 2, n. 410
4°577 3, no. 83, I	**III**, App. pt. I, gr. 5
4°577 3, no. 83, II	**III**, App. pt. I, gr. 5; **III**, App. pt. II, no. 39
4°577/4	viii, B, 2, n. 7; viii, B, 3, nn. 6, 19
4°577/4, f. 4	viii, A, 2, n. 69
f. 27	viii, C, 3, n. 121
f. 98	**III**, App. pt. I, gr. 4; **III**, App. pt. II, no. 67. ix, A, 4, n. 56; ix, B, n. 527
4°577/5, f. 41*v*	**III**, App. pt. II, no. 222
5	iii, F, n. 195. vi, 12, n. 50. vii, B, 3, n. 47. viii, A, 1, n. 39. ix, A, 1, n. 42. x, C, 3, n. 39
7	i, 2, nn. 33, 38. vii, A, 1, n. 5
8	ix, B, n. 170
8°2238	v, D, 1, n. 21
10	iii, D, n. 29; iii, E, n. 57. viii, A, 2, n. 51. ix, A, 1, n. 24; ix, C, 1, n. 110
11	viii, A, 1, n. 61; viii, B, 2, n. 21
12	viii, C, 2, n. 170. x, A, 2, n. 351
83	iii, B, 2, n. 18
83, f. 3	viii, B, 4, n. 28
83, no. 4, item I	**III**, App. pt. II, no. 91. viii, B, 2, nn. 61, 62; viii, B, 3, n. 84
83, no. 4, item II	**III**, App. pt. II, no. 39. viii, B, 2, n. 62
83*c*	vi, 12, n. 52
83*v*	ix, C, 2, n. 12

John Rylands Library, Manchester, Gaster Collection

A 75	v, C, 2, n. 3
A 859	**II**, App. A, sec. 131 b
A 923	**II**, App. B, sec. 30. v, B, 2, n. 101. viii, C, 4, n. 125
A 1192	ii, 4, n. 96
G 21	**II**, App. B, sec. 25
L 213	i, 2, n. 73. viii, C, 2, n. 119. x, A, 2, n. 425

JTS: Jewish Theological Seminary, New York, *see also* ENA

Geniza Misc. 1	v, B, 2, nn. 37, 42
4	ix, C, 1, n. 23
6	ii, 7, n. 25. vi, 3, n. 12. viii, D, nn. 192, 198
13	iii, E, nn. 12, 42, 83. iv, 5, n. 9
15	ii, 4, n. 42
17	viii, C, 3, n. 100
18	**I**, App. C, sec. 19. viii, D, n. 198
21	**II**, App. B, sec. 45
23	**I**, App. D, sec. 35
27	ii, 4, n. 70

Karaite Doc. (not Geniza): D.S. Richards, "Arabic Documents from the Karaite Community in Cairo," *JESHO*, vol. xv (1972)

Karaite Doc. 5	ix, A, 2, nn. 84, 96, 102, 106, 108, 113, 117, 158
17	ix, A, 2, nn. 62, 79, 83, 98, 101, 106, 110, 112, 117, 127, 149, 151, 155, 167; ix, A, 4, n. 67
25	ix, A, 2, n. 154
Maimonides, *Responsa*	*see* Index of Scriptural, Rabbinic, and Maimonidean Citations

Merx: A. Merx, *Documents de paléographie hébraïque et arabe*. Leiden, 1894

pp. 23–35	ix, A, 1, n. 187
25	ix, A, 2, nn. 62, 162
30	ix, A, 2, nn. 38, 83
39	**IV**, App. A, II

39–44 **III**, App. pt. I, gr. 1; **III**, App. pt. II, no. 247. viii, B, 3, n. 76.

Meunier, Private MS
MS Meunier i, 3, n. 12. iii, F, n. 80. iv, 2, n. 36. viii, A, 3, n. 10

Mittheilungen aus der Sammlung der Papyrus Erzherzog Rainer 5 (1892), pp. 127–132 *see* PER H 135

Mosseri: Mosseri Collection, Paris (see *Catalogue of the Jack Mosseri Collection*. Jerusalem, 1990)

Mosseri A 1 viii, C, 4, n. 66
2 **III**, App. pt. II, no. 191. viii, B, 1, n. 38
4.3 viii, C, 1, n. 108
6.2 ix, A, 2, nn. 101, 113, 116, 128
7 viii, A, 1, n. 17
7*v* **III**, App. pt. II, no. 158. viii, B, 2, n. 53
10.1 **III**, App. pt. II, no. 161. viii, B, 4, n. 101; viii, B, 5, nn. 39, 62, 84
11 **I**, App. C, sec. 18. vii, D, 1, n. 13. **III**, App. pt. II, no. 272. viii, D, 4, n. 17; viii, C, 4, n. 28. x, A, 3, n. 29
16 viii, C, 1, nn. 73, 132. x, A, 2, n. 415
17 iii, B, 2, n. 35. vi, 2, n. 5. ix, C, 2, n. 12
18 **I**, App. D, sec. 77. **III**, App. pt. II, no. 239. viii, C, 3, n. 110
21 viii, C, 3, n. 121
27 viii, B, 2, n. 54; viii, C, 1, n. 227; viii, C, 3, nn. 100, 102
28 x, B, 1, n. 84
30 **III**, App. pt. II, no. 255. viii, C, 3, n. 119. x, D, n. 30
37, 2 viii, B, 3, n. 49
37 + 76 viii, B, 2, n. 91; viii, B, 3, n. 84; viii, C, 1, n. 211
40.2 viii, C, 1, n. 143
43 v, A, 1, n. 8. vi, 7, n. 3. vii, D, 1, n. 32
52.1 **III**, App. pt. II, no. 88. ix, B, n. 480
55 ix, B, nn. 90, 143, 147
56 viii, C, 3, n. 133
67.2 viii, A, 3, n. 20. x, C, 5, n. 20
68 viii, B, 1, n. 22. x, B, 5, n. 14
69 ix, A, 5, n. 42
71 iii, F, n. 176
74 x, B, 1, n. 138
75 viii, C, 3, n. 77
76 + 37 viii, B, 2, n. 91; viii, B, 3, nn. 49, 84; viii, C, 1, n. 211
77 viii, C, 3, n. 53
80 viii, C, 3, n. 121
82 viii, A, 3, n. 13. **IV**, App. A, VII. ix, A, 1, n. 88
89.4 **III**, App. pt. II, no. 254. viii, C, 3, nn. 32, 156; viii, C, 4, n. 18
90.1 **III**, App. pt. II, no. 154
101 x, B, 1, n. 115
108 ix, A, 2, n. 47
111 iii, D, n. 29. v, B, 1, n. 121
124 viii, C, 3, n. 128
125 viii, A, 3, n. 36
134 **II**, App. C, sec. 1
156 viii, A, 2, n. 80
178 viii, D, n. 87

Mosseri L 5 ix, A, 2, n. 104
7 viii, B, 3, n. 80
10 vi, 11, n. 43
12 ix, A, 2, n. 164
19 x, A, 1, n. 80

21 ii, 3, n. 21. v, A, 1, n. 35. x, B, 3, n. 45
21*v* **II**, App. A, sec. 114
24 ii, 2, n. 2
39 x, A, 2, n. 298
39*a* iv, 3, n. 76
39*b* iv, 3, n. 76
39*c* iv, 3, nn. 14, 76
39*e* vii, D, 1, n. 41
49 iii, A, 2, n. 6. viii, A, 2, n. 38
52 **I**, App. D, sec. 7. iii, E, n. 28. iv, 3, n. 23; iv, 8, n. 37. ix, C, 1, n. 116
76, slips
1 and 2 ix, C, 1, n. 195
86 iii, G, n. 12
87 ii, 4, n. 87
95 ix, A, 2, n. 104; ix, A, 3, n. 63
101 i, 3, n. 44
127.2 ix, C, 1, n. 159
129.1 x, A, 1, n. 80
130 ii, 4, n. 8; ii, 5, n. 86. vii, B, 1, n. 14
133 iv, 3, n. 35. x, C, 2, n. 26
135 v, D, 2, n. 3. vii, A, 2, n. 1; vii, C, 1, b, n. 1
159, frag. 3 ix, A, 5, n. 13; ix, B, n. 256
161 iii, E, n. 39. iv, 4, n. 12. vii, C, 1, c, n. 17
162 x, B, 1, n. 120
183 x, D, n. 91
191 iii, C, n. 18
197 viii, B, 1, n. 21; viii, C, 1, nn. 43, 100; viii, C, 3, n. 100. ix, A, 1, nn. 151, 242; ix, C, 1, n. 86. x, B, 2, n. 10; x, B, 3, n. 19
199 iv, 3, n. 13
206, 2 viii, A, 2, n. 42
209 vii, A, 2, n. 19
224, item 3 x, A, 2, n. 414
227 x, A, 2, n. 153
230 viii, C, 1, n. 157. ix, A, 5, nn. 6, 12
245 ii, 4, n. 52
268 ii, 7, n. 33. vi, 6, n. 7; vi, 12, n. 28. x, C, 2, n. 24
279 v, A, 1, n. 24
288 x, B, 1, n. 59
290 vii, B, 1, n. 7. x, B, 3, n. 28; x, C, 1, n. 10; x, D, n. 88
Mosseri V 8 **I**, App. D, sec. 80. **III**, App. pt. II, no. 115. viii, B, 3, nn. 19, 84
IX 163 ix, A, 4, n. 115
X 107 viii, A, 2, n. 23
PER: Papyrus-sammlung Erzherzog Rainer, Vienna
PER H 1 **III**, App. pt. II, no. 21. viii, A, Introduction, n. 1; viii, B, 1, n. 19; viii, B, 3, n. 34; viii, B, 4, n. 18. ix, A, 4, n. 146
2 vii, B, 1, n. 51. viii, B, 1, n. 19; viii, B, 4, n. 73. ix, A, 4, n. 99
17 B iv, 8, n. 76
18 **III**, App. pt. I, gr. 4; **III**, App. pt. II, no. 355. viii, B, 1, n. 19; viii, B, 3, n. 5
19 **IV**, App. D, n. 222
20 **III**, App. pt. I, gr. 1; **III**, App. pt. II, no. 359. viii, B, 4, n. 44. ix, A, 4, nn. 7, 21, 57, 196; ix, A, 5, nn. 2, 9, 32; ix, B, nn. 222, 532
21 x, A, 3, n. 10; x, B, 1, n. 53; x, B, 4, n. 150

22 iii, B, 2, nn. 5, 39. viii, C, 1, n. 17. ix, A, 4, n. 181; ix, A, 5, nn. 74, 81; ix, B, nn. 433, 448. x, A, 3, n. 129; x, B, 1, n. 105
23 viii, D, n. 81
24 ii, 5, n. 14. vii, B, 2, n. 3. **III**, App. pt. I, gr. 7; **III**, App. pt. II, no. 107. viii, B, 3, n. 84. ix, A, 4, n. 159; ix, B, nn. 85, 472. **IV**, App. D, n. 172
31 viii, B, 5, n. 63; viii, D, n. 177
45 ii, 4, n. 53
60 v, B, 2, n. 97
82 viii, C, 1, n. 236
85 viii, C, 1, nn. 2, 3
89 viii, C, 2, n. 54; viii, C, 4, n. 7. **IV**, App. A, V
90 viii, B, 1, n. 60; viii, C, 4, n. 48
91 iii, F, n. 132. v, B, 1, nn. 16, 19, 37
92 x, C, 4, n. 45
93 v, B, 1, nn. 12, 104. vi, 4, n. 10
94 v, B, 1, n. 113. vii, D, 1, n. 13. viii, C, 4, n. 111
129*v* x, B, 4, n. 116
135 v, B, 1, n. 124. vi, 7, n. 10; vi, 11, n. 38. viii, B, 1, n. 13
136 iv, 9, n. 3
160 v, A, 1, n. 6; v, B, 1, n. 104. vii, B, 1, n. 54; vii, B, 2, n. 11; vii, B, 3, nn. 1, 14
181 **II**, App. C, sec. 114. viii, C, 1, n. 120

P. Heid.: Papyrus-sammlung der Universitat Heidelberg
P. Heid. 898 iii, F, n. 140
910*v* vi, 7, nn. 17, 21
913 iv, 12, n. 33. v, B, 2, n. 23. viii, B, 1, n. 27. ix, A, 2, n. 45; ix, A, 3, n. 48. x, B, 2, n. 61
915 **I**, App. D, sec. 22. vii, A, 1, n. 49
917 iii, D, n. 73; iii, F, nn. 106, 114
1451 vii, A, 2, n. 5. viii, C, 2, n. 136. ix, A, 1, nn. 85, 103; ix, A, 2, nn. 9, 66, 82, 92, 93, 102, 111, 112, 113, 114, 144

PSR: Papyrus-sammlung Schott-Reinhardt, Heidelberg
PSR 1453 iii, F, n. 110

Sassoon: Sassoon Collection, Letchworth, England
Sassoon 713 ii, 7, n. 24. iii, A, 1, n. 5. v, A, 1, n. 5. vi, 6, n. 5; vi, 7, n. 29; vi, 9, n. 8. vii, A, 3, n. 3; vii, B, 1, n. 14; vii, C, 1, c, nn. 5, 48. viii, C, 2, n. 125. ix, A, 2, n. 140; ix, A, 5, n. 84; ix, B, n. 331. x, A, 2, nn. 71, 337
MS Schechter 4 v, B, 2, n. 56
9 vi, 7, n. 28

TS: Taylor Schechter Collection, University Library, Cambridge, England
TS Box G 1, f. 1 vii, C, 1, c, n. 55; vii, C, 2, n. 51. ix, B, n. 47; ix, C, 1, n. 103
f. 52 x, A, 2, n. 353
f. 61 viii, A, 2, n. 4. x, B, 5, n. 19
Box H 11, f. 78 viii, B, 3, n. 11
Box H 12, f. 11 v, D, 1, nn. 11, 12 (cited as Box H 12, f. 11*a*)
f. 11*a* v, D, 1, nn. 11, 12 (mistake for Box H 12, f. 11)
Box J 1, f. 1 **I**, App. D, sec. 17. ii, 5, n. 58. iii, B, 2, n. 9; iii, D, nn. 10, 25, 59, 74, 78; iii, E, nn. 61, 81; iii, F, nn. 8, 40
f. 1, col. I ix, B, n. 411
f. 1, col. III ix, A, 1, n. 131
f. 1*v* ix, B, n. 194
f. 4 i, 2, n. 88. ii, 4, n. 58. **II**, App. B, sec. 23. v, B, 2, n. 57
f. 11 ii, 7, n. 108
f. 15*d* ix, A, 4, n. 185

f. 26 **II**, App. B, sec. 67. v, C, 1, n. 26. ix, B, n. 200; ix, C, 1, n. 54
f. 29 ii, 7, n. 22. **III**, App. pt. I, gr. 6; **III**, App. pt. II, no. 320. viii, B, 4, nn. 43, 62, 97; viii, D, n. 203. **IV**, App. C, 1, 2. ix, A, 4, nn. 52, 53, 56, 61, 63, 190, 197, 206, 208, 214; ix, A, 5, nn. 4, 10, 47, 64, 78; ix, B, nn. 59, 115, 195, 540
f. 31 ix, B, n. 72. x, A, 3, nn. 138, 185, 203
f. 32 **II**, App. A, sec. 46. vii, C, 1, c, n. 37
f. 34 **II**, App. B, sec. 100
f. 42 ix, A, 5, n. 75
f. 47 ii, 4, nn. 46, 88. **II**, App. A, sec. 94. v, D, 1, n. 30. vi, 4, n. 15. vii, A, 1, n. 12; vii, A, 2, n. 9; vii, B, 1, n. 30; vii, C, 1, c, n. 37. ix, A, 2, n. 43
f. 48 **III**, App. pt. II, no. 370. **IV**, App. C, 2, 4. ix, A, 4, nn. 2, 44, 162, 163
f. 50 ix, A, 4, n. 217
f. 52 **II**, App. A, sec. 150
f. 53 ix, B, nn. 148, 153, 154
f. 54 **I**, App. D, sec. 10. iii, D, nn. 25, 74, 75; iii, E, n. 67; iii, F, n. 10. iv, 6, n. 11; iv, 7, nn. 3, 22; iv, 10, nn. 14, 20; iv, 11, nn. 13, 26
Box J 2 ii, 7, n. 96 (mistake for Box J 3, f. 44)
f. 25 **II**, App. C, sec. 118
f. 26 viii, C, 1, n. 182
f. 63*a-b* **II**, App. A, sec. 33. **IV**, App. B, II
f. 63*c-d* **II**, App. A, sec. 28
f. 66 iii, F, n. 88. iv, 10, n. 6
f. 74 x, A, 2, n. 298
Box J 3, f. 16 x, A, 3, n. 120
f. 25(*x*) viii, B, 3, n. 76
f. 27(*z*) vii, B, 3, n. 58. viii, B, 4, n. 77; viii, B, 5, nn. 18, 39
f. 44 ii, 7, n. 96 (cited as Box J 2)
f. 46 viii, C, 1, n. 223
f. 47 (was 13 J 32) iii, F, n. 196. **III**, App. pt. I, gr. 4; **III**, App. pt. II, no. 196. viii, B, 4, n. 96. ix, B, n. 279
Box J 6, f. 4 ix, C, 1, n. 68
Box K 1, f. 91*c* viii, C, 1, n. 58
f. 117 iv, 8, n. 78
f. 121 iv, 12, nn. 3, 14
Box K 3, f. 1 vi, 8, n. 1
f. 6 **II**, App. C, sec. 58
f. 11 ii, 2, n. 40; ii, 3, nn. 5, 20; ii, 5, n. 28. **II**, App. A, secs. 30, 31. v, B, 2, n. 91. ix, C, 1, n. 72.
f. 11*a* ix, A, 1, n. 107
f. 21 **II**, App. A, sec. 142. ix, A, 3, n. 74
f. 22 ii, 5, n. 27. **II**, App. C, sec. 41
f. 26 ix, A, 5, n. 88
f. 28 ix, A, 5, n. 37
f. 32 i, 3, n. 31. vi, 9, n. 26; vi, 11, n. 15. viii, C, 4, n. 34
f. 34 i, 2, n. 86. **II**, App. B, sec. 28. v, B, 2, n. 101
f. 36 ii, 7, n. 106. iv, 10, n. 1
Box K 5 vi, 2, n. 21
f. 41 vii, A, 3, n. 45
f. 76 ii, 3, n. 19; ii, 4, n. 89
Box K 6, f. 24 viii, B, 5, n. 18
f. 44 ii, 4, n. 61; ii, 5, n. 77. iii, A, 1, n. 14; iii, B, 4, n. 6. iv, 7, n. 17. **II**, App. A, sec. 95. vii, C, 1, c, n. 36. **IV**, App. B, III
f. 44*v* ix, A, 1, n. 193

f. 47 vii, B, 1, n. 36. **IV**, App. A, IV
f. 54 **II**, App. A, sec. 40
f. 106 ii, 4, n. 73. **II**, App. A, sec. 16. v, B, 2, n. 72. ix, A, 1, nn. 94, 95
f. 118 **III**, App. pt. I, gr. 6. viii, C, 2, n. 146; viii, C, 4, n. 24. x, A, 3, n. 316
f. 146 iii, G, n. 2 (mistake, *see* Reif)
f. 149 **I**, App. D, sec. 57. ii, 1, nn. 11, 13. **II**, App. C, sec. 30. v, B, 2, n. 100
f. 177 ii, 1, nn. 11, 13; ii, 4, n. 46. iii, G, n. 2. **II**, App. C, sec. 31
f. 189 iii, D, n. 69. x, C, 2, n. 13

Box K 15, f. 2 ii, 4, n. 97; ii, 5, n. 29. **II**, App. B, sec. 43. v, B, 2, n. 96. vii, A, 3, n. 12. viii, C, 1, n. 129
f. 3 **II**, App. A, sec. 42. ix, A, 2, n. 159
f. 4*v* viii, A, 1, nn. 10, 12
f. 5 i, 2, n. 56. ii, 4, n. 94. **II**, App. B, secs. 19–22. vi, 11, n. 9
f. 6 ii, 1, n. 16; ii, 2, n. 10; ii, 5, n. 7. iii, A, 1, n. 42; iii, G, n. 2. **II**, App. C, sec. 33. vi, 10, n. 34. x, A, 1, n. 164
f. 7 viii, A, 1, n. 16. x, B, 2, n. 20
f. 8 vi, 9, n. 19; vi, 10, n. 34. vii, B, 1, n. 23
f. 9 ii, 4, n. 68
f. 9*v* vi, 12, n. 60
f. 10 ii, 4, n. 61. **II**, App. C, sec. 75
f. 12 **II**, App. C, sec. 63
f. 13 ii, 4, n. 101; ii, 7, n. 112 (cited as Box 15, f. 13). **II**, App. A, secs. 34, 36. ix, A, 1, n. 115
f. 14 i, 2, n. 49. ii, 3, n. 7; ii, 4, nn. 2, 81, 99, 100. iii, F, n. 117. **II**, App. B, secs. 4, 5. v, B, 2, n. 102. x, A, 1, n. 164; x, A, 3, n. 206
f. 15 i, 2, nn. 49, 88, 94. ii, 6, n. 18. vi, 12, n. 75
f. 16 **II**, App. C, sec. 65
f. 17 ii, 7, n. 112 (cited as Box 15, f. 17). **II**, App. B, sec. 10
f. 18 ii, 4, nn. 80, 91; ii, 5, n. 71. **II**, App. C, sec. 69. vi, 9, n. 22
f. 21 ii, 5, n. 68. iii, A, 1, n. 13. **II**, App. A, sec. 47
f. 25 **II**, App. B, sec. 50. viii, C, 1, n. 134
f. 27 viii, A, Introd., n. 2 (mistake for Box K 15, f. 28)
f. 28 **II**, App. C, sec. 11. viii, A, Introd., n. 2 (cited as Box K 15, f. 27)
f. 29 ii, 4, n. 53
f. 30 **II**, App. B, sec. 35
f. 32 **II**, App. C, sec. 56
f. 34 ii, 4, n. 101; ii, 6, n. 6. **II**, App. C, sec. 71
f. 36 ii, 1, n. 14; ii, 2, nn. 10, 33; ii, 4, nn. 100, 101; ii, 5, nn. 40, 68. iii, A, 1, n. 14. **II**, App. C, sec. 39. v, B, 2, n. 32. viii, A, 1, n. 83
f. 39 i, 2, nn. 56, 87, 89, 94. v, B, 2, n. 57
f. 43 ii, 4, nn. 2, 95; ii, 5, n. 27. iii, A, 1, n. 42; iii, F, n. 123. **II**, App. C, sec. 62. v, B, 2, n. 101
f. 45 ii, 2, nn. 41, 42; ii, 3, n. 21; ii, 4, nn. 87, 89. **II**, App. A, sec. 7. vi, 13, n. 2. **IV**, App. B, I. ix, A, 2, nn. 141, 161
f. 47 ii, 4, nn. 55, 107. ix, A, 1, n. 220. x, B, 3, n. 38
f. 48 ii, 3, n. 14; ii, 4, nn. 2, 54, 62; ii, 5, n. 60; ii, 6, n. 10. **II**, App. B, sec. 25. v, B, 2, n. 57. viii, B, 1, n. 79. ix, B, n. 30
f. 49 **II**, App. B, sec. 87
f. 50 ii, 4, nn. 58, 94, 100; ii, 6, nn. 9, 18. **II**, App. B, sec. 31. v, B, 2, nn. 96, 101. vi, 10, n. 37; vi, 12, n. 75. viii, A, 1, n. 82; viii, C, 1, n. 214. ix, C, 2, n. 53

f. 53 **I**, App. D, sec. 12. ii, 3, nn. 8, 21; ii, 5, n. 25. iii, B, 4, n. 5; iii, D, n. 73, 77; iii, E, n. 77. iv, 11, n. 22. vii, A, 2, n. 18; vii, C, 1, b, n. 16; vii, C, 1, d, n. 22. ix, B, n. 100

f. 54 ii, 4, n. 95; ii, 5, n. 67. **II**, App. A, sec. 43. **IV**, App. B, II, III. ix, A, 2, n. 117

f. 55 iii, D, n. 73

f. 58 ii, 4, n. 90; ii, 5, n. 68. **II**, App. C, sec. 67. v, A, 2, n. 19. vii, C, 1, d, n. 26. ix, A, 1, n. 220

f. 60 ii, 2, n. 33

f. 60*v* **II**, App. C, sec. 49

f. 61 ii, 2, n. 11; ii, 5, n. 40. **II**, App. C, sec. 40. vii, C, 1, c, n. 6

f. 62 **II**, App. C, sec. 64

f. 63 **II**, App. B, sec. 42. v, B, 2, n. 54

f. 63*v* viii, A, Introd., n. 2 (mistake for Box K 15, f. 68)

f. 64 ii, 5, n. 68. **II**, App. C, sec. 57

f. 65 ii, 7, n. 104. **III**, App. pt. I, gr. 1; **III**, App. pt. II, no. 76. viii, B, 4, n. 50. ix, B, n. 74

f. 65, col. I ix, B, nn. 378, 439, 453, 518

col. II **III**, App. pt. I, gr. 1; **III**, App. pt. II, no. 131. **IV**, App. C, 3. ix, A, 4, nn. 165, 192, 196; ix, B, n. 532

col. III ix, B, nn. 426, 438

col. IV **IV**, App. C, 1, 2. ix, A, 4, nn. 28, 32, 192, 196, 208; ix, A, 5, nn. 4, 32

f. 65*v*, col. III ix, B, n. 125

f. 66 i, 2, n. 49. ii, 3, nn. 7, 9; ii, 4, nn. 2, 5, 46, 52, 78, 106; ii, 6, n. 8. **II**, App. B, secs. 4, 5. vi, 10, n. 37

f. 68 v, D, 2, n. 30. viii, A, Introd., n. 2 (cited as Box K 15, f. 63*v*). x, D, n. 302

f. 68*v* ii, 1, n. 9. iv, 8, n. 58

f. 69 viii, B, 4, n. 94. x, B, 3, n. 64

f. 70 i, 2, n. 70. ii, 4, nn. 12, 100. **II**, App. B, sec. 13. vi, 11, n. 9; vi, 12, n. 75. viii, A, 1, nn. 82, 84

f. 71 ii, 4, n. 38

f. 74 **II**, App. C, sec. 42

f. 77 ix, B, n. 396

f. 79 **III**, App. pt. II, no. 90. ix, A, 4, nn. 7, 32, 48, 50; ix, B, nn. 115, 417, 447, 455

f. 82 **II**, App. C, sec. 78

f. 85 ii, 4, nn. 2, 55. **II**, App. B, sec. 34

f. 86 **II**, App. C, sec. 76

f. 87 **II**, App. A, sec. 111

f. 88 **II**, App. C, sec. 43

f. 89 iii, F, n. 12

f. 90 iii, C, n. 12 (mistake for Box K 25, f. 90). **II**, App. B, sec. 40

f. 91 ii, F, nn. 128, 207. **II**, App. C, sec. 23. vii, C, 1, b, n. 47. viii, A, 1, n. 64. ix, A, 3, n. 98; ix, A, 4, n. 205; ix, A, 5, n. 79; ix, B, n. 448. x, A, 3, n. 255; x, B, 4, n. 149

f. 92 viii, C, 2, n. 113

f. 93 ii, 3, n. 9; ii, 4, n. 2. **II**, App. B, sec. 6. v, B, 2, n. 96. viii, C, 4, n. 179. x, A, 1, n. 164

f. 94 **II**, App. B, sec. 59. **II**, App. C, sec. 14

f. 95 vii, A, 3, n. 6; vii, C, 1, c, n. 7. viii, C, 4, n. 71. ix, B, n. 209

f. 96 ii, 2, n. 10; ii, 4, nn. 56, 78, 93, 101; ii, 6, n. 8. iv, 3, n. 17. **II**, App. B, sec. 8. vi, 5, n. 7

f. 97 **I**, App. D, sec. 45. i, 2, n. 89. ii, 6, n. 9. **II**, App. B, sec. 29. viii, A, 1, n. 82; viii, C, 4, n. 125

f. 98*v* ix, B, n. 147
f. 99 ii, 4, n. 19. ix, A, 4, nn. 34, 61; ix, A, 5, nn. 10, 17, 39, 49; ix, B, nn. 29, 273, 453, 540. **IV**, App. D, nn. 83, 160
f. 100 ii, 3, nn. 18, 35; ii, 4, nn. 73, 89. **II**, App. A, sec. 144. **III**, App. pt. II, no. 145. **IV**, App. C, 2
f. 102 i, 2, n. 89. ii, 1, nn. 7, 18, 19; ii, 4, nn. 57, 84. iii, F, n. 123. **II**, App. B, sec. 31. vi, 11, n. 46. viii, C, 1, n. 214; viii, C, 4, n. 125
f. 105 x, A, 2, n. 383
f. 106 ii, 5, n. 56. iii, A, 1, n. 1. **II**, App. C, sec. 16. ix, B, n. 166. x, B, 3, n. 72
f. 107 **II**, App. C, sec. 60. x, A, 1, n. 102
f. 109 **II**, App. C, sec. 13
f. 110 **II**, App. A, sec. 45
f. 111 **III**, App. pt. II, nos. 367, 368. ix, A, 5, n. 31
f. 111, col. I **IV**, App. C, 2. ix, B, nn. 422, 523. **IV**, App. D, n. 263
f. 113 **II**, App. B, sec. 26
f. 114 ii, 2, n. 21. iii, D, nn. 25, 35; iii, E, n. 8. viii, D, n. 143. ix, B, nn. 148, 166
f. 153 ix, C, 1, n. 18
Box K 21, f. 21 v, A, 2, n. 40
f. 29 x, C, 5, n. 50
f. 35 v, D, 2, n. 28
f. 98*v* ix, A, 1, n. 78; ix, A, 2, n. 21
Box K 25, f. 42 ix, A, 4, nn. 27, 33, 47, 201; ix, A, 5, nn. 2, 11, 33, 44, 45; ix, B, n. 553. **IV**, App. D, nn. 6, 7, 226
f. 64 v, A, 2, n. 46. vi, 12, nn. 35, 46
f. 84 **II**, App. A, sec. 120
f. 90 iii, C, n. 12 (cited as Box K 15, f. 90)
f. 153 **I**, App. C, sec. 20. ii, 4, n. 48
f. 161 **II**, App. C, sec. 122
f. 166 vii, A, 3, n. 33. **III**, App. pt. II, no. 24; **IV**, App. C, 2
f. 169 ii, 4, nn. 2, 39. **II**, App. A, sec. 8. **IV**, App. B, I
f. 171 viii, B, 4, n. 54. ix, B, nn. 499, 518
f. 183 **III**, App. pt. II, no. 319
f. 190 **I**, Introduction, n. 46. ix, A, 2, n. 168
f. 191 viii, C, 3, n. 140
f. 205 viii, C, 1, n. 56
f. 208 **II**, App. A, sec. 118
f. 240, no. 1 iii, D, n. 81. vii, C, 2, n. 48
no. 11 iii, D, n. 81. vii, C, 2, n. 48
no.12 iii, D, n. 81. vii, C, 2, n. 48
nos. 11–38, 40–56 **II**, App. A, secs. 48–92
no. 17 i, 2, n. 92
no. 18 i, 2, n. 95
no. 19 i, 2, n. 95. v, C, 1, n. 19
no. 20 i, 2, n. 95
no. 26 vi, 4, n. 16
nos. 33–37 v, C, 4, n. 37
no. 38 **II**, App. B, sec. 39
no. 40 ii, 2, n. 43
f. 244 ii, 4, n. 74. v, B, 1, nn. 119, 132, 142. viii, C, 1, n. 77. x, C, 5, n. 82
f. 251 i, 4, n. 6. vii, A, 2, n. 5. viii, A, 3, n. 16. ix, A, 1, nn. 47, 49, 51, 87, 103, 194. ix, A, 2, nn. 52, 62, 80, 91, 94, 97, 102, 112, 116, 125, 145, 156
f. 269 **III**, App. pt. II, no. 373. viii, B, 4, n. 63. **IV**, App. C. ix, A,

	4, nn. 19, 27, 47, 208; ix, A, 5, nn. 2, 11, 60, 61; ix, B, nn. 125, 409, 429, 440, 488, 524, 532, 539. **IV**, App. D, nn. 155, 220
f. 284	vii, A, 2, n. 5. viii, A, 3, n. 16. **IV**, App. A, VII. ix, A, 1, n. 79; ix, A, 2, nn. 67, 99, 149, 154, 160
Box K 27	x, A, 3, n. 305
f. 45	vii, B, 3, n. 42 (mistake for NS 246, f. 28). ix, A, 1, n. 100
BOUND VOLUMES	
TS 6 J 1, f. 1	**II**, App. A, sec. 105. ix, A, 2, n. 140
f. 5	x, C, 2, n. 9
f. 23	mistake for 6 J 1, f. 32
f. 32	**I**, App. D, sec. 78. ii, 7, n. 62 (cited as 6 J 1, f. 32)
6 J 2, f. 1	viii, C, 1, n. 223
f. 2	viii, B, 5, n. 54; viii, C, 1, n. 132
f. 5	**IV**, App. D, n. 134
f. 10	v, B, 2, n. 113
f. 14	ii, 5, n. 52
f. 17	x, C, 4, n. 34
f. 22	ix, A, 3, n. 68
f. 26	viii, C, 4, n. 45
6 J 3, f. 5	x, A, 3, n. 243
f. 16	viii, C, 1, n. 92
f. 18	ix, C, 1, n. 112
f. 22	viii, C, 1, n. 90
f. 33	iii, F, n. 163. iv, 5, n. 1
6 J 4, f. 14	x, B, 4, n. 130
6 J 5, f. 10	ix, A, 4, n. 96
6 J 6, f. 17	viii, C, 2, n. 58
f. 21	viii, C, 4, n. 126. ix, A, 2, n. 111
6 J 7, f. 3	**II**, App. D, sec. 31. vi, 6, n. 8. vii, A, 1, n. 56
6 J 8, f. 4	**II**, App. B, sec. 91. ix, C, 1, n. 74
6 J 9, f. 1	*see* TS 10 G 5, f. 7
6 J 10, f. 2	mistake for 6 J 10, f. 12
f. 12	iii, A, 1, n. 42 (cited as 6 J 10, f. 2)
6 Ja, f. 2	**III**, App. pt. I, gr. 4; **III**, App. pt. II, no. 321
TS 8 J 1, f. 1	viii, C, 1, n. 39
8 J 2, f. 11	ix, A, 3, n. 120
8 J 4, fs. 1–2	v, B, 1, n. 110. vii, B, 3, n. 11
f. 2	viii, A, 1, n. 60
f. 2*b*	**III**, App. pt. I, gr. 4; **III**, App. pt. II, no. 219. viii, B, 2, n. 83
f. 3	iii, F, n. 145
f. 3*v*	vii, B, 3, n. 40. ix, A, 5, n. 42
f. 3*b*, *v*	viii, C, 3, n. 116. ix, A, 4, nn. 34, 215, 217; ix, A, 5, n. 62
f. 9*d*	v, B, 1, n. 115; v, B, 2, nn. 6, 71, 77, 80, 91; v, C, 4, n. 25. vii, B, 3, n. 15
f. 12*v*	vii, C, 1, a, n. 26
f. 13	viii, A, 3, n. 23. ix, A, 1, n. 94; ix, A, 2, nn. 41, 45, 75
f. 14*a*	vii, C, 1, b, n. 7. ix, A, 2, n. 149. x, B, 1, nn. 130, 137
f. 14*c*	iii, E, n. 57
f. 14*d*	ii, 5, n. 71. x, B, 1, n. 136
f. 15*a*	v, B, 2, n. 83. viii, C, 1, n. 235
f. 16	ix, A, 4, n. 48; ix, B, n. 481
f. 17	vii, D, 1, nn. 17, 26. viii, C, 2, n. 168
f. 18*c*	**I**, App. D, sec. 48. ii, 4, n. 92. viii, C, 1, n. 145. ix, C, 1, nn. 49, 78
f. 19	iii, C, nn. 5, 14. v, B, 1, n. 41
f. 20	viii, C, 4, n. 5

f. 21	viii, C, 4, n. 43
f. 22	**IV**, App. D, n. 240
f. 22*v*	**III**, App. pt. I, gr. 5; **III**, App. pt. II, no. 71. viii, B, 2, n. 76; viii, B, 5, n. 47
f. 23*v* (*c*)	**III**, App. pt. I, gr. 5; **III**, App. pt. II, no. 72. viii, B, 2, n. 77
f. 23*d*	viii, D, n. 68. x, A, 3, n. 75
f. 25	iii, F, n. 95
f. 25*v*	viii, C, 1, n. 199
8 J 5, f. 1	i, 2, n. 67. iii, F, nn. 99, 213. **II**, App. D, sec. 14. vii, B, 3, n. 49. **III**, App. pt. II, no. 298. viii, C, 4, n. 32. ix, A, 4, n. 207; ix, A, 5, nn. 7, 54, 78, 82. **IV**, App. D, nn. 180, 197. x, A, 3, nn. 163, 233
f. 2	viii, C, 3, n. 128
f. 2*a-c*	**III**, App. pt. I, gr. 5; **III**, App. pt. II, no. 37. viii, B, 3, n. 82; viii, B, 4, n. 13; viii, B, 5, n. 54; viii, D, n. 113. ix, A, 1, n. 25
f. 2*c-d*	**III**, App. pt I, gr. 5; **III**, App. pt. II, no. 38. viii, B, 4, n. 16; viii, B, 5, nn. 10, 77, 84; viii, C, 1, n. 132
f. 3*a-b*	**III**, App. pt. I, gr. 5; **III**, App. pt. II, no. 127. viii, C, 1, n. 207
f. 3*c*	**III**, App. pt. I, gr. 5
f. 4*a*	viii, D, n. 4
f. 4*c*	ii, 3, n. 26. viii, A, 3, n. 67
f. 4*d*	ii, 1, n. 17; ii, 5, n. 86. v, B, 2, nn. 84, 91
f. 4*v*, item IV	viii, B, 5, n. 71; viii, C, 1, n. 146
f. 5*b-c*	viii, D, nn. 159, 169
f. 7	viii, B, 5, n. 66
f. 8	viii, C, 1, n. 171. x, C, 2, n. 1
f. 9	ix, A, 1, n. 199; ix, A, 2, n. 45
f. 10	ii, 5, n. 50. iii, F, n. 65. vii, B, 2, n. 28
f. 10, II	ix, A, 2, n. 140; ix, A, 3, n. 10
f. 12	ii, 4, n. 88. ix, A, 1, n. 195; ix, A, 2, n. 60
f. 13	viii, A, 1, n. 70. ix, A, 1, n. 210. x, C, 2, n. 7
f. 14	**II**, App. B, sec. 36
f. 14*c*	ii, 3, n. 9
f. 14*d*	i, 2, n. 3
f. 15	**II**, App. A, sec. 132
f. 16	**III**, App. pt. II, no. 215. viii, A, 1, n. 37; viii, C, 1, n. 85; viii, D, n. 163
f. 18	ii, 4, nn. 14, 21, 22. v, B, 1, nn. 25, 31.
f. 18*c*	vii, A, 3, n. 6
f. 18*d*	**III**, App. pt. I, gr. 1; **III**, App. pt. II, no. 136. ix, B, nn. 396, 416, 440, 478, 488
f. 21	**III**, App. pt. I, gr. 7; **III**, App. pt. II, no. 168. viii, B, 5, n. 49
f. 22	**III**, App. pt. I, gr. 1; **III**, App. pt. II, no. 113. viii, B, 2, n. 63; viii, B, 3, n. 84; viii, B, 5, n. 35
f. 22*v*	**II**, App. A, sec. 134. ix, A, 3, n. 32
f. 23	viii, C, 1, n. 150
f. 24	x, B, 1, n. 93
f. 25	**II**, App. C, sec. 59. vi, 9, n. 44. viii, C, 1, n. 134; viii, C, 4, n. 48
8 J 6, fs. 2 and 3	viii, D, n. 62
f. 3*v*	**II**, App. B, sec. 85
f. 4	viii, C, 4, n. 54
f. 6	viii, C, 4, n. 56
f. 7	vi, 4, n. 27. viii, A, 1, n. 84
f. 8	iii, C, n. 27

f. 9 iii, B, 2, n. 27. vi, 11, n. 8
f. 9*v* **I**, App. D, sec. 70. vi, 11, n. 60
f. 12 **III**, App. pt. I, gr. 7. viii, C, 4, n. 9. ix, A, 1, n. 37
f. 14 ii, 5, n. 59. **II**, App. C, sec. 89. **III**, App. pt. II, no. 238. viii, C, 3, n. 6. x, A, 3, nn. 60, 63
f. 14*v* **IV**, App. A, III. ix, A, 1, n. 53; ix, A, 3, n. 33
f. 15 **IV**, App. A, II
f. 16 viii, C, 1, n. 134
f. 18 ii, 4, n. 87. v, A, 1, n. 34. **III**, App. pt. I, gr. 4; **III**, App. pt. II, no. 218
f. 18*d* viii, A, 2, n. 78; viii, C, 4, n. 52
f. 19 **I**, Introduction, n. 48
8 J 7, f. 5 iii, C, n. 5
f. 7 viii, C, 4, n. 24. **IV**, App. A, I
f. 9 v, D, 2, n. 28
f. 15 x, A, 2, n. 29; x, B, 1, n. 115
f. 18 ii, 2, nn. 16, 25; ii, 4, n. 89. vii, A, 2, n. 22; vii, B, 2, n. 10
f. 23 vi, 5, n. 9. ix, A, 4, nn. 206, 217; ix, A, 5, n. 65
f. 27 viii, B, 5, n. 60
8 J 8, f. 4 ii, 7, n. 51
f. 5 vi, 4, n. 23
f. 9 x, A, 3, n. 45
f. 12 vii, A, 3, n. 39. viii, C, 3, nn. 9, 38. ix, A, 4, n. 207. x, A, 3, n. 46
8 J 9, f. 2*v* **IV**, App. A, VII. ix, A, 2, nn. 85, 91
f. 3 **IV**, App. A, VII. ix, A, 2, nn. 85, 91; ix, A, 3, nn. 8, 33, 76, 112; ix, D, n. 35
f. 6 ix, A, 1, n. 221. x, C, 5, n. 31
f. 9 **III**, App. pt. II, no. 182. viii, B, 2, n. 78; viii, B, 5, n. 9
f. 11 ix, A, 3, n. 34
f. 13 **III**, App. pt. II, no. 144a, 337. viii, B, 2, n. 29
f. 15 x, B, 1, n. 38
f. 16 x, D, n. 333
f. 17 ix, B, n. 440
f. 17*a* **III**, App. pt. I, gr. 1; **III**, App. pt. II, no. 75. **IV**, App. C, 2
f. 17*c*, I ix, A, 2, n. 121. **IV**, App. A, II
f. 17*c*, item II **III**, App. pt. I, gr. 1; **III**, App. pt. II, no. 246
f. 17*d*, item I **III**, App. pt. I, gr. 1; **III**, App. pt. II, no. 246
f. 19 **I**, App. D, sec. 54. ix, A, 5, n. 34
f. 24 x, B, 1, n. 109
f. 27 ii, 5, n. 35 (mistake for TS 8 J 19, f. 27)
8 J 10, f. 9 iii, E, n. 10
f. 17 ii, 4, n. 92; ii, 6, n. 2. vii, B, 1, n. 3. viii, C, 1, n. 147. ix, C, 1, n. 80
f. 18 vii, B, 1, n. 3
f. 19 vii, B, 2, n. 31. x, D, n. 321
8 J 11, f. 2*v* x, B, 3, n. 41
f. 4 iii, F, n. 22. **II**, App. A, sec. 29. ix, A, 1, n. 116
f. 7*a-b* ii, 4, n. 87; ii, 5, n. 28; ii, 6, n. 9. **II**, App. A, sec. 32. vi, 3, n. 15. **IV**, App. B, II
f. 7*d* **II**, App. A, sec. 27. vii, C, 2, n. 34
f. 9 iii, F, n. 93. **II**, App. A, sec. 19. ix, A, 3, n. 115
f. 9*v* **II**, App. A, sec. 20
f. 10 x, D, n. 39
f. 14 iii, B, 2, nn. 7, 14. x, B, 1, n. 34
f. 15 viii, B, 3, n. 74; viii, D, n. 25. **IV**, App. A, I
f. 16 viii, B, 3, n. 21

f. 18 ix, A, 1, n. 88; ix, A, 3, n. 45
f. 19 vii, A, 3, n. 8. viii, C, 3, n. 92
8 J 12, f. 1 ii, 7, nn. 43, 97
f. 2 ii, 7, n. 97. x, A, 3, n. 120
f. 3 ii, 7, nn. 66 (cited as TS 8 J 12, f. 13), 97. **II**, App. B, sec. 36
f. 4 ii, 7, n. 97
f. 13 ii, 7, n. 66 (mistake for 8 J 12, f. 3)
8 J 13, f. 1 x, B, 4, n. 62
f. 3 ix, B, n. 266
f. 7 v, C, 2, n. 17
f. 14*v* **II**, App. C, sec. 48
f. 15 v, D, 2, n. 15
f. 18 ii, 4, n. 61. **II**, App. A, sec. 9. ix, A, 1, n. 200
f. 25 vi, 10, n. 42
8 J 14, f. 2 viii, C, 1, n. 203; viii, C, 3, n. 112
f. 3 vi, 12, n. 63. ix, A, 5, n. 72
f. 3*v* **IV**, App. A, I
f. 5 vi, 12, n. 59
f. 6 vii, A, 3, nn. 34, 41
f. 9 iii, F, n. 178
f. 12 x, A, 1, n. 10
f. 18 ix, A, 2, n. 107; ix, A, 4, n. 77. **IV**, App. D, n. 81. x, A, 2, n. 85
f. 25 viii, B, 2, n. 40
f. 25*v* viii, B, 2, nn. 1, 15
f. 27 viii, C, 1, n. 9
8 J 15, f. 3 v, C, 2, n. 29. x, A, 2, n. 339
f. 5 x, A, 1, n. 69
f. 8 v, D, 2, n. 16
f. 9 x, B, 1, n. 54
f. 14 ix, B, n. 45; ix, C, 1, n. 193
f. 17 **II**, App. A, sec. 97. vi, 7, n. 4. ix, A, 1, n. 192
f. 18 x, A, 2, n. 420; x, B, 2, n. 121
f. 20 x, A, 3, n. 304
f. 20*v* vi, 12, n. 63
f. 23*v* vi, 11, n. 36
f. 24 iii, D, n. 29. x, C, 2, n. 2
f. 25 ix, B, n. 166; ix, D, n. 19
f. 28 x, A, 1, n. 40
f. 32 ii, 4, n. 19
8 J 16, f. 1 viii, C, 4, n. 137
f. 3 v, C, 1, n. 16. x, B, 2, n. 59
f. 4 ii, 7, n. 105. v, A, 1, n. 2 (cited as TS 18 J16, f. 4). vii, C, 1, b, n. 44. x, D, n. 314
f. 6 ix, A, 1, n. 167
f. 7 x, A, 2, nn. 205, 206, 208
f. 13 **II**, App. C, sec. 84. v, C, 2, n. 9
f. 18 x, B, 3, n. 85
f. 19 ix, C, 1, n. 132
f. 22 iii, F, n. 15
f. 25 ix, B, n. 251
f. 27 ii, 4, n. 62. vi, 12, n. 71
f. 29 x, A, 1, n. 129; x, A, 2, n. 228
f. 31 **I**, App. D, sec. 32. iii, D, nn. 10, 11; iii, E, n. 74. iv, 4, nn. 1, 2; iv, 7, n. 15; iv, 10, nn. 26, 28; iv, 11, n. 23. ix, A, 1, n. 142. x, B, 1, n. 112

8 J 17, f. 3 v, D, 1, n. 6
f. 5 x, A, 1, n. 21
f. 6 **II**, App. D, sec. 29. v, B, 1, n. 38; v, C, 2, n. 8. viii, B, 5, n. 48; viii, C, 4, n. 127
f. 9*a-c* **III**, App. pt. I, gr. 5; **III**, App. pt. II, no. 155. viii, B, 2, n. 80; viii, B, 4, n. 22; viii, B, 5, nn. 9, 48
f. 9*d* **III**, App. pt. I, gr. 5; **III**, App. pt. II, no. 198. viii, B, 2, n. 81
f. 13 v, A, 2, n. 66; v, C, 4, n. 54. x, A, 1, n. 125
f. 15 x, B, 2, n. 16
f. 16 iii, F, n. 38. x, B, 2, n. 145
f. 17 viii, C, 3, n. 52. x, B, 2, n. 82
f. 18 **I**, App. D, sec. 56. **II**, App. C, sec. 29. v, B, 1, n. 33
f. 20*v* ix, B, n. 528
f. 22 ix, C, 1, n. 115. x, B, 2, n. 124; x, C, 2, n. 19
f. 27 v, A, 2, n. 66; v, C, 2, n. 13
f. 33 x, B, 2, n. 128
8 J 18, f. 2 iv, 7, n. 26. ix, B, nn. 304, 371
f. 8 iv, 5, n. 19; iv, 10, n. 30
f. 14 iii, A, 2, n. 10; iii, D, n. 20. iv, 7, n. 20. vii, A, 2, n. 18. viii, A, 2, n. 67. ix, B, n. 36
f. 18 iii, F, n. 146. iv, 3, n. 64. vii, B, 3, n. 23
f. 20 x, A, 2, n. 299
f. 21 iii, D, n. 12. iv, 7, n. 16; iv, 10, n. 37
f. 22 x, A, 1, n. 123
f. 23 x, A, 2, n. 350
f. 27 **I**, App. D, sec. 39. iii, E, n. 54; iii, F, n. 45. iv, 8, n. 31
f. 28 x, A, 1, n. 127
f. 29 iv, 12, n. 24. vi, 6, n. 4
f. 33 iv, 3, n. 47. v, A, 1, n. 2. vii, A, 2, n. 14. ix, B, n. 186
8 J 19, f. 1 ii, 3, n. 31. iv, 10, n. 26. vii, C, 2, n. 27
f. 4 iii, E, n. 48
f. 7 iii, D, n. 9
f. 8 x, A, 2, n. 357
f. 9 iv, 4, n. 14
f. 11 ii, 5, n. 12
f. 12 iv, 8, n. 6
f. 15 x, B, 2, n. 75
f. 19 ix, A, 4, n. 99
f. 21 ix, A, 3, n. 43
f. 21*v* ix, A, 5, n. 49
f. 23 iii, F, n. 44. iv, 3, n. 71. vi, 3, n. 12
f. 24 **I**, App. D, sec. 40. ii, 4, n. 60; ii, 5, n. 35. iii, D, n. 3; iii, F, n. 18. vii, A, 2, n. 20. ix, A, 1, n. 127
f. 25 ii, 5, n. 81. iii, E, n. 76; iii, F, nn. 73, 137. iv, 4, nn. 9, 10; iv, 7, n. 24; iv, 10, n. 26. vii, C, 1, c, n. 43; vii, C, 1, d, n. 26. viii, A, 2, n. 66
f. 26 iii, D, n. 29. iv, 10, n. 32. ix, B, n. 170
f. 27 ii, 5, n. 35 (cited as TS 8 J 9, f. 27). iii, C, nn. 25, 26; iii, E, n. 23; iii, F, n. 49. iv, 8, n. 54
f. 29 viii, C, 4, n. 145
f. 32 iii, E, n. 61
f. 33 viii, C, 1, n. 155
8 J 20, f. 1 x, A, 2, n. 277
f. 2 i, 2, n. 33. iii, E, nn. 18, 25. iv, 8, n. 80. ix, C, 1, n. 107
f. 4 x, B, 1, n. 51
f. 5 ix, B, n. 27
f. 8 ii, 4, n. 3. ix, A, 4, n. 138

f. 11 x, B, 4, n. 7
f. 16 vii, C, 2, n. 53. viii, C, 1, n. 96. ix, A, 2, n. 154
f. 17 iv, 8, n. 36
f. 18 iv, 12, n. 18. ix, A, 2, n. 45; ix, A, 3, n. 42
f. 20 x, D, n. 276
f. 24 x, A, 2, n. 143
f. 26 vi, 12, n. 54. x, A, 2, n. 47; x, B, 1, n. 9
8 J 21, f. 2 iii, E, n. 48; iii, F, n. 88
f. 3 v, D, 2, n. 28
f. 4 viii, C, 3, n. 38. **IV**, App. D, n. 41. x, A, 3, n. 46
f. 6 i, 2, n. 71. v, A, 2, n. 32. vi, 4, n. 34. vii, C, 2, n. 36
f. 7 iii, D, n. 27. viii, D, n. 130
f. 12 v, D, 2, n. 21. x, B, 1, n. 32
f. 14 iii, A, 1, n. 42. viii, C, 3, n. 30. ix, A, 4, n. 207
f. 20 x, A, 2, n. 296
f. 21 x, A, 1, n. 4
f. 22 i, 2, n. 82
f. 23 ix, B, n. 425
f. 28 ix, B, n. 405
f. 29 ii, 5, n. 28. iii, D, nn. 3, 14, 29. iv, 6, n. 13; iv, 7, n. 24. vii, B, 1, n. 23. ix, A, 1, n. 135
f. 30 x, A, 2, n. 226
f. 33 x, A, 2, n. 263
8 J 22, f. 3 v, D, 2, n. 24
f. 6 vii, B, 2, n. 12. viii, C, 2, n. 50. ix, B, n. 151. x, A, 2, nn. 110, 112, 125, 377
f. 7 v, D, 2, n. 42. x, C, 3, n. 18; x, C, 5, n. 16
f. 8 i, 2, n. 52. ii, 4, nn. 37, 84; ii, 5, n. 86 (cited as TS 8 J 22, f. 18). iii, A, 1, n. 17; iii, D, n. 14. ix, B, n. 92
f. 9 x, B, 3, n. 13
f. 10 ii, 4, n. 60. iii, E, n. 62. vii, C, 1, c, n. 16. viii, A, 1, n. 47
f. 11 ix, C, 2, n. 9
f. 14 **II**, App. B, sec. 57b
f. 14*v* vii, B, 2, n. 21
f. 18 ii, 4, nn. 37, 84; ii, 5, n. 86 (mistake for TS 8 J 22, f. 8). ix, B, n. 92. x, B, 2, n. 116
f. 22 vii, C, 1, b, n. 24. viii, C, 3, n. 120. x, D, n. 327
f. 23 iii, E, n. 19. vii, C, 1, a, n. 16. viii, C, 2, n. 111. x, B, 1, n. 125
f. 24 ix, A, 2, n. 154
f. 25 v, D, 2, n. 54. x, B, 5, n. 37
f. 27 viii, C, 1, n. 128. x, B, 1, n. 19
f. 30 iii, F, nn. 108, 111, 190. vii, C, 1, c, n. 55
8 J 23, f. 7 x, A, 2, n. 110
f. 10 ix, A, 3, n. 80
f. 17 ix, A, 1, n. 63
f. 20*v* x, B, 1, n. 42
f. 27 x, C, 3, n. 16; x, C, 5, n. 14
f. 30 ix, B, n. 331
8 J 24, f.1 x, C, 2, n. 4
f. 4 viii, C, 1, n. 62; viii, C, 2, n. 49; viii, C, 3, n. 151
f. 7 iii, D, n. 40. vii, A, 3, n. 31
f. 10 iii, B, 4, n. 9
f. 11 iv, 3, n. 12
f. 15 iii, F, n. 201
f. 17 x, A, 2, n. 209; x, C, 3, n. 17; x, C, 5, n. 13

f. 21 iii, A, 2, n. 11. iv, 6, n. 24; iv, 8, n. 39; iv, 9, n. 19. **IV**, App. D, n. 205
8 J 25, f. 2 ix, B, n. 200
f. 3 i, 2, n. 61. ii, 5, n. 29. vi, 7, n. 24. vii, B, 3, n. 33
f. 4 ix, A, 4, n. 145
f. 6 ii, 4, n. 2. iv, 3, n. 84. x, B, 2, n. 63
f. 13 ii, 2, n. 35. vii, C, 1, c, n. 17. viii, C, 1, n. 146. ix, B, n. 205
f. 15 ii, 4, n. 40. x, B, 4, n. 28
f. 16 x, B, 2, n. 107
f. 19 ii, 4, n. 84. iii, B, 1, n. 20
f. 20 ix, A, 5, n. 48
f. 21 ix, C, 1, n. 163
8 J 26, f. 1 x, A, 1, n. 121
f. 2 x, C, 4, n. 29; x, C, 4, n. 29
f. 3 vii, D, 2, n. 4
f. 4 iii, D, n. 68. x, C, 2, n. 71
f. 5 ii, 5, n. 39. viii, C, 1, n. 154. ix, A, 4, n. 158
f. 6 iii, D, n. 84
f. 17 viii, C, 1, n. 146
f. 18 iii, A, 1, n. 42. vii, C, 2, n. 11. ix, C, 1, n. 120
f. 19 ii, 4, n. 59. vi, 12, nn. 19, 56, 78. vii, A, 1, n. 10
f. 20 x, B, 4, n. 112
8 J 27, f. 1 x, B, 4, n. 27
f. 2 ii, 5, n. 35. iii, G, n. 31. iv, 4, n. 8; iv, 6, n. 1; iv, 7, n. 10; iv, 9, nn. 25, 28. viii, A, 2, n. 66
f. 3 vii, A, 3, n. 53
f. 5 **I**, App. D, sec. 38. viii, C, 2, n. 80
f. 8*v* x, C, 5, n. 53
f. 9 x, A, 2, n. 287
f. 11 **I**, App. C, sec. 27. ii, 5, n. 66. iii, C, n. 17 (mistake for TS 8 J 27, f. 12); iii, G, n. 20
f. 12 iii, C, n. 17 (cited as TS 8 J 27, f. 11)
f. 15 ix, A, 1, n. 68
f. 19 iv, 3, n. 82
f. 22 x, B, 2, n. 105
8 J 28, f. 5 x, B, 4, nn. 27, 28
f. 7 vi, 3, n. 3
f. 9 iv, 2, n. 14; iv, 7, n. 21
f. 12 iv, 2, nn. 27, 34
8 J 29, f. 7 **IV**, App. C, 2. ix, A, 4, nn. 15, 22; ix, B, nn. 504, 541. **IV**, App. D, nn. 172, 253
f. 9 ix, A, 2, nn. 125, 154
f. 13 viii, C, 1, n. 238. x, A, 1, n. 74
f. 15 **IV**, App. D, n. 92
8 J 31, f. 4 ix, A, 4, n. 136
f. 6 ix, D, n. 24
8 J 32, f. 1 **III**, App. pt. I, gr. 5; **III**, App. pt. II, no. 203. viii, B, 4, n. 15; viii, B, 5, n. 25
f. 3 ii, 2, n. 36; ii, 4, n. 14; ii, 5, n. 52. iii, B, 2, n. 15; iii, D, n. 58. vii, B, 3, n. 50
f. 4 vii, A, 2, n. 7; vii, B, 3, n. 50. **IV**, App. A, II. ix, A, 3, n. 24
f. 6 vii, B, 2, n. 22
8 J 33, f. 4 x, A, 3, n. 306
f. 8*v* iii, D, n. 10 (cited as TS 8 J 33, f. 38*v*). ix, A, 1, n. 138
f. 10 **II**, App. A, sec. 133; **II**, App. B, sec 69. v, B, 2, n. 78
f. 10*v*, sec. *a* ii, 5, n. 50. **II**, App. A, sec. 22
f. 10*v*, sec. *b* iii, F, n. 92. **II**, App. A, sec. 23

f. 38 iii, D, n. 10 (mistake for TS 8 J 33, f. 8*v*)
8 J 34, f. 1 viii, C, 1, n. 141
f. 4 viii, A, 3, n. 17. ix, A, 1, n. 92
f. 10 **III**, App. pt. II, no. 283. viii, C, 1, n. 50; viii, C, 3, n. 7. x, A, 3, n. 62
8 J 35, f. 1 vii, C, 1, c, n. 47
f. 5 **IV**, App. A, I
f. 11 viii, D, n. 54
8 J 36, f. 2 iii, B, 3, n. 5. x, B, 2, n. 88
f. 5 vii, A, 3, n. 42
8 J 37, f. 1 ii, 4, n. 67. ix, A, 5, n. 52
f. 5 ix, A, 2, n. 164
f. 11 x, A, 2, n. 227
8 J 39, f. 12 iii, A, 1, n. 26. iv, 7, n. 28. vii, A, 2, n. 29
8 J 40, f. 1 x, B, 2, n. 143
f. 8 iii, A, 1, n. 1. x, A, 1, n. 94; x, A, 2, n. 371
8 J 41, f. 1*v* **II**, App. C, sec. 86
f. 2 iii, D, n. 39
f. 8 viii, C, 1, n. 229
f. 11 v, B, 1, nn. 136, 142; v, B, 2, n. 66; v, D, 1, n. 12; v, D, 2, nn. 26, 48. vi, 2, n. 15. ix, A, 4, n. 141
f. 12*v* ix, A, 5, n. 50
f. 13 ix, A, 1, n. 112; ix, A, 3, n. 82. x, A, 2, n. 352
f. 13*v* **II**, App. B, sec. 75. viii, C, 4, n. 185
8 Ja 1, f. 2 vi, 12, n. 32
f. 3*v* viii, A, 1, n. 57
f. 4 iv, 3, n. 62. x, B, 1, n. 40
f. 5 iii, E, n. 23. iv, 8, n. 80
8 Ja 2, f. 1n **II**, App. D, sec. 7. viii, A, 1, n. 75
8 K 10, f. 5 v, B, 2, n. 98
8 K 20, f. 1 vii, B, 3, n. 11
f. 1*v* viii, C, 3, n. 118
8 K 22, f. 1 ii, 4, n. 53 (mistake for TS 8 K 22, f. 6). **II**, App. D, sec. 32. vi, 9, n. 22. viii, B, 4, n. 94. x, B, 3, n. 64
f. 6 ii, 4, n. 53 (cited as TS 8 K 22, f. 1). viii, A, 1, n. 54. x, D, n. 303 (cited as TS 8 K 22)
f. 12*v* vi, 12, n. 98
TS 10 G 5, f. 7 x, C, 4, n. 122 (formerly TS 6 J 9, f. 1)
10 H 3, fs. 11–12 v, A, 2, n. 40. vii, C, 1, a, n. 33
10 J 1 vi, 7, n. 22; vi, 8, n. 9
10 J 2, f. 1 vi, 10, nn. 27, 45. x, A, 2, n. 305
fs. 1–40 viii, C, 3, n. 64
f. 4 viii, C, n. 30
f. 6 viii, C, 3, n. 121
f. 7*v* viii, C, 3, n. 95
f. 8 viii, C, 3, n. 121
f. 11 viii, C, 3, n. 121
f. 12 vi, 11, n. 17
f. 15 ii, 7, n. 101. viii, C, 3, n. 95
f. 17 viii, C, 3, n. 95
f. 35 viii, C, 3, n. 121
f. 37 viii, C, 3, n. 121
f. 38 viii, C, 3, n. 121
f. 39 viii, C, 3, n. 84
10 J 4, f. 1 iii, F, n. 84
f. 2 iii, E, n. 13. iv, 7, n. 15
f. 3 viii, C, 4, n. 107

f. 4 x, D, n. 320
f. 7 iii, B, 3, n. 12. **II**, App. D, sec. 23. vii, C, 2, n. 8. viii, A, 3, n. 30
f. 9 ii, 7, n. 42. viii, A, 2, n. 66
f. 10 vi, 13, n. 6. viii, C, 3, n. 31
f. 11 ii, 5, n. 49. viii, C, 1, n. 55
f. 11*v* **II**, App. A, sec. 100. v, B, 1, n. 115. x, A, 1, n. 64; x, B, 3, n. 74
f. 12 v, C, 4, n. 16
f. 15 iii, F, n. 186
10 J 5, f. 1 **I**, App. D, n. 17
f. 2 viii, C, 3, n. 24; viii, D, n. 73
f. 4 viii, C, 4, n. 127. ix, B, n. 151
f. 5 vii, B, 1, n. 54
f. 6 x, C, 4, nn. 72, 76, 90, 92, 93
f. 8 ii, 6, n. 20
f. 9 viii, C, 4, n. 22. x, B, 1, n. 104
f. 10 iv, 3, n. 71. viii, C, 3, n. 67. x, C, 5, n. 93
f. 11 **II**, App. C, sec. 3. v, B, 1, n. 110. viii, A, 1, n. 60
f. 12 i, 3, n. 5. iv, 9, n. 29. vii, C, 1, c, n. 16. x, B, 2, nn. 63, 85
f. 14 vi, 13, n. 53
f. 15 ii, 2, n. 36. vi, 11, n. 53. viii, A, 1, n. 60. **IV**, App. D, n. 229
f. 16 viii, D, n. 162. ix, A, 2, n. 120
f. 17 vii, C, 1, b, n. 40
f. 19 viii, D, n. 86
f. 21 iii, F, n. 89. vi, 9, n. 17
f. 24 i, 2, n. 51. ix, A, 4, n. 65
f. 25 vi, 13, n. 7
10 J 6, f. 2 ii, 5, n. 37. iv, 3, n. 80. vii, C, 1, d, n. 23
f. 3 viii, D, n. 96
f. 4 ix, C, 1, n. 72; ix, C, 2, n. 5
f. 4*v* x, A, 3, n. 10
f. 5 viii, C, 2, n. 60. x, A, 2, n. 369; x, A, 3, n. 286
f. 6 viii, A, 3, n. 58; viii, C, 1, n. 211
f. 7 x, A, 3, n. 41
f. 14 ii, 5, n. 65
f. 16 viii, C, 3, n. 113
10 J 7, f. 3 viii, C, 2, n. 117
f. 4 vii, C, 1, c, n. 55. viii, A, 2, n. 47. ix, A, 1, n. 162
f. 5 viii, B, 3, n. 85; viii, C, 2, n. 83
f. 6 x, A, 3, n. 196
f. 6, sec. *a* viii, A, 3, n. 41
f. 6, p. 2, item *a* viii, B, 2, n. 43
f. 6*b* ix, A, 1, n. 142
f. 6*b*, col. I **II**, App. D, secs. 19, 20
f. 6*b*, sec. 2 iii, D, n. 11
f. 6*b*, sec. 3 **I**, App. C, sec. 13
f. 6*c* **III**, App. pt. II, no. 64. x, A, 3, n. 197
f. 6*d*, sec. 1 ii, 5, n. 64
f. 6*d*, sec. 2 ii, 7, n. 33. iii, F, n. 123
f. 6*d*, sec. 4 iii, F, n. 196
f. 10*c* x, A, 3, n. 61
f. 10*v* viii, D, n. 186
f. 13 **III**, App. pt. II, no. 134. viii, B, 4, n. 54. ix, A, 2, nn. 114, 133
f. 14*v* vi, 4, n. 4
f. 17 viii, C, 4, n. 86

f. 18 ix, C, 2, n. 11
f. 27 x, B, 1, n. 103
f. 27*v* ix, C, 1, n. 174
10 J 8, f. 2 ix, A, 1, n. 31
f. 7 ix, C, 1, n. 139
f. 9 viii, A, 3, n. 54. x, C, 3, n. 38
f. 10*v* vii, A, 2, n. 37
10 J 9, f. 1 viii, A, 2, n. 39; viii, C, 2, n. 131. x, A, 3, n. 289
f. 2 iii, C, n. 5
f. 3 **I**, App. D, n. 7. iii, B, 1, n. 12; iii, B, 4, n. 5; iii, G, n. 5. iv, 5, n. 8; iv, 8, n. 70; iv, 11, n. 17. x, C, 3, n. 10
f. 5 iii, A, 1, n. 31. iv, 3, n. 58; iv, 4, n. 3. vii, A, 2, n. 16
f. 9 ii, 4, n. 2. iv, 8, n. 80
f. 13 viii, A, 2, n. 79; viii, C, 1, n. 82
f. 15 viii, A, 2, n. 18
f. 16 ii, 5, n. 17. v, B, 2, n. 55. viii, C, 1, n. 214
f. 18 iv, 8, n. 68
f. 21 iii, D, n. 12. iv, 4, n. 42; iv, 12, n. 18. vii, C, 1, c, n. 38. x, A, 1, n. 8
f. 24 vi, 5, n. 9
f. 24*v* vi, 6, n. 13. ix, B, nn. 437, 481
f. 26 iv, 8, n. 26. v, A, 2, n. 5. x, B, 1, n. 125
f. 27 viii, A, 2, n. 14
f. 28 v, D, 2, n. 42
f. 30 **I**, App. C, sec. 10. iii, G, n. 21
f. 32 vi, 9, n. 41. viii, A, 2, n. 48; viii, C, 1, n. 119
10 J 10, f. 2 v, C, 4, n. 21
f. 3 i, 3, n. 46. iv, 3, n. 42. vii, A, 3, n. 14. x, A, 2, n. 290
f. 5 ix, A, 4, n. 57; ix, B, n. 52
f. 7 v, B, 1, n. 46. vii, C, 1, b, n. 13
f. 9 v, C, 2, n. 18
f. 10 vii, C, 2, n. 25
f. 13 vi, 10, n. 1. viii, C, 1, n. 231
f. 14 iv, 8, n. 10. x, C, 1, n. 44
f. 15 viii, C, 1, n. 210
f. 18 viii, C, 1, n. 154
f. 20 x, A, 3, n. 310
f. 23 i, 3, n. 10 (cited as *India Book* 251). iii, E, n. 53; iii, G, n. 8. iv, 8, n. 33. viii, C, 4, n. 130
f. 24 iv, 3, n. 68. ix, B, n. 392
f. 25 iii, E, n. 13. iv, 5, n. 20; iv, 7, n. 24
f. 27 x, B, 4, n. 30
f. 29 ii, 3, n. 4. **IV**, App. D, n. 95. ix, A, 4, n. 204; ix, C, 1, n. 154
f. 30 iv, 3, n. 76. viii, C, 1, n. 155
10 J 11, f. 1 x, D, nn. 192, 229
f. 2 **IV**, App. D, n. 229
f. 3 ix, A, 5, n. 18
f. 4 **II**, App. A, sec. 155
f. 12 x, A, 2, n. 279
f. 13 viii, A, 2, n. 80; viii, C, 2, n. 71; viii, C, 3, n. 67; viii, C, 4, nn. 107, 123; viii, D, n. 56. x, B, 2, n. 84; x, C, 5, n. 93
f. 15 ix, A, 5, n. 35. x, C, 5, n. 12
f. 17 iii, B, 1, n. 9. iv, 3, n. 55
f. 22 iv, 5, n. 16. viii, C, 2, n. 126
f. 23 iv, 7, n. 2
f. 26 **II**, App. A, sec. 113. ix, A, 1, n. 200
f. 27 iv, 12, n. 18

f. 30 viii, C, 1, n. 178
f. 31 ii, 7, nn. 49, 64
10 J 12, f. 1 viii, C, 1, n. 120; viii, C, 4, n. 172; viii, D, n. 221. ix, A, 1, n. 37; ix, B, n. 123
f. 3 ix, C, 1, nn. 67, 69
f. 4 iv, 12, n. 42. viii, A, 3, n. 39
f. 5 ix, C, 1, n. 164
f. 8 x, A, 1, n. 24
f. 10 vi, 12, n. 37. **IV**, App. C, 2. ix, A, 4, nn. 33, 145; ix, A, 5, nn. 18, 79. x, A, 2, n. 266
f. 14 viii, C, 3, nn. 131, 142. x, A, 2, n. 421
f. 16 ix, A, 1, n. 54; ix, B, n. 547; ix, C, 2, n. 43
f. 17 v, B, 2, n. 104
f. 18 viii, C, 1, n. 87
f. 20 ii, 3, n. 1. iv, 12, n. 34. vii, A, 1, n. 3. x, B, 2, nn. 105, 129
f. 22 iv, 5, n. 17. v, C, 1, n. 18
f. 24 ii, 7, n. 37. viii, C, 1, n. 25
f. 25 v, C, 2, n. 37. vi, 9, n. 17
f. 26 ii, 5, n. 81. iii, D, nn. 11, 25, 78; iii, F, n. 120; iii, G, n. 1. iv, 11, n. 19. ix, B, n. 223
f. 27 x, D, n. 332
f. 28 viii, C, 1, n. 26
10 J 13, f. 1 **II**, App. B, sec. 60. vii, A, 3, n. 34
f. 3 ii, 4, n. 100. vii, C, 1, b, n. 24
f. 4 viii, B, 1, n. 27
f. 5*v* viii, B, 3, n. 86. ix, B, n. 222
f. 8 x, D, n. 307
f. 10 ii, 5, n. 60 (mistake for 10 J 30, f. 10). iv, 1, n. 4. vii, C, 1, d, n. 27. viii, C, 2, n. 130. ix, C, 1, n. 119. x, B, 1, n. 17
f. 11 vii, B, 1, n. 38; vii, D, 2, n. 8. x, C, 1, n. 19
f. 12 viii, C, 2, n. 106
f. 13 viii, A, Introd., n. 3. x, B, 1, n. 74
f. 14 x, D, n. 305
f. 15 x, B, 1, n. 27
f. 16 ix, C, 1, n. 23
f. 18 viii, C, 2, n. 27
f. 21 iii, G, n. 13
f. 23 ix, A, 2, n. 123. x, C, 3, n. 18
f. 24 viii, C, 2, n. 132. ix, C, 1, n. 7
10 J 14, f. 4 **I**, App. C, sec. 21. ii, 2, n. 19
f. 5 vi, 12, n. 46. x, D, n. 310
f. 6 viii, C, 2, n. 124
f. 9 viii, B, 1, n. 27. x, C, 3, n. 18; x, C, 5, n. 16
f. 11 x, A, 2, n. 340; x, B, 2, n. 146
f. 12 iv, 1, n. 4. vii, C, 1, d, n. 27. ix, C, 1, n. 119. x, B, 1, n. 17
f. 13 ix, B, n. 202
f. 16 vii, A, 1, n. 47
f. 20 ii, 6, n. 12. iii, F, n. 182. iv, 3, n. 28; iv, 5, n. 14; iv, 8, n. 32; iv, 12, n. 4. v, B, 2, n. 81. viii, A, 2, n. 36 (cited as TS 10 J 24, f. 20) ix, B, n. 51; ix, C, 1, n. 145. x, A, 2, n. 264
f. 24 vi, 12, n. 57
f. 27 iii, F, nn. 59, 111; iii, G, n. 16. ix, A, 2, nn. 36, 41; ix, B, n. 75
f. 29 viii, A, 2, n. 11
f. 30 v, D, 2, n. 55
10 J 15, f. 2 ix, A, 1, n. 209. x, A, 1, n. 32
f. 3 iv, 7, n. 26. ix, B, n. 304. x, D, n. 209

f. 4 ii, 4, n. 106; ii, 5, n. 42. iii, D, n. 11
f. 5 iv, 2, n. 9; iv, 3, n. 83; iv, 8, n. 31
f. 6 iii, D, nn. 22, 44. iv, 3, nn. 74, 75
f. 8 viii, A, 2, n. 37
f. 9 viii, C, 3, n. 69. x, B, 1, n. 15
f. 11 iv, 3, n. 21
f. 12 viii, C, 1, nn. 11, 248
f. 14*v* ix, B, n. 166
f. 15 iv, 3, n. 40. vii, B, 1, n. 14. viii, C, 2, n. 151
f. 19 ii, 5, n. 70. iv, 3, nn. 68, 74
f. 19*v* ix, B, n. 145
f. 23 viii, C, 2, n. 30. x, B, 2, n. 9
f. 25 iii, E, n. 48; iii, F, n. 41
f. 26 viii, A, 2, n. 79; viii, B, 3, n. 96 (cited as TS 13 J 15, f. 26); viii, B, 5, n. 33. **IV**, App. A, IV. ix, A, 1, n. 211; ix, C, 1, n. 124. **IV**, App. D, n. 134 (cited as TS 10 J 25, f. 26)
f. 27 **II**, App. C, sec. 91. v, C, 2, n. 18. viii, C, 4, n. 134. x, A, 2, n. 216
f. 29 v, B, 1, n. 30
f. 32 v, B, 1, n. 30
f. 33 iii, E, n. 10. x, A, 2, n. 16. x, C, 2, n. 15
10 J 16, f. 1 viii, A, 2, n. 61
f. 2 i, 2, n. 17. iv, 10, n. 3. x, A, 3, n. 88
f. 4 viii, C, 3, n. 60
f. 6 **II**, App. C, sec. 53. v, C, 2, n. 411. viii, C, 1, n. 201. ix, A, 4, n. 211
f. 8 vii, D, 2, n. 7
f. 10 iv, 8, n. 28. **IV**, App. C, 2
f. 11 x, B, 1, n. 24
f. 12 v, A, 2, n. 43; v, B, 1, n. 108. vi, 4, n. 32
f. 14 viii, C, 1, n. 53; viii, C, 2, n. 79
f. 15 iv, 8, n. 73. ix, C, 1, nn. 68, 94
f. 16 x, A, 2, n. 248; x, B, 1, n. 33
f. 17 iv, 8, n. 40. viii, B, 1, n. 40. x, B, 4, n. 71; x, D, n. 177
f. 18 viii, C, 2, n. 12. ix, B, n. 224
f. 19 viii, C, 2, n. 155
f. 25 ii, 4, n. 79
10 J 17, f. 3 vi, 13, n. 6. viii, C, 2, n. 116
f. 4 x, A, 1, n. 147
f. 6 vii, B, 3, n. 32
f. 7*v* x, B, 1, n. 23; x, B, 2, n. 104
f. 8 viii, C, 2, n. 117. x, B, 2, n. 95; x, D, n. 38
f. 9 **II**, App. D, sec. 20
f. 10 ix, C, 1, n. 90. x, A, 1, n. 9
f. 12 vi, 13, n. 61
f. 13 vii, C, 1, a, n. 36
f. 14 vi, 11, n. 35. viii, C, 2, n. 101
f. 16 vii, A, 3, n. 9. viii, B, 2, n. 45; viii, D, n. 12. x, A, 2, nn. 344, 356
f. 17 x, A, 2, nn. 301, 348
f. 18 ii, 2, n. 25; ii, 6, n. 22. iv, 12, n. 35
f. 19 vii, C, 2, n. 41
f. 20 vii, C, 2, n. 43
f. 21 ix, A, 2, n. 155; ix, A, 3, n. 47. x, B, 4, n. 30
f. 22 vi, 12, n. 73. viii, A, 2, n. 54. x, B, 2, n. 84
f. 23 ii, 5, n. 10
f. 25 vi, 6, n. 3; vi, 7, n. 19; vi, 9, n. 21. vii, D, 1, n. 32. viii, C, 4, n. 38. x, B, 3, n. 65; x, C, 3, n. 15; x, C, 5, n. 14

10 J 18, f. 1	iv, 12, n. 35. viii, A, 1, n. 14; viii, C, 2, n. 94
f. 2	x, B, 4, n. 152
f. 3	ix, A, 1, n. 54
f. 5	v, B, 2, n. 31. vi, 4, n. 11
f. 6	viii, C, 1, n. 2
f. 10	viii, A, 3, n. 7; viii, C, 2, n. 123. x, B, 1, n. 10
f. 11	vi, 13, n. 61
f. 13	vii, C, 1, b, nn. 13, 32
f. 14	iii, F, n. 100
f. 15	v, A, 2, n. 67
f. 16	iv, 4, n. 18; iv, 7, n. 23 (cited as 10 J 18, f. 19). ix, C, 2, n. 53
f. 19	iv, 7, n. 23 (mistake for 10 J 18, f. 16)
f. 21	iv, 12, n. 18
f. 22*v*	vi, 7, n. 27. vii, C, 2, n. 41
10 J 19, f. 3	iv, 10, n. 12
f. 5	iv, 3, n. 74 (mistake for 10 J 29, f. 5)
f. 7	vi, 13, n. 14. viii, A, 2, n. 69. x, A, 1, nn. 77, 130
f. 8	ix, B, n. 166
f. 10	vi, 2, n. 4. ix, C, 1, n. 109
f. 15	viii, B, 2, n. 69
f. 16	ii, 5, n. 65. iii, D, n. 44. iv, 3, n. 66. v, B, 2, n. 53
f. 19	iii, E, n. 30. iv, 8, n. 44; iv, 10, n. 30; iv, 12, n. 18
f. 20	iii, F, n. 182. v, B, 2, n. 81
f. 26	iv, 4, n. 25. x, C, 1, n. 30
10 J 20, f. 2	x, B, 4, n. 149
f. 3	viii, C, 4, n. 18
f. 4	iv, 3, nn. 15, 46; iv, 8, nn. 49, 80
f. 5	ii, 3, n. 22; ii, 5, n. 50. **II**, App. A, sec. 104
f. 5*v*	**II**, App. A, sec. 103. v, A, 2, n. 67. vi, 12, n. 55. ix, A, 1, n. 178. x, A, 1, n. 64
f. 6	viii, C, 4, n. 35
f. 7	iv, 3, n. 85
f. 9	iv, 3, n. 83
f. 13	iv, 3, n. 85
f. 16	iii, F, nn. 74, 119
f. 18	viii, B, 3, n. 87
f. 19	x, C, 3, n. 14
f. 21	viii, D, n. 112
10 J 21, f. 1	ii, 4, n. 12
f. 2	iii, D, n. 24
f. 4*a*	ix, B, nn. 418, 446, 453, 508
f. 4*b*	**IV**, App. C, 2. ix, A, 4, nn. 2, 28, 49, 51; ix, A, 5, n. 40
f. 4*c*	ix, A, 4, nn. 176, 196, 219
f. 4*d*	**III**, App. pt. II, no. 167. viii, B, 2, n. 65; viii, B, 5, n. 17
f. 4*e*	ix, A, 4, n. 208
f. 5	**III**, App. pt. II, no. 86. viii, B, 4, n. 57. ix, A, 4, n. 192; ix, B, nn. 409, 447, 524
f. 6	viii, B, 4, n. 53
f. 10	vi, 12, n. 50. viii, C, 4, n. 4
f. 13	**III**, App. pt. II, no. 232. viii, B, 4, n. 38
f. 14	viii, C, 4, n. 5
f. 16	viii, C, 3, n. 33
f. 17	**IV**, App. A, II. ix, A, 3, nn. 24, 33
10 J 22, f. 7 (was 12.857)	**II**, App. B, sec. 55. v, A, 2, n. 32; v, B, 1, n. 3
10 J 23, f. 1	ii, 7, n. 108
10 J 24, f. 1 *c-d*	viii, C, 1, n. 223

f. 2 x, B, 4, n. 142
f. 4 iv, 2, n. 30; iv, 3, n. 19. vii, A, 3, n. 17. ix, B, n. 276. x, A, 2, n. 303
f. 6 now TS 13 J 4, f. 4
f. 7 v, C, 4, n. 6. vi, 10, n. 49
f. 8*v* vii, D, 2, n. 11
f. 9 v, B, 1, n. 5; v, C, 4, n. 60
f. 20 viii, A, 2, n. 36 (mistake for TS 10 J 14, f. 20)
10 J 25, f. 3 viii, A, 1, n. 56. x, A, 1, n. 148
f. 8 viii, A, 2, n. 66; viii, D, n. 173
f. 26 **IV**, App. D, n. 134 (mistake for TS 10 J 15, f. 26)
10 J 26, f. 1 vi, 12, n. 27. viii, C, 1, n. 175
f. 2 vi, 12, n. 21. viii, A, 1, n. 42
f. 4 viii, C, 3, nn. 45, 152
f. 5 **I**, App. D, sec. 73
f. 7 vi, 10, n. 16. x, A, 2, n. 205
f. 9 **II**, App. D, sec. 9
f. 10 iii, F, n. 188. vi, 13, n. 14
f. 13*v* **II**, App. C, sec. 35
10 J 27, f. 3*a* v, A, 1, n. 1; v, B, 1, n. 40. **III**, App. pt. I, gr. 5; **III**, App. pt. II, no. 126. viii, B, 2, n. 75; viii, B, 5, nn. 36, 39, 47
f. 3, item II viii, C, 3, n. 111
f. 3*c* **I**, App. C, sec. 6. ii, 2, n. 19. x, C, 2, n. 28
f. 4 iii, C, n. 22
f. 8 iv, 9, nn. 7, 12
f. 12 viii, B, 4, n. 34; viii, C, 3, n. 114
10 J 28, f. 1 **III**, App. pt. II, no. 209
f. 2 v, B, 1, n. 142. vii, D, 2, n. 2
f. 9 ix, B, n. 545
f. 11*v* viii, D, n. 11
f. 13 **I**, App. D, sec. 59. **II**, App. A, sec. 143. ix, A, 2, n. 122; ix, A, 3, n. 81
f. 16 ii, 7, nn. 47, 97. **IV**, App. D, n. 112
f. 18 vi, 10, n. 44
10 J 29, f. 1 vii, B, 1, n. 47. viii, B, 1, n. 58
f. 4 v, B, 2, n. 95; v, C, 4, n. 6. vi, 10, n. 49
f. 5 ii, 5, n. 19. iii, C, nn. 22, 26; iii, D, nn. 44, 84. iv, 3, nn. 74 (cited as TS 10 J 19, f. 5), 75. v, A, 2, n. 55; v, B, 2, n. 53. vii, B, 3, n. 40. viii, C, 4, n. 39
f. 13 v, D, 2, n. 44
f. 15 viii, A, 2, n. 13; viii, C, 1, n. 66
10 J 30, f. 7 viii, C, 4, n. 82. x, B, 1, n. 21
f. 8 x, A, 3, n. 308
f. 9 vi, 2, n. 39. x, A, 2, n. 248
f. 10*v* ii, 5, n. 60 (cited as 10 J 13, f. 10*v*). vii, A, 3, n. 44
f. 11 viii, B, 1, n. 43. x, D, n. 311
f. 14 v, A, 1, n. 34
f. 15 iii, F, n. 134
10 J 31, f. 3 x, B, 4, nn. 103, 105
f. 6 x, A, 2, n. 55
f. 9 x, B, 1, n. 22
f. 10*v* ix, D, n. 17
f. 13 iv, 5, n. 1. vii, A, 3, n. 25. ix, C, 1, n. 73
f. 14 viii, C, 1, n. 96
10 J 32, f. 8 v, B, 1, n. 124. vii, B, 1, n. 32
f. 9 v, B, 1, nn. 124, 145. vii, B, 1, n. 32
f. 10 **I**, App. D, sec. 37. ii, 5, n. 34. iii, A, 2, n. 11. iv, 8, n. 31. viii, D, n. 118

f. 12	**II**, App. C, sec. 36. x, A, 1, n. 64
TS 10 K 7, f. 1	vii, A, 3, n. 28. viii, C, 3, n. 72
f. 2	vi, 8, n. 11
10 K 8, f. 13	ii, 7, n. 19
10 K 16, f. 12	vi, 13, n. 53
10 K 20, f. 1	**II**, App. C, sec. 28. v, D, 2, n. 45
f. 2	v, B, 1, n. 106
TS 13 J 1, f. 2	vii, B, 1, n. 7. **III**, App. pt. I, gr. 4; **III**, App. pt. II, no. 243. viii, C, 1, n. 180; viii, D, n. 5
f. 3	**I**, App. C, sec. 1. **II**, App. C, sec. 1. **II**, App. D, secs. 4, 5. vii, A, 3, n. 1; vii, B, 2, n. 2; vii, B, 3, nn. 22, 50
f. 4	vii, B, 3, nn. 20, 50
f. 5	viii, D, n. 105. ix, A, 1, n. 73; ix, A, 3, n. 86
f. 6	viii, C, 1, n. 181
f. 7	ii, 1, n. 19. v, A, 1, n. 3. vi, 10, n. 42. vii, B, 2, n. 8; vii, B, 3, n. 3. viii, B, 2, n. 34
f. 8	**I**, App. D, sec. 85. ix, C, 1, n. 112. x, B, 5, n. 49
f. 9	**II**, App. C, sec. 1. **II**, App. D, sec. 5
f. 10	vi, 11, n. 59. vii, B, 3, nn. 22, 44
f. 12	vi, 11, n. 43. viii, C, 1, nn. 103, 118. **IV**, App. D, n. 267
f. 13	ii, 3, n. 16. v, B, 1, n. 80. vi, 11, n. 43
f. 14	vii, B, 3, n. 21. x, A, 2, n. 390
f. 15	vii, B, 1, n. 48
f. 17	viii, C, 2, n. 169
f. 18	**II**, App. D, sec. 10. viii, D, n. 15
f. 20	iii, F, n. 199
f. 21	**II**, App. D, sec. 22. vi, 13, n. 9. vii, B, 1, n. 43. viii, D, nn. 27, 165. ix, A, 2, n. 149; ix, A, 3, n. 110. **IV**, App. D, n. 135
f. 22	ii, 6, n. 11. vii, B, 3, n. 52. x, A, 2, n. 212
f. 23	v, B, 2, n. 33. viii, D, n. 158
13 J 2, f. 1	viii, C, 4, n. 167
f. 2	iii, C, nn. 5, 16. viii, C, 4, n. 108
f. 3	**II**, App. D, sec. 10. v, A, 1, n. 43; v, A, 2, n. 51. vi, 13, n. 2. **III**, App. pt. II, no. 143. viii, B, 2, n. 79; viii, B, 4, n. 22; viii, B, 5, n. 36. ix, A, 1, n. 191; ix, A, 3, n. 77
f. 4	i, 3, n. 45
f. 5	ii, 1, n. 10. iii, B, 2, n. 30; iii, F, n. 5
f. 6*v*	x, A, 3, n. 25
f. 8	viii, B, 1, n. 59; viii, B, 2, n. 78; viii, C, 4, n. 62
f. 10	ii, 5, n. 71. vi, 11, n. 17
f. 12	ii, 5, n. 71. viii, C, 1, n. 223
f. 13	vii, B, 1, n. 42
f. 14	v, B, 2, n. 84. viii, B, 3, n. 72. ix, B, n. 545
f. 15	iii, F, nn. 124, 176
f. 16	viii, C, 1, n. 66; viii, C, 3, n. 59. ix, A, 2, n. 45; ix, A, 5, n. 36
f. 17	**III**, App. pt. I, gr. 7. viii, C, 4, n. 171; viii, D, nn. 97, 98, 101
f. 18	**I**, App. D, sec. 82. ix, B, n. 442
f. 19	v, A, 1, n. 8. vii, B, 3, n. 21
f. 20	ii, 7, n. 41
f. 22	viii, C, 1, nn. 72, 132, 167
f. 24	vii, B, 1, n. 12; vii, C, 1, b, n. 24
f. 25	i, 3, n. 40. vii, C, 1, b, nn. 1, 12. viii, B, 5, n. 21; viii, C, 1, nn. 22, 207; viii, D, n. 164. **IV**, App. A, III. ix, A, 1, n. 92
13 J 3, f. 1	**III**, App. pt. I, gr. 6. viii, C, 1, n. 207. ix, A, 4, n. 181; ix, A, 5, n. 83

f. 2 iii, A, 1, n. 15; iii, F, n. 97. vi, 12, n. 52. vii, C, 2, n. 9. **III**, App. pt. I, gr. 6; **III**, App. pt. II, no. 269. ix, B, nn. 250, 286. x, A, 2, n. 411; x, A, 3, nn. 24, 65, 191, 193
f. 3 ii, 7, n. 56. viii, A, 2, n. 80; viii, A, 3, n. 25; viii, B, 2, n. 33; viii, B, 5, n. 36; viii, C, 1, n. 149. ix, A, 1, n. 167; ix, B, n. 293; ix, C, 1, n. 76. x, A, 2, n. 422; x, A, 3, nn. 130, 193
f. 4 **I**, App. D, sec. 52. i, 3, n. 21. ii, 4, n. 26. iii, D, n. 14. iv, 8, n. 43; iv, 10, nn. 5, 26; iv, 11, n. 14. vi, 12, n. 21. vii, C, 1, c, nn. 2, 23; vii, D, 1, n. 11. viii, C, 4, n. 47
f. 5 **I**, App. C, sec. 12
f. 6 ii, 4, n. 111. iii, F, n. 197. vii, C, 1, b, n. 27; vii, C, 1, d, n. 14. **IV**, App. A, VI
f. 7 ii, 7, nn. 58, 71, 72. iii, B, 4, n. 6; iii, F, n. 5. viii, D, n. 188
f. 8 vi, 11, n. 15
f. 9 ii, 4, n. 90
f. 10 vi, 12, n. 50. vii, B, 3, n. 37. ix, A, 4, n. 7
f. 10, item II viii, C, 4, n. 89
item III **III**, App. pt. I, gr. 1; **III**, App. pt. II, no. 170. ix, A, 4, n. 49; ix, B, nn. 435, 531
f. 10*c* ix, B, n. 460
f. 10*c*, col. I ix, B, n. 408. **IV**, App.D, n. 172.
col. III ix, A, 4, n. 57; ix, A, 5, n. 28
f. 10, item IV **III**, App. pt. I, gr. 1; **III**, App. pt. II, no. 66. viii, B, 3, n. 81
item V **III**, App. pt. I, gr. 1; **III**, App. pt. II, no. 275. viii, B, 4, n. 53
f. 10(*e*) **III**, App. pt. II, no. 309. viii, C, 3, n. 31. ix, A, 4, n. 81; ix, A, 5, nn. 6, 8, 18, 44, 88
f. 11 viii, C, 3, n. 45
f. 12 **II**, App. D, sec. 23. vi, 12, n. 50. vii, C, 1, b, n. 24. viii, A, 1, n. 39. ix, A, 3, n. 68. x, C, n. 40; x, D, n. 80
f. 13 **III**, App. pt. I, gr. 8. viii, C, 1, n. 106
f. 14 **III**, App. pt. I, gr. 1; **III**, App. pt. II, no. 248 viii, C, 3, n. 110
f. 15 **I**, App. C, sec. 14
f. 16 ii, 7, nn. 64, 65, 71. **II**, App. D, sec. 25
f. 17 vi, 12, nn. 25, 88. **III**, App. pt. II, no. 240. viii, A, 1, n. 84; viii, C, 3, n. 8
f. 18 ii, 5, nn. 31, 82 (cited as 13 J 6, f. 11). iii, F, n. 212; iii, G, n. 2. x, A, 3, n. 40
f. 19 **I**, App. D, sec. 66
f. 20 v, B, 1, nn. 3, 104, 146
f. 21 **I**, App. D, sec. 67. iii, F, n. 155. vi, 9, n. 22; vi, 10, n. 22. vii, B, 1, n. 70. x, D, n. 319
f. 22 v, A, 2, n. 18. viii, C, 3, n. 113
f. 23 **I**, App. D, sec. 63
f. 24 iii, F, n. 156
f. 25 v, A, 2, n. 18. vii, B, 2, n. 8. viii, C, 4, n. 60
f. 26 viii, B, 2, n. 47
f. 27 i, 2, nn. 48, 56. iii, B, 2, n. 52
f. 27*v* vii, B, 1, n. 70. viii, D, n. 84. x, D, n. 322
13 J 4, f. 1 **I**, App. D, sec. 68. v, B, 1, n. 53. vi, 10, n. 34. viii, B, 4, n. 37. x, A, 1, n. 36
f. 2 ii, 5, n. 66; ii, 7, n. 49
f. 4 ii, 5, n. 60. iii, F, n. 127
f. 4*v* **I**, App. D, sec. 69. ii, 5, n. 46. vii, A, 2, n. 17. ix, A, 2, nn. 8, 136; ix, A, 3, nn. 54, 68
f. 7 vi, 5, n. 3. vii, C, 2, n. 6. viii, C, 1, n. 243. x, A, 3, n. 312
f. 8 i, 2, n. 33. vi, 4, n. 25

f. 9 ii, 5, n. 76
f. 10 x, A, 3, n. 222
f. 11 ii, 4, n. 47
f. 12 vii, B, 3, n. 42
f. 13 iii, F, nn. 124, 136
f. 14 v, D, 2, n. 21. ix, A, 2, n. 58
f. 15 I, App. D, sec. 84. **III**, App. pt. II, no. 93. viii, B, 4, nn. 5, 87; viii, C, 4, n. 164
f. 16 I, Introduction, n. 48. v, A, 2, n. 82. viii, C, 1, n. 224. x, A, 1, n. 67
13 J 5, f. 1 iii, F, nn. 145, 185. vii, B, 1, nn. 11, 44, 53, 54; vii, B, 3, n. 10; vii, D, 1, n. 32. viii, C, 4, n. 85
f. 1*c* viii, C, 3, n. 117
f. 2 iii, F, n. 66. **II**, App. A, sec. 13. vii, B, 1, n. 7
f. 3 ii, 7, n. 64. iii, F, n. 210. vii, D, 1, n. 33
f. 3, item II ix, C, 2, n. 16
f. 3*v*, item I ix, C, 2, n. 16
f. 4 vii, B, 3, n. 42
f. 5 **III**, App. pt. I, gr. 7; **III**, App. pt. II, no. 294. viii, B, 4, n. 48; viii, C, 3, n. 45
13 J 6, f. 3 iv, 2, n. 20. v, A, 1, n. 28. vi, 11, n. 59
f. 5 ii, 2, n. 4. iii, B, 2, n. 53; iii, F, nn. 23, 105, 111, 171. vii, C, 1, d, n. 10
f. 6 v, B, 1, n. 7
f. 7 ii, 7, nn. 64, 74
f. 9 **III**, App. pt. II, no. 379. viii, B, 4, nn. 34, 37
f. 9, col. I ix, B, n. 434
f. 9*v* ix, A, 4, n. 216; ix, A, 5, nn. 15, 70; ix, B, nn. 310, 311, 446, 447, 472. **IV**, App. D, n. 142. x, A, 3, n. 306
f. 9*v*, col. I ix, B, nn. 465, 543
f. 10 ii, 5, n. 38. iii, F, n. 129
f. 11 ii, 5, n. 82 (mistake for 13 J 3, f. 18). iii, F, n. 204. viii, C, 3, n. 129
f. 14 v, C, 5, n. 5. vi, 11, n. 25; vi, 12, n. 63. **III**, App. pt. I, gr. 4. viii, B, 5, n. 37; viii, C, 2, n. 147
f. 15 x, A, 2, n. 231
f. 16 **II**, App. C, sec. 46. vi, 12, nn. 83, 88. x, A, 2, n. 203
f. 20 **II**, App. B, sec. 7
f. 21 v, B, 2, n. 38; vi, 9, n. 18; vi, 11, n. 29. viii, D, n. 98
f. 22 ii, 4, n. 21. viii, A, 2, n. 29. ix, A, 2, nn. 45, 136; ix, A, 4, n. 151; ix, B, n. 139
f. 26 v, B, 2, n. 28. viii, B, 4, n. 35
f. 27 ii, 4, n. 100. v, C, 4, n. 15. vi, 3, n. 15; vi, 4, nn. 11, 28; vi, 10, n. 4. viii, C, 4, n. 141; viii, D, n. 204. x, D, n. 77
f. 30 vii, C, 2, n. 13
f. 32 vii, A, 1, n. 11
f. 33 v, C, 2, n. 36. viii, B, 5, nn. 40, 77. x, C, 4, n. 48
13 J 7, f. 2 ix, A, 4, n. 130
f. 5 iii, D, n. 14. vii, C, 1, c, n. 38
f. 6 v, D, 1, n. 4
f. 8 **III**, App. pt. II, no. 372. ix, A, 4, nn. 40, 64, 164, 168. **IV**, App. D, n. 286
f. 10 iii, G, n. 2. x, B, 2, n. 64
f. 11 i, 3, n. 45
f. 17 x, B, 1, n. 141
f. 25 v, B, 1, nn. 13, 101, 144; v, B, 2, n. 14
f. 29 x, C, 4, n. 50

13 J 8, f. 1 iii, A, 1, n. 13. vii, D, 1, n. 20. viii, D, n. 102
f. 2 **I**, App. D, sec. 4. v, A, 1, n. 8. viii, C, 1, n. 197
f. 3 ii, 7, n. 55
f. 4 viii, A, 1, n. 95
f. 5 ii, 4, n. 12. iii, E, nn. 52, 73, 83 (cited as TS 13 J 18, f. 5). iv, 2, n. 2; iv, 3, n. 30. vi, 2, n. 25
f. 9 viii, A, 2, n. 25
f. 11*v* **II**, App. A, sec. 146. **II**, App. B, sec. 37. **II**, App. D, sec. 30. v, C, 4, n. 1. viii, D, n. 191. ix, A, 2, nn. 68, 117
f. 13 **I**, App. D, sec. 15. iii, E, n. 53. vii, A, 2, n. 16. viii, C, 2, n. 13 (cited as TS 13 J 18, f. 13)
f. 14 ii, 4, n. 63. **II**, App.C, sec. 4. v, D, 2, n. 29
f. 15 **II**, App. D, sec. 24
f. 18 iii, D, n. 44
f. 19 viii, C, 1, n. 173
f. 20 viii, A, 3, n. 42; viii, C, 4, n. 26
f. 22 viii, A, 2, n. 79
f. 23 viii, C, 1, nn. 24, 40, 44, 124; viii, C, 3, n. 87. ix, B, n. 537. x, B, 1, n. 36
f. 24 **III**, App. pt. II, no. 176. viii, B, 2, n. 65; viii, B, 3, n. 84; viii, B, 4, n. 32; viii, B, 5, nn. 2, 35, 50, 86
f. 25 ii, 5, nn. 11, 45. **II**, App. A, sec. 107. vi, 9, nn. 3, 22. ix, A, 1, n. 98
f. 25*v* v, B, 2, n. 12
f. 27 viii, A, 1, n. 95; viii, B, 1, n. 46. x, B, 3, n. 16
f. 28 **II**, App. D, sec. 30
f. 31 vii, D, 1, n. 19. viii, B, 2, n. 34; viii, C, 1, n. 225
13 J 9, f. 1 x, B, 1, n. 68
f. 2 v, A, 2, n. 34. vi, 4, n. 34. vii, D, 2, n. 6
f. 3 v, B, 1, n. 44. vi, 7, n. 12; vi, 10, n. 24; vi, 12, n. 14. viii, A, 1, n. 95. x, B, 1, n. 63
f. 4 ii, 5, n. 11. viii, A, 2, n. 21; viii, B, 1, n. 47; viii, C, 2, nn. 109, 122. x, B, 2, n. 45
f. 5 ii, 1, n. 20; ii, 4, nn. 12, 90. vi, 11, n. 41. vii, B, 3, n. 22. x, B, 1, n. 115
f. 6 v, B, 1, n. 94
f. 7 v, A, 1, n. 28. vi, 11, n. 59. vii, D, 1, n. 34
f. 8 viii, C, 4, nn. 121, 131
f. 10 ii, 5, n. 61. x, D, n. 316
f. 15 ix, C, 1, n. 190
f. 17 v, C, 1, n. 17
13 J 10, f. 5 i, 2, n. 58. **II**, App. B, sec. 55. v, B, 1, nn. 58, 69. vi, 11, n. 28
f. 13 ix, D, n. 19
13 J 11, f. 4 iv, 12, n. 2
f. 5 iii, F, n. 167. vii, A, 1, n. 43; vii, C, 1, c, n. 42; vii, C, 2, n. 46
f. 7 x, C, 5, n. 17
f. 9 ii, 5, n. 15. v, A, 1, n. 9. vi, 9, n. 37; vi, 10, n. 32
13 J 12, fs. 1–5 vii, B, 2, n. 27
f. 4 vii, B, 3, n. 40
13 J 13, f. 1 v, A, 2, n. 32. viii, D, n. 85
f. 2 v, A, 2, n. 33; v, B, 1, n. 64. vii, C, 1, a, n. 28
f. 4 x, A, 1, n. 22
f. 10 iv, 4, n. 21; iv, 11, n. 24. vii, C, 1, b, n. 34. viii, A, 2, n. 12
f. 11 **I**, App. D, sec. 33. iii, D, n. 78
f. 12 iv, 4, n. 22. v, A, 2, n. 46. viii, A, 2, n. 9

f. 13 v, A, 2, n. 39; v, D, 2, n. 9. viii, C, 2, nn. 53, 134. ix, C, 1, n. 167. x, A, 2, n. 132
f. 18 ii, 5, n. 71
f. 20 v, B, 1, n. 43
f. 21 iv, 3, n. 81. viii, B, 4, n. 96
f. 24 v, B, 2, n. 33. vii, A, 1, nn. 14, 25; vii, C, 1, c, n. 43
f. 27 ii, 5, n. 47. **IV**, App. A, IV
f. 28 v, B, 2, n. 104
13 J 14, f. 1 iv, 3, n. 19; iv, 10, n. 3. vii, A, 3, nn. 17, 23; vii, D, 1, n. 41
f. 2 i, 3, n. 7. ii, 4, n. 71. iv, 7, n. 12; iv, 12, n. 40. ix, B, nn. 158, 224. x, A, 2, n. 13
f. 3 ii, 6, n. 14. viii, B, 2, n. 19
f. 4 ii, 7, nn. 70, 79. iii, F, nn. 108, 111, 209. v, B, 2, nn. 61, 63. viii, A, 3, n. 61; viii, C, 2, n. 100. x, A, 3, n. 31; x, C, 5, n. 34
f. 5 vi, 12, n. 11. vii, A, 2, n. 32
f. 8 x, D, n. 199
f. 9 iii, E, n. 57; iii, G, n. 1. vii, C, 1, d, n. 21
f. 10 v, B, 1, nn. 7, 115
f. 11 x, C, 5, n. 11
f. 12 viii, A, 3, n. 63
f. 14 ii, 2, n. 17. vii, C, 1, b, nn. 24, 37. x, C, 4, n. 40
f. 16 v, B, 1, n. 95. vi, 9, n. 12
f. 17 ii, 2, n. 2; ii, 4, n. 37. iii, B, 4, n. 9. iv, 3, n. 77
f. 18 iv, 3, n. 68. vii, C, 2, n. 20
f. 20 iii, E, n. 23. iv, 9, n. 11. ix, A, 3, n. 121
f. 21 i, 3, n. 33. iv, 7, n. 9
f. 23 ix, D, n. 22
f. 25 vi, 12, n. 96. viii, A, 2, n. 66
13 J 15, f. 2 iv, 4, n. 41. vii, C, 2, n. 17
f. 3 x, C, 3, n. 11; x, C, 5, n. 11
f. 5 ii, 2, n. 2; ii, 5, n. 28. iii, D, n. 37; iii, F, n. 75. iv, 3, n. 78. ix, B, n. 536
f. 7 iv, 4, n. 38. viii, C, 1, n. 159
f. 8 x, C, 5, n. 21
f. 9 iv, 8, n. 80. ix, C, 1, n. 117
f. 10 vii, C, 1, c, n. 30
f. 12 x, C, 1, n. 40
f. 14 x, B, 1, n. 57; x, B, 4, n. 58
f. 15 ii, 4, n. 34. x, B, 1, n. 75
f. 16 iv, 12, n. 39 (mistake for 13 J 15, f. 20). x, B, 4, n. 163
f. 18 ix, B, n. 61. x, A, 3, n. 11
f. 19 **I**, App. D, sec. 43. ii, 2, n. 38; ii, 4, n. 33; ii, 5, n. 77. ix, B, nn. 62, 216
f. 20 iv, 6, n. 27; iv, 8, n. 34; iv, 12, n. 39 (cited as TS 13 J 15, f. 16). vii, A, 3, n. 17. x, A, 2, n. 314; x, B, 4, n. 163
f. 22 x, C, 1, n. 22
f. 23 viii, C, 1, n. 177
f. 24 vii, A, 2, n. 6. ix, A, 2, n. 69. x, B, 4, n. 148
f. 25 **I**, Introduction, n. 26
f. 26 iv, 8, n. 80 (mistake, *see* Reif). viii, A, 2, n. 79; viii, B, 3, n. 96 (mistake for TS 10 J 15, f. 26). **IV**, App. D, n. 134 (cited as 13 J 25, f. 26)
13 J 16, f. 1 x, C, 5, n. 21
f. 2 ii, 5, n. 39; ii, 6, n. 7. iv, 4, n. 45. ix, A, 4, n. 127
f. 3 vii, B, 1, n. 52. viii, C, 2, n. 171
f. 4 i, 2, n. 77. iv, 3, n. 70. viii, C, 1, n. 86

f. 5 ii, 1, n. 14; ii, 4, n. 39 (cited as 13 J 16, f. 15). iii, A, 1, n. 42; iii, D, n. 8. vi, 9, n. 21. viii, B, 2, n. 17
f. 6 v, B, 2, n. 24. vi, 10, n. 23. ix, A, 1, n. 31
f. 7 iii, F, n. 42. iv, 3, n. 69. viii, A, Introd., n. 2; viii, C, 1, nn. 86, 190. x, B, 2, n. 96
f. 8 v, B, 1, nn. 3, 57. vii, C, 1, b, n. 44
f. 9 x, C, 3, n. 14; x, C, 5, n. 13
f. 10 iv, 4, nn. 36, 44. vii, C, 1, c, n. 38
f. 11 viii, C, 3, n. 63
f. 12 **I**, App. D, sec. 36. ii, 5, n. 34
f. 13 v, B, 1, n. 6
f. 15 ii, 4, n. 39 (mistake for TS 13 J 16, f. 5)
f. 17 v, A, 1, n. 61; v, B, 2, n. 16
f. 19 ii, 2, n. 46; ii, 4, n. 35; ii, 5, nn. 35, 37. iii, C, n. 5; iii, E, n. 24; iii, G, n. 1. iv, 6, n. 8; iv, 7, n. 21; iv, 8, n. 31. ix, C, 1, n. 106
f. 21 v, D, 2, nn. 44, 51
f. 23 iv, 10, n. 1
f. 24 viii, C, 3, n. 76
13 J 17, f. 1 iv, 5, n. 15; iv, 10, nn. 27, 38. ix, A, 5, n. 77
f. 2 i, 2, n. 15. iii, D, n. 14. iv, 8, n. 69; iv, 10, n. 36. x, A, 2, n. 359
f. 3 ii, 4, n. 74; ii, 7, n. 8. iii, A, 2, n. 2; iii, E, n. 30. iv, 6, n. 15; iv, 8, nn. 20, 38; iv, 9, n. 24; iv, 10, nn. 20, 30. vii, A, 1, n. 5; vii, C, 1, c, n. 41
f. 4 i, 3, n. 4
f. 6 iii, C, n. 25; iii, F, n. 75. iv, 3, n. 78. x, A, 2, n. 363
f. 8 x, A, 2, n. 342; x, C, 3, n. 59
f. 9 viii, C, 2, n. 104
f. 10 x, B, 4, n. 113
f. 11 iii, D, n. 1; iii, E, n. 69 (cited as 13 J 27, f. 11). iv, 3, n. 54; iv, 6, n. 7; iv, 7, n. 18; iv, 8, n. 88. vii, A, 2, n. 31
f. 14 i, 2, n. 31. **III**, App. pt. I, gr. 4; **III**, App. pt. II, no. 364. viii, B, 4, n. 51; viii, C, 1, n. 110. ix, A, 4, nn. 44, 64, 89, 92, 168, 215, 216; ix, A, 5, nn. 3, 14, 35, 42. **IV**, App. D, n. 267
f. 15 x, B, 1, n. 41
f. 15*v* ix, A, 1, n. 22
f. 16*v* v, B, 2, n. 61. vi, 7, n. 7. x, A, 1, n. 106; x, A, 3, n. 323
f. 18 iv, 3, n. 81. viii, C, 4, n. 107. ix, B, n. 139
f. 20 ii, 1, n. 7
f. 21 x, B, 3, n. 27
f. 23 iv, 4, n. 39. viii, C, 1, nn. 155, 158; viii, C, 2, n. 12
13 J 18, f. 2 x, A, 1, n. 40
f. 3 v, A, 2, n. 65
f. 4 iv, 8, n. 2. x, A, 2, n. 301
f. 5 iii, E, n. 83 (mistake for TS 13 J 8, f. 5). viii, C, 1, n. 2
f. 6 iii, F, n. 76 (mistake for TS 13 J 18, f. 16). viii, C, 4, n. 179
f. 7 viii, A, 1, n. 66
f. 8 ii, 5, n. 57. iii, B, 4, n. 7; iii, D, n. 16; iii, E, nn. 43, 44, 46, 83; iii, F, n. 134; iii, G, n. 8. iv, 3, n. 34. ix, A, 2, n. 117; ix, A, 3, n. 46; ix, B, nn. 49, 224; ix, C, 2, n. 48
f. 9 viii, C, 2, n. 113
f. 10 viii, C, 4, n. 136
f. 11 viii, A, 2, n. 25. x, C, 3, n. 14; x, C, 5, n. 13
f. 12 viii, C, 1, n. 154

f. 13 viii, A, 2, n. 69; viii, C, 2, nn. 7, 13 (mistake for 13 J 8, f. 13)
f. 14 iii, F, n. 170
f. 15 viii, C, 1, n. 64. x, B, 3, n. 38
f. 16 ii, 4, n. 85. iii, C, n. 25; iii, F, n. 76 (cited as TS 13 J 18, f. 6)
f. 17 viii, C, 2, nn. 4, 9
f. 18 vii, B, 1, nn. 12, 54. viii, C, 1, n. 242
f. 19 vii, A, 3, n. 19. x, A, 1, n. 32
f. 20 iv, 1, n. 1. vii, C, 1, d, n. 32. viii, C, 2, n. 56
f. 21 ix, A, 1, n. 110
f. 22 viii, B, 1, n. 50
f. 25 iii, F, n. 193. v, A, 2, n. 57; v, B, 2, n. 11. vii, B, 1, nn. 19, 27. ix, A, 1, n. 30
f. 26 ii, 2, n. 51. viii, C, 1, n. 154; viii, C, 2, n. 118. ix, A, 2, n. 40
f. 27 iv, 3, n. 64. viii, A, 3, nn. 2, 43; viii, C, 3, n. 113. ix, A, 3, n. 107; ix, C, 1, n. 115. x, A, 2, n. 312; x, B, 2, n. 124
f. 29 ii, 4, n. 100. viii, A, 3, n. 64; viii, C, 2, n. 163. ix, A, 1, n. 54
13 J 19, f. 2 viii, A, 2, n. 78
f. 3 vi, 12, nn. 11, 26, 47. vii, A, 2, n. 9; vii, C, 1, c, nn. 3, 25. ix, A, 2, n. 43
f. 4 ii, 4, n. 57. iv, 12, n. 13. vii, C, 1, b, n. 24. x, A, 1, n. 23
f. 6 iii, B, 3, n. 13. v, A, 1, n. 48; v, B, 1, nn. 6, 122; v, D, 2, n. 48. vi, 10, n. 23
f. 7 x, A, 1, n. 12; x, C, 2, n. 77
f. 9 **I**, App. D, sec. 88. iii, F, n. 48. iv, 3, n. 63. ix, B, nn. 63, 99. x, B, 1, n. 110
f. 10 iii, C, n. 13
f. 12*v* viii, C, 4, n. 180
f. 13 viii, A, 2, n. 12
f. 14 viii, A, 2, n. 26; viii, C, 2, n. 11. x, A, 1, n. 27
f. 15 v, B, 1, n. 1
f. 16 v, A, 1, n. 13; v, C, 2, n. 3; v, D, 2, n. 43. vii, B, 1, n. 2. x, C, 3, n. 31; x, C, 4, nn. 46, 53, 54
f. 17 ii, 5, n. 77. iv, 4, n. 29. vii, A, 3, n. 17; vii, C, 1, c, n. 33. ix, A, 3, n. 41. x, B, 4, n. 37
f. 20 ii, 3, n. 28. iv, 8, nn. 30, 59, 80; iv, 12, n. 39
f. 21 x, B, 1, n. 66; x, B, 4, n. 66
f. 23 x, A, 2, n. 314
f. 27 i, 2, n. 22. ii, 4, nn. 19, 35; ii, 5, n. 57. iii, E, nn. 52, 53. iv, 6, n. 19; iv, 7, n. 18; iv, 8, n. 46. vi, 10, n. 32. ix, B, nn. 128, 150
f. 29 iii, B, 1, n. 10; iii, E, nn. 52, 69, 83. iv, 3, n. 52; iv, 4, nn. 4, 8; iv, 9, n. 22; iv, 10, n. 26. vii, C, 1, c, n. 41. x, A, 2, n. 41
f. 30 ii, 4, n. 101. x, A, 2, n. 257
13 J 20, f. 1 v, D, 1, n. 31
f. 2 v, A, 2, n. 59. vii, C, 1, b, n. 43. viii, A, 1, n. 64. x, B, 2, n. 81
f. 3 v, B, 1, n. 46. vi, 2, n. 34. viii, C, 2, n. 75. x, A, 2, n. 288
f. 5 iii, A, 1, n. 1; iii, G, n. 17. **II**, App. D, sec. 17. vii, C, 1, a, n. 39; vii, C, 1, c, nn. 27, 44, 48. ix, A, 1, n. 67. **IV**, App. D, n. 10
f. 6 vii, C, 1, b, n. 4. viii, A, 2, n. 9; viii, C, 1, n. 7; viii, C, 2, n. 155. x, A, 1, n. 22; x, B, 1, n. 27; x, B, 2, n. 112
f. 7 **I**, App. D, n. 19 (mistake for TS 13 J 29, f. 17)
f. 8*v* ix, B, n. 201. x, B, 1, n. 11
f. 9 viii, C, 1, n. 255

f. 10 iii, D, n. 17
f. 11 ii, 4, n. 84. vi, 11, nn. 50, 54. vii, C, 1, b, n. 23
f. 12 ix, A, 2, n. 164
f. 13 iv, 4, n. 15. v, B, 1, nn. 60, 61, 72. vi, 9, nn. 2, 39
f. 15 **II**, App. A, sec. 106
f. 16 x, A, 2, n. 333
f. 17 **I**, App. D, n. 19 (cited as TS 13 J 20, f. 7). vi, 11, n. 10. vii, A, 3, n. 33. **III**, App. pt. I, gr. 8. viii, C, 1, n. 200
f. 18 v, B, 2, n. 93. vi, 11, n. 21. viii, D, n. 143. ix, B, nn. 200, 201. x, B, 2, n. 93
f. 19 iv, 6, n. 13. ix, A, 5, n. 37
f. 20 viii, B, 1, n. 31. x, A, 1, n. 28; x, C, 1, nn. 39, 40
f. 21 iii, F, n. 66. vii, D, 1, n. 42
f. 22 i, 2, n. 69. ii, 2, n. 34.vi, 3, n. 2. vii, C, 1, a, n. 1. viii, A, 2, nn. 27, 28. x, B, 2, n. 113
f. 23 **I**, App. D, sec. 50
f. 24 v, C, 1, n. 17; v, C, 4, n. 7
f. 25 iv, 9, n. 8. viii, D, n. 133
f. 26 ii, 2, n. 2. iv, 10, n. 10. ix, A, 1, n. 19. x, C, 3, n. 18
f. 27 v, C, 1, n. 4. viii, C, 3, n. 149. **IV**, App. A, II. ix, A, 2, n. 38
f. 28 **II**, App. C, sec. 85. viii, B, 1, n. 3. x, C, 1, n. 39
f. 28*v* viii, A, 2, n. 25
13 J 21, f. 1 x, C, 3, n. 18
f. 2 vi, 9, n. 31. vii, B, 1, n. 66. viii, C, 1, n. 174
f. 3 vi, 4, n. 18. x, A, 2, nn. 217, 295; x, C, 3, n. 18
f. 5 i, 3, n. 22. v, C, 1, n. 16. vii, C, 1, c, n. 55; vii, D, 1, n. 12. viii, A, Introduction, n. 3; viii, A, 3, n. 68; viii, C, 3, n. 81. x, B, 4, n. 19
f. 8 **II**, App. D, sec. 26. v, A, 1, n. 49
f. 11*v* x, D, n. 326
f. 12 iii, E, n. 5. iv, 3, n. 49; iv, 10, n. 8. ix, A, 2, n. 43; ix, B, n. 143
f. 13 ii, 4, n. 14; ii, 5, n. 57
f. 14 iv, 4, n. 35. vii, C, 1, a, n. 28. viii, A, 2, n. 79. x, B, 1, n. 29
f. 17 **I**, Introduction, n. 56. i, 1, n. 14; i, 2, n. 35. ii, 2, n. 52; ii, 4, n. 104. iii, F, n. 175. v, B, 1, n. 67. vi, 12, n. 1. vii, C, 1, d, n. 29. **IV**, App. A, V. ix, C, 2, n. 30
f. 18 ii, 7, n. 30. iii, F, n. 219. vii, C, 1, c, n. 18. viii, A, Introd., n. 2; viii, A, 2, n. 44; viii, C, 2, n. 48. ix, A, 1, n. 36
f. 21 v, B, 2, n. 118. vi, 11, n. 31
f. 23 viii, C, 1, n. 7
f. 24 iii, D, n. 8. v, B, 2, n. 33; v, C, 2, n. 17; vii, C, 1, c, n. 31. x, A, 2, n. 110
f. 25 v, C, 4, n. 59. vi, 10, n. 6
f. 25*v* **II**, App. A, sec. 184
f. 26 iii, D, n. 44
f. 27 iv, 4, n. 23. x, A, 1, n. 138
f. 28 x, B, 2, n. 99
f. 29 ix, A, 1, n. 219; ix, C, 1, n. 177
f. 30 v, B, 1, nn. 97, 111; v, C, 2, n. 1. viii, C, 4, n. 185
f. 31 **II**, App. A, sec. 96. v, B, 1, n. 147
f. 32 viii, C, 2, n. 19
f. 35 viii, C, 2, n. 108. ix, D, n. 21
f. 36 viii, B, 1, n. 4; viii, C, 1, n. 25
13 J 22, f. 2 ii, 4, n. 101; ii, 7, nn. 27, 42. **II**, App. A, sec. 18. vi, 10, n. 36; vi, 12, n. 15. vii, A, 2, n. 5. **III**, App. pt. II, no. 285. viii, A, 3, n. 15; viii, C, 3, n. 146; viii, D, n. 25. ix, A, 1,

nn. 102, 194; ix, A, 3, nn. 3, 6, 26; ix, B, n. 29. x, A, 3, nn. 63, 106; x, C, 5, n. 53
f. 5 vi, 3, n. 2
f. 7 viii, C, 4, n. 124
f. 9 v, C, 2, n. 11; v, C, 4, n. 1. vi, 4, nn. 4, 25. vii, C, 2, n. 2
f. 10 ii, 4, nn. 19, 42, 72. x, B, 2, n. 85
f. 12 x, B, 1, n. 76
f. 12*v* ix, B, n. 460
f. 13 x, A, 1, n. 19
f. 14 ix, C, 1, n. 168
f. 15 v, B, 1, n. 1. x, A, 1, n. 20
f. 16 ix, A, 1, n. 219
f. 19 x, C, 5, n. 41
f. 20 viii, A, 1, n. 46; viii, C, 3, n. 17
f. 21 viii, C, 1, n. 103; viii, C, 3, n. 63
f. 22 iii, E, n. 6. viii, C, 2, n. 158. ix, C, 2, n. 35
f. 23 iv, 4, n. 20; iv, 12, n. 8. vii, A, 1, n. 22. x, A, 2, n. 349
f. 24 vii, C, 1, a, n. 6. ix, A, 1, nn. 26, 161. x, A, 3, n. 260
f. 25 viii, C, 4, n. 147
f. 26 viii, C, 1, n. 8
f. 28 viii, C, 3, n. 17
f. 29 viii, A, 2, n. 15; viii, C, 2, n. 106. x, A, 3, n. 152; x, D, n. 39
f. 30 i, 2, n. 34. ii, 4, nn. 15, 25. iii, E, n. 57. iv, 5, n. 11; iv, 8, n. 31
f. 33 ii, 7, n. 3
13 J 23, f. 2 iv, 8, n. 6
f. 3 i, 3, n. 24. v, A, 2, n. 42; v, B, 1, nn. 108, 148. vii, A, 3, n. 5. x, A, 2, n. 263; x, B, 1, nn. 23, 26, 58; x, B, 4, n. 143
f. 5 viii, C, 2, nn. 23, 24. x, B, 2, nn. 23, 44
f. 7 v, A, 1, n. 28; vi, 11, n. 59. viii, B, 5, n. 57
f. 8 x, B, 1, n. 44
f. 9 v, B, 1, n. 1 (mistake for 13 J 33, f. 9)
f. 10 x, A, 2, n. 432; x, C, 1, n. 31
f. 14 ii, 2, n. 2. ix, C, 1, n. 67. x, A, 1, nn. 33, 37; x, A, 2, n. 8
f. 15 viii, A, 1, n. 44. x, A, 2, n. 398; x, B, 3, n. 8
f. 16 ii, 4, n. 30. v, B, 1, n. 24
f. 17 **II**, App. C, sec. 29. x, B, 1, n. 47
f. 18 iii, A, 2, n. 11; iii, E, nn. 13, 52. iv, 8, n. 31. viii, A, 2, n. 41
f. 20 v, C, 2, n. 40. vi, 2, n. 20; vi, 10, n. 32
f. 21 ii, 5, n. 29. iii, E, n. 57. ix, B, n. 222
f. 22 i, 3, n. 47. x, B, 2, n. 63
f. 24 iv, 12, n. 27 (mistake, *see* Reif)
13 J 24, f. 1 viii, C, 2, n. 74
f. 3 x, A, 2, n. 7
f. 4 ii, 5, n. 87 (mistake for 13 J 24, f. 14). iii, D, n. 81. v, A, 2, n. 73; v, C, 1, n. 31. vii, B, 2, n. 26. x, B, 1, n. 100; x, B, 3, n. 73
f. 7 vii, C, 1, a, n. 16
f. 8 iv, 8, n. 1. vii, B, 1, n. 14. ix, A, 2, n. 114. x, B, 2, n. 96
f. 10*v* vi, 12, n. 49. viii, C, 1, n. 63
f. 14 ii, 4, nn. 46, 95; ii, 5, n. 87 (cited as TS 13 J 24, f. 4). vi, 12, n. 58. x, B, 4, n. 63
f. 17 ii, 5, n. 66
f. 18 x, B, 3, n. 15
f. 20*v* x, B, 4, n. 115
f. 22 viii, C, 2, nn. 116, 118. x, B, 2, n. 17
f. 23 viii, A, 2, n. 65

TS 13 J 25, f. 1 iii, F, n. 180
f. 2 ii, 4, nn. 78, 93. ix, C, 1, nn. 129, 138. x, A, 1, n. 137; x, A, 2, n. 219
f. 3 **II**, App. D, sec. 6. viii, B, 3, n. 101
f. 6 ix, B, n. 273
f. 8 iii, D, n. 47; iii, F, nn. 13, 29. iv, 10, n. 28. ix, A, 4, n. 152. x, B, 4, n. 28
f. 9 ii, 4, n. 2 (cited as TS 13 J 25, f. 19). iii, E, n. 13; iii, F, n. 43. iv, 7, n. 10. **IV**, App. C. ix, A, 2, n. 9; ix, B, nn. 267, 301
f. 11 vi, 4, n. 20. vii, A, 1, n. 38
f. 12 iv, 3, nn. 74, 75. x, A, 2, n. 22; x, B, 1, n. 23; x, B, 4, nn. 156, 157; x, C, 1, n. 22
f. 13 ix, B, n. 153
f. 14 iii, D, n. 69; iii, E, n. 57; iii, F, n. 76
f. 15 ii, 4, nn. 32, 36. vi, 12, n. 68. vii, A, 1, n. 39; vii, B, 1, n. 34. x, A, 2, nn. 110, 322
f. 16 v, A, 2, n. 79; v, B, 1, nn. 11, 146
f. 18 i, 2, n. 50. iii, B, 1, n. 1; iii, B, 3, n. 5; iii, E, n. 53. x, B, 2, n. 88
f. 19 ii, 4, nn. 2 (mistake for TS 13 J 25, f. 9), 91. iv, 6, n. 12. viii, C, 2, n. 78; viii, D, nn. 64, 91. **IV**, App. A, III
f. 20 i, 2, n. 41. viii, B, 1, n. 39
f. 26 **IV**, App. D, n. 134 (mistake for TS 13 J 15, f. 26)
13 J 26, f. 1 x, A, 1, n. 129
f. 2 iii, F, n. 87
f. 4 iv, 3, n. 68
f. 6 ii, 2, n. 14. **II**, App. B, sec. 16. vii, A, 3, n. 42; vii, B, 2, nn. 26, 29. viii, A, 2, n. 10. ix, A, 4, n. 155. x, A, 1, n. 63
f. 7 i, 2, n. 72. iv, 4, n. 17. vi, 4, nn. 2, 20. x, A, 1, n. 71; x, C, 5, n. 18
f. 8 ii, 5, n. 69. iv, 7, n.13; iv, 8, n. 46. v, A, 2, n. 76. vi, 12, n. 13. viii, A, 1, n. 46. ix, A, 4, n. 154; ix, A, 5, n. 23; ix, B, n. 411
f. 8*v* x, A, 2, n. 113
f. 9 iii, D, nn. 9, 29; iii, F, n. 218. iv, 3, n. 59; iv, 6, n. 6
f. 10 iv, 1, n. 2; iv, 8, nn. 62, 80. ix, C, 1, n. 145
f. 11 vi, 8, n. 7
f. 13 vii, C, 2, n. 38
f. 15 x, C, 5, n. 17
f. 16 v, A, 1, n. 23. vii, B, 1, n. 16
f. 18 ii, 4, n. 74. iv, 8, n. 24. v, A, 1, n. 47; v, B, 1, n. 137; v, C, 2, n. 3. vii, C, 1, b, n. 30. viii, A, 2, n. 1; viii, B, 4, n. 96; viii, C, 3, n. 32. x, A, 1, n. 76
f. 19 ii, 5, nn. 17, 73 (cited as TS 13 J 26, f. 29). iii, E, n. 6. v, A, 2, n. 75. vii, C, 1, b, n. 24
f. 21 iii, G, n. 25. vii, C, 1, d, n. 23; vii, D, 1, n. 40
f. 22 i, 3, n. 17. iv, 11, n. 21. x, B, 1, n. 20
f. 24 **I**, Introduction, n. 53. v, A, 1, n. 6; v, B, 1, n. 75. x, C, 5, n. 20
f. 29 ii, 5, n. 73 (mistake for TS 13 J 26, f. 19)
13 J 27, f. 4 **I**, App. D, sec. 90. ii, 4, n. 46. iii, E, nn. 53, 57; iii, G, nn. 6, 7
f. 5 ix, C, 1, n. 167. x, A, 2, n. 132
f. 6 iv, 3, nn. 48, 81
f. 9 iii, D, n. 12. iv, 8, n. 4; iv, 12, n. 18
f. 11 i, 3, n. 37. iii, E, n. 69 (mistake for TS 13 J 17, f. 11). vi, 4, n. 22; vi, 10, nn. 15, 21. viii, C, 1, n. 256

f. 14 I, Introduction, n. 53
f. 15 viii, A, 3, n. 70. x, B, 2, n. 73
f. 16 iv, 3, n. 74
f. 17 ii, 4, n. 76. iv, 6, nn. 21, 26
f. 18 ii, 4, nn. 30, 31. iii, E, n. 61
f. 20 x, B, 3, n. 20; x, B, 4, n. 146
f. 21 viii, D, n. 120
f. 22 iv, 10, n. 5. vi, 2, n. 40
13 J 28, f. 2 ii, 2, n. 46; ii, 7, n. 13. ix, A, 5, nn. 42, 53, 82; ix, B, nn. 533, 534
f. 4 ix, B, n. 290
f. 6 ii, 5, n. 71. iv, 3, n. 80
f. 8 vi, 4, n. 7
f. 9 ii, 4, n. 8. iii, E, n. 83. iv, 8, n. 80
f. 10 ii, 6, n. 8. **II**, App. B, sec. 27. x, B, 1, n. 55
f. 11 i, 3, n. 47. iv, 5, n. 18. x, B, 2, n. 63
f. 12 v, B, 1, n. 24. x, A, 1, n. 154
f. 15 iv, 11, n. 20; iv, 12, n. 4. v, B, 1, n. 122. vii, A, 2, n. 19; vii, C, 2, n. 14. viii, A, 2, n. 3; viii, B, 1, n. 53
f. 16 iii, D, n. 19. viii, C, 1, n. 159; viii, D, n. 119
f. 17 iv, 6, n. 14. x, B, 1, n. 39
f. 19 viii, C, 1, nn. 49, 88, 97
f. 24 ii, 4, n. 87. ix, D, n. 6
f. 29 ix, B, n. 273
13 J 29 vi, 5, n. 6 (mistake for 13 J 29, f. 9)
f. 1 iii, A, 2, n. 4; iii, F, n. 179. iv, 7, n. 22; iv, 8, n. 16; iv, 12, n. 18
f. 2 ii, 4, n. 12. iii, B, 4, n. 9; iii, D, n. 18; iii, E, nn. 61, 69. viii, B, 3, n. 97. ix, C, 1, n. 159
f. 3 x, B, 4, n. 31
f. 7 viii, C, 1, n. 194
f. 9 vi, 5, n. 6 (cited as 13 J 29). ix, B, n. 127
f. 10 iii, E, n. 51. iv, 12, n. 18. ix, C, 2, n. 53. x, C, 1, n. 26
13 J 30, f. 2 iii, F, n. 134. viii, A, 1, n. 39. ix, C, 2, n. 18
f. 3 vii, B, 2, n. 19; vii, D, 1, n. 14
f. 4*v* viii, D, n. 67
f. 5 v, B, 1, nn. 103, 144
f. 6 vi, 3, n. 1. vii, A, 2, n. 12. ix, A, 2, n. 68. x, B, 1, n. 49
f. 7 ii, 7, n. 97
13 J 31, f. 5 v, B, 1, n. 103
f. 6 iii, F, nn. 196, 203. v, B, 2, n. 58
f. 6*v* v, B, 2, n. 79
13 J 32 *see* Box J 3, f. 47 (new classmark)
13 J 33, f. 1 i, 2, n. 23. viii, B, 1, n. 62
f. 3 v, B, 1, n. 47. x, A, 2, n. 158
f. 5 ii, 4, n. 65
f. 7 vi, 12, n. 109. x, A, 2, nn. 165, 173
f. 8 v, B, 1, n. 47. vi, 4, n. 7. x, A, 2, n. 167
f. 9 v, A, 2, n. 69; v, B, 1, nn. 1 (cited as TS 13 J 23, f. 9), 89. vii, A, 1, n. 26; vii, C, 1, d, n. 22; vii, C, 2, nn. 49, 50
f. 10 ii, 7, n. 83; iii, F, n. 111. viii, C, 2, n. 153
13 J 34, f. 3 v, B, 1, n. 6; v, C, 4, n. 60; v, D, 2, n. 40
f. 4 **II**, App. D, sec. 24. viii, B, 5, n. 65
f. 5 viii, A, 2, n. 23; viii, C, 2, n. 113
f. 5*v* x, A, 3, n. 94
f. 8 vii, C, 2, n. 41. viii, C, 2, n. 8. x, C, 4, n. 60
f. 9 viii, B, 3, n. 94

f. 12 x, B, 2, n. 60
13 J 35, f. 2 iv, 3, n. 76. v, A, 2, n. 28. vi, 10, nn. 9, 19
f. 3 v, B, 1, n. 116
f. 5 ii, 5, n. 61
f. 6 viii, C, 2, n. 5
f. 7 ii, 4, n. 80. iii, D, n. 12
f. 7*v* **II**, App. C, sec. 8
f. 10 ii, 4, n. 38
f. 14 vi, 10, n. 28. viii, B, 1, n. 45
f. 15 iii, E, n. 55
13 J 36, f. 1 iii, B, 3, n. 5. iv, 2, n. 17. v, A, 1, n. 32. vii, B, 1, n. 15. viii, A, 2, n. 19; viii, C, 3, n. 71. x, B, 2, n. 73
f. 2 vii, C, 2, nn. 24, 43. x, C, 1, n. 36
f. 3 x, B, 2, n. 114
f. 4*v* viii, C, 2, n. 57
f. 5 v, C, 2, n. 3. vi, 7, n. 13. ix, B, n. 273
f. 6 iv, 3, n. 83; iv, 8, nn. 53, 80. **II**, App. A, sec. 11*c*. v, B, 2, n. 7; v, D, 2, n. 8. vi, 12, n. 66. x, A, 3, n. 21
f. 11 ii, 4, n. 75; ii, 7, n. 81. ix, A, 1, n. 54. x, A, 2, n. 291
13 J 37, f. 2 viii, C, 1, n. 150
f. 3 v, B, 1, n. 125
f. 4 iii, F, n. 196
f. 6 **I**, App. C, sec. 25. x, A, 1, n. 102
f. 10 viii, A, 3, n. 52
f. 11 **III**, App. pt. II, no. 376. ix, A, 4, n. 21; ix, A, 5, n. 88
f. 12 ii, 7, nn. 64, 69, 71
13 Ja 1, f. 1 viii, B, 2, n. 22 (cited as 13 Ja 1)
13 Ja 1, f. 2 ii, 4, n. 26 (cited as 13 Ja 2)
13 Ja 2 ii, 4, n. 26 (mistake for 13 Ja 1, f. 2)
TS 18 J 1, f. 1 vii, B, 3, nn. 2, 40. viii, C, 3, n. 47
f. 2 vi, 10, n. 34. viii, C, 4, n. 52
f. 3 ii, 4, n. 61 (mistake for 18 J 1, f. 4). **III**, App. pt. I, gr. 4; **III**, App. pt. II, no. 190. viii, B, 2, n. 71
f. 4 ii, 4, n. 61 (cited as 18 J 1, f. 3). **III**, App. pt. II, no. 279. viii, C, 3, nn. 5, 156; viii, C, 4, n. 31
f. 5 v, B, 1, n. 129. x, B, 1, n. 1
f. 6 ii, 4, n. 99. vi, 9, n. 42; vi, 10, nn. 36, 41. vii, B, 1, n. 23; vii, B, 2, n. 9. x, C, 5, n. 24
f. 7 viii, A, 1, n. 60; viii, C, 4, n. 64
f. 8 iii, A, 1, n. 33. vii, B, 1, n. 68 (mistake for 18 J 1, f. 18). x, A, 2, n. 29
f. 9 iii, A, 1, n. 1; iii, E, n. 9. **II**, App. D, sec. 19. viii, A, 1, n. 55. ix, C, 1, n. 67
f. 10 iv, 7, n. 17; iv, 10, nn. 9, 10. vi, 11, n. 43. ix, A, 5, nn. 32, 72. ix, B, n. 147. x, A, 3, n. 47
f. 11 ii, 2, n. 8. iii, F, n. 8. vii, A, 3, n. 31; vii, B, 2, n. 24; vii, C, 1, c, nn. 26, 39, 53
f. 12 ii, 7, n. 39
f. 13 vi, 4, n. 23
f. 14 **III**, App. pt. II, no. 188
f. 15 **III**, App. pt. II, no. 242. x, A, 3, n. 33 (cited as 18 J 1, f. 17)
f. 17 ii, 7, n. 39. viii, C, 3, n. 140. x, A, 3, n. 33 (mistake for 18 J 1, f. 15)
f. 18 **II**, App. D, sec. 14. vii, B, 1, n. 68 (cited as 18 J 1, f. 8). viii, C, 3, n. 45
f. 20 **III**, App. pt. II, no 296. viii, C, 3, n. 39

f. 21	x, A, 3, n. 45
f. 22	viii, C, 4, n. 69
f. 23	viii, C, 3, nn. 58, 146
f. 24	x, A, 3, n. 39
f. 25	v, C, 2, n. 39; v, C, 3, n. 13. vii, B, 3, n. 52. viii, D, n. 166
f. 26	v, B, 2, n. 117. ix, B, nn. 366, 432, 493
f. 27	viii, C, 3, n. 13. ix, A, 1, n. 219
f. 28	viii, B, 2, n. 3; viii, B, 3, n. 80; viii, C, 4, n. 148
f. 29	**I**, App. D, sec. 71. iii, F, n. 130
f. 30	ii, 7, n. 65
f. 32	viii, A, 3, n. 55
18 J 2, f. 1	**II**, App. A, sec. 116. v, B, 1, n. 82. vi, 12, n. 80. ix, A, 2, n. 168
f. 3	v, A, 2, n. 51; v, B, 1, n. 142. vii, B, 1, n. 36. x, B, 2, n. 99
f. 4	**II**, App. B, sec. 52
f. 5	vii, B, 2, n. 18. viii, A, 3, nn. 18, 67
f. 6	ii, 5, n. 16. v, B, 1, n. 139. vii, C, 1, b, n. 33. ix, A, 2, n. 73; ix, A, 3, n. 36
f. 8	ii, 4, n. 87 (cited as 18 J 2, f. 18). v, B, 1, n. 126. ix, A, 2, n. 156
f. 10	i, 2, n. 99. ix, C, 1, n. 17. x, A, 1, n. 161; x, B, 1, n. 30
f. 11	v, B, 1, n. 20; v, B, 2, n. 10. x, A, 2, n. 365
f. 12	viii, C, 4, n. 17. ix, A, 1, n. 4
f. 13	ii, 5, n. 86. v, A, 2, n. 3. viii, C, 3, nn. 97, 122. ix, A, 2, n. 103
f. 16	**II**, App. C, sec. 1. viii, A, 1, n. 60; viii, C, 4, nn. 77, 80. x, A, 3, n. 21
f. 18	ii, 4, n. 87 (mistake for 18 J 2, f. 8)
18 J 3, f. 1	ii, 5, nn. 6, 10. vii, C, 2, n. 24. x, B, 1, n. 102
f. 2	vii, B, 1, n. 54. viii, A, 2, n. 78; viii, C, 1, nn. 99, 168, 242
f. 4	viii, A, 2, nn. 70, 79
f. 5	ii, 5, n. 87. iii, A, 1, n. 5. v, B, 2, nn. 104, 10; v, D, 2, n. 48. vii, C, 1, d, n. 31. viii, A, Introduction, n. 2; viii, C, 2, n. 102. x, B, 4, n. 147
f. 9	vii, C, 1, b, n. 1. x, A, 2, n. 83
f. 11	x, D, n. 330
f. 12	vii, C, 1, b, n. 24. viii, C, 3, n. 120. x, D, n. 327
f. 13	iii, C, n. 5; iii, D, n. 78. vii, A, 2, n. 14
f. 15	i, 3, n. 36. v, B, 2, n. 15. viii, C, 1, n. 3; viii, C, 2, n. 8. x, B, 3, n. 67
f. 19	i, 2, n. 76. vi, 2, n. 2. vii, C, 1, a, n. 16. viii, C, 2, nn. 10, 51, 110. x, B, 2, n. 44
f. 20	vi, 10, n. 33
18 J 4, f. 1	v, B, 2, n. 21. vi, 12, n. 87. ix, D, n. 13
f. 2	viii, C, 2, n. 8
f. 3	vi, 8, n. 4; vi, 10, n. 7. x, B, 2, n. 93
f. 4	vii, B, 1, n. 36. viii, C, 2, n. 178
f. 5	i, 2, n. 39. v, A, 2, n. 28. vii, C, 1, a, n. 21
f. 6	iv, 7, nn. 5, 17. **II**, App. C, sec. 18. vii, A, 1, n. 21; vii, C, 1, a, n. 21; vii, C, 2, n. 58
f. 10	ii, 2, n. 14. vii, B, 1, n. 27; vii, C, 1, c, n. 37. x, A, 2, n. 315
f. 11	viii, B, 3, n. 102
f. 12	v, A, 2, n. 37; v, B, 1, nn. 76, 92, 136; v, B, 2, nn. 75, 88; v, D, 2, n. 13. vi, 2, n. 9. vii, B, 1, n. 35. ix, A, 2, nn. 103, 168
f. 13	x, A, 3, n. 21
f. 14	i, 2, n. 78. iv, 2, n. 31
f. 19	v, B, 1, nn. 47, 149. vii, C, 1, c, n. 30. x, C, 3, n. 13

f. 21 viii, C, 3, n. 32; viii, C, 4, n. 18
f. 24 ii, 5, n. 13. iv, 2, n. 33
f. 26 vii, A, 1, n. 17. vii, C, 1, a, nn. 13, 26; vii, D, 2, n. 6
18 J 5, f. 5 ii, 5, n. 56. vii, A, 1, nn. 3, 37. ix, A, 5, n. 51; ix, B, n. 119. x, A, 2, n. 103
f. 9 ii, 5, n. 29. **II**, App. C, sec. 1
f. 10 viii, D, n. 7
18 J 16, f. 4 v, A, 1, n. 2 (mistake for TS 8 J 16, f. 4)
ARABIC BOXES (Mostly Arabic and Judeo-Arabic fragments originally kept in boxes and now in binders)
Arabic Box 4, f. 2 vi, 10, n. 47
f. 4 ix, A, 4, nn. 146, 171, 201; ix, A, 5, nn. 6, 21, 45, 49, 59, 60, 68, 91; ix, B, n. 425, 444, 464, 474, 488, 553. **IV**, App. D, nn. 6, 7
f. 5 iii, F, nn. 2, 187, 215. v, C, 2, n. 38. viii, D, n. 175. ix, B, nn. 292, 427, 470. x, A, 3, nn. 204, 319
f. 7 **II**, App. A, sec. 183
f. 10 vi, 12, n. 83
Arabic Box 5, f.1 x, B, 2, n. 69
f. 1, sec. A iii, D, n. 17
f. 1, sec. B ix, A, 2, nn. 8, 91, 117, 141; ix, A, 3, nn. 51, 52
f. 2, col. III ix, A, 5, n. 52
f. 4 vi, 10, n. 47
Arabic Box 6, f. 1*a* iii, F, n. 173
f. 2 **III**, App. pt. II, no. 150. **IV**, App. C, 2. ix, A, 4, nn. 2, 30, 163, 219
f. 3 **II**, App. A, sec. 122
f. 8 **II**, App. C, sec. 25
f. 28 ii, 2, n. 49; ii, 4, n. 100. viii, A, 1, nn. 10, 18; viii, A, 2, n. 80; viii, C, 1, n. 208. ix, A, 1, n. 220
Arabic Box 7,
f. 3 (1) ix, B, n. 245
f. 3 (2), cols. I-II ix, B, n. 90
f. 5 ix, A, 3, n. 80
f. 9 viii, B, 3, n. 75. x, A, 1, n. 30
f. 13 ii, 7, n. 111. **II**, App. C., sec. 127. vi, 6, n. 12
f. 18 iv, 10, n. 35
f. 22 iii, F, n. 185. viii, B, 3, n. 88
f. 22*v* vi, 4, n. 17
f. 29 **III**, App. pt. II, no. 266. viii, C, 3, n. 125
f. 32 iii, A, 2, n. 9 (mistake, *see* Reif)
Arabic Box 18(1),
f. 3 ix, A, 2, n. 141
f. 10 ix, C, 1, n. 7
f. 33 vi, 4, n. 16
f. 34 v, A, 2, n. 44. vi, 10, n. 25
f. 35 **II**, App. A, sec. 3
f. 76 v, B, 2, n. 62
f. 101 ii, 4, n. 83. iii, B, 1, n. 13. ix, A, 2, n. 118
f. 113 **I**, Introduction, n. 35
f. 127 ix, A, 2, n. 157; ix, C, 2, n. 37
f. 128 vi, 2, n. 26
f. 130*v* ix, A, 1, n. 166
f. 132 iii, F, n. 170. vi, 11, n. 45
f. 137 vii, C, 1, d, n. 27. x, B, 1, n. 17
f. 155 **II**, App. A, sec. 24. ix, A, 1, n. 114; ix, A, 2, n. 40; ix, A, 3, n. 116; ix, D, n. 29

f. 164 ii, 5, n. 39. iii, E, n. 16. ix, B, n. 166; ix, C, 1, n. 152
f. 181 **II**, App. A, sec. 4. ix, A, 2, n. 161
f. 183 ii, 5, n. 17
Arabic Box 18(2),
f. 4 ii, 4, n. 86. v, B, 1, n. 97; v, B, 2, n. 20; v, C, 4, n. 5. vii, A, 1, n. 41. viii, A, 1, n. 23
Arabic Box 25, f. 53 ix, A, 5, n. 37
Arabic Box 30, f. 2 iii, F, n. 33
f. 8 **III**, App. pt. II, no. 197. viii, B, 4, nn. 5, 16; viii, C, 4, n. 154
f. 30 iii, A, 1, n. 42; iii, F, n. 46. vii, A, 2, n. 5. ix, A, 1, n. 53; ix, A, 2, nn. 92, 115, 164; ix, A, 3, nn. 53, 68
f. 32 **I**, App. D, sec. 87. iii, F, nn. 101, 104
f. 36 vi, 2, nn. 11, 14
f. 40 x, B, 3, n. 78
f. 53 ix, A, 2, nn. 87, 167
f. 65*v* vi, 12, n. 63; vi, 13, nn. 1, 30
f. 67 ii, 4, n. 62; ii, 6, nn. 14, 24. **II**, App. B, sec. 65. x, A, 2, n. 225
f. 84 ix, C, 2, n. 23
f. 95*v* ix, C, 1, n. 48
f. 129 vii, C, 2, n. 35
f. 145 ix, B, n. 155
f. 146 v, C, 4, n. 52
f. 156 x, B, 3, n. 70
f. 163 ii, 1, n. 17; ii, 2, n. 17. **II**, App. B, sec. 104
f. 165 vi, 13, n. 57
f. 177 ix, C, 2, n. 36
f. 184 iii, F, n. 61. **II**, App. C, sec. 23
f. 201 ix, A, 5, nn. 4, 14, 78, 79; ix, B, nn. 530, 539
f. 215 **I**, App. D, sec. 89. ii, 4, n. 37; ii, 5, n. 39. iii, F, nn. 8, 171, 189. ix, A, 3, n. 45
f. 250 vi, 10, n. 10. x, D, n. 58
f. 255 ii, 4, n. 37
f. 258 ix, A, 3, n. 65
f. 263 ix, A, 1, n. 50
f. 274 vi, 13, n. 51
f. 278 v, A, 1, n. 37; v, A, 2, n. 36. vii, D, 2, n. 5
f. 284 **I**, App. D, sec. 2
Arabic Box 36,
f. 119 ix, D, n. 10
Arabic Box 38, f. 1 vi, 2, n. 37
f. 2 iii, F, n. 152
f. 11 viii, B, 3, n. 84
f. 14 viii, C, 1, nn. 165, 192
f. 41 x, B, 2, n. 91
f. 81 iii, F, n. 150
f. 86 ix, A, 1, n. 140; ix, A, 2, nn. 43, 151
f. 87 vii, D, 2, n. 14
f. 88 x, A, 2, n. 110
f. 93 v, A, 2, n. 41
f. 95 **II**, App. B, sec. 110
f. 98 iii, A, 1, n. 42
f. 102 viii, A, 3, n. 22; viii, C, 2, n. 139. ix, A, 2, nn. 102, 117, 148, 163
f. 115 ix, A, 2, n. 147
f. 116 viii, D, nn. 25, 61. ix, A, 1, n. 103; ix, A, 2, nn. 37, 62, 167

f. 117 ix, A, 2, nn. 75, 102, 154. x, B, 3, n. 78
f. 119 v, C, 1, n. 35. ix, A, 2, nn. 38, 98, 117; ix, A, 3, nn. 55, 68
f. 131 v, A, 2, n. 82; v, D, 2, n. 53. vii, B, 1, n. 72
f. 138 i, 2, n. 32
Arabic Box 39, f. 17 ix, A, 3, nn. 53, 65
f. 57 v, A, 2, n. 66. viii, C, 1, n. 202
f. 79 **II**, App. C, sec. 131. x, A, 1, n. 164
f. 170 vii, B, 1, n. 40
f. 173 vii, D, 2, n. 14
f. 338 viii, C, 1, n. 58
f. 449 **II**, App. C, sec. 139
fs. 452, 453 v, A, 2, n. 41
f. 476 vii, B, 3, n. 42
Arabic Box 40, f. 9 x, A, 1, n. 167
f. 16 vi, 12, n. 84
f. 29 vi, 13, n. 10. viii, D, n. 60
f. 48 v, A, 1, n. 48. x, A, 1, n. 172
f. 53 (col. II) **II**, App. C, sec. 137. ix, A, 1, n. 167. x, A, 1, n. 164
f. 56 viii, C, 3, n. 94. x, B, 2, n. 127
f. 96 vii, A, 3, n. 8. viii, C, 1, n. 187; viii, C, 3, n. 93
f. 103 iii, A, 1, n. 12
f. 113 ix, A, 1, n. 42
f. 126 iii, C, n. 6. vii, C, 1, b, n. 50
f. 153 vii, C, 1, b, n. 24
f. 161 **II**, App. B, sec. 108
f. 187 x, A, 2, n. 221
Arabic Box 41, f. 53 x, B, 4, n. 125
f. 79 vii, B, 3, n. 40. viii, C, 3, n. 48
f. 105 vii, D, 2, n. 14
f. 109 vii, C, 2, n. 18. x, A, 3, n. 229
f. 141 viii, A, 1, n. 67
Arabic Box 42,
f. 130 ix, A, 1, n. 151
f. 158 iv, 4, nn. 7, 40; iv, 7, n. 28
f. 165 x, A, 2, n. 423
Arabic Box 43, f. 71 ix, B, n. 339; ix, C, 2, n. 52
Arabic Box 44, f. 54,
fol. 3*a*, no. 4 x, B, 4, n. 99
fol. 5*a*, no. 5 x, B, 4, n. 100
fol. 8*a*, no. 5 x, B, 4, n. 101
f. 223 **II**, App. A, sec. 178
Arabic Box 46,
f. 253 **II**, App. C, sec. 140
Arabic Box 47, f. 244 viii, B, 2, n. 29
Arabic Box 48, f. 42 **II**, App. C, sec. 138
f. 42*v* **II**, App. A, sec. 181
f. 121 **II**, App. D, sec. 18
f. 270 ii, 1, n. 7. v, A, 1, n. 56. vii, C, 1, a, n. 2. ix, A, 1, n. 42
Arabic Box 49, f. 166 vii, B, 2, n. 7. viii, B, 3, n. 9; viii, C, 4, nn. 76, 79
f. 166*v* **II**, App. A, sec. 179
Arabic Box 50,
f. 181*b* **III**, App. pt. II, no. 347
f. 197 viii, B, 2, nn. 2, 82; viii, C, 1, n. 226
Arabic Box 51, f. 103 **III**, App. pt. I, gr. 5. viii, A, 3, n. 24; viii, B, 4, n. 41
f. 107 ii, 4, n. 94. iii, F, n. 202. ix, A, 1, n. 231
f. 111 **II**, App. C, sec. 36. v, A, 2, n. 50; v, C, 5, n. 9. vii, C, 1, a, n. 7; vii, D, 2, n. 15. x, A, 3, n. 141; x, D, n. 336

f. 118 **IV**, App. A, II. ix, A, 2, n. 166
f. 140 **II**, App. C, sec. 79
f. 144 **II**, App. A, sec. 145
Arabic Box 52,
f. 247*a-b* **II**, App. B, sec. 72
f. 247*d* **II**, App. A, sec. 137. **II**, App. B, sec. 72. ix, A, 1, n. 174. x, A, 1, n. 68
f. 248 **II**, App. B, sec. 69. viii, C, 2, n. 177
Arabic Box 53, f. 11 iii, E, n. 83; iii, F, nn. 30, 40
f. 19 v, B, 1, nn. 21, 52. vii, A, 2, n. 5. ix, A, 1, n. 109; ix, A, 2, nn. 43, 57, 62, 116, 167
f. 29 iii, E, n. 31
f. 32 ix, B, n. 319
f. 33 vi, 12, n. 63; vi, 13, n. 29
f. 37 i, 1, n. 14; i, 2, n. 96. ii, 1, n. 8. viii, B, 1, n. 55; viii, B, 2, n. 1. ix, A, 3, n. 125. x, D, n. 121
f. 51 iv, 10, n. 21. ix, B, n. 258
f. 53 viii, C, 4, n. 45
f. 60 viii, A, 3, n. 21. ix, A, 1, nn. 50, 104, 150; ix, A, 2, n. 72
f. 61 vi, 13, nn. 2, 11. vii, A, 2, n. 9. viii, D, n. 55. **IV**, App. A, VI. ix, A, 1, n. 50; ix, A, 2, nn. 11, 72
f. 65 vi, 2, n. 36
f. 66 ix, A, 1, nn. 50, 167; ix, A, 3, n. 3
f. 70 **IV**, App. A, IV. ix, A, 1, n. 103; ix, A, 2, nn. 88, 95, 153
f. 73 ix, A, 2, nn. 62, 102, 112, 146; ix, A, 3, n. 35
Arabic Box 54
f. 15*a* **I**, App. D, sec. 86; ii, 3, n. 25. **II**, App. A, sec. 139
f. 15*b* iii, F, nn. 8, 35, 55. ix, A, 1, n. 136
f. 19 iii, A, 1, n. 10. vi, 13, n. 66
f. 20 ix, A, 1, n. 112; ix, A, 3, n. 78
f. 21 iii, G, n. 2. **II**, App. C, sec. 27
f. 25 vi, 2, n. 26
f. 39 ix, B, n. 397
f. 44 vi, 13, n. 54
f. 45 **II**, App. A, sec. 117
f. 46 vi, 2, n. 26. viii, C, 2, n. 19
f. 48 x, A, 1, n. 173; x, A, 2, n. 289
f. 49*v* viii, C, 4, n. 49
f. 52 **II**, App. B, sec. 93. viii, C, 4, n. 126
f. 56 ii, 4, n. 73 (mistake for Ar. Box 54, f. 66)
f. 59 ii, 2, n. 8. **II**, App. C, sec. 45
f. 60 v, A, 2, n. 46; v, B, 1, n. 118
f. 61 **II**, App. A, sec. 148
f. 66 ii, 4, n. 73 (cited as Ar. Box 54, f. 56), 84. vii, B, 1, n. 65. ix, A, 3, n. 40. x, A, 1, nn. 64, 81
f. 69 viii, C, 3, n. 104; viii, D, n. 15
f. 74 viii, C, 2, n. 61
f. 78 viii, B, 2, n. 60; viii, B, 4, n. 33
f. 88 ii, 4, n. 79. ix, B, nn. 224, 319
f. 91 v, B, 1, n. 31. viii, C, 1, n. 14. x, A, 2, nn. 370, 375
f. 92 **IV**, App. A, II, V. ix, A, 2, nn. 38, 166; ix, A, 3, n. 39
f. 93 **I**, App. D, sec. 85. iii, E, n. 41. iv, 3, n. 38. vii, C, 1, b, n. 22. ix, A, 4, n. 219; ix, C, 1, n. 112. x, B, 5, n. 49
MISCELLANEOUS BOXES (Fragments originally kept in boxes and now stored in binders)
TS Misc. Box 8, f. 2 ix, C, 1, n. 155
f. 9 ii, 6, n. 17. iv, 12, n. 12. **II**, App. B, sec. 18. v, B, 2, n. 96. vi, 9, n. 4; vi, 10, n. 37. viii, C, 1, n. 214

f. 10	**II**, App. A, sec. 121
f. 18	v, B, 1, n. 147. vi, 10, n. 29. vii, C, 1, b, n. 29
f. 22*a*	ix, A, 1, n. 97
f. 25	**II**, App. B, sec. 24. v, B, 2, n. 49. viii, B, 1, n. 77
f. 29	**II**, App. C, sec. 17. viii, C, 4, n. 179
f. 61	**II**, App. B, sec. 46. v, D, 1, n. 27. vi, 10, n. 36. vii, A, 2, n. 5
f. 62	iii, D, nn. 70, 77, 83; iii, F, nn. 9, 17, 53, 54, 57
f. 65	**I**, App. D, sec. 16. iii, C, n. 18; iii, D, n. 76; iii, E, n. 80. ix, B, n. 394
f. 66	**I**, App. D, sec. 55. ii, 2, n. 12. iii, A, 1, n. 12; iii, E, n. 54; iii, F, nn. 21, 58. v, C, 2, n. 24; v, C, 4, n. 6. ix, C, 1, n. 189
f. 72	viii, C, 4, n. 49
f. 76	ii, 3, n. 25. **II**, App. A, sec. 15
f. 86	**II**, App.A, sec. 10. ix, A, 1, n. 113
f. 90	iii, E, n. 1. vii, A, 2, n. 28
f. 97	**III**, App. pt. II no. 55. viii, B, 5, n. 35. **IV**, App. C, 2. ix, B, nn. 121, 308
f. 99	iii, A, 1, n. 4. **II**, App. C, sec. 55. vi, 13, n. 2. viii, D, n. 15. ix, A, 5, n. 87. x, A, 1, n. 151
f. 100	**II**, App. B, sec. 41. v, B, 2, n. 86. viii, C, 1, n. 129
f. 102	iii, F, nn. 98, 111. **II**, App. C, sec. 19. vi, 13, n. 2. viii, D, n. 189. x, B, 3, n. 72
f. 103	iii, B, 4, n. 5; iii, D, nn. 68, 70, 76. iv, 8, nn. 25, 80
Misc. Box 20, f. 153	i, 2, n. 14. ix, A, 1, n. 162.
Misc. Box 24, f. 5	vi, 11, n. 17. ix, A, 2, n. 73
f. 28	x, D, n. 51
f. 42	vii, B, 3, n. 411
f. 66	vii, A, 2, n. 27
f. 137	v, C, 2, n. 31. vi, 10, nn. 36, 40
f. 137, p. 4*v*	viii, A, 3, n. 19; viii, B, 2, n. 47. ix, A, 4, n. 181. **IV**, App. D, nn. 110, 121. x, A, 3, nn. 23, 42; x, D, n. 81
Misc. Box 25, f. 6	viii, C, 1, n. 57
f. 14	**III**, App. pt. II, no. 328. ix, A, 4, nn. 87, 199
f. 19	iii, D, n. 1; iii, E, nn. 7, 61. iv, 10, nn. 11, 26
f. 20	ix, D, n. 20
f. 25	**II**, App. B, sec. 69. viii, B, 2, n. 44
f. 30	vi, 12, n. 65 (mistake for Misc. Box 25, f. 130)
f. 38	**II**, App. A, sec. 159
f. 53	viii, C, 4, n. 32. ix, A, 5, n. 79; ix, B, nn. 287, 330. **IV**, App. D, nn. 196, 202. x, A, 3, n. 255
f. 62	vii, C, 1, c, n. 40; vii, C, 2, n. 19. viii, B, 3, n. 99
f. 63	viii, B, 2, n. 45
f. 84	**II**, App. B, sec. 80
f. 103	ii, 4, n. 54
f. 106	**I**, Introduction, n. 53. v, D, 2, n. 18. vi, 9, n. 34
f. 107	ii, 7, n. 94
f. 124	x, C, 5, n. 2
f. 129	**II**, App. A, sec. 162. viii, D, n. 14
f. 130	iii, A, 1, n. 18. vi, 12, n. 65 (cited as Misc. Box 25, f. 30). x, A, 2, n. 345
f. 132	v, D, 1, n. 13. vii, B, 2, n. 14
f. 138	viii, C, 4, n. 59
f. 139	v, D, 1, n. 13. vii, B, 2, n. 14
f. 140	**III**, App. pt. I, grs. 5 and 8. viii, B, 5, n. 34
Misc. Box 27, f. 1	vii, A, 1, n. 28
f. 4.22	**III**, App. pt. II, no. 140 (cited as Misc. Box 27, f. 22*a*)
f. 4.26	**III**, App. pt. II, no. 142 (cited as Misc. Box 27, f. 26)

f. 4.31 viii, D, n. 107 (cited as Misc. Box 27, f. 31)
f. 22*a* **III**, App. pt. II, no. 140 (mistake for Misc. Box 27, f. 4.22)
f. 26 **III**, App. pt. II, no. 142 (mistake for Misc. Box 27, f. 4.26)
f. 31 viii, D, n. 107 (mistake for Misc. Box 27, f. 4.31)
Misc. Box 28, f. 5 x, A, 3, n. 78
f. 26 **III**, App. pt. II, no. 346. viii, B, 4, nn. 24, 87; viii, B, 5, n. 85
f. 29 ix, B, n. 166
f. 33*v* **IV**, App. A, III
f. 37 ii, 5, nn. 39, 79. iii, C, n. 19; iii, D, n. 23. iv, 10, n. 15. x, C, 5, n. 5
f. 40 **II**, App. B, sec. 94
f. 42 i, 2, n. 70. **II**, App. B, sec. 14. v, B, 2, n. 101. vi, 12, n. 75
f. 44 viii, C, 4, n. 48
f. 51 v, D, 1, n. 19. ix, A, 4, nn. 111, 209; ix, B, n. 419
f. 52 **II**, App. A, sec. 168
f. 71 **III**, App. pt. I, gr. 7; **III**, App. pt. II, no. 41
f. 72 ix, A, 3, n. 44; ix, C, 1, n. 74
f. 79 viii, C, 1, n. 74
f. 79, sec. 12 **II**, App. A, sec. 180
f. 131 vi, 10, n. 17
f. 137 vii, C, 1, c, nn. 44, 48. ix, A, 2, n. 159
f. 155 ix, C, 1, n. 69
f. 184 **II**, App. B, sec. 66. viii, C, 4, n. 115; viii, D, n. 192. x, A, 3, nn. 197, 206
f. 199 ii, 5, n. 41. v, C, 4, n. 46. x, A, 3, n. 230
f. 217 **III**, App. pt. II, no. 234. viii, B, 4, nn. 24, 87. ix, 1, 4, n. 16; ix, A, 5, n. 60; ix, B, n. 387
f. 225 vii, A, 2, n. 14. ix, B, n. 158. x, A, 1, n. 37; x, B, 2, n. 79
f. 228 iii, C, nn. 6, 24. iv, 4, n. 46 (cited as Misc. Box 28, f. 288); iv, 6, n. 13. ix, B, n. 148
f. 234 **IV**, App. A, I
f. 240 i, 2, n. 5
f. 246 **I**, App. D, sec. 34. vii, D, 1, n. 23
f. 249 ii, 7, n. 99
f. 256 x, A, 2, n. 110
f. 263 iii, B, 3, n. 1. viii, A, 3, n. 35
f. 264 **III**, App. pt. II, no. 81
f. 266 **III**, App. pt. II, no. 175. viii, B, 2, n. 2; viii, B, 3, nn. 19, 29, 71; viii, B, 4, nn. 66, 88
f. 267 viii, B, 4, nn. 49, 86
f. 288 iv, 4, n. 46 (mistake for Misc. Box 28, f. 228)
Misc. Box 29, f. 6 *see* TS 16.377
f. 23 **IV**, App. A, V
f. 29 **III**, App. pt. II, no. 147. viii, A, 2, n. 78; viii, B, 3, nn. 19, 20; viii, B, 4, nn. 49, 86. ix, A, 4, n. 16; ix, B, n. 503. **IV**, App. D, n. 6
f. 44 vii, B, 3, n. 37
f. 58 **III**, App. pt. II, no. 193. viii, B, 1, n. 33; viii, B, 4, n. 93
Misc. Box 35 and 36 *see* TS Loan
TS LOAN (fragments originally lent by the library to Solomon Schechter for study while he was in the United States): Nos. 1–108 are now marked TS Misc. Box 35; nos. 109–209 are now marked TS Misc. Box 36
4, f. 5 vi, 8, n. 8
10 viii, B, 3, n. 5
20 i, 3, n. 42
32 x, A, 1, n. 117

35 i, 2, n. 71
40 v, A, 1, n. 40; v, B, 2, n. 106
43 v, B, 2, n. 109
48 **II**, App. D, sec. 18
137 **II**, App. C, sec. 1
149 ii, 2, n. 2
170 x, B, 5, n. 39
174 **II**, App. D, sec. 11. vii, C, 1, a, n. 26
206 v, B, 1, nn. 7, 123

GLASSES (Fragments originally kept under glass, arranged according to size, and now in binders)

TS 8.4 v, B, 1, n. 29. vii, A, 2, n. 9
.9 viii, C, 2, n. 162. x, B, 2, n. 33
.11 v, B, 2, n. 4. x, A, 2, n. 346
.12 ii, 7, n. 106. iii, D, n. 43; iii, E, n. 20; iii, F, n. 12. iv, 2, n. 13. ix, B, n. 167
.13 v, B, 1, n. 5. viii, C, 4, n. 77
.14 vii, B, 3, n. 12; vii, C, 1, d, n. 20
.18 iii, E, n. 57
.20 viii, A, 1, n. 86
.21 vii, C, 1, b, n. 35
.23 ii, 6, n. 23; v, B, 1, n. 31
.26 iii, F, n. 14
.28 iv, 4, n. 18
.29 vi, 6, n. 11
.32 x, A, 2, n. 15; x, B, 4, n. 161
.33 x, A, 2, n. 121
.38 iii, B, 3, n. 5
.58 ii, 5, n. 18
.60 x, C, 1, n. 11
.72 iii, D, n. 11
.73 iv, 10, n. 10. ix, A, 4, n. 175
.79*v* v, A, 2, n. 15; v, B, 2, nn. 30, 94
.86 vi, 11, n. 30
.89 **III**, App. pt. I, gr. 8
.90 viii, B, 3, n. 69
.97 **III**, App. pt. I, gr. 4; **III**, App. pt. II, no. 325. **IV**, App. C, 3. ix, A, 4, nn. 37, 54, 97, 169, 193
.101 viii, C, 4, n. 113
.102 **III**, App. pt. II, no. 169
.104 viii, C, 2, nn. 21, 98; viii, C, 3, n. 20
.106 ii, 2, n. 3. x, C, 4, n. 55
.110 **III**, App. pt. II, n. 262. viii, C, 1, n. 94
.111 viii, B, 2, n. 41
.112 **III**, App. pt. II, no. 183. viii, B, 2, n. 32
.115 v, A, 1, n. 43
.116 **III**, App. pt. I, gr. 5; **III**, App. pt. II, no. 300. viii, B, 3, n. 77; viii, C, 1, n. 207
.121 viii, C, 1, n. 95
.127 **III**, App. pt. II, no. 310
.129 **III**, App. pt. II, no. 195. viii, B, 4, n. 94
.131 viii, C, 1, n. 113
.133 **III**, App. pt. II, no. 267
.138 **III**, App. pt. I, gr. 5
.139 viii, C, 3, n. 74
.143 viii, C, 4, n. 27. x, A, 3, n. 43
.143*v* vii, B, 3, n. 57

.147 **III**, App. pt. II, no. 316
.149 v, A, 2, n. 15
.150 vii, A, 2, n. 9. ix, A, 2, n. 116; ix, A, 3, nn. 3, 5
.152 viii, C, 2, n. 13
.154 ii, 7, n. 99. viii, C, 3, n. 80
.161 v, D, 2, n. 23
.162 ix, A, 2, n. 35
.166 ii, 6, n. 8. viii, B, 4, n. 44; viii, C, 1, n. 114; viii, C, 4, n. 169. ix, B, n. 369
.168 **III**, App. pt. I, gr. 6; **III**, App. pt. II, no. 174. viii, C, 3, n. 45
.173 **III**, App. pt. II, no. 263
.183 v, A, 2, n. 60
.184 viii, B, 4, n. 103; viii, C, 3, n. 73
.187 vi, 9, n. 15
.193 v, C, 3, n. 1
.199 viii, B, 5, n. 26
.200 x, A, 2, n. 217
.206 viii, C, 2, n. 144
.208 **III**, App. pt. I, gr. 5; **III**, App. pt. II, no. 1. viii, B, 4, nn. 5, 14
.210 **III**, App. pt. I, gr. 5; **III**, App. pt. II, no. 330. viii, B, 4, n. 78
.213*v* x, A, 3, n. 263
.223 **III**, App. pt. I, gr. 8
.224 viii, D, nn. 14, 111. ix, A, 3, n. 93
.225 **III**, App. pt. I, gr. 5; **III**, App. pt. II, no. 125
.228 **III**, App. pt. I, gr. 8. viii, B, 4, n. 79
.238 **III**, App. pt. II, no. 200. viii, B, 4, n. 15
.239 **III**, App. pt. I, gr. 7; **III**, App. pt. II, no. 306
.245 vii, B, 1, n. 23
.251 vii, B, 1, n. 67
.257 ix, A, 2, n. 116; ix, A, 3, n. 47
.260 ix, A, 3, n. 52
.260*v* viii, C, 3, n. 42
.265 v, A, 1, nn. 12, 25; v, A, 2, n. 10
.268 iii, F, n. 29
.271 vii, A, 3, n. 45
TS 12.1 ii, 2, n. 8. iii, F, nn. 4, 8. vii, C, 1, a, n. 19; vii, C, 1, c, nn. 38, 41
.1*v* **III**, App. pt. II, no. 369. viii, B, 3, n. 79
.2 iii, E, n. 61; iii, F, n. 72. viii, C, 4, n. 107
.3 i, 2, n. 55; i, 3, n. 23. ii, 4, n. 53. vi, 4, n. 20. vii, C, 2, n. 3. ix, C, 1, n. 17. x, A, 2, n. 143
.5 **I**, App. B, II, 5. iii, A, 1, n. 42; iii, B, 2, n. 28; iii, B, 4, nn. 4, 9. vi, 10, n. 26; vi, 11, n. 40; vi, 13, n. 32. vii, D, 1, n. 1
.6 v, B, 2, n. 22
.7 viii, A, 2, n. 61
.8 ii, 7, n. 42. viii, A, 2, n. 66
.9 v, B, 2, n. 17. vi, 6, n. 2. viii, C, 2, n. 92
.12 i, 2, n. 30. ii, 4, n. 45. **III**, App. pt. I, gr. 4; **III**, App. pt. II, no. 344. viii, B, 4, nn. 33, 56. **IV**, App. C, 2, 4. ix, A, 4, nn. 5, 26, 46, 54, 57, 64, 92, 140, 164, 174, 178, 214; ix, A, 5, n. 42; ix, B, nn. 115, 405, 474, 534. **IV**, App. D, nn. 119, 226
.13 viii, C, 2, n. 112. ix, C, 1, n. 176. x, B, 1, n. 53
.16 vi, 7, n. 13. vii, B, 1, nn. 23, 34; vii, C, 1, c, n. 9. viii, A, 3, n. 44

.17 v, A, 1, n. 61
.18 x, C, 2, n. 17
.21 x, B, 2, nn. 70, 76
.23 **II**, App. A, sec. 124
.24*v* ix, C, 2, n. 56
.26 i, 2, n. 72. ii, 1, n. 6. v, D, 2, n. 37. vii, B, 1, n. 64
.31 ii, 3, n. 40; ii, 5, nn. 16, 30
.33 vi, 12, n. 63
.34 vi, 7, n. 18 (mistake for 12.43)
.34*v* ix, B, nn. 273, 338. x, B, 2, n. 106; x, C, 2, n. 59
.39 **I**, App. D, sec. 81. v, A, 1, n. 58. vi, 4, n. 25. **III**, App. pt. I, gr. 7; **III**, App. pt. II, no. 338. viii, B, 2, n. 5; viii, B, 5, n. 52; viii, C, 4, n. 173
.41 x, C, 2, n. 33
.43 v, A, 2, n. 24. vi, 7, n. 18 (cited as 12.34)
.50 vii, A, 2, n. 5. viii, C, 2, n. 137. ix, A, 2, n. 160
.53 vii, B, 3, n. 21
.55 **II**, App. D, sec. 32. vi, 4, n. 4; vi, 10, n. 36
.56 v, B, 1, nn. 21, 29, 45; v, B, 2, n. 52. ix, A, 5, n. 33. x, A, 1, n. 171; x, C, 3, n. 18; x, C, 5, n. 15
.57 x, A, 2, n. 297
.58 iv, 3, n. 66. v, B, 1, n. 139; v, B, 2, n. 53. x, A, 1, n. 27
.62 **I**, App. D, n. 18. **II**, App. D, sec. 31. vi, 4, n. 23
.64 viii, B, 4, n. 14. x, B, 2, n. 58
.65 x, C, 2, n. 18
.66 x, B, 4, n. 80
.69*v* viii, A, 2, n. 79. x, B, 1, n. 19
.74 vii, A, 1, n. 9
.80 ix, C, 1, n. 185
.81 x, C, 3, n. 12
.88 viii, C, 3, n. 11
.91 vii, A, 1, n. 34
.92 iv, 8, n. 32. viii, C, 1, n. 155. ix, B, n. 227. x, A, 2, n. 355; x, B, 4, n. 32
.95 **III**, App. pt. II, no. 307
.98 **III**, App. pt. I, gr. 8; **III**, App. pt. II, no. 14. viii, B, 3, n. 45. ix, A, 5, n. 21
.108 v, B, 2, n. 63
.114 iv, 8, nn. 12, 56
.115 ix, A, 3, n. 12
.116*v* viii, B, 3, n. 15
.118 **III**, App. pt. I, gr. 3; **III**, App. pt. II, no. 230. ix, A, 5, n. 73
.119 **III**, App. pt. II, no. 289. viii, B, 5, n. 41. ix, B, n. 475. **IV**, App. D, n. 222
.121 **III**, App. pt. II, no. 144. viii, B, 2, nn. 4, 13
.122 ix, A, 1, n. 3
.124 **I**, App. D, sec. 8. iii, D, n. 27; iii, E, nn. 5, 66. iv, 7, n. 23; iv, 8, n. 32; iv, 12, n. 23. viii, A, 2, n. 67
.125 vii, B, 1, n. 26. viii, C, 3, n. 44. ix, B, n. 486
.125*v* ix, B, nn. 465, 472, 486, 487, 488, 510, 514
.126 **I**, App. C, sec. 23
.128 iii, B, 3, n. 6 (mistake for 12.218). **III**, App. pt. I, gr. 4; **III**, App. pt. II, no. 58. viii, B, 3, n. 91
.129 v, B, 1, n. 80; v, C, 2, n. 34. viii, C, 1, n. 135
.131 **III**, App. pt. II, no. 225
.133 i, 3, n. 10. ii, 1, n. 8; ii, 4, nn. 41, 43. iii, B, 3, n. 5. iv, 1, n. 3; iv, 2, nn. 11, 14, 39. vi, 5, n. 4. viii, C, 2, n. 155. ix, B, n. 233. x, B, 2, n. 88

.134 ix, A, 5, n. 63
.140 ii, 7, nn. 28, 49. viii, C, 3, n. 36
.141 **IV**, App. C, 2
.144 **III**, App. pt. II, no. 94
.146 viii, A, Introd., n. 3
.147 ii, 5, nn. 1, 21. iii, E, n. 147. ix, B, n. 363
.150 iii, A, 2, n. 11
.153 v, A, 2, nn. 26, 27; v, B, 1, n. 7
.154 **III**, App. pt. I, gr. 7; **III**, App. pt. II, no. 17. viii, B, 1, n. 7; viii, B, 3, n. 35; viii, B, 4, n. 18. ix, A, 4, n. 56
.155 vii, A, 3, n. 1; vii, B, 3, n. 2. **III**, App. pt. I, gr. 4; **III**, App. pt. II, no. 20. viii, B, 3, n. 76; viii, B, 4, n. 104
.156 viii, C, 4, n. 23. **IV**, App. A, V. **IV**, App. C, 3
.159 **III**, App. pt. II, no. 132
.160 ix, A, 4, n. 170
.163 **III**, App. pt. I, gr. 5; **III**, App. pt. II, no. 313. viii, B, 3, n. 84. ix, B, n. 364
.163*v* vii, B, 1, n. 48. **III**, App. I, 8
.164 v, A, 2, n. 15. **III**, App. pt. I, gr. 5; **III**, App. pt. II, no. 329. viii, B, 4, n. 78
.165 **III**, App. pt. II, no. 69
.166 vii, A, 2, n. 1. **IV**, App. A, III
.167 **III**, App. pt. I, gr. 4; **III**, App. pt. II, no. 305. **IV**, App. C, 3; ix, A, 4, n. 54
.167*v* **IV**, App. C, 2
.171 iv, 3, n. 5; iv, 8, n. 32. x, B, 2, n. 89
.172*v* ix, A, 2, nn. 37, 58, 65, 160, 162
.174 ix, A, 1, n. 141
.175 i, 2, n. 42. ii, 7, nn. 4, 102, 106. iii, B, n. 5. iv, 2, n. 11; iv, 8, n. 32. viii, A, 2, n. 19. x, A, 2, n. 1; x, B, 2, n. 89 x, B, 4, n. 47
.176 viii, D, n. 58. **IV**, App. A, VI. ix, A, 3, n. 7
.177, top v, B, 2, n. 107
.177 vi, 11, n. 44. viii, C, 2, n. 140. ix, A, 3, n. 12
.178 vii, B, 2, n. 2
.179 i, 2, n. 98. x, C, 1, n. 8
.180 iv, 2, nn. 28, 29, 42 (mistakes for 20.180). **III**, App. pt. I, gr. 4; **III**, App. pt. II, no. 59. ix, A, 4, n. 64
.190 vi, 6, n. 13
.192 **II**, App. C, sec. 82(b). v, B, 1, n. 35. vii, C, 2, n. 5
.198 viii, C, 1, n. 236
.204 vii, B, 3, n. 9
.215 iii, E, n. 61. v, B, 1, n. 84; v, D, 2, n. 40. vii, C, 1, a, n. 10; vii, C, 1, c, n. 18; vii, D, 1, n. 23. ix, C, 1, n. 16; ix, D, n. 5
.217 v, A, 1, n. 29. x, A, 2, n. 402
.218 iii, B, 1, n. 16; iii, B, 3, n. 6 (cited as 12.128). iv, 3, n. 60
.223 iii, B, 1, n. 15; iii, G, n. 11. iv, 8, n. 32; iv, 10, n. 35
.224 iii, G, n. 34. iv, 7, n. 24. x, B, 1, n. 26
.227 ii, 2, n. 26. iii, E, n. 75. ix, B, n. 223. x, A, 2, n. 5
.229 i, 2, n. 21. iii, A, 2, n. 11; iii, F, nn. 30, 37. viii, A, 1, n. 44. ix, A, 4, n. 119; ix, B, n. 224
.230 vii, C, 1, a, n. 31
.231*v* **IV**, App. A, II. ix, A, 2, n. 159
.234 viii, C, 1, n. 223
.238 **II**, App. D, sec. 22. v, C, 4, n. 60
.239 v, A, 1, n. 47; v, B, 1, n. 112. vii, B, 2, n. 20
.241 iv, 8, nn. 56, 80

.242 viii, B, 2, n. 28; viii, C, 1, n. 207; viii, C, 4, n. 146. x, B, 5, n. 21
.243 ii, 5, n. 12. iv, 10, n. 4. vi, 2, n. 3. ix, C, 1, n. 72
.244 v, C, 4, n. 24. vii, A, 3, n. 34. ix, C, 1, n. 26
.245 vii, C, 2, n. 25. x, C, 1, n. 8
.246 iv, 3, n. 80. viii, C, 1, n. 35
.247 x, C, 2, n. 43
.248 I, App. B, sec. 7 (cited as 12.284). iii, B, 1, n. 7; iii, C, n. 23; iii, E, n. 61. iv, 10, nn. 5, 7. vii, C, 1, c, n. 49. ix, C, 1, n. 125
.250 iii, B, 2, n. 16; iii, E, n. 83. iv, 2, n. 16; iv, 7, n. 30; iv, 8, nn. 32, 80; iv, 10, nn. 5, 9. viii, C, 2, n. 25. x, C, 1, n. 48
.251 iii, E, nn. 3, 52, 60, 83. ix, B, n. 94
.252 vi, 7, n. 28. viii, A, 2, n. 79; viii, C, 1, n. 2. ix, C, 1, n. 144. x, D, nn. 45, 91
.254 ii, 5, n. 85; ii, 7, n. 23. iii, D, n. 72; iii, E, nn. 34, 48. iv, 3, n. 23; iv, 10, n. 12
.258 x, C, 1, n. 8
.262 iv, 3, n. 26; iv, 12, n. 37. vi, 3, n. 2. viii, A, 2, n. 40; viii, B, 1, n. 5; viii, B, 3, n. 95; viii, C, 1, n. 47; viii, C, 2, n. 19; viii, D, nn. 11, 27, 29
.263*v* ix, C, 2, n. 45
.264 ii, 4, n. 78. iii, A, 1, n. 33
.270*v* x, A, 3, n. 13; x, C, 1, n. 28
.274*v* ix, B, n. 166
.275 iii, D, n. 21. viii, A, 1, n. 86. ix, B, n. 63
.279 iv, 3, n. 74. ix, B, n. 393. x, A, 1, n. 37; x, B, 2, n. 96
.280 x, A, 1, n. 32; x, D, n. 228
.281 iii, F, nn. 12, 77, 121. vii, C, 1, d, n. 24
.282 I, App. D, sec. 5
.284 I, App. B, sec. 7 (mistake for 12.248)
.284*v* x, A, 3, n. 155
.285 ix, B, n. 200
.287 x, B, 2, n. 100
.288 I, App. D, sec. 92. iii, D, n. 23. viii, C, 1, n. 83; viii, C, 3, n. 113
.289 v, B, 1, n. 36; v, C, 1, n. 12; v, C, 4, nn. 45, 49. vii, C, 2, n. 41. viii, C, 4, nn. 133, 150. ix, B, n. 28. x, D, n. 308
.290 iii, D, nn. 23, 35, 48; iii, F, n. 64. iv, 2, n. 32; iv, 7, n. 9; iv, 8, n. 29. v, B, 2, n. 33. vii, A, 1, nn. 6, 30; vii, C, 1, c, nn. 20, 30; vii, C, 2, n. 30
.291 ii, 2, n. 22; ii, 4, n. 55. iii, B, 2, n. 40; iii, C, n. 15; iii, G, n. 10. iv, 7, n. 29; iv, 10, n. 22. vii, A, 2, n. 19. x, B, 2, n. 98
.296 iii, E, n. 57
.298 x, A, 2, n. 257
.299 viii, C, 1, n. 166. x, A, 1, n. 90; x, A, 3, n. 287
TS 12.300*v* ix, A, 1, n. 105
.301 v, C, 2, n. 2
.303 x, B, 2, n. 71; x, B, 3, n. 21
.305*v* ix, C, 1, n. 91. x, B, 2, n. 70
.307*v* ix, B, n. 411
.312 ii, 5, nn. 2, 69. v, B, 2, n. 67. ix, B, nn. 47, 200. x, A, 1, n. 150
.320*v* vii, B, 2, n. 17. ix, C, 1, n. 164
.322 viii, A, 1, n. 15
.328 v, B, 1, n. 96. vi, 9, n. 6
.335 iii, D, nn. 13, 67. iv, 4, n. 32; iv, 5, n. 9; iv, 7, nn. 14, 20; iv, 8, n. 72; iv, 10, n. 37

.337 iv, 10, n. 22. viii, B, 1, n. 32; viii, B, 2, n. 1. x, B, 1, n. 29
.338 iv, 9, n. 14 (cited as 12.388). vii, A, 1, n. 19; vii, B, 1, n. 15
.340 ix, C, 1, n. 155
.345 ix, C, 2, n. 35
.347 i, 3, n. 25. viii, C, 1, n. 190; viii, C, 2, n. 37. ix, A, 1, n. 206
.348 x, B, 4, n. 113
.350 viii, C, 3, n. 17
.352 v, A, 1, n. 49
.357 x, C, 1, n. 29
.360 v, B, 1, n. 53. vi, 4, n. 8
.362 i, 3, n. 5. ii, 4, nn. 62, 83. x, B, 1, n. 99
.364 iii, F, n. 51. iv, 3, n. 68
.365 v, B, 1, n. 138
.366 iii, B, 1, n. 11; iii, D, n. 40; iii, E, nn. 52, 61, 73, 83. iv, 5, n. 6; iv, 7, n. 27; iv, 8, nn. 36, 46. ix, B, n. 316
.367 **I**, App. D, sec. 6. ii, 4, n. 16. iii, D, n. 14; iii, E, n. 54. viii, A, 1, n. 76. ix, A, 1, n. 124
.368 iv, 3, n. 80
.369 iii, E, n. 14. ix, B, n. 231
.371 iii, A, 1, n. 2. v, B, 1, nn. 98, 148. vii, B, 1, n. 66; vii, B, 3, n. 31
.372 ii, 4, n. 41. iii, E, nn. 61, 73; iii, G, n. 10. iv, 6, n. 13; iv, 9, n. 17. vii, A, 3, n. 5; vii, C, 1, d, n. 23. viii, A, 1, n. 44
.373 iii, F, n. 28. viii, C, 1, n. 2. ix, A, 5, n. 72; ix, B, n. 380. x, A, 2, n. 262
.374 iv, 3, n. 74. **II**, App. C, sec. 6. ix, A, 1, n. 137. x, A, 2, n. 270
.378 iv, 10, n. 25. x, C, 2, n. 27
.383 ii, 2, n. 2. iii, B, 3, n. 5. iv, 7, n. 27; iv, 10, n. 6. ix, A, 1, n. 19. x, B, 2, n. 87
.386 iv, 6, n. 12; iv, 8, n. 76; iv, 12, n. 40. x, C, 5, n. 12
.388 iv, 4, n. 8; iv, 8, n. 46; iv, 9, n. 14 (mistake for 12.338). v, B, 1, n. 93
.389 ix, B, n. 224
.391 iv, 4, n. 17
.392 i, 2, n. 8. x, B, 2, n. 136; x, C, 2, n. 58
.394 i, 2, n. 56. vi, 11, n. 47
.404 ix, A, 4, n. 133
.405 x, B, 4, n. 119
.405*v* x, B, 1, n. 31
.413*v* x, B, 3, n. 77
.415 ix, C, 1, n. 119. x, B, 1, n. 17; x, B, 4, n. 160
.417 vii, A, 2, n. 5. ix, A, 3, n. 110
.419*v* **II**, App. C, sec. 36
.421 vi, 10, n. 1
.424 iv, 2, n. 40
.425 vi, 4, n. 14. vii, C, 1, b, n. 5. viii, A, 1, n. 30. x, A, 2, n. 167; x, C, 3, n. 18
.427 vi, 10, n. 42
.428 x, A, 2, n. 283
.433*v* x, A, 2, n. 18
.434 ii, 1, n. 12; ii, 5, n. 30. iii, C, n. 6; iii, D, nn. 2, 46, 50; iii, E, n. 47. iv, 10, n. 18; iv, 11, nn. 14, 25. ix, A, 5, n. 23; ix, B, n. 170. x, A, 2, n. 137
.435 i, 3, n. 13. iii, E, nn. 2, 27. iv, 2, n. 18; iv, 5, n. 14; iv, 11, n. 19. vii, A, 1, n. 17; vii, C, 1, c, n. 43. ix, B, n. 254. x, B, 2, n. 117
.438 viii, B, 3, n. 71

.440 **III**, App. pt. II, no. 98. viii, B, 3, n. 84; viii, B, 4, n. 25. ix, B, nn. 438, 525
.442 **III**, App. pt. II, no. 8. viii, B, 4, n. 20
.443 **III**, App. pt. I, gr. 1; **III**, App. pt. II, no. 117. viii, B, 3, n. 66
.445 viii, C, 4, n. 162
.449 viii, B, 3, n. 68
.451*v* x, D, n. 161
.452 **III**, App. pt. I, gr. 4; **III**, App. pt. II, no. 323. ix, A, 5, n. 27
.453 **III**, App. pt. I, gr. 5; **III**, App. pt. II, no. 73
.457 **III**, App. pt. I, gr. 1; **III**, App. pt. II, no. 74
.458 vii, A, 3, n. 29
.459 x, C, 5, n. 26
.459*v* ix, A, 4, n. 99
.461 iii, B, 2, n. 25. viii, D, n. 11
.462 ii, 4, n. 61. ix, A, 3, n. 88
.464 x, C, 1, n. 48; x, C, 2, n. 30
.465 ix, A, 4, nn. 83, 216
.466 x, A, 2, n. 419
.468 iv, 10, n. 7. vii, B, 3, n. 51. ix, B, n. 167
.474 ix, B, nn. 472, 473, 480
.477 ix, A, 3, n. 55
.479 ii, 4, n. 37. iii, D, nn. 40, 70. ix, A, 1, n. 222
.482 **IV**, App. A, III. ix, A, 3, n. 24
.485 ix, A, 3, n. 24
.487 ii, 2, n. 20. **II**, App. A, sec. 102. ix, A, 3, n. 57. x, D, n. 161
.488 **III**, App. pt. I, gr. 5; **III**, App. pt. II, no. 102. **IV**, App. C, 2. ix, A, 4, n. 31
.489 **III**, App. pt. II, no. 214. viii, B, 3, n. 73
.490 **III**, App. pt. II, no. 13. viii, B, 4, n. 13
.493 ii, 6, n. 9. vi, 3, n. 5. viii, A, 1, n. 82; viii, C, 2, n. 84
.494 v, B, 1, n. 41. vi, 5, n. 2. **III**, App. pt. I, gr. 7; **III**, App. pt. II, no. 12. viii, B, 3, n. 26; viii, B, 4, n. 13; viii, C, 2, n. 72; viii, C, 4, n. 164
.499 vi, 11, n. 43. vii, A, 2, n. 5. viii, A, 3, n. 15. **IV**, App. A, III. ix, A, 1, n. 72; ix, A, 3, n. 17
.502 **IV**, App. A, III
.512 viii, C, 2, n. 62. x, A, 1, n. 82
.513 iii, E, n. 69
.515 iii, F, n. 141. **I**, App. D, n. 15
.519 **III**, App. pt. II, no. 378. ix, A, 5, nn. 15, 32, 71
.520*v* **IV**, App. D, n. 229
.523 iii, F, n. 25
.525 ii, 2, n. 8; ii, 4, nn. 68, 90; ii, 5, nn. 28, 42. iii, A, 1, n. 7
.526 **III**, App. pt. I, gr. 1; **III**, App. pt. II, no. 116. **IV**, App. C, 2. ix, A, 4, n. 192; ix, B, n. 74
.528 v, B, 1, n. 41
.530 viii, A, 1, n. 86; viii, C, 4, n. 32. **IV**, App. D, n. 195. x, A, 3, n. 165
.530*v*, col. I ix, A, 4, n. 205; ix, A, 5, nn. 10, 49; ix, B, nn. 395, 443, 469, 520, 554
.530*v*, col. II ix, A, 4, nn. 34, 107, 119, 205; ix, A, 5, n. 40
.531 ii, 2, n. 25. vii, B, 3, n. 49. viii, C, 3, n. 25
.532 v, C, 1, n. 8
.537 viii, B, 4, n. 86
.538 iii, D, n. 10. ix, A, 3, n. 16
.541 **III**, App. pt. II, no. 29
.543 **I**, Introduction, n. 45. **II**, App. C, sec. 99. v, B, 1, nn. 14,

18, 21, 31, 33; v, C, 4, n. 62. vi, 12, n. 27. vii, C, 1, b, n. 12. ix, A, 1, n. 37
.544 **II**, App. C, sec. 24. vii, A, 2, n. 9. **III**, App. pt. I, gr. 6; **III**, App. pt. II, no. 277. viii, D, nn. 25, 100. **IV**, App. A, VI. ix, A, 3, n. 14
.545 ii, 4, n. 80
.547 **III**, App. pt. I, gr. 7; **III**, App. pt. II, no. 314
.549 *see* 16.355
.551 *see* 16.356
.552 **III**, App. pt. I, gr. 1; **III**, App. pt. II, no. 221. ix, A, 4, nn. 162, 196
.553 viii, C, 3, n. 27
.558 **III**, App. pt. II, no. 84
.562 *see* 16.356
.564 *see* 16.355
.566 **I**, App. D, sec. 9. iv, 4, n. 8. vi, 5, nn. 4, 7
.568 x, C, 2, n. 17
.569 **II**, App. D, sec. 18
.570 vii, B, 3, n. 51
.573 vi, 12, n. 22
.573*v* **II**, App. C, sec. 73
.575 viii, C, 1, n. 218; viii, C, 4, n. 116
.576 viii, D, n. 15
.577 **IV**, App. A, II
.579 iii, F, n. 40. vi, 11, n. 59
.580 ii, 3, n. 16. v, B, 1, n. 80
.581 ii, 3, n. 9; ii, 5, n. 76. **II**, App. B, sec. 38. v, B, 1, nn. 26, 27, 32, 56; v, C, 4, n. 11. vii, A, 1, n. 5; vii, C, 2, n. 32. ix, A, 2, n. 156. x, A, 3, n. 200
.582 ii, 7, n. 10
.583 iii, F, nn. 124, 200. **I**, App. D, n. 28. v, B, 2, n. 58. vi, 11, n. 22
.585 ii, 7, n. 88. **III**, App. pt. I, gr. 1; **III**, App. pt. II, no. 293. viii, C, 1, n. 150
.586 ix, A, 1, n. 53; ix, A, 2, n. 43; ix, A, 4, n. 170; ix, A, 5, n. 70
.587 iii, B, 3, n. 14. vii, B, 1, n. 49. ix, C, 2, n. 21
.588 ix, A, 1, n. 38
.591 viii, C, 4, nn. 38, 47, 99
.594 iii, F, n. 126. vii, D, 1, n. 26
.594*v* x, A, 3, n. 314
.596 viii, B, 3, n. 71
.597 v, B, 1, nn. 53, 74; v, B, 2, n. 27. viii, C, 1, n. 22
.601 ix, A, 3, n. 9
.606 **I**, App. C, sec. 4. ii, 4, n. 57. iii, D, n. 84
.608 v, B, 2, n. 90. vi, 9, n. 43
.613 **III**, App. pt. I, gr. 5. viii, C, 3, n. 135. x, A, 3, n. 26
.615 ix, B, n. 411
.616 ii, 2, n. 8. iii, A, 1, n. 7
.617 ii, 3, n. 16
.618 viii, D, n. 4
.619 ix, A, 4, nn. 84, 92, 191, 212
.620 i, 2, n. 33
.621 viii, B, 1, n. 33. ix, A, 4, n. 174
.624 viii, B, 3, n. 67; viii, B, 5, n. 66 (cited as 12.634). ix, A, 3, n. 79
.628 ix, A, 1, n. 151
.631 viii, C, 3, n. 26. x, A, 3, nn. 26, 202

.633 **IV**, App. D, n. 196
.634 iii, C, n. 11. vii, B, 1, n. 67. viii, B, 5, n. 66 (mistake for 12.624); viii, C, 4, n. 58
.635 ii, 7, n. 60. ix, A, 4, nn. 92, 174
.636 ii, 5, n. 71. x, A, 3, nn. 179, 182
.640 **III**, App. pt. II, no. 208
.641 vii, A, 2, n. 5
.644 x, C, 4, n. 61; x, C, 5, n. 53
.646*v* ix, B, nn. 363, 365
.647 viii, B, 4, n. 46
.651 iii, B, 3, n. 8
.652 v, C, 4, n. 56. x, B, 1, n. 50
.653 **III**, App. pt. I, gr. 5; **III**, App. pt. II, no. 202. viii, B, 4, n. 15. ix, A, 4, n. 49
.654 v, A, 1, n. 49; v, B, 1, n. 74. x, A, 1, n. 18; x, A, 2, nn. 263, 300, 307; x, B, 4, n. 136
.655*v* ix, D, n. 18
.656 **III**, App. pt. II, no. 261
.657 v, A, 1, n. 57. vii, B, 2, n. 25. x, A, 2, n. 389
.658 viii, D, n. 15. ix, A, 4, n. 150. **IV**, App. D, n. 105
.659 viii, B, 4, n. 24
.660 ii, 5, n. 26. vii, A, 2, n. 5. ix, A, 2, n. 63
.664 **II**, App. D, sec. 29
.666 vii, D, 1, n. 9
.668 ix, A, 3, n. 3
.670 iii, B, 2, nn. 5, 23. vi, 13, n. 4
.673 **III**, App. pt. I, gr. 6; **III**, App. pt. II, no. 23
.678 viii, A, 2, n. 78; viii, C, 1, n. 223
.681 viii, C, 1, n. 188
.683 x, B, 1, n. 140
.684 ii, 4, n. 61. viii, A, 3, n. 58; viii, C, 1, n. 218
.685 **III**, App. pt. II, no. 47
.688 viii, B, 3, n. 76
.689 viii, B, 3, nn. 51, 52
.690 **IV**, App. C, 3
.693 i, 2, n. 16. x, A, 2, n. 310
.694 iii, A, 1, n. 38; iii, B, 4, n. 5. **IV**, App. A, III. ix, A, 1, nn. 51, 53, 80, 103; ix, A, 2, nn. 11, 64
.695 ix, A, 1, n. 38
.708 ii, 5, nn. 16, 63. ix, D, n. 11
.714 viii, C, 4, n. 50
.715 viii, B, 3, n. 53
.719 x, C, 5, n. 25
.722 v, B, 1, n. 69. vi, 9, n. 6
.732 vii, A, 3, nn. 38, 47
.762 **III**, App. pt. II, no. 52
.763 viii, C, 4, n. 177. ix, A, 4, n. 47; ix, B, n. 494
.771 **III**, App. pt. I, grs. 6 and 8; **III**, App. pt. II, no. 268. viii, B, 4, n. 80. ix, A, 3, n. 92
.773 viii, D, n. 48. ix, A, 2, nn. 9, 62, 72, 75, 157
.777 iii, D, n. 8. ix, A, 3, nn. 53, 66
.780 viii, A, 1, n. 8; viii, A, 3, n. 29; viii, C, 2, n. 128. x, A, 2, n. 399
.781 iii, C, n. 21. ix, A, 4, n. 92
.784 iii, B, 2, n. 22; iii, F, nn. 96, 103, 105, 111, 112
.789 viii, A, 2, n. 79
.791 vi, 11, n. 51
.792 ii, 5, n. 70. ix, A, 2, n. 39

.793 ii, 1, n. 12; ii, 4, n. 93. iii, D, nn. 14, 16. x, A, 2, n. 137
.794 **I**, App. D, n. 27
.815 (was 8.88, 8.249) **III**, App. pt. I, gr. 8. viii, A, 1, n. 43
.816 x, B, 4, n. 80
.822 v, A, 2, n. 49
.825 ii, 7, n. 55. iv, 3, n. 16
.829 iii, B, 3, n. 5. viii, A, 2, n. 18
.830 x, C, 2, n. 7
.834*v* vi, 10, n. 46
.857 *see* TS 10 J 22, f. 7
TS 16.1 vi, 12, n. 21
.2 **III**, App. pt. II, no. 40
.3 viii, B, 3, n. 91
.5 viii, A, 3, n. 18. ix, A, 3, nn. 52, 75
.6*v* x, A, 3, n. 229
.7 ii, 5, n. 39. iii, B, 1, n. 12; iii, E, nn. 6, 32, 41, 42, 61, 73; iii, F, n. 42. iv, 3, n. 27; iv, 7, n. 23; iv, 8, nn. 32, 59. vi, 5, n. 5; vi, 13, n. 31
.9 v, C, 4, n. 60. x, A, 2, n. 45
.11 vii, A, 2, n. 17. viii, B, 5, n. 74. x, Notes on Sources, n. 4; x, A, 3, n. 313
.13 ii, 4, n. 8. iii, D, n. 71; iii, E, n. 61. iv, 6, nn. 11, 12; iv, 7, n. 15; iv, 8, n. 36; iv, 9, nn. 5, 6; iv, 10, n. 30; iv, 11, n. 19; iv, 12, nn. 15, 17. v, A, 2, n. 11. vi, 2, n. 7. viii, D, n. 132. x, A, 2, n. 14; x, B, 2, n. 109
.14 vii, B, 1, n. 21. viii, A, 1, n. 49; viii, C, 4, n. 45
.15 ii, 7, nn. 17, 64
.19 ii, 4, n. 84
.20 ii, 7, n. 53
.22 iii, A, 1, n. 43. vii, C, 1, b, n. 40
.23 viii, C, 3, n. 24; viii, D, n. 11
.24 ii, 2, n. 17
.26 v, A, 1, n. 5
.27 viii, C, 4, n. 82. x, B, 1, n. 21
.30 ix, A, 4, n. 169
.32 **III**, App. pt. II, no. 224. viii, D, n. 15. ix, A, 4, nn. 54, 191; ix, B, n. 63. **IV**, App. D, n. 229
.34 x, C, 5, n. 32
.35 viii, C, 1, n. 71. ix, A, 2, n. 79; ix, A, 4, n. 213
.36 v, A, 1, n. 49
.39 **I**, App. B, I, 10. **I**, App. D, sec. 58. v, C, 4, n. 3. vi, 10, n. 46. vii, C, 2, n. 33
.41 vii, A, 2, n. 5. ix, A, 3, n. 3
.42 viii, A, 1, n. 76; viii, A, 2, n. 19. x, B, 1, n. 22
.44 vii, B, 3, n. 37. **III**, App. pt. I, gr. 5. x, A, 3, n. 26
.45 vii, B, 1, n. 45
.47 vi, 10, n. 26. vii, B, 3, n. 16
.49 ii, 4, n. 61. viii, C, 3, n. 45
.50 **III**, App. pt. II, no. 192. viii, B, 4, n. 92; viii, D, n. 7. ix, B, n. 280
.51 **II**, App. D, sec. 18. vi, 13, n. 6. ix, A, 3, n. 92
.52 v, A, 2, n. 15. **III**, App. pt. I, gr. 5; **III**, App. pt. II, nos. 49, 332. viii, B, 3, nn. 45, 56
.53 **III**, App. pt. I, gr. 7; **III**, App. pt. II, no. 22. viii, B, 4, n. 13
.54 iv, 2, nn. 7, 23; iv, 6, n. 8; iv, 7, n. 24; iv, 8, nn. 12, 19, 40, 56, 80. vi, 12, n. 82. x, B, 2, n. 139; x, D, n. 189
.56 iii, F, n. 142

.57 iii, F, nn. 108, 111. v, A, 2, nn. 15, 52; v, C, 1, n. 40. viii, C, 2, n. 65. x, A, 3, n. 10; x, B, 1, n. 83
.58 **III**, App. pt. II, no. 311. ix, A, 4, n. 57
.60 iii, F, nn. 40, 143
.61 vii, C, 1, b, n. 2
.63 **II**, App. A, secs. 129, 157. vii, B, 3, n. 54
.64 vii, D, 2, n. 1. viii, A, 1, n. 50; viii, A, 2, n. 19; viii, B, 1, n. 34. x, B, 1, nn. 120, 121, 125, 128
.65 vii, A, 2, n. 5. viii, C, 2, n. 141. ix, A, 1, n. 169
.67 vii, D, 1, n. 21. **III**, App. pt. II, no. 252. viii, B, 1, n. 8; viii, B, 3, nn. 13, 29, 84; viii, B, 4, n. 15
.68 iv, 12, n. 5
.70 ii, 7, n. 45. vi, 13, n. 4. **III**, App. pt. I, gr. 4; **III**, App. pt. II, no. 317. viii, D, n. 11. ix, A, 4, nn. 55, 217; ix, B, nn. 278, 536, 554
.71 **I**, App. D, n. 26. **III**, App. pt. II, no. 56. viii, B, 3, n. 47. x, D, n. 32
.72 ii, 4, n. 90. ix, A, 1, nn. 51, 88; ix, A, 3, nn. 3, 47
.73 viii, B, 3, n. 61. ix, B, n. 411
.74 **III**, App. pt. II, no. 35. viii, B, 4, n. 60
.75 **III**, App. pt. II, no. 54
.76 v, B, 1, n. 4. viii, B, 1, n. 7; viii, B, 3, n. 45
.77 **II**, App. D, sec. 12. vi, 9, n. 4
.78 **III**, App. pt. II, no. 104. viii, B, 3, n. 49
.79 ii, 4, n. 106. v, B, 1, n. 80; v, C, 2, n. 33. vi, 13, n. 2. viii, D, n. 23. ix, A, 3, n. 3
.80 **III**, App. pt. I, gr. 4; **III**, App. pt. II, no. 366. ix, A, 4, nn. 97, 129, 219; ix, A, 5, nn. 3, 6, 11, 32, 43, 48, 55, 69, 85; ix, B, n. 221. **IV**, App. D, nn. 29, 46, 59, 128
..83 **IV**, App. A, VI. ix, A, 1, n. 95; ix, A, 2, n. 37
.85 **III**, App. pt. I, gr. 7; **III**, App. pt. II, no. 259. viii, B, 4, n. 50
.86 **III**, App. pt. I, gr. 1. viii, B, 4, n. 56. **IV**, App. C, 2. ix, A, 4, n. 196; ix, B, n. 74
.87 iii, B, 2, n. 26; iii, C, nn. 5, 18. vii, A, 2, n. 18; vii, C, 1, c, n. 17. ix, B, n. 166
.89 iii, F, n. 156
.90 viii, C, 2, n. 172; viii, C, 3, n. 45
.91 viii, B, 3, nn. 42, 45
.95 v, A, 1, n. 19
.102 iii, G, n. 3. ix, A, 1, n. 230
.104 viii, B, 3, p. 111
.105 **I**, App. D, sec. 1. ii, 7, n. 99. **III**, App. pt. I, gr. 4; **III**, App. pt. II, no. 57. viii, B, 3, n. 84
.106 **III**, App. pt. II, no. 133. ix, A, 1, n. 212
.107 **III**, App. pt. I, gr. 5; **III**, App. pt. II, no. 236. viii, B, 3, nn. 62, 91; viii, B, 4, n. 57. ix, B, nn. 487, 526
.109 viii, B, 2, n. 2; viii, B, 3, nn. 38, 46. x.C, 4, n. 61
.111 vi, 9, n. 15
.112 v, B, 1, n. 4. viii, B, 3, nn. 50, 76
.115 **II**, App. A, sec. 1. vii, B, 3, n. 2. viii, C, 4, n. 154. **IV**, App. A, V; ix, A, 1, n. 183; ix, A, 3, nn. 32, 113. x, A, 3, nn. 67, 97
.116 ii, 4, nn. 53, 69. iii, F, n. 109. vii, A, 2, n. 5. ix, A, 1, n. 76; ix, A, 2, nn. 9, 35, 92
.117 vi, 13, n. 12. vii, A, 2, n. 9. **IV**, App. A, III. ix, A, 3, n. 3
.119 **II**, App. C, sec. 18. viii, B, 2, n. 74; viii, D, n. 99. **IV**, App. D, n. 109

.122 I, App. D, sec. 53. **II**, App. A, sec. 17. v, B, 1, n. 115. vi, 9, n. 17. vii, B, 1, n. 36. ix, A, 3, n. 63
.123 vii, B, 2, n. 1. **III**, App. pt. I, gr. 8; **III**, App. pt. II, no. 18. viii, B, 1, nn. 19; viii, B, 3, n. 29; viii, B, 4, n. 10. ix, B, n. 445
.124 iii, F, n. 144. **II**, App. D, sec. 6. vii, B, 1, n. 3. x, A, 3, n. 305
.125 viii, B, 3, n. 82
.126 **II**, App. D, sec. 29. **IV**, App. A, V
.127 viii, C, 4, n. 167
.128 x, A, 1, n. 88
.130 v, B, 1, n. 1; v, B, 2, n. 33
.132 iii, F, n. 8. **III**, App. pt. I, gr. 7. viii, A, 3, n. 27. **IV**, App. A, II; ix, A, 2, nn. 9, 35
.133 ii, 7, n. 110. vii, D, 1, n. 2
.134 ii, 4, nn. 2, 64; ii, 7, n. 26. v, A, 2, n. 64. viii, C, 3, n. 110
.134*v* vi, 2, n. 7. viii, C, 4, n. 158
.137 ix, A, 2, nn. 155, 156, 158
.138 ii, 4, n. 53. iii, B, 2, n. 54. x, A, 3, n. 305
.140 vii, A, 2, n. 3; vii, A, 3, n. 27. ix, A, 2, nn. 56, 74, 89, 112, 116, 153, 154; ix, A, 3, nn. 9, 11
.141 viii, C, 4, nn. 19, 51
.142 ii, 4, n. 87. **III**, App. pt. I, gr. 4; **III**, App. pt. II, no. 357. viii, B, 4, n. 65; viii, B, 5, n. 91. ix, B, n. 367
.144 viii, C, 1, n. 111
.146 ii, 5, n. 77. iii, D, n. 8; iii, F, n. 123. viii, D, n. 58. **IV**, App. A, VI. ix, A, 1, n. 65; ix, A, 3, n. 7
.147 **III**, App. pt. I, gr. 5; **III**, App. pt. II, no. 349. viii, B, 3, n. 73
.148 I, App. C, sec. 1. iii, F, nn. 6, 216. vii, C, 1, b, n. 18. viii, A, 3, n. 66
.149 v, B, 1, n. 99; v, B, 2, n. 15. vi, 9, n. 38. x, A, 1, nn. 96, 112
.150 viii, A, 1, nn. 45, 59; viii, C, 4, n. 67
.151 vi, 4, n. 26
.153 viii, B, 3, n. 39; viii, C, 4, n. 165; viii, D, n. 15
.154 v, B, 2, n. 29. vii, A, 3, n. 41; vii, B, 2, n. 30
.155 **III**, App. pt. II, no. 100. viii, B, 3, n. 76. **IV**, App. A, IV. ix, A, 5, nn. 17, 32 (*see* Dropsie 333)
.159 ii, 5, n. 71. iii, F, n. 156
.162 **II**, App. D, sec. 7. viii, C, 4, n. 19
.163 i, 2, nn. 22, 65. iii, A, 2, n. 11; iii, D, nn. 44, 62; iii, E, nn. 52, 61, 83; iii, F, n. 39. iv, 6, nn. 2, 11; iv, 7, nn. 10, 15, 17, 20; iv, 8, n. 32; iv, 10, nn. 28, 29, 30. ix, C, 2, n. 56
.164 vi, 11, n. 14
.169 **III**, App. pt. II, no. 89. viii, B, 2, n. 78
.170 iii, B, 2, n. 19. x, C, 1, n. 48
.171 ii, 1, n. 4. viii, C, 2, n. 86. x, A, 2, n. 405
.172 viii, D, n. 59
.172*v* viii, D, nn. 12, 66, 92
.173 **III**, App. pt. II, no. 165. ix, B, n. 472
.176 vi, 12, n. 26. **IV**, App. A, IV. ix, A, 3, n. 22
.177 ii, 1, n. 14. vi, 12, n. 27. x, C, 5, n. 53
.178 viii, B, 3, n. 49. ix, A, 4, n. 172
.179 i, 2, n. 46. ii, 7, n. 83. iii, A, 1, n. 33. iv, 3, n. 51; iv, 7, n. 30. v, A, 2, nn. 11, 78; v, B, 1, n. 118. vi, 2, n. 28; vi, 6, n. 6; vi, 12, n. 93. vii, A, 1, n. 7; vii, C, 1, c, n. 18. viii, A, 2, n. 6; viii, C, 1, n. 5; viii, C, 2, nn. 8, 9, 17, 31, 64. x, A, 1, n. 160
.181 v, A, 1, n. 3. vii, B, 1, n. 21. viii, B, 1, n. 7; viii, B, 2, n. 84. **IV**, App. A, IV. ix, A, 2, nn. 35, 43; ix, B, n. 259
.181, I **III**, App. pt. I, gr. 3; **III**, App. pt. II, no. 162

.181, II **III**, App. pt. I, gr. 3; **III**, App. pt. II, no. 180
.181, III **III**, App. pt. I, gr. 3; **III**, App. pt. II, no. 103
.181, IV ix, A, 5, n. 83. ix, B, n. 253
.181*v*, II viii, B, 3, n. 33
.181*v*, III ix, A, 2, n. 150; ix, A, 4, n. 214; ix, A, 5, n. 70
.181*v*, IV **III**, App. pt. I, gr. 3; **III**, App. pt. II, no. 163. viii, B, 4, n. 31
.181*d* ix, B, n. 534
.184 vi, 9, n. 15. **III**, App. pt. II, no. 281. ix, A, 4, nn. 57, 170, 199, 219
.185 v, B, 2, n. 63. viii, C, 1, n. 214. ix, A, 2, nn. 36, 67
.186 v, B, 1, n. 128; v, B, 2, n. 33. vi, 10, n. 34. x, A, 2, n. 391
.187 v, A, 1, n. 57; v, A, 2, n. 50; v, B, 1, nn. 110, 142; v, D, 2, nn. 44, 46. x, D, nn. 301, 334
.188 ii, 7, n. 40. vi, 10, n. 22. viii, D, n. 11. ix, A, 1, n. 41
.189 **III**, App. pt. I, gr. 4; **III**, App. pt. II, no. 260
.191 **II**, App. C, sec. 1. vii, B, 1, n. 30. viii, A, 3, n. 67
.196 v, B, 2, n. 17. vi, 6, n. 2. x, A, 2, n. 24; x, A, 3, n. 35; x, B, 1, nn. 24, 136
.198 **III**, App. pt. II, no. 210. viii, C, 1, n. 145. ix, A, 4, n. 192; ix, A, 5, nn. 23, 38, 48; ix, B, nn. 370, 472
.200 **I**, App. D, sec. 74. iii, F, n. 134. v, D, 2, n. 21. ix, A, 1, n. 18; ix, C, 1, n. 153
.203 iii, B, 2, n. 38; iii, B, 4, nn. 3, 10
.206 **I**, App. D, sec. 82. ix, B, n. 503
.207 ix, A, 3, n. 91
.208 iii, F, n. 154. vii, A, 1, n. 29
.209 viii, B, 3, n. 91
.209*v* **II**, App. C, sec. 9
.210 **III**, App. pt. II, no. 267
.211 viii, B, 3, n. 51
.213 iii, F, n. 191. v, B, 1, n. 57. vii, B, 2, n. 16
.214 **III**, App. pt. II, no. 284. viii, C, 1, n. 207
.215 i, 3, n. 2 (cited as India Book No. 187). iv, 8, n. 3. ix, A, 5, n. 81
.217 **III**, App. pt. I, gr. 5; **III**, App. pt. II, no. 125
.218 viii, C, 3, n. 111
.220 viii, C, 1, n. 115
.222 ii, 5, n. 48. **II**, App. A, sec. 99
.230 **II**, App. B, sec. 109
.231 vii, C, 1, c, n. 45. viii, B, 2, nn. 21, 83
.232 ii, 5, n. 16. ix, C, 1, n. 141
.233 **III**, App. pt. I, gr. 5; **III**, App. pt. II, no. 301
.235 v, B, 1, n. 152
.238 vii, D, 1, n. 27. viii, D, nn. 14, 111
.239 ii, 7, n. 46. iii, A, 1, n. 43. ix, B, n. 536. **IV**, App. D, n. 113
.241 viii, C, 2, nn. 99, 108, 148
.243 vii, B, 3, n. 37
.244 iii, D, n. 45. iv, 6, n. 14; iv, 8, n. 6
.245 vii, A, 3, n. 1. viii, B, 3, nn. 14, 39, 84
.246 **III**, App. pt. I, gr. 6. viii, B, 3, n. 45
.246*v* **III**, App. pt. I, grs. 6 and 8; **III**, App. pt. II, no. 352. viii, B, 3, n. 73; viii, B, 5, n. 73
.250 x, A, 2, n. 433; x, D, n. 37
.251 v, B, 1, nn. 1, 7. vii, B, 1, n. 15
.253 **II**, App. B, sec. 16
.255 x, B, 1, n. 64
.256 iii, B, 3, n. 8; iii, C, n. 22. viii, C, 4, nn. 74, 87, 112
.261 vi, 12, n. 20

.262 vii, A, 2, n. 19. viii, C, 2, n. 97. ix, A, 1, n. 233. x, A, 3, nn. 13, 30
.263 I, App. D, sec. 31. iv, 6, n. 11; iv, 7, n. 15
.264 iii, D, n. 38. iv, 10, n. 39; iv, 11, n. 11; iv, 12, n. 26. viii, A, 2, n. 13
.265 viii, C, 2, n. 116
.267 v, B, 2, n. 35. vii, B, 1, n. 30
.269 viii, A, 3, n. 68. x, B, 4, n. 53
.272 ii, 4, nn. 46, 108; ii, 5, n. 87. v, B, 1, nn. 118, 130; v, B, 2, n. 104; v, C, 2, n. 7. vi, 10, n. 30. vii, A, 2, n. 36; vii, C, 1, c, nn. 8, 19; vii, C, 2, n. 27; vii, D, 2, n. 9. viii, C, 2, n. 92
.274 viii, C, 1, n. 12. ix, B, n. 166. x, B, 4, n. 24
.276 ii, 2, n. 2 (mistake for 16.279)
.277 v, B, 1, n. 74. vii, B, 3, n. 28; vii, C, 1, c, n. 30. viii, C, 1, nn. 21, 31, 38; viii, C, 2, nn. 120, 153. x, B, 5, n. 4
.278 v, B, 2, n. 101. vi, 10, n. 26. viii, C, 1, n. 267. x, B, 2, n. 42
.279 I, App. D, sec. 25. ii, 2, n. 2 (cited as 16.276). viii, A, 3, n. 40. ix, B, n. 95. x, A, 3, nn. 6, 21
.281 x, B, 2, n. 130
.283 vi, 11, n. 36
.286 ii, 3, n. 43. iii, B, 4, n. 6. II, App. D, sec. 26. v, C, 2, n. 14. vii, C, 2, nn. 35, 52. viii, A, 2, nn. 28, 46, 79; viii, B, 5, n. 70. ix, A, 1, n. 41. x, A, 2, nn. 12, 30, 46, 127, 310; x, B, 1, n. 10; x, B, 2, n. 118; x, B, 4, n. 162
.287 v, C, 4, n. 59. viii, A, 3, n. 53; viii, C, 1, n. 78. x, A, 3, n. 287
.290 vi, 12, n. 55
.291 vi, 12, n. 37. viii, C, 2, n. 10; viii, C, 4, n. 183. x, B, 1, n. 65; x, B, 3, n. 62, 79
.291*v* vi, 12, n. 63
.292 ix, B, n. 346
.293 vi, 7, n. 30. vii, C, 1, b, n. 45. viii, A, 2, n. 62; viii, A, 3, n. 48; viii, B, 1, n. 43. x, B, 2, nn. 82, 85; x, B, 3, n. 67; x, D, n. 14
.294 v, B, 1, n. 55. x, B, 1, nn. 13, 35; x, B, 4, nn. 3, 57
.296 v, A, 2, nn. 62, 74. vii, C, 1, d, n. 22; vii, C, 2, nn. 37, 49
.298 ix, A, 4, n. 157. x, B, 3, nn. 71, 83
.301 i, 2, n. 63
.303 x, B, 1, n. 15
.305 v, A, 2, nn. 43, 61. vi, 12, n. 21. vii, A, 1, n. 6. x, A, 1, n. 148; x, A, 2, n. 376; x, D, n. 329
.307 x, D, n. 31
.309 v, B, 2, n. 91
.318 v, A, 1, n. 7
.330 v, B, 1, n. 4. viii, B, 3, n. 42
.334 vi, 13, nn. 5, 52. x, C, 4, n. 45
.335 viii, C, 3, n. 158. ix, A, 1, n. 37
.339 I, App. D, sec. 24. i, 2, n. 22. iii, B, 3, n. 9; iii, D, n. 71; iii, E, nn. 45, 52, 61, 73, 83; iii, F, n. 19. vi, 11, n. 53. x, A, 3, n. 13; x, B, 2, nn. 86, 90; x, C, 2, n. 9
.341 iii, F, n. 185. ix, B, n. 273
.347 x, C, 4, n. 43
.353 vii, C, 2, n. 25
.355 (was 12.549, 12.564) I, App. D, sec. 76. vi, 4, n. 23
.356 (was 12.551, 12.562) I, App. D, p. 396 (Conclusions). II, App. C, sec. 134. viii, A, 3, n. 18. ix, A, 1, n. 103; ix, A, 2, nn. 9, 62, 92, 95, 97, 101, 112, 113, 117, 148; ix, A, 3, nn. 53, 75

.357 viii, B, 3, n. 82
.370 vii, B, 3, n. 2. viii, C, 3, n. 47
.374 **I**, App. D, sec. 3a. vii, B, 2, n. 4. viii, B, 3, n. 4; viii, B, 4, n. 23
.377 viii, B, 3, n. 78. ix, C, 1, n. 90 (cited as TS Misc. Box 29, f. 6)
TS 20.1 **III**, App. pt. II, no. 85. viii, B, 3, n. 25; viii, B, 4, nn. 57, 104; viii, C, 4, n. 175; viii, D, n. 23. ix, A, 2, n. 45; ix, A, 5, n. 36
.2 ix, B, nn. 118, 122
.3 **II**, App. A, sec. 176. vii, A, 2, n. 10. ix, A, 1, n. 190; ix, A, 2, nn. 37, 154; ix, A, 3, n. 28
.4 ii, 4, n. 6
.5 **III**, App. pt. II, no. 122
.6 i, 2, n. 39. ii, 4, n. 61. vi, 9, n. 42. vii, B, 1, n. 21; vii, B, 3, n. 11. **III**, App. pt. I, gr. 4; **III**, App. pt. II, no. 229. viii, B, 3, n. 40; viii, B, 4, n. 100. **IV**, App. C, 3. ix, A, 2, n. 44; ix, A, 3, n. 88; ix, A, 4, nn. 57, 64; ix, B, n. 517. **IV**, App. D, n. 4
.7 i, 2, nn. 30, 31. **II**, App. D, sec. 8, 10. vi, 9, nn. 5, 15. vii, B, 1, n. 67. **III**, App. pt. II, no. 166. viii, B, 3, nn. 30, 41; viii, B, 4, nn. 57, 59, 99. **IV**, App. C, 2. ix, A, 4, nn. 9, 30, 45, 56, 57, 64, 93, 165, 170, 174, 178, 205; ix, A, 5, n. 14; ix, B, nn. 116, 222. **IV**, App. D, n. 263. x, B, 3, n. 59
.8 i, 2, n. 31. v, B, 1, n. 15. **III**, App. pt. I, gr. 1; **III**, App. pt. II, no. 221. **IV**, App. C, 2, 3. ix, A, 4, nn. 2, 10, 29, 162; ix, A, 5, nn. 9, 27, 70; ix, B, nn. 478, 485, 525. **IV**, App. D, n. 155
.9 i, 2, n. 62. ix, B, n. 319
.10 **III**, App. pt. I, gr. 8; **III**, App. pt. II, no. 96. viii, B, 4, n. 87. ix, B, n. 386
.12 **III**, App. pt. II, no. 45
.16 vii, B, 1, n. 23; vii, B, 3, n. 3
.19 v, A, 1, n. 33; v, B, 1, n. 80; v, C, 2, n. 3. vi, 10, n. 36. ix, C, 1, n. 165
.21 iii, B, 3, n. 8; iii, D, n. 54; iii, F, nn. 25, 111
.23 ii, 6, n. 13. viii, C, 4, n. 53
.23*v* **II**, App. B, sec. 3
.24 i, 2, n. 93; iv, 12, n. 5. v, A, 2, n. 12. vii, C, 1, a, n. 38
.25*v* **III**, App. pt. II, no. 299. ix, B, nn. 497, 526
.28 v, C, 2, n. 14. x, A, 1, n. 126; x, B, 1, n. 52
.31 iii, F, n. 198. **II**, App. D, sec. 12. vi, 9, n. 4. vii, B, 1, n. 4
.32 vii, D, 1, n. 26. viii, D, n. 79
.33 **III**, App. pt. I, gr. 6; **III**, App. pt. II, no. 326. viii, B, 3, n. 68. ix, A, 5, n. 64; ix, B, n. 543
.36 viii, B, 5, n. 35
.37 v, A, 1, nn. 46, 56. ix, A, 5, n. 86. x, A, 1, n. 116; x, A, 2, n. 302
.38 **II**, App. D, sec. 9. v, B, 2, n. 62. x, B, 5, n. 24
.39 viii, C, 4, n. 161
.41 ii, 7, nn. 64, 78
.42 viii, B, 3, n. 54
.44 **I**, App. D, no. 60. **II**, App. D, sec. 31. vi, 12, n. 40. x, D, n. 300
.47 ii, 5, n. 29; ii, 7, n. 107. v, D, 1, n. 18. ix, A, 4, n. 73; ix, B, n. 332
.47*v* **III**, App. pt. II, no. 371. viii, B, 2, n. 2; viii, B, 3, n. 18; viii, C, 1, n. 41. **IV**, App. C, 1, 2. ix, B, nn. 17, 359

.48 viii, B, 4, nn. 35, 38. ix, A, 4, n. 204; ix, A, 5, nn. 58, 90; ix, B, nn. 74, 98, 124, 464, 543
.49 vi, 8, n. 10
.60 iii, F, n. 109. viii, C, 4, n. 83
.62 **III**, App. pt. I, gr. 5; **III**, App. pt. II, no. 99. viii, B, 3, n. 65; viii, B, 4, n. 25; viii, B, 5, nn. 72, 91
.64 **III**, App. pt. II, no. 16. x, B, 2, n. 58
.66 viii, C, 2, n. 59. x, C, 5, n. 19
.69 **I**, App. D, no. 14. ii, 4, nn. 16, 26, 41. iii, A, 1, n. 33; iii, A, 2, n. 7; iii, B, 1, nn. 2, 3, 18; iii, B, 2, n. 12 (cited as TS 20.96); iii, D, nn. 45, 52, 68; iii, E, nn. 33, 53, 59; iii, F, n. 18. iv, 5, n. 5; iv, 6, n. 7; iv, 7, nn. 3, 6; iv, 10, n. 29. vii, A, 2, n. 16. ix, A, 4, n. 131; ix, B, n. 229; ix, D, n. 17. x, B, 1, n. 28; x, C, 5, n. 8
.75 iii, A, 1, n. 4 (mistake, *see* Reif)
.76 i, 2, n. 61. ii, 4, nn. 35, 100; ii, 5, nn. 39, 85; ii, 7, n. 106. iii, B, 1, n. 7; iii, B, 3, n. 9; iii, D, n. 44; iii, E, nn. 6, 42. iv, 7, n. 7; iv, 8, nn. 32, 59; iv, 10, nn. 10, 23, 30. vi, 5, nn. 5, 10. ix, A, 4, n. 175; ix, B, n. 119
.77 **III**, App. pt. II, no. 228. viii, B, 3, n. 33. ix, B, n. 80
.78 x, C, 5, n. 14
.80 **I**, App. D, sec. 51. i, 2, n. 2. ii, 4, n. 14; ii, 5, n. 29. iii, A, 1, n. 25; iii, C, nn. 6, 22; iii, F, n. 161. v, B, 1, nn. 24, 25. vi, 11, n. 32. vii, A, 2, n. 17; vii, C, 1, d, n. 8. viii, A, 1, n. 64. ix, A, 5, n. 43; ix, B, n. 222. x, A, 3, n. 166; x, C, 1, n. 43; x, C, 3, n. 43
.83 iii, F, n. 148. vii, B, 1, n. 23. viii, A, 1, n. 86. ix, C, 1, n. 152. x, A, 1, n. 35
.85 vii, A, 2, n. 5. ix, A, 1, n. 71
.86 viii, B, 3, n. 56
.87 **II**, App. A, sec. 177. viii, B, 5, nn. 63, 64
.89 vii, B, 1, n. 6
.90 vii, A, 1, n. 16
.92 ii, 4, nn. 40, 46. iii, F, n. 116. vi, 4, n. 6. viii, A, 3, n. 23. ix, A, 1, nn. 94, 103; ix, A, 2, nn. 41, 43, 150
.93 A vii, A, 3, n. 13; vii, C, 1, a, n. 17
.93, sec. 2 ii, 7, n. 40
.94 v, B, 2, n. 102. vi, 9, n. 22. x, B, 3, n. 61; x, C, 5, n. 53
.96 iii, B, 2, n. 12 (mistake for 20.69). **II**, App. A, sec. 3. **II**, App. D, sec. 1. v, A, 2, n. 23; v, B, 1, n. 114; v, B, 2, nn. 52, 59, 61, 64; v, C, 1, n. 20. viii, D, n. 119. ix, A, 1, n. 77; ix, A, 2, nn. 61, 68, 156; ix, A, 3, n. 119
.99 ii, 3, n. 12; ii, 5, n. 3. iii, B, 3, n. 3. ix, B, nn. 33, 556. x, A, 3, n. 52
.100 v, B, 2, n. 124. vi, 10, n. 23. viii, C, 4, n. 106
.101 **III**, App. pt. II, no. 274. ix, B, n. 388
.102 x, A, 3, n. 319
.103 vi, 11, n. 25. x, A, 2, n. 389
.104 v, B, 1, nn. 8, 100, 110, 144; v, B, 2, nn. 8, 52, 123. vi, 9, n. 45; vi, 10, nn. 36, 39, 45. vii, B, 1, n. 21. ix, A, 1, n. 147
.109 **III**, App. pt. II, no. 83. viii, B, 3, n. 12; viii, B, 4, nn. 5, 85; viii, B, 5, n. 52
.110 **I**, App. C, sec. 5. iii, B, 2, n. 25; iii, D, n. 11
.111 x, C, 5, n. 19; x, D, n. 43
.112 ii, 6, n. 6. **II**, App. B, secs. 2*a*, 52
.113 iv, 2, n. 37. viii, A, 1, n. 48. x, A, 2, nn. 44, 363; x, B, 1, n. 23; x, C, 4, nn. 71, 76, 90, 93
.114 iv, 12, n. 7. v, C, 4, n. 29. vii, C, 1, c, n. 11

.116 iii, F, n. 135. v, A, 1, n. 48. vii, C, 1, b, n. 2
.116*v*, item I **III**, App. pt. II, no. 109
.116*v*, item II **III**, App. pt. II, no. 19. viii, B, 4, n. 14; viii, D, n. 176. ix, A, 4, nn. 52, 105. ix, A, 5, nn. 21, 32, 37, 49
.117 v, D, 2, n. 11. x, B, 5, n. 36
.117*v* v, B, 1, nn. 9, 143; v, D, 2, n. 3. viii, D, n. 116. x, A, 1, n. 52
.118 **II**, App. D, sec. 25. vi, 9, n. 21
.119 vi, 10, n. 22
.121 iii, D, n. 73; iii, F, nn. 34, 46; **I**, App. D, n. 21. vi, 10, n. 22; vi, 11, n. 26. ix, A, 3, n. 79
.122 **I**, App. D, sec. 22. i, 2, n. 47. ii, 4, n. 16; ii, 5, n. 23. iii, E, n. 56; iii, F, n. 29. iv, 10, nn. 1, 8, 26, 30. vii, C, 1, c, n. 43. viii, A, 1, n. 86; viii, B, 2, n. 18. ix, B, n. 264
.124 v, B, 1, n. 42
.125 iii, D, n. 25 (mistake for 20.152). v, A, 1, n. 2; v, B, 2, n. 17. vi, 6, n. 2. x, A, 1, n. 13
.126 vii, B, 1, n. 7. viii, D, n. 57. **IV**, App. A, IV. ix, A, 1, n. 82; ix, A, 4, n. 139
.127 **I**, App. D, sec. 28. iii, B, 1, nn. 13, 22; iii, B, 2, n. 41; iii, D, n. 10; iii, E, nn. 6, 32, 52, 61, 63, 64, 71; iii, F, nn. 14, 30, 147. iv, 1, n. 3. vi, 5, n. 5. x, B, 1, n. 12
.128 ii, 4, nn. 53, 77. v, A, 1, n. 49. vii, A, 2, n. 1. ix, A, 2, nn. 103, 164. x, A, 2, n. 87; x, B, 3, n. 77
.129 vii, B, 1, n. 15. ix, A, 3, n. 79
.130 x, A, 2, n. 38
.131 vi, 2, n. 29
.133 ii, 1, n. 12. iii, C, nn. 12, 25. iv, 5, n. 2. v, B, 1, n. 1. vii, C, 2, n. 52. x, A, 2, n. 137
.135 vii, B, 1, n. 72. viii, C, 1, n. 16
.137 x, A, 2, n. 95
.138 iii, E, n. 14. iv, 3, n. 36
.138*v* vi, 6, n. 9
.140*v* viii, C, 1, n. 185
.141 vi, 9, nn. 25, 33. vii, C, 2, n. 8. ix, C, 1, n. 1
.142 ix, A, 4, n. 84
.145 iv, 7, n. 22; iv, 9, n. 15. v, A, 2, n. 71
.148*v* ix, B, n. 81. x, A, 2, n. 206
.149 ix, B, n. 273. x, A, 2, nn. 196, 199
.151 **III**, App. pt. II, no. 212
.152 **I**, App. B, II, 5. iii, A, 1, n. 42; iii, B, 2, n. 28; iii, B, 4, n. 4; iii, D, n. 25 (cited as 20.125). v, B, 1, n. 138. vi, 10, n. 26; vi, 11, n. 40. vii, D, 1, n. 1
.156 **III**, App. pt. II, no. 211. ix, A, 4, nn. 37, 54
.160 vii, B, 2, n. 2. viii, B, 5, nn. 17, 69, 75. x, A, 1, n. 164
.162 iii, B, 2, n. 14. viii, C, 4, n. 19
.163 ii, 4, n. 60
.166*v* ix, A, 5, n. 19
.168 ii, 5, n. 86. **II**, App. A, sec. 6. vi, 13, n. 2. **IV**, App. B, I. ix, A, 1, n. 113; ix, A, 2, n. 141; ix, A, 3, n. 56
.169 ii, 5, n. 86. iii, C, n. 12. viii, A, 2, n. 56; viii, A, 3, nn. 45, 54; viii, C, 2, n. 96; viii, D, n. 47. ix, A, 2, n. 161. x, C, 3, n. 38
.170 iii, A, 1, n. 5. v, B, 1, n. 132
.171 x, A, 3, n. 90
.173 x, C, 5, n. 9
.174 i, 3, n. 29. viii, A, Introduction, n. 2; viii, A, 3, n. 31
.175 ii, 2, n. 27; ii, 4, nn. 2, 101; ii, 6, n. 16. iv, 3, n. 18. v, A, 1, n. 49. ix, A, 4, n. 33

.177 i, 2, nn. 36, 67. v, B, 1, n. 134
.180 **I**, App. D, sec. 13. ii, 1, n. 12. iii, D, nn. 19, 37, 42. iv, 2, nn. 28, 29, 42 (cited as 12.180); iv, 7, n. 15; iv, 10, n. 11. vii, A, 2, nn. 16, 19. ix, B, nn. 130, 411
.181 v, B, 2, n. 108
.187 i, 2, n. 9. ii, 4, n. 80. vii, B, 3, n. 22; vii, C, 1, d, n. 20. viii, A, 2, n. 83; viii, B, 4, n. 52. ix, A, 4, nn. 146, 184, 187; ix, A, 5, nn. 14, 32, 38, 40; ix, B, n. 536; ix, D, n. 16
TS 24.1 **II**, App. D, sec. 11. **III**, App. pt. II, no. 194. viii, B, 4, n. 95. **IV**, App. C, 1. ix, B, n. 368
.2 **III**, App. pt. I, gr. 4; **III**, App. pt. II, no. 43. viii, B, 3, n. 39; viii, B, 4, n. 70. ix, A, 4, nn. 41, 44, 54, 84, 169, 215; ix, B, n. 526
.3 i, 2, n. 30. v, A, 2, n. 15. **III**, App. pt. I, gr. 5; **III**, App. pt. II, no. 48. viii, B, 1, n. 7; viii, B, 3, nn. 45, 56. ix, A, 5, n. 58
.5 ii, 7, n. 108. v, A, 2, n. 15. **III**, App. pt. I, gr. 5; **III**, App. pt. II, no. 33. viii, B, 3, nn. 45, 56; viii, B, 4, n. 18. **IV**, App. A, II. **IV**, App. C, 2
.6 iv, 11, n. 19. v, A, 2, n. 8; v, B, 1, nn. 5, 120. vi, 7, n. 24. x, C, 5, n. 22
.7 **III**, App. pt. I, gr. 4; **III**, App. pt. II, no. 237. viii, A, 2, n. 78; viii, B, 3, nn. 20, 46
.8 **I**, App. D, sec. 83. **III**, App. pt. II, no. 233. viii, B, 3, n. 33; viii, B, 4, nn. 24, 85. ix, A, 5, n. 59; ix, B, nn. 442, 503
.9 viii, B, 4, n. 85. ix, A, 5, nn. 5, 45, 47; ix, B, nn. 440, 465, 499, 545, 552. **IV**, App. D, nn. 142, 155
.11 **II**, App. C, sec. 1
.12 i, 2, n. 31. **III**, App. pt. I, gr. 4; **III**, App. pt. II, no. 318. ix, A, 4, nn. 56, 61, 64, 90; ix, A, 5, n. 42; ix, B, n. 337. **IV**, App. D, n. 83
.13 i, 2, n. 31. viii, B, 3, n. 46
.14 ii, 4, n. 101. viii, B, 4, n. 27. ix, A, 1, n. 232. x, A, 2, n. 409
.15 **III**, App. pt. I, gr. 5; **III**, App. pt. II, n. 99. viii, B, 3, n. 73; viii, B, 4, n. 25; viii, B, 5, nn. 72, 91. **IV**, App. C, 2, 3. ix, A, 4, nn. 2, 163, 165, 179; ix, B, nn. 465, 541
.15*v*, item II **III**, App. pt. I, grs. 5 and 8; **III**, App. pt. II, no. 333.
.16 **III**, App. pt. II, no. 213. viii, B, 3, n. 65. ix, A, 4, n. 61; ix, A, 5, n. 15; ix, B, n. 470. **IV**, App. D, n. 83
.17 vi, 10, n. 22. viii, B, 3, n. 70; viii, D, n. 23. ix, B, n. 532
.18 iii, C, n. 11. vii, B, 1, n. 67. viii, C, 4, n. 58
.21*v* v, B, 2, n. 15
.25 ii, 4, n. 115; ii, 5, n. 80. iii, F, nn. 196, 205. v, B, 1, n. 29; v, B, 2, nn. 24, 62; v, C, 1, n. 28. vi, 11, n. 15. vii, C, 1, b, n. 24. viii, A, 2, n. 49
.25*v* ix, C, 2, n. 19
.26 iii, F, n. 194. vi, 11, n. 39
.27 viii, B, 1, n. 57. ix, B, n. 44. x, A, 2, n. 165; x, A, 3, n. 11; x, C, 3, n. 14
.28 viii, C, 1, n. 105
.29 i, 3, n. 19. iv, 3, n. 43; iv, 8, n. 21. vi, 4, n. 23. x, B, 4, n. 158; x, D, n. 41
.30 **IV**, App. C, 2. ix, A, 4, n. 214
.34 ii, 2, n. 45. v, B, 1, n. 122. **III**, App. pt. II, no. 271. viii, C, 3, n. 106
.35 **III**, App. pt. I, gr. 4; **III**, App. pt. II, no. 223. viii, D, n. 26
.37 iii, C, n. 2. ix, B, n. 539
.38 i, 2, n. 72; i, 3, n. 28. v, B, 1, nn. 56, 142; v, B, 2, n. 13. vi, 4, n. 24; vi, 12, n. 97

.40 ii, 4, n. 87
.43 v, A, 1, n. 38; v, D, 2, n. 36. x, B, 2, n. 72; x, C, 3, n. 31; x, C, 5, n. 21
.44 vi, 4, n. 26. vii, A, 2, n. 5. **IV**, App. A, IV; ix, A, 2, n. 62
.45 **III**, App. pt. II, no. 189
.46 iii, D, n. 54. v, C, 4, n. 9. vi, 10, n. 19. x, C, 3, n. 19
.49 i, 2, n. 10. v, C, 4, n. 57. vi, 11, n. 20. viii, C, 2, nn. 123, 178. x, B, 4, n. 61; x, C, 5, n. 53
.51 vii, B, 3, n. 35
.55 v, A, 2, n. 15. viii, B, 3, n. 90
.56 v, A, 2, n. 35. x, A, 1, n. 81; x, B, 4, n. 60; x, B, 5, n. 46
.63 **II**, App. C, secs. 101–112
.64 ix, A, 4, n. 205
.65 x, B, 4, n. 28; x, C, 4, n. 82
.66*v* ix, A, 4, nn. 109, 156
.67 vi, 12, n. 44. vii, C, 1, a, n. 4. viii, A, 2, n. 79
.70 iii, F, n. 109
.72 vii, C, 1, a, n. 5. ix, A, 4, n. 214; ix, B, n. 295. x, A, 3, n. 262
.73 vii, B, 1, n. 20. viii, A, 1, n. 38; viii, D, n. 5
.75 **III**, App. pt. I, gr. 5. viii, B, 5, n. 88. x, B, 3, n. 38
.76 ii, 4, nn. 78, 93; ii, 6, nn. 8, 15. iii, F, n. 117. **II**, App. B, sec. 1. viii, B, 1, n. 75; viii, C, 3, n. 61; viii, D, nn. 19, 191. ix, A, 1, nn. 26, 220. x, A, 1, n. 165
.77 i, 2, n. 45
.78 i, 2, n. 33. ii, 5, n. 20. iii, D, n. 14; iii, G, n. 12. iv, 2, nn. 19, 35; iv, 7, n. 25; iv, 8, n. 20; iv, 8, nn. 39, 47. vi, 9, n. 11; vi, 11, n. 7. vii, A, 1, n. 34; vii, C, 1, b, n. 26; vii, C, 1, c, n. 24; vii, C, 1, d, nn. 18, 25. viii, C, 2, n. 167. ix, A, 1, nn. 32, 36, 194; ix, C, 1, n. 132. x, A, 1, nn. 152, 162; x, B, 1, n. 2; x, B, 2, n. 150
.80 i, 2, n. 30. **III**, App. pt. I, gr. 4; **III**, App. pt. II, no. 105. viii, B, n. 89. **IV**, App. C, 4. ix, A, 4, nn. 38, 169
.81 iii, F, n. 5. v, B, 2, n. 64. vi, 11, n. 43. vii, B, 1, n. 41; vii, C, 1, b, n. 2. **III**, App. pt. II, no. 302. viii, C, 4, nn. 36, 72; viii, D, n. 4. ix, A, 3, n. 33
TS 28.1 i, 2, n. 65
.3 iii, C, n. 26; iii, F, n. 40. vii, B, 3, n. 44. viii, A, 3, n. 12; viii, D, nn. 48, 104. **IV**, App. A, V. ix, A, 1, n. 73; ix, A, 2, nn. 9, 72; ix, A, 3, n. 86
.4 x, B, 1, nn. 137, 138, 140; x, B, 4, n. 61
.5 v, B, 2, n. 82
.6 ii, 5, n. 4. iii, B, 4, n. 6. vii, B, 1, n. 30; vii, B, 3, n. 52. **IV**, App. C, 1. ix, A, 4, n. 178
.6 A viii, A, 3, n. 55. ix, B, n. 396. x, C, 2, n. 10
.6 B **I**, App. C, sec. 3. ii, 2, n. 19. iii, B, 2, n. 42
.6 C ii, 5, n. 31. vii, B, 1, n. 48. viii, A, 2, n. 83; viii, B, 4, n. 52; viii, C, 2, n. 144. ix, B, n. 499
.7 iii, B, 3, n. 15. vii, B, 3, n. 21. viii, C, 1, n. 213. x, A, 3, n. 312
.8 ii, 7, n. 86
.10 v, D, 1, n. 31. vi, 6, n. 3. x, C, 5, n. 5
.11 iv, 3, n. 16
.17 i, 1, n. 2. ii, 2, n. 36. iii, B, 2, n. 20; iii, D, n. 57. x, B, 3, n. 10
.19 vii, A, 2, n. 17; vii, C, 1, c, n. 29; vii, D, 1, n. 38. **III**, App. pt. II, no. 292. viii, C, 3, n. 51; viii, D, n. 87

.20 viii, C, 1, n. 2. x, A, 3, n. 75
.22 ix, A, 4, nn. 4, 157; ix, B, nn. 152, 154. x, A, 1, n. 124
.23 v, B, 1, n. 40. **III**, App. pt. I, gr. 5; **III**, App. pt. II, no. 125. viii, B, 4, n. 55. **IV**, App. C, 2. ix, B, n. 520
TS 32.4 vii, C, 1, a, n. 41
.8 v, B, 1, n. 44
.10 i, 3, n. 40. x, C, 5, n. 5
TS NS: Taylor-Schechter New Series (fragments sorted since 1954, stored in binders)
TS NS Box 31, f. 7 vi, 10, n. 30. viii, C, 4, n. 126. ix, A, 2, n. 111
f. 8 **II**, App. C, sec. 95. viii, C, 2, n. 103. ix, B, n. 34
NS Box 99, f. 45 viii, B, 1, n. 19
NS Box 108, f. 50 x, A, 2, n. 358
NS Box 110, f. 20 viii, B, 3, n. 11
f. 26 v, A, 1, n. 50; v, D, 2, n. 34. vii, C, 1, a, n. 25. x, B, 3, n. 75
NS Box 135 x, A, 3, n. 311
NS Box 143, f. 46 x, D, n. 247
NS Box 154, f. 165 viii, C, 4, n. 13
NS Box 164, f. 13 viii, B, 4, n. 57
NS Box 169, f. 11 v, A, 1, n. 52
NS Box 184, f. 49 ix, B, n. 548
f. 50 viii, A, 2, n. 80; viii, B, 2, n. 20
f. 54 viii, B, 5, n. 23
f. 57 viii, D, n. 55
f. 58 viii, A, 2, n. 80; viii, B, 2, n. 20; viii, D, n. 4. ix, D, n. 35
f. 62 viii, A, 2, n. 80; viii, B, 2, n. 20; viii, D, n. 4. ix, D, n. 35
f. 65 viii, B, 3, n. 88
f. 70 viii, A, 2, n. 80; viii, B, 2, n. 20; viii, D, n. 4. ix, D, n. 35
f. 71 viii, A, 2, n. 80; viii, B, 2, n. 20; viii, D, n. 4. ix, D, n. 35
f. 72 viii, A, 2, n. 80; viii, B, 2, n. 20; viii, D, n. 4. ix, D, n. 35
f. 74 viii, A, 2, n. 80; viii, B, 2, n. 20; viii, D, n. 4. ix, D, n. 35
f. 90 **III**, App. pt. II, no. 201
f. 98 viii, A, 2, n. 80; viii, B, 2, n. 20; viii, D, n. 4. ix, D, n. 35
NS Box 200, f. 55 x, B, 5, n. 42
NS Box 225, f. 25 ix, A, 2, n. 147
NS Box 226, f. 8 **II**, App. B, sec. 53
f. 10 **III**, App. pt. I, gr. 5. viii, B, 5, n. 9
f. 11 **III**, App. pt. I, gr. 5. viii, B, 5, n. 11
f. 12 viii, C, 4, n. 21
NS Box 228, f. 3 vi, 7, n. 4
NS Box 235, f. 11 iii, B, 3, n. 1 (mistake for NS Box 325, f. 11)
NS Box 246, f. 22 **II**, App. C, sec. 26. vi, 7, n. 20; vi, 9, n. 20. viii, A, 1, n. 82 (mistake for NS Box 246.26, f. 12). **IV**, App. D, n. 109. x, B, 3, n. 38
f. 28 vii, B, 3, n. 42 (cited as Box K 27, f. 45)
NS Box 246.26, f. 12 viii, A, 1, n. 82 (cited as NS Box 246, f. 22)
NS Box 264, f. 1 x, C, 1, n. 13
f. 13 ix, A, 4, n. 215
NS Box 297, f. 1 vii, B, 1, n. 40. viii, C, 4, n. 2
297*d* vii, C, 1, b, n. 24 (mistake for NS J 297 *b*)
NS Box 298, f. 6 ix, B, n. 88
f. 27 viii, C, 2, n. 118
NS Box 306, f. 1 iii, D, n. 14. **II**, App. A, sec. 39. viii, D, n. 69. **IV**, App. A, III. ix, A, 1, n. 141; ix, A, 2, n. 38
NS Box 308, f. 25 viii, C, 3, n. 65
f. 114 iii, F, n. 52
f. 119 ix, B, n. 170
NS Box 311, f. 23 ii, 7, n. 64

NS Box 312, f. 82 v, A, 1, n. 47. viii, A, 2, n. 59
NS Box 313, f. 4 **III**, App. pt. II, no. 108. viii, B, 5, n. 84
NS Box 320, f. 6 vi, 2, nn. 4, 35; vi, 11, n. 13
f. 7 ii, 6, n. 15. v, C, 5, n. 7. ix, D, n. 19. x, A, 2, n. 383
f. 15 **II**, App. A, sec. 123 (mistake for NS Box 320, f. 141). viii, B, 4, n. 22
f. 15*v* viii, B, 3, n. 84
f. 16 v, A, 1, n. 52; v, B, 2, n. 7; v, D, 2, n. 23. vi, 7, n. 17. viii, A, 2, n. 20. x, B, 1, n. 125
f. 17 ii, 7, n. 52. iii, F, n. 52. ix, B, n. 486
f. 19 ix, C, 1, n. 142
f. 20 viii, C, 1, nn. 201, 217
f. 23 x, A, 3, nn. 58, 75
f. 26 v, B, 1, n. 110
f. 27 **II**, App. A, sec. 136 (cited as NS Box 320, f. 27*v*). v, A, 1, n. 48
f. 28 v, A, 1, n. 48
f. 29 viii, D, n. 81
f. 30 ii, 6, n. 24. **II**, App. B, sec. 63. vi, 3, n. 16
f. 31 **II**, App. A, sec. 154
f. 32*v* **II**, App. A, sec. 136 (mistake for NS Box 320, f. 27*v*)
f. 33 **II**, App. B, sec. 88. viii, C, 2, n. 55
f. 34 ix, A, 4, nn. 54, 167, 174, 205; ix, B, n. 526
f. 35 **II**, App. C, sec. 52
f. 41 **II**, App. B, sec. 74. v, B, 2, n. 100. viii, A, 1, n. 82
f. 42 ii, 7, nn. 64, 65 (mistake, *see* Reif)
f. 44 x, D, n. 47
f. 45 v, B, 2, n. 16
f. 46 viii, C, 3, n. 156
f. 52 ix, A, 4, n. 130. x, A, 3, n. 87
f. 54 viii, C, 1, n. 152
f. 55 ix, C, 1, n. 186
f. 57 viii, C, 1, n. 152
f. 58 x, B, 4, n. 130
f. 62 **II**, App. C, sec. 2
f. 108 **III**, App. pt. I, gr. 3; **III**, App. pt. II, no. 366
f. 141 **II**, App. A, sec. 123 (cited as NS Box 320, f. 15)
NS Box 321, f. 1 iv, 4, n. 27. x, A, 1, n. 104 (now NS Box 329, f. 999)
f. 6 **II**, App. B, sec. 64. viii, A, 1, n. 82
f. 8 iii, B, 1, n. 18
f. 14 **II**, App. B, sec. 70
f. 22 v, D, 2, n. 15
f. 23 viii, C, 1, n. 2. x, B, 3, n. 83
f. 28 vi, 4, n. 11
f. 50 viii, A, 3, n. 35
f. 54 viii, D, n. 214
f. 79 **I**, App. D, sec. 75
f. 93 x, A, 2, n. 375
f. 100 viii, C, 1, n. 140
NS Box 323, f. 1 ix, B, n. 224
f. 3 v, A, 1, n. 3
f. 4 **III**, App. pt. I, gr. 5; **III**, App. pt. II, no. 7. viii, B, 3, n. 56; viii, B, 4, n. 14
f. 7 v, B, 1, n. 19 (mistake for NS Box 323, f. 17)
f. 13 vi, 2, n. 24
f. 17 v, B, 1, n. 19 (cited as NS Box 323, f. 7)
f. 19 viii, C, 3, n. 27
f. 29 ix, B, n. 480

NS Box 324, f. 17 v, B, 1, n. 109
f. 104 v, B, 1, n. 7
f. 107 **III**, App. pt. I, gr. 4; **III**, App. pt. II, no. 308
f. 132 **II**, App. B, sec. 71. vi, 10, n. 2
f. 144 **III**, App. pt. II, no. 288. ix, B, nn. 416, 488. **IV**, App. D, n. 142
NS Box 325, f. 7 vii, A, 3, n. 37
f. 8 iii, F, n. 208. viii, B, 2, n. 40
f. 11 iii, B, 3, n. 1 (cited as NS Box 235, f. 11)
f. 13 ix, B, n. 222. **IV**, App. D, n. 261
f. 50 vii, A, 3, n. 54
f. 64 vii, A, 3, n. 54
NS Box 329, f. 999 (was NS Box 321, f. 1) iv, 4, n. 27. x, A, 1, n. 104
TS NS J (fragments originally in TS NS 94 and 95)
1 x, B, 2, n. 142
2 v, C, 4, n. 53. vi, 2, n. 16. viii, A, 2, n. 53
3 i, 2, n. 7. ii, 5, n. 69. iv, 12, n. 3. vii, A, 2, n. 5; vii, C, 2, n. 15. ix, A, 1, nn. 153, 202
4 vii, C, 1, c, n. 57. ix, A, 2, n. 116. x, A, 2, n. 273
6 ii, 7, n. 10. iii, B, 2, nn. 36, 47. **II**, App. D, sec. 11. ix, A, 1, n. 20
7 vii, B, 3, nn. 34, 36; vii, C, 1, b, nn. 28, 34. viii, A, 2, n. 9. ix, D, n. 15
8 iii, F, n. 62
9 ii, 3, n. 36. vi, 12, n. 29. viii, A, 1, n. 53
12 **I**, App. D, sec. 23
13 ii, 5, n. 12
14 viii, C, 2, n. 160. x, C, 4, n. 51
16 ii, 7, n. 24. x, B, 1, n. 55; x, B, 2, n. 111
23 x, B, 1, n. 37
24 i, 1, n. 6. ii, 3, n. 10; ii, 6, n. 17. v, B, 1, n. 133; v, B, 2, n. 15. vii, A, 1, n. 15. viii, A, 2, n. 11. x, A, 1, n. 155
27 ii, 4, n. 2; ii, 5, nn. 5, 34. iii, D, n. 22. **II**, App. A, sec. 108. vi, 13, n. 22. vii, D, 1, n. 33. ix, A, 4, nn. 63, 121, 187, 209; ix, A, 5, nn. 4, 8, 10, 18, 39, 43, 57, 76; ix, D, n. 16. x, A, 3, n. 255
27 IV **III**, App. pt. I, gr. 6; **III**, App. pt. II, no. 112. viii, D, n. 25
27, p. III, item 4 **IV**, App. A, V. ix, A, 1, n. 101; ix, A, 2, n. 11
27*v*, col. II b **IV**, App. D, n. 127
28 **I**, App. D, sec. 19. iii, A, 1, n. 21; iii, B, 4, n. 7; iii, D, nn. 73, 77. ix, B, n. 159
29 i, 3, n. 30. vi, 12, n. 49. vii, B, 1, n. 33; vii, C, 1, a, n. 37; vii, C, 1, d, n. 31; vii, D, 2, n. 12. viii, A, 2, n. 29; viii, A, 3, n. 31
30 **I**, App. C, sec. 24. **I**, App.D, sec. 61. v, B, 1, nn. 21, 31
32 ii, 7, n. 76. viii, A, 2, n. 80
35 i, 2, n. 72. v, B, 1, nn. 58, 65; v, C, 2, n. 15. vi, 4, n. 20
36 v, B, 2, n. 33. vii, C, 1, c, n. 52. ix, A, 1, n. 54
38*v* vi, 12, n. 63
39 v, B, 1, n. 1; v, D, 2, n. 28
41 **II**, App. B, sec. 17. vii, C, 1, d, n. 26. viii, C, 1, n. 214
42 ii, 5, nn. 17, 33, 36. vii, C, 1, b, n. 49. viii, C, 2, n. 14
47 viii, D, n. 12
51 ii, 4, n. 87; ii, 6, n. 17. v, A, 2, n. 27. vii, B, 1, nn. 42, 43. viii, C, 1, n. 223
52 vii, C, 1, a, n. 40

54 vi, 10, n. 47
58 ii, 4, n. 22. viii, C, 2, n. 160
59 ix, A, 1, n. 44. x, D, n. 338
60 x, B, 2, n. 168
66 v, D, 2, n. 23
68 ii, 6, n. 3. viii, C, 4, n. 149. x, B, 1, n. 91
73 vii, C, 2, n. 25. viii, D, n. 89
76 ii, 4, n. 46. **II**, App. B, sec. 38. **II**, App. C, sec. 87. x, A, 1, n. 164
78 ix, C, 2, nn. 17, 31
84 x, C, 3, n. 18; x, C, 5, n. 17
86 viii, C, 4, n. 168. ix, A, 4, nn. 93, 178, 217; ix, A, 5, n. 82; ix, B, n. 546
87 x, B, 1, n. 93; x, B, 4, n. 175
90 viii, C, 4, n. 102
92 v, B, 1, n. 5
94 x, A, 3, n. 62
97 viii, C, 1, n. 7
98 ii, 4, n. 46. **II**, App. B, sec. 47. viii, A, 1, n. 81. x, A, 2, n. 223
102 viii, B, 2, n. 50
105 **II**, App. B, sec. 49
108 **II**, App. C, sec. 61
111 **I**, App. D, sec. 18. iii, D, nn. 73, 78; iii, F, n. 8. ix, B, n. 258. x, B, 1, n. 115
112 viii, B, 4, n. 44
117 vii, C, 1, b, n. 34
118 viii, C, 1, n. 129
119 **II**, App. A, sec. 11 b
120 v, C, 4, n. 58. viii, C, 1, n. 230. x, B, 1, nn. 21, 54, 74; x, C, 2, n. 17
121 vi, 10, n. 18
125 x, C, 4, n. 121
127 **I**, App. D, sec. 20. ii, 5, n. 37. iii, D, nn. 73, 75, 78. ix, B, n. 224
128 ix, A, 4, n. 128; ix, B, n. 319
131 ii, 2, n. 12
133 ii, 4, n. 64. vii, B, 1, n. 54. viii, C, 1, n. 137
134 x, A, 2, n. 431; x, B, 1, n. 33
137 i, 2, nn. 26, 36. iii, D, n. 6
138 vii, C, 1, b, n. 42 (cited as NS 138)
145 iii, F, n. 182
149 viii, C, 1, n. 197
150 ii, 2, n. 16; ii, 4, n. 48. vii, A, 2, n. 25. ix, B, n. 163
151 ii, 2, n. 33; ii, 4, n. 62; ii, 5, n. 56. **II**, App. C, sec. 47
162 iii, F, n. 3. iv, 12, n. 43
163 viii, C, 4, n. 95. ix, A, 5, nn. 44, 55, 88
164 **II**, App. D, sec. 22
165 v, D, 2, n. 35
170 iv, 4, n. 1
171 ii, 7, n. 33. vi, 12, n. 45
172 i, 2, n. 46
173 ii, 4, n. 101. vi, 12, n. 41. x, D, n. 53
174 v, B, 2, nn. 62, 73; v, D, 2, n. 3. x, A, 2, n. 110
176 iii, D, n. 70
179 ii, 3, n. 9; ii, 6, n. 13. iii, A, 1, n. 13; iii, C, n. 26. **II**, App. B, sec. 11. viii, A, 1, n. 63. ix, B, n. 258; ix, C, 1, n. 151
180 x, A, 2, n. 27

183 v, B, 2, n. 45. viii, A, 2, n. 78. ix, C, 2, n. 39
184 viii, C, 4, n. 33. ix, A, 4, nn. 186, 213; ix, A, 5, nn. 20, 22, 34, 48; ix, B, nn. 29, 83, 548. **IV**, App. D, n. 143
185 **III**, App. pt. I, gr. 5. viii, C, 1, n. 136. ix, A, 2, n. 45; ix, A, 3, n. 13
189 **II**, App. A, sec. 153
190 **IV**, App. A, VII
190*v* **IV**, App. A, VI. ix, A, 1, n. 66
191 **II**, App. B, sec. 9. vi, 4, n. 20. viii, C, 1, n. 214
193 v, A, 2, n. 79
197 ii, 4, n. 37. iv, 11, n. 15
198 I, App. D, sec. 21. ii, 2, nn. 5, 14. iii, D, nn. 73, 78; iii, F, nn. 17, 35, 56. iv, 6, n. 25. viii, B, 5, n. 74
199 ii, 3, nn. 11, 29; ii, 4, n. 2. iii, D, n. 78
200 iii, D, nn. 73, 78
205 **II**, App. C, sec. 70
208 ix, A, 4, nn. 52, 185; ix, A, 5, nn. 26, 32, 44, 64, 88, 91; ix, B, n. 473
209 x, A, 3, n. 243
215 ii, 2, n. 32. ix, A, 1, n. 184
221 **II**, App. A, sec. 152. **II**, App. B, sec. 48
222 iii, A, 1, n. 12. **II**, App. C, sec. 88
226 viii, B, 4, n. 42. ix, A, 5, n. 60; ix, B, n. 543
226*v*, item I viii, B, 2, n. 92; viii, C, 4, n. 166; viii, D, n. 121
item II viii, C, 3, n. 78
item III viii, B, 4, n. 32
227 **II**, App. B, sec. 93. viii, C, 1, n. 46
228 **III**, App. pt. I, gr. 7; **III**, App. pt. II, no. 97. viii, B, 4, n. 25. **IV**, App. C. ix, A, 4, n. 98; ix, A, 5, n. 31
230 **II**, App.A, sec. 115
231 **III**, App. pt. II, no. 92. **IV**, App. C. ix, A, 4, n. 202; ix, A, 5, n. 61; ix, B, nn. 412, 430, 523
235 iii, A, 1, n. 43 (mistake for NS J 325). **II**, App. C, sec. 51
236 vi, 9, n. 27. viii, C, 1, n. 67. x, A, 3, n. 215
239 v, B, 2, n. 96. viii, A, 1, n. 81
239*v* **II**, App. B, sec. 83*a*
241 x, B, 2, n. 136
242 x, B, 3, n. 80; x, C, 2, n. 5
243 iii, F, n. 68. ix, C, 1, n. 105
245 **II**, App. B, sec. 84
247 viii, C, 3, n. 121
249 viii, C, 4, nn. 120, 132
251 **II**, App. B, sec. 77
256 **II**, App. C, sec. 44. v, B, 2, n. 100
257 vii, C, 1, b, n. 24
259 iii, G, n. 2. **II**, App. D, sec. 13. vii, B, 1, n. 71; vii, C, 1, b, nn. 17, 19
260 x, A, 2, n. 311
261 i, 2, n. 56
262 v, A, 2, n. 64
264 **II**, App. A, sec. 119. ix, A, 1, n. 78 (mistakes for NS J 264*a*)
264*a* **II**, App. A, sec. 119. ix, A, 1, n. 78 (cited in both places as NS J 264)
267 **II**, App. B, sec. 81
268 iii, B, 2, n. 27. vi, 11, n. 60
269 iii, F, n. 149. viii, A, 1, n. 86
270 iii, F, n. 181. **II**, App.C, sec. 93. v, D, 2, n. 56. x, A, 2, n. 9
272 vii, A, 1, n. 34; vii, C, 1, a, n. 21. x, C, 2, n. 16

273 ii, 1, n. 14; ii, 2, n. 25
275 ii, 6, n. 11 (mistake, *see* Reif)
277 ii, 3, n. 27. iii, F, n. 193. v, A, 2, n. 60. vii, A, 2, n. 23; vii, A, 3, n. 11; vii, C, 1, a, n. 20
278 **III**, App. pt. II, no. 220. viii, B, 2, nn. 2, 17
279 iv, 2, n. 24. v, D, 2, n. 26. vii, A, 1, n. 58. ix, C, 1, n. 6
282 viii, C, 3, n. 82
283 vii, A, 2, n. 5; vii, B, 2, n. 3
284 ix, B, nn. 70, 118. x, A, 3, nn. 193, 224
285 x, A, 2, nn. 28, 363
287 viii, B, 4, n. 82; viii, B, 5, n. 13
288 **II**, App. B, sec. 16
289 iv, 4, n. 35
290 vii, C, 2, n. 49
291 ii, 4, n. 2. iii, E, n. 52. iv, 8, n. 80
292*v* **II**, App. A, sec. 125. x, B, 3, n. 72
293 ii, 4, n. 94 (mistake, *see* Reif); ii, 5, n. 50; ii, 6, nn. 21, 25. **II**, App. B, sec. 33. vi, 10, n. 37. vii, C, 1, d, n. 26. viii, C, 1, n. 57
294 **II**, App. C, sec. 97
295 iv, 4, n. 35
296 v, B, 1, n. 115; v, B, 2, n. 91; v, D, 1, n. 19. vi, 12, n. 73. ix, A, 4, nn. 111, 209; ix, B, nn. 419, 453. x, D, n. 152
297 **I**, App. D, sec. 79. vi, 10, n. 27. viii, B, 5, n. 51; viii, C, 3, n. 84
297 *b* vii, C, 1, b, n. 24 (cited as 297*d*)
299 iii, A, 1, n. 40
300 ii, 2, n. 46. ix, B, n. 224
305 **II**, App. A, sec. 158
306 viii, B, 4, n. 50. ix, B, nn. 370, 525, 546
315 **II**, App. C, sec. 20
317 ix, C, 1, n. 33
318 **II**, App. A, sec. 127
321, f. 7*a* ix, C, 2, n. 24
323 x, A, 2, n. 223
325 iii, A, 1, n. 43 (cited as NS J 235). viii, D, n. 15
326 vi, 9, n. 31
327*v* ix, C, 1, nn. 68, 121
330 **II**, App. C, sec. 74
337 x, C, 3, n. 25
338 vi, 11, n. 44. viii, C, 2, n. 140. ix, A, 2, nn. 116, 150; ix, A, 3, n. 12
341 ii, 4, n. 2
342*v* **II**, App. A, sec. 126
344 v, A, 2, n. 76. vii, B, 1, n. 65; vii, C, 1, c, n. 21. ix, B, n. 166
347 viii, C, 3, n. 10. x, A, 3, n. 53
354 vi, 12, n. 50. x, A, 2, n. 413
356 viii, C, 3, n. 14
357 viii, C, 3, n. 35
358 **III**, App. pt. II, no. 253. viii, B, 5, n. 82
359 ix, A, 4, n. 160; ix, A, 5, nn. 44, 64, 90; ix, B, n. 251
362 **II**, App. B, sec. 61
363 viii, B, 4, n. 85; viii, B, 5, n. 51
364 **III**, App. pt. II, no. 280
366 vii, B, 3, n. 17
373 iv, 2, n. 25
375 **II**, App. A, sec. 93. v, B, 2, n. 91; v, D, 1, n. 28. ix, C, 1, n. 72

376 x, A, 1, n. 7
378 **III**, App. pt. II, no. 235. viii, B, 5, nn. 7, 44, 67, 77. ix, A, 3, n. 67
380 viii, C, 1, n. 216. x, A, 2, n. 124
382 vi, 11, n. 44. viii, C, 2, n. 140. ix, A, 2, nn. 43, 159; ix, A, 3, n. 12
383 v, B, 2, n. 117. viii, C, 2, n. 99; viii, D, n. 109
384 **II**, App.C, sec. 83
385 viii, C, 4, n. 47
389 **II**, App. C, sec. 90. v, D, 2, n. 45
390 i, 2, n. 53. **III**, App. pt. II, no. 227. viii, C, 1, n. 41. **IV**, App. C, 2. ix, A, 4, nn. 11, 30, 32, 85, 174, 205; ix, B, nn. 117, 417, 530. **IV**, App. D, nn. 226, 266, 286
392 viii, C, 3, n. 31. ix, A, 4, n. 32; ix, A, 5, nn. 10, 21, 39, 83; ix, B, nn. 29, 124, 261
396 ii, 4, n. 114
397 vii, A, 3, n. 48
400 **II**, App. C, sec. 10
401 viii, D, n. 157 (mistake for NS J 401b)
401, no. 2 viii, B, 2, nn. 3, 94 (mistake for NS J 401q)
401, no. 6 viii, C, 1, n. 153 (mistake for NS J 401k)
401, no. 10 iii, F, n. 109 (mistake for NS J 401b)
401, no. 21 vi, 2, n. 19 (mistake for NS J 401l)
401b iii, F, n. 109 (cited as NS J 401, no. 10). viii, D, n. 157 (cited as NS J 401)
401k viii, C, 1, n. 153 (cited as NS J 401, no. 6)
401l vi, 2, n. 19 (cited as NS J 401, no. 21)
401q viii, B, 2, nn. 3, 94 (cited as NS J 401, no. 2)
403 **II**, App. C, sec. 18. x, A, 3, n. 229
404 **II**, App.C, sec. 66
405 ii, 3, n. 27
409 ii, 7, n. 64. ix, A, 4, nn. 176, 202, 208; ix, A, 5, nn. 2, 32, 61
410 **III**, App. pt. II, no. 118. viii, B, 4, n. 63. **IV**, App. C, 2. ix, A, 4, nn. 217, 219. **IV**, App. D, n. 263
411 v, B, 2, n. 120
412 **I**, App. D, sec. 64. **III**, App. pt. II, no. 258. viii, C, 3, n. 110
413 viii, C, 3, n. 57
414 ix, B, nn. 143, 144, 425, 499, 518
416 **II**, App. C, sec. 34. vi, 12, n. 77; vi, 13, nn. 19, 70
419 x, A, 3, nn. 148, 152
420 **II**, App. B, sec. 55
422 **II**, App. C, sec. 24. vi, 12, n. 73. x, D, n. 152
424 **II**, App. C, sec. 77
425 vi, 2, n. 32
430 iii, F, n. 183. **II**, App. C, sec. 96
432 ix, B, n. 95
433 **II**, App. A, sec. 140
434 ii, 4, n. 46 (mistake for NS J 434). v, C, 1, n. 27. vi, 4, nn. 11, 15
434a ii, 4, n. 46 (cited as NS J 434)
437 ix, C, 1, n. 32
438 **II**, App. B, sec. 78. ix, C, 1, n. 16
440 **II**, App. B, sec. 86
441 **II**, App. C, sec. 72
443 **III**, App. pt. II, no. 264. ix, B, n. 263
444 **II**, App. C, sec. 22
446 ix, C, 1, n. 162
453 viii, C, 3, n. 143. ix, A, 5, n. 47

455 viii, C, 3, n. 77
457 **III**, App. pt. II, no. 336. viii, C, 4, n. 175
458 ix, C, 1, n. 172
459 viii, C, 3, n. 63
460 ix, D, n. 35
461 **III**, App. pt. II, no. 36. viii, C, 3, n. 29
465 viii, C, 4, n. 94
469 viii, C, 4, n. 2
473 x, C, 2, n. 27
475 **III**, App. pt. II, no. 135. viii, B, 3, n. 88
484 x, A, 3, n. 120
488 ix, B, n. 119
490 viii, C, 1, n. 207
496 viii, C, 3, n. 33

TS AS: Taylor-Schechter Additional Series (fragments sorted in 1974 and stored in binders)

TS AS 145, f. 1 **III**, App. pt. II, no. 4
f. 3 viii, D, n. 162
f. 7 viii, C, 4, n. 20; viii, D, n. 21
f. 9 viii, C, 3, n. 17
f. 10 ix, A, 4, nn. 199, 219
f. 13 viii, D, n. 187
f. 14*b* x, C, 3, n. 18
f. 17 viii, C, 4, n. 118
f. 22 viii, C, 2, n. 121. x, A, 1, n. 31
f. 24 viii, C, 1, n. 33
f. 25 viii, C, 4, n. 101
f. 76 ix, C, 1, n. 195
AS 146, f. 2 x, A, 3, n. 44
f. 3 x, C, 4, n. 69; x, D, n. 44
f. 4 viii, C, 1, n. 166
f. 5 viii, C, 2, n. 177
f. 7 viii, B, 2, n. 74. **IV**, App. D, n. 266
f. 9 x, A, 1, n. 131
f. 13 ix, A, 5, n. 78; ix, B, n. 530
f. 18 viii, D, n. 43
f. 66, item I **III**, App. pt. I, gr. 3; **III**, App. pt. II, no. 343
item II **III**, App. pt. I, gr. 3; **III**, App. pt. II, no. 365
f. 183 **III**, App. pt. II, no. 351
AS 147, f. 1 **III**, App. pt. II, no. 50
f. 2 viii, A, 1, n. 17; viii, B, 2, n. 79. x, A, 2, n. 108; x, B, 2, n. 67; x, C, 4, n. 44
f. 4 viii, C, 2, n. 92. ix, C, 1, n. 127. x, A, 2, n. 436; x, B, 1, n. 108
f. 8 viii, D, n. 82
f. 9 **III**, App. pt. I, gr. 6; **III**, App. pt. II, no. 146
f. 12 **III**, App. pt. II, no. 149. viii, B, 2, n. 4; viii, B, 5, n. 52
f. 17 viii, C, 3, n. 112
f. 20 ix, A, 4, n. 169; ix, A, 5, n. 82
f. 22 viii, D, n. 139
f. 23 viii, C, 4, n. 65
f. 24 ix, C, 1, n. 184
f. 25 **III**, App. pt. II, no. 63
f. 38 ix, A, 3, n. 53. **IV**, App. D, n. 196
AS 148, f. 2 x, B, 4, n. 114
f. 3 x, B, 2, n. 75
f. 6 **III**, App. pt. II, no. 276
f. 7 ix, A, 5, n. 42

f. 9 ix, B, n. 154. x, A, 2, n. 26
f. 15 **IV**, App. A, V. ix, A, 5, n. 87
f. 17 x, B, 1, n. 24
AS 149, f. 3 ix, A, 4, n. 175. x, A, 2, nn. 105, 302
f. 7 x, C, 2, n. 27
f. 10*v* ix, C, 1, nn. 155, 176
AS 150, f. 1 ix, A, 1, n. 238
f. 2*v* x, B, 2, n. 78
f. 6 x, A, 3, n. 151
f. 13 x, A, 2, n. 230
AS 151, f. 2 x, A, 2, n. 416
f. 3 ix, A, 4, n. 192
f. 4 ix, A, 3, n. 56; ix, A, 4, n. 149
AS 152, f. 1 viii, C, 3, n. 83
f. 4 x, A, 2, n. 321
f. 360 ix, C, 4, n. 13
AS 153, f. 1 viii, C, 4, n. 13
AS 155, f. 207 ix, C, 2, n. 12
AS 156, fs. 237
and 238 x, B, 2, n. 16
MS Toledano: Three manuscripts in the possession of J. M. Toledano and edited by him in *Mizrah u-Maʿarav*, 1 (1920), 344–350 (Hebrew)
viii, A, 1, n. 40
Turner, Justin G.
(Private MS), G.-TB ix, B, n. 518
ULC: University Library, Cambridge (usually cited as CUL)
Oriental Collection (Fragments acquired separately from T-S collection)
ULC Or 1080 Box
1, f. 2 viii, B, 3, n. 11
1, f. 3*v* viii, B, 1, n. 6
4, f. 15 vi, 11, n. 10. viii, C, 1, n. 200
5, f. 15 vi, 13, n. 57. **III**, App. pt. I, gr. 1; **III**, App. pt. II, no. 286. viii, B, 4, n. 44. **IV**, App. C, 2. ix, A, 4, nn. 61, 189
5, f. 17 **III**, App. pt. II, no. 6. viii, B, 4, n. 20. ix, A, 5, n. 41
6, f. 25 v, B, 1, n. 141; v, B, 2, n. 61. viii, C, 4, n. 181. x, A, 1, n. 106; x, A, 3, n. 323
ULC Or 1080 J 1 vi, 12, n. 81
2 i, 2, n. 81. **II**, App. C, sec. 113. vi, 13, n. 18. viii, D, n. 117. x, A, 1, n.102; x, B, 3, n. 82
6 i, 2, n. 44. ii, 3, n. 5. v, B, 1, nn. 5, 104. viii, B, 2, n. 73; viii, C, 1, n. 83; viii, C, 2, nn. 99, 173; viii, C, 3, n. 40
7 i, 2, n. 100. vi, 7, n. 24. **III**, App. pt. I, gr. 4; **III**, App. pt. II, no. 303. viii, C, 1, n. 195. **IV**, App. A, VII. ix, A, 1, n. 93; ix, A, 2, n. 35
8 viii, C, 4, nn. 100, 121
9 iii, A, 1, n. 13
10 **II**, App. A, sec. 101. ix, A, 3, n. 52
11 **II**, App. D, sec. 30
13 iv, 2, n. 1
14 i, 2, n. 12. iii, F, n. 47
15 iv, 3, n. 67. x, B, 5, n. 3
17 ii, 4, n. 35; ii, 5, nn. 24, 35. iii, A, 1, n. 33. iv, 8, n. 9
21 x, A, 2, n. 11
22 i, 3, n. 15. ii, 4, n. 16. iii, E, n. 55. iv, 8, n. 36. viii, C, 1, n. 144. x, A, 3, n. 9
23 i, 2, n. 72. v, B, 2, n. 126. vi, 9, n. 40. viii, C, 1, nn. 33, 37, 90, 244. ix, A, 1, n. 65; ix, A, 4, n. 132
24 viii, B, 1, n. 62. ix, B, n. 123. x, A, 2, n. 397

25 ii, 7, n. 33. viii, C, 1, n. 62; viii, C, 2, n. 49; viii, C, 3, n. 151. ix, A, 2, n. 151. x, B, 2, n. 43
26 iv, 3, n. 45; iv, 4, nn. 6, 28. vii, C, 1, c, n. 1; vii, D, 1, n. 7
27 vii, C, 1, a, n. 32. ix, A, 1, n. 194. x, A, 2, n. 354
28 viii, C, 1, n. 15; viii, C, 2, n. 13; viii, D, n. 15. x, A, 1, n. 9; x, B, 3, n. 22; x, C, 5, n. 10
29 ii, 2, n. 49; ii, 4, n. 73. iv, 11, n. 4. vi, 12, n. 77. vii, B, 1, nn. 29, 38; vii, B, 3, n. 54. ix, D, n. 17. x, A, 1, n. 9
30 ii, 7, n. 35. viii, A, 3, n. 28
31 v, D, 1, n. 24
33 v, B, 2, n. 117. vi, 12, n. 31
34 v, B, 1, nn. 1, 89; v, C, 4, n. 55
35 iii, B, 3, n. 7. iv, 4, n. 12; iv, 8, n. 5; iv, 11, n. 11. viii, C, 1, n. 48. ix, B, n. 306. x, C, 3, n. 26
36 iv, 6, n. 4; iv, 7, n. 4; iv, 10, n. 38. vii, C, 1, c, n. 54. ix, A, 1, n. 126. x, B, 4, n. 33
37 iv, 4, n. 8
39 ii, 4, n. 40. vii, C, 1, c, n. 4. x, B, 2, n. 131
40 v, B, 2, n. 46. viii, A, 2, n. 52. x, C, 5, n. 20
42 ii, 2, n. 2; ii, 5, n. 39. iii, F, n. 21. iv, 1, n. 7; iv, 2, n. 26; iv, 3, nn. 37, 76; iv, 10, n. 23 (mistake, *see* Reif). x, C, 2, n. 14
45 i, 2, n. 66. v, A, 1, n. 36; v, C, 3, n. 14. vii, B, 1, n. 33
46 ii, 4, n. 2. **II**, App. B, sec. 51. v, B, 2, n. 54
47 viii, C, 1, n. 223. ix, C, 1, n. 79
48 **II**, App. B, sec. 57 a. vi, 10, n. 30
48*v* ix, A, 4, nn. 52, 106; ix, A, 5, n. 6
49 ii, 7, n. 47. **III**, App. pt. I, gr. 6; **III**, App. pt. II, no. 363. viii, B, 4, n. 53. **IV**, App. C, 3. ix, A, 4, nn. 163, 174, 196; ix, B, nn. 116, 411, 459
50 ix, A, 4, n. 100. x, A, 1, n. 139
55 iii, B, 4, n. 9; iii, D, nn. 1, 3. ix, A, 5, nn. 7, 64, 82; ix, B, n. 516. x, B, 2, nn. 50, 105
57 i, 2, n. 80
62 x, A, 3, n. 32
64 iii, A, 1, n. 40. ix, B, n. 74
65 **III**, App. pt. I, gr. 6
66 ix, A, 1, n. 167; ix, A, 2, n. 126
67 **II**, App. D, sec. 30. vi, 9, n. 31. viii, C, 3, n. 153
68 viii, C, 1, n. 223
70 iv, 3, n. 62. x, B, 4, n. 129
71 ii, 7, nn. 83, 90. iii, A, 1, n. 35. viii, C, 1, n. 10. ix, A, 2, n. 152; ix, C, 1, n. 122. x, B, 2, n. 15
73 iii, B, 2, n. 21
74 vi, 10, n. 22
77 ii, 4, nn. 40, 41, 42, 81. iii, E, n. 6. ix, A, 4, nn. 102, 120; ix, B, nn. 96, 137, 172, 181, 233
78 iv, 3, n. 67. x, B, 1, n. 30
79 iii, B, 4, n. 7. iv, 5, n. 10
80 vii, C, 2, n. 35. viii, C, 1, n. 3. ix, A, 2, n. 44
81 iii, F, n. 140. vi, 4, n. 23
82 ix, C, 1, n. 169
85 v, B, 1, n. 62
86 v, B, 2, n. 81. vii, C, 1, a, n. 19; vii, C, 1, c, n. 32; vii, C, 1, d, n. 17. x, A, 1, n. 156
87 **II**, App. C, sec. 7. v, C, 1, n. 11
88 i, 2, n. 72
89*v* ix, D, n. 14
90 viii, A, 2, n. 80; viii, B, 3, n. 80

91 **I**, App. D, sec. 49
92 iii, F, n. 26
93 vi, 12, n. 59; vi, 13, n. 1. vii, A, 1, n. 46; vii, A, 2, n. 24; vii, A, 3, n. 15; vii, B, 2, n. 13. x, B, 5, n. 23
94 x, D, n. 176
95 ix, B, n. 154
96 iii, F, n. 21
100 **III**, App. pt. II, no. 119. ix, A, 4, n. 54
101 ii, 5, n. 43. vi, 13, n. 61
104 ii, 2, n. 26; ii, 3, n. 5; ii, 4, n. 89. iii, E, n. 31; iii, F, n. 10. iv, 2, n. 12
104*v* **II**, App. A, sec. 170
105 viii, C, 1, n. 183
106 v, A, 1, n. 26; v, B, 2, n. 112; v, C, 2, n. 3; v, C, 4, n. 19. vii, B, 1, n. 35
107 viii, C, 1, n. 183
109 ii, 5, n. 75
110 ii, 7, n. 32. x, C, 4, n. 34; x, D, n. 313
111 iii, B, 1, n. 11; iii, C, nn. 2, 26. ix, C, 2, n. 53
112 v, A, 2, n. 57. vii, B, 1, nn. 12, 14, 29, 56
113 ii, 4, nn. 59, 87. vii, A, 3, n. 11
115 vii, A, 3, n. 43
117 vi, 11, n. 12; vi, 13, n. 13. vii, A, 2, n. 5. **IV**, App. A, III. ix, A, 2, nn. 58, 82, 103, 116, 134, 141, 160, 166; ix, A, 3, nn. 35, 52
117*v* viii, C, 2, n. 138
119 ii, 4, n. 112. iii, D, nn. 73, 77; iii, E, nn. 53, 57
121 iii, B, 2, n. 24
122 **II**, App. C, sec. 98
126 ix, A, 4, nn. 18, 49; ix, A, 5, n. 79; ix, B, n. 490
126*v* **II**, App. A, sec. 131*a*
130 iii, A, 2, n. 4; iii, D, nn. 10, 81. **I**, App. D, n. 20. ix, A, 1, n. 141
132 vi, 9, n. 42. x, C, 5, n. 21
137 iii, B, 2, n. 3
138 iii, F, n. 131. vii, C, 1, d, n. 30
138*v* ix, D, n. 12
140 **III**, App. pt. II, no. 68. viii, B, 2, n. 92. ix, A, 4, nn. 54, 164, 169, 193
141 viii, C, 3, nn. 109, 114
142 viii, C, 4, n. 32. ix, A, 4, nn. 90, 116; ix, B, nn. 260, 287, 330. **IV**, App. D, n. 205. x, A, 3, n. 255
145 viii, C, 1, n. 2
148 iii, C, n. 12. v, D, 2, n. 28
149 viii, A, 1, n. 7
152 ii, 4, n. 60
154 iv, 3, n. 57. x, A, 2, n. 1
160 iii, G, n. 15 (mistake for 1080 J 180)
161 x, A, 2, n. 379
167 iv, 9, n. 25. vii, C, 1, c, n. 47
169 iv, 5, n. 21
170 ix, A, 2, n. 103
172 viii, C, 4, n. 170
173 viii, C, 1, n. 218
175 viii, D, n. 98
176 iv, 3, nn. 48, 81. vi, 13, n. 20
178 iv, 8, n. 48. ix, B, n. 166
180 iii, G, n. 15 (cited as 1080 J 160)

181*v* x, C, 2, n. 80
185 viii, B, 4, n. 44. ix, A, 4, n. 202
186 **III**, App. pt. II, no. 251. viii, B, 3, n. 12
187 **III**, App. pt. I, gr. 8
190 viii, C, 2, nn. 46, 66
200 vi, 11, nn. 8, 49. vii, C, 2, n. 56
206 **III**, App. pt. I, gr. 8. viii, B, 3, nn. 45, 82; viii, D, n. 11
211 v, B, 1, n. 7
214 v, B, 1, n. 49
223 viii, D, n. 213
237 v, B, 2, n. 46
239 **I**, App. D, sec. 72. iii, F, n. 184. vii, A, 2, n. 9. ix, A, 1, n. 82
244 x, D, n. 276
248 iii, B, 3, nn. 5, 7
255 x, C, 5, n. 9
258 ii, 7, n. 113. iii, E, n. 53. iv, 5, n. 3; iv, 8, nn. 7, 29. v, B, 2, n. 5. vii, A, 3, n. 23; vii, C, 1, b, n. 22; vii, C, 2, n. 29. viii, C, 4, n. 47. x, D, nn. 203, 206
260 **III**, App. pt. I, gr. 8; **III**, App. pt. II, no. 9. viii, B, 3, n. 45
262 viii, C, 3, n. 18; viii, C, 4, n. 82; viii, D, n. 110
264 ii, 7, n. 98. iii, B, 1, n. 18. iv, 3, n. 23. ix, A, 1, n. 222; ix, B, n. 273. x, A, 2, n. 377
265 v, A, 1, n. 34. x, C, 5, n. 21
271*v* vi, 12, n. 70
273 ii, 7, n. 49. iii, F, n. 5
276 viii, C, 1, n. 89. ix, A, 1, n. 29
278 ii, 2, n. 34
280 iii, B, 2, n. 51
281 ii, 7, n. 20. x, D, nn. 304, 309, 315
283 **IV**, App. A, VI
284 ii, 4, n. 24
285 viii, C, 3, n. 120. x, D, n. 327
286 **III**, App. pt. I, gr. 6; **III**, App. pt. II, no. 2. viii, B, 4, n. 19
287 x, D, n. 323
288 iii, B, 2, n. 53
289 **III**, App. pt. II, no. 10
290 iii, A, 2, n. 8; iii, B, 1, n. 20. vi, 10, n. 48
291 **I**, App. D, sec. 3. ii, 3, n. 21. iii, B, 3, n. 7; iii, D, nn. 74, 75; iii, E, nn. 4, 33, 72. iv, 10, nn. 2, 18, 30; iv, 11, n. 14. ix, B, nn. 203, 226
ULC Or 1081 J 1 vi, 12, n. 92
3 ix, A, 5, n. 52. x, B, 2, n. 141
4 vi, 2, nn. 13, 38
5 vi, 12, n. 89. viii, A, 2, n. 79; viii, C, 2, n. 116; viii, D, n. 15
8 **II**, App. C, sec. 92. v, D, 2, n. 59. x, A, 2, n. 400
9 i, 2, n. 54
10 v, A, 2, n. 66
13 vii, C, 1, c, nn. 39, 55; vii, C, 1, d, n. 19; vii, C, 2, n. 4
16 v, A, 2, nn. 56, 69
17 viii, C, 1, nn. 211, 213, 215
18 i, 1, n. 3. v, A, 2, n. 76; v, B, 1, n. 142; v, D, 2, n. 48
23 iii, D, n. 32
24 ii, 7, nn. 8, 9. iii, A, 1, nn. 29, 35; iii, B, 3, n. 6; iii, E, n. 57. iv, 2, n. 11. x, A, 2, n. 368
25 ix, B, n. 170
27 iv, 6, n. 23; iv, 9, n. 16
30 viii, C, 1, n. 200
31 **IV**, App. A, III

35 i, 2, n. 48
36 iii, B, 2, n. 46
38 **II**, App. A, sec. 116. viii, C, 1, n. 233
39 vi, 12, n. 63; vi, 13, n. 29
40 **III**, App. pt. I, gr. 8; **III**, App. pt. II, no. 199. viii, C, 3, n. 133
43 ii, 2, n. 29
50 **II**, App. B, sec. 76
56 **III**, App. pt. II, no. 377. viii, C, 3, n. 114. ix, A, 4, nn. 163, 199
61 **II**, App. B, sec. 96. vii, C, 2, n. 44
63 **II**, App. C, sec. 89
67 **II**, App. B, sec. 89. viii, C, 1, n. 75

Additional (Fragments acquired before major Geniza collections)
ULC Add. 2586 **IV**, App. A, III
3335 v, B, 1, n. 90. vii, A, 1, n. 33; vii, C, 1, a, nn. 31, 35
3336 x, B, 4, n. 144
3337 iii, F, n. 122. viii, A, 3, n. 56
3339 vii, B, 1, n. 9; vii, B, 3, n. 39. **III**, App. pt. I, gr. 7; **III**, App. pt. II, nos. 273, 295. viii, C, 2, n. 89; viii, C, 3, nn. 3, 7; viii, C, 4, n. 96. ix, B, n. 160. x, A, 3, n. 27
3339 (c) iii, F, n. 169
3340 ii, 1, n. 5; ii, 4, n. 73. x, B, 1, nn. 60, 106; x, B, 4, n. 71
3341 v, B, 1, n. 17. x, B, 1, n. 77
3342 x, A, 2, n. 357
3343 viii, A, 1, n. 15; viii, B, 3, n. 94; viii, D, n. 15
3345 vii, A, 3, n. 40. x, B, 1, nn. 42, 46; x, B, 4, n. 137; x, C, 1, n. 35
3348 viii, A, 1, n. 9
3349 iii, F, n. 36. **III**, App. pt. II, no. 138. viii, B, 2, n. 13
3358 ii, 5, n. 29. **II**, App. A, sec. 98. v, A, 1, n. 3; v, B, 1, n. 10
3388 viii, B, 3, n. 15
3412 iii, D, n. 84
3413 **II**, App. D, sec. 11. ix, C, 2, n. 14
3415 ix, B, n. 222
3416*a*, *b* vii, B, 3, n. 25
3416*c* iii, A, 1, n. 33. vii, B, 3, n. 16. x, A, 2, n. 29
3416*d* **II**, App. D, sec. 14
3417 vii, C, 2, n. 32. viii, C, 2, nn. 92, 124. x, A, 2, n. 417
3418 iii, C, n. 23. ix, A, 4, nn. 44, 175; ix, A, 5, nn. 7, 78, 82
3420 ii, 6, n. 16
3420*c* ix, A, 5, n. 42
3420*d* vii, D, 1, n. 32. viii, D, nn. 167, 174
3422 iii, F, n. 192. vii, B, 3, n. 29
3423 iii, D, n. 64. v, B, 1, n. 48. **IV**, App. D, n. 196
3430 **III**, App. pt. I, gr. 4; **III**, App. pt. II, no. 95. viii, B, 1, n. 8. **IV**, App. C, 2. ix, A, 4, nn. 56, 208, 219; ix, A, 5, nn. 6, 9, 14, 32; ix, B, nn. 58, 103; ix, C, 1, n. 165. x, C, 5, n. 53

University Museum, Philadelphia,
E. 16309 viii, B, 1, n. 15; viii, D, n. 14
16510 viii, D, nn. 7, 11. ix, A, 3, n. 75. x, A, 3, n. 231
16516 viii, C, 1, n. 193. x, A, 3, n. 90
16517 ii, 4, n. 71
16522 i, 2, n. 13; i, 3, n. 39. iii, E, n. 23. iv, 7, n. 17; iv, 8, n. 74

Westminster College: Westminster College, Cambridge
Liturgy II, f. 140 x, C, 5, n. 18
Arabica I, f. 28*v* **II**, App. B, sec. 99
f. 40*b* **III**, App. pt. I, gr. 4; **III**, App. pt. II, no. 205

f. 49 II, App. A, sec. 166
f. 53 II, App. C, sec. 117. viii, D, n. 15
fs. 55–63 iii, A, 1, n. 10. vi, 13, n. 66 (cited as Frag. Cairens. 55–63)
f. 76 III, App. pt. I, gr. 4; III, App. pt. II, no. 205
Arabica II, f. 51 viii, C, 1, nn. 52, 169
f. 79 ii, 4, n. 88
f. 129 viii, C, 2, n. 49; viii, C, 3, n. 151
f. 160 II, App. A, sec. 182
West. Coll. Misc. 5 ix, A, 4, n. 36 (cited as Frag. Cairens. 5)
9 ii, 4, n. 65. ix, A, 5, nn. 37, 42, 50, 72, 81; ix, B, nn. 122, 140, 237, 289, 336. x, B, 1, n. 59 (cited as Frag. Cairens. 9)
11 viii, B, 5, n. 57 (cited as Frag. Cairens. 11)
13 ii, 6, n. 19. ix, B, n. 149 (cited as Frag. Cairens. 13)
16, col. III x, A, 2, n. 364 (cited as Frag. Cairens. 16, col. III)
18 viii, C, 1, n. 151 (cited as Frag. Cairens. 18)
25 iv, 5, n. 17 (cited as Frag. Cairens. 25)
35 x, A, 1, n. 95; x, A, 2, n. 175 (cited as Frag. Cairens. 35)
42 III, App. pt. I, gr. 5 (cited as Frag. Cairens. 42)
43 ii, 5, n. 71. vii, C, 2, n. 41; vii, D, 1, n. 8. viii, A, 2, n. 66. x, B, 4, n. 26 (cited as Frag. Cairens. 43)
45 x, B, 1, n. 139 (cited as Frag. Cairens. 45)
46 viii, D, n. 25 (cited as Frag. Cairens. 46)
47 III, App. pt. II, no. 111. ix, B, n. 368 (cited as Frag. Cairens. 47)
50 v, A, 2, n. 51
50a iii, D, n. 29. iv, 10, n. 9
51 I, App. D, sec. 44. v, A, 2, nn. 42, 68; v, B, 1, n. 127; v, B, 2, n. 69. vii, A, 1, nn. 12, 42; vii, C, 1, d, n. 23. ix, A, 1, n. 194; ix, A, 3, n. 62 (cited as Frag. Cairens. 51)
58 II, App. B, sec. 83 b (cited as Frag. Cairens. 58)
77 viii, B, 3, n. 71 (cited as Frag. Cairens. 77)
98 III, App. pt. II, no. 231 (cited as Frag. Cairens. 98)
100 x, B, 1, n. 26 (cited as Frag. Cairens. 100)
103A vi, 7, n. 3 (cited as Frag. Cairens. 103*b*)
104 x, A, 1, n. 144 (cited as Frag. Cairens. 104)
105 III, App. pt. I, gr. 4; III, App. pt. II, no. 205 (cited as Frag. Cairens. 105)
106 viii, B, 3, n. 71 (cited as Frag. Cairens. 106)
109 x, A, 1, n. 29 (cited as Frag. Cairens. 109)
113 III, App. pt. II, no. 291. viii, C, 3, nn. 7, 9, 21; viii, C, 4, n. 176. x, A, 2, n. 400; x, A, 3, n. 28; x, B, 1, n. 105; x, C, 2, n. 12 (cited as Frag. Cairens. 113)
115 viii, C, 3, nn. 7, 9, 15, 16. x, A, 3, n. 28 (cited as Frag. Cairens. 115)
119 viii, B, 3, n. 71. ix, A, 4, n. 47 (cited as Frag. Cairens. 119)
120 viii, B, 4, n. 49. ix, A, 5, n. 62; ix, B, n. 496 (cited as Frag. Cairens. 120)
125 III, App. pt. I, gr. 4; III, App. pt. II, no. 217 (cited as Frag. Cairens. 125)
West. Coll. Glass 1 x, D, n. 57
3 viii, C, 1, n. 151
39 viii, D, n. 20
Frag. Cairens. 5 *see* West. Coll. Misc. 5
9 *see* West. Coll. Misc. 9
11 *see* West. Coll. Misc. 11
13 *see* West. Coll. Misc. 13
16, col. III *see* West. Coll. Misc. 16, col. III
18 *see* West. Coll. Misc. 18

25	*see* West. Coll. Misc. 25
35	*see* West. Coll. Misc. 35
42	*see* West. Coll. Misc. 42
43	*see* West. Coll. Misc. 43
45	*see* West. Coll. Misc. 45
46	*see* West. Coll. Misc. 46
47	*see* West. Coll. Misc. 47
50	*see* West. Coll. Misc. 50
50a	*see* West. Coll. Misc. 50a
51	*see* West. Coll. Misc. 51
55–63	*see* Arabica I, fs. 55–63
58	*see* West. Coll. Misc. 58
77	*see* West. Coll. Misc. 77
98	*see* West. Coll. Misc. 98
100	*see* West. Coll. Misc. 100
103*b*	*see* West. Coll. Misc. 103A
104	*see* West. Coll. Misc. 104
105	*see* West. Coll. Misc. 105
106	*see* West. Coll. Misc. 106
109	*see* West. Coll. Misc. 109
113	*see* West. Coll. Misc. 113
115	*see* West. Coll. Misc. 115
119	*see* West. Coll. Misc. 119
120	*see* West. Coll. Misc. 120
125	*see* West. Coll. Misc. 125
Lewis-Gibson no. 4	**II**, App. D, sec. 22 (mistake, *see* Reif)

Index of Scriptural, Rabbinic, and Maimonidean Citations

Includes references to Hebrew Bible, Yemenite Pentateuch, New Testament, Koran, Mishna, Tosefta, Palestinian Talmud, Babylonian Talmud, Midrash, Abraham Maimonides, and Moses Maimonides. Upper case bold roman numerals indicate volumes; plain Arabic numerals indicate page and note numbers.

SCRIPTURE

Hebrew Bible

Genesis	1:3	**V**, 381
	1:28	**III**, 48, 54
	1:29	**IV**, 442 n. 165
	2:1	**V**, 595 n. 14
	2:1–3	**V**, 349
	2:2	**V**, 603 n. 6
	2:9	**V**, 381
	2:11	**IV**, 418 n. 357
	2:18	**III**, 48, 109, 319, 437 n. 10, 451 n. 24
	2:21–24	**V**, 593 n. 34
	2:24	**V**, 608 n. 33
	2:23	**III**, 194
	2:24	**III**, 302; **V**, 583 n. 11
	3:16	**III**, 437 n. 11
	3:19	**V**, 119
	5:2	**V**, 593 n. 34
	9:3	**IV**, 442 n. 165
	11:1	**V**, 381
	13:6	**III**, 35
	14:22	**V**, 296
	14:23	**IV**, 185
	15:16	**V**, 589 n. 122
	16:5	**V**, 300
	18:16	**V**, 34
	21:4	**V**, 609 n. 35
	21:8	**III**, 233
	21:9–12	**III**, 210
	21:12	**V**, 597 n. 49
	21:33	**V**, 514 n. 122
	24	**II**, 578 n. 9
	24:1	**V**, 128
	24:1–27	**III**, 462 n. 18
	24:22	**IV**, 451 n. 28
	24:50	**III**, 23
	24:67	**III**, 62, 165; **V**, 184

	25:20	**III**, 62
	27:26–29	**III**, 244
	31:17	**III**, 229
	31:50	**III**, 149
	32 and 33	**V**, 520 n. 35
	33:33	**II**, 225
	36:7	**III**, 35
	37:35	**IV**, 244; **V**, 184
	38	**IV**, 456 n. 108
	39:3–4	**V**, 281
	40:20–21	**V**, 27
	41:39	**V**, 605 n. 46
	41:42	**IV**, 184; **V**, 469
	42:1–2	**IV**, 253
	43:34	**V**, 515 n. 141
	44:30	**III**, 463 n. 63
	44:39	**V**, 633 n. 149
	45:27	**III**, 474 n. 24
	46:3	**III**, 136; **V**, 331
	46:16	**V**, 576 n. 162
	48:15–20	**III**, 244
	49:1–28	**III**, 244
	49:9	**III**, 9
	49:10	**V**, 618 n. 29
	50:23	**III**, 224
Exodus	1:1	**V**, 569 n. 32
	1:13	**V**, 370
	1:17	**II**, 569 n. 11
	1:19	**III**, 231
	10:9	**IV**, 155
	12:2–14	**V**, 351
	12:14	**IV**, 155
	12:30	**II**, 45
	13:6	**IV**, 155
	14:8	**IV**, 398 n. 65
	15	**II**, 161
	15:3	**V**, 325
	15:25	**V**, 536 n. 346
	15:26	**V**, 109
	16:3	**IV**, 253
	18:20	**V**, 197
	18:21	**V**, 602 n. 85
	18:24	**V**, 602 n. 85
	19:4	**V**, 405
	19:6	**II**, 40
	20:7	**II**, 340
	20:8–11	**V**, 344
	20:10	**I**, 124; **V**, 343
	20:12	**III**, 244
	20:24	**II**, 169
	21:5	**II**, 89
	21:10	**III**, 217
	21:17	**V**, 301
	22:16	**III**, 445 n. 86
	22:21	**III**, 258
	22:25–26	**V**, 8
	23:9	**IV**, 92; **V**, 233

	23:26	V, 131
	24:10–11	V, 602 n. 85
	24:11	V, 406, 621 n. 65
	31:17	V, 349
	33:4	V, 171
	33:14	V, 343
	34:5	V, 594 n. 4
	34:5–7	V, 324
	34:6	V, 182, 537 n. 367
Leviticus	2:11	V, 40
	5:11	V, 544 n. 58
	16:17	III, 462 n. 23
	16:30	V, 349
	19:1	V, 323
	19:17	V, 295
	19:32	V, 117
	20:13	V, 592 n. 11
	21:13	III, 101
	23:42–43	V, 350
	25:46	V, 545 n. 80
	26:44	V, 525 n. 128
Numbers	1:16–17	V, 581 n. 75
	4:6–9, 11–13	IV, 409 n. 221
	6:23–26	V, 266, 631 n. 117
	6:23–27	III, 101; V, 546 n. 109
	6:24	IV, 417 n. 335
	11:1	V, 602 n. 85
	11:5	I, 126
	11:16	V, 346, 602 nn. 85, 86
	11:17	II, 212
	12:3	V, 197
	12:10–15	V, 590 n. 154
	12:13–15	V, 109
	14:14	V, 394
	14:17–19	V, 324
	15:37–41	IV, 152, 198
	15:38	II, 599 n. 7
	15:39	V, 318
	15:39–41	V, 601 n. 68
	16	II, 88
	18:12	IV, 434 n. 58
	22:21	IV, 448 n. 24
	22:34	II, 89
	23:27	II, 569 n. 11
	25:12	V, 631 n. 117
	25:26	I, 134
	32:14	V, 301, 576 n. 184
	32:20 ff.	V, 546 n. 102
	35:24	II, 323
Deuteronomy	1:11	III, 218
	1:13	II, 4
	1:17	II, 196
	1:18	II, 4
	1:44	II, 568 n. 6
	3:28	V, 571 n. 82
	4:2	V, 360
	4:7–8	V, 348

4:9	**III**, 7
4:9–10	**V**, 417
4:24	**V**, 407
5:14	**IV**, 155
6:4	**V**, 45
6:4–9	**II**, 184; **III**, 226
6:4–10	**V**, 601 n. 68
6:5	**V**, 325
6:8	**V**, 28
7:15	**V**, 612 n. 79
8:5	**V**, 326
10:14	**V**, 389
10:17	**V**, 326, 450, 562 n. 62
11:13–21	**III**, 226
11:13–22	**V**, 601 n. 68
12:16	**IV**, 248
13:1	**V**, 360
13:17	**V**, 583 n. 7
14:10	**V**, 619 n. 37
15:6	**V**, 527 n. 142
15:11	**II**, 119
15:14	**V**, 143
16:11, 14	**II**, 547 n. 22
16:14–15	**V**, 507 n. 26
16:15	**V**, 507 n. 29
16:17	**V**, 77
16:18	**II**, 71; **V**, 535 n. 306
17:8–10	**II**, 71
18:4	**IV**, 423 n. 433
18:7	**II**, 539 n. 68
18:17–18	**V**, 328
20:5–7	**IV**, 360 n. 1
20:7	**III**, 441 n. 2
20:19	**IV**, 77
22:6	**V**, 604 n. 25
22:7	**V**, 408
22:13–21	**III**, 101
22:19	**III**, 102
22:29	**III**, 102
24:1	**III**, 264
24:15	**I**, 98
25:5	**III**, 210
25:7–9	**III**, 210; **V**, 157
25:9	**II**, 452, App. B, n. 46
25:9–10	**IV**, 164
26:17–18	**V**, 343
28:4	**IV**, 263
28:6	**IV**, 123; **V**, 37
28:11	**IV**, 263; **V**, 435
28:12	**V**, 527 n. 142
28:15–68	**V**, 531 n. 232
29:10	**III**, 321
30:4	**V**, 394, 525 n. 128
31:12	**III**, 321, 474 n. 20 (BT Hagiga 3a)
32:4	**V**, 60
32:25	**I**, 305
32:43	**V**, 393

	33:11	**V**, 298
	33:21	**V**, 377
	33:25	**V**, 631 n. 108
Joshua	1:5	**V**, 297
	1:8	**II**, 171, 181
Judges	2:10	**V**, 166
	9:8	**I**, 120
	9:13	**V**, 38
	19:20	**V**, 82
	31:5	**V**, 307
I Samuel	1:8	**III**, 109, 320
	1:16	**V**, 79
	2:7	**V**, 530 n. 200
	10:5–6	**V**, 583 n. 9
	11:14	**IV**, 445 n. 8
	12:73	**IV**, 448 n. 24
	14:27–29	**IV**, 442 n. 160
	18:1–3	**V**, 272
	18:3	**V**, 583 n. 7
	19:13	**IV**, 409 n. 221
	19:20–24	**V**, 583 n. 9
	22:1	**V**, 65
	24:3 ff.	**V**, 65
	25:6	**III**, 161, 462 n. 7; **V**, 65
	25:29	**V**, 623 n. 103
	26:10	**V**, 576 n. 180
II Samuel	1:17–21	**V**, 583 n. 21
	3:12	**V**, 431
	12:23	**V**, 184
	13:1–22	**V**, 272
	13:3	**V**, 583 n. 6
	14:20	**V**, 239, 572 n. 85
	15:37 and 16:16–17	**V**, 583 n. 5
	20:3	**III**, 469 n. 188
	20:19	**IV**, 44
	21:2	**V**, 301
I Kings	1:1	**IV**, 409 n. 221
	1:47	**III**, 245
	2:40	**IV**, 448 n. 24
	3:6	**III**, 225
	4:5	**V**, 583 n. 5
	8:46	**V**, 557 n. 309
	12	**II**, 87
	12:7	**II**, 87
	12:8	**V**, 583 n. 6
	12:19	**II**, 300
	17:14	**IV**, 142
	19:19	**V**, 608 n. 25
	19:19–21	**V**, 583 n. 10
	21:3	**IV**, 41
	21:10, 13	**V**, 70
II Kings	2:12	**III**, 249; **V**, 430
	2:14	**V**, 608 n. 25
	2:19–22	**V**, 536 n. 346
	4:10	**IV**, 108
	5:13	**III**, 249
	6:21	**III**, 249

	22:13–20	**III**, 320
	24:15	**III**, 446 n. 5
Isaiah	1:9	**V**, 612 n. 89
	2:2	**V**, 406
	3:5	**II**, 61
	3:16	**IV**, 418 n. 362
	3:16–24	**IV**, 151
	3:20	**IV**, 159
	4:3	**V**, 351
	6:3	**V**, 325, 381, 413
	8:2	**II**, 367
	9:4	**V**, 398
	9:5	**V**, 404
	9:15	**V**, 396
	10:13	**IV**, 192
	10:14	**V**, 423
	11:7	**V**, 179
	11:10	**IV**, 457 n. 135; **V**, 302
	12:2	**V**, 589 n. 118
	12:3	**V**, 351
	14:2	**V**, 378
	17:10	**III**, 321
	19:1	**III**, 472 n. 247
	19:24	**V**, 258
	21:3	**V**, 108
	24:1	**V**, 63
	24:2	**V**, 63
	24:8–9	**V**, 38
	25:8	**V**, 187, 559 n. 323, 621 n. 63
	26:20	**V**, 242
	26:21	**V**, 599 n. 23
	27:13	**V**, 350
	28:7–8	**V**, 515 n. 143
	32:8	**V**, 83
	33:24	**V**, 520 n. 34
	37:4	**V**, 339
	38:1–22	**V**, 109
	38:9–22	**V**, 109
	38:17	**III**, 472 n. 245
	42:19	**V**, 396, 613 n. 95
	45:25	**II**, 324
	45:25	**IV**, 451 n. 14
	49:15	**V**, 324
	51:21	**V**, 242
	52:7	**V**, 396, 402
	53:7	**V**, 351
	52:8	**V**, 351
	52:10	**V**, 394
	58	**V**, 350
	58:1–8	**II**, 547 n. 22
	58:7	**III**, 436 n. 48
	58:10	**V**, 89
	58:13–14	**IV**, 155
	58:14	**V**, 475
	61:1	**II**, 87; **V**, 55
	61:9	**V**, 378
	62:6	**V**, 361, 362

	63:14	**II**, 551 n. 14
	64:3	**V**, 408
	65:1	**II**, 222, 569 n. 17
	65:23	**II**, 467 sec. 108
	66:7	**III**, 231
	66:13	**V**, 185, 324, 555 n. 275, 556 n. 290
	66:22	**V**, 395, 400, 401, 449
Jeremiah	2:32	**IV**, 186
	6:24	**V**, 576 n. 176
	7:18	**III**, 321
	8:3	**V**, 392
	8:22	**V**, 640 n. 276
	9:16–20	**V**, 163
	9:19	**V**, 361
	9:22–23	**V**, 305
	10:2	**V**, 329, 421
	10:10	**V**, 63
	10:11	**V**, 421
	10:23	**V**, 245, 329
	12:2	**V**, 335
	13:18	**V**, 421
	17:7	**IV**, 382 n. 99
	19:4	**V**, 60
	22:10	**V**, 557 n. 298
	22:14	**IV**, 65
	22:24	**V**, 469
	23:1	**IV**, 423 n. 433
	23:5	**IV**, 453 n. 62; **V**, 396
	23:9	**V**, 576 n. 176
	25:26	**V**, 628 n. 67
	29:6	**III**, 123
	29:7	**IV**, 359 n. 214
	31:19	**V**, 576 n. 176
	31:30	**V**, 396
	31:31	**II**, 568 n. 42
	31:35–37	**V**, 449
	39:8	**II**, 155
	44:15–19	**III**, 321
	44:15, 19, 20, 24	**III**, 499 n. 31
	46:13–28	**V**, 509 n. 45
	48:36	**V**, 548 n. 154
	50:33–34	**V**, 378
	51:9	**II**, 260
Ezekiel	8:14	**III**, 321
	11:16	**II**, 155
	16:11	**V**, 469
	16:44	**V**, 228
	21:31	**V**, 421
	24:17–23	**IV**, 159
	24:25	**III**, 225
	26:16	**V**, 64
	27:4–9	**V**, 18
	35:10	**II**, 89
	37:1–14	**V**, 406
	37:10	**V**, 501
	44:15	**V**, 282
Hosea	2:19	**III**, 109

	2:21	**III**, 78
	3:19–20	**III**, 320
	4:3	**V**, 522 n. 78
	5:15	**V**, 599 n. 23
	6:1	**II**, 260; **V**, 64
	6:1–2	**V**, 109
	12:2	**IV**, 252
	13:14	**V**, 559 n. 323
	14:1	**V**, 506 n. 18
Joel	1:6	**V**, 525 n. 128
	2:13	**V**, 64
	2:31	**II**, 309
	3:4	**II**, 309
	4:17	**V**, 350
Amos	3:2	**V**, 449
	6:4	**IV**, 395 n. 9
	9:5	**V**, 522 n. 78
Jonah	—	**V**, 350
	1:5	**I**, 323
	3:9	**V**, 64
	4:11	**V**, 64
Micah	1:8	**V**, 60
	2:10	**V**, 623 n. 105
	5:8	**V**, 297
	7:18	**V**, 601 n. 59
Nahum	1:6	**V**, 63
Habakkuk	2:4	**V**, 245
	3:2	**V**, 64
Zephaniah	1:8	**IV**, 195
	3:9	**V**, 381
	3:20	**V**, 374
Haggai	1:6	**V**, 38
	1:9	**II**, 203
	2:6	**IV**, 189
Zechariah	1:3	**V**, 362
	1:4	**V**, 364
	3:8	**III**, 444 n. 57
	4:13–15	**V**, 77, 528 n. 171
	6:12	**V**, 396
	8:12	**II**, 62
	8:19	**V**, 604 n. 19
	9:9	**V**, 398
	12:4	**V**, 578 n. 26
	14:9	**V**, 343
Malachi	2:5	**V**, 584 n. 28
	2:5–6	**V**, 631 n. 117
	2:14	**III**, 320, 436 n. 9; **IV**, 451 n. 23; **V**, 583 n. 8
	2:16	**III**, 260
	3:1 and 23	**V**, 402
	3:7	**V**, 362, 392
	3:17	**III**, 240; **V**, 127
	4:5 (Heb. 3:24)	**II**, 62
Psalms	3	**V**, 528 n. 165
	3:4	**V**, 298
	8:6	**V**, 452
	9	**V**, 528 n. 165
	9:10	**IV**, 440 n. 144

11:7	**V**, 631 n. 116
16:6–7	**III**, 57
17:15	**V**, 142
18:43	**IV**, 162
20:10	**V**, 45
24	**V**, 528 n. 165
24:3	**V**, 346
24:3–4	**V**, 346
24:8–10	**V**, 325
24:10	**V**, 595 n. 14
25:13	**V**, 605 n. 53, 631 n. 108
26:9	**V**, 590 n. 146
27:4	**V**, 351, 394, 411, 414
27:13	**V**, 408
31:2	**V**, 199, 428
31:11	**V**, 90
31:20	**V**, 407
34:9	**V**, 450
34:9–10	**IV**, 382 n. 99
36:10	**V**, 407
37:11	**V**, 197, 286
38:21	**V**, 302
39:1	**V**, 285
39:7	**V**, 120
39:14	**V**, 120
41:4–5	**V**, 108
42:4	**V**, 245
44:12–13	**V**, 612 n. 89
44:22	**V**, 314
45:3	**V**, 630 n. 95
45:3–5	**II**, 527 n. 40
45:8	**V**, 399, 435
45:14	**III**, 153
45:16	**III**, 225
45:17	**V**, 236, 301
49:8	**III**, 18; **V**, 538 n. 374
50:22	**V**, 323
51:18–19	**V**, 197
51:19	**V**, 623 n. 88
55:15	**II**, 155
57:1	**V**, 65
61:8	**V**, 532 n. 243
68:21	**II**, 522 n. 28
69:2	**V**, 73
69:34	**V**, 81
72:15	**V**, 589 n. 124
73	**V**, 332, 598 n. 3
73:28	**III**, 468 n. 171
75:4	**V**, 64
78:8	**V**, 364
79:8	**V**, 64
82:1	**II**, 168; **V**, 630 n. 94
85:12	**I**, 241; **II**, 500 App. C, 500 ??
87:5	**IV**, 359 n. 212
89:1	**III**, 221; **V**, 586 n. 64
89:24	**V**, 298
91	**V**, 599 n. 34

	91:11	**V**, 337
	92:13, 15	**V**, 128
	94:17	**III**, 464 n. 78
	98:1	**II**, 159
	102:8	**V**, 26
	102:27	**IV**, 158
	103:1–5	**V**, 414
	104	**V**, 614 n. 114
	104:22–23	**III**, 106
	106:3	**III**, 249
	106:4	**IV**, 382 n. 99; **V**, 396
	107:23–32	**I**, 352, 490 n. 44
	109:31	**V**, 93
	112:1	**IV**, 382 n. 99
	115:17	**III**, 464 n. 78
	116:7	**V**, 412, 415
	116:13 and 3–4	**V**, 282
	118:6	**V**, 223
	119:68	**V**, 325
	119:77	**V**, 442
	119:165	**V**, 286
	119:174	**V**, 37
	121:2	**V**, 77
	121:4	**V**, 336
	121:7–8	**V**, 77
	121:8	**V**, 37
	127:3–5	**III**, 226
	128:2	**V**, 283
	128:4	**III**, 7
	133:1	**III**, 35
	137:5	**V**, 401
	137:6	**III**, 108
	139:5	**V**, 593 n. 34
	142:1	**V**, 65
	144:15	**II**, 137
	145	**V**, 595 n. 7
	145:1	**V**, 45
	145:9	**V**, 324
	146:8	**V**, 342
	149:5	**V**, 557 n. 306
	150	**V**, 38
Proverbs	1:8	**III**, 320, 479 n. 133; **V**, 416
	1:33	**V**, 65
	3:2	**III**, 241
	3:4	**V**, 257, 333, 577 n. 21
	3:12	**V**, 109
	5:15–21	**III**, 438 n. 26; **V**, 312
	6:27–28	**V**, 643 n. 339
	9:11	**V**, 131, 410, 541 n. 11
	10:2	**V**, 93, 142, 354
	10:7	**V**, 410
	10:12	**V**, 295
	10:22	**I**, 208; **IV**, 28; **V**, 599 n. 27
	11:4	**V**, 93, 142, 354, 606 n. 59
	11:17	**III**, 194
	11:26	**V**, 71
	12:25	**V**, 522 n. 75, 576 n. 187

	13:12	**V**, 236, 269
	13:24	**V**, 591 n. 176
	17:6	**III**, 427 n. 29
	17:17	**V**, 583 n. 27
	17:24	**I**, 274; **V**, 340
	18:22	**III**, 108, 164
	18:24	**V**, 279
	19:14	**III**, 108
	19:21	**V**, 328
	20:5	**II**, 240
	20:7	**V**, 130
	20:14	**V**, 206
	20:24	**III**, 108
	20:27	**IV**, 135
	20:29	**V**, 116
	21:1	**II**, 348
	21:14	**II**, 495; **V**, 605 n. 59
	22:2	**II**, 142
	22:7	**I**, 170
	22:23	**III**, 195
	23:11	**III**, 258
	23:26	**V**, 318
	24:11	**V**, 237
	26:11	**II**, 291
	27:2	**III**, 59
	27:6	**V**, 295
	27:10	**V**, 280, 589 n. 121
	27:19	**V**, 283, 585 n. 52
	27:21	**III**, 465 n. 111
	31:10–31	**III**, 106, 319; **IV**, 432 n. 11
Job	1:2	**III**, 474 n. 16
	1:16–18	**II**, 523 n. 49
	1:20	**V**, 245
	1:20–22	**V**, 173
	1:21	**V**, 555 n. 275
	2:4	**II**, 241
	2:9–10	**V**, 173
	3:1	**IV**, 409 n. 218
	3:21	**V**, 244, 392
	6:3	**V**, 427
	6:24	**V**, 427
	7:2	**V**, 427
	7:8	**V**, 427
	9:6	**V**, 63
	9:12	**V**, 273
	12:10	**V**, 296
	12:14	**V**, 427
	14:22	**V**, 622 n. 84
	23:28	**V**, 194, 562 n. 51
	25:2	**V**, 115
	29:16	**V**, 93
	32:7	**V**, 116
	32:20	**V**, 576 n. 189
	34:11	**V**, 303
	42:12	**V**, 126
	42:16	**III**, 224
Songs	1:3	**IV**, 225

	1:8	**V**, 282, 585 n. 49
	1:10–11	**IV**, 202
	2:14	**II**, 184, 235
	3:4	**III**, 171
	4:10	**IV**, 225
	4:12	**V**, 345
	5:16	**V**, 423
	7:1	**V**, 414
	8:2	**III**, 171
	8:13	**V**, 323
Ruth	1:16–17	**III**, 320
	2:17	**V**, 544 n. 58
	2:19	**V**, 531 n. 238
	3:9	**V**, 583 n. 11
	3:18	**V**, 192
	4:7–8	**IV**, 164
	4:11	**III**, 57; **IV**, 451 n. 13; **V**, 622 n. 82
	4:11–12	**III**, 109
Lamen.	—	**V**, 556 n. 287
	4:2	**III**, 225
	5:20	**V**, 405
Eccles.	1:17	**V**, 387
	2:1–2	**V**, 387
	2:4 ff.	**V**, 387
	3:1, 17	**V**, 623 n. 107
	3:21	**V**, 387
	5:1	**V**, 614 n. 112
	5:4	**V**, 269
	7:1	**V**, 156
	7:18	**V**, 387
	7:20	**V**, 182, 326
	7:26	**III**, 164
	8:1	**V**, 528 n. 171
	8:4	**V**, 60, 180
	9:3	**V**, 387
	9:4–6	**V**, 387
	9:11	**V**, 242
	10:5	**V**, 173
	11:2	**III**, 474 n. 16; **V**, 631 n. 116
	11:6	**III**, 439 n. 46
	11:9	**V**, 387
	12:7	**V**, 387
	12:13	**V**, 557 n. 295
Esther	1:9	**IV**, 360 n. 2
	2:12	**IV**, 225
	2:17	**II**, 352
	3:13	**V**, 301
	3:13, 15	**I**, 470 n. 13
	4:16	**II**, 160
	5:2, 8	**II**, 352
	5:3	**V**, 468
	5:8	**II**, 352
	6:8	**IV**, 184
	7:3	**II**, 352
	7:9	**III**, 440 n. 71
	9:22	**V**, 528 n. 162
Daniel	1:6	**V**, 633 n. 145

	2:21	V, 421
	2:44	V, 400, 401
	5:25	I, 360
	9:33	V, 609 n. 58
	12:2	V, 603 n. 2
	12:13	V, 184, 557 n. 308
Ezra	4:7	II, 522 n. 38
	6:1	I, 1
	6:14	IV, 451 n. 15
	7:6	II, 230; V, 580 n. 60, 609 n. 43
	10:1	III, 321
	10:13	V, 534 n. 294
	11:6	II, 552 n. 3
	13:17–23	III, 505 n. 190
Nehemiah	2:3	V, 552 n. 225
	5:1	III, 321, 499 n. 31
	6:14	III, 320
	8:2–3	III, 499 n. 31
	8:10	IV, 434 n. 58
	8:23	III, 321
	9:33	V, 116
	11:1–2	V, 607 n. 6
	12:43	III, 321
	13:24	V, 381
I Chron.	17:21	V, 343
	27:33	V, 583 n. 5
	29:23	II, 527 n. 40
II Chron.	14:6	III, 50; IV, 451 n. 13
	15:7	V, 29
	19:5	II, 571 n. 42
	24:7	V, 637 n. 208
TAJ, Yemenite Pentateuch,		
	II, 5a	V, 544 n. 58
New Testament		
John	20:5–11	V, 621 n. 63
	20:12	V, 621 n. 63
	21:3–4	V, 621 n. 63
Matthew	9:6	V, 594 n. 3
Acts	5:34	I, 382
	22:3	I, 382; III, 8
Romans	13:1	II, 87
I Corinthians	6:1–4	II, 312
	11:1–13	IV, 159
	14:34–35	III, 322
	15:55	V, 559 n. 323
Galatians	1:3	V, 79
Koran		
	2:96	V, 131, 541 n. 15
	2:111	V, 541 n. 15
	2:228	III, 51
	2:229	III, 267
	3:104	V, 316
	5:33	III, 185
	7:200	V, 337
	9:11	IV, 31
	9:12	V, 583 n. 14
	9:129	V, 600 n. 56
	12:92	III, 474 n. 24

	15:17	V, 590 n. 139
	15:30–33	V, 590 n. 140
	16:98	V, 337
	17:81	I, 436
	21:85	V, 508 n. 40
	33:5	IV, 31
	41:36	V, 337
	49:10	V, 583 n. 14
	75:22	V, 557 n. 308
	81:35	V, 590 n. 139
	89	V, 415
	90:6	V, 512 n. 86
	96:4	I, 112
	113:5	V, 590 n. 139
	—	V, 300

RABBINIC LITERATURE

Mishna		
Berakhot	9:5	V, 324, 518 n. 12, 585 n. 40
Pe'a	1:1	V, 535 n. 324
	8:8	III, 451 n. 6
Shabbat	–	V, 620 n. 54
Sheqalim	5:2	II, 539 n. 51
Yoma	1:1	III, 462 n. 23
	3:7	IV, 416 n. 312
	4:4	IV, 417 n. 336
	8:1	V, 534 n. 281
	8:8	V, 541 n. 9
Megilla	1:3	II, 565 n. 1
Ketubbot	1:1	III, 450 n. 84
	4:4	V, 548 n. 153
	5:5	IV, 432 n. 1
	5:8	IV, 414 n. 283
	9:4	III, 146
Sota	3:4	III, 499 n. 34
Gittin	5:1	III, 482 n. 28
	6:1	V, 548 n. 154
	8:5	III, 446 n. 5
Qiddushin	4:1–2	III, 443 n. 46
	4:13	III, 504 n. 155
Bava Mesi'a	5:7	I, 453
	6:2	IV, 371 n. 185
Sanhedrin	6:2	V, 541 n. 9
Makkot	3:16	V, 601 n. 63
Shevu'ot	7:8	III, 146
Eduyot	5:7	V, 623 n. 109
Avot	1:2	V, 624 n. 1
	1:4	V, 570 n. 59
	1:7	V, 583 n. 18
	1:14	V, 623 n. 108
	2:5	III, 506 n. 193
	2:17	V, 623 n. 112
	3:3	IV, 432 n. 15
	3:5	II, 546 n. 4
	3:16	I, 438
	5:6	I, 112
	5:16	V, 582 n. 3, 585 n. 57

	6:2	**II**, 546 n. 4
	6:4	**IV**, 433 n. 24
	6:6	**V**, 578 n. 30
Horayot	3:7	**IV**, 395 n. 14
Tohorot	11:9	**IV**, 426 n. 475

Tosefta

Berakhot	2:23	**V**, 534 n. 276
Ketubbot	4:9	**III**, 451 n. 1
	6:8	**III**, 451 n. 2
Qiddushin	1:4	**III**, 433 n. 76
	1:11	**III**, 479 n. 135
Sanhedrin	13:2	**V**, 616 n. 140

Palestinian Talmud

Berakhot	9:1, f. 13a	**V**, 599 n. 31
Pe'a	I	**III**, 479 n. 133
	21b	**IV**, 397 n. 48
Shabbat	1:2	**III**, 473 n. 5
	2:3, fol. 5b	**V**, 601 n. 60
Megilla,	ch. 2, end	**V**, 525 n. 119
Yevamot	6:6	**III**, 474 n. 22
	8:10, f. 49c	**V**, 593 n. 31
Nedarim	9:1	**V**, 539 n. 416
Sota	19a	**III**, 499 n. 34
Qiddushin	4:1, f. 65a	**V**, 605 n. 57

Babylonian Talmud

Berakhot	6b	**II**, 547 n. 2
	8a	**V**, 585 n. 51
	13a	**V**, 520 n. 41, 573 n. 103
	16b	**V**, 600 n. 40
	17a	**V**, 541 n. 2, 621 n. 65, 623 n. 111, 628 n. 65
	18b	**V**, 622 n. 84
	29b	**V**, 597 n. 46
	32b	**III**, 472 n. 249
	34b	**V**, 622 n. 77, 623 n. 89
	42b–43a	**IV**, 388 n. 215
	43b	**IV**, 389 n. 220
	46a	**V**, 563 n. 83, 600 n. 39
	53b	**IV**, 432 n. 7
	57b	**IV**, 360 n. 1; **V**, 601 n. 69
	58a	**V**, 597 n. 52
	60b	**IV**, 398 n. 66; **V**, 519 n. 30, 540 n. 2 595 n. 9, 601 n. 66
	63a	**V**, 594 n. 2
	64a	**V**, 640 n. 276
Shabbat	32b	**III**, 474 n. 25
	33b	**V**, 585 n. 49
	58a	**IV**, 413 n. 269
	88b	**V**, 591 n. 176
	97a	**V**, 590 n. 154
	113b	**IV**, 395 n. 10
	119a	**IV**, 397 n. 38; **V**, 602 n. 74
	119b	**V**, 603 n. 5
	127a	**V**, 512 n. 87
	129b	**V**, 534 n. 277
	151b	**V**, 518 n. 17

	152b	**V**, 540 n. 1, 623 n. 103
	156a–b	**V**, 596 n. 33
ʿEruvin	55b	**III**, 360 n. 244; **IV**, 434 n. 60
	100b	**V**, 568 n. 13
Pesahim	8a	**III**, 473 n. 2
	49a	**V**, 577 n. 17
	49b	**III**, 439 nn. 44, 45
	50b	**III**, 455 n. 75
	68b	**IV**, 397 n. 42; **V**, 507 n. 26
	78a	**III**, 462 n. 19; **V**, 623 n. 114
	109	**V**, 507 n. 29
	114a	**IV**, 360 n. 3, 434 n. 56
Yoma	66b	**III**, 499 n. 35
	75a	**V**, 522 n. 75, 576 n. 187, 602 n. 73
Sukkot	27b	**V**, 507 n. 31
	53a	**V**, 638 n. 230
Rosh Ha-shana	17a	**V**, 601 n. 59
	17b	**V**, 594 n. 5
Taʿanit	5b	**IV**, 432 n. 15
	8b	**V**, 541 n. 17
	21a	**V**, 545 n. 85, 595 n. 9
	23a	**IV**, 360 n. 246; **V**, 511 n. 75
Megilla	15a	**V**, 556 n. 294
	26b	**IV**, 463 n. 229
Moʿed Qatan	8b	**III**, 450 n. 84
	27b	**V**, 548 n. 149, 554 nn. 258–259
	28a	**V**, 597 n. 42
	end	**V**, 559 n. 323
Hagiga	3a	**III**, 474 n. 20
	5b	**V**, 600 n. 46
	12b	**V**, 623 n. 103
	27a	**III**, 438 n. 28
Yevamot	39b	**III**, 496 n. 4
	44a	**V**, 592 n. 18
	62b	**III**, 436 n. 3, 439 n. 46
	63a–b	**III**, 438 n. 26
	63b	**III**, 440 n. 63; **IV**, 396 n. 22
	76a	**V**, 593 n. 31
	79a	**V**, 563 n. 79, 605 n. 57
	117a	**V**, 585 n. 52
Ketubbot	7b	**III**, 438 n. 26
	17a	**III**, 461 n. 93; **V**, 514 n. 120
	47b	**III**, 455 n. 76
	54a	**III**, 457 n. 106
	64b ff.	**IV**, 414 n. 283
	67b	**II**, 550 n. 14; **V**, 528 n. 159, 623 n. 106
	68a	**III**, 490 n. 30
	72a	**III**, 488 n. 150
	103b	**V**, 541 n. 8
	104a	**V**, 614 n. 106
	110a–b	**III**, 459 n. 48
	110b	**IV**, 360 n. 239
	111a	**V**, 520 n. 34, 617 n. 9
	111b	**V**, 550 n. 189
Nedarim	8b	**V**, 621 n. 66
	20a	**V**, 563 n. 79
	49b–50a	**IV**, 396 n. 25
	66a	**IV**, 395 n. 12

	81a		V, 633 n. 139
Sota	5a		V, 606 n. 59
	13b		V, 631 n. 108
	44a		IV, 360 n. 1
	49a		V, 538 n. 386
	49b		V, 594 n. 3
Gittin	6b–7a		V, 561 n. 36
	14b		V, 545 n. 85
	17a		III, 432 n. 67
	26b		III, 432 n. 67
	37a		III, 492 n. 75
	37b		I, 98
	58a		IV, 396 n. 24
	61a		V, 606 n. 60
	62a		V, 608 n. 27
	84b–85a		III, 427 n. 36
Qiddushin	19a		II, 560
	30b		III, 453 n. 30
	31b		V, 624 n. 5, 640 n. 276
	40b		V, 624 n. 4
	41a		III, 442 n. 23
	70a		V, 590 n. 151, 603 n. 87
Bava Qamma	92a		V, 531 n. 231, 537 n. 356
Bava Mesiʿa	49a		V, 581 n. 70
	52a		IV, 395 n. 1
	65b		IV, 372 n. 23
	70a		III, 493 n. 92
	83b		V, 513 n. 97
	85a		III, 427 n. 29
	87a		V, 515 n. 135
	104b		III, 454 n. 46
Bava Bathra	9a		V, 605 n. 58
	10a		V, 545 n. 76
	16b		V, 573 n. 106
	57b		IV, 395 n. 18
	110a		III, 432 n. 62
	119b		III, 440 n. 64
	139a		V, 538 n. 386
	141a		III, 474 n. 28, 475 n. 32
Sanhedrin	29a		V, 541 n. 12
	46b		V, 548 n. 150
	98b		V, 618 n. 29
	105a		V, 528 n. 166
	110a		V, 640 n. 276
Makkot	23a		V, 571 n. 82
Shevuʿot	15b		V, 599 n. 34
	47b		V, 571 n. 69
ʿAvoda Zara	18b		V, 590 n. 158
	20b		V, 563 n. 71
Hullin	9a		II, 572 n. 1
	84b		IV, 395 n. 2
	95b		III, 450 n. 101, 451 n. 101; IV, 373 n. 40
	142		V, 604 n. 25, 622 n. 74
Midrash			
Bereshit Rabba		8:1	V, 593 n. 34
		sec. 11	IV, 396 n. 23
Shemot Rabba		31:14	V, 531 n. 232

Wayyiqra Rabba 24:6 V, 594 n. 50
34:8 V, 531 n. 238
34:9 V, 518 n. 17, 531 n. 240
34:13 V, 531 n. 232
Bamidbar Rabba 7:7 V, 571 n. 82
Midrash Esther Rabba 3:10 IV, 360 n. 2
Midrash Tanhuma Yelamdenu, Mishpatim 9 V, 532 n. 243

MAIMONIDEAN SOURCES

Abraham Maimonides

Commentary of Abraham Maimonides on Genesis & Exodus, ed. S. D. Sassoon, trans. E. Wiesenberg. London, 1959, p. 57 III, 432 n. 45

Abraham Maimuni, *Responsa*, ed. A. H. Freimann, trans. S. D. Goitein. Jerusalem, 1937. Arabic and Hebrew.

p. 15 i, 3, n. 34
p. 18 x, D, n. 286
p. 19 x, D, n. 290
26 vii, B, 2, n. 15
54 viii, B, 2, n. 39
55 vii, A, 3, n. 11
56 ii, 5, n. 55
62 x, D, n. 290
72–80 iii, F, n. 158
104–105 x, C, 4, n. 34
123 x, D, n. 291
124 x, D, n. 297
126 x, D, n. 297
131 x, D, n. 291
133 x, D, nn. 291, 297
146 x, D, n. 291
149–153 ii, 7, nn. 77, 103
150 vii, C, 1, b, n. 25
158–160 ix, A, 1, n. 99
161–162 vii, C, 2, n. 7
161–167 x, A, 3, n. 56
162–164 x, A, 2, n. 406
163–164 v, B, 1, n. 121
164–165 iii, F, n. 25
165 iii, F, n. 2
173–175 viii, B, 3, n. 10
177 vii, A, 3, n. 7
182 viii, B, 2, n. 48. x, D, n. 16
182–189 v, B, 2, nn. 15, 27
196 iii, A, 1, n. 37. vii, A, 2, n. 12. ix, A, 3, n. 38
203 IV, App. A, I
206 x, A, 2, n. 211
207–209 iii, B, 2, n. 32
231 viii, B, 3, n. 27

Moses Maimonides

The Code of Maimonides

Book I

Foundations of the Torah 4:9 V, 622 n. 71
Moral dispositions and ethical conduct (*Deᶜot*) 5:11 III, 448 n. 32
Study of the Torah 1:1 III, 506 n. 200
2:4 III, 504 n. 155; V, 532 n. 244

Return to God	3:5	V, 616 n. 140
	ch. 8	V, 622 n. 73
Book II		
Prayer	11:5	IV, 384 n. 141
	7:3	V, 540 n. 2
	7:9	V, 601 n. 67
Fringes	3:11	IV, 417 n. 338
Benedictions	4:12	IV, 444 n. 6
Book III		
Sabbath,	ch. 29:29	IV, 389 n. 220
Book IV		
Marriage	3:19	III, 442 n. 24
	13:1–5	IV, 414 n. 283
	13:11	III, 459 n. 58
	15:3	III, 440 n. 64
	20:1–5	III, 490 n. 30
	ch. 21	III, 455 n. 72
	21:10	III, 465 n. 123
Book V		
Forbidden Relations	21:8	V, 593 n. 31
Book VIII		
Temple Service		V, 622 n. 78
Book XII		
Sale	1:1	II, 599 n. 7
	18:1	II, 590 n. 28
	29:12–17	III, 477 n. 88
Book XIII		
Loans	4:14	III, 493 n. 92
Book XIV		
Sanhedrin	2:11	II, 594 n. 2
	2:13	II, 594 n. 4
	21:9	II, 601 n. 15
	23:9	II, 600 n. 6
Mourning	4:4	V, 550 n. 193
	5:3	IV, 413 n. 262

Commentary on the Mishna, Introduction to Sanhedrin, 10:1, ed. J. Qafih. Jerusalem, 1964

	IV, 197 and 207	V, 532 n. 242, 550 n. 191, 621 n. 60
	IV, 204	V, 591 n. 165
	IV, 206–207	V, 562 n. 61
Avot	1:2	
	IV, 408	V, 624 n. 1
Guide of the Perplexed, III:8		V, 515 n. 143

Maimonides, *Responsa*, ed. Jehoshua Blau. Vols. I–III. Jerusalem, 1957-1961. Arabic and Hebrew.

Responsa, I,

2	i, 4, n. 6. ix, A, 2, n. 92; ix, A, 3, n. 72
3	ix, A, 2, nn. 67, 116, 135
8–9	ix, A, 3, n. 69
10, 31, 69–70	vii, A, 2, n. 10
19	ix, A, 3, n. 85
20	viii, C, 1, n. 170
22–24	viii, B, 2, n. 49
32	IV, App. A, VII. ix, A, 3, n. 3
36	viii, C, 1, n. 186
36–37	vii, C, 2, n. 13
37	iii, B, 2, n. 11

38	iii, B, 2, n. 3. vii, D, 1, n. 27
40	viii, C, 2, n. 42
41	iii, B, 2, n. 48
44–45	viii, C, 1, n. 148
45	iii, B, 2, n. 3
47	v, B, 1, n. 1
49	viii, B, 2, n. 26
49–53	viii, D, n. 152
50	viii, D, n. 154
50, no. 34	x, A, 2, nn. 213, 215
50–54	vi, 2, n. 6; vi, 3, n. 14; vi, 4, n. 15. vii, B, 1, n. 25; vii, C, 2, n. 7
51	viii, C, 3, n. 100
56–57	vii, B, 2, n. 7; vii, B, 3, n. 9
70	iii, D, n. 34
71–73	viii, D, n. 152
78	v, B, 2, n. 10
83–85	iii, F, n. 159
85–86	ii, 2, n. 24; ii, 6, n. 11
89	iii, D, n. 28
92	vii, C, 2, n. 39
94	viii, C, 4, n. 30
101–102	vii, B, 3, n. 38; vii, D, 1, n. 3
103	vii, C, 2, n. 10. **IV**, App. A, II. x, A, 3, n. 199
104	iii, D, n. 7
104–105	iii, F, n. 160
108–109	viii, C, 4, n. 170
116	iii, F, n. 160. vii, C, 2, n. 39
117	ix, A, 3, nn. 54, 109
120	iii, B, 2, n. 4
123	ix, A, 3, nn. 55, 60
128	vii, C, 1, b, n. 17
129	viii, C, 4, n. 180
132	vii, B, 1, n. 25
135–136	ix, A, 5, n. 43
136	iii, F, n. 162
137	ii, 4, n. 68
138–139	iv, 9, n. 21
138–144	viii, B, 2, pp. 65-69. **III**, App. pt. II, no. 179.
148	iii, B, 2, n. 4. vii, B, 1, n. 25
150	iii, B, 3, n. 11
150–151	iii, B, 2, n. 48
151 and 155	ix, A, 2, n. 115; ix, A, 3, nn. 11, 12
152–153	vii, B, 1, n. 25
153	iii, B, 4, n. 1
155	iii, B, 3, n. 11
162	ix, A, 2, nn. 65, 80, 160
164	ii, 7, n. 31
167	x, A, 1, n. 146
175	vii, C, 1, b, n. 25
177–178	ix, A, 2, n. 121
178	vii, D, 1, n. 29
178–182	ii, 7, n. 76
179	vii, C, 1, c, n. 25
182	viii, C, 2, n. 101
189	v, B, 2, n. 10

	195	ix, A, 2, n. 167
	199	vii, C, 2, n. 54
	243	ii, 4, n. 14
Responsa, II,		
	302–304	vi, 12, n. 64
	314, 316	vi, 10, n. 20
	317	viii, C, 2, n. 87
	340	x, A, 1, n. 149
	352–354	viii, B, 2, n. 35
	353	vii, D, 1, n. 39
	360	ii, 2, n. 16. vii, A, 2, n. 21
	366	viii, B, 3, n. 11
	367	v, B, 2, n. 6
	366–370	x, C, 4, n. 113
	373–375	ii, 7, n. 36
	379–380	ix, A, 4, n. 93
	386–388	viii, C, 3, n. 155
	410	viii, C, 1, n. 34
	424	vi, 2, n. 32
	433	ii, 2, n. 39; ii, 4, n. 53
	448–451	v, B, 1, n. 28
	457	vii, C, 1, c, n. 38
	488	vii, C, 1, c, n. 23
	492	v, B, 2, n. 18
	496	v, B, 2, n. 18
	497–498	v, B, 2, n. 36
	516	x, A, 1, n. 149
	518	v, B, 1, n. 11
	519	v, B, 1, n. 110
	524–525	vi, 3, n. 4
	533–534	iii, A, 1, n. 39; iii, E, n. 1. vii, A, 2, n. 28; vii, B, 3, n. 40
	545	vi, 7, n. 26
	547	viii, B, 4, n. 48
	548–550	vii, A, 3, n. 24
	576	i, 2, n. 6. iii, E, n. 18
	591–592	vi, 9, n. 9
	613–614	v, C, 4, n. 34
	624–625	v, B, 1, n. 74; v, B, 2, n. 27. vii, D, 1, nn. 18, 31. viii, B, 2, n. 48
	625–627	viii, B, 2, n. 50
	650–655	viii, C, 1, n. 221
	657–8	vii, A, 3, n. 7
	676	iii, B, 2, n. 4
	685	vii, C, 1, c, n. 25; vii, D, 1, n. 33
	710	vii, A, 2, n. 11
	725–728	vii, A, 3, n. 24
	729–732	x, C, 4, n. 35
	733	iv, 9, n. 13
Responsa, III,		
	137	vii, C, 1, b, n. 35
	184	ii, 7, n. 75
	217	iv, 9, n. 1